THE COMPLETE
Google
MANUAL

🔍 How do I use Google apps, Papercut? 📷

The world's most popular apps are not only completely free but it is very likely that you have been using one or more of them for years now, without really thinking about it. From Gmail to Trends, Google have been continually expanding their app suite with must-have tools. Did you know that you can also use Google to explore the earth, build yourself a blog, or plan your week? Google is about much more than search and this guide is here to help you discover just what you can do with these free, browser-based tools, products and services. Learn how to manage and share your images with Photos, discover the best way to configure your Gmail email account, find and download apps, music, books and movies easily on Google Play and take the first steps towards building yourself a free blog or Google Site. And this is just the start.

Contents

6 Get Started with Google

- 8 Google Account Set Up
- 8 Use Across Devices
- 11 Multiple Google & Family Accounts
- 12 Online Passwords
- 12 Improving Your Google Security
- 13 Enable/Disable Cookies
- 14 Cyber Bullying
- 15 Using Google Family Link
- 16 Protecting Your Privacy on Google
- 18 Improving Your Google Searches
- 19 Google Lens Search
- 21 Google Safe Search
- 22 Using Specialised Google Search
- 23 How To Use Google Lens Mobile
- 24 How to Create Google Alerts
- 25 Delete Google Alerts
- 26 How to Personalise Google Trends
- 28 Getting Started with Chrome
- 29 Installing Google Chrome
- 30 Customising the Chrome Browser
- 32 How to Save and Sync Chrome
- 34 Using the Chrome Web Store
- 36 How to Use Chrome Plug-ins
- 38 Setting Up Chrome Autofill
- 39 Chrome's Trusted Sites
- 40 Chrome Tips and Tricks

42 Using Google Apps

- 44 Get Started with Gmail
- 44 Creating a Gmail Account
- 45 Gmail On Android & iOS
- 46 How to Customise Gmail
- 47 Importance Markers
- 48 Dealing with Gmail Spam
- 49 Protect Your Email Address
- 50 Instant Chat in Gmail
- 51 Chat Status
- 52 How to Use Gmail Conversations
- 53 Using Gmail Keyboard Shortcuts
- 54 Create Tasks from Gmail
- 55 Gmail Tasks Shortcuts
- 56 Schedule Your Gmail Messages
- 58 Gmail User Tips and Tricks
- 59 Instant Unsubscribe
- 60 Improving the Google Calendar
- 61 Create a New Calendar
- 62 Sharing Your Calendar
- 63 SMS Reminders
- 64 Get Started with Google Maps
- 65 Your Places
- 66 Planning a Route with Maps
- 68 Using Google Street View
- 69 Route Plan with Street View
- 70 Share and Embed Maps

Contents

72	Explore Deeper with Maps
74	Google Maps Tips and Tricks
76	Explore with Google Earth
77	Google Earth Mobile
78	How to Use Google Translate
79	Translate Documents
80	How to Use Google Flights
82	Getting Started with Photos
84	Using Photo Collages and Animations
85	Linking to Pinterest
86	Editing Images Using Photos
87	Image Processing
88	Using Your Photo Albums
89	Sharing Web Albums
90	Getting Started with YouTube
91	Manage Playlists
92	Using the YouTube App
93	Using YouTube Kids
94	Uploading Videos to YouTube
96	How to Use Google Drive
97	Free Google Storage
98	Restore Deleted Drive Files
99	Permanently Delete Files
100	Set Up and Use Google Docs
101	Using Time Machine
102	How to Use Google Sheets
103	Uploading Spreadsheets
104	Set Up and Use Google Drawing

106	How to Use Google Slides
107	Viewing Presentations
108	Use Templates and Forms
109	Using Google Forms
110	How to Use Google Cloud Print
112	Set Up and Use Google Keep
114	How to Use Google Pay
115	Security Advantages
116	Get Inside the Google Play Store
117	Google Play Family Sharing
118	Create a Blog with Blogger
119	Using a Custom Domain
121	Template Designer

122 Google Hardware Guides

124	Google Home First Time Setup
126	Play Music on Google Home
127	Streaming Music & Podcasts
128	Using Google Home Routines
130	Play Audio Using Bluetooth
132	Google Home Tips and Tricks
134	Essential Google Mobile Hardware
136	Google Pixel Tips and Tricks
138	How To Use Google Chromecast
139	The Google Home App
140	Getting Started with Chromebook
142	The Chromebook Keyboard
144	The Chromebook Desktop Explained

Get Started with Google

Get Started With Google

There are many reasons (all of which are covered in this publication) to delve into the Google app suite. Yet before you start to explore these amazing tools and discover just how much you can do with them, you need to get to grips with the basics. What follows details how to set up your all-important Google account and also teaches you some important safety tips to ensure all of your online Google adventures are secure ones.

Get Started with Google

Google Account Set Up

In the past, using several different Google apps would have meant having several different usernames and passwords. Thankfully, Google took steps to merge all of these different accounts into one main Google account. This means that you only have to remember one username and password to access almost any Google product, plus it is much easier to share information, images and other data between your devices.

Use Across Devices

One of the regular questions we receive regarding Google's applications is: "Can I use my Google account sign in details on both my smartphone and my computer? Thankfully, the answer to that question is yes, follow the information below to set up your Google Account details and then you will be able to use them on all compatible devices and apps.

Creating a Google Account

Step 1
❱ Using any Internet browser, navigate to www.accounts.google.com and click on Create account in the bottom left corner of the screen. Now choose to set up either an individual or a business account.

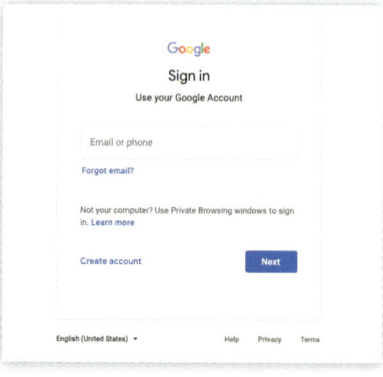

Step 2
❱ Enter your name into the boxes provided and choose your preferred gmail.com email address. If the name you want is already taken, you will be shown some alternatives; or you can try another of your own.

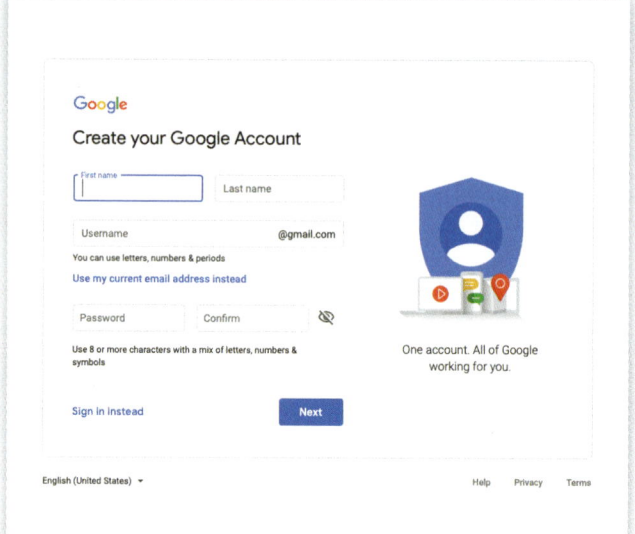

Step 3
❱ Complete the remainder of the information, including a phone number and alternative email address. Next click Express personalisation and Confirm (We are going back to this later!) and agree to Google Terms of Service to progress forward.

8   www.pclpublications.com

Google Account Set Up

Step 4
❯ After completing the initial sign up process, you are taken to the core My Account page. From this page you can customise your entire Google user experience as follows.

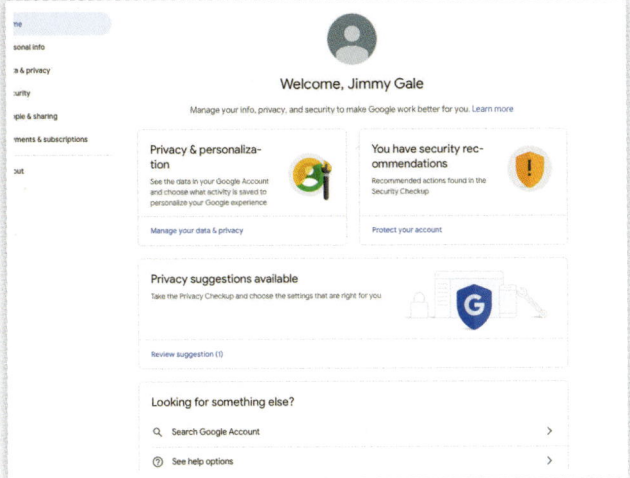

Step 5
❯ Starting with the Protect Your Account option, you can, from here, check the activity of your account, confirming that you are the only user, list devices that are logged in via your account and explore recovery options.

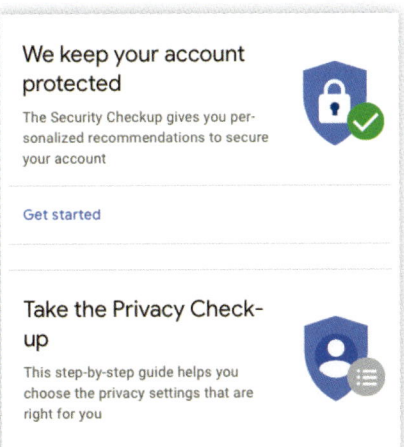

Step 6
❯ There are key areas of the Security options available that can rapidly give you an insight into the uses of your account. Beginning with the Your Devices option, which is important.

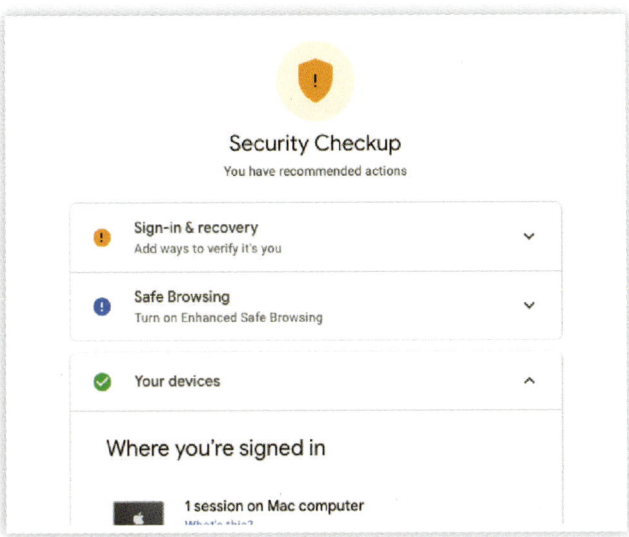

Step 7
❯ These links show any devices that have, or are currently, accessing your account. If these details don't match yours, you can change your password via the Personal Info link.

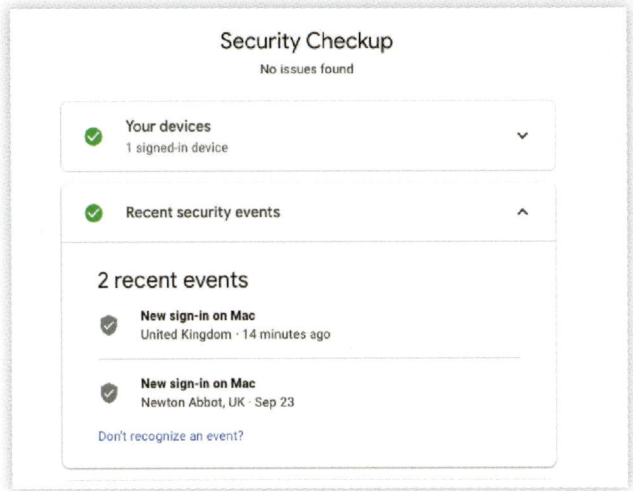

Step 8
❯ Return to the Google account page where the next option, Privacy & Personalisation link, enables you to manage and edit all of your data and details used during this initial setup process.

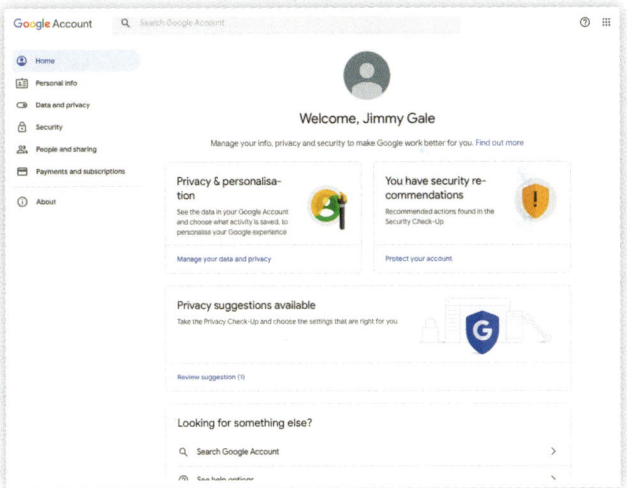

Step 9
❯ The Personal info link, left side bar, opens a page that holds a complete record of the information you have shared with Google. Check to ensure it is correct. Any issues are shown as a triangle symbol containing a "!" icon, click or tap to correct them.

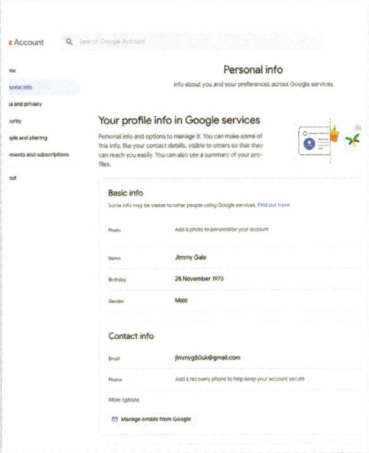

www.pclpublications.com

Get Started with Google

Google Account Set Up cont.

Step 10
❯ For now, we are going to move past the Privacy & personalisation options as, due to their importance and complexity, they are covered in greater depth in this guide.

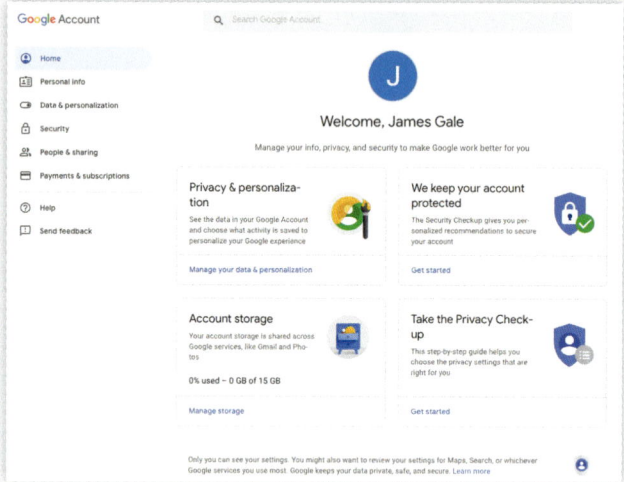

Step 11
❯ Select the Data & personalisation option to view a quick access listing of all your current and historic Google uses. Each section acts as a shortcut link to the app itself, such as Gmail.

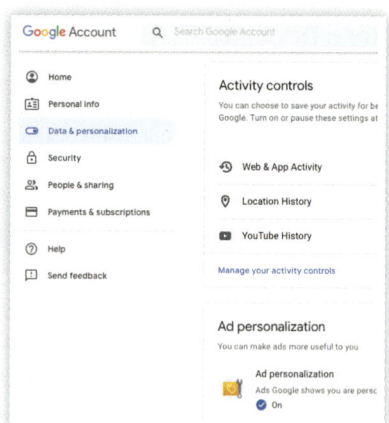

Step 12
❯ Ad personalisation can't completely block any adverts from your Google experience but you can edit the type of adverts you are exposed to, by selecting the topics you like/dislike here.

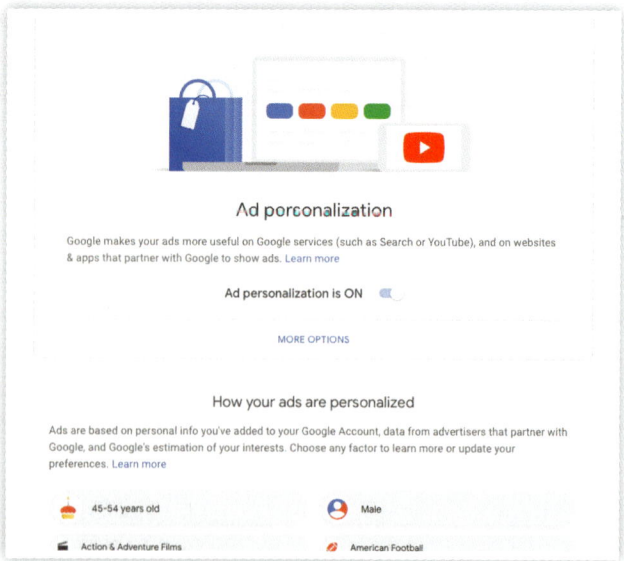

Step 13
❯ You can download or transfer your Google account content such as Internet bookmarks, contents, stored files on Google Drive, etc., should you wish to close your Google account.

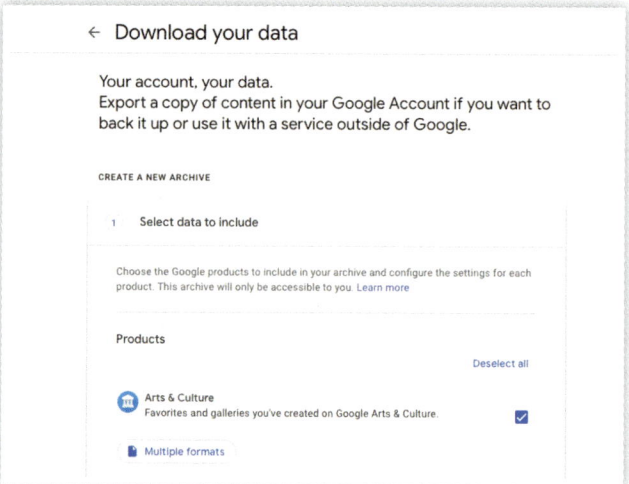

Step 14
❯ Although better suited to a long term user, even as a new user it is advisable to keep an updated archive of your Google data and files should the worst happen to your hardware.

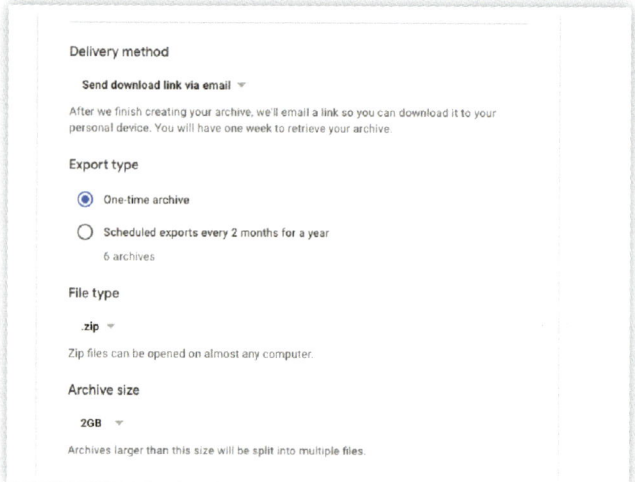

Step 15
❯ Finally, we have the Delete a service or your account option. You can customise everything from how you use your Google account to ultimately deleting your Google account entirely.

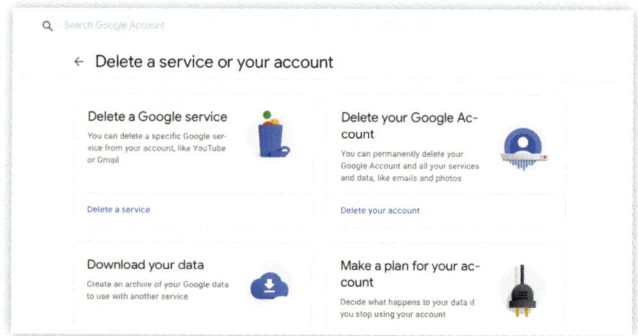

Google Account Set Up

Step 16
› You can change the language of your account using the Language & Input Tools and change the way Google is displayed via the Accessibility tools.

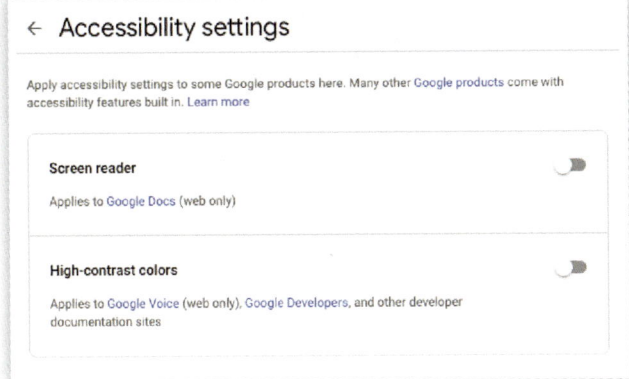

Step 17
› If you wish to give up on Google, we would advise you not to, you can delete your apps and account itself by ticking the two Yes boxes at the bottom of this page.

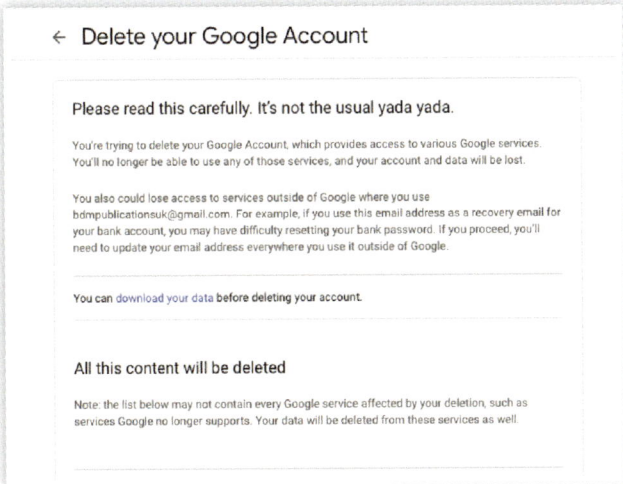

Step 18
› Finally, return to the main Google accounts page. By tapping the icon, top right, you can add a profile picture if you wish. Having a profile picture of yourself will help friends and family find you on their own Google apps.

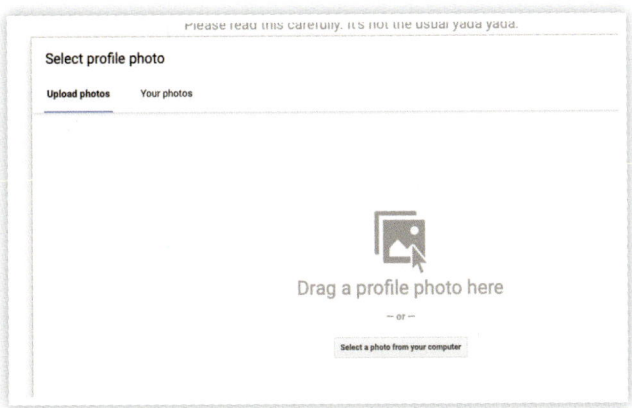

Step 19
› Having set up your Google account, you can return to check/change any settings via the account home page located at: myaccount.google.com.

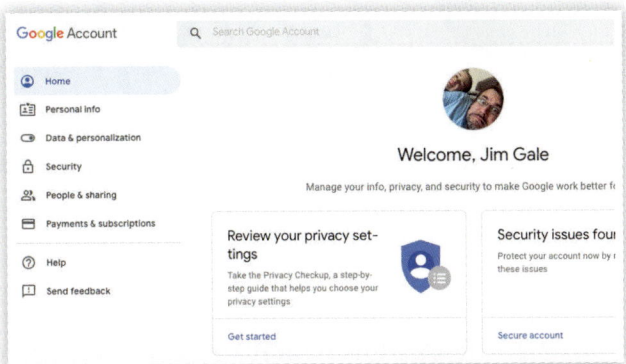

Multiple Google & Family Accounts

It is possible to have more than one Google account and then sync those accounts across your private network of smartphones or tablets.

Adding and syncing a second account will not merge those two accounts anywhere but on your phone (and even here, only in certain apps). Nothing is ever synced between your Google accounts, allowing you to keep things nicely separate for personal and work accounts, for example. To add another account via your phone or tablet, go to Settings > Accounts and then tap the Add Account button. This screen shows all accounts associated with the device. Choose what sort of account you wish to add from the options on the screen; as you can see, it is not just multiple Google accounts that you can add. Next, let's set up a Family Group account.

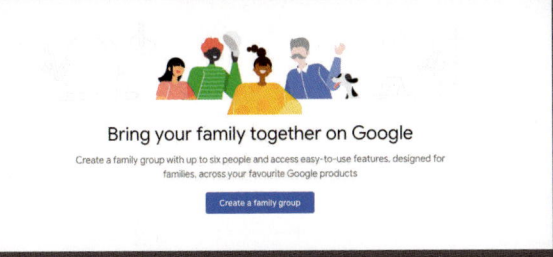

From the People and Sharing link on your Google Account homepage, click on the Family Sharing link. From here you will able to add a further five family members to your account. You will need to set yourself up as the Family manager and you can start the set up process. NOTE: Each family member will need to have a Google Account of their own. Use this account to invite them to join your Family Group using the Send Invitation link. Once accepted you will be able to share your choice of files, content and media with your Family Group.

www.pclpublications.com 11

Get Started with Google

Improving Your Google Security

Keeping yourself and your family safe whilst using your Google apps is just as important as it is when you are sharing your details and your files online. That said it doesn't need to be difficult. While using the Internet and social networks can have its problems, you can reduce them to a minimal level by following a few simple pieces of advice.

Online Passwords

If you are anything like us, the number of passwords that you need to remember grows on an almost daily basis and because of this, it can be tempting to use the same or similar passwords for several different websites. This is a bad idea, particularly if your chosen password is something easy to guess such as your name or date of birth. Here are a few tips to consider when creating passwords.

Keep them Unique

❱ Having a unique password for each website you are required to log in to is a very good idea, particularly for things like email and online banking. Although security on a banking website is likely to be very good, if you use the same password on a website with less stringent security, you risk it being compromised on one and used to gain access to the other. It is not unusual for criminals to harvest passwords from a weak website and then randomly try them on more secure sites.

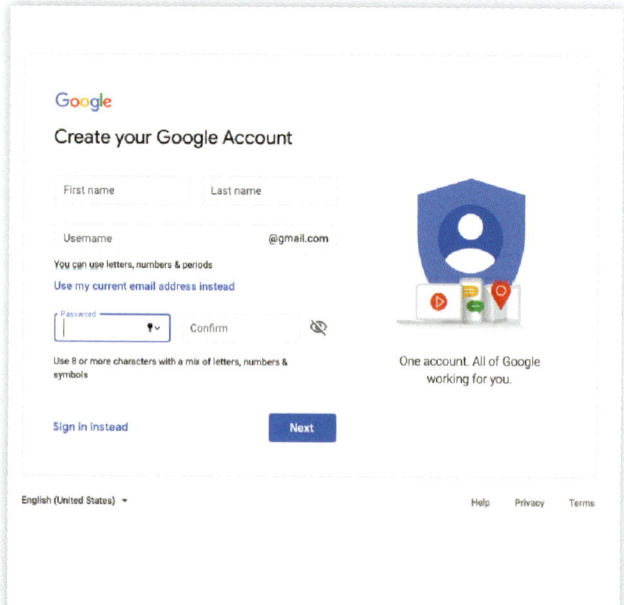

Keep them Random

❱ Try to avoid using anything that is easy to guess, including personal information like your name, date of birth or address. These things are all very easy to discover and often the first things someone will try to get into your accounts. Also avoid, if possible, using real words or sequential strings of numbers, e.g. 123456789 or ABCDEFGHI etc.

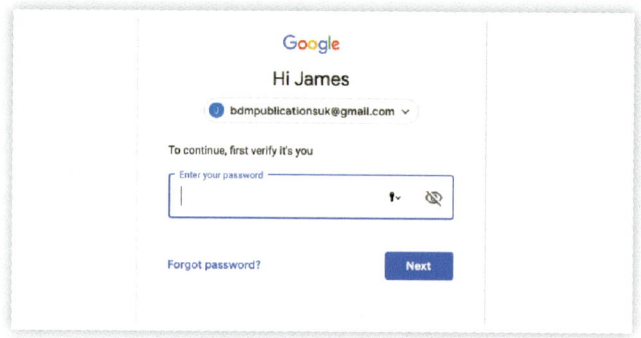

The Longer, the Better

❱ Short passwords are much easier to crack than long ones, so be sure to avoid anything less than eight characters and, if possible, go for something ten characters long at least. There are 4000 times more possible combinations of ten letters and numbers, than there are for eight letters and numbers. Most good websites require at least 8 character passwords nowadays.

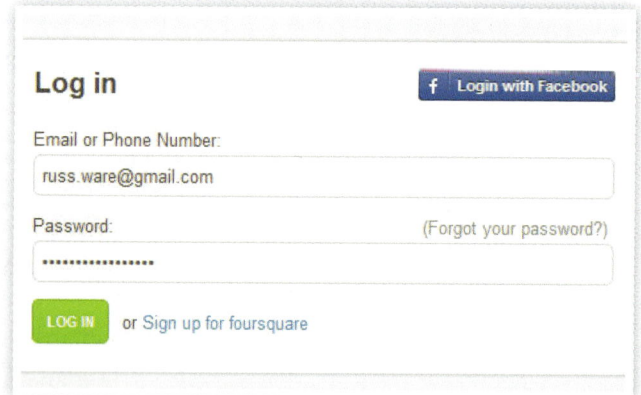

Improving Your Google Security

Mix it Up
❯ Once you start adding in symbols and mixed case letters, along with numbers, into your passwords, the possible variations rise to over six quadrillion (for an eight character password). The password A1z7yDbP is many thousands of times more secure than a1z7ydbp.

Use a Password Manager
❯ For most people, keeping a written list of their passwords is perfectly okay as long as you make sure that it is not left in plain sight on your desk, etc. Even keeping a text document on your computer with your passwords listed is not usually a risk. Just don't call the file 'Passwords' and leave in on the desktop. A much safer way, however, is to use a good Password Manager. These simple bits of software let you store your passwords in a locked file on your computer. Just as long as you have a very good password to get into the manager, your other passwords will be safe. You then only need to remember one password, instead of 10 or 20.

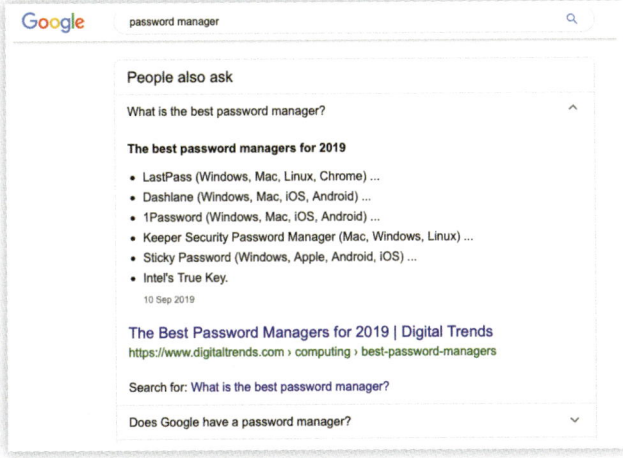

Enable/Disable Cookies in Chrome

❯ To disable cookies in Chrome web browser, click the Three dots icon or Menu button in the top right corner of the browser window. Select Settings, scroll to the bottom and click Advanced settings. Now click Site settings, in the Privacy section, and then Cookies.

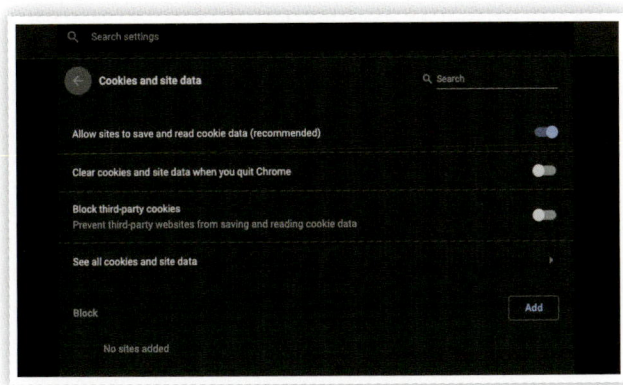

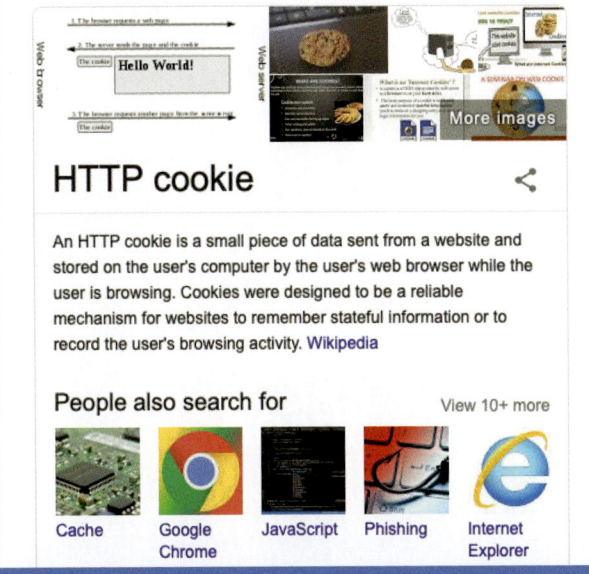

What are Cookies?

Cookies (or HTML Cookies) are small files used by websites to recognise individual users (or rather, recognise their computer). When you visit a website, a cookie is stored in a temporary folder on your computer. When you next visit that site, the cookie will be checked for. Different sites use cookies to store different information but a good example is information in a form being automatically filled when visiting a site you have used recently to order something.

Almost all modern browsers, including Internet Explorer, Chrome and Safari, allow you to block cookies from being downloaded. However, it is worth remembering that many websites now need cookies to work properly, and so blocking them could mean your browsing experience is a frustrating one. Cookies are nothing to be afraid of, they are simply used to make the Internet work better.

❯ Select Allow local data to be set to allow both first-party and third-party cookies. If you only want to accept first-party cookies, check the box next to "Block all third-party cookies without exception."

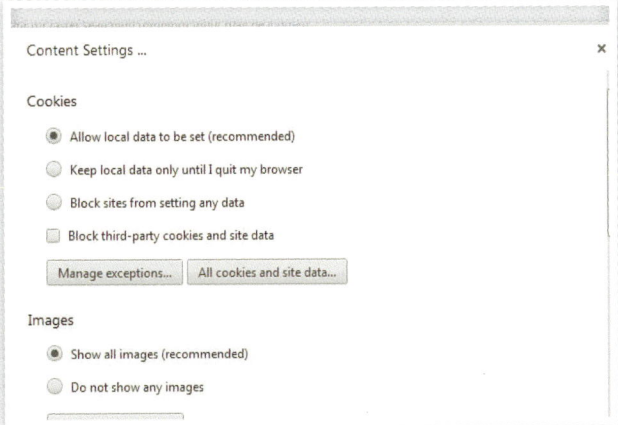

www.pclpublications.com 13

Get Started with Google

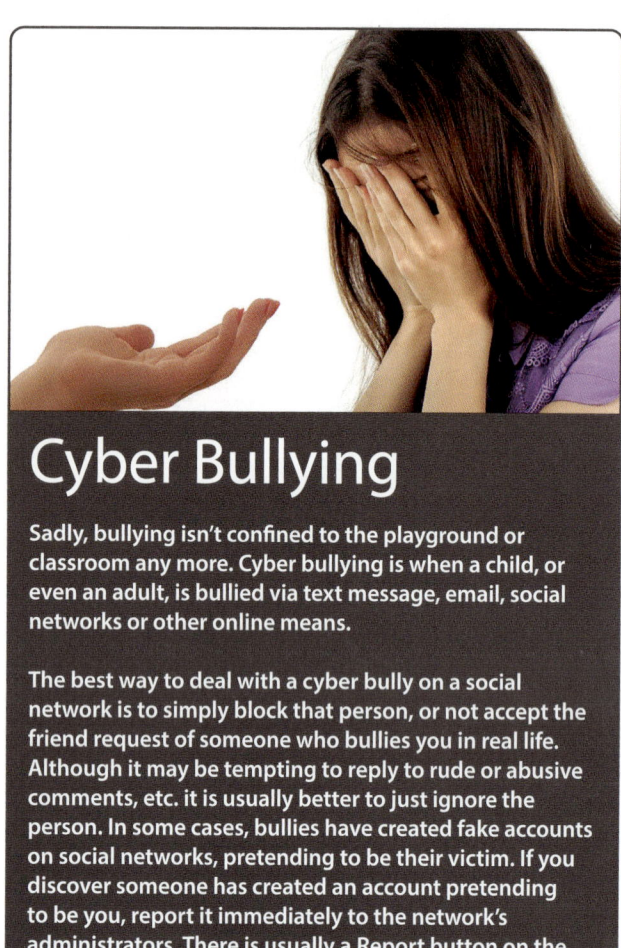

Cyber Bullying

Sadly, bullying isn't confined to the playground or classroom any more. Cyber bullying is when a child, or even an adult, is bullied via text message, email, social networks or other online means.

The best way to deal with a cyber bully on a social network is to simply block that person, or not accept the friend request of someone who bullies you in real life. Although it may be tempting to reply to rude or abusive comments, etc. it is usually better to just ignore the person. In some cases, bullies have created fake accounts on social networks, pretending to be their victim. If you discover someone has created an account pretending to be you, report it immediately to the network's administrators. There is usually a Report button on the user profile page.

What is Phishing?

Phishing is the process of trying to find private information such as PIN numbers, passwords and usernames by trickery. Sometimes spammers create fake websites that look like the Facebook login page. When you enter your email and password on one of these pages, the spammer records your information and keeps it.

When someone has been phished, their account will often start automatically sending messages or links to a large number of their friends. These messages or links are often advertisements telling friends to check out videos or products. If you think your friend's account was phished, tell them to change their password and run anti-virus software on their computer.

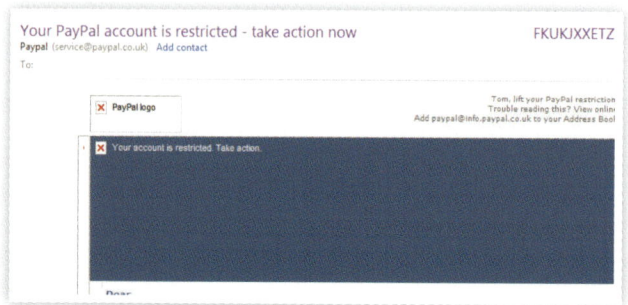

Social Networks – Advice for Parents

Being parents ourselves, we understand the pressure that many people feel to let their children use the Internet and social networks in particular. Many social networking sites, including Facebook, don't allow children under 13 years of age to have accounts. Unfortunately there is little they can do to stop a child below that age entering false details. Rather than a blanket ban on using the Internet and social networks, and potentially have your child visit them behind your back, perhaps a better way to keep your child safe online is to understand the dangers yourself and make sure your children understand them as well.

Do Some Research

❯ Hopefully, if you are reading this, you already want to learn more about social networking and networks. This guide is a great place to start increasing your understanding of what you can do (and therefore what your child can do) on sites such as Facebook, Twitter and Google+. Read as much as you can about the networks your children use and remember that one of the best sources of information is often the children themselves.

Get Involved

❯ Take the next step and create an account for yourself on the social networks your child uses. This not only helps you to understand how things work and what features could be a potential problem but it also allows you to more easily see what your child is doing on there. You will be far better informed when asking questions about the site.

14   www.pclpublications.com

Improving Your Google Security

Privacy Settings

❱ Nearly all the well known social networking sites offer several levels of privacy settings. Ensure your child selects the strongest privacy setting available when they create their account. This will help to make sure that their personal information is only seen by people they want to share it with. Be aware, however, that some sites are totally open to the public.

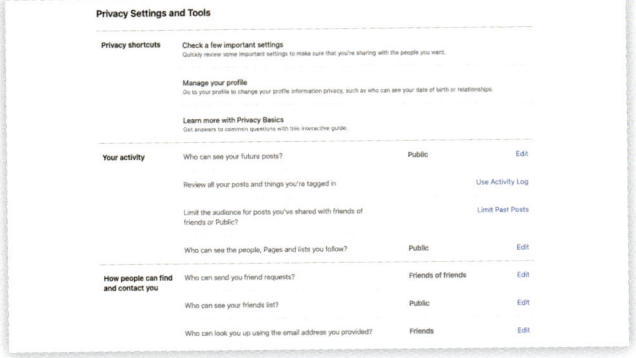

Internet Safety Tips

- Make sure that your child doesn't publish personal information like their location, email address, phone number or date of birth.

- Make sure they are very careful about what images and messages they post, even among trusted friends: once they are online they can be shared widely and are extremely difficult to get removed.

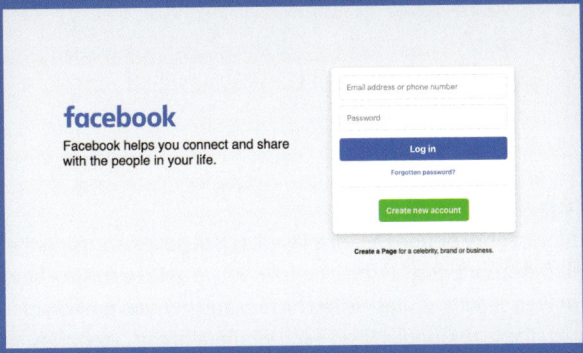

- Encourage your child to talk to you if they come across anything they find offensive or upsetting. Keep a record of anything abusive or offensive they've received and report any trouble to the site management: most sites have a simple reporting procedure, normally activated by clicking on a link on the page.

- If your child makes an online friend and wants to meet up with them in real life, you should go along with them to check the person is who they say they are.

- Tell them to be aware of online scams. Offers which seem too good to be true usually are. Make them aware also that clicking links they are unsure about can be unwise.

Using Family Link

Family link is a fantastic mobile and web app that allows parents to monitor and manage their children online, habits and most important their mobile security. What follows is a brief guide on how to set up and use it.

Step 1
❱ Firstly install the Family Link app for your child's smartphone, it is compatible with Android and iPhone and is listed on both Google Play and the App Store.

Step 2
❱ You will now need to input the Google Account that is linked to your child's device into the app on your device. If they don't have an account you can set one up here. This will generate a code that you will need to enter into your child's Family Link app on their device, tap Join.

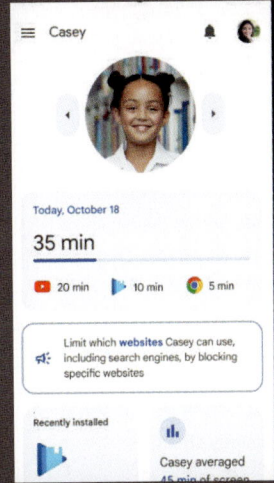 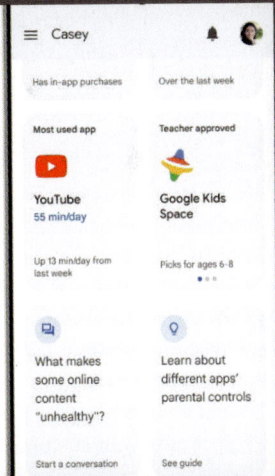

Step 3
❱ On your child's device you can now select which apps, features and uses you wish to monitor via your device using parental controls. Once you have made your choices, you will be notified of any changes/uses that apply to your choices above.

Step 4
❱ You are now able to make the decision should your child wish to install new apps, set screentime limits, apply age rating settings to the devices use and even monitor their location and the device's battery power.

www.pclpublications.com 15

Get Started with Google

Protecting Your Privacy on Google

Online privacy is an extremely important issue when it comes to using your Google apps. Google has included a comprehensive privacy tool to help you take control of, and monitor, how the company uses your information. This guide will reinforce your privacy rules when using Google.

Step 1
❱ Start by opening your main Google Accounts page, this can be accessed by entering https://myaccount.google.com into a browser. From the main account home page, you're able to check on the current levels of privacy, information and security.

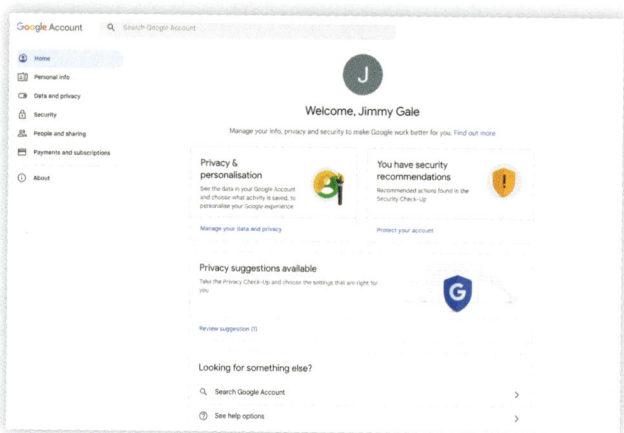

Step 2
❱ The Privacy suggestions available/Privacy Check Up box, located in the bar below the top two links, is a good place to start. What follows is a scrollable selection of options that will help you choose your customised privacy settings.

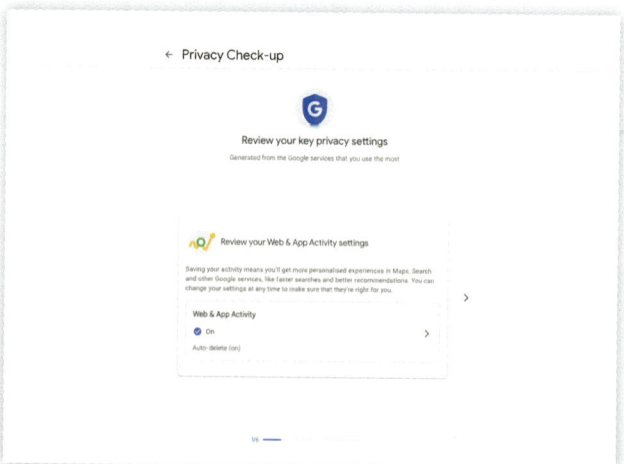

Step 3
❱ The Privacy Check-Up section is broken down into six sub-categories, offering you the chance to review the key settings that determine how Google controls its activity toward you, what ads are displayed, how others will connect to you, what privacy settings are available and what you share with Google themselves, starting with Web & App Activity.

Step 4
❱ The category options are displayed as tick boxes, so, using the Web & App category as the example, you're able to control how your web searches, sites visited history and remain private, or are available to Google. Read each element of the categories carefully to enhance or lower your online privacy. We suggest turning everything off to start to see how it effects your use.

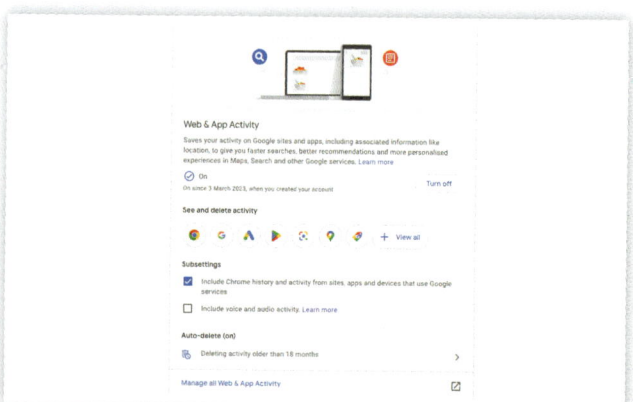

Protecting Your Privacy on Google

Step 5
❱ Going back to the main Google Account home page, by first clicking the back arrow and then Home on the left column, take a moment to look through the other options available. Check on the Privacy & Personalisation box; click the Manage your Data & Personalisation link in the bottom of the box.

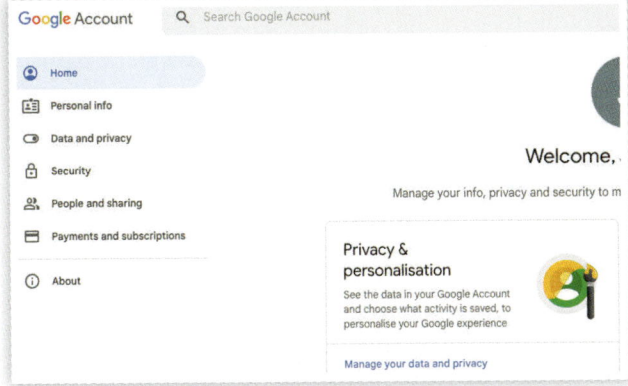

Step 6
❱ The Data & Personalisation category is quite expansive and covers a lot of the content that transpires between you and Google's many services and apps. Each area within this category can be expanded further, such as Location History and so on. It's important to take the time to trawl through these sections to fine-tune your privacy settings.

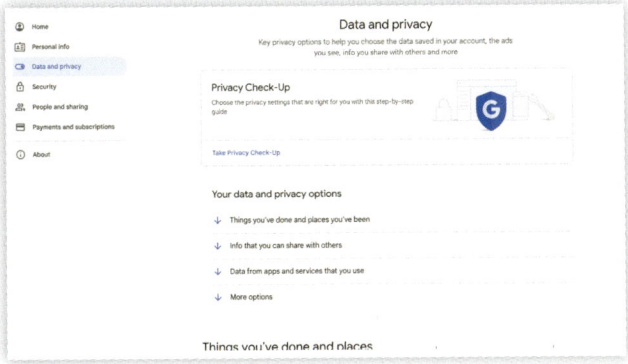

Step 7
❱ To the left you'll see the quick access column, where you're able to navigate back to the Account Home page; click on the Security link. This will open the Security page where, in the event of someone gaining access to your Google password, you're able to lock down your account. Here you can opt for 2-Step Verification, create an Account recovery option and protect its privacy.

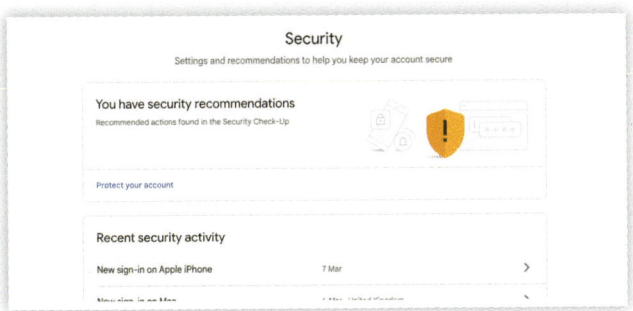

Step 8
❱ The People & Sharing option, found via the left-hand column again, is also worth investigating. In here, you're able to define your contacts, block any users and, most importantly, manage your location sharing, as well as choose what personal info about you is visible to others across the Google services.

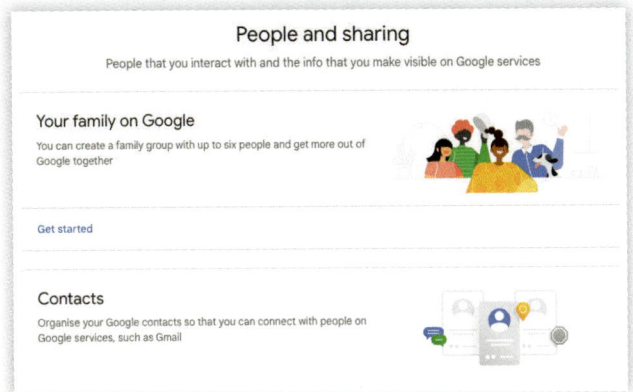

Step 9
❱ Finally we have the Payments and Subscriptions option, here you can check that your Google Account is secure and not being used by a third party! If you ever become confused over any of this information, or simply don't know where to turn next, the Help option will walk you through common issues and offer guided steps on how to proceed.

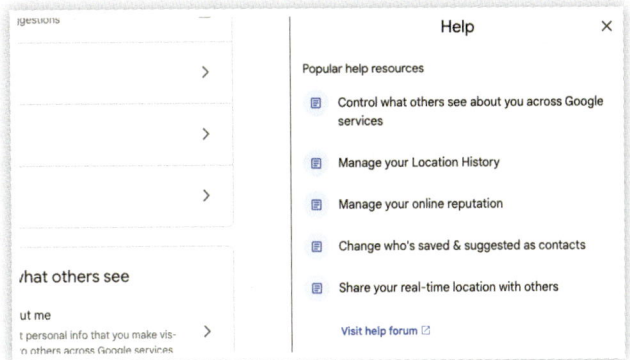

Step 10
❱ One final aspect of privacy that's worth looking up is the Google Privacy & Terms. These are in a constant state of flux and will change depending on the laws of the country in which you're currently resident. Navigate to https://policies.google.com/privacy, to view the latest Google Privacy Policy.

www.pclpublications.com   17

Get Started with Google

Improving Your Google Searches

Google has the ability to search through billions of pages to supply you with the most relevant results for any search you desire. Google has different versions for different countries and, while they all work in basically the same way, by using the version for your home country you can be sure of both local and international results.

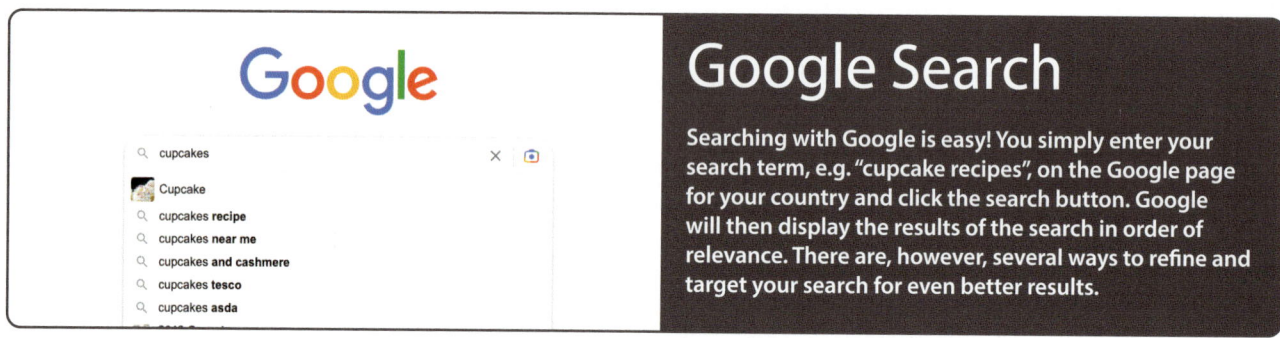

Google Search

Searching with Google is easy! You simply enter your search term, e.g. "cupcake recipes", on the Google page for your country and click the search button. Google will then display the results of the search in order of relevance. There are, however, several ways to refine and target your search for even better results.

Understanding Google Search Results

When you perform a search on Google the results are split into two categories: Paid and Organic results. Paid results can be thought of more like adverts, with their position on the results page determined by how much the advertiser has paid. The organic results are those which are most relevant, respected or popular for your search term.

1 Search Options   **2** Paid Results   **3** Organic Results

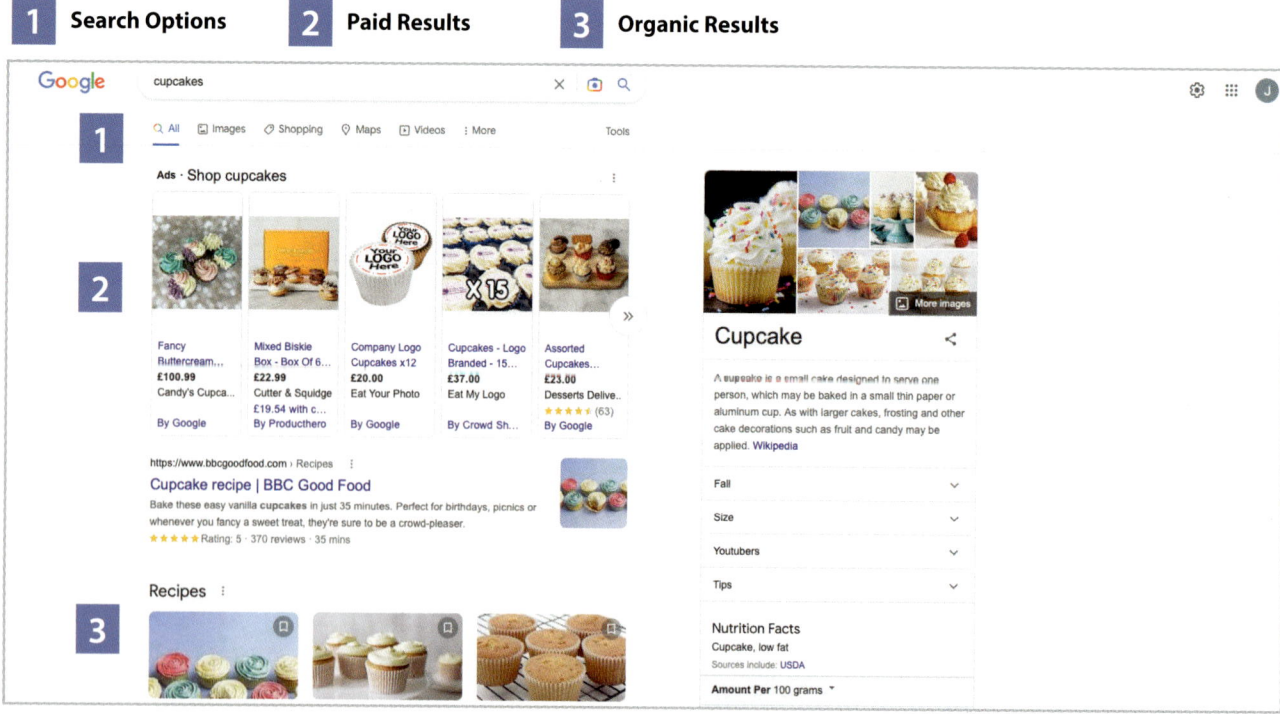

18   www.pclpublications.com

Improving Your Google Searches

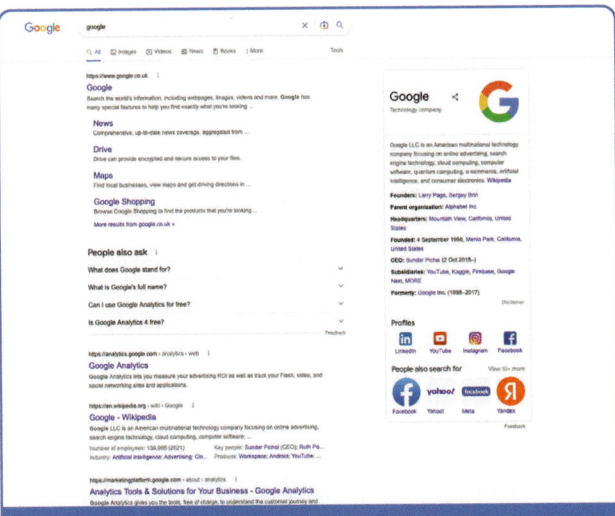

The Knowledge Graph

Certain search terms (people, places or animals, for example) will activate the Google Knowledge Graph. This boxout, shown on the left of the standard search results, highlights facts, photos and other snippets of information about your search. Use this section to find quick information and facts about the subject or to start exploring related subjects. Knowledge Graph results are gathered from a variety of sources, including Wikipedia, World Bank, Freebase and Weather Underground, to name but a few.

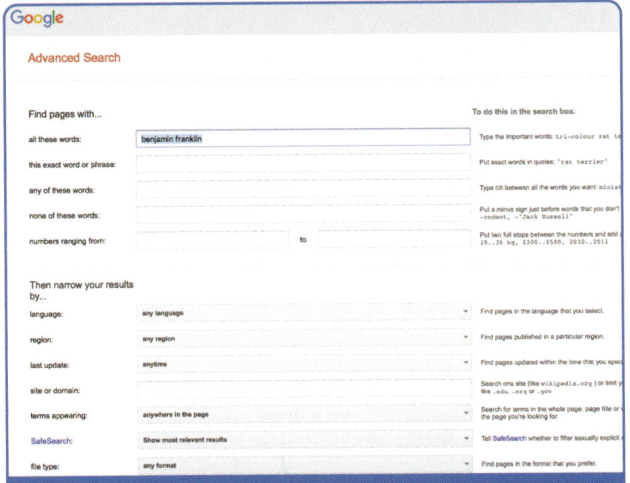

Advanced Search

After searching, while on the results page, notice the Settings link under the search bar. Clicking this allows you to select Advanced Search from the dropdown menu. On the advanced search screen you can refine your search even further so that the results only show pages which feature all the words in your search term, or by country and language. Once you have selected your advanced search options, scroll to the bottom of the page and click the blue Advanced Search button.

Searching Images and Videos

As well as being able to search for text in web pages, you can also search for images and videos amongst other things.

Step 1
⟩ Open the Google search page for your country in your Internet browser. To perform a standard search, type your search term in the box and click Google Search.

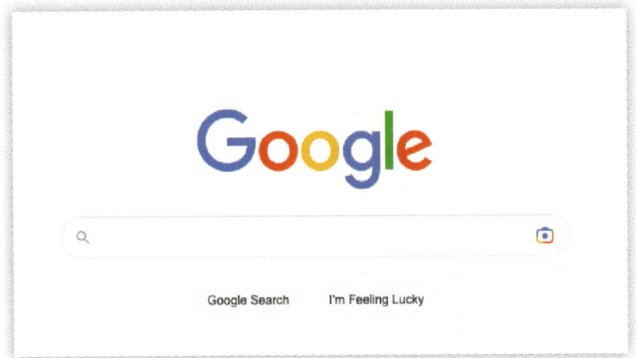

Google Lens Search

To access the desktop version of this fantastic mobile app, visit image.google.com Click on the "Search by Image" camera icon on the search bar and drag and drop or locate the image you wish to use. Once this image has been uploaded, Google Search will display said image on the right of the screen with your search options/tools. These tools are displayed at the bottom of the screen, comprising of Search, Text and Translate. Let's start with the former. Having selected from the above you can then use the entire image or choose to focus on a key area of the image by clicking directly on this point. You can also move the focus frame over the image to focus on other key points you wish to search for. The results of the image search is displayed on the left side of the screen in the familiar Google search manner.
By clicking the Text option at the bottom of the screen, you will be able to highlight any text that is displayed on the main image and drag and drop it to the left side of the screen. This acts like a regular manually inputed text search with the results shown below. You can also copy the selected text via the Copy link and paste it into the search bar manually.
Finally the Translate option will translate any on screen text into the language of your choice using the controls at the top of the right side screen. The translated text will appear in full on the left side of the screen. Here you can choose to Select all, Listen or Open in Translate. The latter will open the text in the Translate web app, while Listen will translate the text to audio and play out loud and Select all enables you to manually cut and paste the text into another app.

www.pclpublications.com

Get Started with Google

Searching Images and Videos cont.

Step 2

❭ To perform a Voice search, using dictation, click the Microphone icon on the right side of the Search bar and then simply say the subject you wish to search for on this screen, your speech will appear on screen and the search will start.

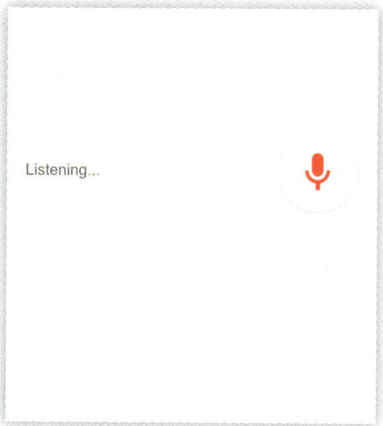

Step 3

❭ The results will now be displayed on screen. At the top of the results page there are several links including Maps, News and Images. Click on the Images link.

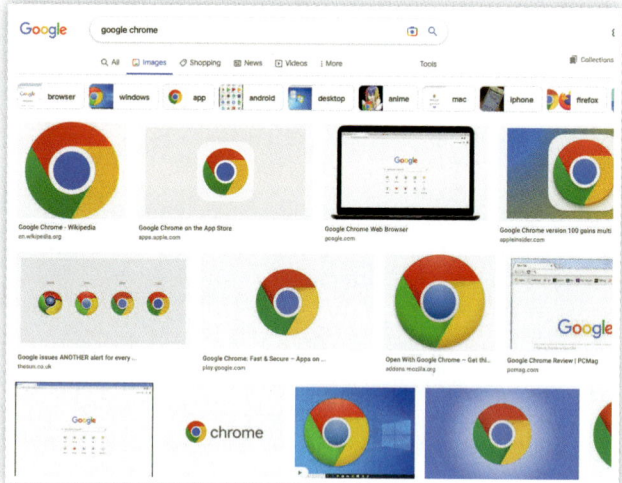

Step 4

❭ Image results for the original search term will now be displayed. Move the mouse over any of the images to see a short description, image dimensions and other image details.

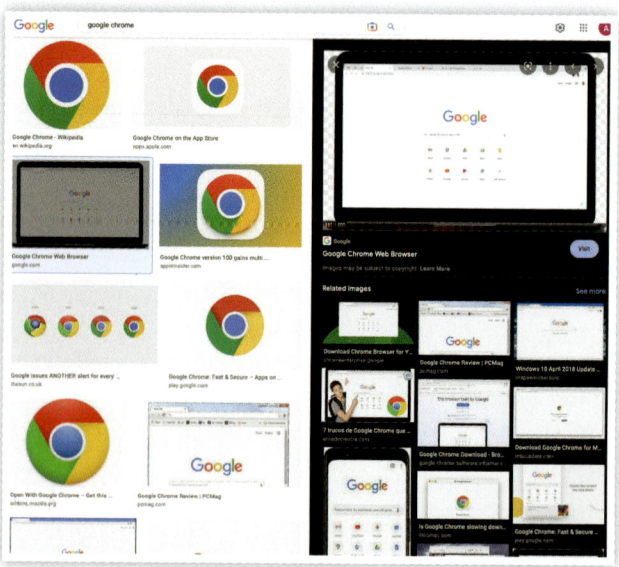

Step 5

❭ Alongside the search links (Web, Images, etc.) you will see a link for Search Tools. Clicking this will allow you to further refine your search by image size, date it was uploaded and image type.

Step 6

❭ Clicking on the image will open it at a larger size and also display a link that will allow you to open the web page where the image was found. Click the image again to close it.

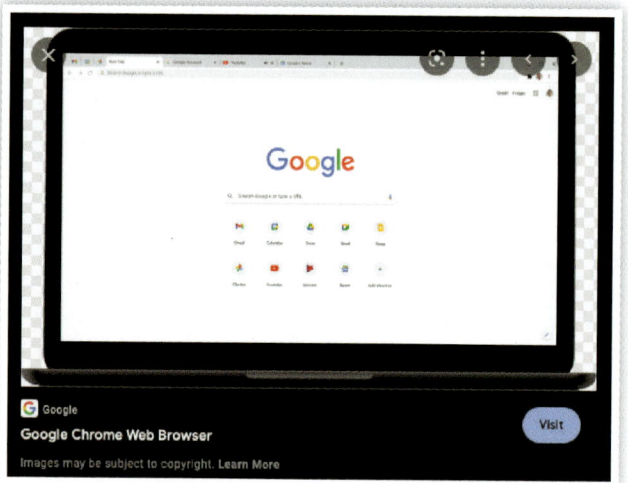

Step 7

❭ To search for videos instead of images, click the More link and then select Videos from the menu that drops down. Videos have their own search tools, including duration and quality.

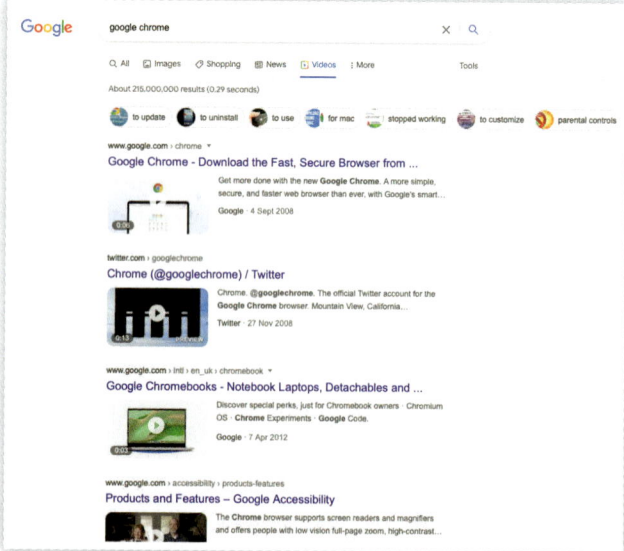

20   www.pclpublications.com

Improving Your Google Searches

Safe Search

Google features a Safe Search option which allows you to select the age rating of the search results. This applies to web search results, as well as images, videos and books and can help to remove sexually explicit content. No filter is 100 per cent accurate, but Safe Search should help you avoid most of this type of material.

Step 1
❯ Perform a search and check the results. If there are websites listed that you think are inappropriate, click the Setting link in the top right beneath the search bar and select Search Settings.

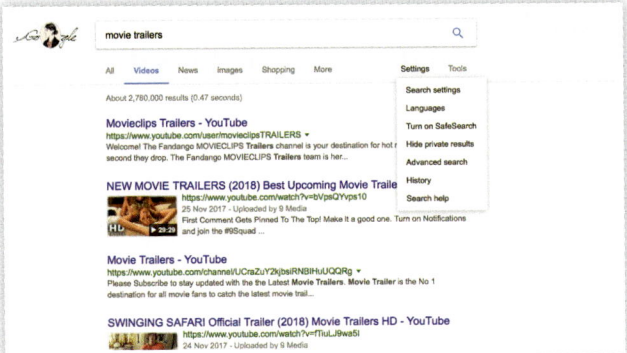

Step 2
❯ At the top of the search settings screen you should see a Safe Search on/off link. Click the turn on Safe Search link to activate it. You can lock Safe Search on by selecting this option too.

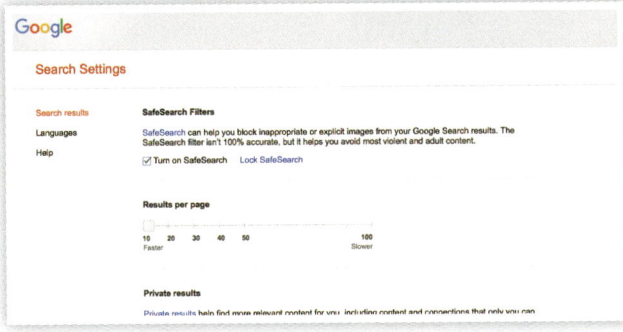

Step 3
❯ If you want the page to display all results, regardless of content, DO NOT activate Safe Search. If you have changed your mind you can deactivate via the Settings link.

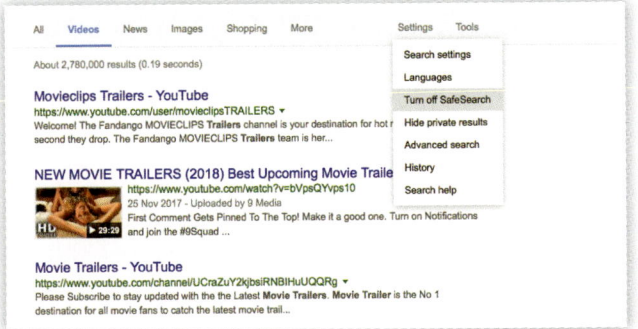

Step 4
❯ Your browser should remember the setting when you next use Google search. If you want to make sure that the safe search setting is not changed, you will have to sign in to a Google account.

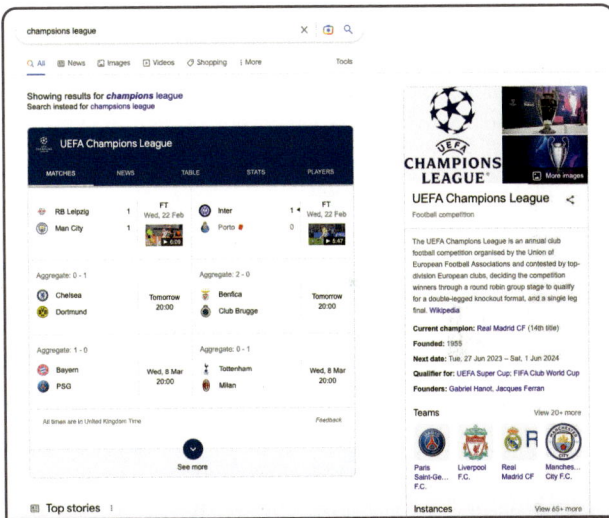

Instant Updates

Based upon your search results, you will receive additional information that is relevant to the subject. For this example we searched for a sports team and results also shows their latest fixtures and results.
Specific search results also contain a downward pointing arrow at the end of the web link, click to show these.

Cached: Google trawls the web and takes snapshots of each page. When you click Cached, you will see the web page as it looked when last indexed by Google. The "Cached" link won't appear for sites that haven't been indexed or for any sites whose owners requested that their content isn't cached.

Similar: Click Similar to see other websites that are related to that result.

www.pclpublications.com

Get Started with Google

Advanced Google Search

There are several specialised search tools, letting you cut through all the unwanted information and just see results from, for example, blogs, shopping sites or scholarly papers. You can access these search pages at any time from the Chrome browser or Google Home page.

Shopping Search

This feature allows you to search only shopping results for any term you enter into the search box on Google.

Step 1
❯ You can open the Shopping search screen by typing www.google.co.uk/shopping into your browser address field. Your browser should automatically detect your location and filter any results to your own currency.

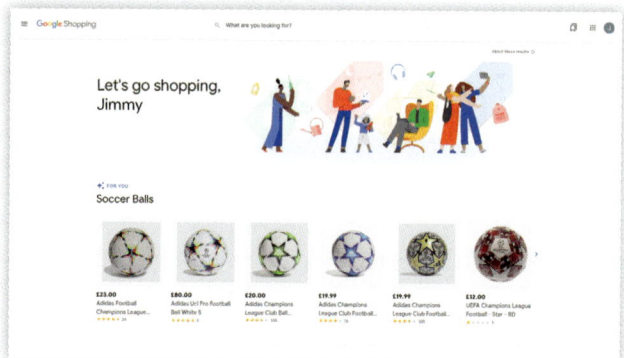

Step 2
❯ You will see that the shopping search screen is very different from a standard Google search screen, with products shown in sections such as electronics, clothing and even as specific as Nexus 7. What is shown depends on what items are found in your search history in Google.

Step 3
❯ Clicking on one of the products shown will display a list of results for that type of product. Alternatively, you can type a search term into the search field at the top in Google.

Step 4
❯ Once the results are shown, you will see that there are several filters down the left-hand side of the screen. These allow you to filter results by specific manufacturer, price, size (depending on the product type) and several others.

Step 5
❯ Click the title of a product you are interested in and a box will expand to show more information, including a range of prices. You can then add the item to a shortlist by clicking the Shortlist button. This allows you to refer back to it easily later.

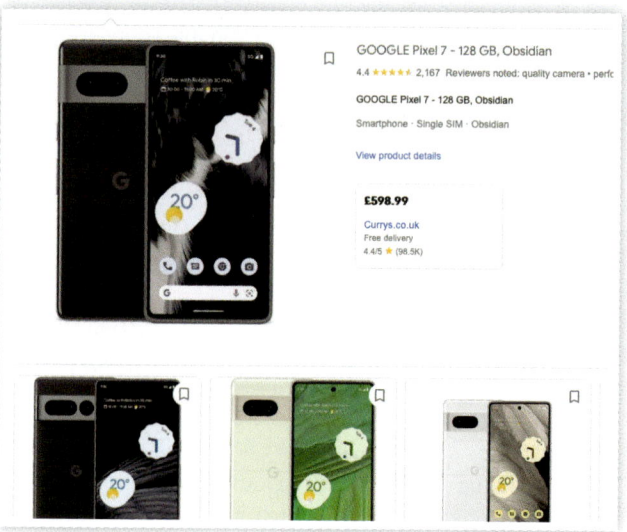

Step 6
❯ If you click the product title a second time when the box is open, it will expand into a full screen page. This page lists all available prices and sellers, along with reviews of the product if they are available online.

Step 7
❯ You can click directly to the item, via your preferred retailer, by clicking the link from the list at the bottom of the page. NOTE: On rare occasions the price linked may not match that of the retailer, so take care to check.

Using Specialised Google Search

How to Use Google Lens Mobile

Google Lens is a fantastic addition to the App Suite, offering functionality on both your mobile and desktop devices. We will be looking at the mobile version, explaining the core functionality and why you really need to download this from your choice of app store right away.

Using Google Lens on your Smartphone

Using your mobile device's camera you are able to access this unique alternative to the traditional Google search engine entry. So let's take a step into the future of online searches. Keyboards? We don't need keyboards where Google is going!

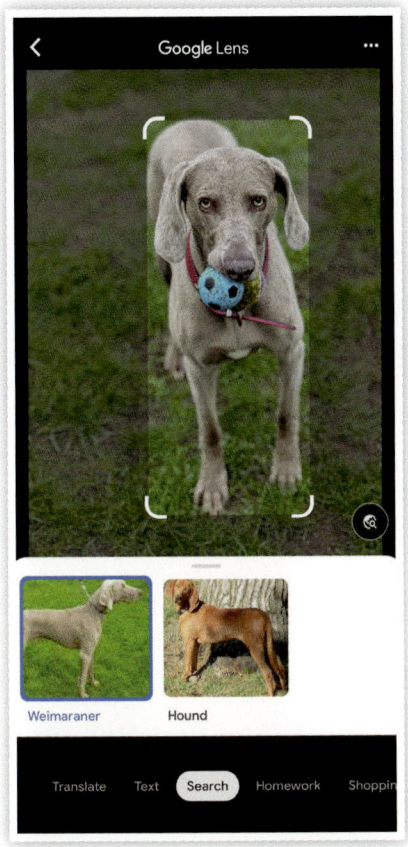

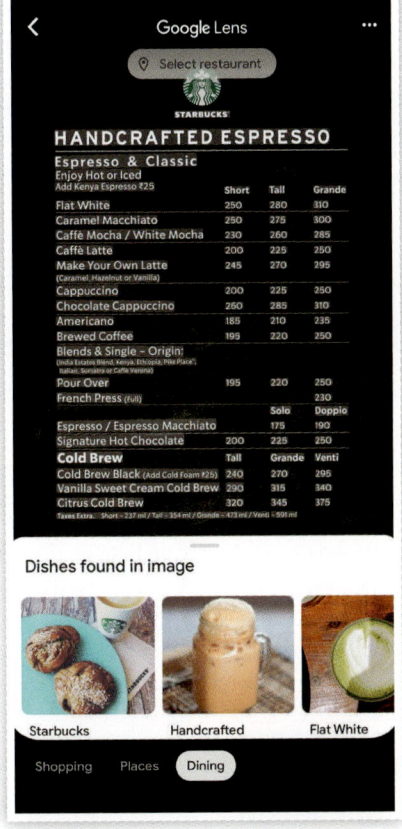

Step 1
❱ At the base of the app UI, you will find your search options; Translate, Text, Search, Homework, Shopping, Places and Dining. To select your choice, simply scroll them, stopping on your choice. Let's start with Search. This is simply Google search and will find you information on your camera's target.

Step 2
❱ Moving on to Dining, this feature will show you images and give detail on items found on a menu (as shown above). Homework is a unique feature that will help the user find the solution to basic Math's problems. Shopping links you to purchase links for the item you have captured on your camera app.

Step 3
❱ Places links your camera view finder to your location giving you background and details on it. Translate and Text will pull text based content from your camera lens, which can be translated into an array of languages or use it as a search term. NOTE: Your search data will be saved to your Google search history.

www.pclpublications.com

Get Started with Google

How to Create Google Alerts

You can use Google Alerts to monitor anything on the web and then have links to any matching content sent directly to your email address each day, or when new content is available.

Setting Up Alerts

Step 1
▶ To get started setting up an alert, navigate to www.google.co.uk/alerts. Enter your query just as if you were doing a normal Google search. You can use the various Google search options, including quotes, minus sign, to exclude words and the site prefix to find specific types of website.

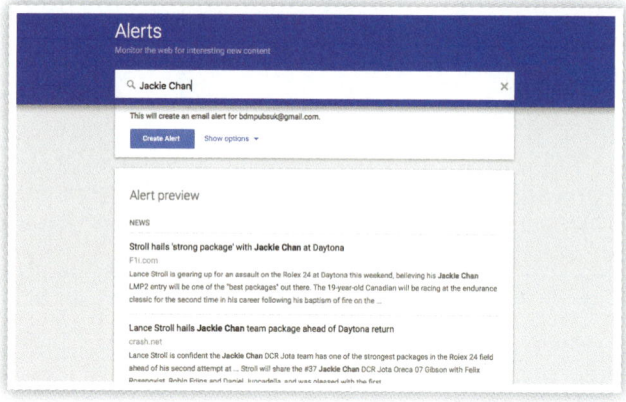

Step 2
▶ Using the Show options menu, you can choose to tell Google to only provide content of a specific type (videos, for example) or you can request that every type of result is sent to you. Everything alerts include results from Google Web Search, Google Blog Search and Google News.

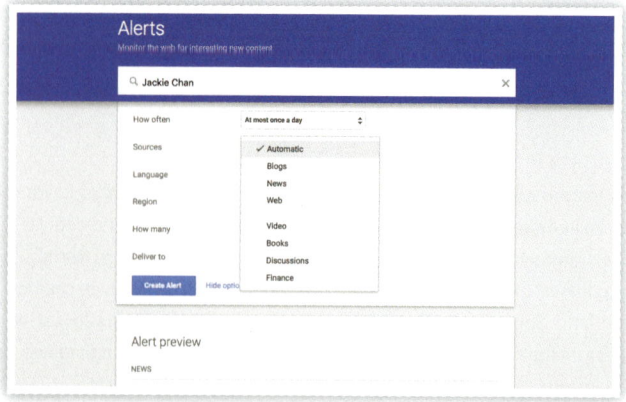

Step 3
▶ The next step is to choose a delivery rate. The default is once a day: Google Alerts checks for new results once per day and emails you if it finds new results. Depending on the subject, Google may not be able to deliver alerts daily. Alerts on these subjects will be sent, when they are available for you.

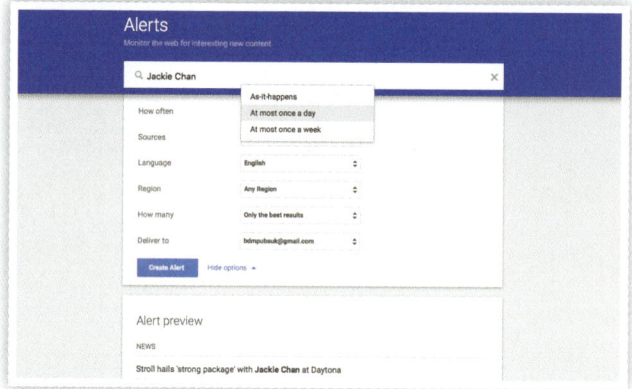

Step 4
▶ To help you avoid an alert email full of low quality results, you can change the volume of the alerts to "Only the best results". This allows Google to filter results to those most relevant to your query and those of high quality. If you prefer, you can change this setting to "All results".

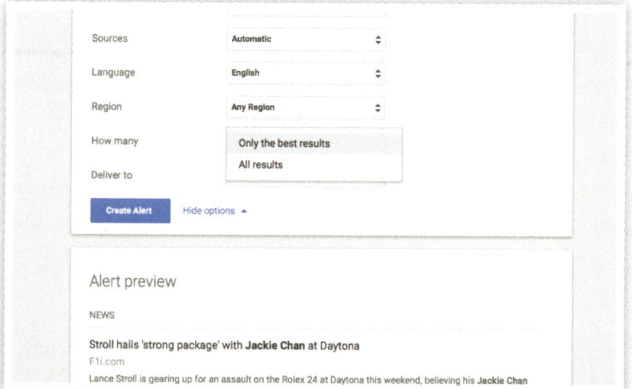

How to Create Google Alerts

Step 5
> Enter the email address to which you want your alerts delivered. Google will protect your email address and will not use it to spam you with offers for any other product or service. If you aren't signed in to a Google Account when you create an alert, Google will send you a verification email.

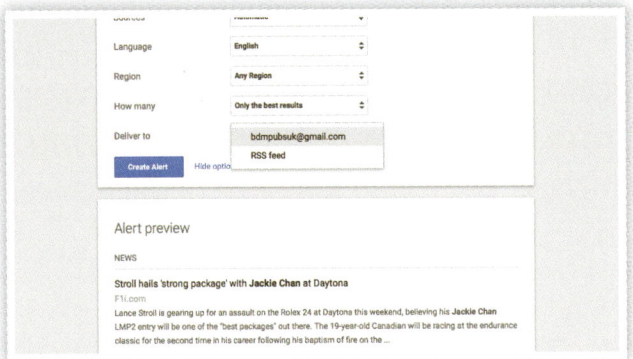

Step 6
> If you prefer, and if you are signed in to a Google account when creating the alert, you can choose to have the results sent via an RSS feed. Simply sign in and choose the Feed option in the Deliver to field. You can read yours in any RSS feed reader.

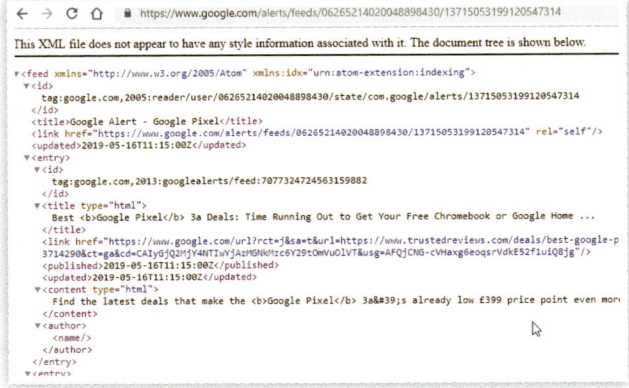

Step 7
> To view any of these Google Alerts, you have to open your email application and check the email addresses that you linked to your Google Account during initial set up. You can check this information at anytime via your account link, top right of your browser.

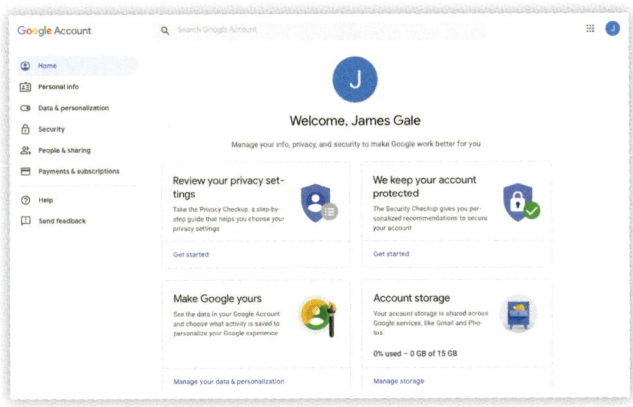

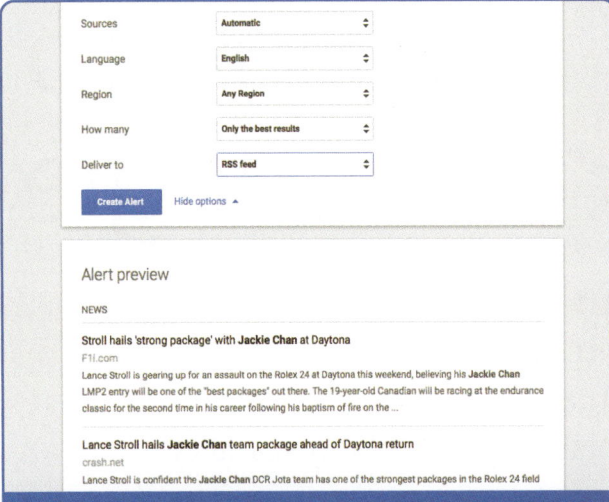

Manage Google Alerts

Users with Google Accounts can view, create, edit and delete their alerts using the Manage your Alerts page. Click on the Edit button and you will be able to alter any of the original settings using the simple drop-down menus. You can manage alerts for more than one email address by adding your other email address to your existing Google Account. To add an email address to your Google Account, visit your Google account page and use the Email addresses section.

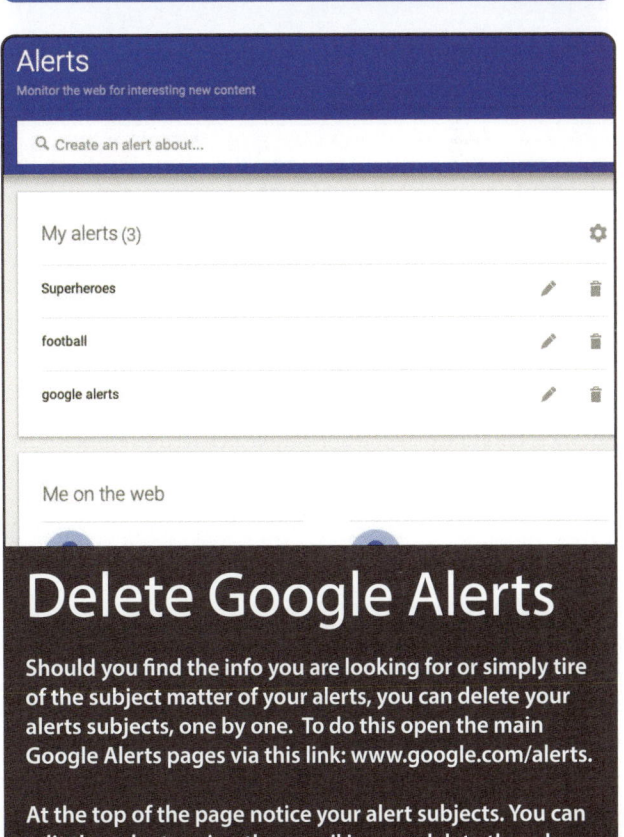

Delete Google Alerts

Should you find the info you are looking for or simply tire of the subject matter of your alerts, you can delete your alerts subjects, one by one. To do this open the main Google Alerts pages via this link: www.google.com/alerts.

At the top of the page notice your alert subjects. You can edit these by tapping the pencil icon or delete them by tapping the Bin icon. Please note you are not given any confirmation window, the alerts are deleted instantly.

www.pclpublications.com 25

Get Started with Google

How to Personalise Google Trends

The Google Trends app brings you the world's most popular search terms or topics. Breaking down the results by country and region, while also offering insights and keeping you updated to the latest trends. Users can also browse history data giving you a clearer view of the world's online habits.

Step 1
❱ Navigate to the Google trends website trends.google.com to be presented with this home page. This is a far complex application so be advised to take a few moments to get used to the layout and the control options you will find here.

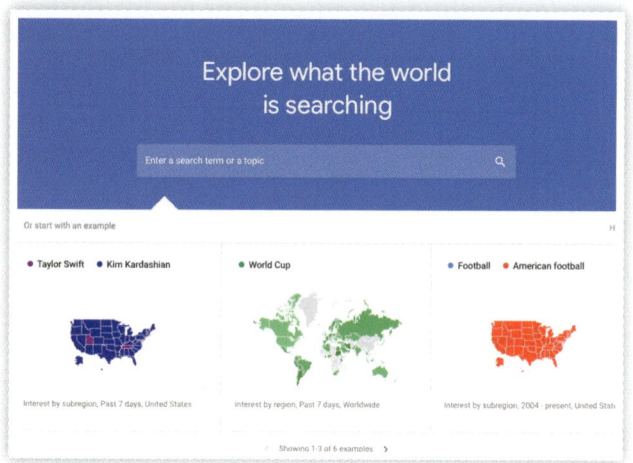

Step 2
❱ Scrolling down through the home page you will find the various options including latest stories, insights and updates, historical data and recently trending search results. We will look at all of these but to start let's focus on the main search bar.

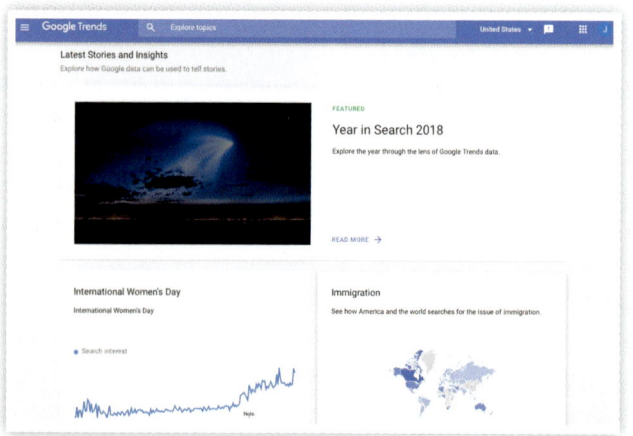

Step 3
❱ In the search bar, enter your term and click on the magnifying glass to activate your search. Some will bring a variety of different searches or similar terms, if this is the case a drop down menu will appear enabling you to select specifically for you.

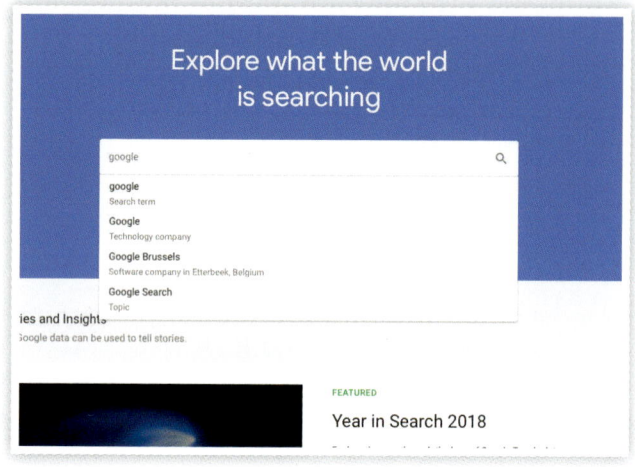

Step 4
❱ Your search will show your results as follows; location, time period, search type and category. You can adjust each of these as you wish to further focus your results. You may wish to check Shopping when looking for most popular selling item etc.

How to Personalise Google Trends

Step 5
❱ Your results will also be broken down by sub region for your area of search. With the most popular area listed first and so on. Notice that related searches and queries are also listed here. You can share each of these search results by clicking the share icon.

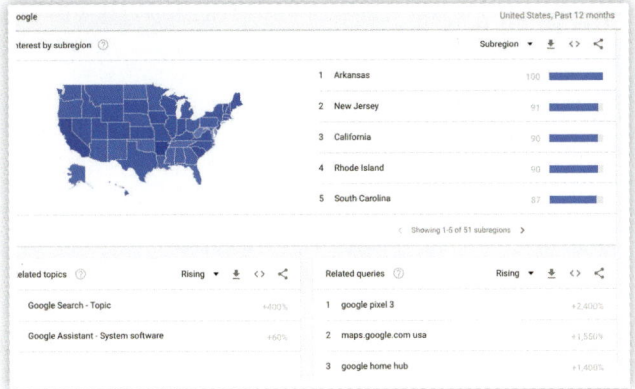

Step 6
❱ If you are looking for an online time machine, Google have one. On the home screen, scroll down and select the year you wish visit and you will be given the most popular search terms from that time period, spread across numerous categories.

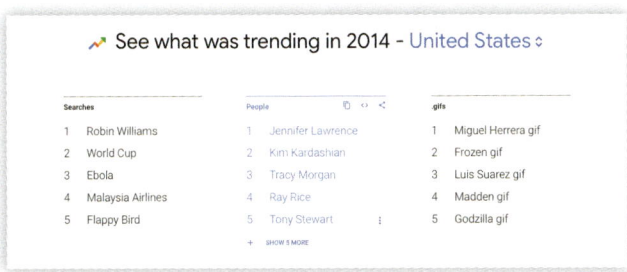

Step 7
❱ All the information found via this app can exported from the web browser to a large variety of spreadsheet software, including Microsoft Excel and Apple's Pages. To save your information as a csv doc click the download icon.

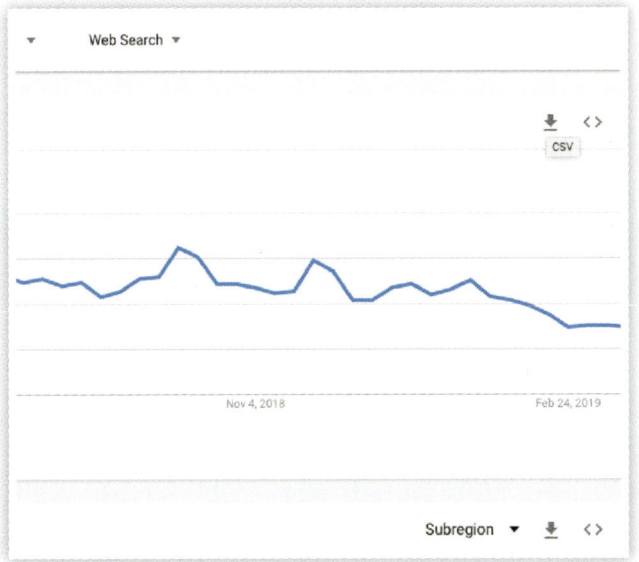

Step 8
❱ One of the best features of this app is the ability to compare two topics and how the results match up with one another. You can add various terms to compare and once again these results can be downloaded as a csv doc or shared via the linked icons.

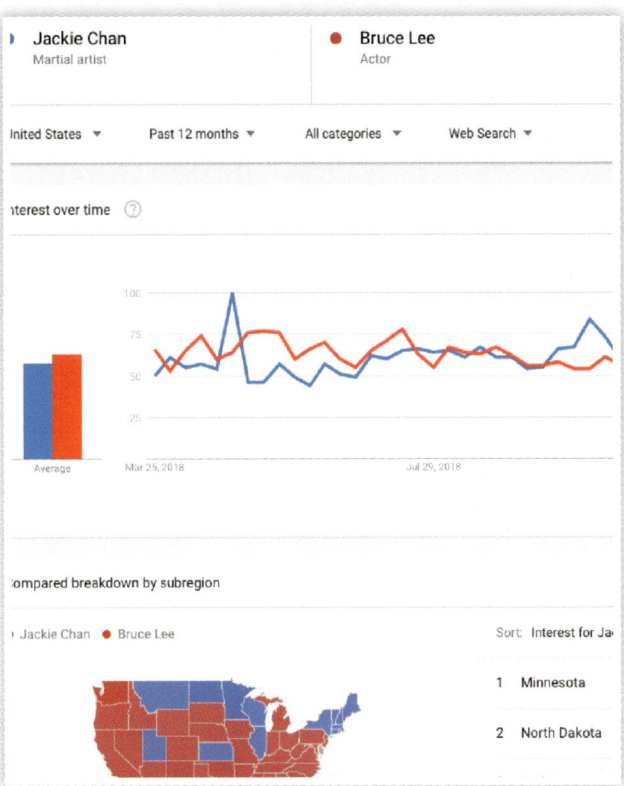

Step 9
❱ You can also subscribe to a regular (weekly or monthly) email which will send you updated data based your key search terms, to sign up click the + icon bottom left and enter the terms you wish to follow. Now simply wait for your email update to arrive.

www.pclpublications.com   27

Get Started with Google

Getting Started with Chrome

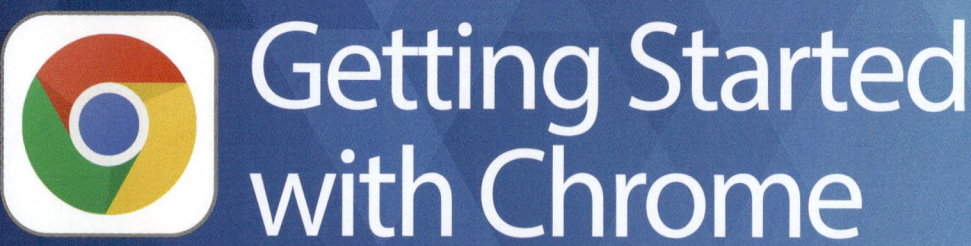

Google Chrome is much more than an alternative web browser. If you are looking to use the Google app suite to any degree we strongly advise you to download Chrome now!

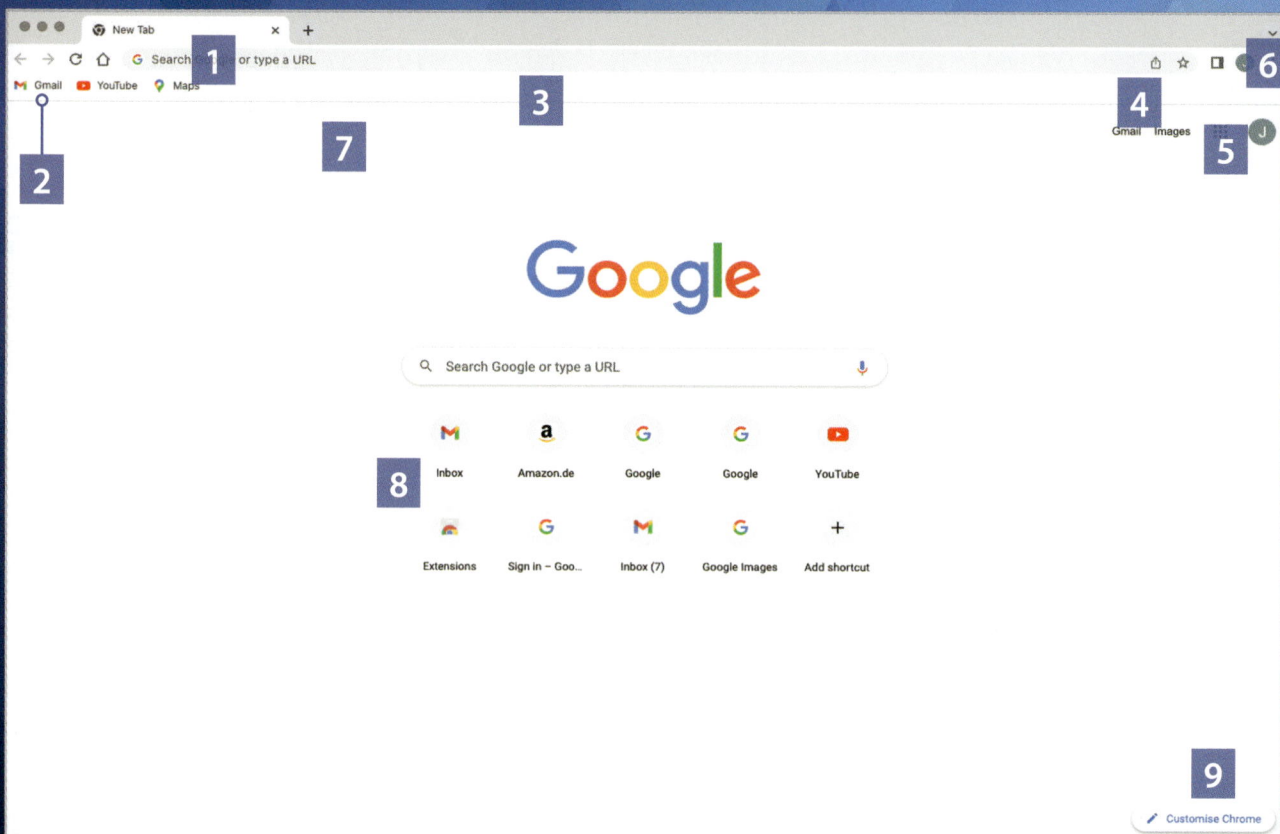

1 Tabs
❱ Just like almost all other browsers, Chrome lets you open multiple web pages at once and display them in tabs. Simply click on any tab to display the page. To add a new tab, click on the small tab to the right of the last one. To remove a tab, click the small X on the right of the tab you want to close. You can also manage tabs from the Chrome options menu.

2 Navigation Controls
❱ From left to right, the main buttons you use when navigating web pages using Chrome are: Back, Forward, Refresh and Home. Click and hold on both the Back and Forward buttons to see your recent navigation history. The Home button may not be displayed here on a brand new install of Chrome but you can turn it on in the settings (Appearance > Show Home Button).

3 Omni Box/Address Box
❱ This is where the URL of the current website is shown. You can use the Omni box to either type a full URL or type a search term. Type a URL and press Return and that web page will open. If you type a search term, Google search results will be shown instead. You can change the default search engine that is used in Settings > Search.

4 Bookmark Button
❱ Clicking on the star while viewing any web page will open a small bookmark option window. This allows you to choose a name for the bookmark, as well as selecting where to save it. If the star is golden, that means you have already bookmarked the page you are viewing. By using the Bookmark Button you will be able to compile a listing of all your favourite websites in a single place.

Getting Started with Chrome

5 Extensions
❱ Many different pieces of software will add extensions to the browser, allowing you to perform specific tasks while viewing websites. The extension shown here is the AVG toolbar, installed as part of the AVG antivirus software. You can disable or remove Chrome browser extensions simply by right-clicking on the icon and choosing from the Action menu.

6 Chrome Options
❱ This is where you will find all of the controls and settings for Chrome, from basic display settings to advanced developer tools. You can also manage your bookmarks, extensions and search history from here. We will look at the Chrome Options in more detail later.

7 Bookmarks Bar
❱ This bar is turned off by default, so must be activated in the Settings if you want to use it. When saving bookmarks, you have the option to Save to Bookmarks Bar. Any pages saved to this will be shown as quick links in the bar. This is very useful for saving those websites you use most often. Depending on the length of the title you give the bookmarks, only about five or six links will be visible here; the remainder are displayed in a drop-down menu.

8 Shortcuts
❱ This section of the Google Chrome homescreen contains a fully customisable Shortcut links to your favourite websites and web apps. To add new shortcuts click on the link, bottom right. Then add the links name and the full url.

9 Customise Chrome
❱ If you have grown tired of the simple and clean look of the Chrome browser, click here. You can edit the background image, change your shortcut links to your most visited websites links and finally change the colour and theme for the entire browser window, including the controls and search bar.

Chrome System Requirements

Chrome is fairly lightweight, so it should run happily even on an old computer. Here are the bare minimum requirements for PC, Mac, Smartphone & Tablet users.

Operating System: Windows 10 or later, macOS High Sierra 10.13 or later, 64-bit Ubuntu 18.04+, Debian 10+, or Fedora Linux 32+, Android 7.0 Nougat, iOS 14 or later.
Free Disk Space: 153MB

Installing Chrome

You may find that Chrome is preinstalled on many new computers but if not, here is how to install it yourself.

Step 1
❱ Visit www.google.co.uk/chrome/browser/desktop/index.html and click on the Download Now button to get the Chrome installer. You can choose to make Chrome your default browser at this point or you can change that setting later.

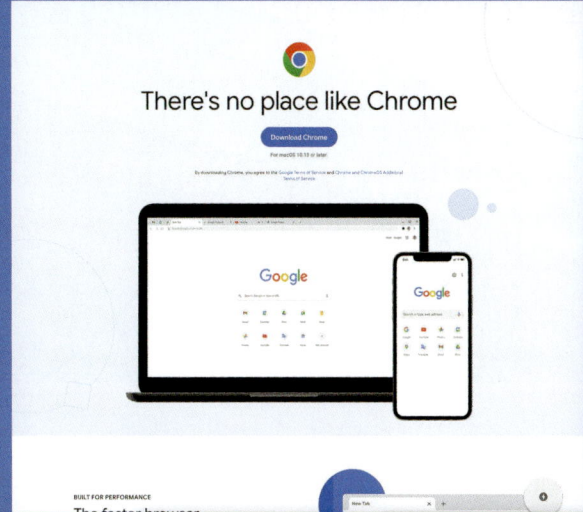

Step 2
❱ Once the download is complete, Chrome will install automatically. When the installation is complete, a Chrome browser window will open, giving you the opportunity to take a tour of Chrome's main features; and that's it, simple eh?

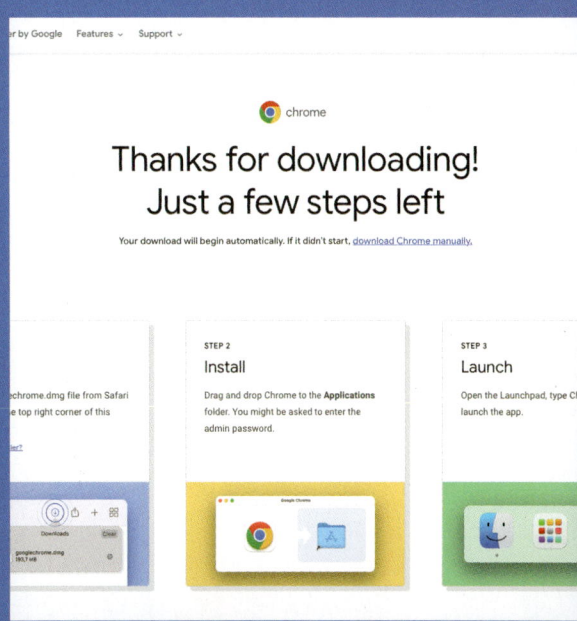

Get Started with Google

Customising the Chrome Browser

There are many different ways you can customise your Chrome experience, from adding extensions to setting the default home page. If you really want to make Chrome personal to you, there is no better way than adding a theme.

Changing the Theme

Step 1
❱ Open Chrome on your computer and click on the Chrome Menu button in the bottom right corner. Look for the Chrome options link, click this and select Settings and this window will open.

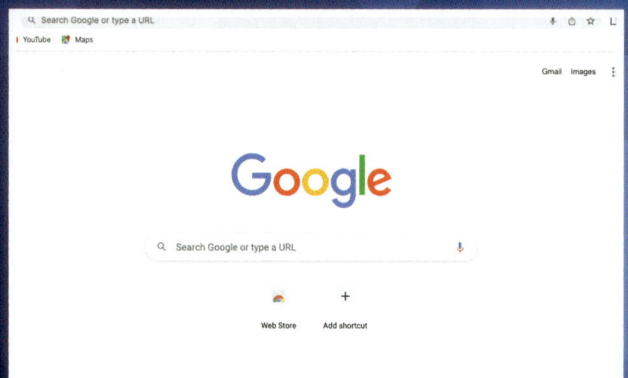

Step 2
❱ From this link you will open the basic customisation options of Chrome. From this pop up you can change the Chrome Browsers' Background image, Chrome's web Shortcuts and the Colour and theme. Click on each option and make your choice, we advise to set your Shortcuts to your Most-visited sites, for ease of use.

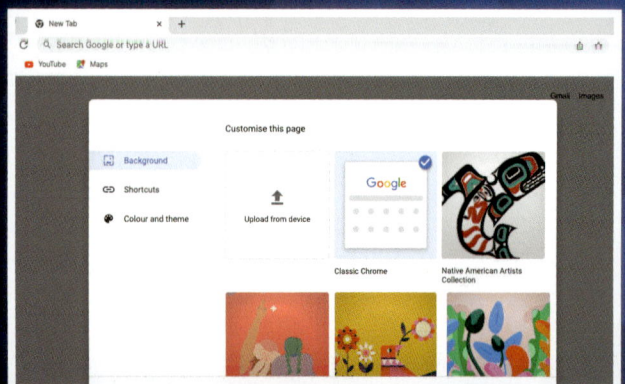

Step 3
❱ For more indepth customisation options, retrun to the Chrome browser home page and select the Chrome Web Store link, which shows web apps and extensions. To view the available themes, scroll down to the left-hand menu and click the Themes link. A selection of themes will now be displayed on screen. Click on your choice to download it.

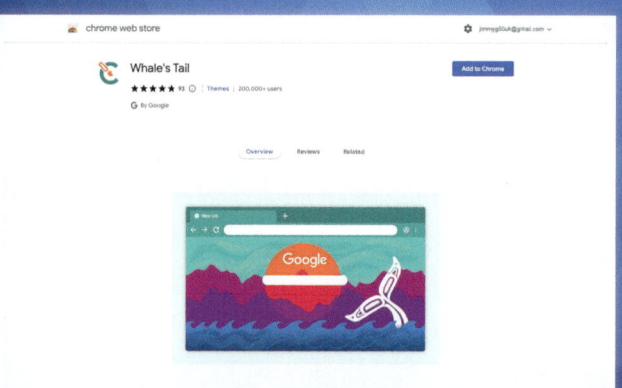

Step 4
❱ Themes you download aren't saved on your computer, so applying a new theme will overwrite the previous one. You can remove a custom theme at any time by clicking the Chrome options button, then selecting Settings. Under the Appearance heading you will see the option to Reset to Default Theme.

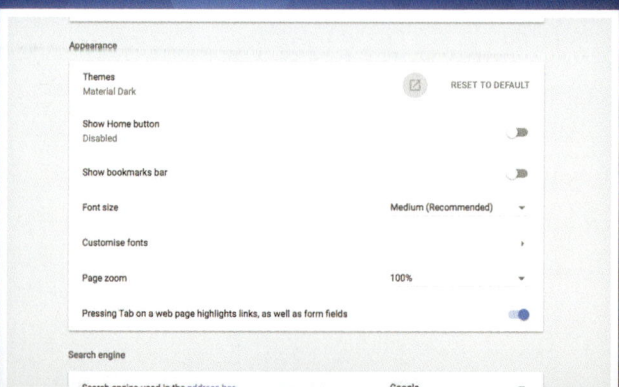

Customising the Chrome Browser

Change the Default Home Page

Chrome gives you several choices for what you see when you start it up. You may decide that you want to always open with the Google home page or you may want to show a selection of your most visited sites. All of these options are accessed through Options > Settings > On Startup.

Open the New Tab Page
❱ This option will display a grid of eight website thumbnails. Each thumbnail relates to one of your eight most visited web pages. Click on any of the thumbnails to go to the page. You can remove any of the thumbnails by hovering the mouse pointer over it and then clicking the X that appears in the top right corner.

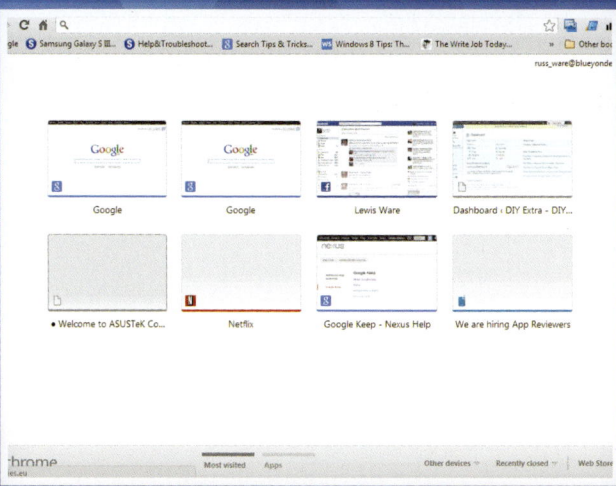

Continue Where I Left Off
❱ If this option is enabled, Chrome will always start up showing the website and tabs you were viewing when you last closed the browser. If you close all of the open tabs individually, rather than clicking the X at the top right to close the entire browser window, when you open Chrome again it will display the New Tab page.

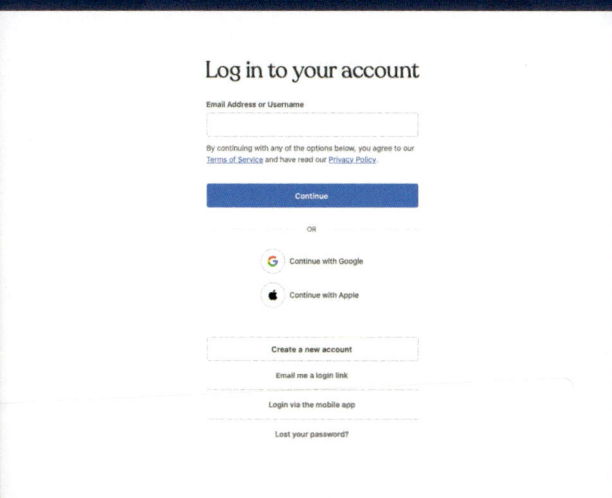

Open a Specific Page or Set of Pages
❱ You can use this option to set a single web page to open whenever you start Chrome. This could be the Google home page for your country, the Facebook login or any other web page you choose. You can also choose a set of pages to open. Click Set Pages and enter the URLs of the sites you want to open. They will each open in a separate tab when you start Chrome.

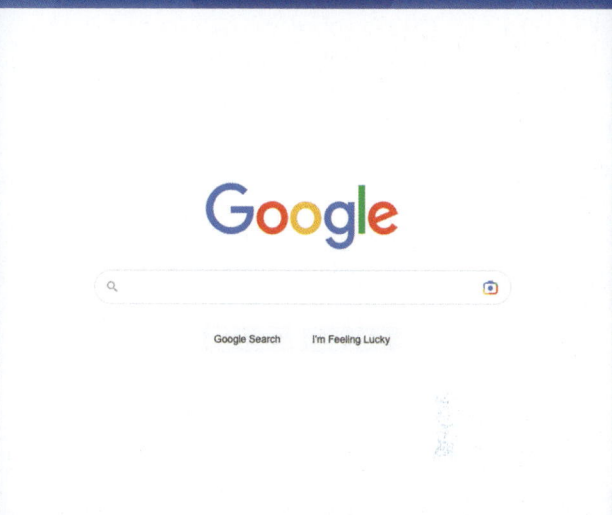

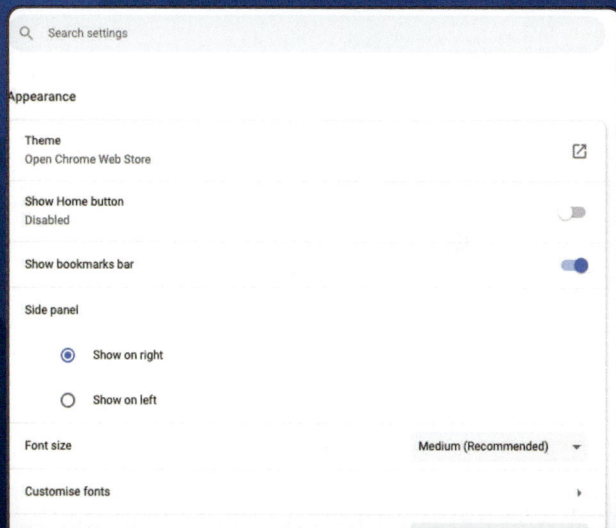

Show the Home Button

When you first install and use Chrome, you will probably notice that there is no Home button in the toolbar. We don't really understand why Google chose to hide the Home button but you can activate it easily, so it's not too much of a problem. To activate the Home button, click the Options button and select Settings. Under the Appearance heading, check the box next to Show Home Button. You can choose which page is displayed when the Home button is clicked (the New Tabs page or another of your choice).

Get Started with Google

How to Save and Sync Chrome

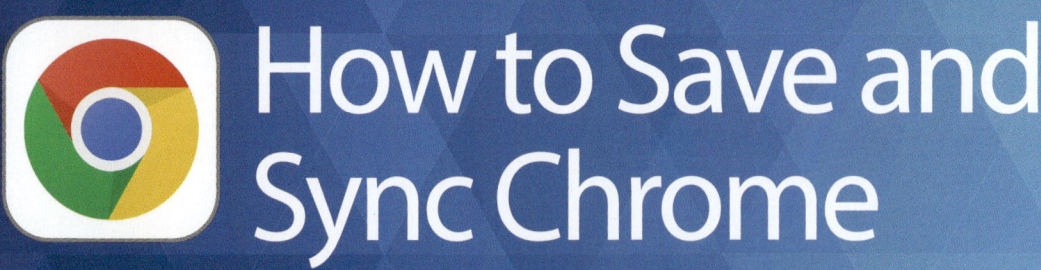

If you use Google Chrome on any device other than just your computer, the ability to sync the browser is a great feature. Chrome lets you save bookmarks, preferences, themes and even extensions and then share those changes with all your mobile devices quickly and easily.

Signing in to Chrome

Before you can sync your Chrome settings, you will need to sign in using a common Google account.

Step 1
❱ Open Chrome on your computer and click on the Chrome User button in the top right corner. Now follow the on-screen instructions and sign into your account. Click this and a new window will open.

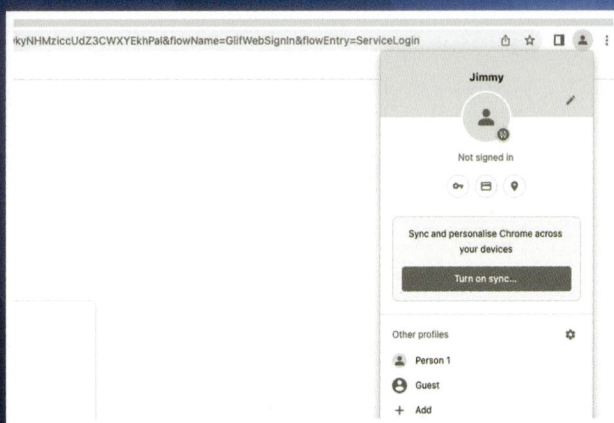

Step 3
❱ A Sync Settings windows should now open but if not, go to Chrome Menu > Settings > You & Google > Sync and Google Serives. Here you can select what is synced between devices. Click on Manage What You Sync and choose what to share.

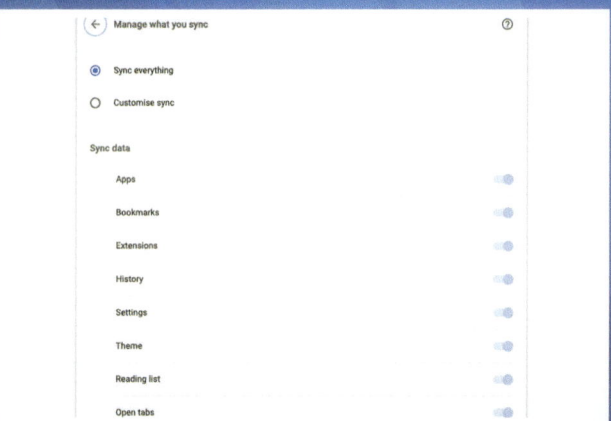

Step 2
❱ You will now need to sign in using the Google account that you use on your other devices (smartphones, tablets, etc.). You probably only have one account but if you have more than one, make sure you check this.

Step 4
❱ You can also choose to encrypt your synced data. By default, your Google Account password is used to encrypt saved passwords. If you want, change this to encrypt all your synced data and then create a custom passphrase for encryption.

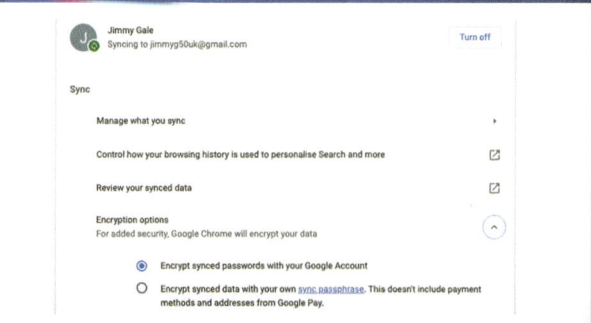

How to Save and Sync Chrome

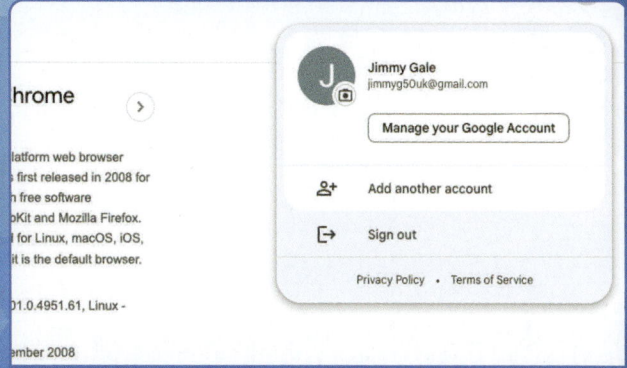

Signing Out of Chrome

You can disconnect your Google account from Chrome and stop syncing with your other devices at any time. Disconnecting your Google account won't wipe the data stored on your computer or in your Google account. However, any future changes you make on your computer will not be reflected on other computers or devices that you have signed in to Chrome on.

Syncing Open Tabs

You can disconnect your Google account from Chrome and stop syncing with your other devices at any time. Disconnecting your Google account won't wipe the data stored on your computer or in your Google account. However, any future changes you make on your computer will not be reflected on other computers or devices that you have signed in to Chrome on.

Step 1
❱ Before you can sync open tabs between devices, you will need to make sure that the setting is enabled on both devices. Sign in to Chrome using the same Google account on the devices you want to sync.

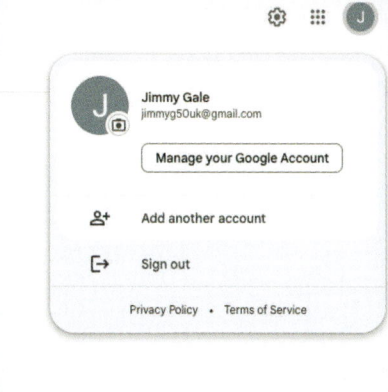

Step 2
❱ Check your sync settings on each device. Open the Chrome Menu > Settings, click the icon to the right of the Sync opinion and then check Open Tabs.

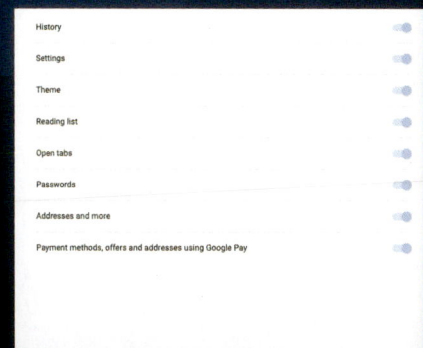

Step 3
❱ On Chrome for Android, tap the Menu button > Settings > Sign in to Chrome. Once signed in, tap Sync and make sure the Open tabs checkbox is selected. You should now be ready to go.

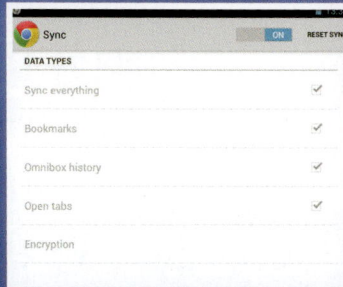

Step 4
❱ Open a new tab on your computer by clicking the New Tab button or Ctrl+T. In the lower right corner of the screen, click Other devices and click the tab you want to open on the current device.

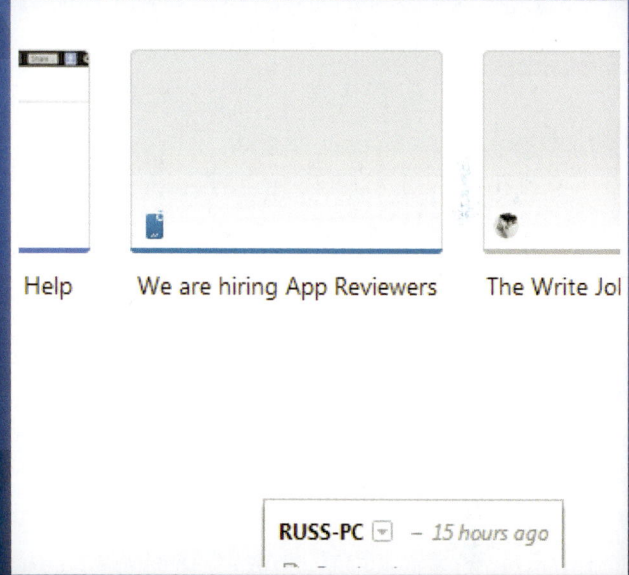

Step 5
❱ Open tabs are grouped together by devices. You can hide a specific one by disabling tab syncing on that particular device. To temporarily hide a device, right-click its name and select Hide.

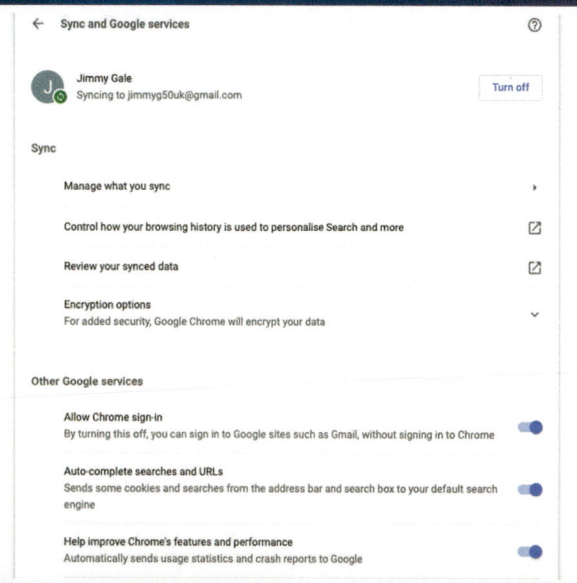

Get Started with Google

Using the Chrome Web Store

The Chrome Web Store gives you the option of adding thousands of different themes and extensions to your browser. Here's how to get started with apps and extensions on Chrome.

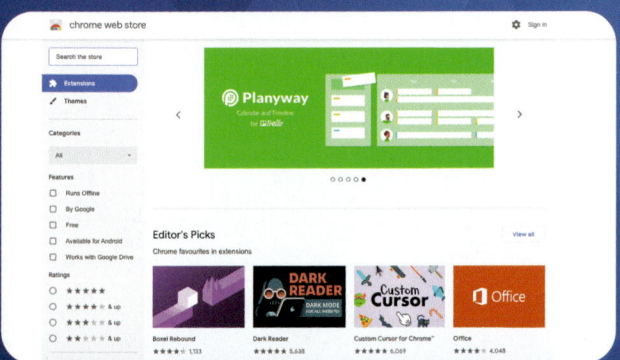

Chrome Themes

Chrome Extensions are web-based programmes that are designed to be used entirely within the browser. Using apps, you can do things like create documents, edit photos and listen to music, without having to install complicated third-party software on your computer. Themes on the other hand are purely aesthetic as they change the look of the Chrome browser and do not add any further functionality. Think of Themes as a way of injecting a little extra bit of your personality into your web browser.

Step 1

❱ You can access the Web Store easily by clicking on the Apps Icon in the top left area of the page when you start Chrome. The Apps page will slide into view, displaying any apps you currently have installed (Gmail and YouTube for example).

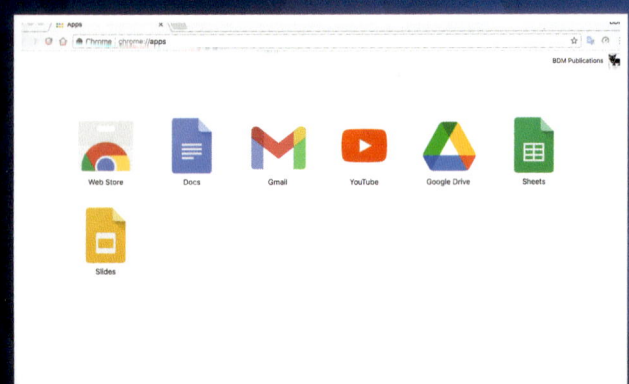

Step 2

❱ Click on the lower right side of the Chrome Web Store icon to open it. The web store home screen shows a selection of popular and trending themes. Roll over any of the images to read a short description. To see more details, click anywhere on the description or theme title.

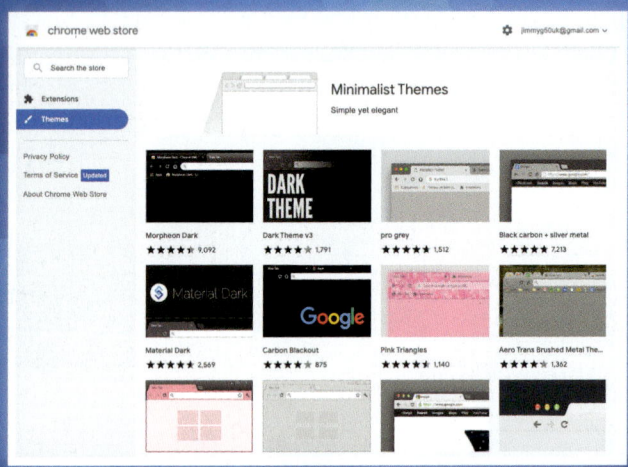

Step 3

❱ To install a theme, click on the Add to Chrome button. Your new theme will instantly install and be present within your current Chrome Browser window. You can also share themes with others by clicking on the Share button next to the Add to Chrome button; or Launch Theme button if already installed. Choose the Share method from the list.

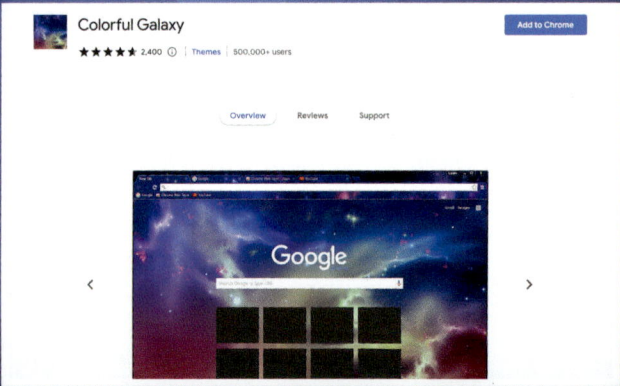

34 www.pclpublications.com

Using the Chrome Web Store

Chrome Extensions

Extensions are extra features and tools that you can add to Google Chrome. Using extensions, you can customise Chrome with the features you want or need, while keeping your browser free of things that you don't. Some extensions add buttons next to the address bar to let you know about certain events. For instance, you can use the Google Mail Checker to get alerts about new emails. Some extensions act like shortcuts. For example, if you use a feed reader, the RSS Subscription Extension lets you know if there's a feed for the site you're on. Click the small icon that appears in the address bar to quickly subscribe to the feed. Here's how to find and install extensions to Google Chrome.

Step 1

❱ You need to return to the Web Store, following the same process as previously covered. Once again the Apps page will be the first thing you view, displaying any apps you currently have installed. Unlike apps, extensions will not be displayed here.

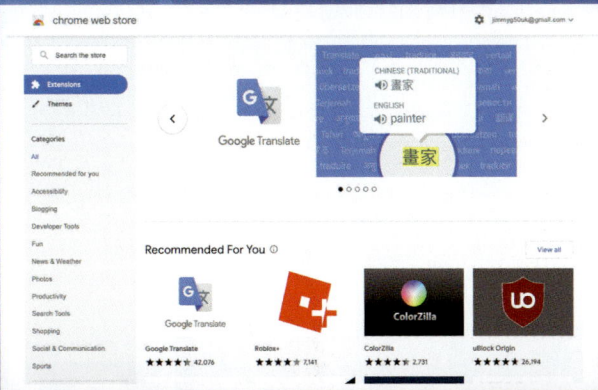

Step 2

❱ Click on the Chrome Web Store icon to open it. The web store Home screen shows a selection of popular and trending extensions and themes. To view available extensions, click the Extensions link at top left. An extended menu will then allow you to choose a category.

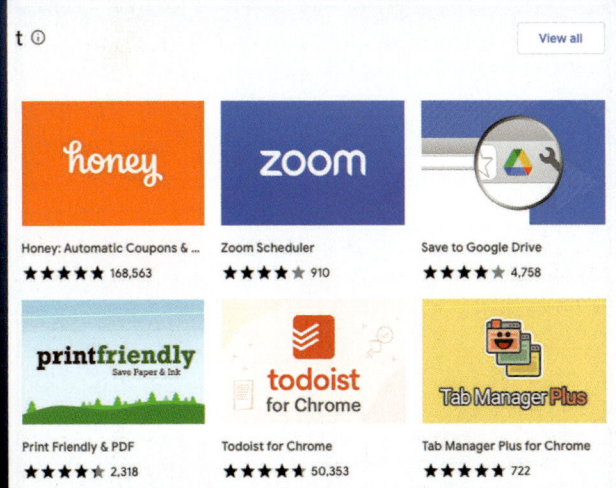

Step 3

❱ Roll over any of the extension images to read a short description. To see more details, click anywhere on the description or extension title. You can then read an overview, details, reviews and see related software. To install an extension, click on the Add to Chrome button.

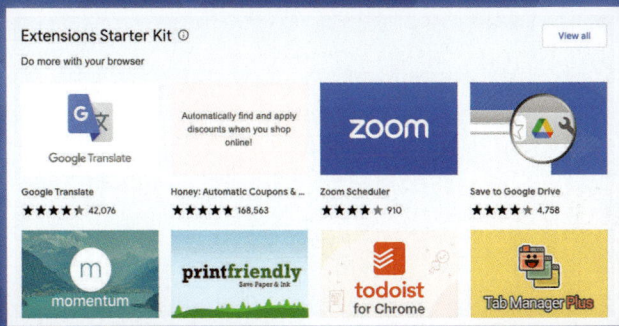

Step 4

❱ When you have confirmed you wish to save it, your new extension will be downloaded and appears as a small icon at the top right of the screen. To open this simply click on the icon.

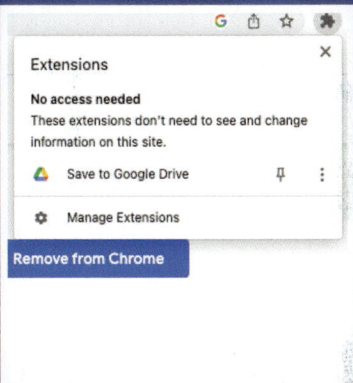

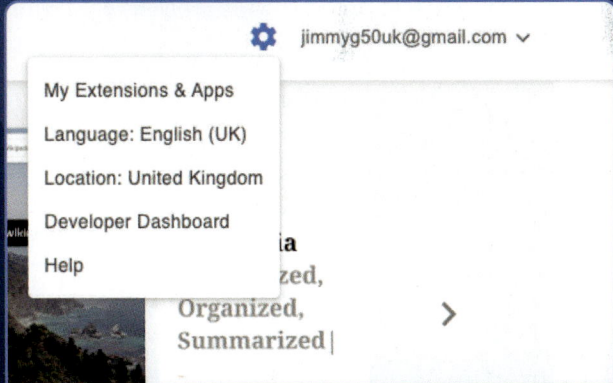

Manage the Toolbar

You can rearrange and customise how the extensions are displayed in the toolbar. To rearrange the icons, simply drag extension icons next to the address bar to rearrange them on the browser toolbar. If you want to see more extension icons on the browser toolbar, you can expand the extension icon area. Click the right border of the address bar and drag it to the left. Similarly, to hide extra extensions, extend the address bar by dragging its right border to the right. You can click the arrow button next to the Chrome menu to see your extra extensions (if they display icons).

Get Started with Google

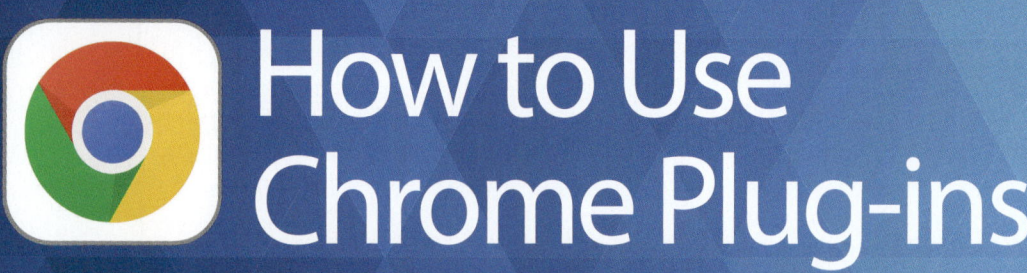

How to Use Chrome Plug-ins

Plug-ins are essential pieces of software that help the browser to read and display certain types of content. Unlike extensions, which add extra features to Chrome, plug-ins are essential to the smooth running of the browser. Here's how to check, install, block and disable plug-ins for Chrome.

Installing Plug-ins

Step 1
❱ Assuming that you allow websites to use plug-ins, if Google Chrome detects that you're missing a particular plug-in for a page you are trying to view, you will see a prompt to install the plug-in at the top of the web page.

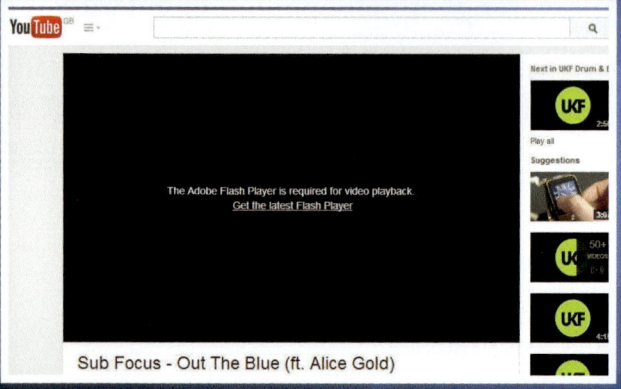

Step 2
❱ Click Install plug-in in the message dialog. Some plug-ins begin the installation process by downloading a setup file to your computer. For those plug-ins, make sure that you confirm the download by clicking Save in the downloads bar that appears.

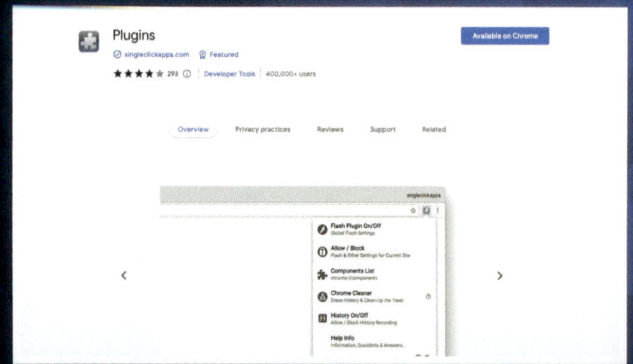

Step 3
❱ Once the download has finished, restart Google Chrome by closing all open windows to complete the installation process. This is an important step as Chrome needs to be restarted or it will continue to look for the plug-in you just downloaded.

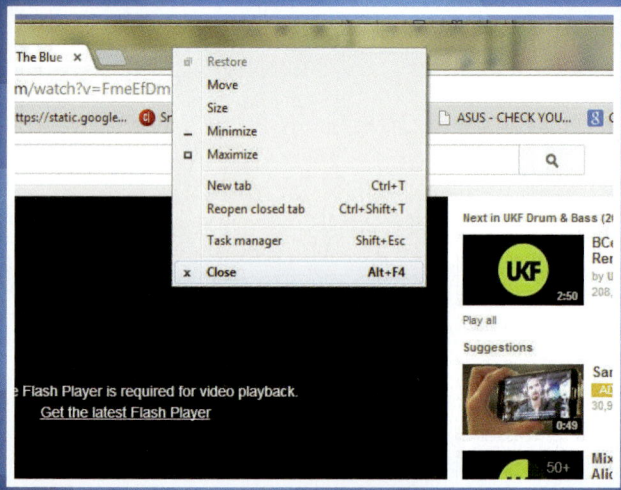

Step 4
❱ NOTE: It is not unusual that a previously installed Chrome Plug-in will require an update to enable functionality. These updates will require you to manually agree to re-install the plug-in, by downloading the new version, via the same process detailed above.

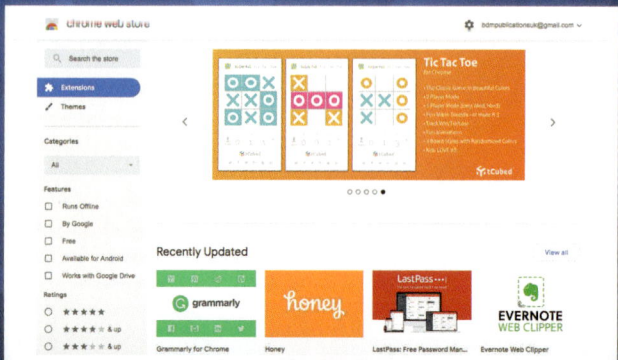

How to Use Chrome Plug-ins

Blocking Chrome's Plug-ins

Step 1
❯ Plug-ins are allowed by default. However, since they can occasionally be a security risk, Google Chrome blocks plug-ins that are outdated or not widely used. Examples include Java, RealPlayer, QuickTime and Shockwave. You can also block all plug-ins on a one by one basis.

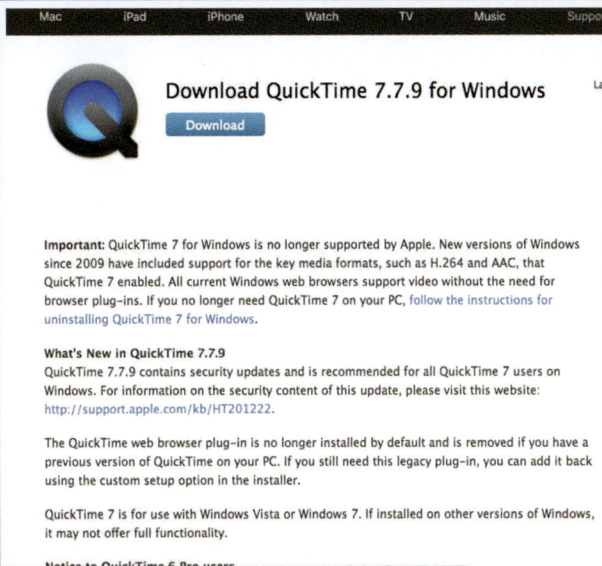

Step 2
❯ To block plug-ins, click the Chrome menu and select Settings. Click Show advanced settings and in the Privacy section click the Content settings button. Click the arrow to the right of the plug-in and select which sites you wish to block from its use.

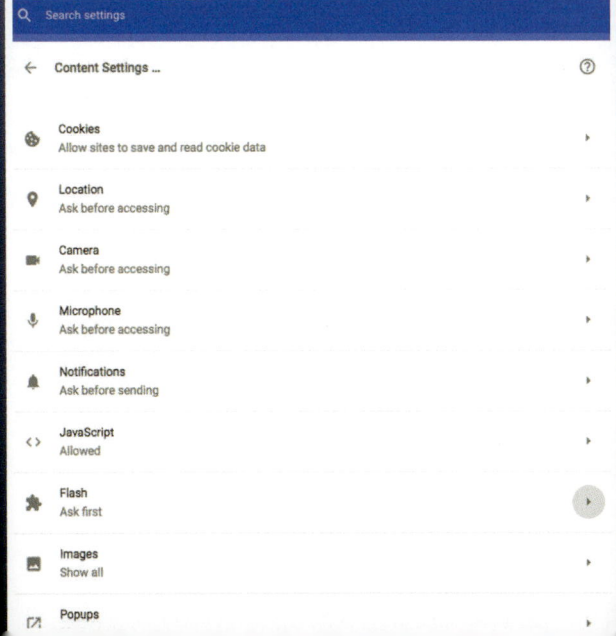

Step 3
❯ To block the website(s) that are causing you an issue with the a specific plug, such as Flash Player for example, click the Add button and enter the URL of the site that has issues and then Click Add again to complete the process.

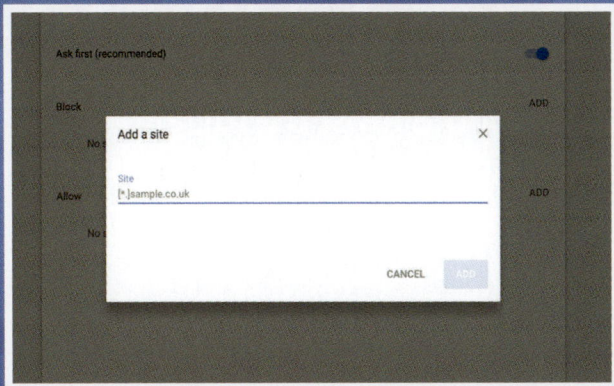

Step 4
❯ If you have used previous versions of the Chrome browser you may notice that you are unable to completely disable a plug-in in the current Chrome build. You are able to block plug-ins as detailed here and there is no limit on the number of sites you can add to the blocked list.

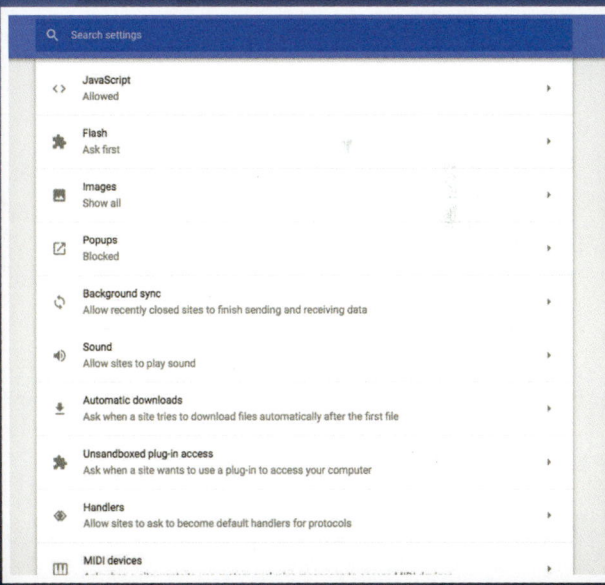

Chrome Plug-ins

Whether using Windows, Linux or Mac, Chrome supports many of the most popular and widely used plug-ins.

These include:

- Honey
- Java
- Real PlayerQuickTime
- Microsoft Silverlight
- Adobe Reader
- Windows Media Player
- QuickTime

Get Started with Google

Setting Up Chrome Autofill

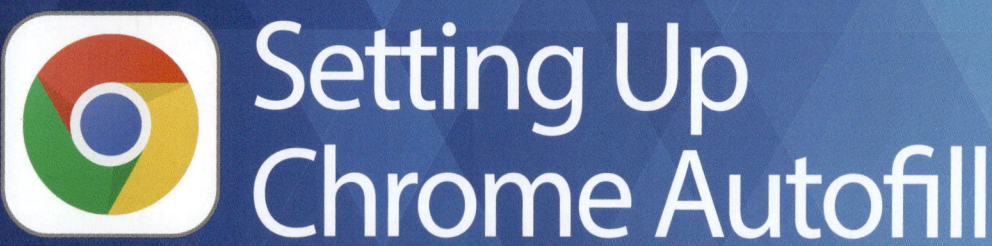

Some of the most useful features of Chrome, like Chrome Autofill, are easy to set up and can make browsing the Internet a much quicker experience, particularly if you find yourself forever filling out online forms.

Step 1
❱ The first time you fill out a form, Google Chrome automatically saves the contact information that you enter, like your name, address, phone number or email address, as an Autofill entry. You can store multiple addresses as separate entries.

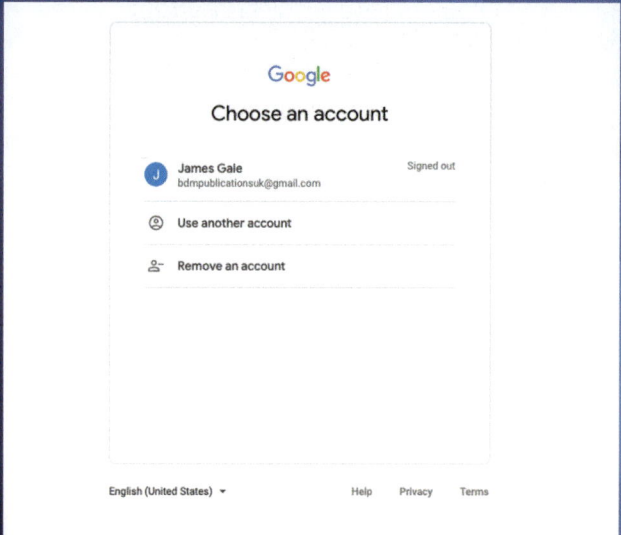

Step 2
❱ Chrome can also save your credit card information, with your permission. When you do this on a form, Chrome asks you at the top of the page whether you'd like to save the information.

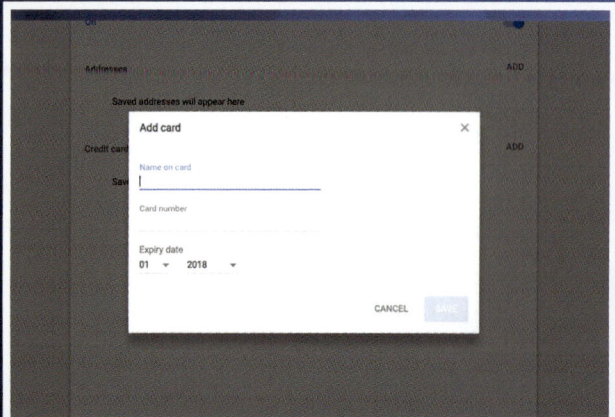

Step 3
❱ If your Chrome Autofill information is correct, you don't need to do anything more. If you have changed address recently, or some of the other information has changed, it can be frustrating for Chrome to keep suggesting the wrong info.

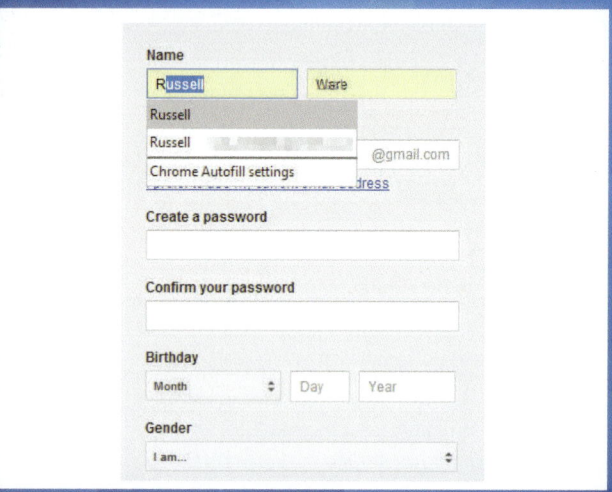

Step 4
❱ To manage your Autofill entries, open Chrome and click on the menu button in the top right corner (icon with the three dots in a column). Select Settings and then click Advanced at the bottom of the page. Find the Passwords and forms section and click Autofill settings.

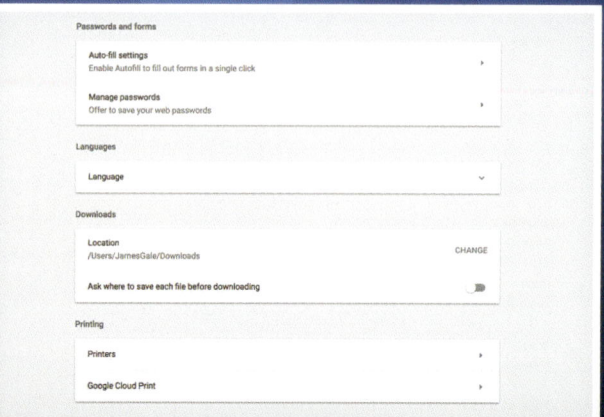

Setting Up Chrome Autofill

Step 5
❯ If you have more than one Autofill entry, click the one you want to edit and then click the Edit button that appears to the right of it. Complete or edit the information form and then click OK to finish. You can also Add a completely new address using the button here.

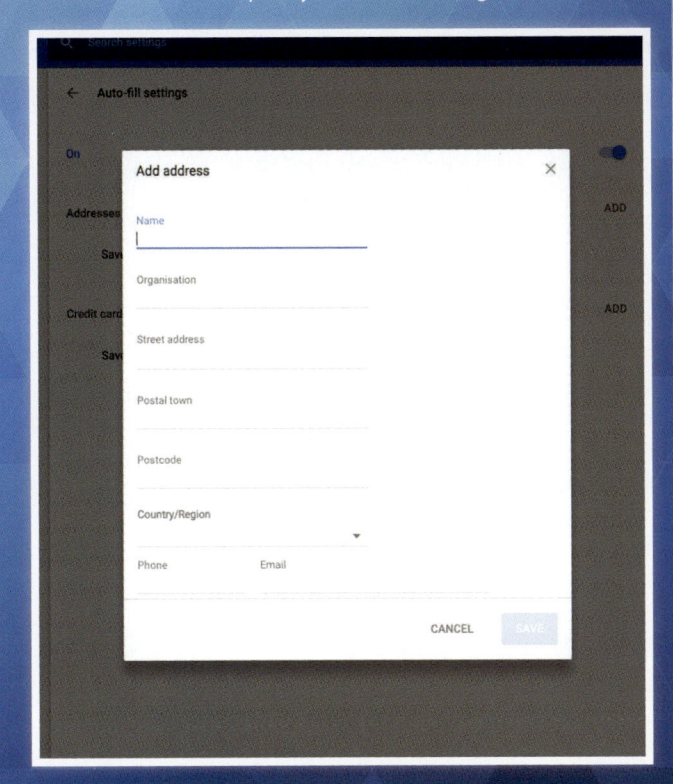

Step 6
❯ To remove an entry, click on it in the Autofill settings and then click the X that appears to the right of the entry. If you want to disable Chrome Autofill altogether, you can do so by unchecking the box next to the option in the Chrome settings.

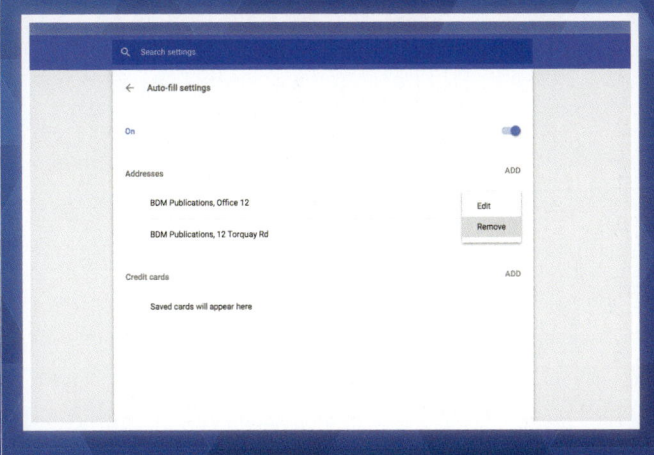

Step 7
❯ Now, when you start filling out a form, the Autofill entries that match what you're typing appear in a menu. Select an entry to automatically complete the form with information from it. This allows you to have multiple entries in Autofill.

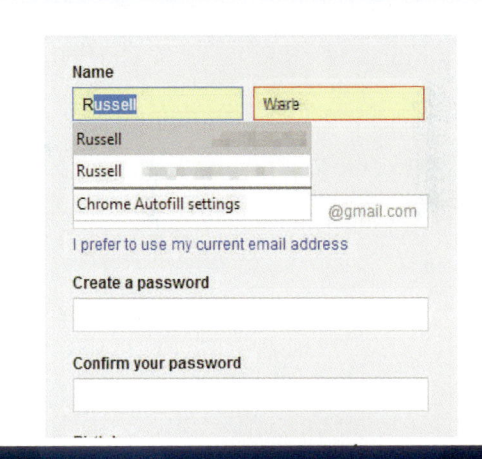

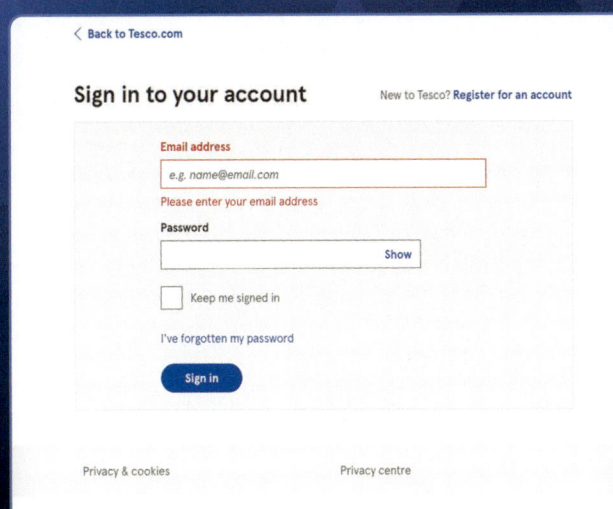

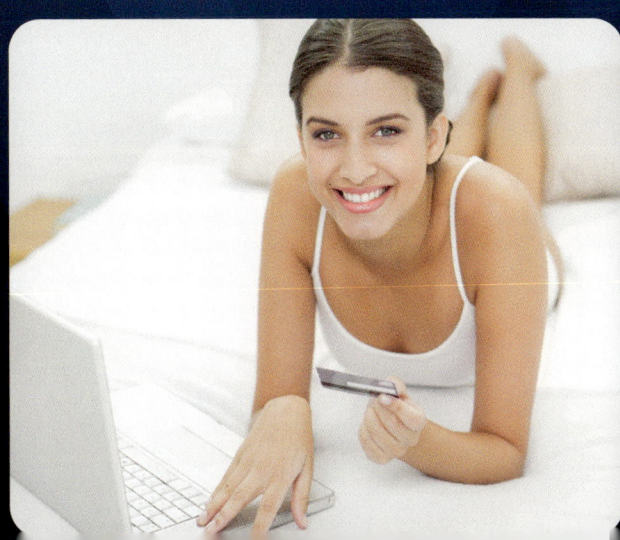

Trusted Sites

It's important that you use Autofill only on websites you trust, as certain websites might try to capture your information in hidden or hard to see fields. Some websites prevent browsers from saving text that you've entered, so Google Chrome won't be able to complete forms on those sites.

Get Started with Google

Chrome Tips and Tricks

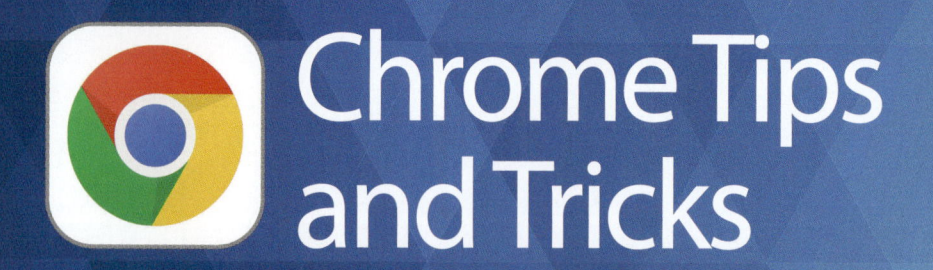

Even if you have been using Chrome for a while, there are probably dozens of tricks that you never even knew were possible. Here are a few tips and tricks to get you started.

Chrome-Casting Your Screen
❱ Have you ever been browsing online and stumbled upon a video, or photograph, that you want to share with those around you on the big screen of your family TV? With the additional purchase of a Google Chromecast you will be able to do just that, by casting content from your Chrome browser, on your desktop or mobile devices, to your TV. The quickest way to do this, on your desktop device, is by right-clicking on the Chrome window and then clicking on "Cast". On a mobile, tap the Three dot icon, top right of the Chrome app, and tap "Cast".

Incognito Window
❱ There are several ways to open a new incognito window for Chrome. If you have a Chrome shortcut pinned to the task bar, you can right-click it and select New Incognito Window. You can also click the Settings menu button at the top right of the browser window and select the same. The quickest way to do it however, is to use the keyboard shortcut Ctrl + Shift + N. Content displayed in an incognito window will not show up in your browser history, nor will cookies be saved.

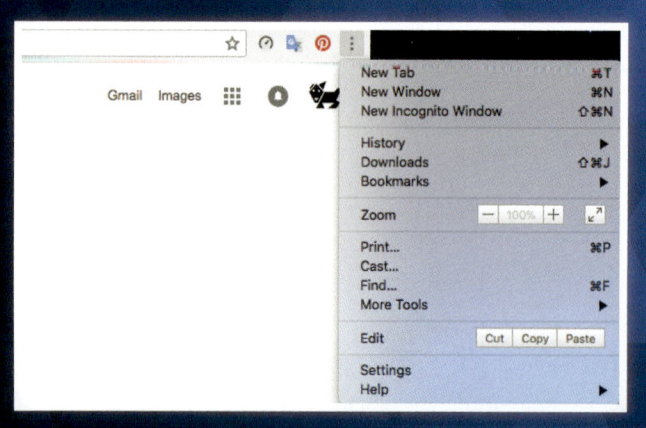

Chrome Keyboard Shortcuts
❱ There are several useful keyboard shortcuts for Chrome. Remember that the browser window must be currently selected for these to work.

Ctrl+Shift+N   New Incognito Window
Alt+Home   Load your Home Page
Ctrl+T   Open a new tab
Ctrl+Shift+T   Open most recently closed tab
Ctrl+Tab   Scroll through open tabs
Ctrl+J   Opens your downloads screen

Chrome Task Manager
❱ The Task Manager is a useful tool to see how much memory your currently open tabs and browser plug-ins are using. To open the task manager, right-click the top of the browser window and select Task Manager from the menu. Highlight one and click End Process to stop it running. You can also press Shift + Esc as a quicker way to bring up the Google Chrome Task Manager.

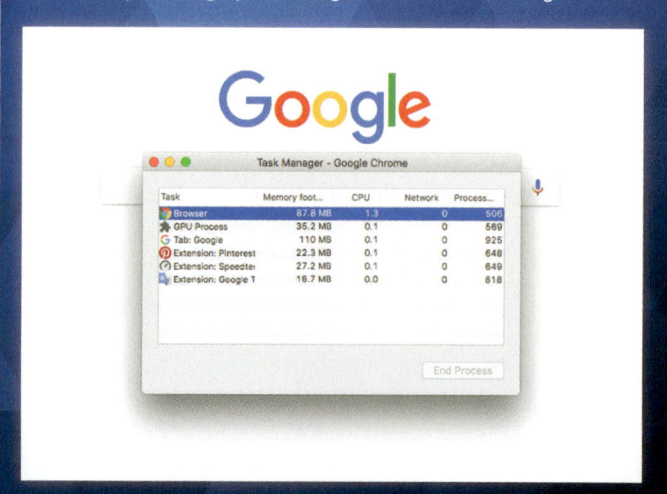

www.pclpublications.com

Chrome Tips and Tricks

Spring Cleaning
❱ To delete cookies, click on the menu button and go to Settings. Scroll down to the Privacy section, and click Content Settings. Now you can click Remove All or Remove Individual Cookies. To clear more data such as the Google Chrome browsing history and cache, click the Tools icon and select Clear Browsing Data. To clear the most visited websites that appear on your Google Chrome Start page, you must clear your browsing history using the method already described. Clearing your Google Chrome browser history will also stop matches from previously browsed sites appearing as suggestions in your address bar.

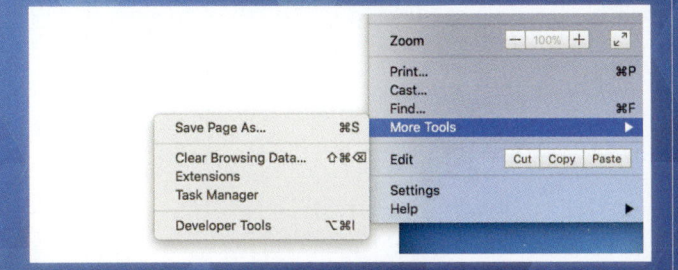

Adjust Text Size
❱ Having trouble reading small text on a page in Chrome? No problem! Chrome lets you easily zoom both in and out, increasing or decreasing the size of both text and images. You can do this a couple of ways. The first is to click the Settings menu button and use the Zoom controls you find there. An easier way to do it is to hold Ctrl and use the scroll wheel on your mouse to zoom in and out; as you do this, a small window will pop out of the address bar to show you the level of zoom.

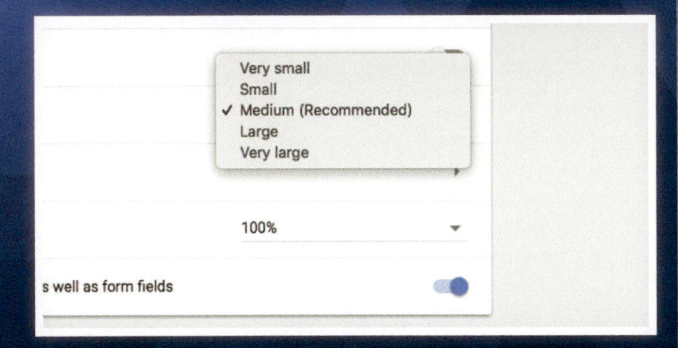

Rearrange Tabs
❱ If you have several tabs open in Chrome, you can rearrange them easily by simply clicking on a tab and dragging it along the row to the position you want. If you want to open one of the tabs as a separate window, click on it and drag it to the desktop. Release the mouse button and a new window will open. Right-click on any tab to see the tab options menu. Here you can reload tabs, close all tabs to the right of the selected one and even reopen closed tabs (Chrome remembers the last ten closed tabs).

Pinning Tabs
❱ Another useful thing you can do with tabs is pin them. Pinning tabs means that whatever is shown on the tab when it is pinned will automatically be loaded when you next open a new Chrome browser window. To pin a tab, right-click on it and select Pin Tab from the menu. Pinned tabs appear smaller in the row than unpinned tabs. To unpin a tab, simply repeat the process and select Unpin Tab from the menu.

Start-up Preferences
❱ By default, when launching a new window in Chrome, the browser displays the New Tab page, which is a blank tab with links to your most visited websites. It is possible to customise this. Click the Settings icon and select Settings. Under the On start-up section, choose the 'Open a specific page or set of pages' radio button and click the Set pages link next to it. Then, either click 'Use current pages' or type an address to set an alternative home page.

Syncing Chrome
❱ With Chrome's sign in feature, you no longer need to fret about your bookmarks or apps being stuck on one computer. When you sign in to the Chrome browser or a Chrome device, your bookmarks, extensions, apps, theme and other browser preferences are saved and synced to your Google Account. You can then load these settings any time you use Chrome on other computers and devices. Signing into Chrome also makes using Google services, like Gmail, YouTube and Maps easier since you generally only need to sign in once from your browser.

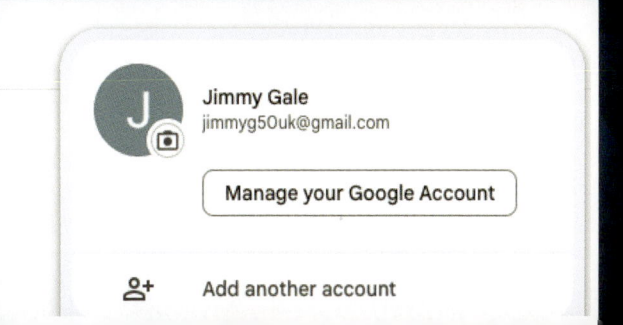

Using Google Apps

Using Google Apps

The Google app suite contains some of the world's most popular and widely used applications. Offering alternatives to operating staples such as email, maps, calendar, photo editing and so much more. Having set up your Google account, you can then access the entire suite for free. Over the following pages, we will take you through our expert tips to ensure that you make the very best of each one.

Using Google Apps

Get Started with Gmail

Gmail is an integral element of the Google app suite, an email platform that works seamlessly on whichever OS you use, quickly becoming a key part of your daily routine.

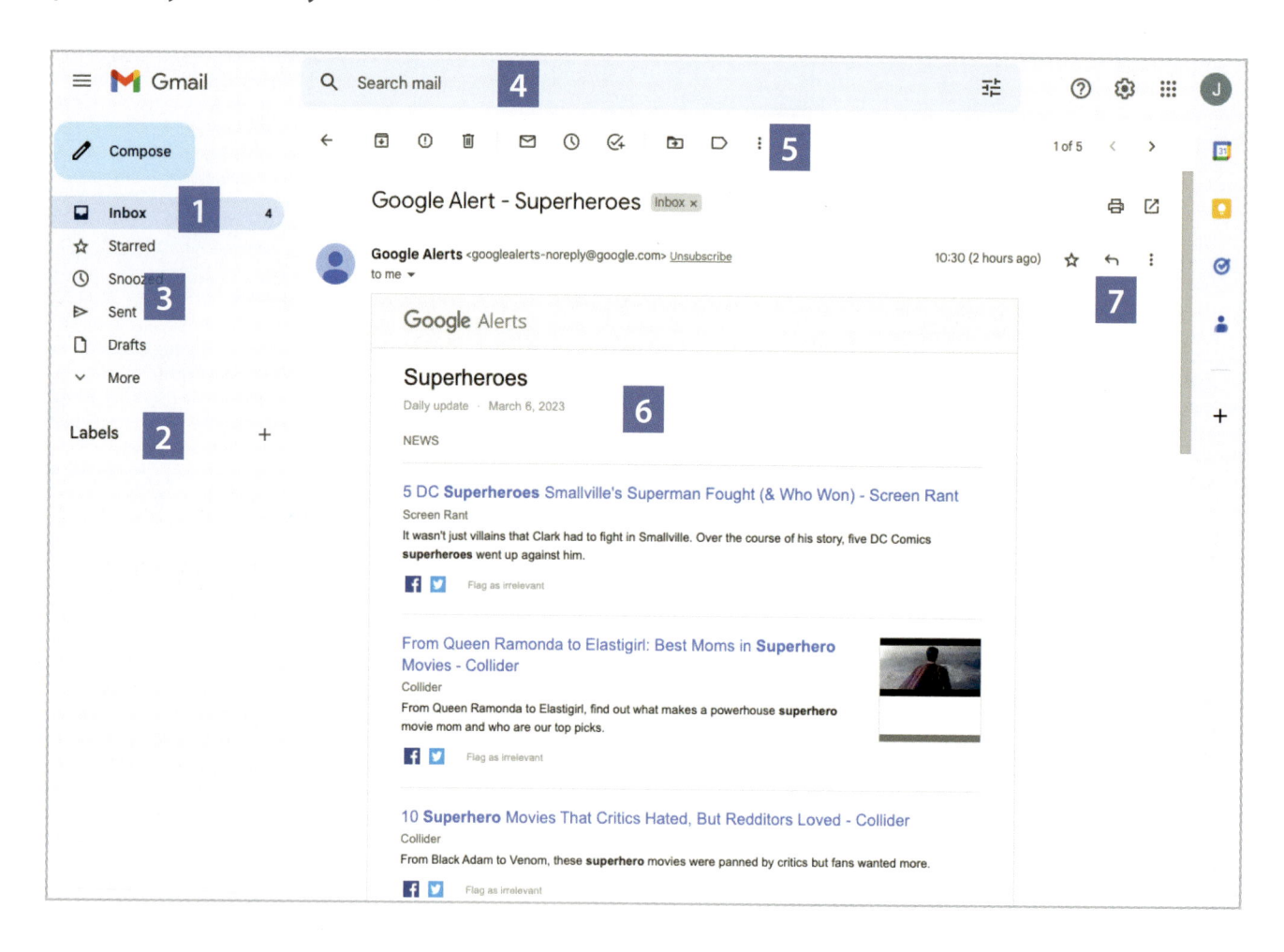

Creating a Gmail Account

You can either connect a Gmail account to your main Google account or you can create a completely new account from scratch. If you connect an account, you will be able to use your new Gmail address or your original Google account email to sign in.

1 Mailboxes
› These links let you display the messages in those mailboxes. A number next to any mailbox shows the amount of unread messages, rather than the total amount in the mailbox.

2 Labels
› Labels allow you to categorise your messages into various pre-set or custom folders. You can save messages under more than one label for better cross-referencing.

Get Started with Gmail

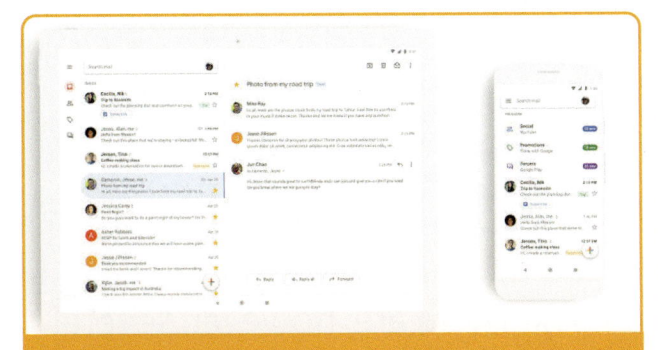

Gmail on Android & iOS

You can download the Gmail app for mobile devices, free of charge, from the Play Store or App Store. This allows you to use Gmail on the go.

Once downloaded, the app should automatically sign in using the same Google account details you entered on your computer (hopefully, this is also the one with which you set up your Android or iOS device).

You will now be able to see all of the folders and emails you use and have sent/received on your computer, albeit on your smartphone or tablet.

3 Chat Controls

❯ This section shows a list of your available Chat contacts, as well as containing the various chat controls: Add Contact, Status Update, etc. You can read more about Gmail Chat later.

4 Search Box

❯ Search for any message or contact in your Gmail inbox. Clicking on the small arrow at the end of the search box allows you to refine your search in several different ways.

5 Message Controls

❯ This set of buttons only appears when viewing a message. They allow you to archive, delete or report the message as spam, as well as letting you move the message to a particular mailbox or apply a label. The More button reveals more controls.

6 Conversation

❯ Gmail displays multiple messages from a contact in a conversation format. If someone replies to your message, both the reply and the original message are shown stacked in the window. Expand the conversation to make it easier to read.

7 Quick Reply

❯ Click anywhere in this box to start a quick reply to the last message in the conversation. To Forward a message, click the Forward tab in the quick reply window that opens. Quick reply offers the same formatting options as a new message does.

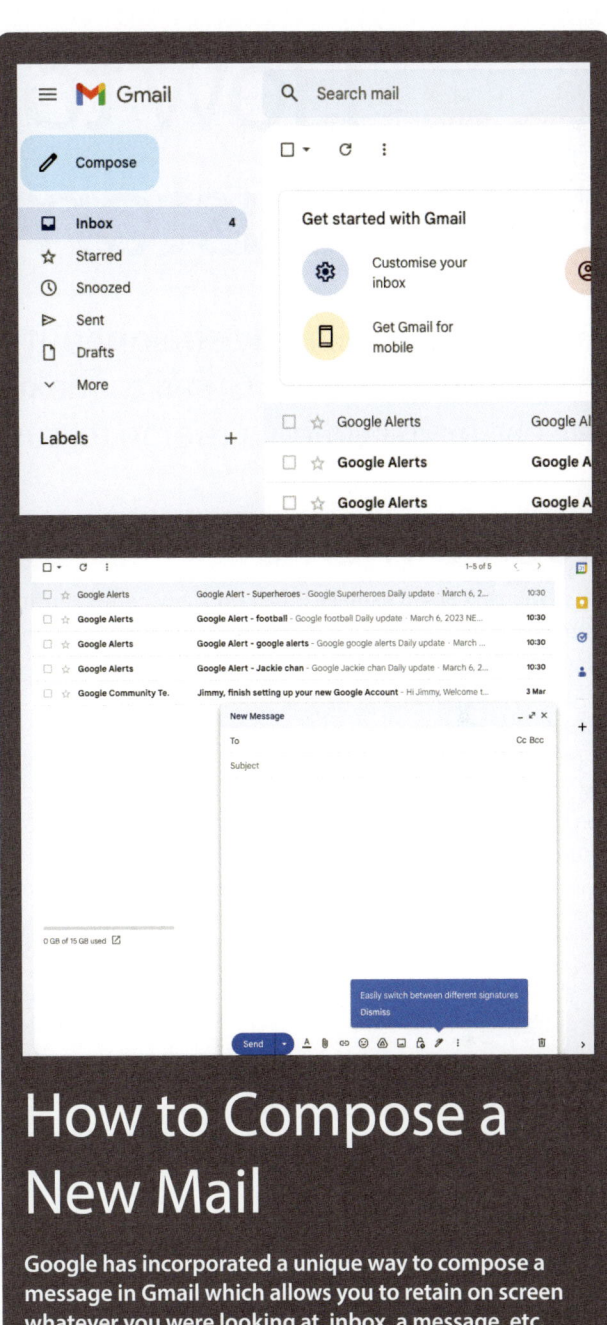

How to Compose a New Mail

Google has incorporated a unique way to compose a message in Gmail which allows you to retain on screen whatever you were looking at, inbox, a message, etc. while composing a new message in a separate window. At the time of writing, this was still an optional feature but could be made standard at any time.

To activate this compose window, click the Compose button and a new window will open at the bottom right of the Gmail window. Whatever you were viewing before you clicked Compose will remain on screen but you can click through into a different mailbox or open a message without the compose window disappearing.

The new compose window contains many of the options. Click in the To field and start to type a name or email address to see a list of known contacts. The icons at the bottom let you control formatting and attachments. If you want to switch back to the old compose method, click the Send icon at the bottom of the window.

www.pclpublications.com 45

Using Google Apps

How to Customise Gmail

Gmail works brilliantly straight out of the box. There are, however, several things you can do to Gmail to make it suit your personal preferences more closely, from adding a theme to customising the layout of the inbox.

Apply a Theme

OK, so this isn't going to make Gmail work any better, run any faster or deliver emails in a different way but it does brighten things up a bit and makes Gmail more personal to you.

Step 1

❱ Sign in to Gmail on your computer and open the main inbox. In the top right corner of the page you will see the Settings icon (the gear icon). Click this and select Themes from the listings displayed on this page.

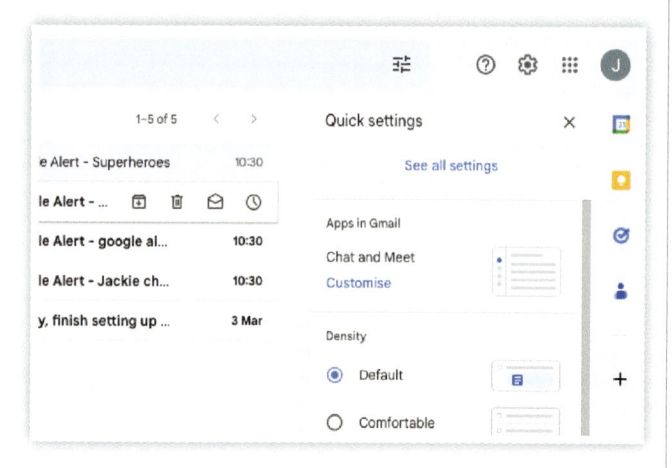

Step 2

❱ The available themes are split up into categories, with basic colour themes at the top of the page, then HD themes that use background images, custom themes and classic Gmail themes.

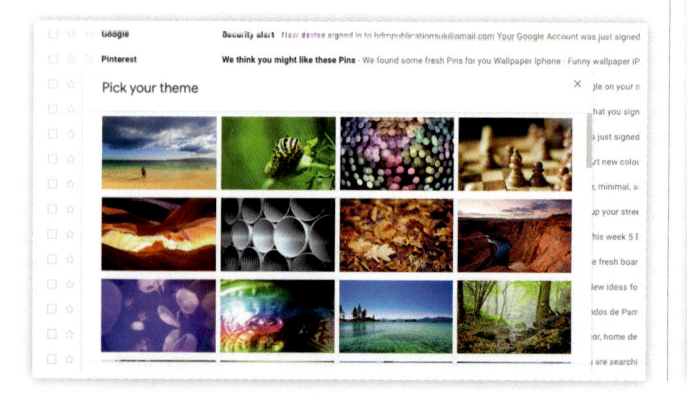

Step 3

❱ Click on any theme to activate it. You will see the background change, allowing you to preview the theme without leaving the themes page. If you find one you like, simply select it and then click back to the inbox.

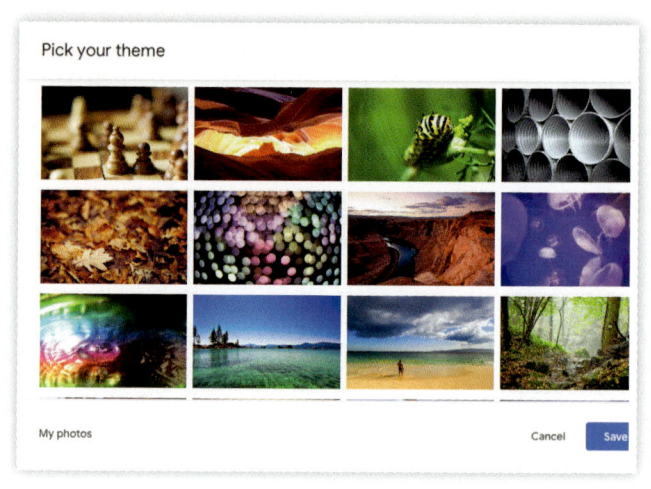

Step 4

❱ Custom themes let you get a bit more creative. Click on either Light or Dark custom and then choose an image. You can use a preselected image or use one of your own via My Photos.

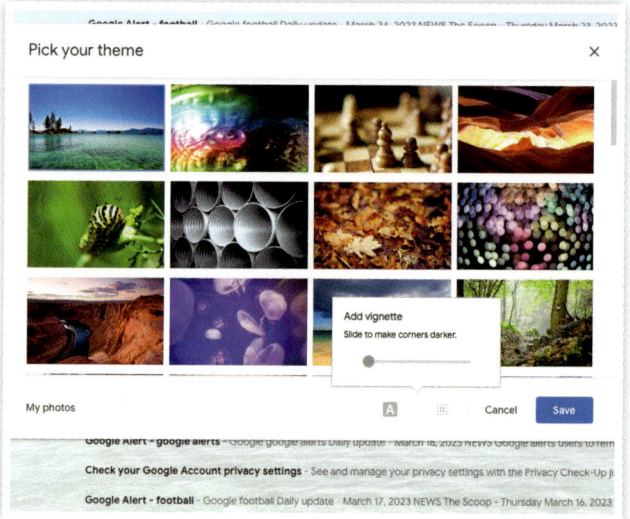

How to Customise Gmail

Step 5
❱ Once you have Chosen the Theme you wish to show on your Google Mail page, you can also add a customisable level of blur to the image which may make some text easier to read. To do this click the third icon to the right of the Cancel button.

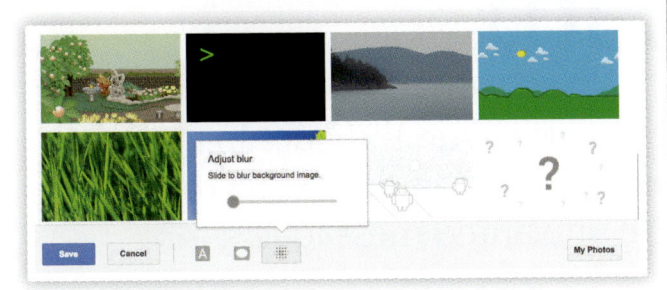

Customise the Inbox
You can easily customise the main inbox to show important or starred emails in a separate section at the top of the page.

Step 1
❱ Log in to Gmail and click on the main inbox to select it. With the main inbox displayed, hover the mouse pointer over the inbox label and you should see a small, down-pointing arrow.

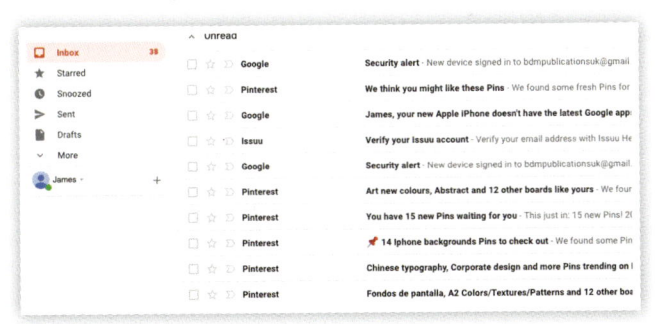

Step 2
❱ Click on the arrow to see a small menu. Here you can choose the way emails are displayed in the inbox. Roll over each of the settings to read a short description of how they work.

Step 3
❱ Choose a display option and you will see the inbox split into sections. At the right-hand side of each section heading, another drop-down menu lets you further customise the section: number of emails to display, etc.

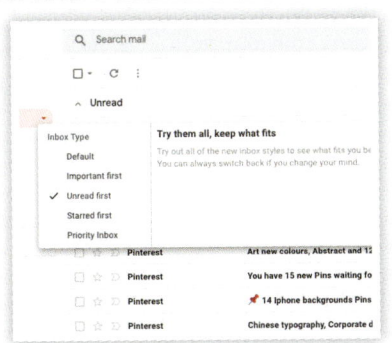

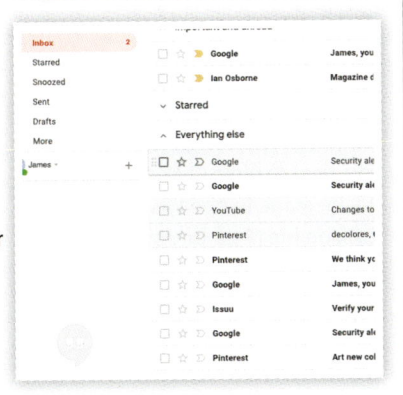

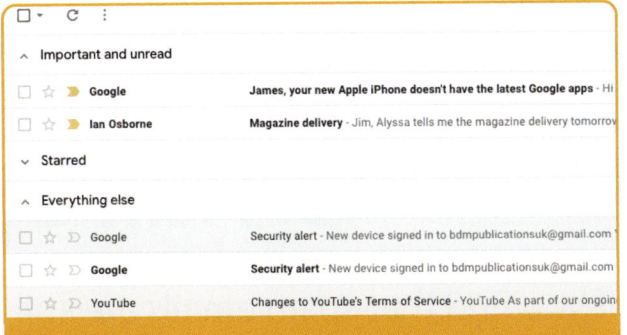

Importance Markers

How exactly does Gmail decide if an email is important to you or not? The answer, is very cleverly and sometimes with a bit of help from you. Gmail displays different coloured markers next to emails to indicate different types of messages. A yellow marker means that a message is important. An empty (white) marker means that the message is not seen as important.

If you want to know why a message was classified as important, you can hover your mouse over the importance marker in order to see the main reason why. To teach Gmail that messages from a certain contact are important, all you need to do is find an email from that person and click on the unfilled importance marker.

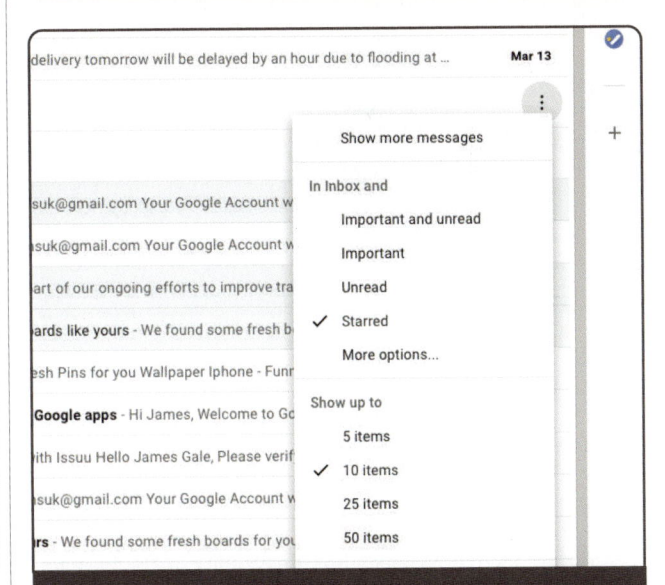

Show or Hide Labels

On the left-hand side of the Gmail interface is a list of your different mailboxes and labels. Preset mailboxes (or System Labels) include Important, Starred, Sent Mail and Drafts. It is useful to have links to your labels displayed here, but you can hide them if you wish. Click on Settings and then click on the Labels tab at the top of the page. You will see a full list of all your labels, with a show and hide link next to each. You can simply go down the list hiding those labels you don't wish to see in the sidebar.

www.pclpublications.com

Using Google Apps

Dealing with Gmail Spam

If you find that spam emails are still getting through the built-in filters and being displayed with your other emails, you can do several things to improve detection and removal of these unwanted messages.

Do I Need to Worry About Spam Emails?

That's a good question with a potentially very long answer, but in short, yes, spam email is best avoided. Junk or spam emails are unsolicited/requested messages sent in bulk by email.

Email spam has steadily grown since the early 1990s and by 2014 were estimated to make up around 90% of email messages sent. Most spam email messages are commercial in nature and albeit harmless, they are annoying. However, some can also be dangerous because they may contain links that lead to phishing web sites, or sites that are hosting malware, or include malware as file attachments.

With this in mind, it is always best to approach spam with caution and following this guide will better equip you to avoid spam as a whole.

Report and Remove Spam

Step 1
❯ Removing spam from your inbox is easy. Click on the message you want to remove and look for the ! button above the message box. Clicking this will remove the spam message and report it to Google.

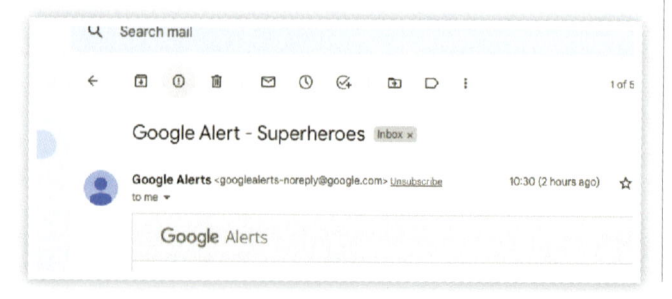

Step 2
❯ If you want to remove the spam that is collecting in the spam mailbox, the spam mailbox will only appear in your labels when spam has been detected and moved into it, click the mailbox and then click "Delete all spam messages now".

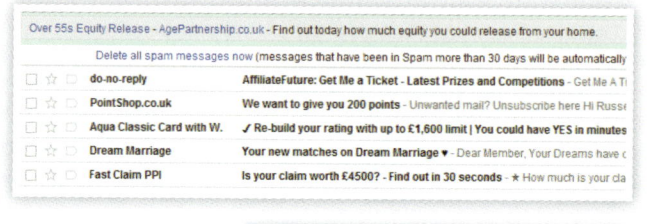

Step 3
❯ If you see a message in the spam mailbox which has been moved there incorrectly (i.e. it is not spam), you can correct the mistake by selecting it and clicking Not Spam from the options above it.

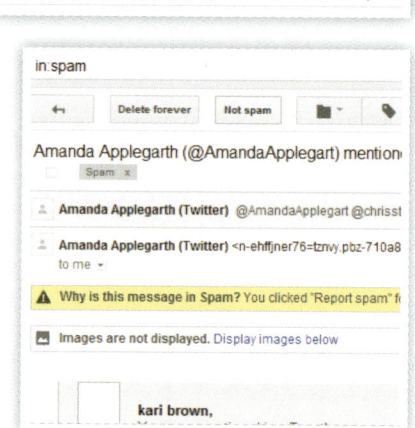

Creating Filters

Another way to deal with unwanted emails, particularly if you are getting lots of emails from one particular address, is to set up a filter.

Step 1
❯ Open the inbox and find a message from the contact you want to filter. Click on the message to open it. Click on the More button to the right of the buttons above the message, and select Filter Messages Like These from the menu.

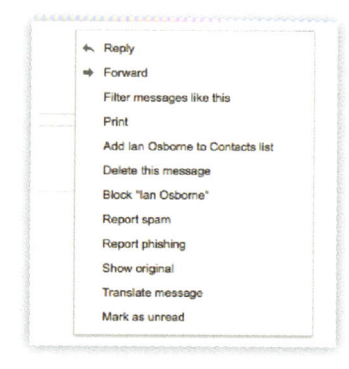

Dealing with Gmail Spam

Step 2
› In the box that appears, the email address of the sender will be automatically entered. You can add extra triggers to the filter such as certain words or recipient addresses. Next, click Create filter for this search.

Step 3
› You can now decide what to do with messages that trigger this filter. There are numerous options, and not just options for spam messages. For the purpose of this guide, choose Delete it. Click Create Filter to finish.

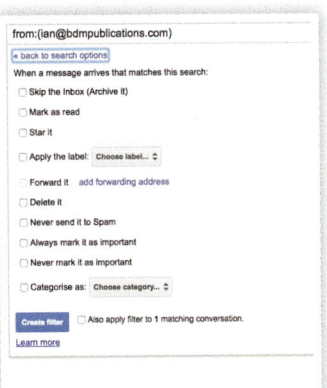

Protect Your Email Address

One of the very best ways of ensuring that spam does not become the bane of your life is to protect your email at all times. Entering your email address onto websites that you don't fully trust or posting the address on blogs and forums, will almost certainly lead to a whole heap of spam heading your way. Automated software (bots) scan through millions of web pages to find email addresses, which are then used by spammers to flood your inbox with unwanted emails.

If you do need to write your email on a blog or forum (in the signature for example), write it in a way that a non-human reader would not understand. For example, you could write it as john dot doe at gmail dot com (instead of john.doe@gmail.com). A human should understand how to write that email address properly.

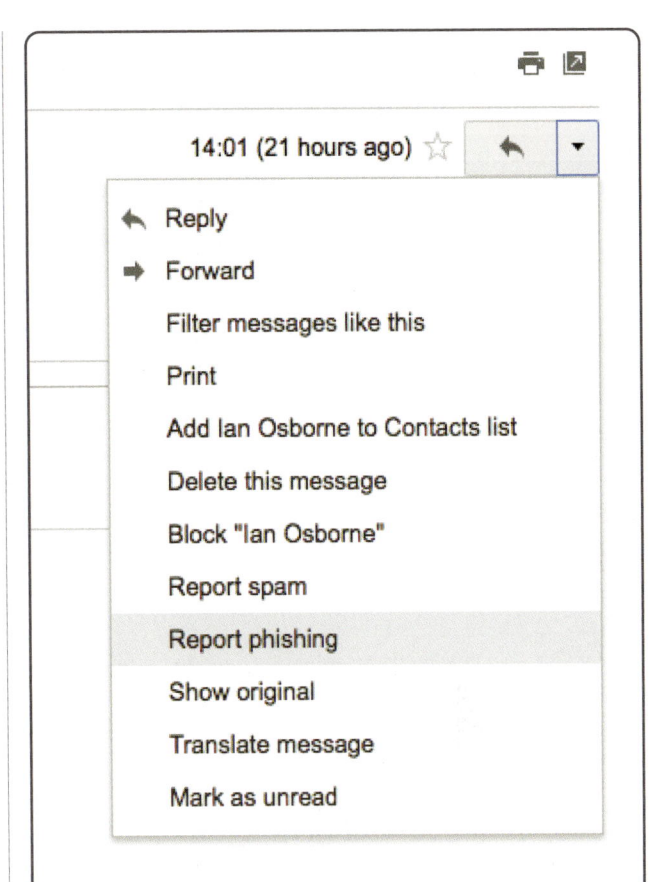

What is Phishing?

Phishing is the process of trying to find private information such as PIN numbers, passwords and user names by trickery. Sometimes spammers create fake websites that look for example, like a well-known bank's login page. You will then get an email pretending to be from that bank, asking you to confirm your login or change some settings by clicking a link to the fake website. When you enter your email and password on one of these pages, the spammer records your information and keeps it.

Remember that banks or credit card companies will never ask you to email them your password or click on links in emails. If you are in any doubt as to the legitimacy of an email and the links within, the first thing to check is the link. Without clicking it, roll your mouse pointer over the link and look at the information that appears at the bottom of the browser window. This will show you the actual link address, letting you check whether it looks OK. If you really want to check your online bank, open a new browser window and navigate to your bank's page normally.

If the message seems like an attempt to get your personal information, click Report Phishing from the message options menu (arrow to the right of the Reply button) to help Gmail and Google learn from such attempts.

www.pclpublications.com 49

Using Google Apps

Google Chat in Gmail

You can add and chat to anyone on the Google network as long as they are using Gmail, iGoogle, Google Talk, Google+ or a third-party client. You can find the Google Chat controls on the left side of the Gmail window.

Using Chat in Gmail

Step 1
❭ Before you can chat with someone, you need to set up Google Chat and then invite them and they will need to accept the invitation. The people you invite will see the invitation above their chat list asking if they'd like to be able to chat with you.

Step 2
❭ Press the + icon, then in the search box at the top of this menu, type your friend's username. If they're already in your Contacts, Gmail will prepopulate their username. If they are not in your contacts, type their email and click Invite to Chat.

Step 3
❭ Once someone has accepted your invitation (and if they are online) you will see a status button to the left of their name in your chat list, which indicates whether they're available (green); their name will show in bold if they have sent you a message.

Step 4
❭ To chat with someone who is available in your list, click on their name and a small chat window will open in the bottom right corner of the Gmail window. Click the arrow to the right of the contact's name to undock the chat window.

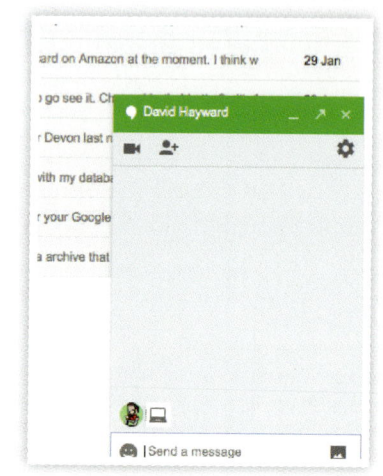

50   www.pclpublications.com

Instant Chat in Gmail

Step 5

> Click in the text box at the bottom of the chat window to start typing. You can type as much as you like, the window will just expand. To add emoticons, either type a recognised emoticon symbol or click the smiley face in the chat box.

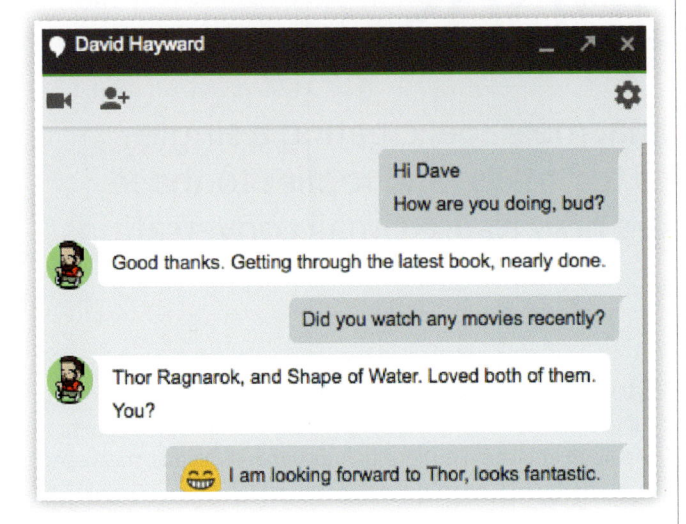

Step 6

> By default, Gmail will store a copy of your chats in the chat history label. These are searchable in exactly the same way as emails. If you prefer not to keep a record of your chats, go to Settings > Chat and turn off the option.

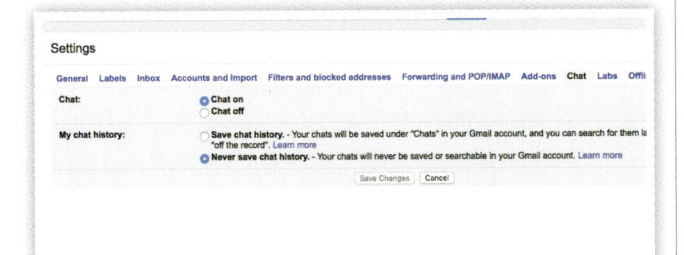

Step 7

> Just as we said previously, you can chat using a variety of Google products. If, for example, you have an Android phone, you will probably also have Google Chat. As long as they use the same Google account, they will share contacts.

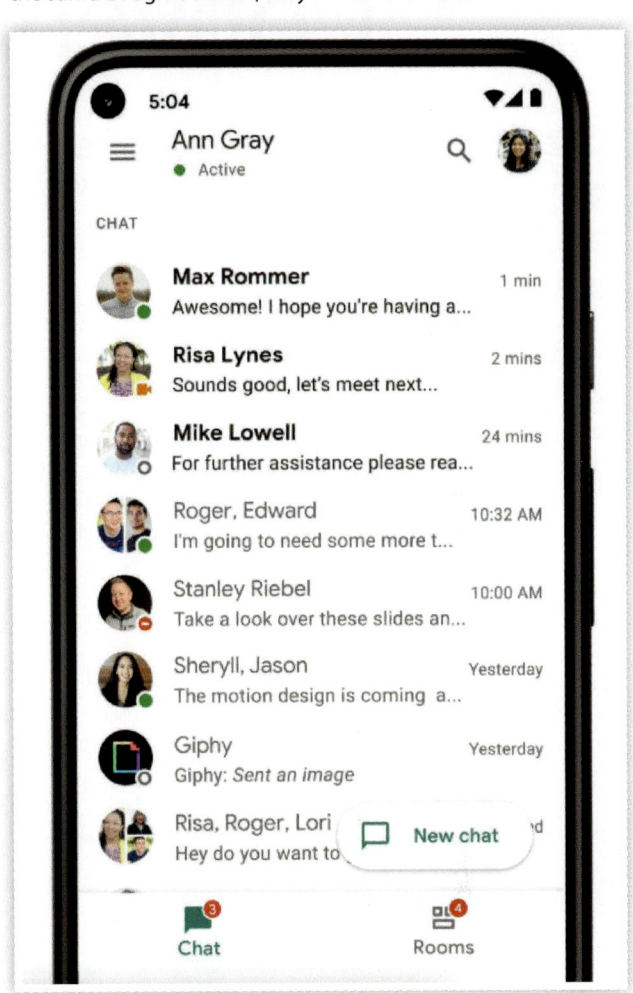

Chat Status

Your chat status controls your availability to chat with your friends. You can manually enter your status which can be viewed by all of your Chat contacts.

To change your status, click the down arrow next to your picture in the Chat list. Select the status you'd like to appear next to your name in your friends' chat lists. By creating a new status message, which appears beneath your name in your contacts chat list, select Custom messages from the status menu.

Your status message can be anything you want, from your favourite quote to a simple note to say you're hard at work or away from the computer. To clear your custom message, click the text under your name in Chat and delete it or select another message from the status drop-down menu.

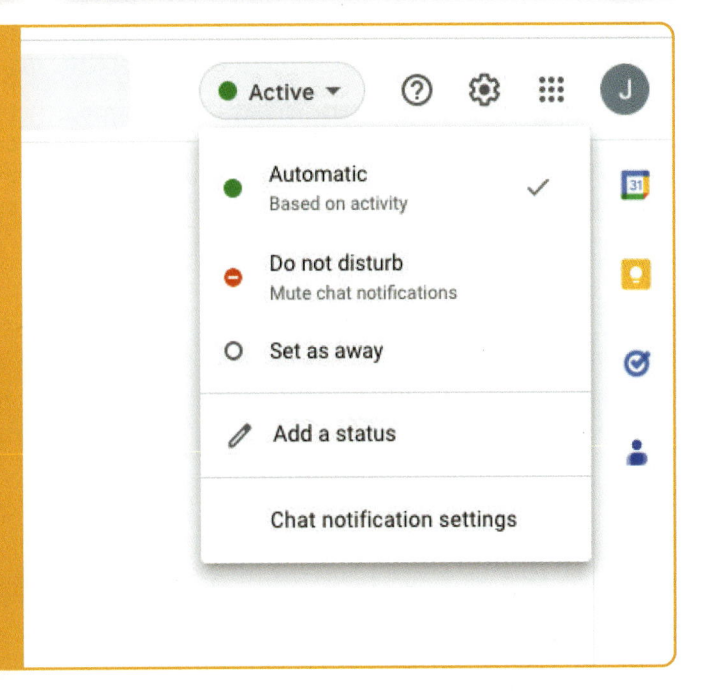

www.pclpublications.com   51

Using Google Apps

How to Use Gmail Conversations

Gmail groups all replies with their original message, creating a single conversation or thread. In Gmail, replies to emails (and replies to those replies) are displayed in one place. Here's how to use Gmail conversations to their best advantage.

Step 1
❱ When you open one message in a conversation, all of your related messages are stacked neatly on top of each other, called Conversation View. In Conversation View, each new message is stacked on top of the ones that arrived before it, so that the newest message is always the one you see first.

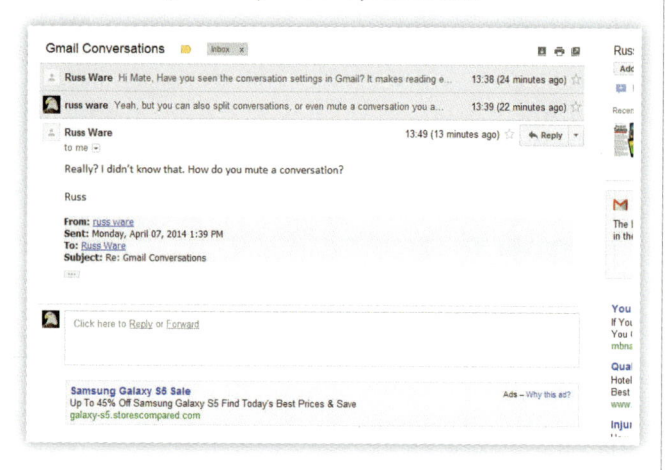

Step 2
❱ To see all the messages in a conversation, just click the Expand all button. A conversation will break off into a new thread if the subject line of the conversation is changed, or if the conversation reaches over 100 messages.

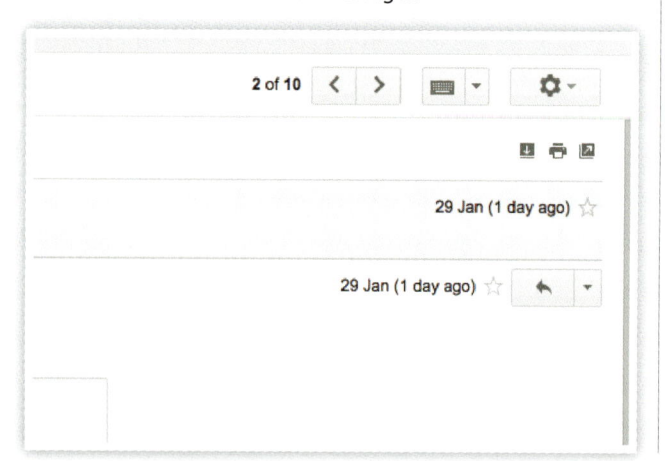

Step 3
❱ If you like, you can change this setting so that replies aren't threaded into conversations but appear as individual messages in your inbox. To do so, go to the General tab of your Gmail Settings and check the box next to Conversation view off.

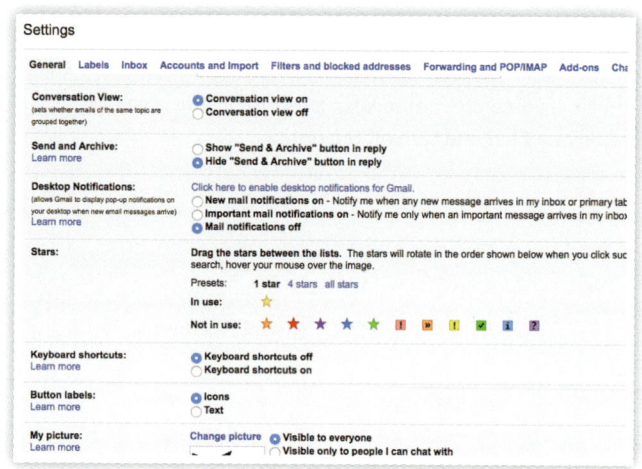

Step 4
❱ You can mute the conversation to keep all future additions out of your inbox. Open or select the conversation and click the More button above your messages. Select Mute from the options, shown below.

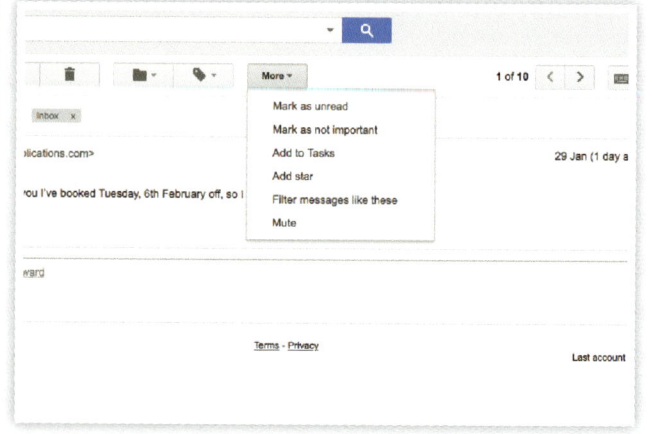

How to Use Gmail Conversations

Step 5
> If you need to find a muted conversation or if you accidentally muted a thread, don't worry. Muted messages are not marked as read and are still searchable. You can type is:muted into your Gmail search box to find all muted conversations.

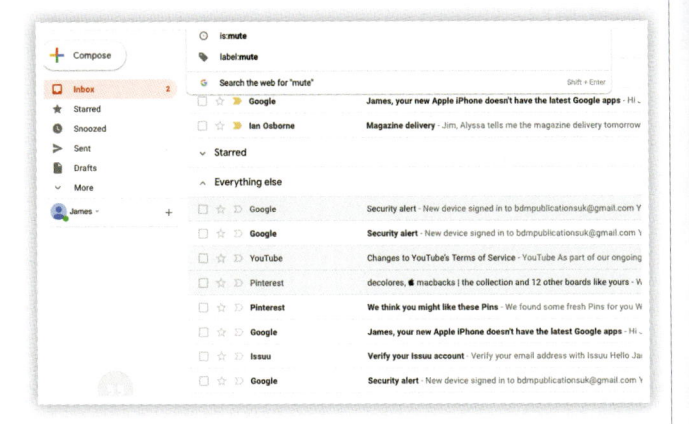

Step 6
> Conversation View in Gmail can be confusing at times. To make things clearer and focus on a single reply, you can open a single email from a conversation string. To do this, open the Conversation and click on the top-right options Arrow (next to the Reply button).

Step 7
> From the menu choose Print. This will open a single email in a new tab or window. Close the print dialog window or press escape. The tab stays open so you can refer to the email and keep it open. To open a whole email conversation in a new tab, press Ctrl when you click on the email.

Using Gmail Keyboard Shortcuts

As you become more accustomed to Gmail and its many features, the use of keyboard shorts will vastly increase your productivity and make your Gmail user experience far easier.

How to turn on Gmail keyboard shortcuts
Click the gear in the top right corner of Gmail and, from there, select the Settings link. Then click on General, scroll down to the Keyboard shortcuts section and switch them on. Finally, select Save Changes at the bottom of the page.

Gmail Keyboard Shortcuts

Shortcut	Action
Shift + Esc	Focus on the main window
Esc	Focus on the latest chat or compose
Ctrl/Cmd +.	Advance to next chat or compose
Ctrl +,	Advance to previous chat or compose
Ctrl/Cmd + Enter	Send
Ctrl/Cmd + Shift + c	Add Cc recipients
Ctrl/Cmd + Shift + b	Add Bcc recipients
Ctrl/Cmd + Shift + f	Access custom from
Ctrl/Cmd + Shift + d	Discard draft
Ctrl/Cmd + k	Insert a link
Ctrl/Cmd + ;	Go to previous misspelled word
Ctrl/Cmd + '	Go to next misspelled word
Ctrl/Cmd + Shift + '	Open spelling suggestions
Ctrl/Cmd + Alt + .	Go to next section
Ctrl/Cmd + Alt + ,	Go to previous section
Ctrl/Cmd + z	Undo
Ctrl/Cmd + y	Redo
Ctrl/Cmd + Shift + -	Decrease text size
Ctrl/Cmd + Shift + +	Increase text size
Ctrl/Cmd + b	Bold text
Ctrl/Cmd + i	Italics text
Ctrl/Cmd + u	Underline text
Ctrl/Cmd + Shift + 8	Bulleted list
Ctrl/Cmd + Shift + 9	Quote
Ctrl/Cmd + Shift + l	Align text left
Ctrl/Cmd + Shift + e	Align text centre
Ctrl/Cmd + Shift + r	Align text right
Ctrl/Cmd + Shift + x	Strikethrough
Ctrl/Cmd + \	Remove formatting
g + I	Go to InBox
g + t	Go to Sent messages
g + d	Go to Drafts
g + c	Go to Contacts
g + k	Go to Tasks

www.pclpublications.com

Using Google Apps

Create Tasks from Gmail

One of the most useful planning tools Gmail includes is the ability to create tasks from any message you receive. This tutorial will show you how to use this little known feature of the Gmail application to its full potential.

Step 1
❱ Open Gmail on your computer and find the email you want to create the task from. Open the email or select it by checking the box next to it in the main inbox list. Both actions will bring up several new options along the top of the email pane.

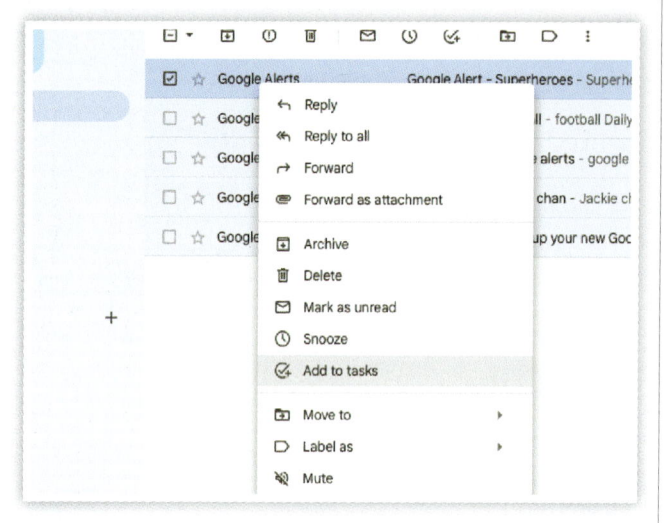

Step 3
❱ The latest task will be shown at the top, labelled using the subject of the email. Click on the arrow next to the task title and you can change details such as the due date, add notes and move it to a different task list if you have one.

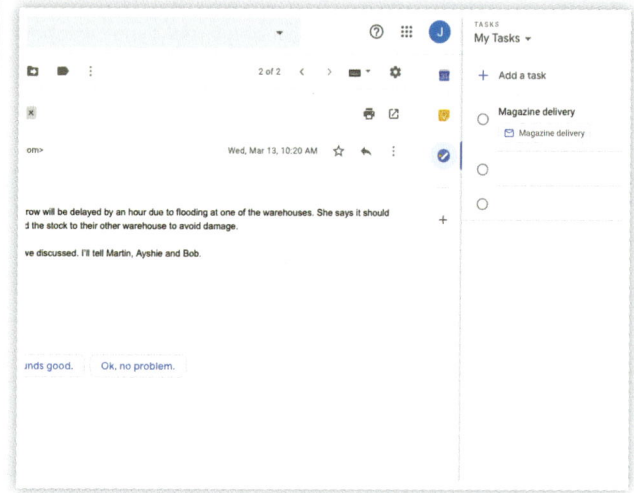

Step 2
❱ Click the More button at the top and then click Add to Tasks. You can also use Shift-T. When you do this a tasks list panel will appear in the bottom right corner of Gmail. Any tasks you have added, from any source, will be listed here.

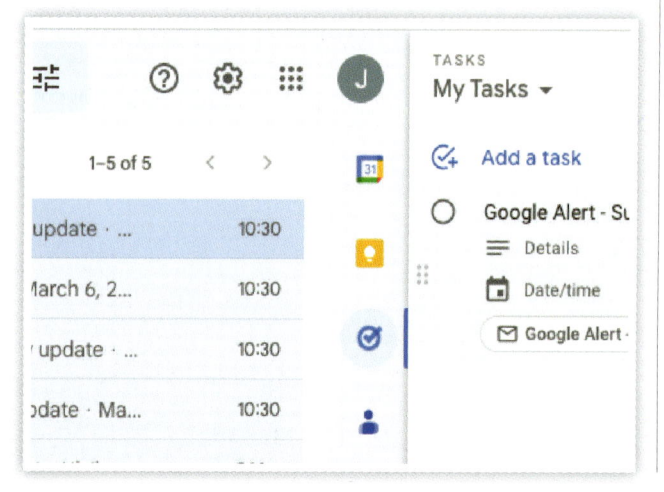

Step 4
❱ To show a task as completed in the list, check the box next to it. The task will stay in the list as a reminder. If you want to remove a task from the list, select it and click the trash icon at the bottom of the Tasks pane. NOTE: It cannot be restored.

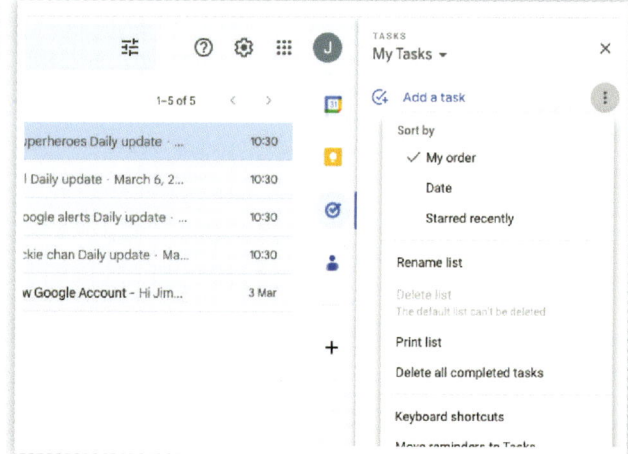

Create Tasks from Gmail

Step 5
❭ Once you add a due date to a created task, it will appear in your Google Calendar on that date. If you go into Calendar and can't see the task, make sure that the Tasks option is highlighted in the left-hand sidebar. You can change the colour of shown tasks using the drop down menu.

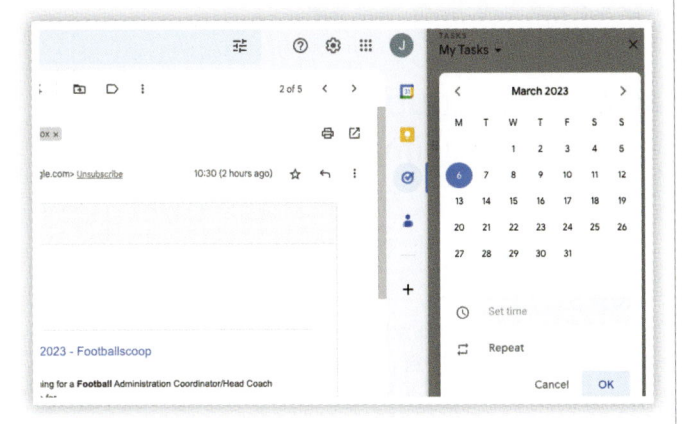

Step 6
❭ When the Tasks option is selected in Calendar, a new sidebar will open on the right to show all tasks. You can manage tasks from here or from in the main Calendar panel. If you don't want the sidebar to be displayed, click the X to close it.

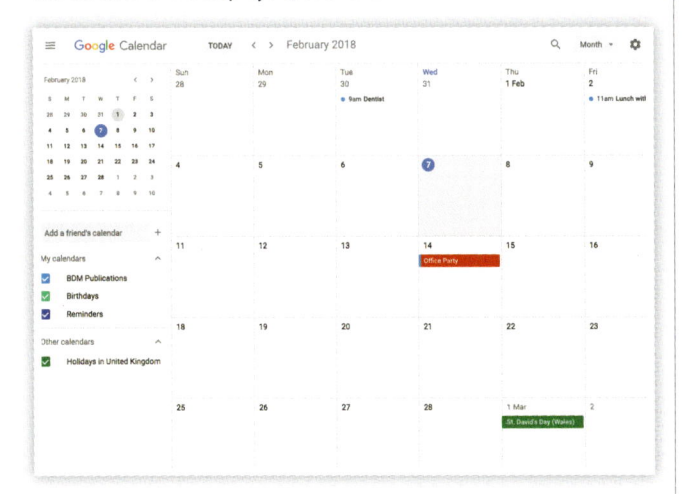

Step 7
❭ Once you have created a task from an email, go back to the Tasks panel in Gmail where you can add additional tasks as part of that main task. To show that the task is a sub-task, you can indent it. Click anywhere in the tasks panel and hit Enter.

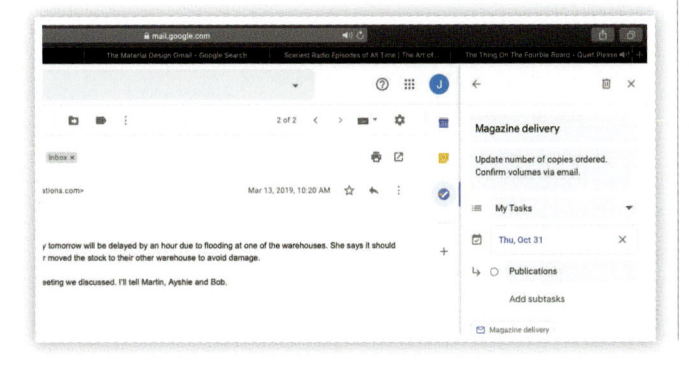

Step 8
❭ Select the new task and type a title. Like any other task, you can use the arrow to go in and set a due date and notes. Go back to the list and highlight the sub-task. Click Actions and then select Indent. The title will indent, showing that it is part of the task above it.

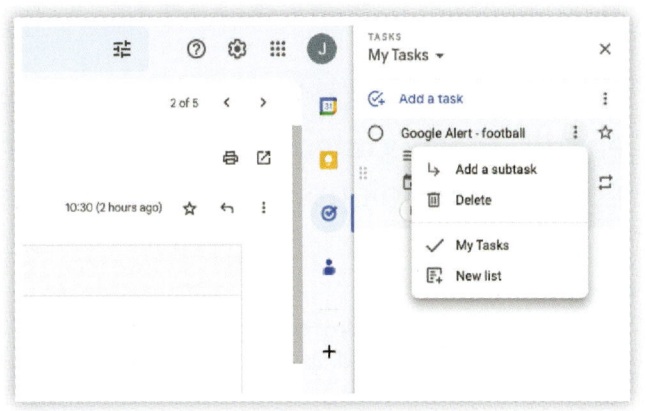

Step 9
❭ To remove an email association from a to-do item in Gmail Tasks, highlight the desired task. Press Shift-Enter and then click the X next to Related email option. Once the related email is removed, it can't be added again.

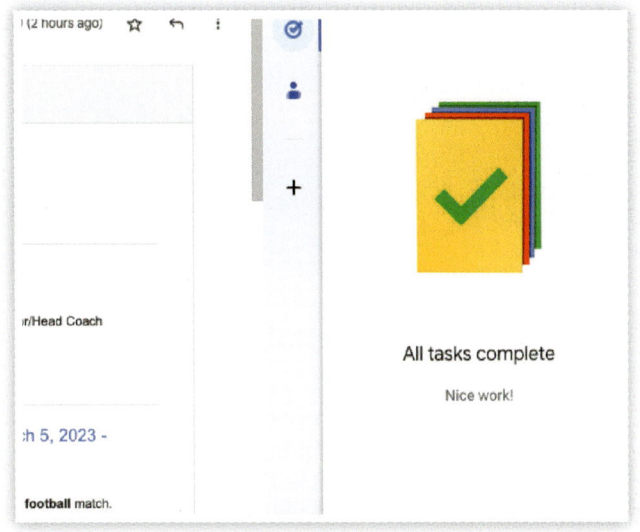

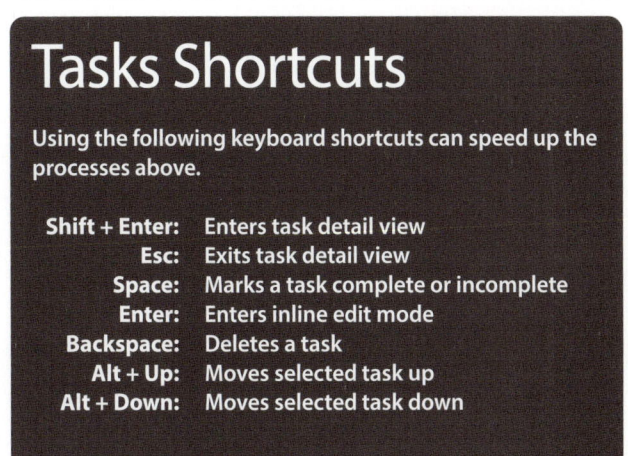

Tasks Shortcuts

Using the following keyboard shortcuts can speed up the processes above.

Shift + Enter:	Enters task detail view
Esc:	Exits task detail view
Space:	Marks a task complete or incomplete
Enter:	Enters inline edit mode
Backspace:	Deletes a task
Alt + Up:	Moves selected task up
Alt + Down:	Moves selected task down

Using Google Apps

Schedule Your Gmail Messages

With an additional bit of software, Gmail can be set up to send specific emails at scheduled times. This is particularly useful if you are sending emails to recipients in different time zones.

Step 1
❯ The first thing you need to do is download and install the Boomerang software for Gmail. Open your Chrome browser and search for "Boomerang for gmail" or point your browser to www.boomeranggmail.com. In addition to letting you schedule emails, Boomerang offers several other features too.

Step 2
❯ With Boomerang installed you will see a new Send Later button with a Boomerang icon. You can now write an email when it's convenient, then schedule it to send automatically. Just write the message, then click the Send Later button.

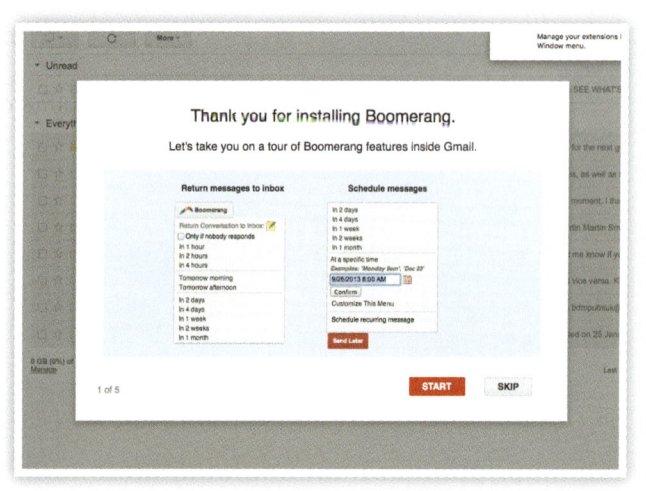

Step 3
❯ From the popup menu, schedule the sending time with either the handy calendar picker or text box. The smart menus display your most frequently used scheduling times for easy access. Boomerang will then automatically send your message at the chosen time, without you having to worry about it.

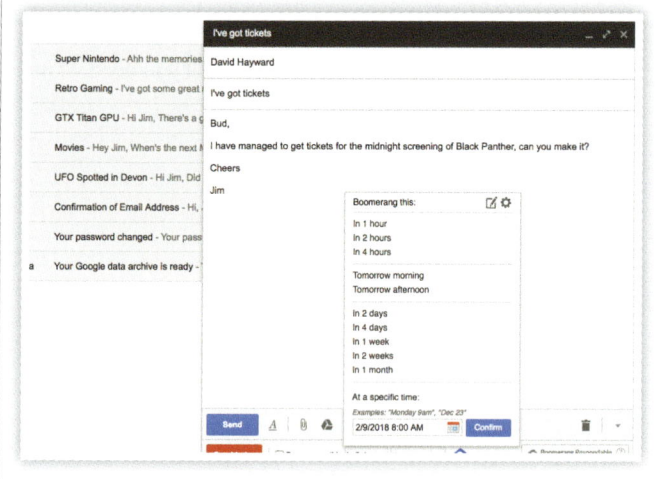

Step 4
❯ You can also set up email reminders. This means taking messages out of your inbox until you actually need them. At the scheduled time you chose, the software will bring it back to your inbox, marked unread, starred or at the top of your list.

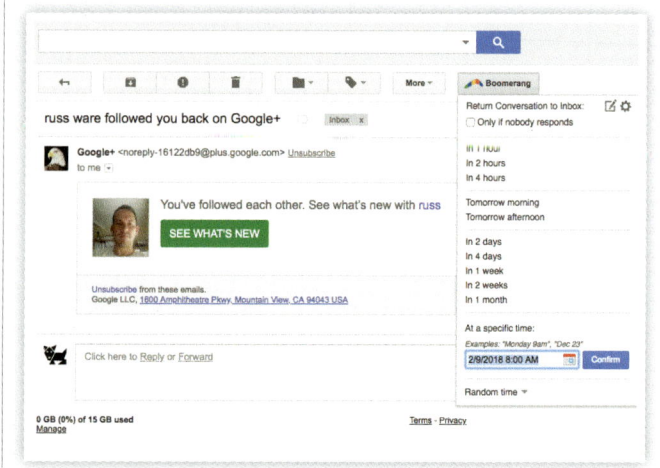

Schedule Your Gmail Messages

Step 5
❭ This function is useful to remind yourself about stuff that is weeks or months away but you may forget why you wanted to keep it in the first place. You can attach a note to the message as you schedule it. When the message returns to your inbox, your note will be added to the email thread.

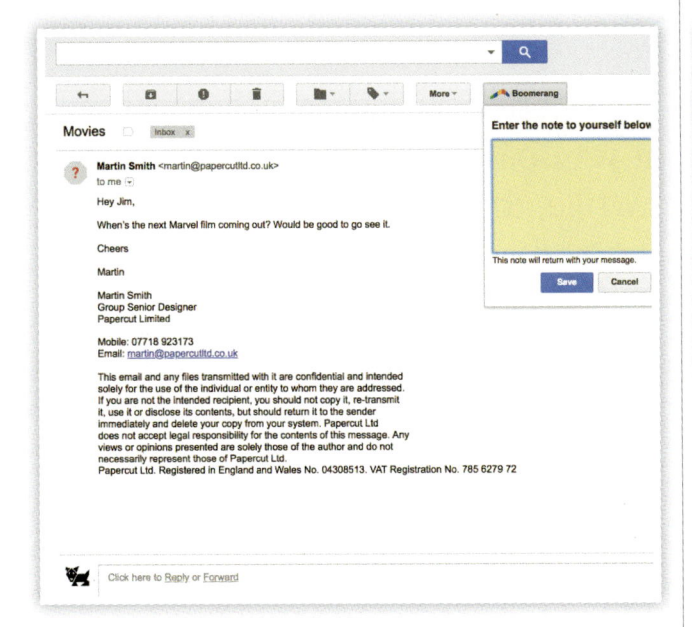

Boomerang Extras

Boomerang is a useful and rather powerful tool that can play an increasingly important part in how you use your Gmail account. Here we will be looking at some of the extra functionality it offers.

Step 1
❭ One of the other useful features here is tracking responses. When writing an email, you can set Boomerang to give you a reminder if you don't get a reply after a certain amount of days. If the message comes back to your inbox without a response, you can then send another email to follow up.

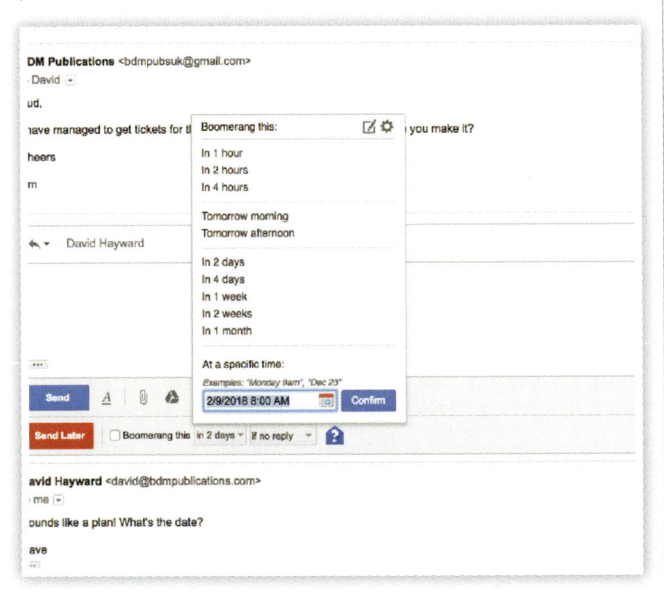

Step 2
❭ You can schedule your follow-up message as you're writing the original email. If the person replies to your original email, Boomerang will detect the response, and will not send the second email. If they don't reply, the software will send the follow-up message automatically.

Step 3
❭ You can also send recurring emails. All you have to do is write a message as you normally would, then click Schedule Recurring Message from the bottom of the Send Later menu. From the menu, you can then choose the start date, frequency, day of the week to send and end date.

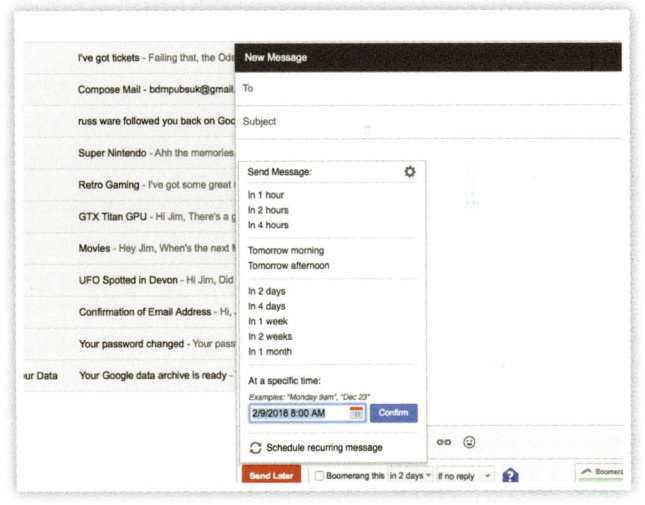

Step 4
❭ To remove Boomerang from your computer, first uninstall the plug-in from your browser. Now revoke Boomerang's access to Gmail data. Right click the Boomerang icon in your browser and click Manage Extensions. Now disable Boomerang and then click the Bin icon to delete it.

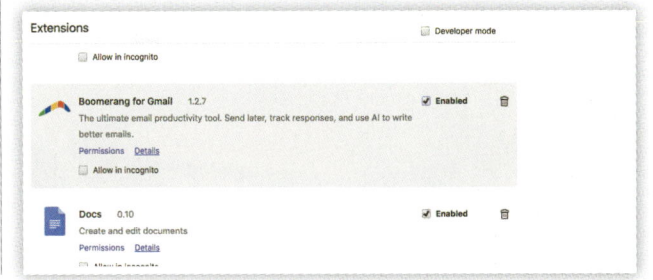

www.pclpublications.com 57

Using Google Apps

Gmail User Tips and Tricks

You can be up and running with the basic Gmail in seconds, or you can spend ages customising it and getting it set up in several different ways. Even if you have been using Gmail for a while, there are probably dozens of tricks that you never even knew were possible.

Add Stars to Messages

❱ You can mark a conversation or message that appears next to the item in your inbox with a star. Stars can be an eye catching way to mark a special message or even a great visual reminder to follow up on an item later. Stars will only appear to you and not to anyone else, so you won't offend your friends by starring their messages rather than reading them. To star a message from your inbox, just click the Star icon next to the sender's name. You can also add a star when reading a message by clicking the icon on the top right of the message.

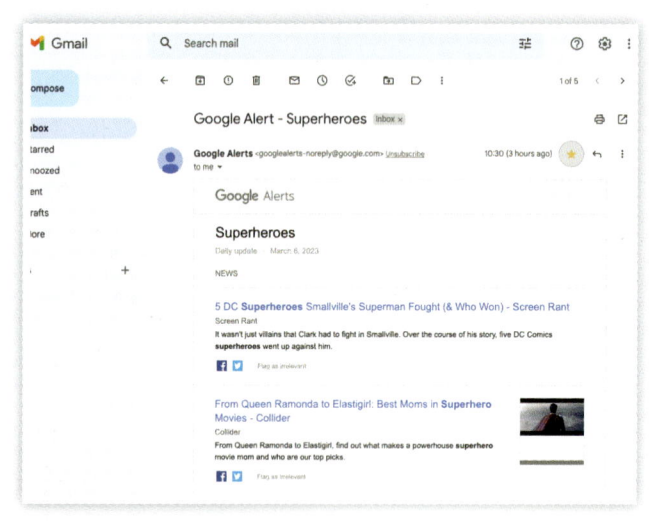

Customise Display Density

❱ Gmail automatically adjusts the amount or "density" of information on a page when you adjust your browser window or when you use different sized screens. If you prefer a denser view whatever size your monitor, you can set a limit on your Default Density. This setting reflects the lowest density (the most space) permitted for your account. Choose how many messages are on your screen at a time by clicking on the gear icon and then selecting from Comfortable, Cosy or Compact.

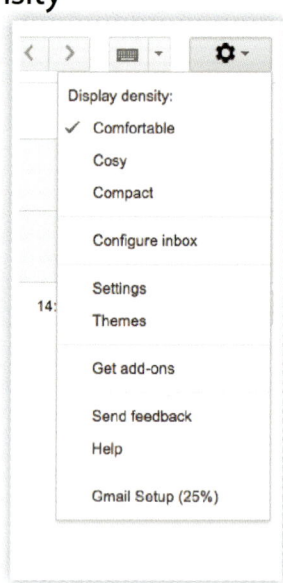

Voice and Video Chat

❱ With Gmail, you can now use voice and video chat services such as Google+. From within these services, you can have an actual conversation with someone or even chat face-to-face over video. To get started, download the voice and video chat plug-in from www.google.com/chat/video, quit all open browser windows and install the plug-in. Sign in to Gmail, Google+ or Chrome OS device.

Gmail User Tips and Tricks

Labelling Your Emails

❭ Labels help you organise your messages into categories such as work, family, to-do, read later, jokes, recipes, etc. Labels do all the work that folders do but with the added bonus that you can add more than one to a message. Only you can see your labels, so whether you mark a message with "Best friend" or "Read later", the sender will never know. You can create a new label for a message in your inbox by selecting the box next to the message, clicking the Label button above your message list and then clicking Create New.

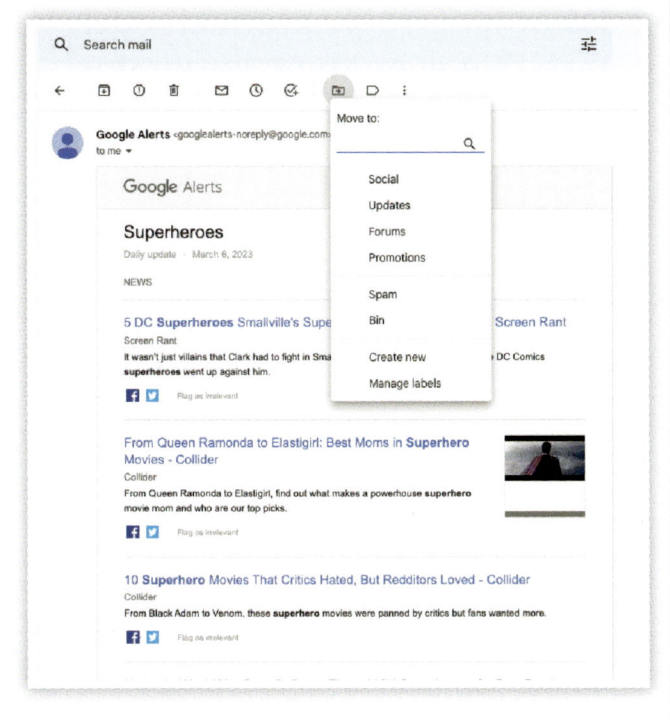

Clean Up Your Inbox

❭ You can use the Move To button at the top of your inbox to easily move a message out of your inbox and add a label at the same time. If you have lots of labels, you can pick the one you want by typing the first couple of characters and letting auto-complete find the right one, or alternatively create a new one.

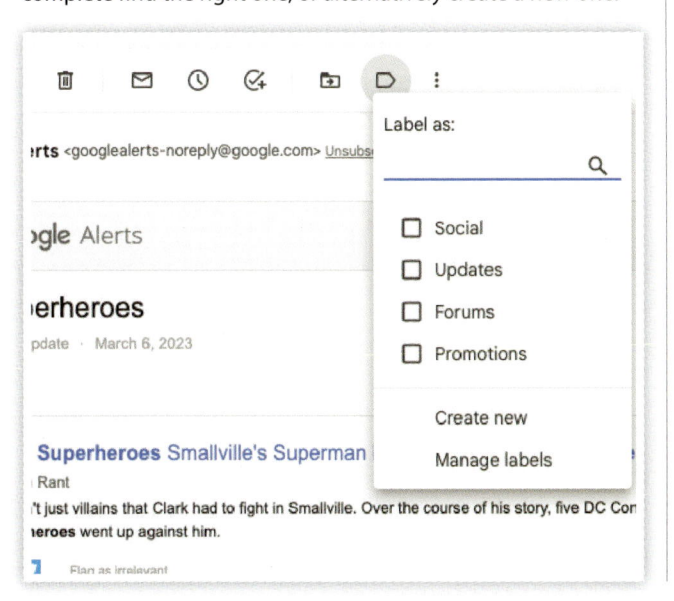

Search Your Mail

❭ It can be a pain to scroll through old emails just to find the one you need, which is why you might want to try searching for it instead. For example, if you're looking for a message that contains the word "shopping", simply type "shopping" in the search field and click the Search button. Your results will be displayed with your search results and within the message highlighted in yellow. If you're having trouble finding the result you want, you can refine your query by clicking the small arrow in the search box and entering your criteria in the appropriate fields.

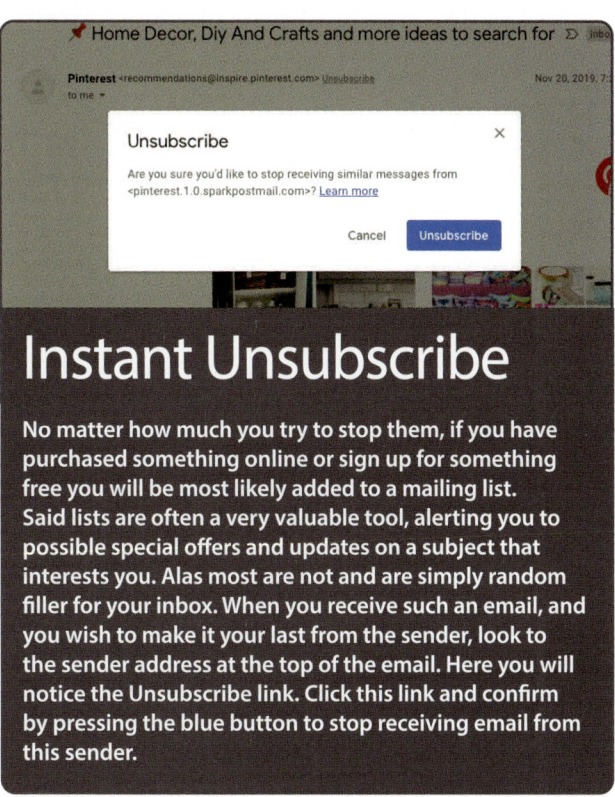

Instant Unsubscribe

No matter how much you try to stop them, if you have purchased something online or sign up for something free you will be most likely added to a mailing list. Said lists are often a very valuable tool, alerting you to possible special offers and updates on a subject that interests you. Alas most are not and are simply random filler for your inbox. When you receive such an email, and you wish to make it your last from the sender, look to the sender address at the top of the email. Here you will notice the Unsubscribe link. Click this link and confirm by pressing the blue button to stop receiving email from this sender.

www.pclpublications.com 59

Using Google Apps

Improving the Google Calendar

Google's free online calendar app is perfect for keeping track of all the important events in your life. And if you use other Google products such as Android or Gmail, you can set things up so that everything integrates and syncs perfectly and with barely any effort.

Creating Events

There are three ways to create a new event on the desktop version of Google Calendar. Which method you use depends entirely on which you find easiest or most convenient.

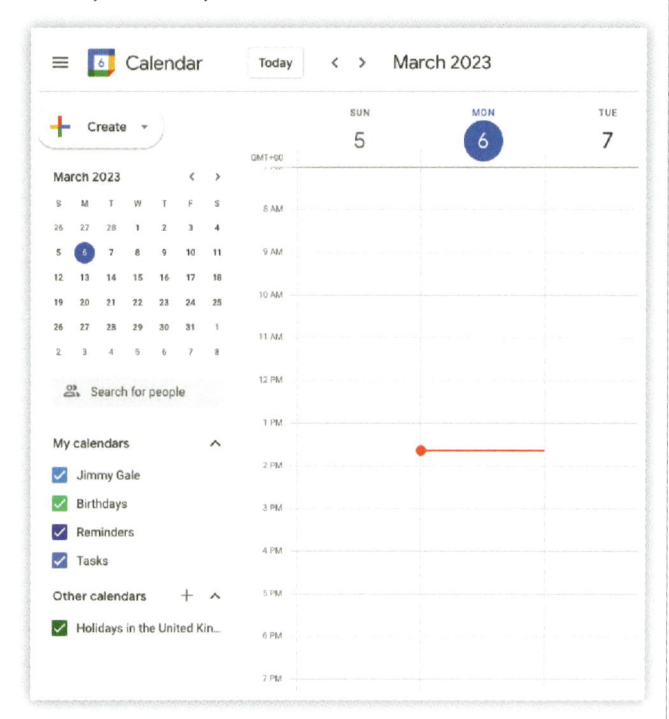

Click on the Date

❯ Open the Google Calendar screen and scroll to the date and time where you want to mark an event. If you need to look far ahead, click on the month view button at the top of the screen. You can then scroll through whole months by clicking the forward and back arrows, also at the top. If in Week view, you can click and drag on the event location if you want it to spread over more than a single hour. If in Month view, you only have the option to click, although you can change the length of the event afterwards. Type the title and event time for your new event in the box. Finally, click Create event to publish the event to your calendar immediately or click Edit.

Using Quick Add

❯ To use Quick Add simply type "Q" while you're in Calendar. Quick Add can almost read your mind. If you type in something like "Lunch with Dad at The Ivy 1pm Friday", Quick Add can figure out what you mean and pop the new event right onto your calendar. Just remember that for Quick Add to work at its best, you need to include: what, event title, e.g. lunch; when, time and date or day; who, if there is anyone else to include in the event; and where, location of the event.

www.pclpublications.com

Improving the Google Calendar

Click the Create Button
❯ Just click on the Plus sign in the bottom right of your Calendar window, this will bring you to a page where you can enter as much information as you'd like about your event. On this page, you can also add guests, change a reminder setting and publish your event to other users. Once you've entered the appropriate information and selected the desired settings, click Save.

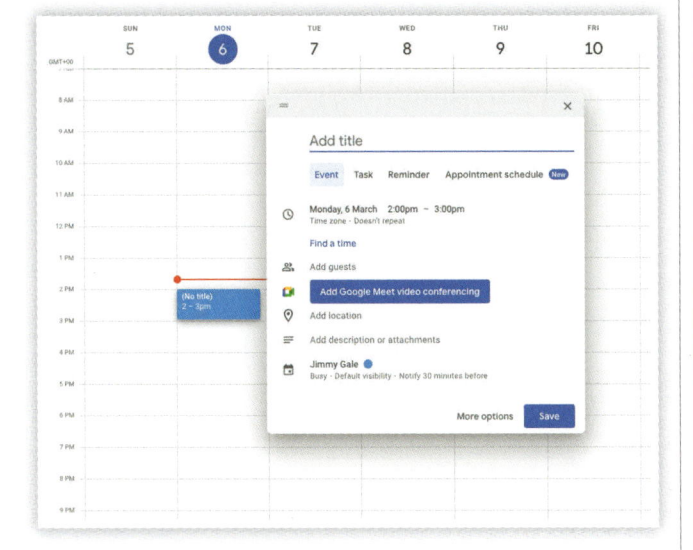

Using Google Tasks
❯ You can access Google Tasks directly from the Calendar application. By linking these apps together you can quickly work between the two as follows. Open Google Calendar and log in if required. Now click the Tasks icon from the sidebar found on the right hand side of the window. Click Add a task and then start to enter your details via the new task link in Google Calendar. You can now add tasks to this listing. You can directly add an item from this list to your Calendar by choosing a date in the properties of the task itself. You can edit a task directly from the Calendar app by clicking the pencil icon. From this link you can change the details and move or delete it.

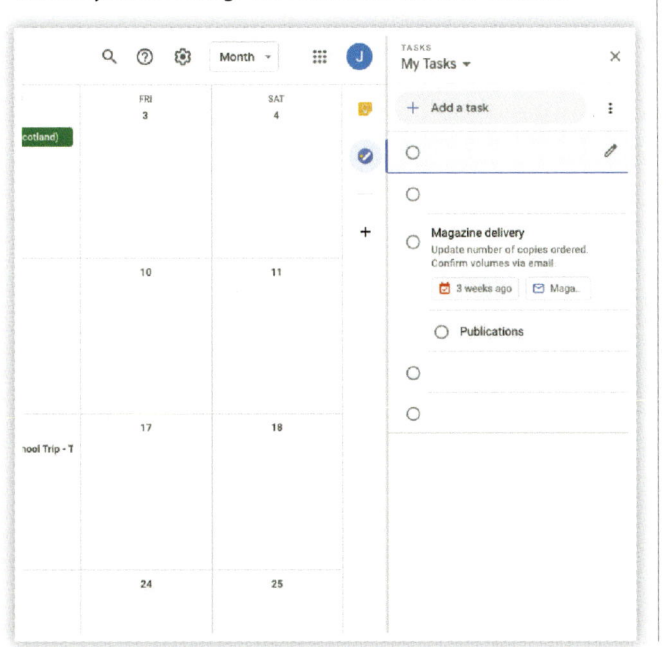

Create a New Calendar

With Google Calendar you are not restricted to having one calendar crammed with all your birthdays, events, appointments and holidays. To make things less messy, it is possible to create several calendars if, for example, you want to keep personal and business entries completely separate.

Step 1
❯ At the left-hand side of the Google Calendars screen, look for the section labelled Other Calendars. Click on the small arrow button and select Create New Calendar.

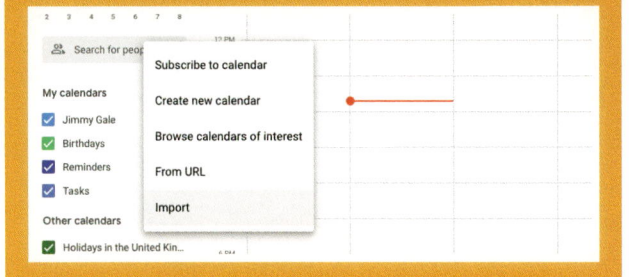

Step 2
❯ Give your new calendar a title and write a description if you wish. The location box is useful if the calendar is to be public, as it makes it easier for your friends or family to find events on it.

Step 3
❯ All of the calendars you create will be listed under My Calendars on the left side of your page. Just click on the name to select it. For each of the calendars, you can add, delete and edit events any time you like.

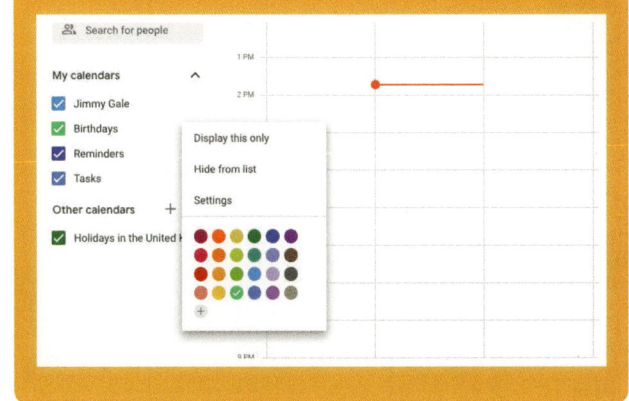

www.pclpublications.com 61

Using Google Apps

Sharing Your Calendar

It is possible to share your different calendars with individuals or groups. An email invitation is sent and the contact will be able to view your calendar alongside theirs.

Step 1

❱ Log in to your Google Calendar and look for the calendar list on the left-hand side of the screen. Roll the mouse over the calendar you want to share and click the small arrow button. Select Share this Calendar from the drop-down menu.

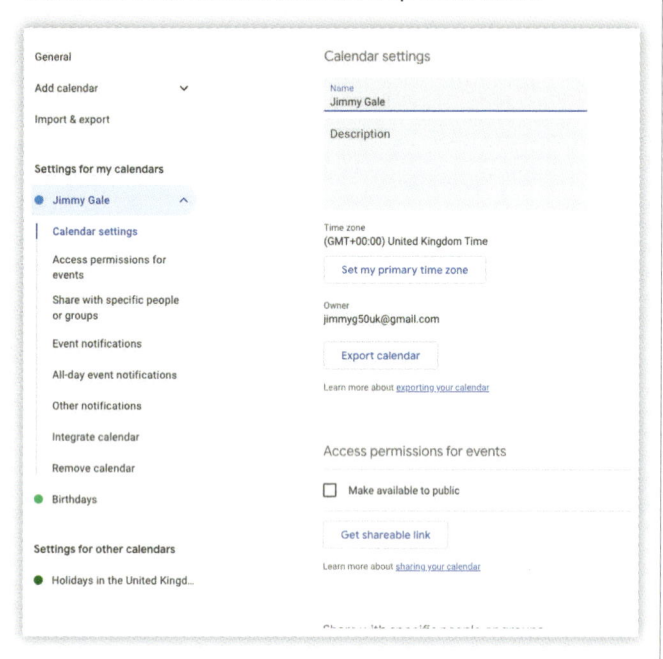

Step 2

❱ Enter the email address of the person with whom you want to share your calendar. From the drop-down menu on the right side, select a level of permission (view only or view and make changes), then click Add Person. Click Save to finish.

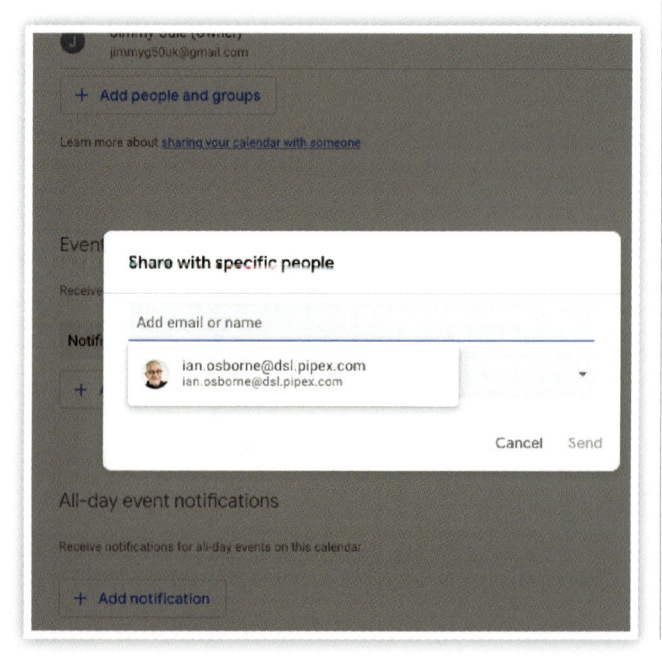

Step 3

❱ Once you click Save, the person with whom you selected to share the calendar will receive an email invitation to view your calendar. The person will need to click on the link contained in the email to add the calendar to his/her Other calendars list.

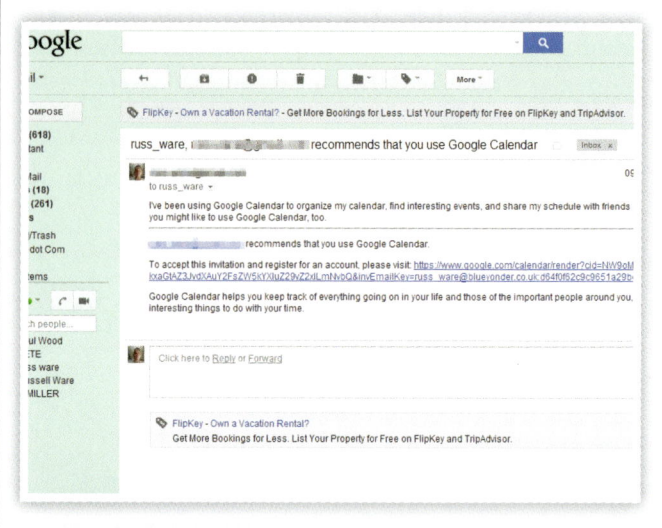

What Platforms are Compatible?

Google Calendar uses the iCalendar (iCal) file format to save/share its calendars and the relevant information. Having been created in 1988, this open source software was quickly adopted by a wide array of developers for use in their platform specific calendar apps. What follows is a listing of the platforms and applications that will be compatible with Google Calendar files.

- Apple
- Yahoo!
- eM Client
- Mozilla
- IBM
- Microsoft Outlook
- Novell GroupWise

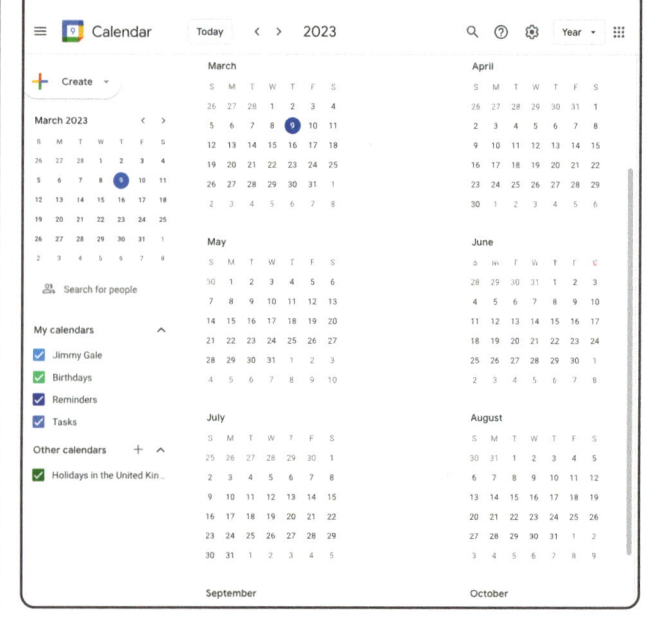

Improving the Google Calendar

SMS Reminders

If you have Google Calendar on your Android smartphone, your events and reminders can be automatically synced between desktop and mobile. If you don't have Google Calendar on your phone, it is still possible to receive reminders on your mobile.

Step 1
> The first thing you need to do is obtain a verification code. This will show you that your phone and carrier is capable of receiving SMS reminders from Google Calendar. Click on the gear icon at the top of the page and select Settings.

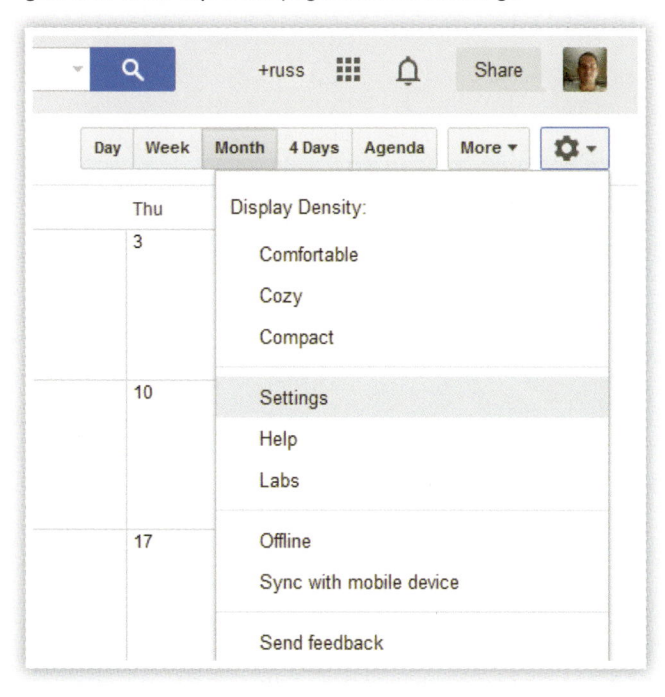

Step 2
> Click on the Mobile Setup tab at the top of the settings page. Select your country from the drop-down list and then enter your full mobile phone number. You may also need to select your carrier from the menu that appears.

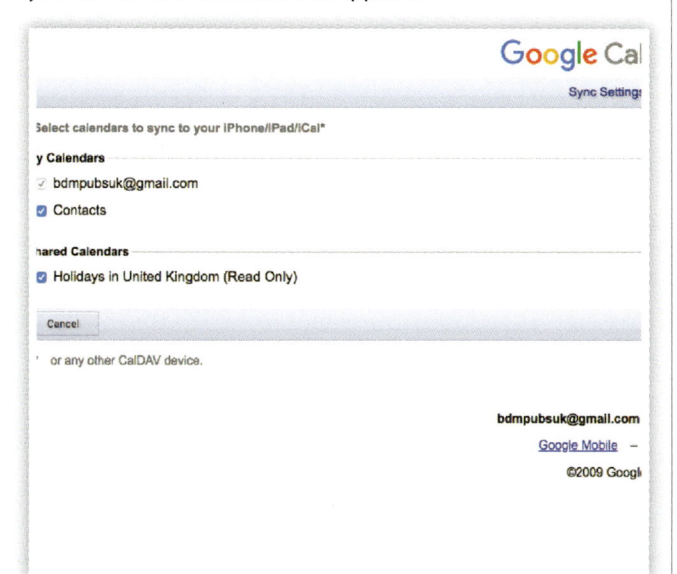

Step 3
> If your carrier is supported, click the Send Verification Code button and you receive a text message on your phone. Once you receive this message, enter the code you received in the Verification code field and click the Finish setup button.

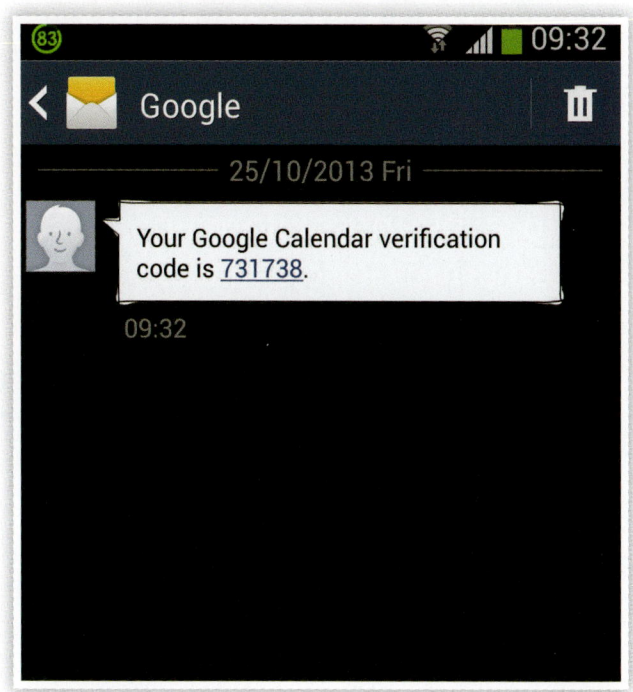

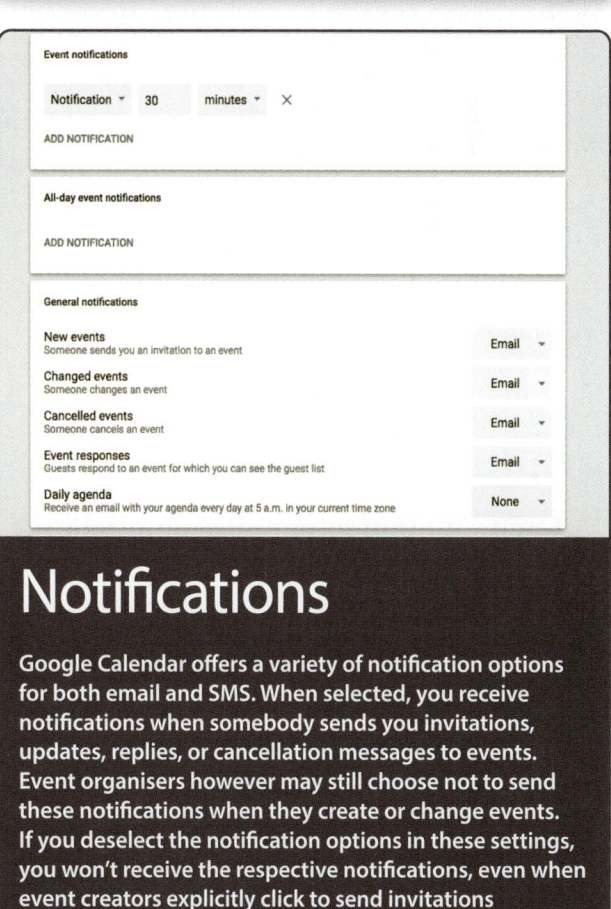

Notifications

Google Calendar offers a variety of notification options for both email and SMS. When selected, you receive notifications when somebody sends you invitations, updates, replies, or cancellation messages to events. Event organisers however may still choose not to send these notifications when they create or change events. If you deselect the notification options in these settings, you won't receive the respective notifications, even when event creators explicitly click to send invitations or updates.

www.pclpublications.com   63

Using Google Apps

Get Started with Google Maps

Google Maps is a great service that you view in your web browser or via the app. Depending on your location, you can view basic or custom maps and local business information, and that's just the start. Here's how to get started using Google Maps.

1 Search Maps

❯ You can search for places (towns, cities, addresses) and businesses using the search box at the top of the page. Search for a location and the view will switch to show that location. Search for businesses and the view will remain the same but red dots will appear to show individual businesses. If you search for "railway stations Devon" the map will zoom to the location (Devon) and show all known railway stations in that area.

You can also search for individual businesses by name. If there is more than one business with that name, a list will appear to the left of the map, showing the addresses of each of the businesses. Click on the business in the list to be taken there.

2 Pan Controls

❯ You can use this control to move the view up, down, left and right. You can also scroll around the map by clicking anywhere on it (you will see the mouse pointer change to a hand) and dragging the map in the direction you want to move.

This is a quick and easy way, not only to show off the impressive visuals this app contains but also make navigating easier too.

To navigate around the world with even greater ease; press and hold the mouse button or press your finger on the touch screen, then move the mouse or swipe around the screen. You can also press the hold the SHIFT key to hold the central position and move on a point.

Get Started with Google Maps

3 Street View
❭ Click on the little man and drag him onto the map. Any road or street that is overlaid in blue can be viewed in Street View. You simply drop the man at the location you want to view. Once in Street View, you can split the map screen so that half shows the map view and half shows the Street View. To do this, click on the box in the bottom right corner of Street View.

4 Zoom Controls
❭ Click the + and – buttons to zoom in and out of the map. You can also click on the slider and drag it up and down to zoom more quickly. If you have a mouse with a scroll wheel on it, you can use this to zoom in and out of the map much more easily.

5 Information Box
❭ Many businesses are shown on the map with an icon next to the name, particularly restaurants, hotels and pubs. Click on the icon to pop up the information box. This will show you the address details, links to reviews and to a website if applicable. You can also click the Directions link to quickly open the Route Planner menu.

6 Map Layers/Map View
❭ These controls let you switch to a flat map view, as well as add layers of information that can be overlaid on the map. These layers include traffic, weather, webcams, photos, public transport information and many others.

MapsGL

You now also have the option to use MapsGL. MapsGL uses new technology called WebGL (Web-based Graphics Library) to enhance the Google Maps experience. WebGL brings 3D graphics to your browser without the need to install additional software. This allows Google to provide seamless transitions between various levels of imagery and different map views. You can view some buildings in 3D and parts of the map using 45 degree aerial images. This is still a beta test of the feature, so it doesn't work everywhere you want to look.

MapsGL requires a certain level of specification in your computer to work. You can check out the recommended specifications at www.maps.google.com.

Your Places

Your Places makes it easy for you to organise content relevant to you on Maps, including maps you have created with My Maps, businesses you have rated in Google+ Local and locations and directions you have previously searched for.

Step 1
❭ To access your content, open Google Maps and click on the Your Places link. If you're not logged in to your Google account, you'll be prompted to sign in before continuing. Your content will appear in the left panel.

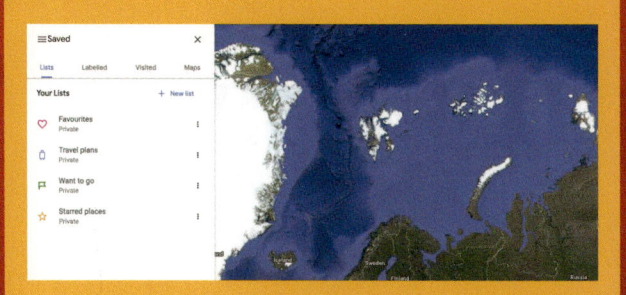

Step 2
❭ Click the tabs at the top to see specific types of information. Your ratings, check-ins, and directions will appear under the More menu. To add a Home and Work location, click on the relevant button.

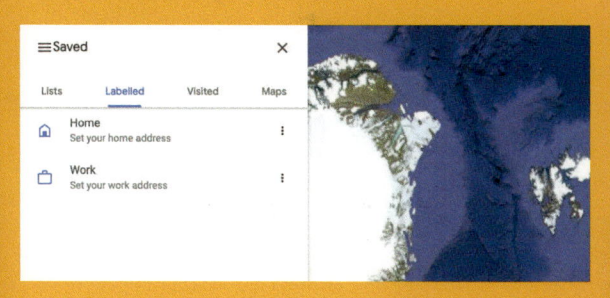

Step 3
❭ To delete content, click on the "X" icon to the right of any item. Note that deleting information from the Your Places tab will also permanently remove it from any related activities.

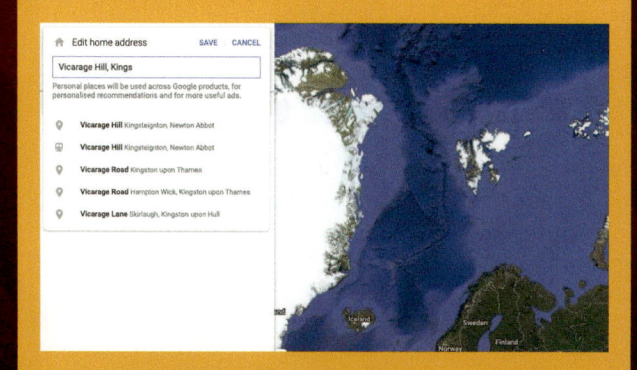

Using Google Apps

Planning a Route with Maps

Google Maps features a very powerful, and normally very accurate, route planner. You can plan a route by car, on foot or even using public transport. If you save your route to My Maps, you can easily access it again on your mobile device.

Step 1

❯ Click on the Apps icon at the top right of the Google Search home page and select Maps. The map, normally zoomed out on the country you live in, will be shown on the page and a search box, which will act as your navigation hub. Note: If you aren't signed in to your Google account, do so now.

Step 2

❯ Click on the blue arrow on the search box. Two boxes will appear in the blue bar, these are start and destination input points, along with buttons to choose your mode of transport. These include travelling by car, on foot, by public transport or by bicycle. Click on the mode of transport you will be using.

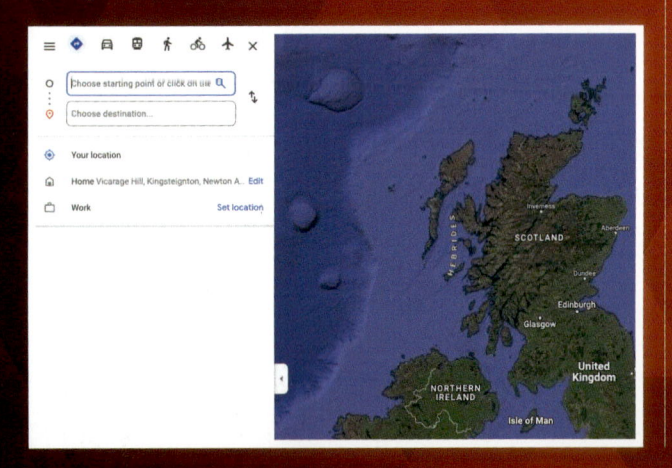

Step 3

❯ In the start box, type the starting point for your journey. If you have added a home address to My Places, and if your journey starts at home, you can simply type Home in the first box. If not, type your preferred starting locations. This can be an address or even just a town or city.

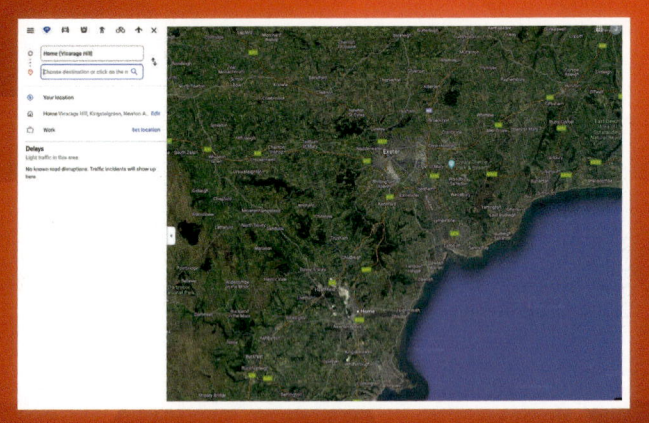

Step 4

❯ Type your destination in the second box. Again, this can be an exact address or a town or city. Suggestions will appear as you type, so make sure you select the correct address; there will almost certainly be more than one instance of your street name to be found.

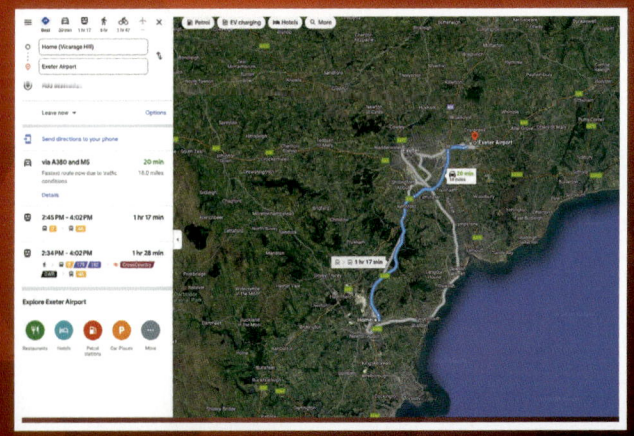

Planning a Route with Maps

Step 5
With both starting point and destination completed, Google Maps will automatically generate your route. If you want to include additional stopping points to your journey, click on Add Destination and a third box will appear. Remove this box by clicking the X next to it.

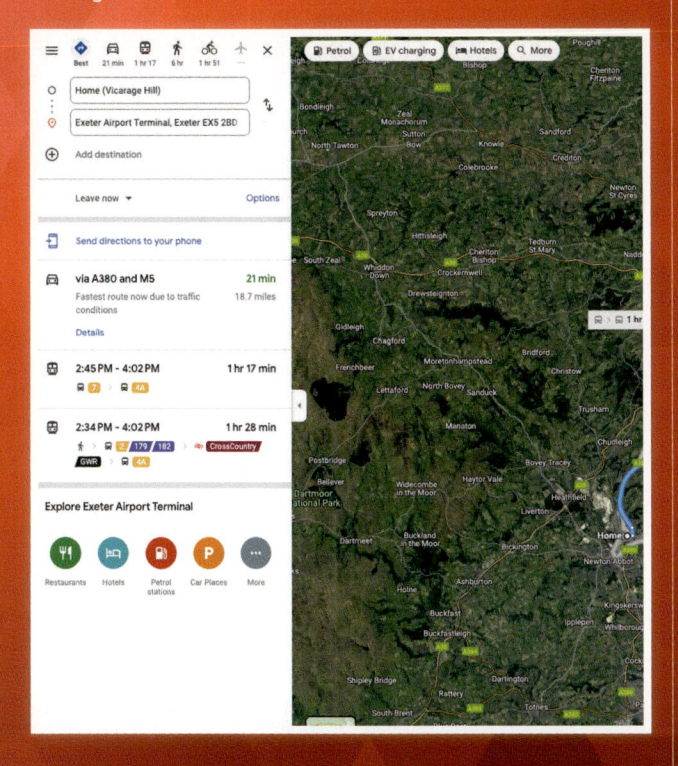

Step 6
Having generated your route, the map screen will zoom in to show the complete journey highlighted in blue. You can zoom in and out as normal if you want to get a closer look at the route. You can also alter the route by clicking on any part of it and dragging the blue line.

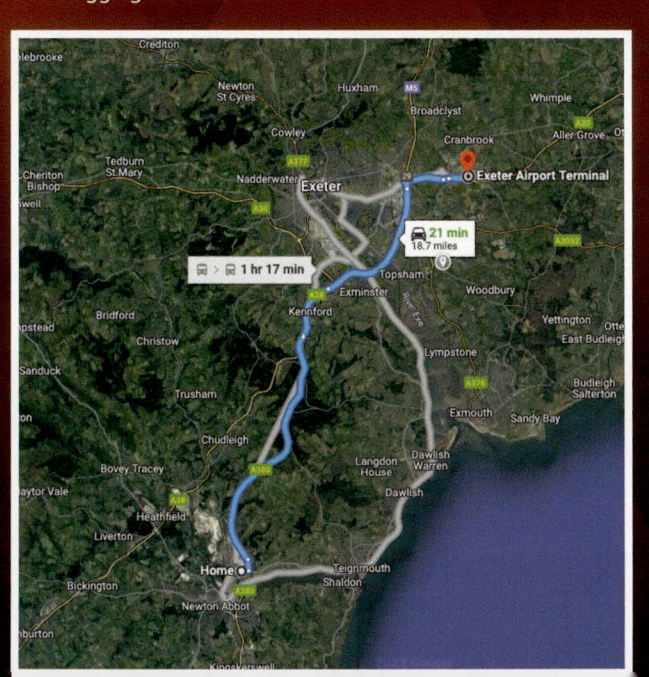

Step 7
The route is shown as a list of directions in the left-hand column which is accessed by clicking the Details icon. At the top of the list the distance and the estimated journey time is displayed. Roll your mouse over the list and you will see a marker displayed on the map at different junctions, roundabouts, etc.

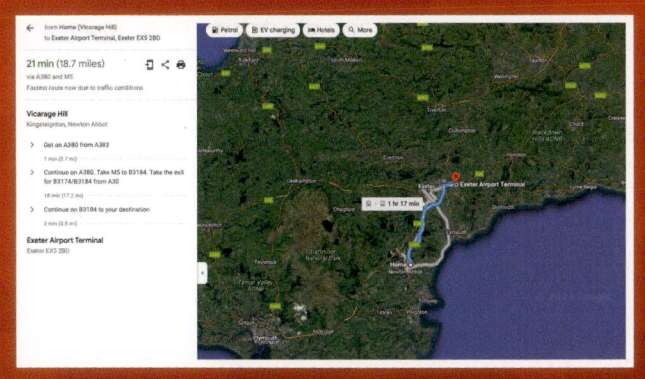

Step 8
Scroll to the top of the directions list and you will see three icons, a link to save the route to My Maps. Share the details and you can also print directions directly by clicking the printer button. You can choose to show the map or just the directions on your printout.

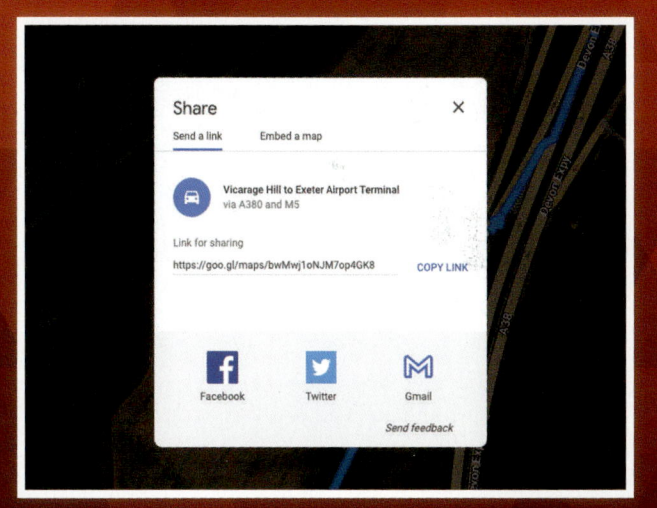

Using Google Apps

Using Google Street View

Street View is a feature of Google Maps that allows you to quickly and easily view and navigate high-resolution, 360-degree street level images of various cities around the world. With this guide you can learn the new ways to enter Street View.

Step 1
❱ To start using Street View, open the Google Maps page by clicking on the Maps link on the Google Search home page. Type the name of the street, town or city you want to start viewing in the search box at the top of the screen.

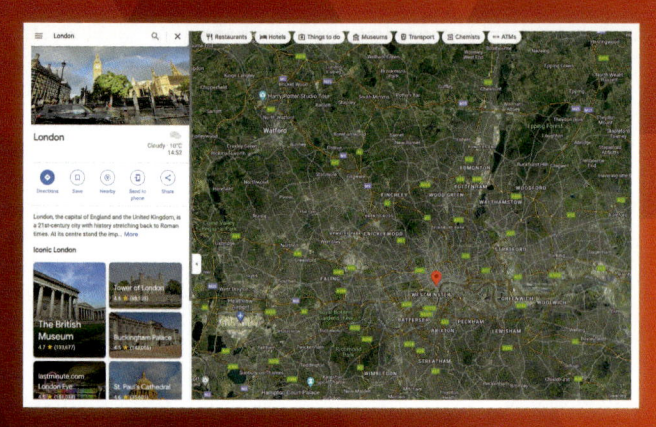

Step 2
❱ When the map has zoomed in to show the area you searched for, click and drag the little yellow man from the bottom of the map zoom controls, onto the map. Blue lines will appear to show which streets and roads have been captured for Street View.

Step 3
❱ Drop the yellow man icon onto any of these blue lines to see that road in Street View. As you hold the man over a marked location, Street View image will remain static, but if you slowly move it you will get additional Street View previews.

Step 4
❱ With Street View now showing, you can move around by moving the mouse pointer onto the road so that it becomes a circle and then clicking. The camera will pan forward to that position. Repeating this action lets you follow roads and streets along their length.

Using Google Street View

Step 5
❱ Move the mouse pointer up onto the side of a building and it turns into a rectangle. Click the mouse and the camera will rotate to show the building centred on the screen. If, when you move the pointer onto a building, it shows a magnifying glass, you can zoom in to the image.

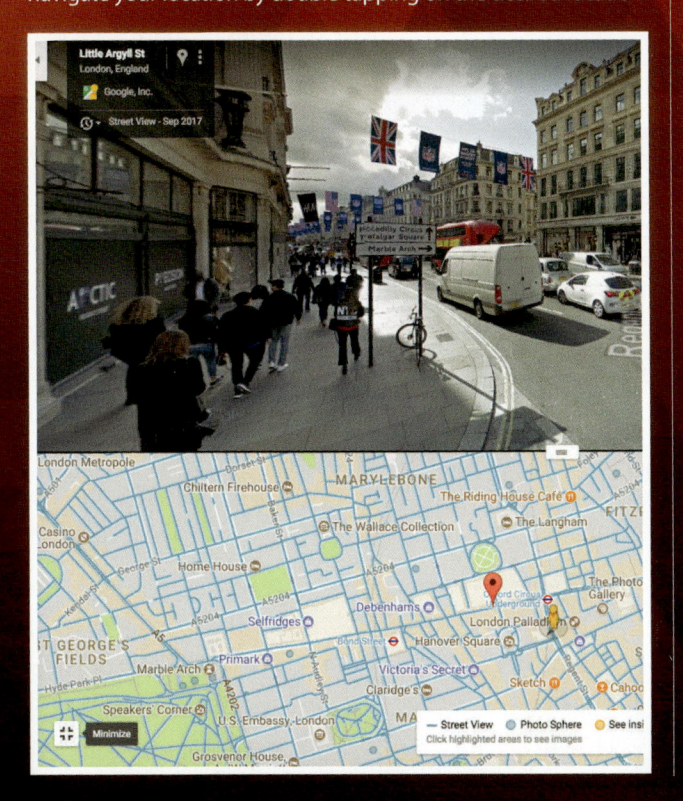

Step 7
❱ You can also use the mouse wheel to zoom in and out of the image in Street View. If you want to view the image in full screen, click in the button with four arrows in the top corner of the window. Click the X next to that to close Street View and return to the normal map view.

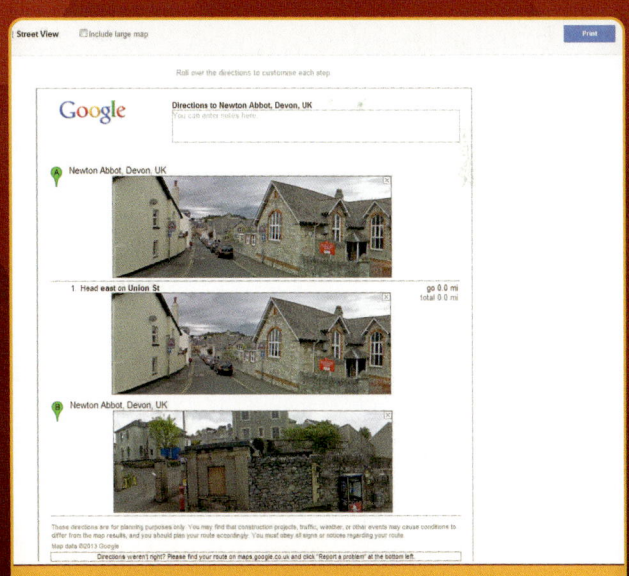

Step 6
❱ In the corner of the Street View window is a small box showing your position on the map. You can expand or minimise it by clicking the icon to the bottom left. When you expand the map box, it will split the screen with Street View. You can also quick navigate your location by double tapping on the desired location.

Route Plan with Street View

When using the route planner feature of Google Maps, it is possible to have the route displayed with a Street View image for each junction, roundabout or major change of direction. To activate this option, plan your route using the steps shown previously, click to print the route and then click the Street View link at the top of the Print screen.

www.pclpublications.com   69

Using Google Apps

Share and Embed Maps

Google Maps is a great tool when used on a phone or tablet for navigating and planning a route in advance. Not only can you use this great tool yourself, you can also share maps with others and even embed them on a website to give your customers directions.

Step 1
❭ Before you share a map, you need to zoom and scroll until the area you want to share is centred on the window. Only the visible portion is shared. You can also choose to share the map in Map view or Earth view.

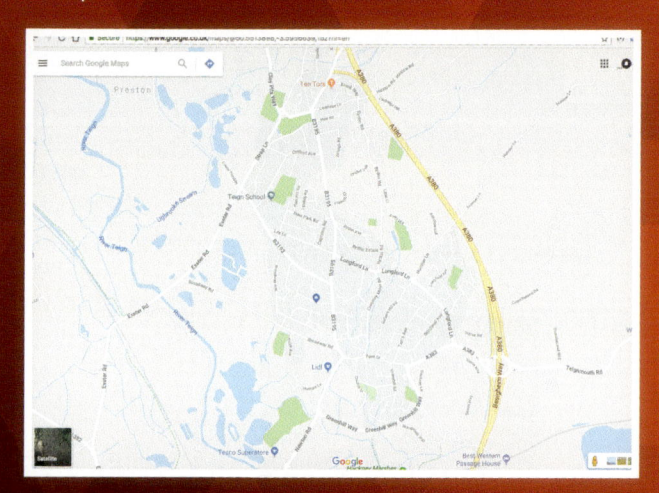

Step 2
❭ If you have saved favourites on a map, only you will see them. Equally, if you embed the map and view it on your site, you see your saved places on the map. Your site's visitors won't see those saved places, they see a map built for them.

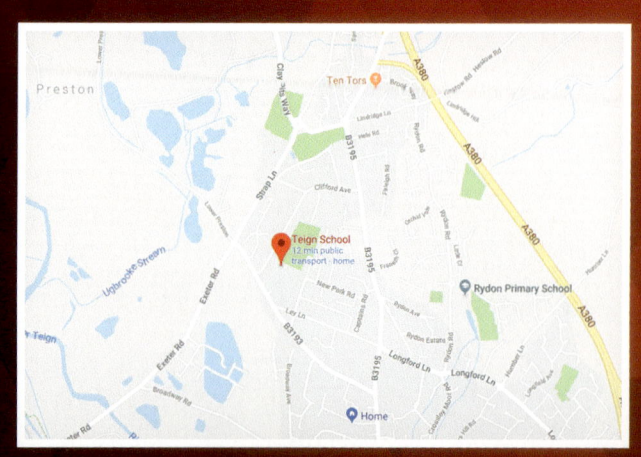

Step 3
❭ Directions can be marked on the map, and will be shared when you send it. Right-click on two points on the map to set your direction to and from those locations. Check that the correct route is selected, if alternatives are available.

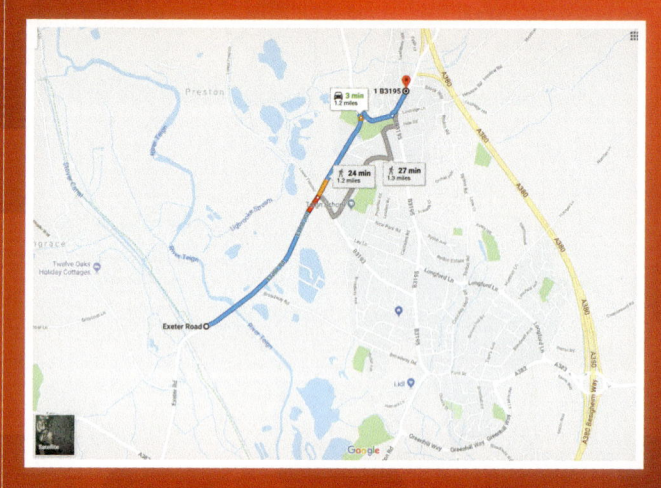

Step 4
❭ In the top left corner of the screen, click the Menu icon. Select Share and embed map. Check the box next to Short URL to create a shorter link. Double-click the link to highlight it, then copy it by pressing Ctrl+c (or Cmd+c on Mac). Paste the link wherever you want to share the map, like an email or Google+ post.

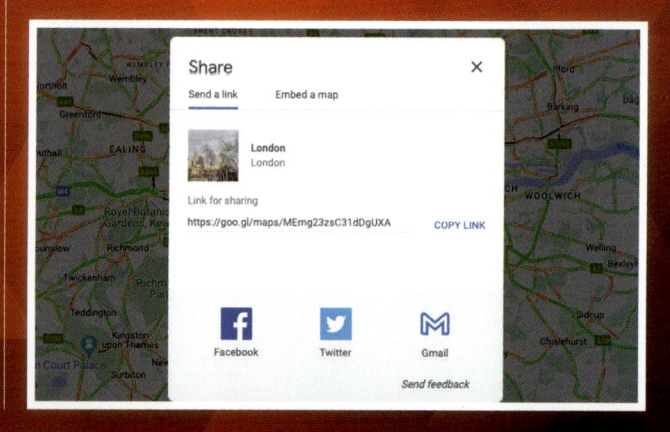

70   www.pclpublications.com

Share and Embed Maps

Step 5
By using a short URL, you can squeeze a long Google Maps link into fewer characters to leave more room for other text. For example, the URL http://goo.gl/l6MS is easier to share than the long URL http://googleblog.blogspot.com/2009/12/making-urls-shorter-for-google-toolbar.html.

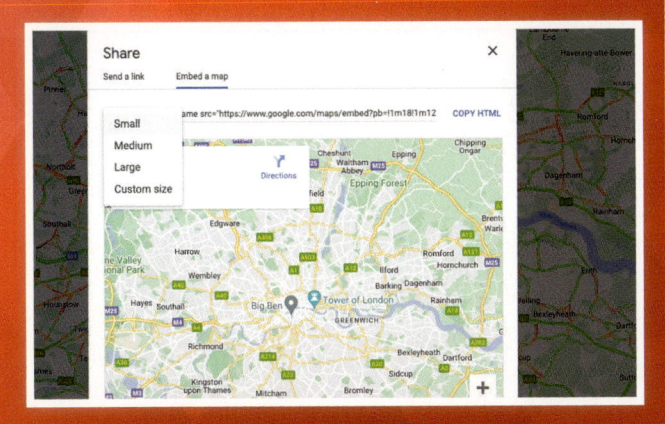

Step 6
When the recipient opens the email, they can paste the link into their browser and see the map, with directions marked and listed in a step-by-step format. They will be able to interact with the map (choose an alternative route, etc.) just as if they created it.

Step 7
You can embed a basic map, driving directions or a local search into your website or blog from the new Google Maps. When your viewers are signed in to Google, they can also see their home and work, saved locations and more in your embedded map.

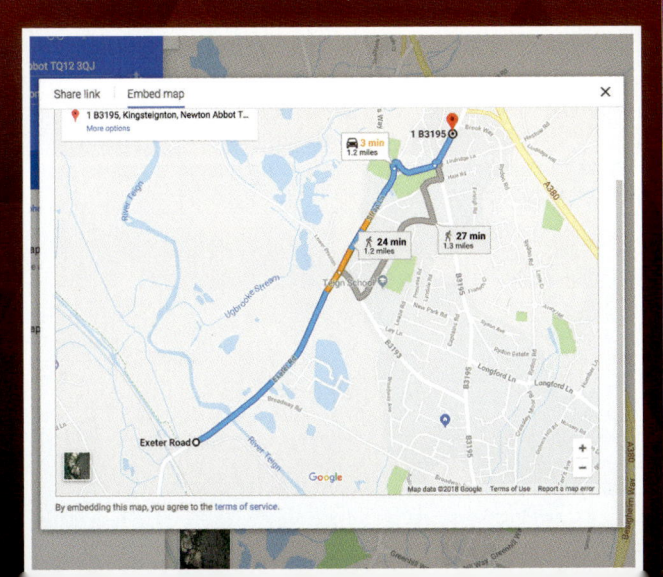

Step 8
Ensure that the map you'd like to embed appears in the current map display. Click the settings gear icon in the bottom right. Click Share and embed map. In the box that appears, make sure the Embed map tab is selected.

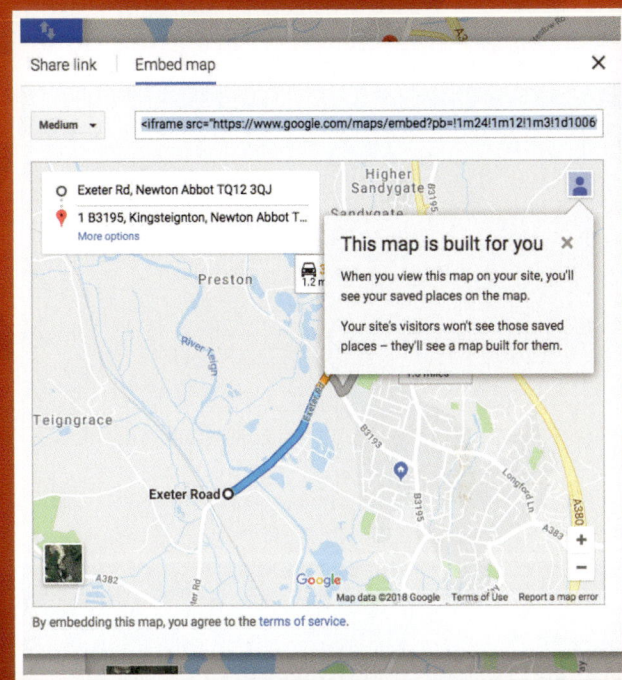

Step 9
Choose the embed size you want, then copy the HTML and paste the code into the source code of your website or blog. Keep in mind that traffic information and some other Maps features may not be available in the embedded map.

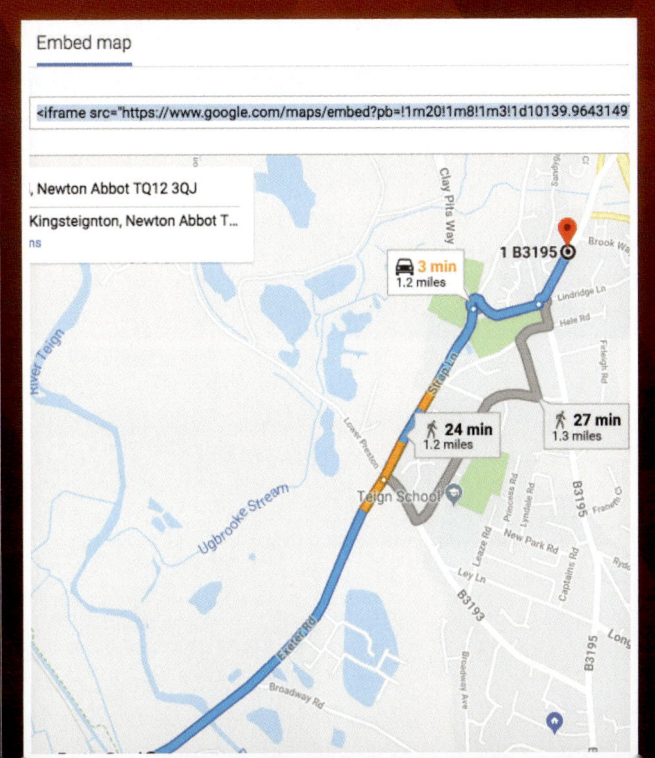

Using Google Apps

Explore Deeper with Maps

From adding more detail to maps to making it more intuitive to find local businesses, some updates may not be immediately noticeable. However, if you know where to look, a host of new features are there to be used. Here we take a look at using these extra options.

Step 1
❱ Open Google Maps on your desktop. The map should be centred on the country you live in, even if you have not shared location information with Google. Photo tours can be found using the satellite imagery (Earth view).

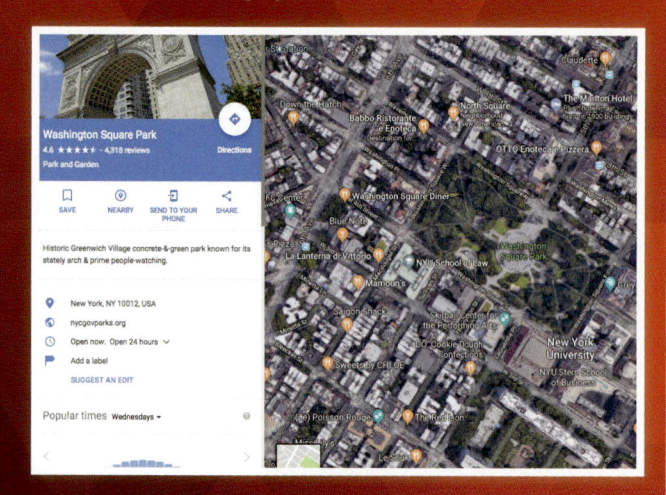

Step 2
❱ Having entered your search criteria, if photo tours of a location are available, they will be displayed as a series of photo thumbnail images on the pop up left side menu. These photos will show a side facing circular arrow icon in the bottom left.

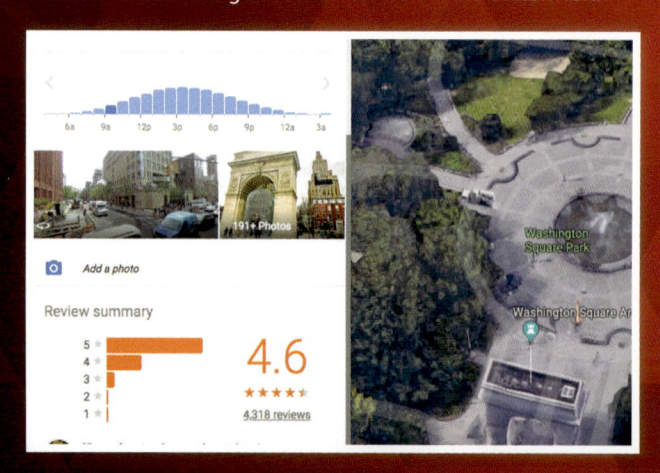

Step 3
❱ Photos, See inside and street views can also be displayed along the bottom of the map, by clicking the Yellow man icon. Photo Spheres are marked with a small blue circle, See Inside with an orange icon and street views with a circular arrow.

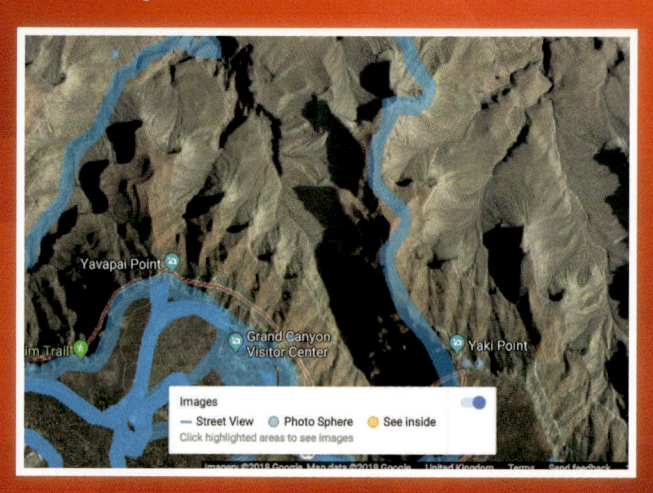

Step 4
❱ Not all areas will feature photo points. They are made available when there are several different views of a particular area. Click on your choice of view and Google Maps will automatically swap to that location and view, here we have selected Photo Sphere.

Explore Deeper with Maps

Step 5
❯ Photo Sphere and See Inside are interactive still photographs that have been uploaded to Google Maps. The latter allows you to do exactly as one would expect and give you a view inside the location, by simply clicking the small orange icon on the map. To exit to Maps click the back arrow top left.

Step 6
❯ If you choose instead to open a photo sphere, you can use your mouse to grab and drag the image around to see a 360 degree image of a location. Photo spheres are created using a smartphone app which, as mentioned, blends multiple photos together as one.

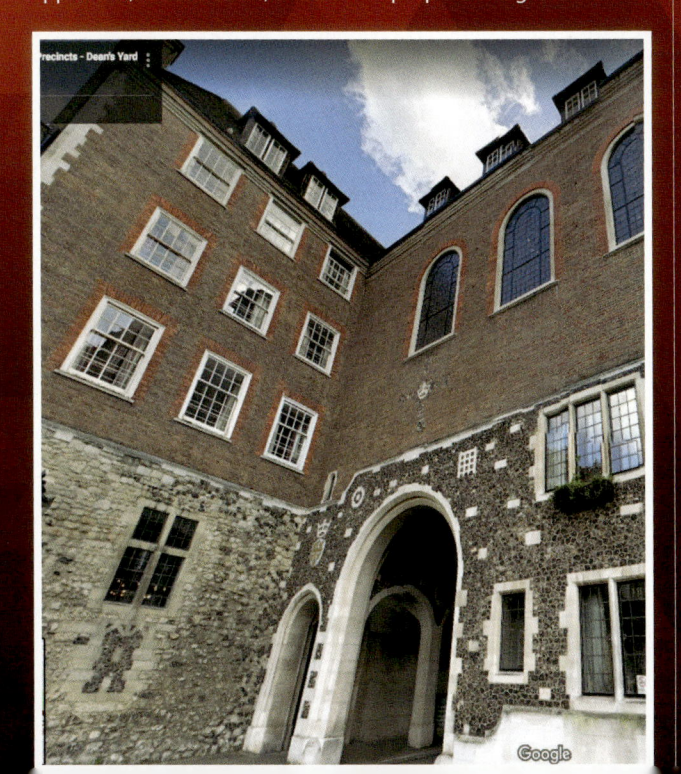

Step 7
❯ Another fantastic feature of Maps is the 3D rendered view point you can access in key locations by clicking the 3D button on the main navigation controls, bottom right. By pressing and holding the Control key you can explore this 3D environment at your will.

Step 8
❯ While in 3D mode, zoom into the screen and your viewpoint will change from the 3D rendered background to Street View automatically. This offers a perfect showcase of view points with a single gesture.

Using Google Apps

Google Maps Tips and Tricks

Google Maps and Google Earth are two of the most powerful and useful tools that Google has ever produced. If you have never done more than check out your house on Maps, here are a few tips and tricks that will help you to see the real possibilities of these tools.

Turn-by-turn Navigation

❯ If you own an Android smartphone, you won't need an extra GPS device for your cross country excursions. Map your road trip and get hands-free, turn-by-turn GPS navigation, complete with voice guidance. You can even get live traffic reports, letting you see current traffic conditions before you set off and while you're on the go. Get estimated travel times and even find alternative routes if things look busy.

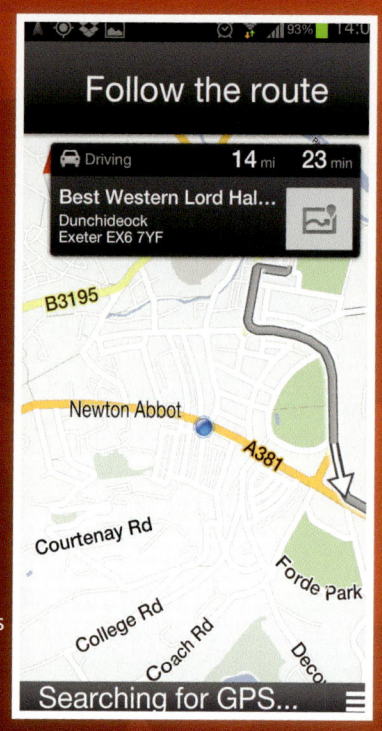

Offline Maps

❯ Get access to a map, with or without a network signal. Download a map of your destination to use offline and maintain GPS functionality even when you lose mobile service. You can save and use certain maps when you're not connected to the Internet. If your mobile device has GPS, the blue dot shows your location so you know where you are. You can even get maps of indoor spaces. The next time you're running through the airport or in a shopping centre, use Google Maps on your mobile phone to get indoor walking directions and find your way around.

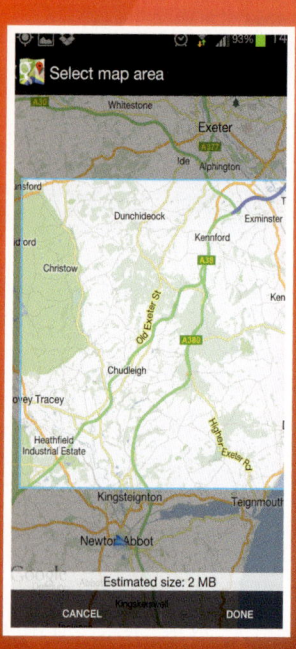

Biking Maps

❯ If you are more of a fan of pedal power than horsepower, you can use the Google Maps Biking Directions beta. Find dedicated bike trails, routes without motor vehicles and the best streets for cycling. Dark green lines indicate bike trails, light green shows dedicated bike lanes and dotted green lines are bicycle-friendly roads. Navigate it all with biking directions in Google Maps Navigation Beta.

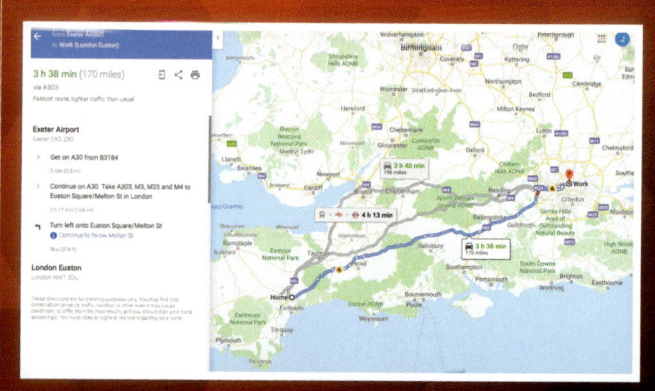

74   www.pclpublications.com

Google Maps Tips and Tricks

Your Places
❱ Want to map out your travel plans or share hiking spots with friends? Try making your own map of what matters to you most with Your Places. Mark locations, add details like photos and links and invite others to collaborate with you on your map; and access it on your Android device. Sign in to your Google account to access your map across all your devices. You can take your map on the go to find your favourite spots easily and even access your desktop location search history on your phone, and vice versa.

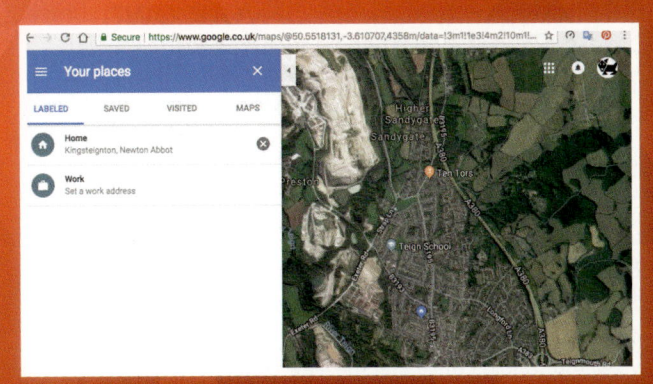

Sharing Maps
❱ You can share maps via a short URL, an HTML embed, email, text message and even send maps to certain GPS units and cars. To generate a customisable embed code or URL, click on the link icon to the top left of your display. Check the Short URL box (or whatever you require) or click the link for Customise and Preview Embedded Map. If you want to send the link out, rather than copy/paste the text that's been generated, click Send for further options.

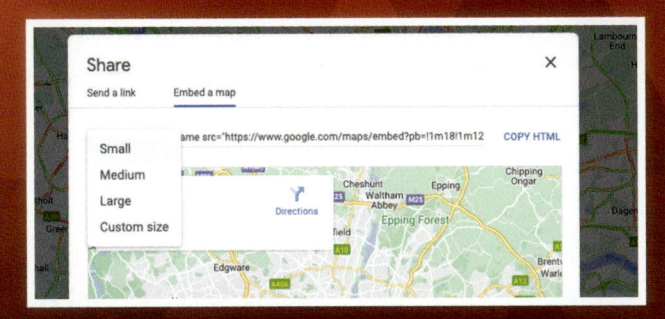

MapsGL
❱ MapsGL uses technology called WebGL (Web-based Graphics Library) to enhance the Google Maps experience. WebGL brings 3D graphics to your browser without the need to install additional software. This allows you to provide seamless transitions between various levels of imagery and different map views. Some of the MapsGL improvements include 3D buildings in Map view mode and 45° aerial imagery, smooth transitions between zoom levels and seamless 45° aerial view rotations and the ability to Swoop quickly from the Map View to Street View imagery. With MapsGL, you can experience all of this in your browser without a plug-in.

Google Arts & Culture
❱ Google Arts & Culture is a platform which brings world heritage sites of the modern and ancient world online. Using Street View, 3D modelling and other Google technologies, these amazing sites are now accessible to everyone across the globe. With videos, photos and in-depth information, you can now explore the wonders of the world from your armchair just as if you were there. A fantastic feature that makes Street View even more unmissable.

Send to Phone
❱ Google Send to Phone enables you to send text messages of Google Maps content to your mobile phone. For example, you might text yourself an address or location you've found.
 To send something you've found on Google Maps to your phone, click the link icon in the left panel. Click Send and choose Phone from the left side. Enter the required information and hit Send. You'll receive a text message with your selection. You can also send a local search result to your phone, by clicking More > Send from the place marker's location information window.

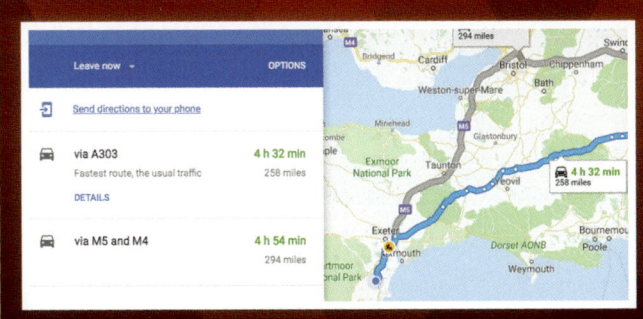

My Places
❱ Using My Places, you can create custom, annotated Google Maps that include place marks, lines and shapes. You can even add descriptive text and embed photos and videos in your map; then share your maps with others. This can be handy for mapping out your favourite restaurants, planning an upcoming holiday or saving hiking routes for future reference.

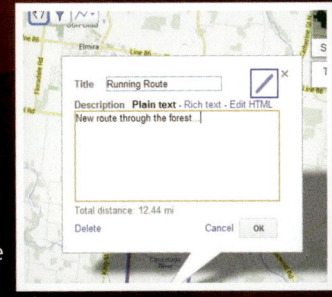

Using Google Apps

Explore with Google Earth

Google Earth lets you explore the world from the comfort of your own home. Featuring high quality satellite imagery, as well as incredible 3D rendered models, Google Earth lets you take a trip to a faraway place, stroll through a 3D forest and even travel back in time.

Step 1
❯ If you have not already installed the Google Earth app on your smartphone or tablet device, you will need to do this before you can begin. Alternatively you can use it from the Google Earth webpage, click on the Learn more link in the bottom left corner of the screen and click on the Earth Pro link to start.

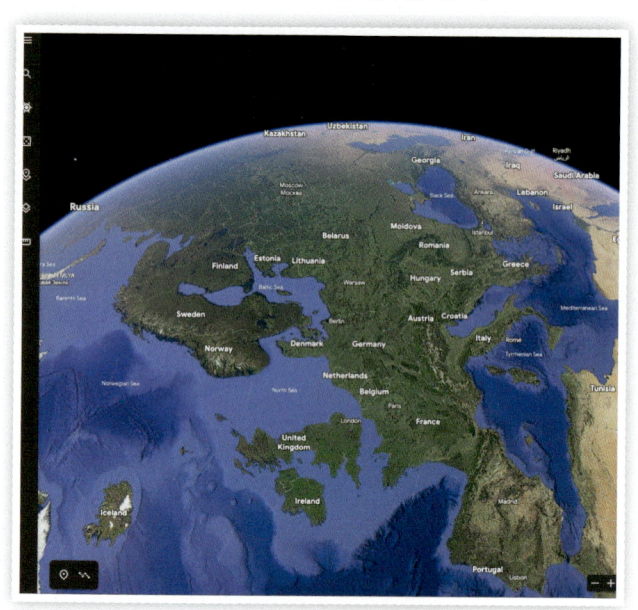

Step 2
❯ Click on the links to install the app. When installation is complete, you will need to refresh the page to load the Earth view. You should notice that the view changes to show detail that is more realistic. You can now zoom right out into space.

Step 3
❯ You can search for locations in Google Earth by clicking the Search icon in the side bar to the left of the screen. Type the name of a street, town or country in the search box and the view will zoom in to show it. Search also for landmarks and businesses.

76   www.pclpublications.com

Explore with Google Earth

Step 4
❯ The view of many locations in Google Earth will be in 3D. To tilt the camera, use the controls at the top left of the window: the control with the eye tilts the camera, the control with the hand pans the camera. You can pan, zoom and tilt by right-clicking on a point and moving the mouse.

Step 5
❯ Switch to view while using Google Earth by clicking the Menu options, top right, and then selecting Map Style. Now you can pick how the Map details are shown. From limited information to in-depth detail or an option between the two.

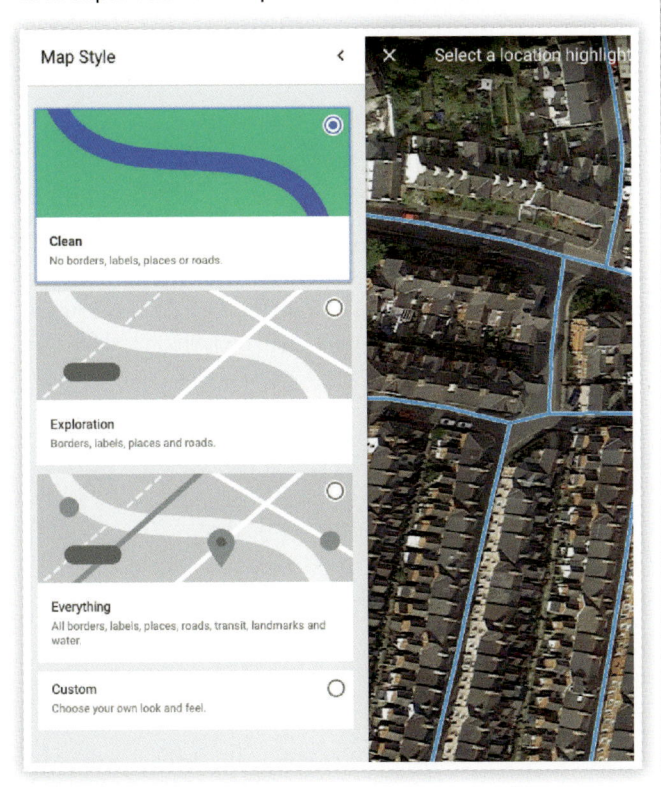

Step 6
❯ You can access news, photos, videos and Wikipedia information via Google Earth. Click on the ship's wheel icon on the left side bar to switch to the Voyager screen. You can then click on individual piece to read it in full. This information is updated regularly so remember to check back.

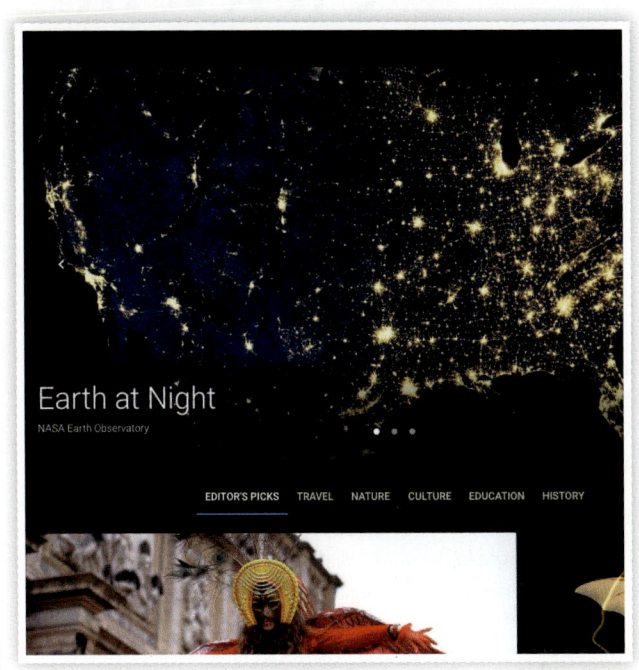

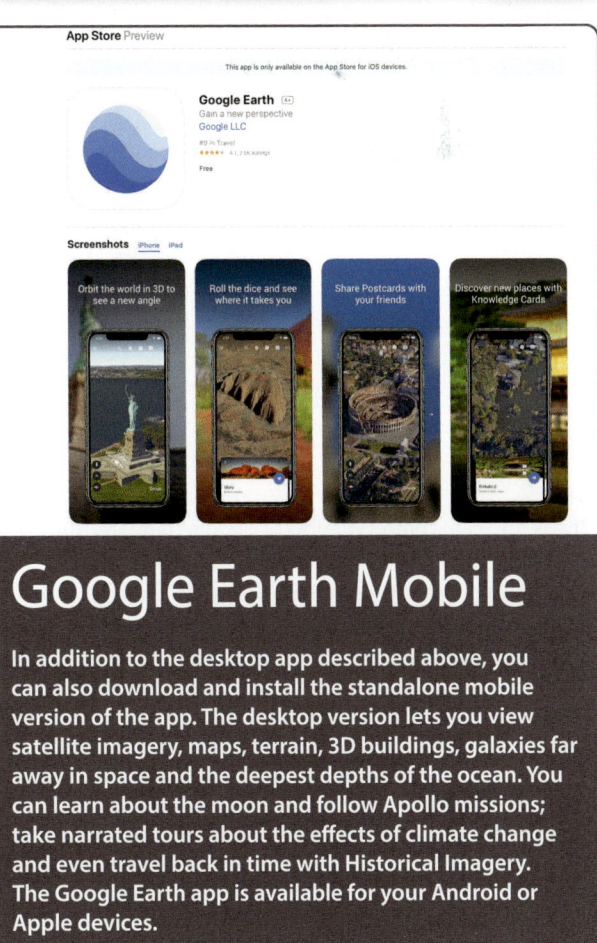

Google Earth Mobile

In addition to the desktop app described above, you can also download and install the standalone mobile version of the app. The desktop version lets you view satellite imagery, maps, terrain, 3D buildings, galaxies far away in space and the deepest depths of the ocean. You can learn about the moon and follow Apollo missions; take narrated tours about the effects of climate change and even travel back in time with Historical Imagery. The Google Earth app is available for your Android or Apple devices.

www.pclpublications.com 77

Using Google Apps

How to Use Google Translate

With the Earth in the palm of your hand or at the end of your keyboard, there are no limits to how far you can explore without barriers. Yet if you have been inspired to open up your world on the other side of your screen, there is one barrier that could limit your travels, that of language.

Setting Up Translate

Google Translate is far more than just a basic translate tool. You can use this in several different ways.

Step 1
❱ Unlike Google Earth or Maps, the Translate app is far less graphically intense but its lack of visual gloss is replaced with a very powerful tool that can prove as essential, so let's take a look. Open the Apps menu on the tool bar and select Translate from the choice of applications.

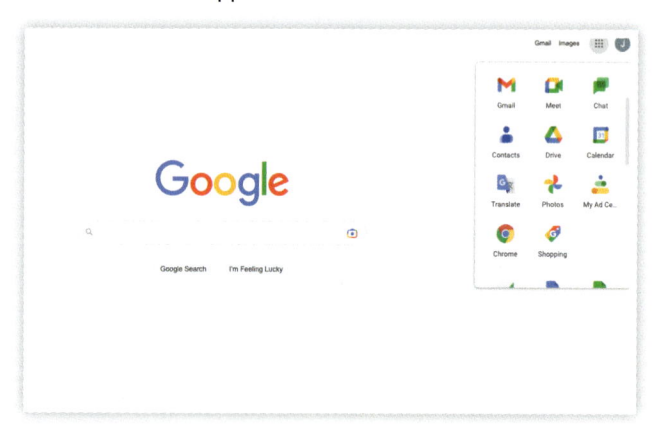

Step 2
❱ This is the main control window of Google Translate, from here you can decipher any communication break downs. Notice the two boxes on screen. The left (input) is where you enter the original text and the right (output) is where it is translated.

Step 3
❱ Just like a standard Google search you can choose to input your text via the keyboard or using voice input. To use the latter, click on the Microphone icon to the left or if you prefer the former, tap the keyboard icon to the right. Your text will now appear in the box to the left. By clicking the double arrow icon between these boxes, you can swap the text.

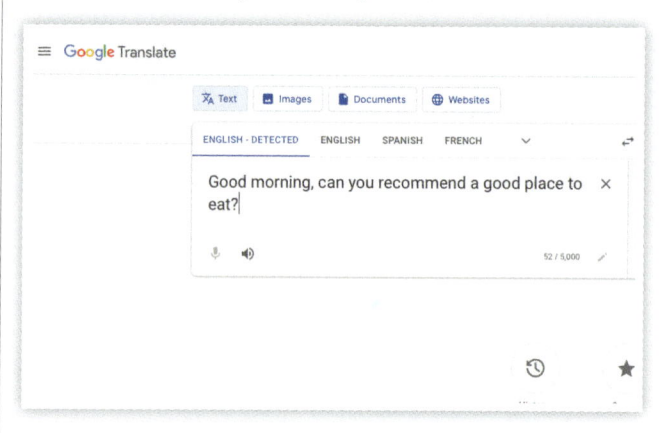

Step 4
❱ NOTE: You are limited 5000 characters per translation so ensure you enter your text in small chunks to avoid missing text. For this first example we have entered an expression in English and selected Norwegian, from the drop down menu, as the translated language. The translation happens in real time.

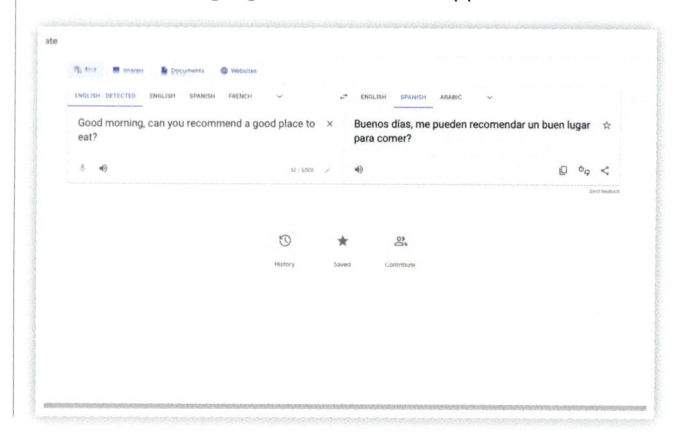

Google Lens Translate

Using the Google Lens feature on your smartphone's camera you can instantly translate text. You do this by selecting the "Translate" option from those displayed at the bottom of the screen and simply holding your camera at the text you wish to translate and tapping Capture. The image will now display in your default language.

78 www.pclpublications.com

How to Use Google Translate

Step 5
❱ If you wish to translate the same piece of text into another language, click on the downward arrow icon and select your language for the list of options. You can also hear both the original and the translated expression by clicking the speaker icon in the bottom left of the input or output windows.

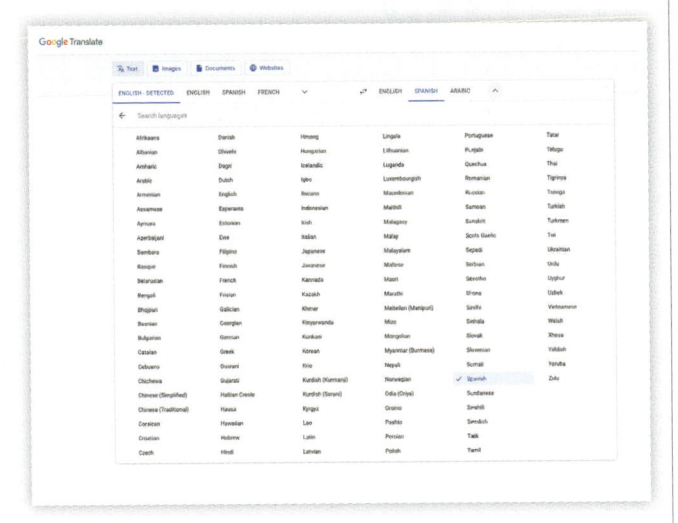

Step 6
❱ You can also use Google Translate for images, documents and websites. Simply select from the above and follow the instructions. For this example let's look at translating a website from English into Spanish. Click website from the links, enter the URL and hit the Blue arrow, it will load in a pop-in in Spanish.

Step 7
❱ Translated text can be Copied, Shared or Saved to Phrasebook, the results using the icon links in the output box. By clicking the Star icon to the top right you can open your Phrasebook and quickly view all your saved translations. You can also save the file by clicking Export to Google Sheets.

Step 8
❱ To translate complete documents and text on images via Google Translate, the process is similar for both formats. Click either Documents or Images from the top bar and then locate the file on your device. Then click on Download Translation to output the translated file to device.

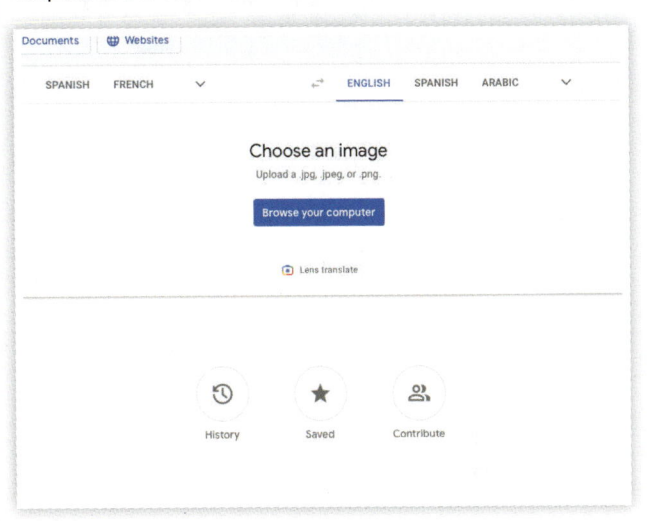

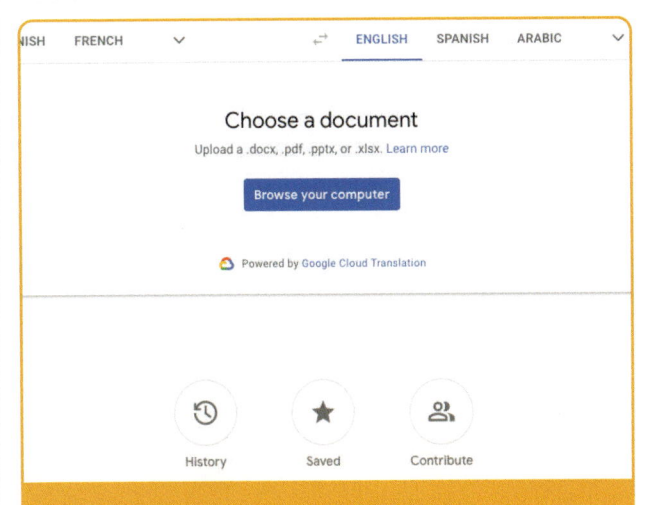

Translate Documents

To translate a piece of text that is larger than 5000 characters you can upload a full document which will be read and translated by the Translate app. Once the process is complete you are free to download the translated document. This process is far from complex as we will detail below.

From the "translate a document" link below the text input box, click on blue text to bring up a small grey box with a Choose file link on the left side. Click this link and locate the file you wish to translate and select as is usual with your OS. You can upload files from a number of formats from Word to HTML files, there is a 1MB file size limit so ensure your doc is compatible. Once your file is uploaded tap the blue Translate icon to load your translated document, leaving you to copy and paste the results as you wish.

www.pclpublications.com

Using Google Apps

How to Use Google Flights

Google have apps for navigating the world around you, and Google Flights is the next logical addition to their app portfolio, giving you quick access to explore the world for real. With this app you can find and book flights for you and your family, making the world more accessible.

Step 1
❱ Navigate to the Google Flights website google.com/flights to be presented with this home page. It is advised that you allow Google to track your location so you will be automatically linked to your nearest airport, based on distance.

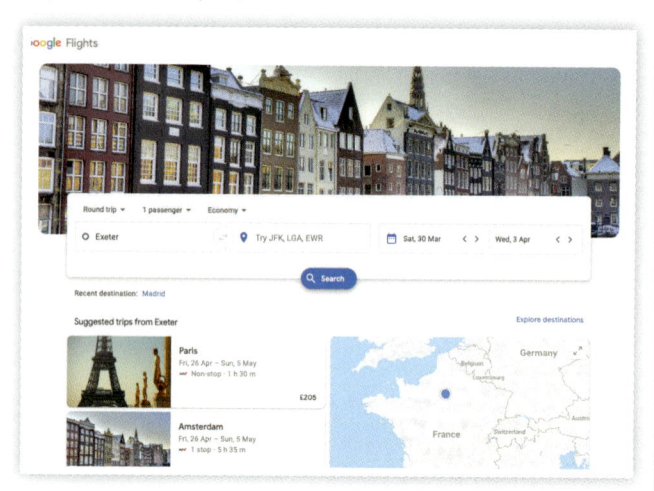

Step 2
❱ Just above the main search bar, you will notice you have three options which are very important to ensure your search results match your requirements. Your options are type of trip, number of passengers and finally type of seat. Enter your picks.

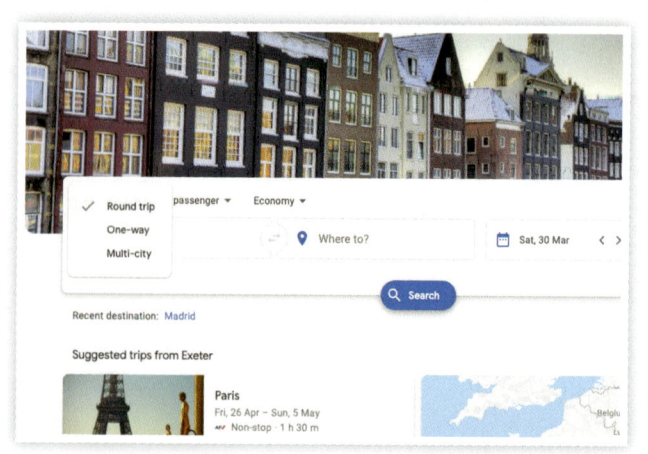

Step 3
❱ In the search bar, first enter the airport you wish to fly from and the destination you wish to travel to. NOTE: if this location doesn't fly to your choice of destination the nearest airport that does, will be selected for you. Next select a travel date.

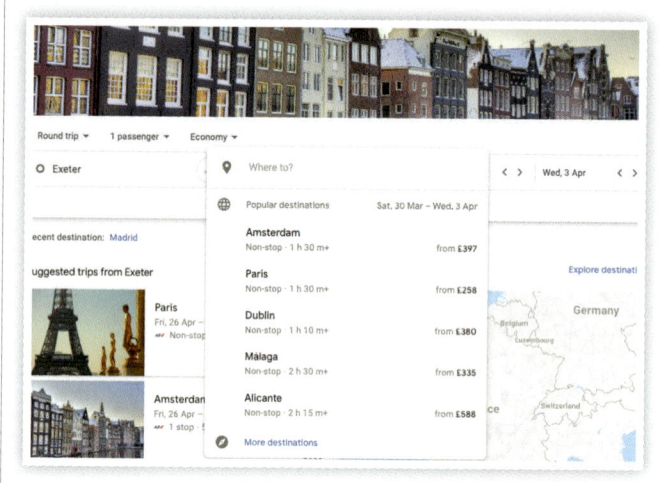

Step 4
❱ Having selected the airport and your destination you can now confirm that your flights are available for the time period you wish to fly. To do this simply enter the departure and return dates to see a listing of all available flights within this time scale.

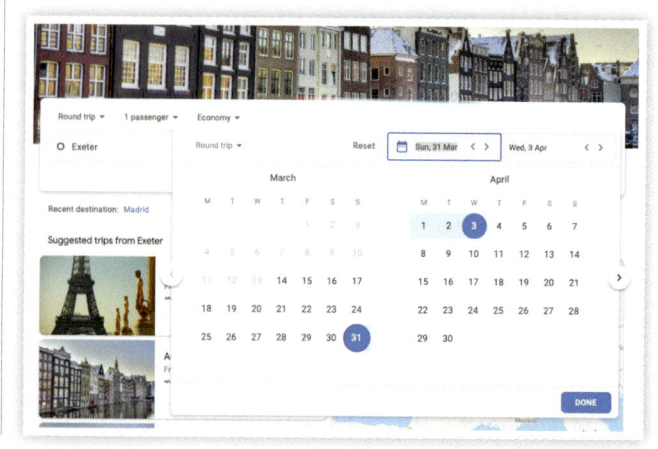

How to Use Google Flights

Step 5
❭ Click the flight that suits your needs to be taken to this window, from here you can view any stop overs or changes required by clicking the small arrow icon to the right of the top bar. If you have happy to move on click anywhere on the listing.

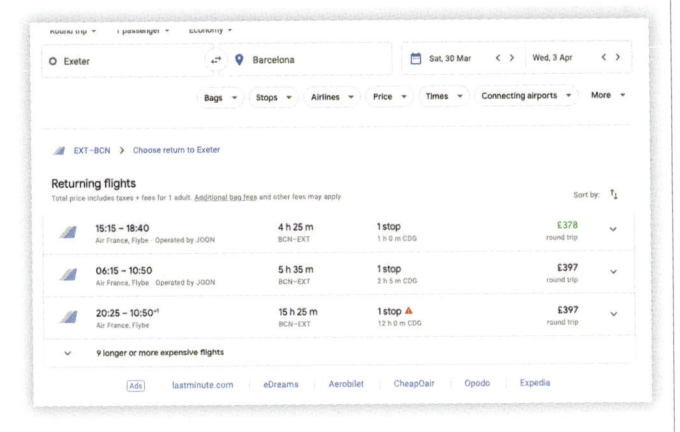

Step 6
❭ This screen is where you actually book the flight and confirm the listed details. When you are happy to proceed, click the Select icon and you will be automatically taken to the airline or ticket vendors' website, where you can complete your booking.

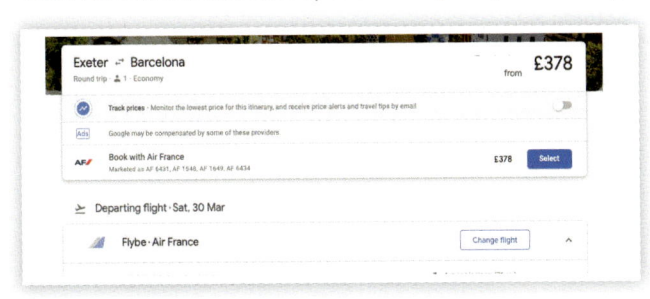

Step 7
❭ If you are more open with your travel plans, and don't have a strict destination you wish to visit you are well covered by this app. From the home page click the Explore Destinations link directly above the world map bottom right.

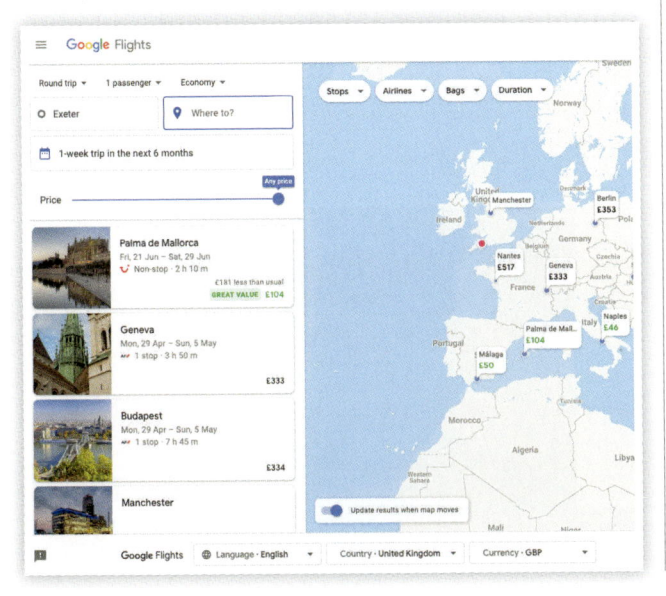

Step 8
❭ From the map screen you will see a selection of locations and flight prices that are available from your choice of airport. Click on any of these to be shown the flight plan, a visual and a brief selection of alternative flights and their costs.

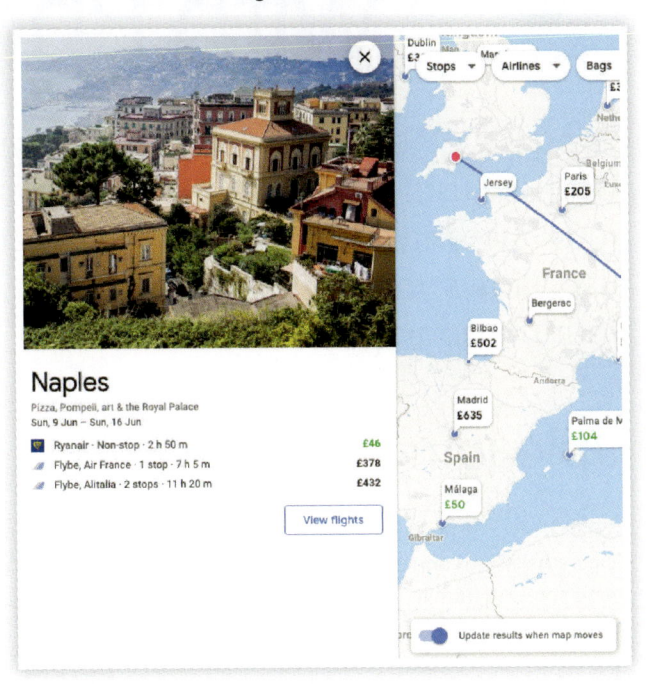

Step 9
❭ You can also choose to change the search parameters based on the price of the flight. You can do this by using the slide bar on the left of the screen and selecting the price you wish to pay. The results are displayed below.

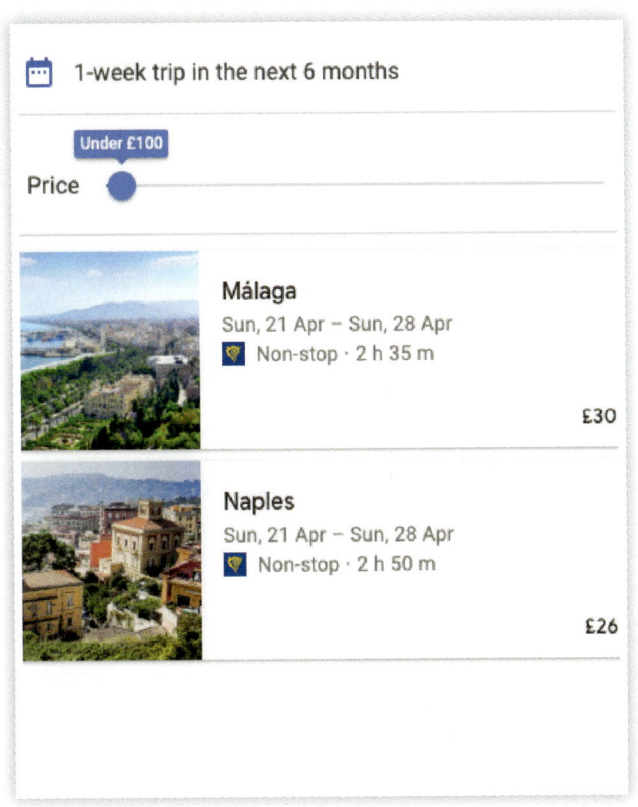

www.pclpublications.com   81

Using Google Apps

Getting Started with Photos

If you have never used Photos before, you may be surprised to discover just how useful this free tool is. It not only lets you create slideshows of your favourite images and share images with your friends and family, it also allows you to edit your images. By making Photos the central hub for your photography those memories will be safe.

Uploading to Photos

Step 1
❭ Open the Photos app via the App icon and the drop down menu accessed from it. The first thing you will need to do with Photos is upload your images and videos into it. Unlike its predecessor Google's Picasa, Photos doesn't search your computer for files thus you will need to organise yours first.

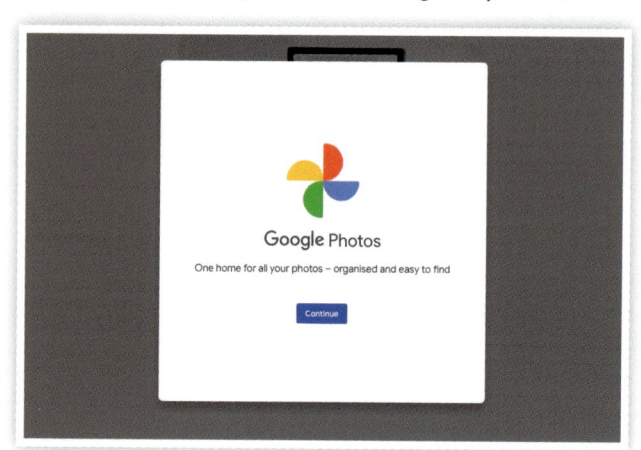

Step 2
❭ Having placed the files you wish to upload to Photos in a folder, the quickest way to transfer them is to simply drag and drop the files on the Photos window as a group. You can choose to resize them from their original size to Storage saver, with a reduction in quality.

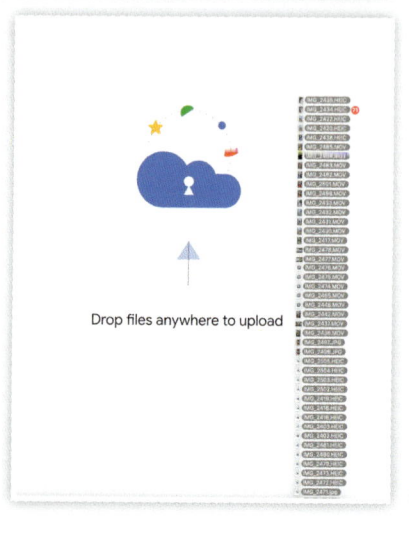

Step 3
❭ When your files have uploaded to Photos, they will be displayed based upon the date the images or videos were captured, newest to oldest being the default setting. Notice the link to the Desktop Uploader, ignore that for now as we will cover it later.

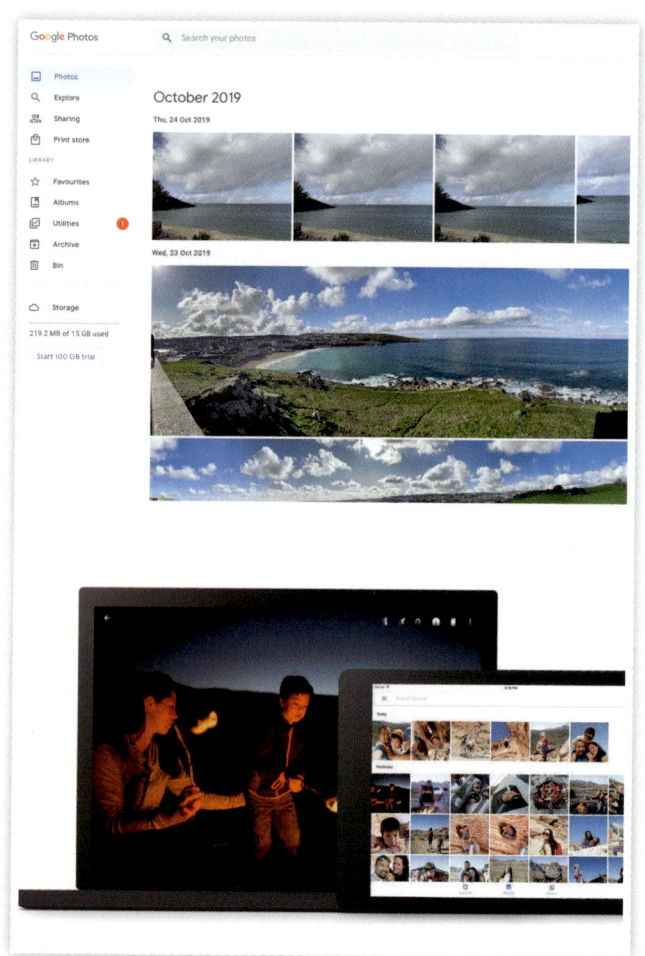

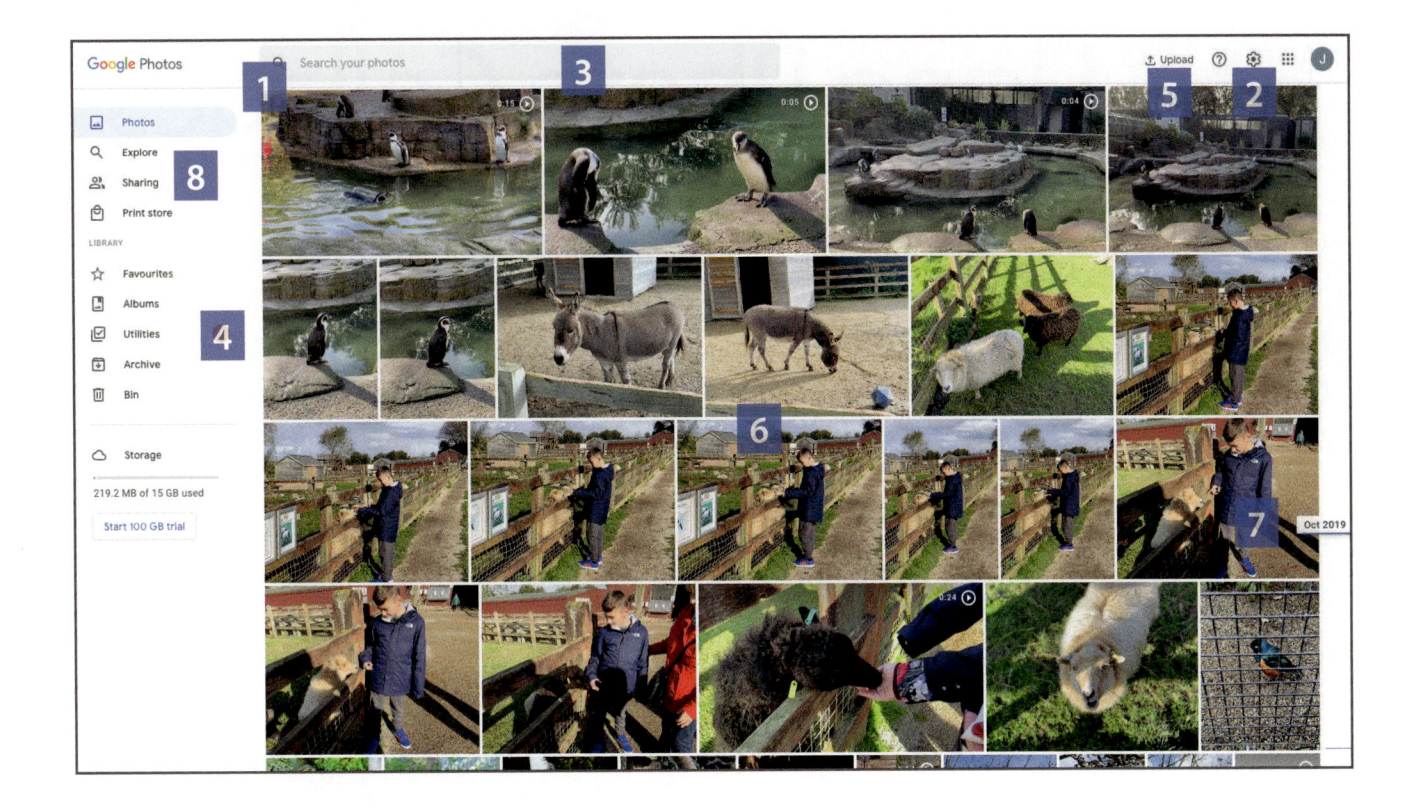

Getting Started with Photos

Using Photos
Below we break down the key features and controls of the Google Photos application, so it's even easier to use.

1 Menu
❱ This is the main Photos menu panel, giving you control of the core uses of the app. Here you can quickly access the key functionality of the application, from sharing your images and videos to clearing out unwanted files.

2 Settings
❱ The Settings link gives you access to Photos customisable features. From this link you can decide upon your storage options, compressed but high quality storage is free, while keeping your files at the original size is limited to 15GB for free.

3 Search
❱ By entering the title of your file you can search your image and video database for it. If you have a large amount of files stored in Photos, you can narrow the criteria of your search to specific files from Videos to 360 photos by double clicking on search.

4 Ulties
❱ Tap this link to open a pop-up menu which contains four additional links, Album, Shared album, Animation and Collage. By click on your choice from these four options you will be taken directly to its specific window.

5 Upload
❱ By tapping this link you will open an upload window, where you can search your computer for any additional photographs or videos that you wish to add to your Photos file collection. Once you have located the files, select them and click Open.

6 Timeline
❱ Here you can control the images and videos that are displayed in the main Preview window based upon the date they were originally captured. To do this simply scroll up or down through the Timeline bar, stopping at the date you wish to view.

7 Preview Window
❱ By default, all images, animations, collages and videos will be displayed in this main window. You can scroll through your collection and by clicking on a file you can view it full screen and add it to your Pinterest account by tapping the icon top left.

8 Sharing
❱ This option is a far more in-depth way of sharing your entire library of files with another user via an email account, for example a family member or friend. You can, however, only share your library with one person.

www.pclpublications.com

Using Google Apps

Using Photo Collages and Animations

One of the great features included with Photos is the ability to make collages and animations of your files, either for yourself or to be shared with your friends and family.

Step 1
❯ Starting with a collage, the first task is to select your photos. You can select a single folder by clicking on it in the folder panel or you can select numerous images by clicking on the tick icon on the top left corner of each of the images you want.

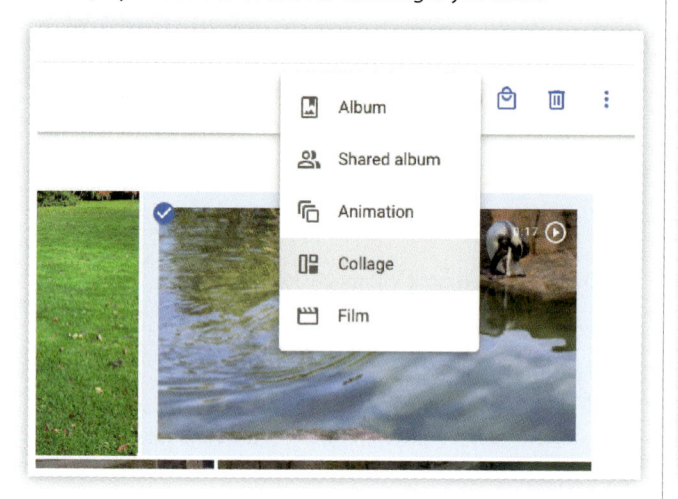

Step 2
❯ Once all the images you want are selected, click the + icon located in the top right of the preview window. A new menu will open; from the options you are given, select Collage. Photos will now auto generate a collage based on your images.

Step 3
❯ You can edit your image collage by tapping the edit icon located to the top right of this screen. You have a series of options and filters that you can apply to your new image. To use a filter click the Edit icon (Top left) and then click on the style.

Step 4
❯ You can also adjust the level of filter use using the slider bar in the middle of the filters listings. The crop and rotate tool enables you to cut out sections of the collage or rotate the image at either 90 degree angles or manually.

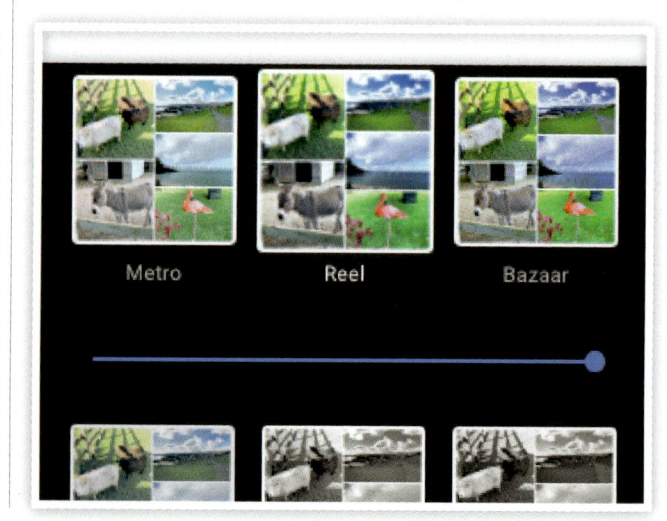

84   www.pclpublications.com

Using Photo Collages and Animations

Step 5
❱ When you are happy with the edits to your collage, tap the Done icon. You have a couple of options for saving it. Click the more options link on the far right corner of the window. Now choose how you wish to store your new collage from this list.

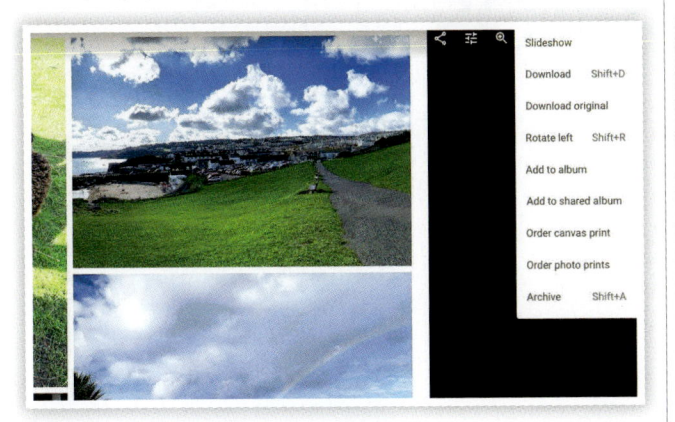

Step 6
❱ Moving on to the Animation option, once again select the images you wish to add and click the + icon and select Animation for your list of options. Now all your have to do is leave the Photos application to do the work for you.

Step 7
❱ Photos will now auto generate an Animation based on your images. This animation is simply a slideshow, moving between a series of still images. This animation is automatically saved to your collection of files within Photos.

Step 8
❱ When you are happy with your collage and or your animated slide-show you can send them to your contacts by tapping the Share icon. When you see this window, choose how you wish to share the file and click the required icon to make your selection.

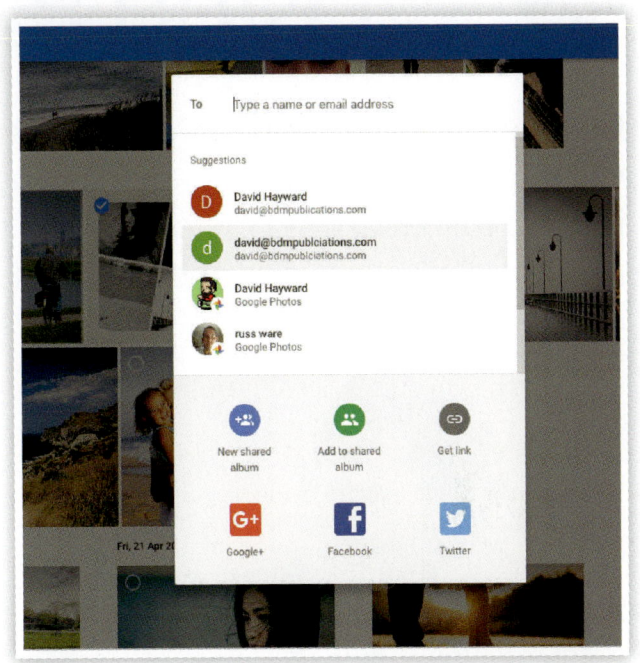

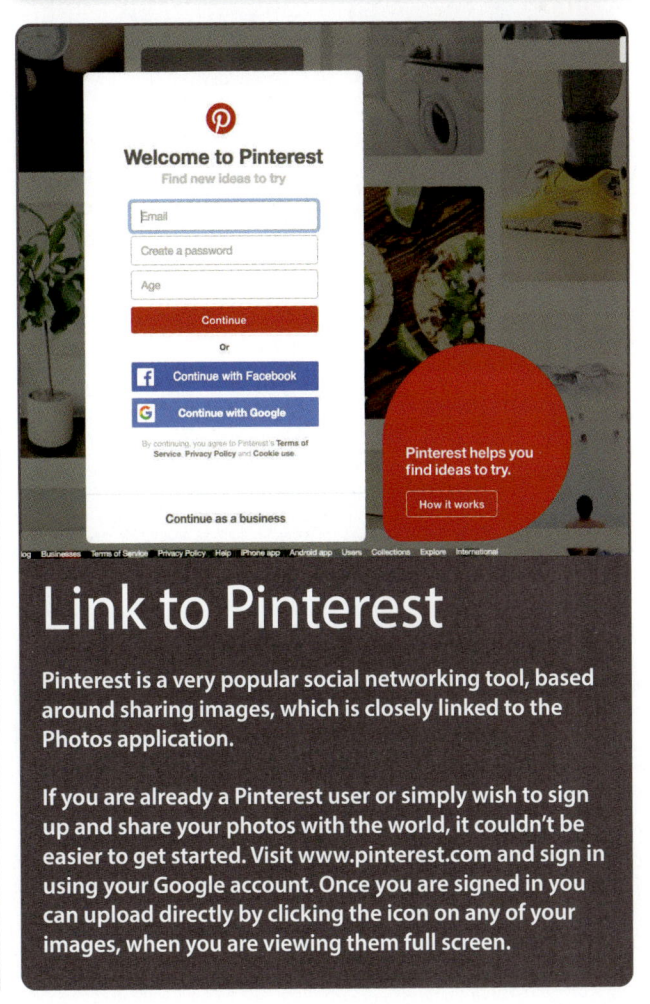

Link to Pinterest

Pinterest is a very popular social networking tool, based around sharing images, which is closely linked to the Photos application.

If you are already a Pinterest user or simply wish to sign up and share your photos with the world, it couldn't be easier to get started. Visit www.pinterest.com and sign in using your Google account. Once you are signed in you can upload directly by clicking the icon on any of your images, when you are viewing them full screen.

Using Google Apps

Editing Images Using Photos

Google Photos not only provides you with storage for your photos and videos in one place, it can also be used to edit your picture. Photos editor is not a fully-featured image editing program but it includes enough to make the most of your photos. It's also free!

Quick Fixes

❱ As stated Google Photo editing isn't a fully optimised and functional Photoshop alternative but with that said, there are more than enough options for you to clean up or enhance your digital photography, with only the most basic understanding of photo-editing. Photos offers simple tools, designed to help fix common problems with a few clicks as follows.

Light and Colour Fixes

❱ These controls let you change the lighting or colour levels of your image. You can either use the sliders to change Light, Colour temperature and Pop. The latter being a fantastic tool that adds greater depth to your images with a simple adjustment to the slider.

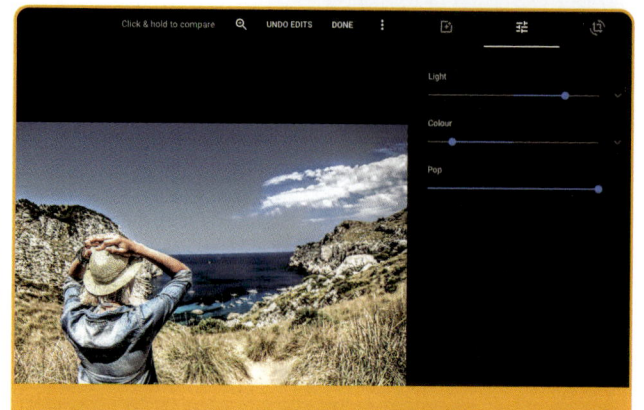

Undo Edits

You can easily remove any edits you have made to your photographs while you are still editing. All you need to do to remove your edits is click on the Undo Edits button located at the top of the editing window. By doing this you will instantly remove any changes you have made to the image, from applying filters to cropping and rotating, so make sure you are happy to do so before clicking. You can copy your edits via the edit menu (three dots) and paste them on any image in your library.

Editing Images Using Photos

Image Processing (Filters)
❯ These controls let you quickly add a range of different filters to your images. These range from sepia and black and white, to soft focus and graduated tint. Click on each filter and you can then control the intensity of the effect using sliders. You can easily undo any effect using the buttons below the filter list.

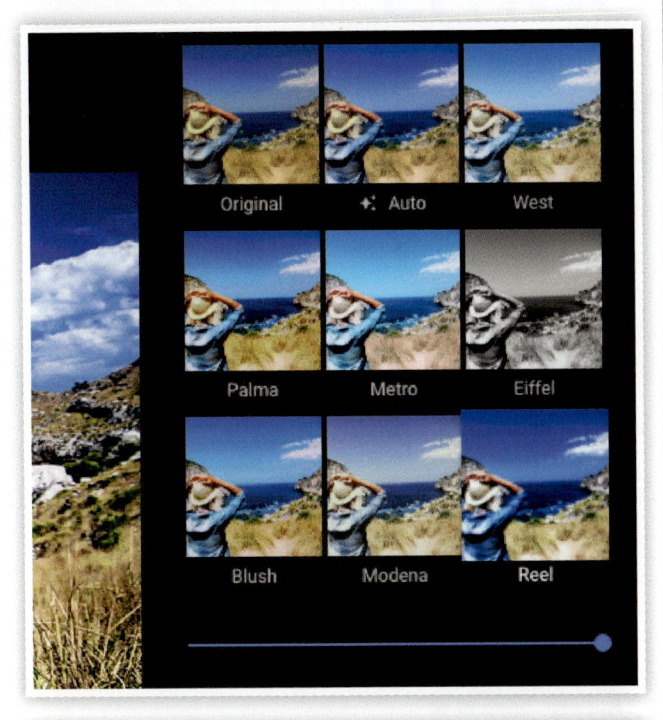

Rotate and Crop
❯ The crop and rotate tool enables you to cut out sections of the collage or rotate the image at either 90 degree angles or manually using the user controls down the right hand side. NOTE: If you are using the crop tool to zoom this could effect image quality.

You can also crop the image to a number of specific aspect ratios, Free (user defined as detailed above), Original, Square, 16:9, 4:3 and 3:2 by clicking the aspect ratio icon in the top bar. Having selected any of these ratio options, Photos will place an adjustable frame on the image, click Done when you are ready to crop the image.

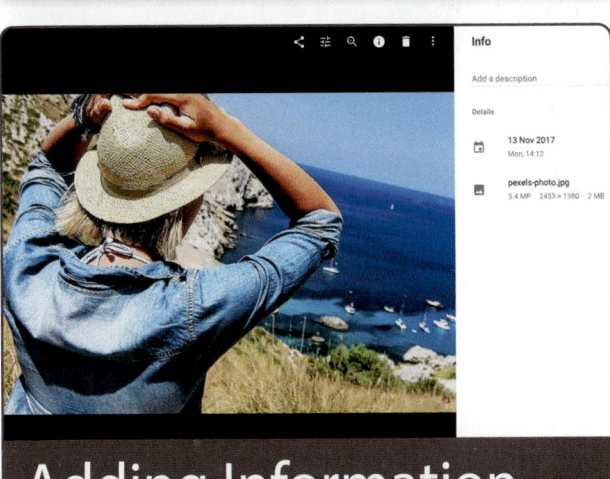

Click and Hold to Compare
❯ When editing or applying filters to your images, it is very important that you don't lose sight of the original image; this ensures that your edits aren't actually detrimental. At anytime during the editing process, you can revert to your original image by pressing and holding on the mouse button or screen. Your altered image can be saved as a copy.

Adding Information
Each photo or movie file in your Photos library contains unique information. This includes file size, resolution, date and time it was captured all as default. This data can be viewed by clicking on the "i" icon on the control bar at the top of the window. You can add a custom description to your files, which will be stored as part of the image's information. To save this new info tap the X Icon in the top right corner of the screen.

www.pclpublications.com

Using Google Apps

Using Your Photo Albums

Google Photos Albums is an easy way to store your photos online and then share them as and when you choose. Google provides free storage that makes sharing your photos quick and easy.

Adding Photos to Web Albums

Adding photos that you have on your computer to your Web Albums is easy using the Google Photos software.

Step 1
❱ Open the Photos app and search through your photo folders to find the images you want. Each file acts as an individual but you can create new albums containing a mix of files if you wish.

Step 2
❱ To create a new album folder, click on the tick icon on the files you want to add to the folder. Now click the + icon in the top right of the main tool bar and select Album from the drop down list in the top right corner, as shown here.

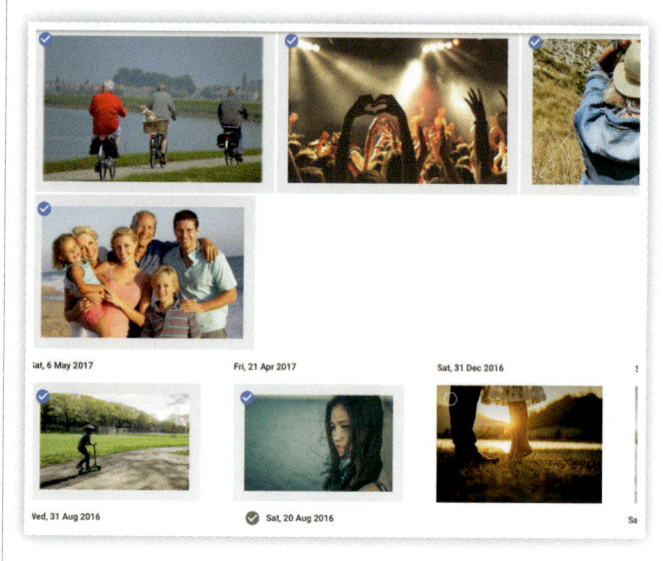

Step 3
❱ You can choose to save to an existing Album to create a new one. Access to these albums is achieved in the same way, by clicking the link of your choice.

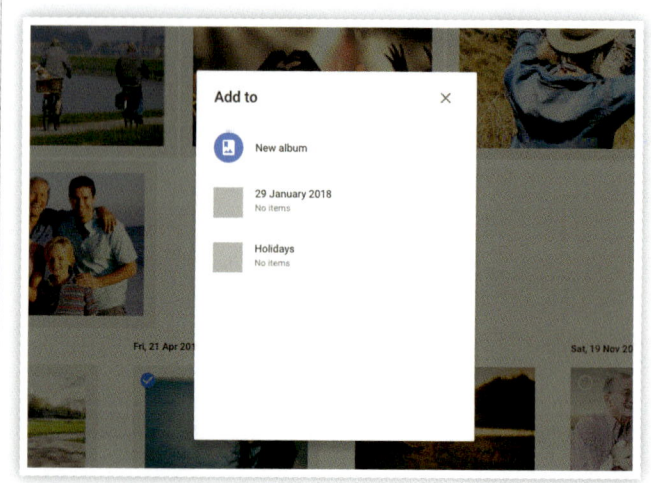

Using Your Photo Albums

Step 4
❱ Having chosen to create a new Album, you can now customise its name by entering your title into the text input box at the top of the collection of files; click the tick icon to finish . You can also add files to this folder by dragging and dropping directly.

Sharing Web Albums
There are a couple of different ways to share your files and albums, depending on whether the recipients have signed up for Google.

Step 1
❱ To share a single file, click on the image to enter full screen view and then tap the Share icon on the right of the screen. From this menu screen you can share with a Google contact by clicking them.

Step 2
❱ Alternatively you can share via your social networks by tapping the link to Facebook or Twitter. To share to a non-Google contact, click Get Link and then copy and paste it into a message or email.

Step 3
❱ To share an album, click on the icon in the top right corner of the album and then click on Share. Once again you can quickly share with Google contacts by clicking on their name.

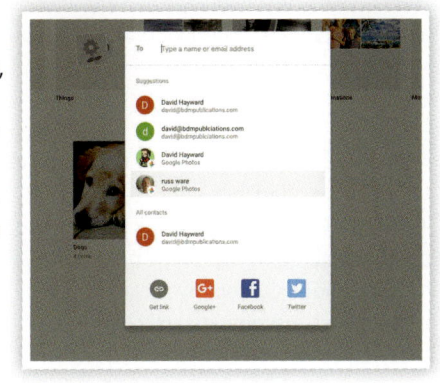

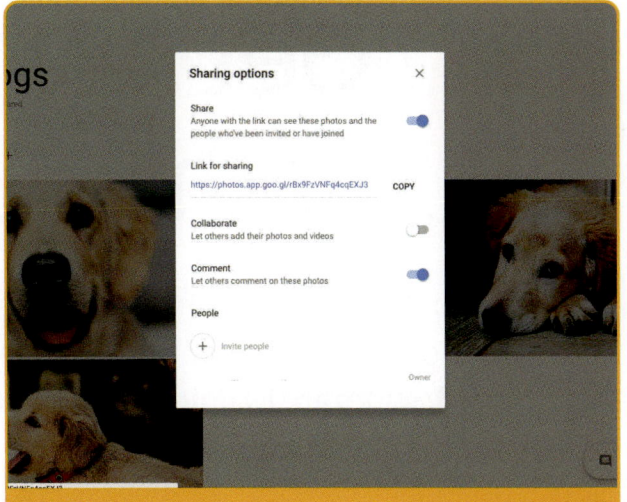

Album Access
The people you share with are added to the Shared with list in Google Photos. These people can do the following:

- If your album visibility is limited, they can view it by signing in to Photos.
- They can see the shared album on your Photos Web gallery, your Google profile and in Google+ (if you've signed up).
- Google+ users: The people you share with have permission to reshare your album. Within Google+, they can also see who else you've shared it with.

Step 4
❱ Alternatively you can also share via your social networks by tapping the link(s). To share to a non-Google contact, click Get Link and then copy and paste it into a message or email and send the link as per usual.

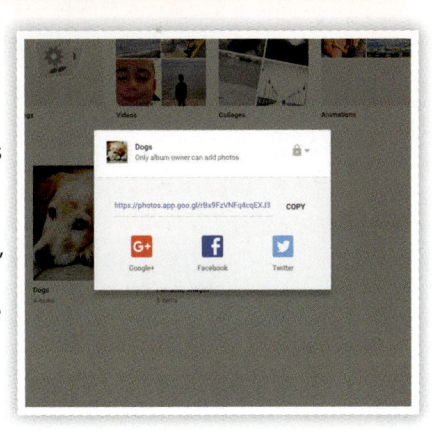

Step 5
❱ Add a comment if you'd like to add context to your photos. This text will be posted with your photos in Google+. Add individual people or email addresses and then click Share.

www.pclpublications.com 89

Using Google Apps

Get Started with YouTube

YouTube provides a forum for people to connect, inform and inspire others across the globe and acts as a distribution platform for original content creators. More than 1 billion unique users visit YouTube, are you one?

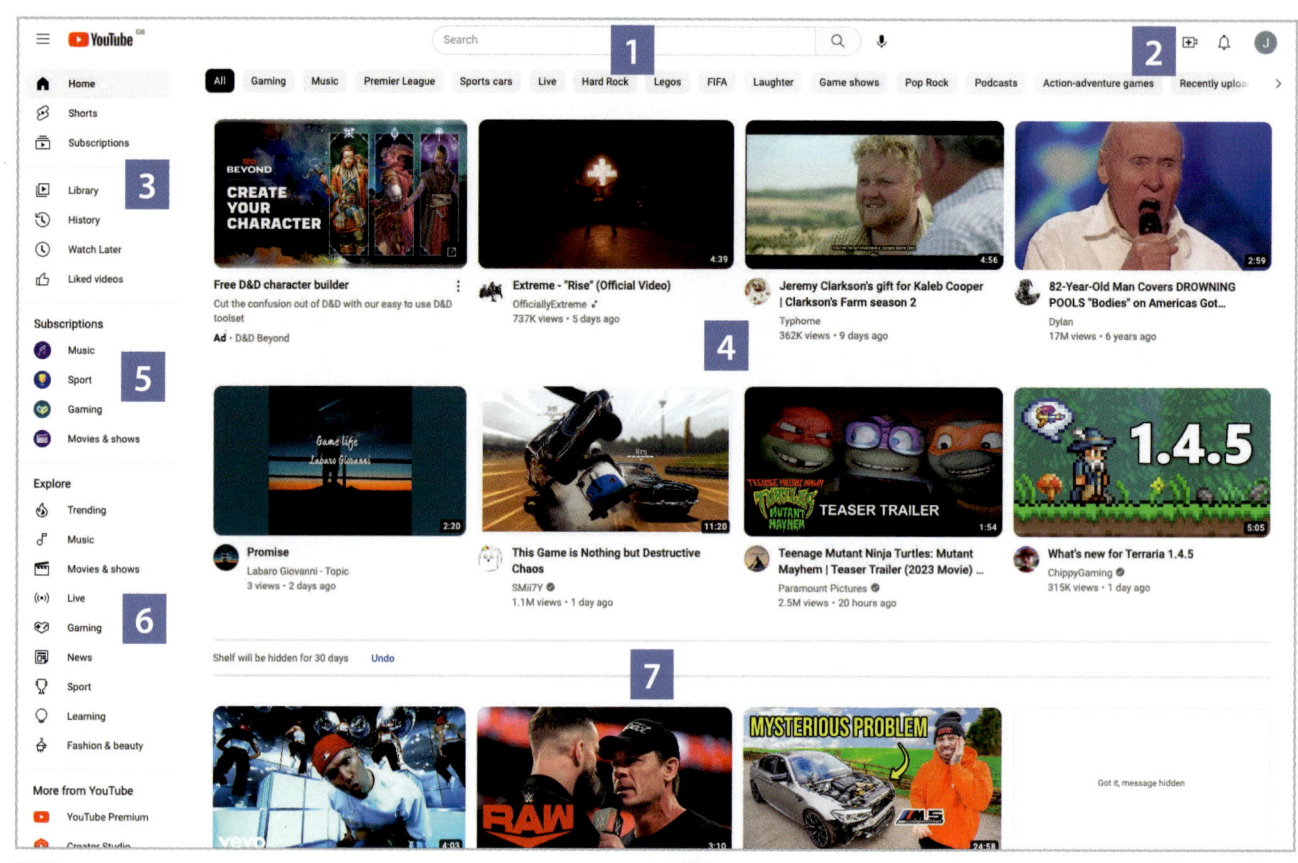

1 Search
> You can search YouTube just as you would search on Google and as you type your search term, suggestions will appear below the search box. Previously searched terms that are similar will show at the top of the suggestions box. Search results are displayed in order of relevance.

2 Upload Controls
> This drop-down menu contains a direct link to the upload screen as well as links to your uploads dashboard; here you can see all of the content you have uploaded and your analytics, which shows how many times your videos have been viewed and, if you have a channel, how many subscribers you have. These controls give access to figures charting your channel.

3 Account Controls
> Here you can see your viewing history, channel subscriptions, playlists you have created and social connections. You can also control or delete channel subscriptions. Social connections allows you to share your content with your Facebook or Twitter.

4 Recommended Content
> If you are signed in to your account, and have viewed any videos previously, content that is recommended for you will be displayed at the top of the home page. You can view more recommended content by clicking the word "recommended". If you have subscribed to any channels, relevant content from those channels will also be included here.

Get Started with YouTube

5 Subscribed Channels

❯ A list of your subscribed channels is shown here. You can click the arrow button just above the list to change how it is displayed: new content, A-Z or most relevant. Just below the channel subscriptions list is a button which takes you to the complete listing of available channels. You will also find the controls for managing channels there as well.

6 Recommended Content

❯ The listing here is based on the videos you have watched and which channels you have previously subscribed to. Roll your mouse over the Subscribe button to see how many subscribers any channel has and click the button to instantly subscribe. A tick next to the name of the channel shows that it is verified as an official channel.

7 Latest Content

❯ The most recent content from your subscribed channels is displayed as a list at the bottom of the screen. If you have not subscribed to any channels, this list will be populated from the most viewed content on YouTube, content that is currently trending and that which is relevant to your geographic location.

Manage Playlists

With playlists, you can put a series of videos all in one handy place. For example, you could create a playlist of all of your favourite music videos or sports clips.

Step 1

❯ To add videos to playlist, click the Add to link underneath a video. You can add it to a playlist that already exists or you can create a new one.

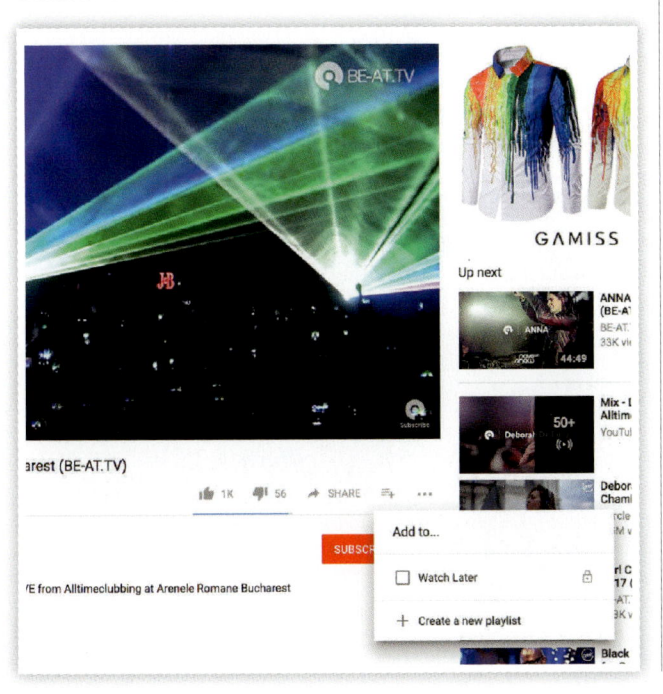

Step 2

❯ You can make changes to your playlists by visiting your Library. This link is found on the left side of the main YouTube user window.

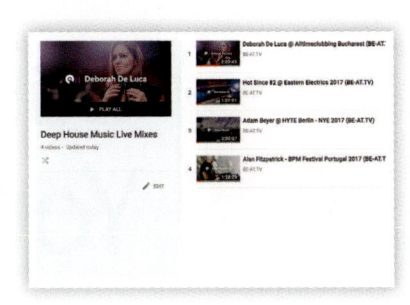

Step 3

❯ Open the playlist you want to change and click the Edit button next to the playlist you want to edit. Click Done to save any changes you make.

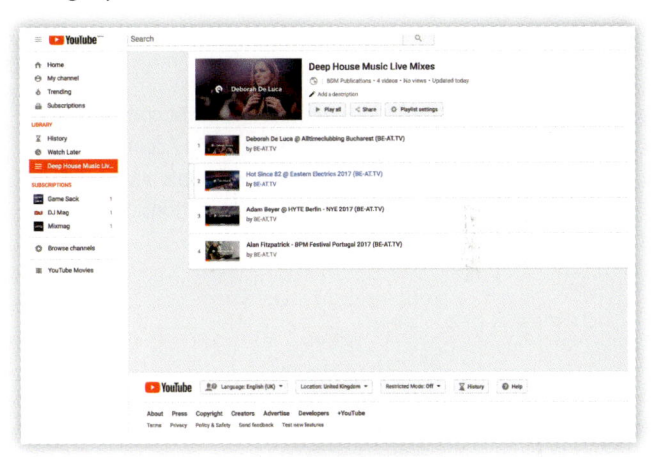

Step 4

❯ Reorder videos in your playlist by hovering your mouse over the video until you see a grey vertical bar to the left of the video. Click the grey bar, then drag and drop the video to rearrange it.

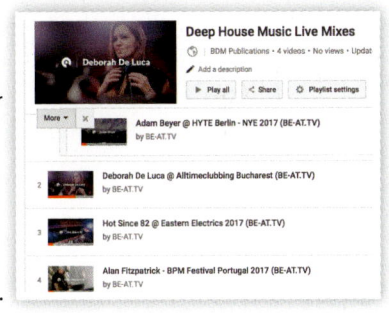

Step 5

❯ To delete an entire playlist, click the More icon at the top right corner of this window, then click Delete Playlist at the top of the list. Once a playlist has been removed, you cannot undo.

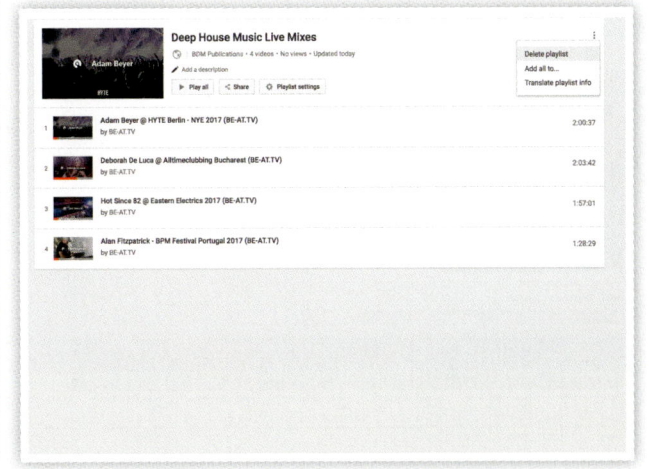

www.pclpublications.com   91

Using Google Apps

Using the YouTube App

The YouTube app gives you access to great videos and shows on all sorts of subjects. It is the gateway to a huge and always expanding world of entertainment. Follow this guide and enjoy YouTube, wherever you are.

Step 1
❱ Log in by tapping the Silhouette icon (top right corner). If you don't, you can set one up (tap Sign In then Add Account). It's a good idea to use YouTube while logged in, as this allows videos you might like to be offered as viewing suggestions.

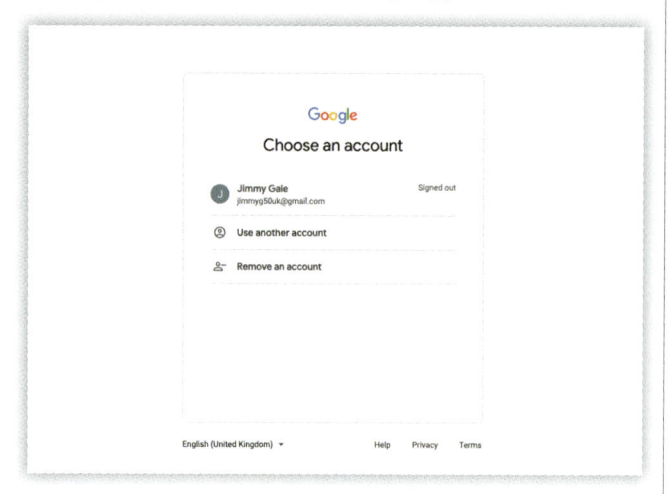

Step 2
❱ You can search for a subject or channel using the Magnifying glass icon. You're then presented with a list of relevant videos, showing how many views they've had, their length and their uploader. Their length, in minutes, is shown in the screenshot.

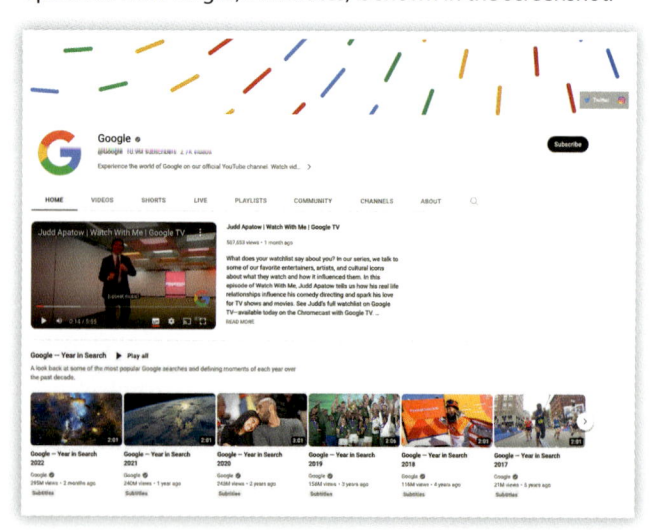

Step 3
❱ Tap on a video to open it. You might have to watch a short advert first. While watching, you can use the Thumbs icons to like or dislike it, the Share icon to share it or you can save it to your Watch Later list. Similar videos are listed below it.

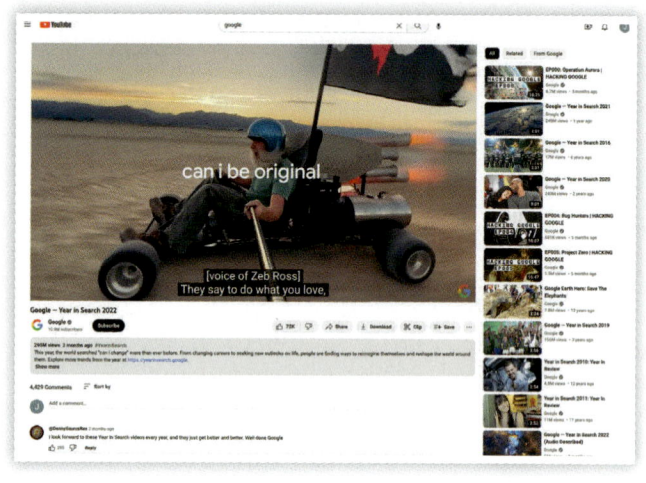

Step 4
❱ Two more controls are worth a mention. The Show More link below the left corner of the video can be tapped to reveal or conceal further information and you can tap the Subscribe button to be informed whenever the YouTuber posts.

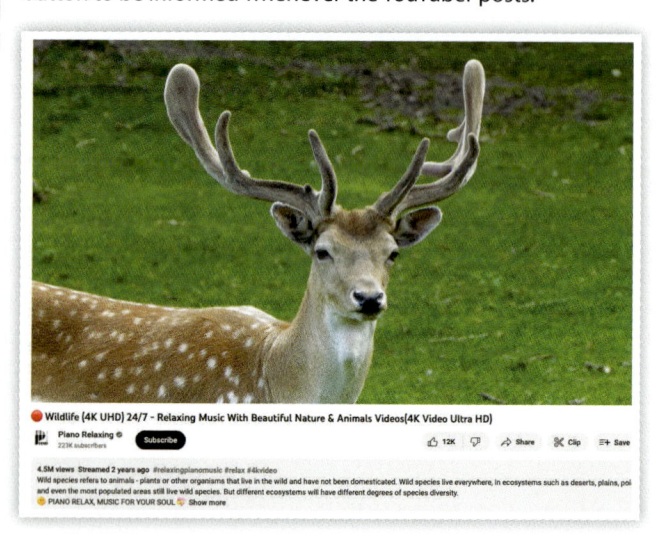

Using the YouTube App

Step 5
❱ Tap the video as it plays and you get these controls. There's the Pause/Play icon and either side are the controls to skip to the next video or restart. Scrub through the video using the red dot, or make it full screen with the icon in the bottom right.

Step 6
❱ The icons, in the bottom right, gives access to further options, such as: reporting the video, adding captions or changing the resolution. Tap the video at the top of the screen, anywhere there's no icons, to hide the controls and go back to viewing.

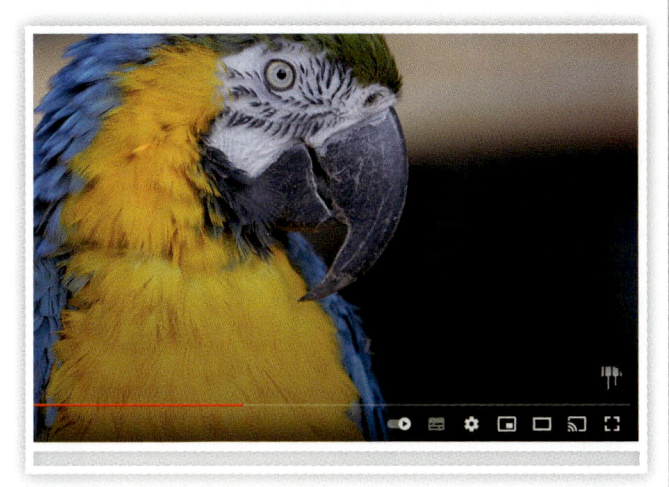

Step 7
❱ Notice the rectangular icon with the Wi-Fi icon within it. Tap this icon to stream YouTube from your tablet to a TV, using Chromecast or Airplay. Simply select the device you wish to cast to from the list and your video will instantly play on that device.

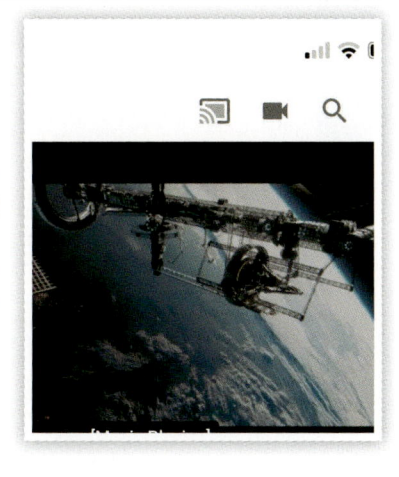

Step 8
❱ The YouTube app also features the ability to "Go Live" with your content. This is available directly through your device if you have a camera and microphone attached or built in. To start your live stream click the camera icon and select "Go Live" to share your stream with the world. Once complete your stream will be save to your YouTube video uploads.

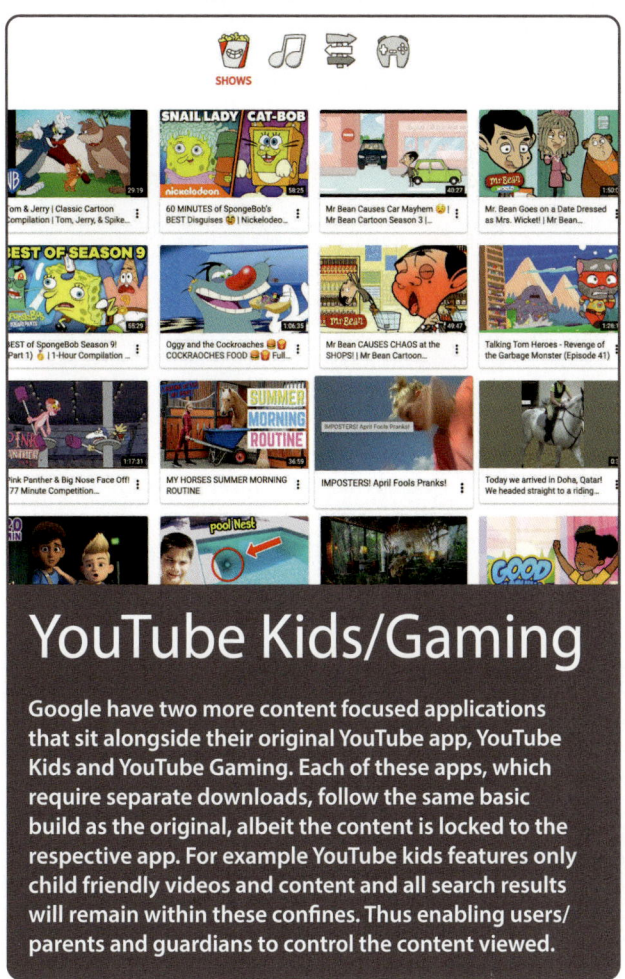

YouTube Kids/Gaming

Google have two more content focused applications that sit alongside their original YouTube app, YouTube Kids and YouTube Gaming. Each of these apps, which require separate downloads, follow the same basic build as the original, albeit the content is locked to the respective app. For example YouTube kids features only child friendly videos and content and all search results will remain within these confines. Thus enabling users/parents and guardians to control the content viewed.

www.pclpublications.com   93

Using Google Apps

Uploading & Live Streaming Videos

It may sometimes seem like the whole world is uploading videos to YouTube, from the random ramblings of retro gamers to budding musicians. If you want to add your own voice to the varied world of YouTube, here's how to get started.

Step 1
❱ Sign in to your YouTube account if you haven't already done so. At the top right of the screen, wherever you are in YouTube, you will see a Camera Icon. Click this to get started. Firstly you will need to create a Youtube Channel to upload your videos and, more importantly, allow others to find them and if they like them, subscribed to see more. Be careful to pick the right name as this is the your introduction to other Youtubers!

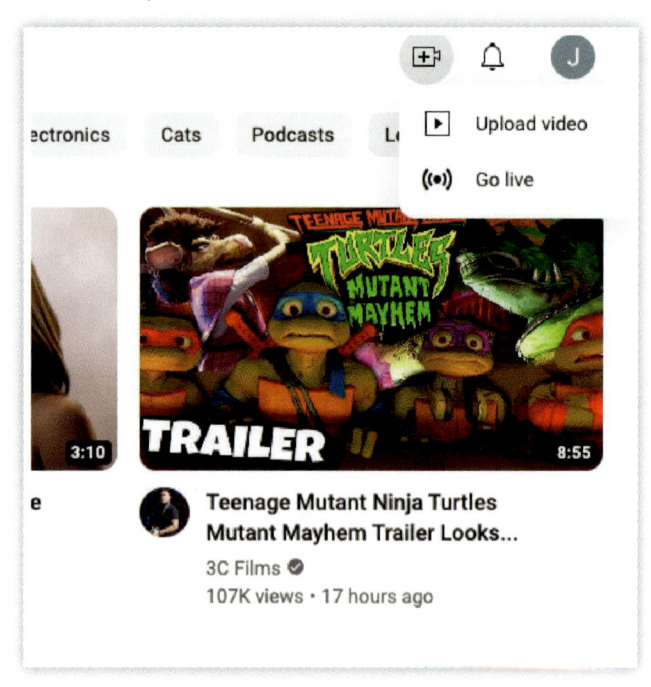

Step 2
❱ Click anywhere in the upload window on the next screen to start browsing for your videos. Alternatively, you can drag videos onto the browser window from any open folder.

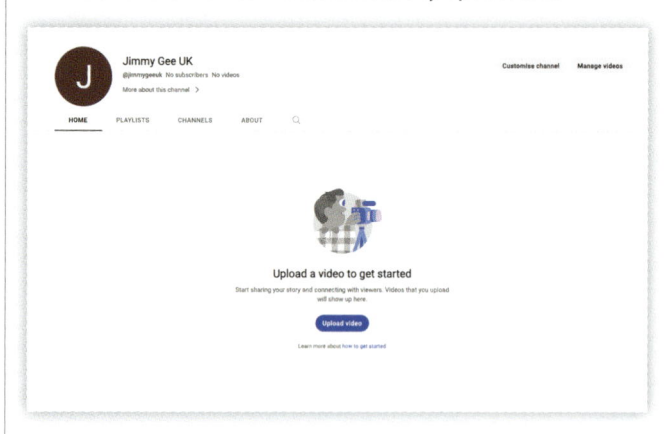

Step 3
❱ Once you have added a video to the upload window, using either method, a new page will open. If the video file has a title, it will automatically be entered in the title box or you can edit it.

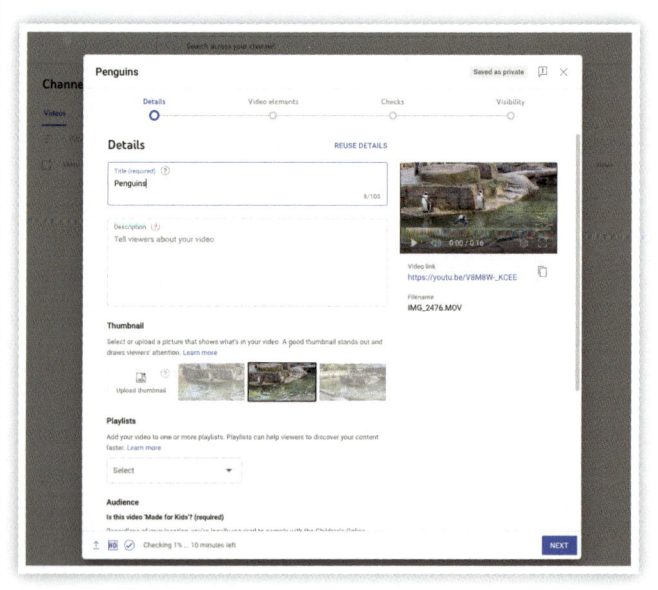

Video Formats

Not sure which format to save your video? If you receive an "invalid file format" error message when you're uploading, make sure that you're using one of the following formats:

.MOV, .MPEG4, .AVI, .WMV, .MPEGPS, .FLV, 3GPP or WebM

Uploading Videos to YouTube

Step 4
❯ Fill out the rest of the information, including the description and the tags, as these help make it easier for the video to be found by searchers. Try to give as much information as you can as this will widen the search and get you more views.

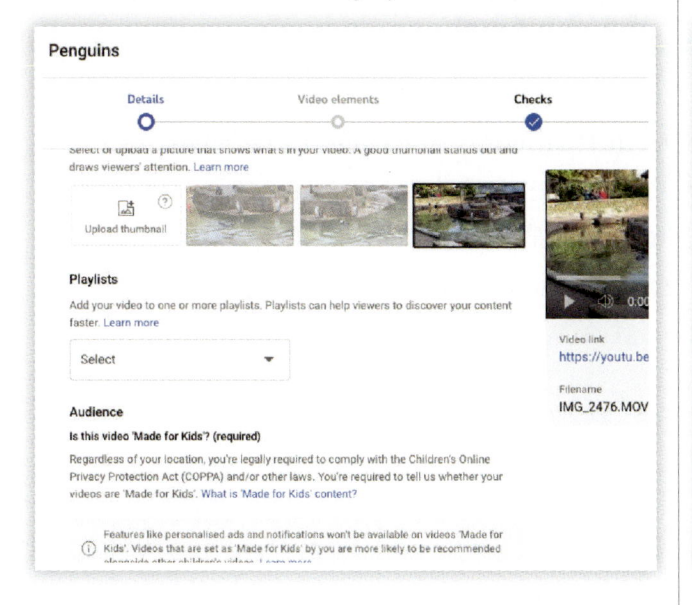

Step 5
❯ When the video has finished processing, several thumbnails will automatically be grabbed from it and displayed. Click on the one you want to use as the display thumbnail on YouTube: select the one that sums up your video clip or add your own.

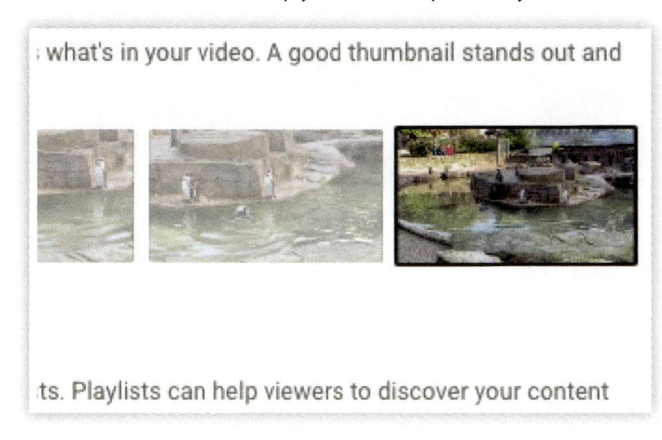

Step 6
❯ The next stages are Checks and Visibility. Checks allows you to add your own subtitles, an end screen and in video cards to promote your channel etc. These options only appear for videos over 25 seconds in length and user generated.

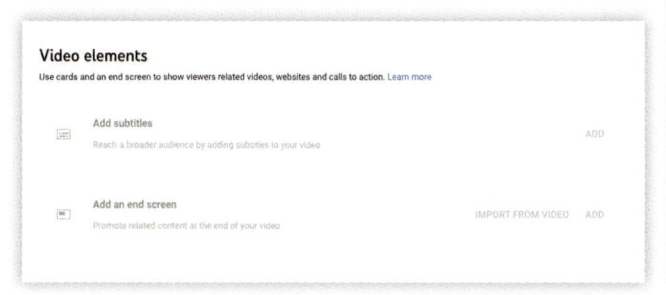

Step 7
❯ This final stage, allows you to select Visibility, your audience for the video, you can choose, Private, Unlisted or Public. Private videos are only viewable by invite, unlisted videos aren't listed in searches and public videos are viewable by all.

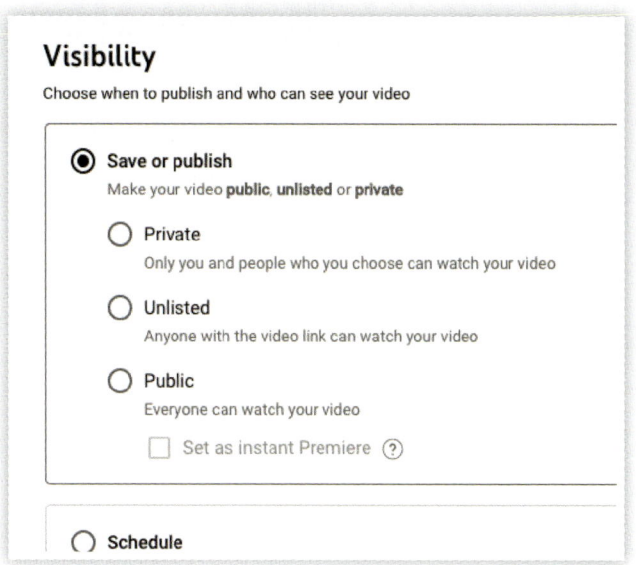

Step 8
❯ You are now taken to the Channel Content screen, here you can view all of your videos, change some settings such as Visibility and Restrictions and check your video's stats, such as views and likes.

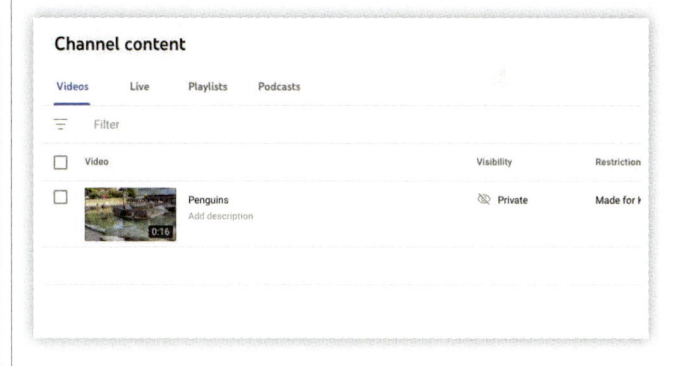

Step 9
❯ Once your Channel is verified by adding a Phone number, you can request to Live Stream, this will take 24 hours to confirm. Once confirmed you can live stream via the Create Link and your webcam or external camera and mic to the world. Be nice!

www.pclpublications.com   95

Using Google Apps

How to Use Google Drive

Google Drive is a free storage service which allows you to store images, folders and documents in the Cloud. These files and documents can then be accessed from any tablet, phone or computer via the Google Drive software. Not only is this a great way to free up space on your devices, it also lets you access your files from almost anywhere.

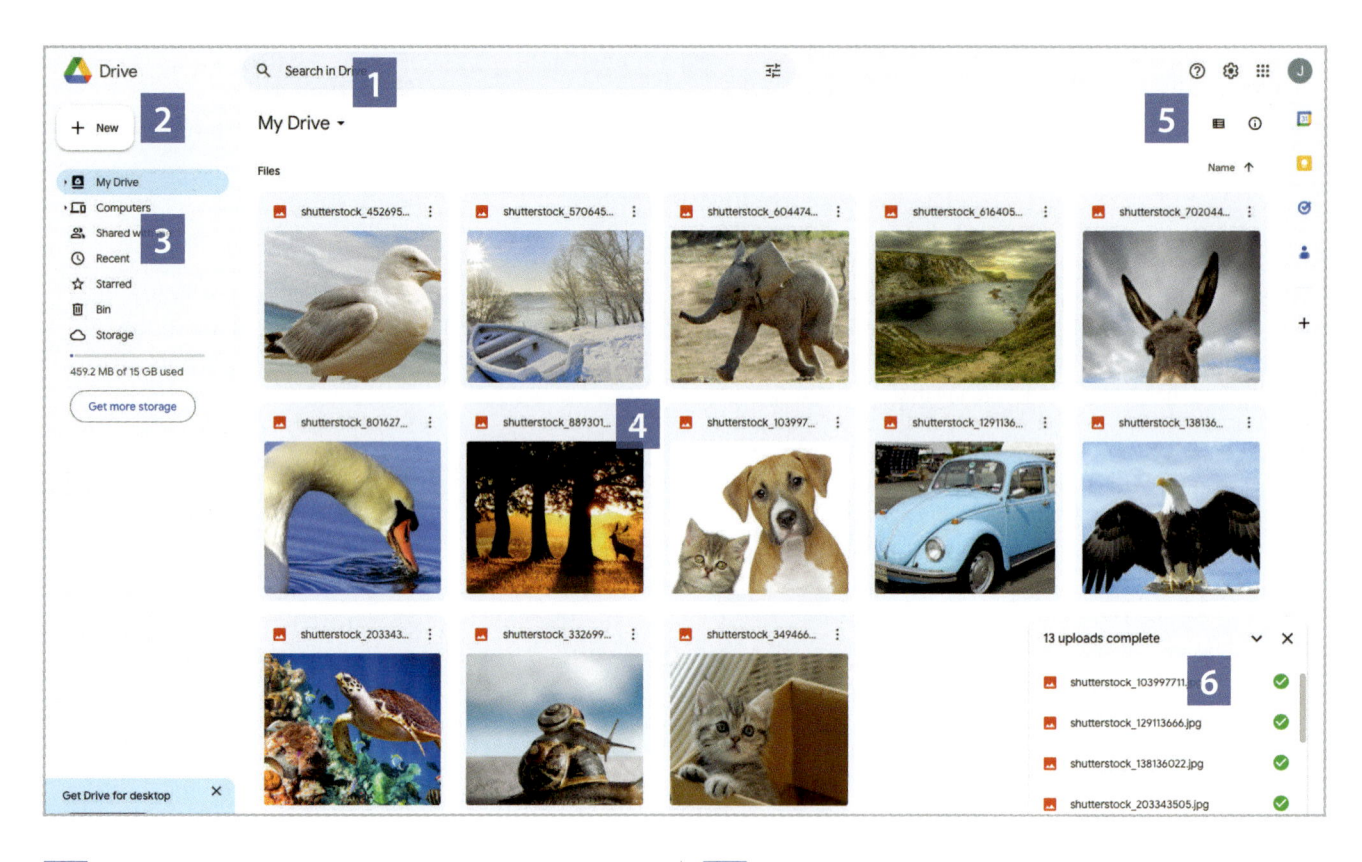

1 Search
› You can search Google Drive in the same way that you can search Gmail or one of the other Google products.

2 New
› Click the New button to open a new document, spreadsheet, presentation, form or drawing.

3 Folders
› Your preset Google Drive folders are shown here, along with any that you have created. Click More to see Labels.

4 Current Folder
› The contents of the currently selected folder are shown here. You can change how items are displayed (List or Grid).

5 Display Controls
› Change how items in your folders are displayed and how they are sorted. The gear icon lets you access the G Drive settings.

6 Upload List
› When you upload multiple items to Google Drive, the Upload box appears, to show you the progress of each item.

How to Use Google Drive

Free Google Storage

Google Drive, Google+ Photos and Gmail give you storage space for nothing so you can keep your files, emails and photos accessible from any device, anywhere. If you reach the free storage limit, everything in Google Drive, Google+ Photos, and Gmail will still be accessible but you won't be able to create or add anything new. You'll still be able to create Google Docs, since they don't take up any storage space. For G+ Photos, you will only be able to upload new photos and videos under certain size limits.

Installing Backup and Sync – PC/Mac

Step 1
❱ The first thing you need to do is check your Google Drive access status. You can do this at drive.google.com/start. If you have access, you will see a blue Download button.

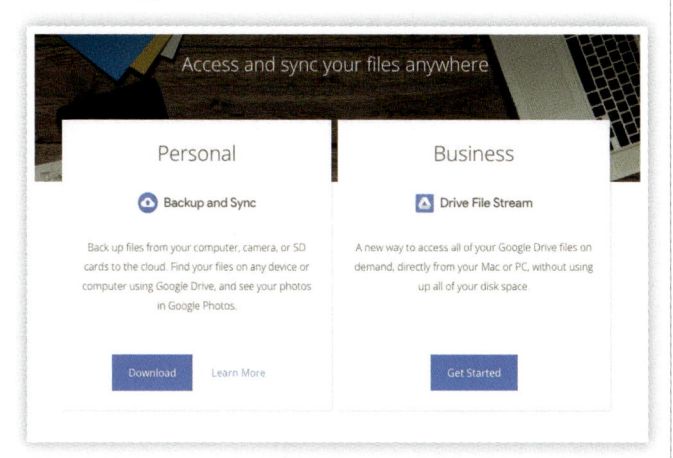

Step 2
❱ Click on the Download button and when asked to, Agree to the Google Terms of Service. You must do this before you start the download.

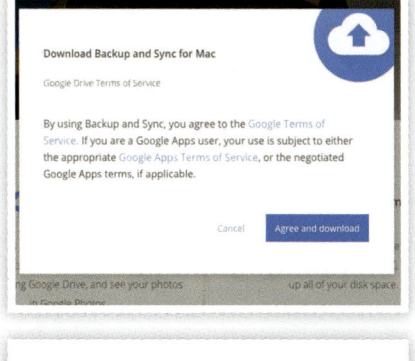

Step 3
❱ Click on Download Backup and sync and follow the instructions to install the software on your computer. The site will automatically detect whether it is PC or Mac.

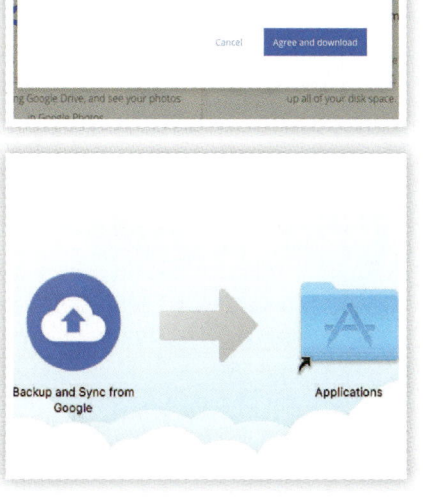

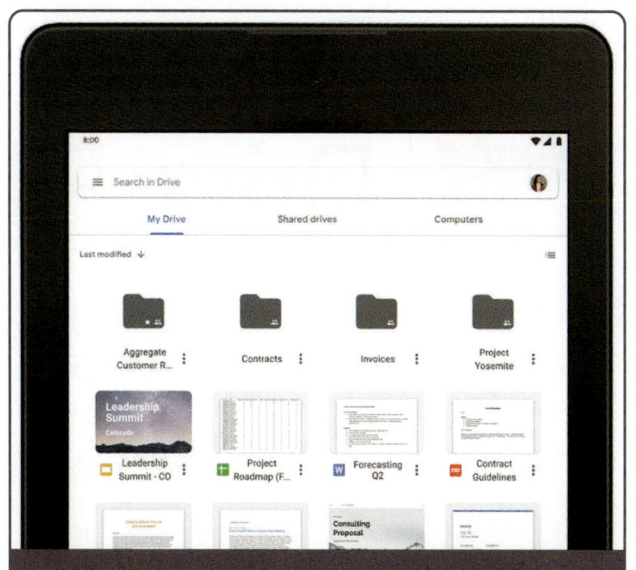

Google Drive on Android and iOS

You can download the Google Drive app for mobile devices free of charge, from the Play Store or App Store. This allows you to both view and edit files in your Google Drive folders.

Once downloaded, the app should automatically sign in using the same Google account details you entered on your computer (which is also, hopefully, the one with which you set up your Android or iOS device).

You will now be able to see any files you placed in the Google Drive folder on your computer. If you had the Google Docs app installed, this will now be replaced by Google Drive. To create a new doc, tap Menu > New > Document, or Spreadsheet, etc.

Step 4
❱ You will be asked to sign in again and will then be asked to sync. This creates a new folder on your computer which is used as the storage folder.

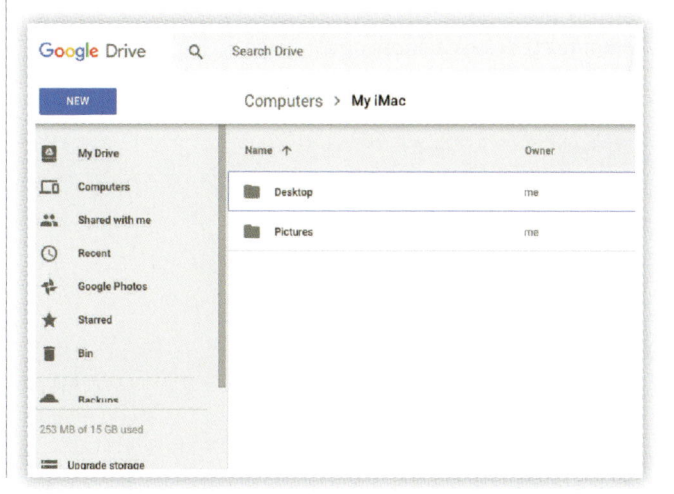

www.pclpublications.com   97

Using Google Apps

Restore Deleted Drive Files

Deleting files from Drive is a very quick process but a file you remove might not always be gone forever. You have the chance to restore deleted files before they are deleted permanently. Here is how you restore, remove and permanently delete files in Google Drive.

Restoring Incorrectly Deleted Documents

Step 1
❯ If you decide that you don't want to delete a file or folder that you've moved to the trash, you can restore it so that you can access it again. Once you restore a file, it will be recovered wherever you use Drive or Docs, Sheets and Slides.

Step 2
❯ At the moment, you can't restore a file or folder from the Drive mobile apps or from the Docs, Sheets or Slides home screens. You can restore your files from Drive on the web or on your computer. Let's look at those options here.

Step 3
❯ Sign in to Drive at www.drive.google.com. Go to the Bin section on the left side of your screen and right-click the file or folder you want to restore. Click Restore to return it to its previous location. To restore a file from the trash that you don't own, you need to contact the owner of the file.

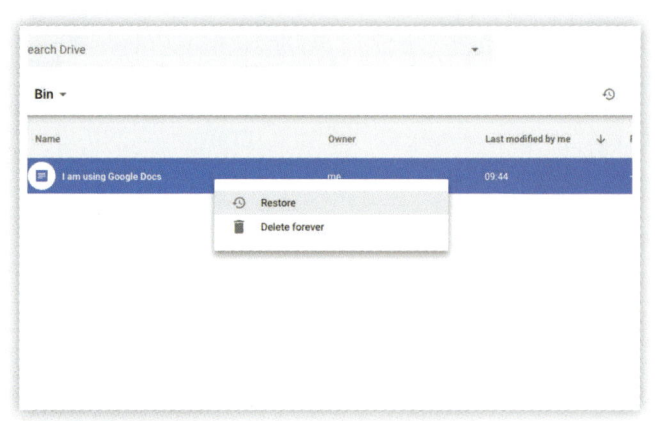

Restore Deleted Drive Files

Step 4
❯ If you permanently delete a file or folder that you realise you need access to, Google is able to help you recover it for a limited time. However, after the file has been deleted from Google's systems, it's gone forever. You can request recovery from Google themselves at www.support.google.com.

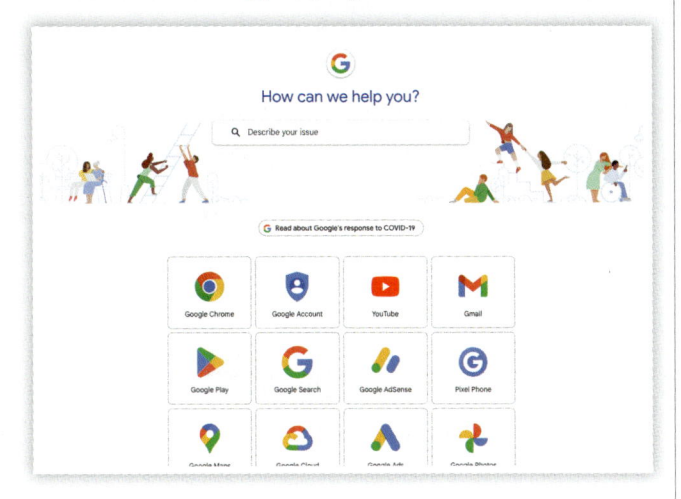

Step 2
❯ To remove files in Drive online, sign into Drive at www.drive.google.com. Now click or right-click the file or folder you want to remove and then click the Remove icon; as with removing files on your computer, anything removed is deleted.

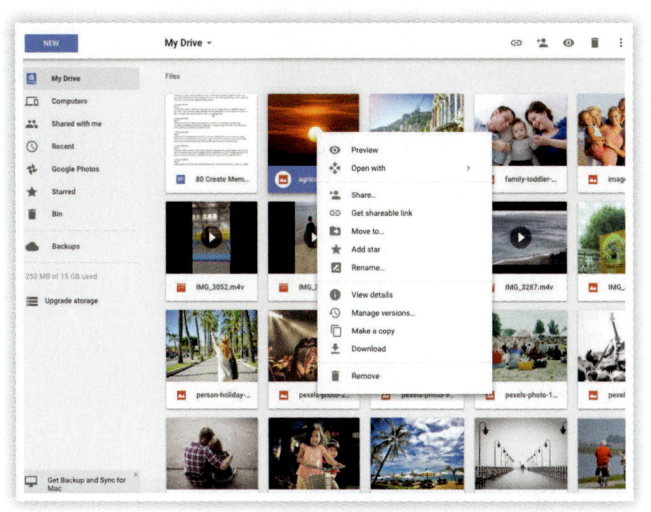

Removing Files

Step 1
❯ Open the Google Drive folder on the desktop of your computer, select the file or folder you want to remove and drag it to the trash on your computer. A file you remove from the Drive folder on your computer will be moved to the trash in Drive on the web and in the Drive, Docs, Sheets and Slides.

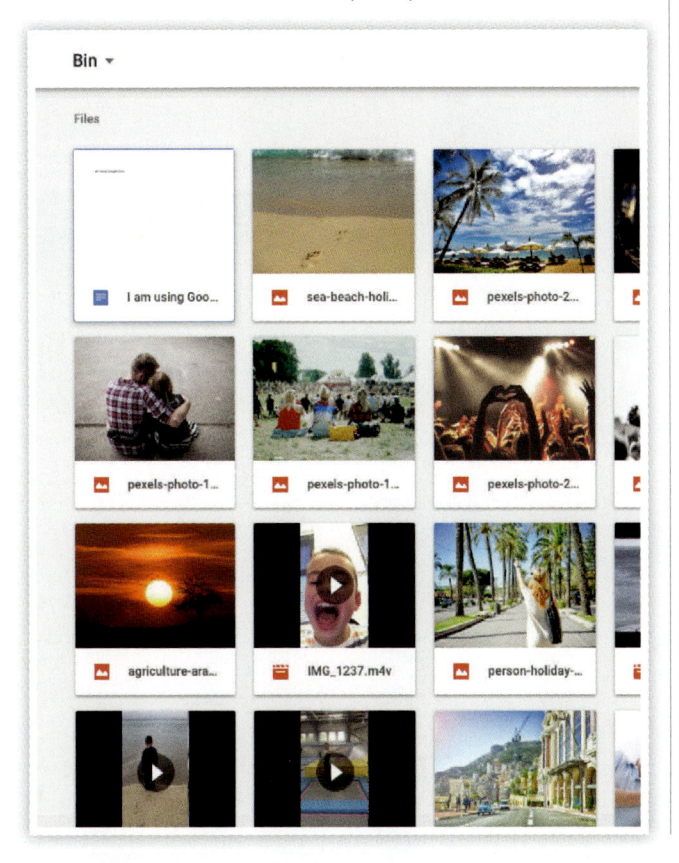

Permanently Delete Files

Step 1
❯ If you want to permanently delete a file or folder you own, you can delete an individual file or empty your entire trash to delete all files you have removed. Once a file has been deleted, anyone you've shared the file with will lose access to the file as well.

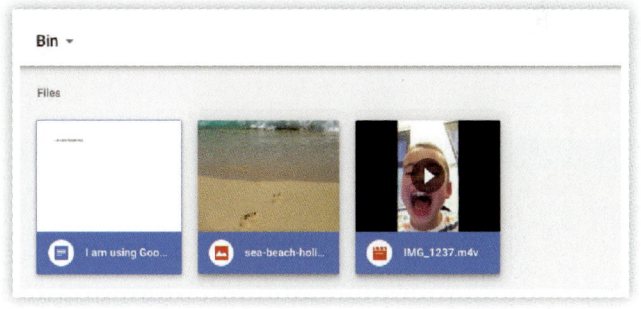

Step 2
❯ To permanently delete files you added to the trash from the Drive folder on your computer, simply empty the trash on your desktop. The files, along with anything else you trashed, will be deleted. On the web, sign in to Drive, go to Bin and select the file. Click Delete Forever. The file is now been deleted for good.

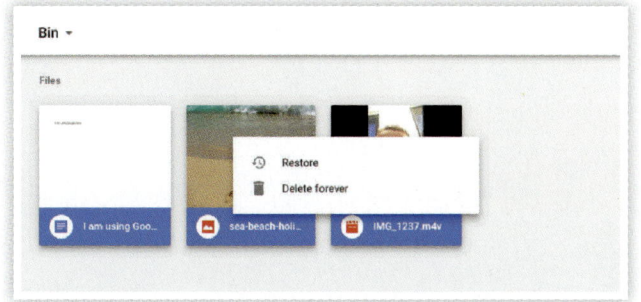

Using Google Apps

Set Up and Use Google Docs

Google Docs is a free, web-based office suite. Using this software you can create text documents, spreadsheets, complex forms and even presentations. Everything you create is stored via your Google Drive account. Here's how to make the most of Google Docs.

Creating New Documents

Step 1
❱ There are several different ways of getting started with Google Docs. You can create a new online document, you can upload an existing document to edit or you can use a template from the templates gallery. Let's start with a new Google doc.

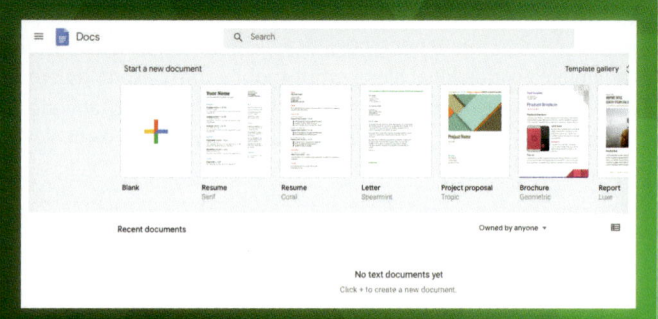

Step 2
❱ To create a new document, go to your Drive, click the downward pointing arrow and select Google Docs from the menu, then pick either Blank or Template. Name the document by entering the text in the top left corner, this will also start auto-save.

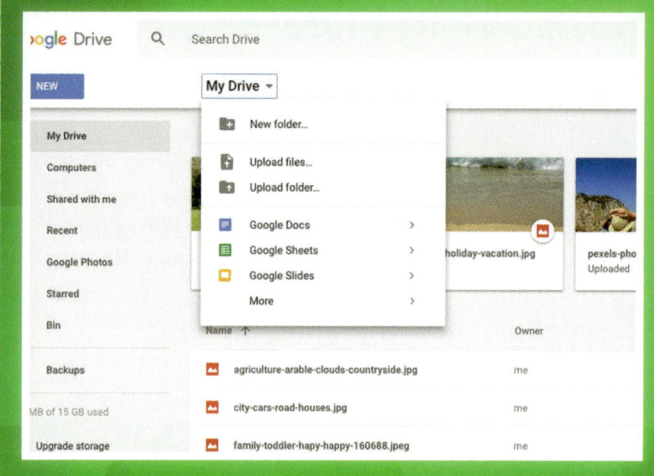

Step 3
❱ Along the top of the document you will find the editing and formatting tools. If you have ever used Microsoft Word or OpenOffice Writer, you should be familiar with most of the formatting options here.

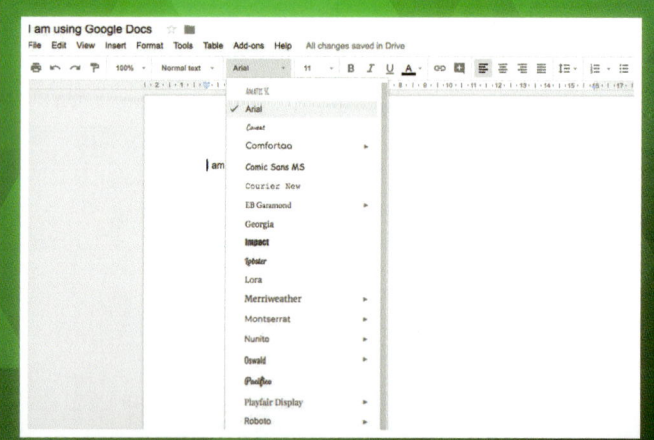

100   www.pclpublications.com

Set Up and Use Google Docs

Step 4
› You can also save a copy of any document to your computer if you wish. To save a copy of any document in the Drive, open it and go to the File menu. Roll the mouse pointer over the Download As... option.

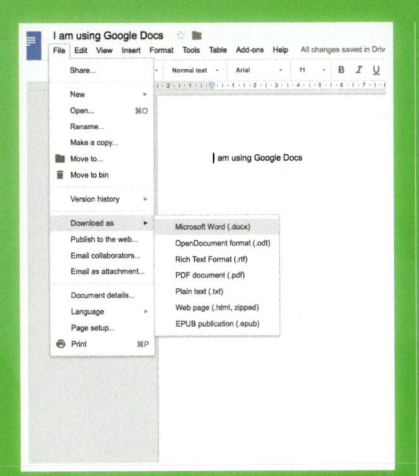

Step 5
› Select one of the following file types: HTML (zipped), RTF, Word, Open Office, PDF or plain text. Your document will then download to your computer. The original document will remain in Google Drive.

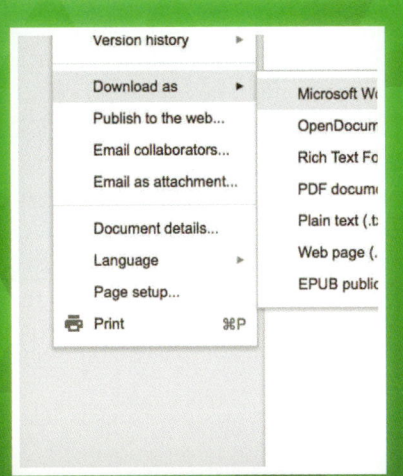

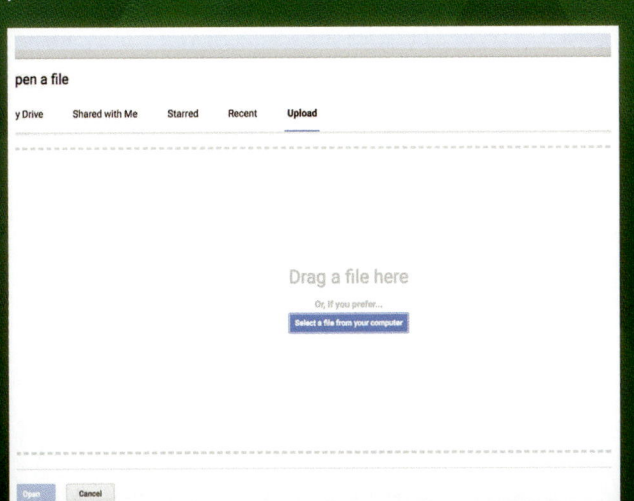

Step 2
› When the document has uploaded, click the File option, as before. From these links click on Email collaborators and enter the details of those you wish to share the file. This allows you to edit and collaborate on the document online.

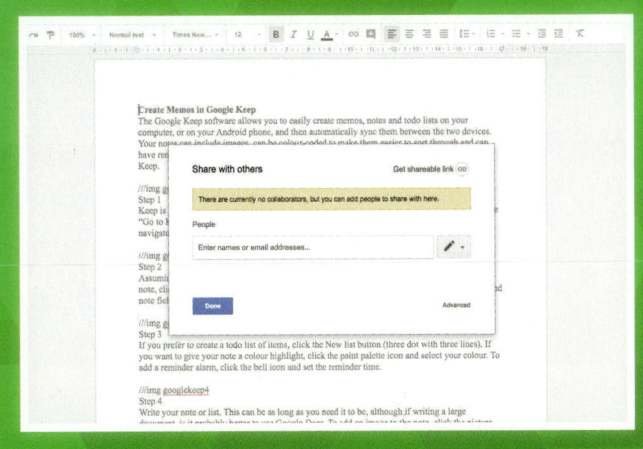

Step 3
› Having uploaded a compatible document to Google Docs, said file will instantly be saved to your Google Drive. These files are then accessible from the main Google docs menu screen, shown here. NOTE: Files to be converted by Docs can't be larger than 1 MB.

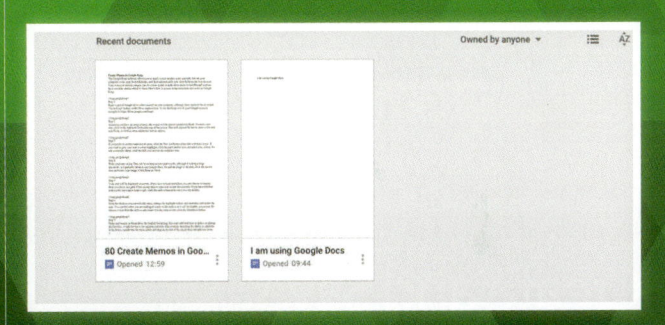

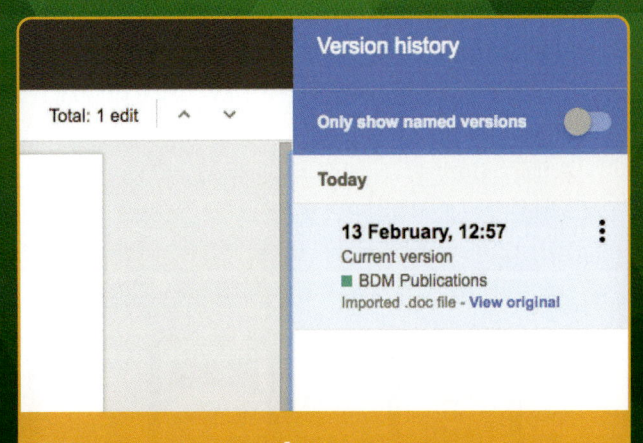

Import Documents

You can import a variety of documents into Google Drive and then either keep them as they were originally formatted or convert them into Google Docs.

Step 1
› Open a new Google Doc and click the File link at the top left of your documents options list. Click Open and then click Upload. The Upload window will appear leaving you to drag and drop your file into this window. The file will open automatically.

Time Machine

Google Drive tracks every change you make to files and documents you store there, so when you hit the Save button a new revision is saved. You can use the tools in Google Drive to look back as far as 30 days automatically, or choose a specific revision to save forever.

Using Google Apps

How to Use Google Sheets

With Google Sheets you can create spreadsheets online, work on them with others in real-time and then store them online in Google Drive. Google Sheets, for most users, is more than capable of replacing the corresponding software in something like Microsoft Office.

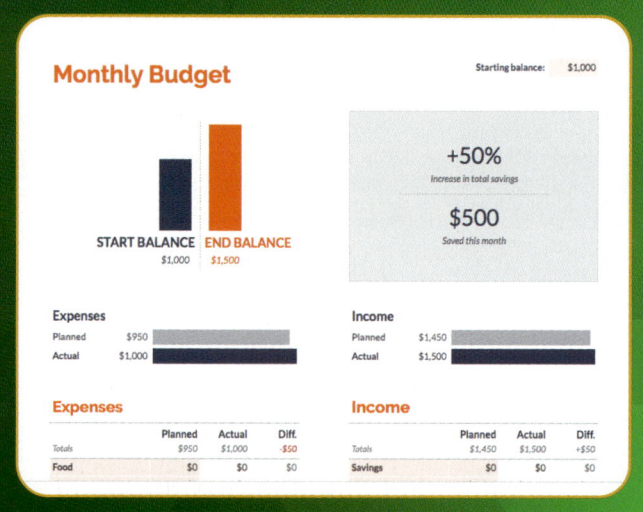

Create and Save Spreadsheets

Step 1
❱ There are different ways of getting started with Google Sheets. You can create a new spreadsheet, upload an existing spreadsheet from a computer or use a template from the templates gallery, to create a spreadsheet with a specific purpose.

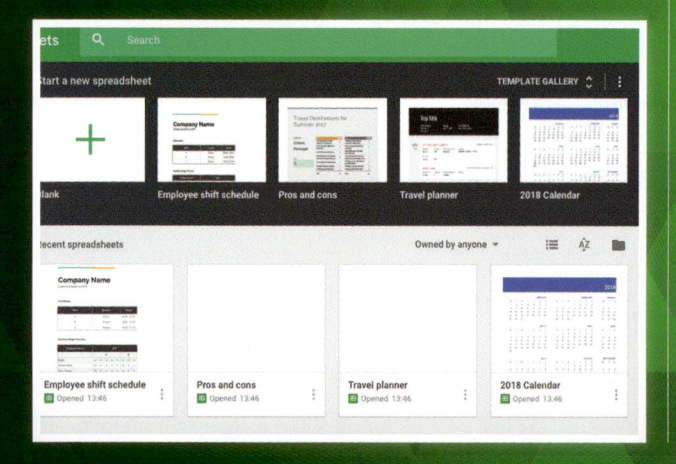

Step 2
❱ To create a new spreadsheet, go to your Google Drive, click the NEW button and select Google Sheet from the drop-down menu. Once you name the spreadsheet or start typing, Google Sheets will automatically save your work every few seconds.

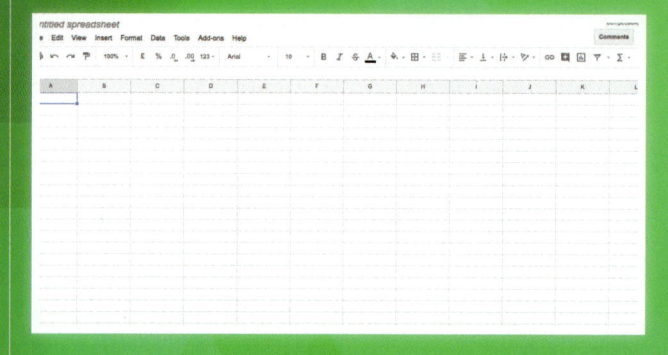

Step 3
❱ Give your Sheet a title. At the top of the spreadsheet, you will see text that indicates when your spreadsheet was last saved. You can access your spreadsheet at any time by opening your Drive at www.drive.google.com. Here you will see it as a saved file.

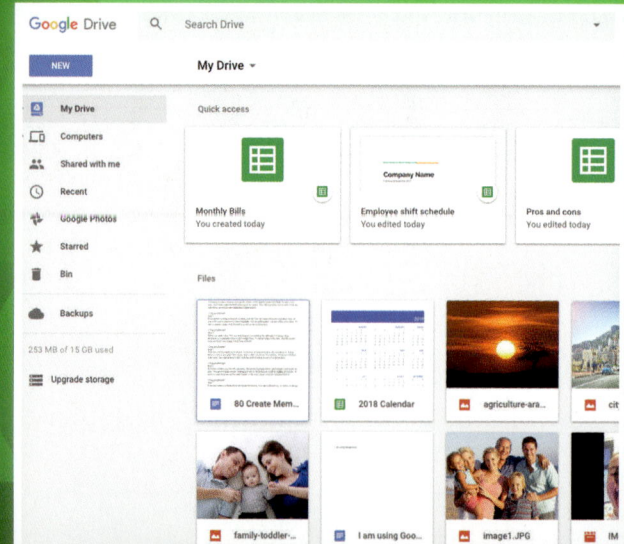

102 www.pclpublications.com

How to Use Google Sheets

Uploading Spreadsheets

Step 1
❯ When you upload a spreadsheet into Google Drive, you have the choice to keep your spreadsheet in the original format or convert it into the Google Docs format. If you don't convert the spreadsheet, you may not be able to access it collaboratively.

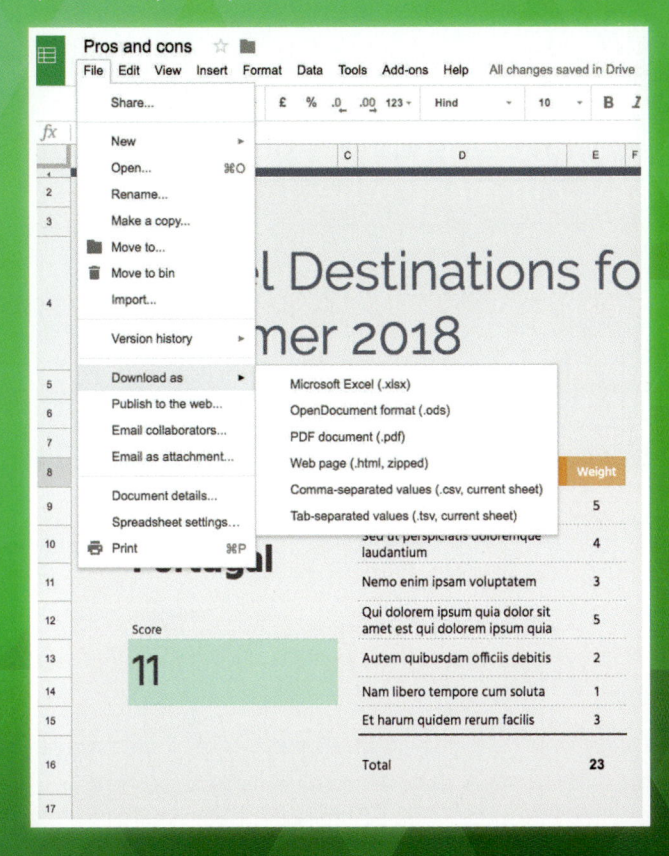

Step 2
❯ Open a new Google Sheet and click the File link at the top left of your documents options list. Click Open and then Upload. The Upload window will appear leaving you to drag and drop your file into this window. The file will open automatically.

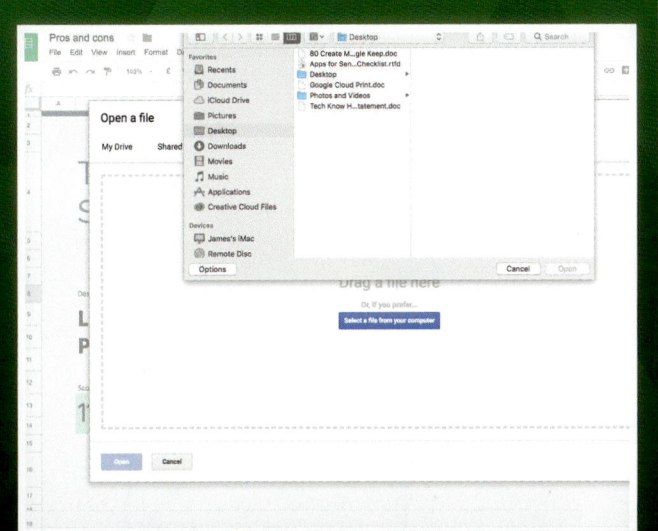

Step 3
❯ When the document has uploaded, click the File option, as before. From these links click on Email collaborators and enter the details of those with whom you wish to share the file. This allows you to edit and collaborate on the Google Sheet document online.

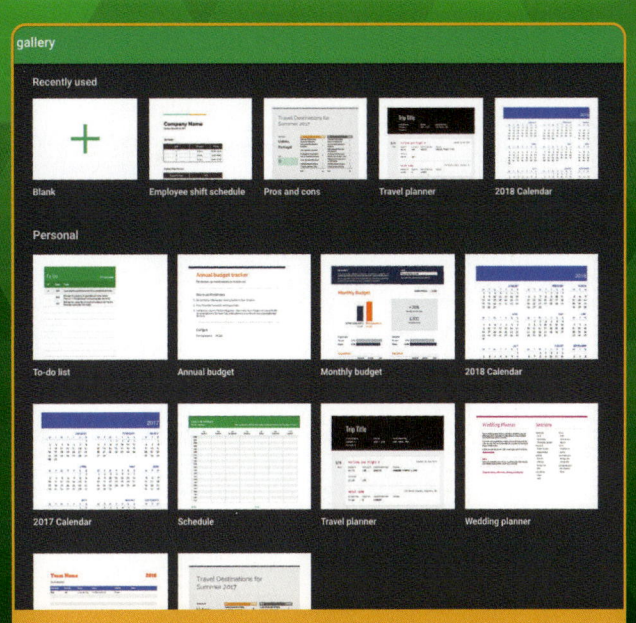

Using Sheets Templates

If you want to quickly create a spreadsheet, you can pick one of the templates in the templates gallery. Each template has standard text that you can replace with your own, and preset formatting that you can reuse. You can also create a spreadsheet with a template directly from your Documents List. Click the red Create button and select From template....

Using Google Apps

Set Up and Use Google Drawings

Google Drawings allows you to create, share and edit documents online and collaborate with others by inviting them to view your edits. You can even chat with others from within the app, in real-time, before you save or publish your drawings online as an image or in many other image formats.

Create a New Drawing

Step 1
❱ To start creating drawings in Google Docs, go to your Docs list, click the NEW button and select Drawing from the More menu. Then, using the menu options and buttons in the toolbar, you can create flow charts, design diagrams and other drawings.

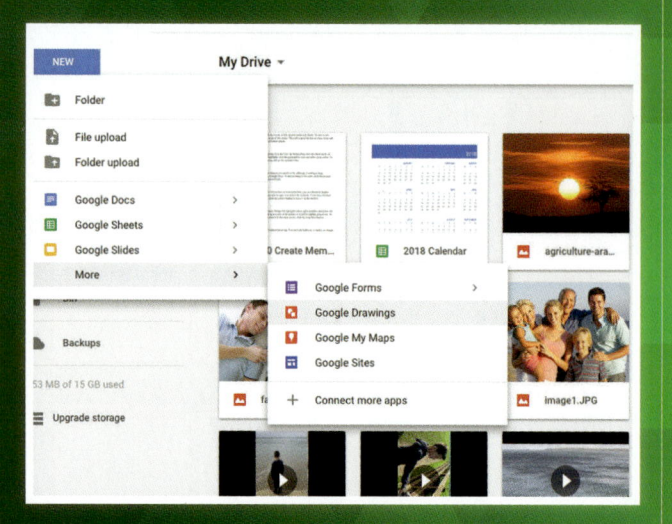

Step 2
❱ Click on the tools at the top of the screen to select them. These range from arrows, lines and poly-lines, to shapes and text boxes. You can also insert images or photos using the image button. To place a line, for example, click to place one end of the line and drag to the other end.

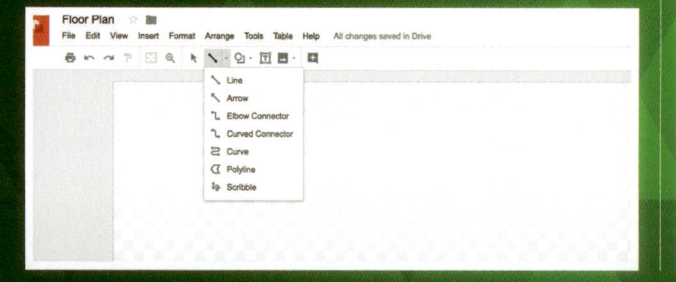

Step 3
❱ In line, arrow and scribble modes, you can keep adding lines until you go back to select mode by clicking the Select button from the toolbar (the small arrow to the left of the Shapes button) or pressing the Esc key.

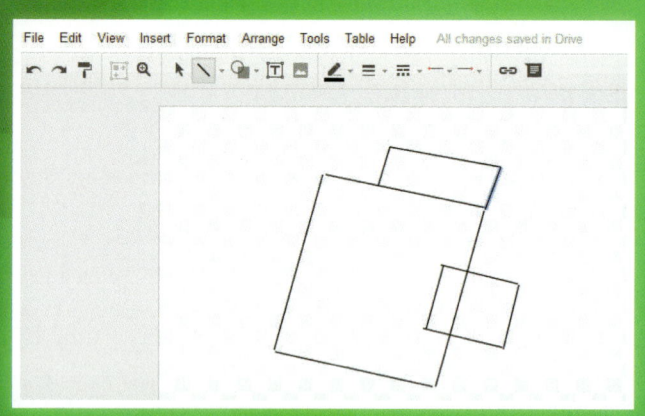

Step 4
❱ To insert a text box, select it and click where you want to add the text box. Enter your text and press Enter. Your text will be added to your drawing. Use text boxes instead of word art if you'd like to use word wrap or specify a different text size.

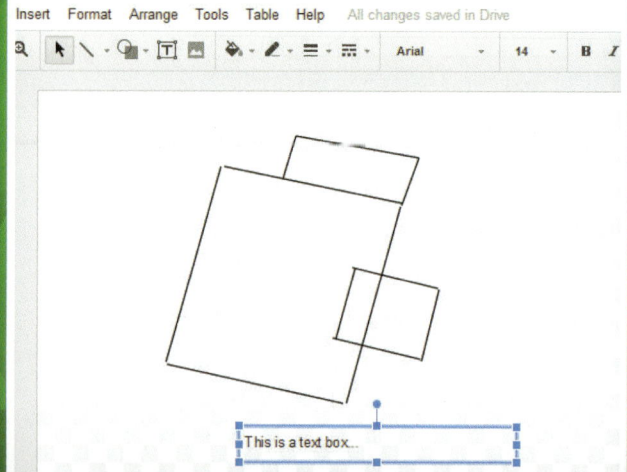

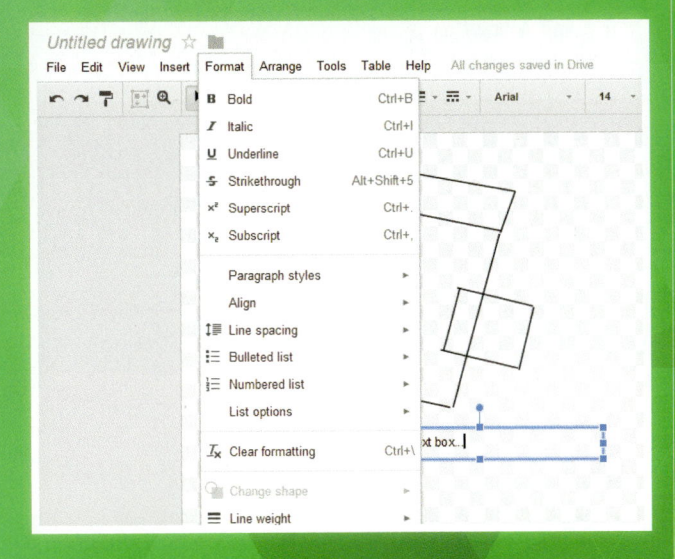

Set Up and Use Google Drawing

Step 5
❱ The Format menu lets you change the background of your drawing, align and rotate items, select snap to grid or snap to guide, change the order of the items (for example, bring a shape forward) and group items.

Step 6
❱ You can undo and redo changes by clicking the two arrows to the left end of the toolbar. To zoom in and out on your drawings, click the Zoom button in the toolbar.

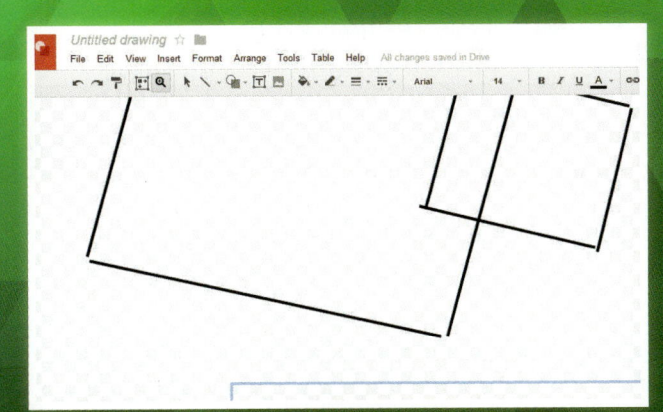

Step 7
❱ Some editing options are available only when you've selected a specific item. For example, when you insert a text box or word art, you can see the Edit text button at the right end of the toolbar. Click it to change the selected text.

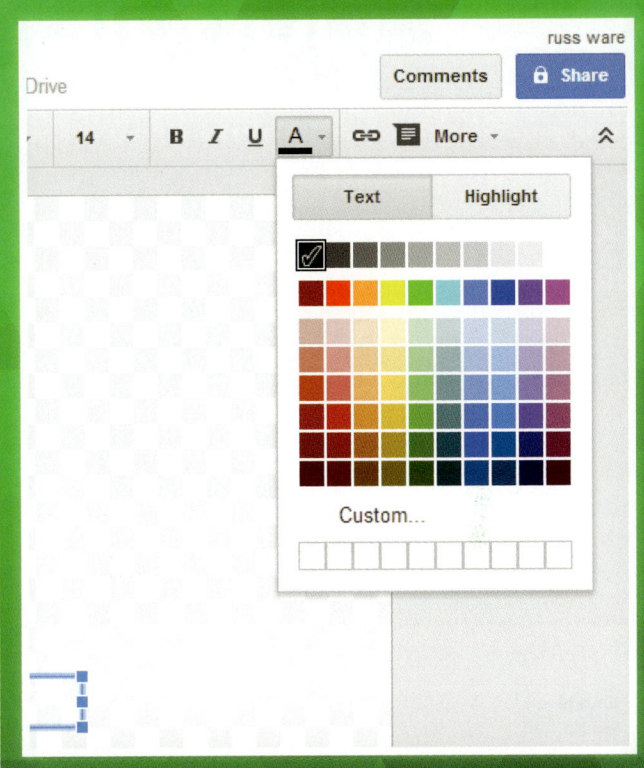

Step 8
❱ Once you're done, your drawing is automatically saved. You can then add it to a document, presentation or spreadsheet. To do this, open the document you want to add the drawing to, click Insert and then select Drawing.

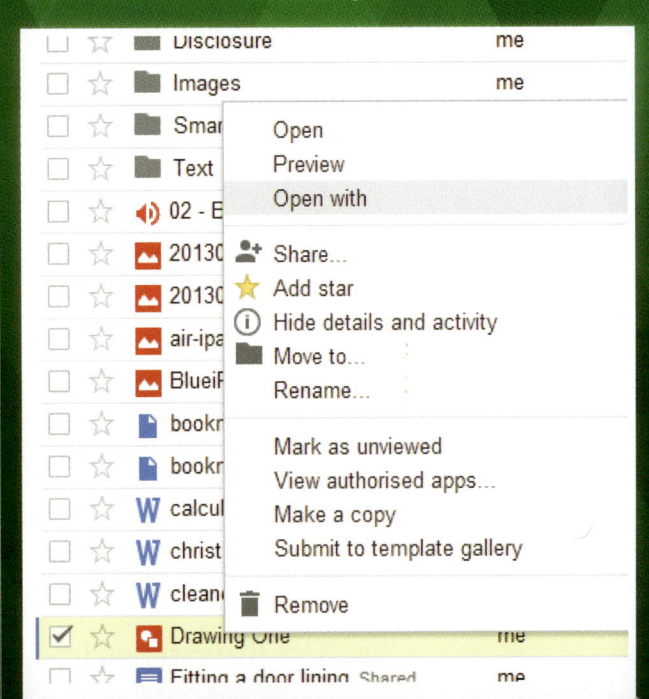

Using Google Apps

How to Use Google Slides

Google Slides is an online presentation app that allows you to show off your work in a visual way. There are different ways of getting started using Google Slides: you can create a new online presentation, you can upload an existing one or you can use a template from the gallery.

Creating a Presentation

Step 1
❱ Just like creating any new document in Google Docs, to create a new presentation go to your Documents List, click the NEW button and select Google Slides from the drop-down menu.

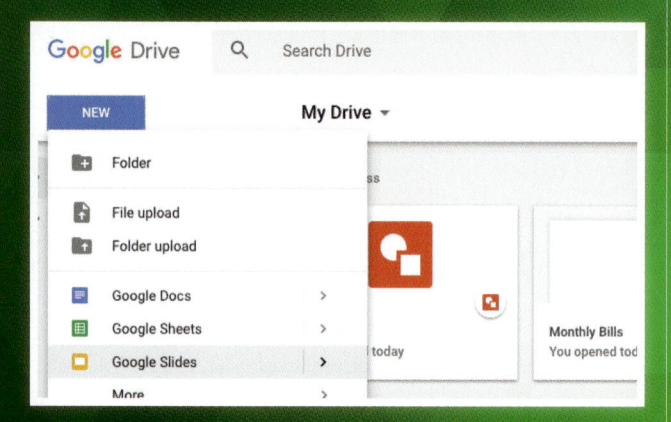

Step 2
❱ When you give your document a name and start typing, Google Docs will automatically save your work. Auto-save will continue to save at intervals whenever the document is open and being worked on. You can work from a template or free hand.

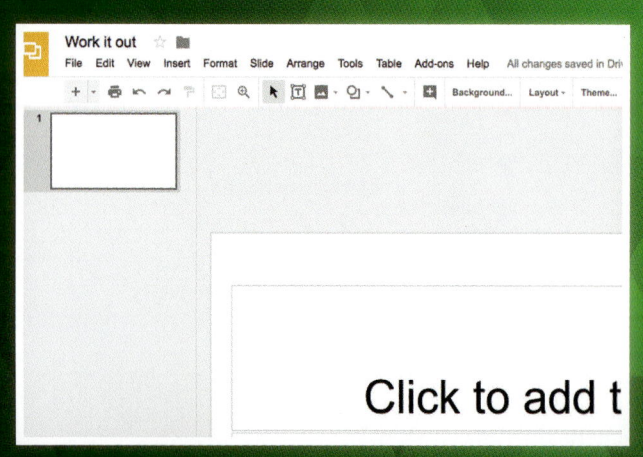

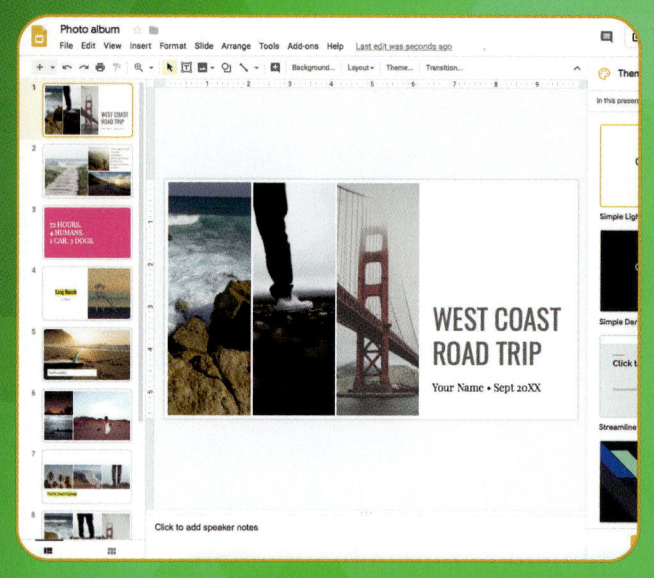

Step 3
❱ There are several ways to format text and objects on a slide. To get started, click on the object you want to format, resize or move. To add custom formatting to text or to an object, you can use the Format menu or the Edit toolbar.

106 www.pclpublications.com

How to Use Google Slides

Step 4
❱ To select multiple objects, hold the Shift key while selecting each object or drag your mouse over all of the objects you'd like to select. To deselect one or more objects, press the Shift key and click the objects.

Step 5
❱ To change or add a theme to your presentation in real time, go to the Slide menu, and select Change theme. Select the theme you'd like to use and it is automatically applied to all of the slides in your presentation.

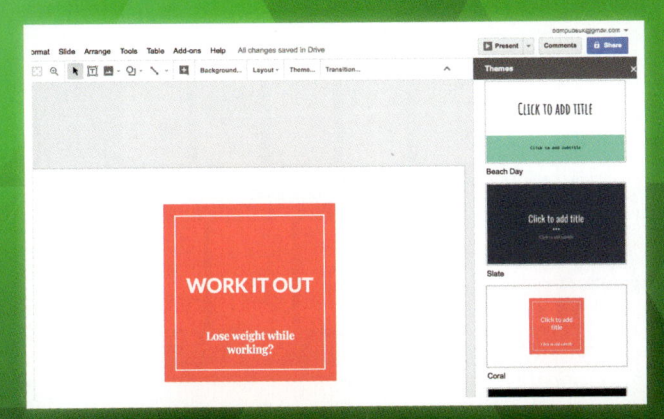

Step 6
❱ Transitions are a way to make your presentations look more dynamic. You can animate elements such as bullet points or even a list of images; for example, making them slide in from off screen. Go to the View menu and select Transitions.

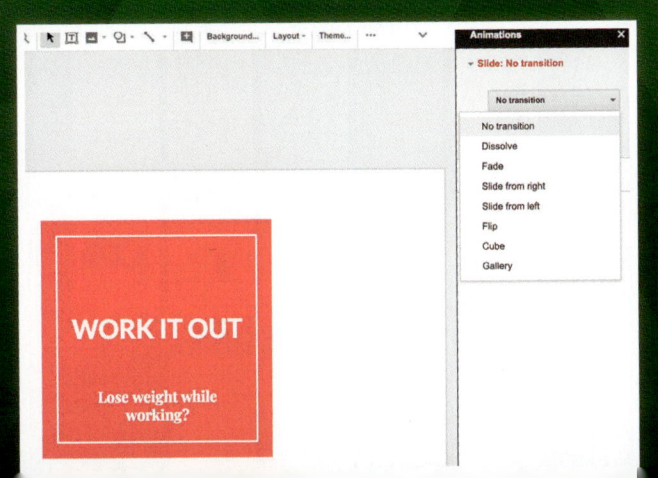

Step 7
❱ To save a copy of a presentation to your computer rather than online, you can download it. In your document, go to the File menu and point your mouse to the Download as option. Select a file type and your presentation will download.

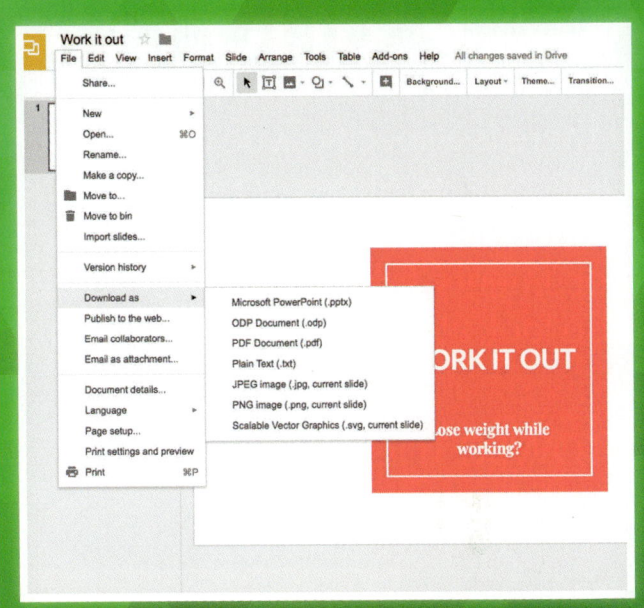

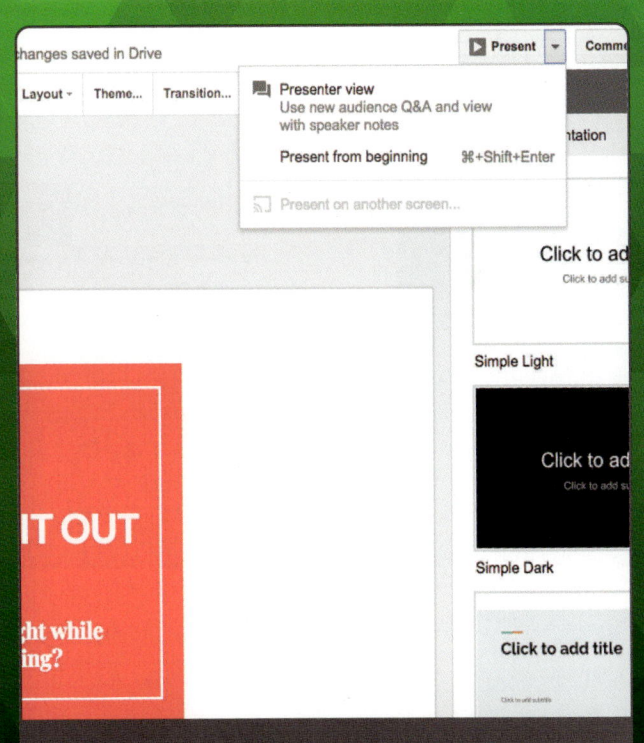

Viewing Presentations

To show a finished presentation, select Start Presentation in the top right of the screen. A new window opens, displaying your presentation one slide at a time. To skip from one slide to the next, use the arrow keys on your keyboard or click the arrow icon in the grey bar at the bottom of your presentation. To close the presentation viewer, press the Esc key.

Using Google Apps

Use Templates and Forms

If there is a specific type of document you want to create in Google Docs, Sheets, Slides or Forms, check the template gallery to see if there is one available. The template gallery includes hundreds of pre-made documents, from a simple CV to multi-page company presentations. We also look at the Google Forms app and see how it can be used.

Browse the Template Gallery

Step 1
❱ Open Google Drive and click on the NEW button on the left of the window. Select Document, Presentation, Spreadsheet or Form from the drop-down menu (depending on what type of document you want to create).

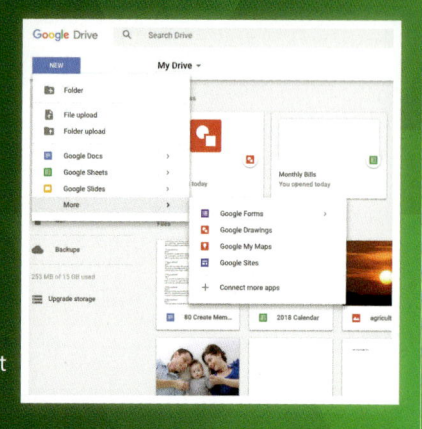

Step 2
❱ From within one of these document types, click File > New > From Template. This will open the main Google Docs template gallery. You can now scroll down through the listings to see which one would be the best fit for your project.

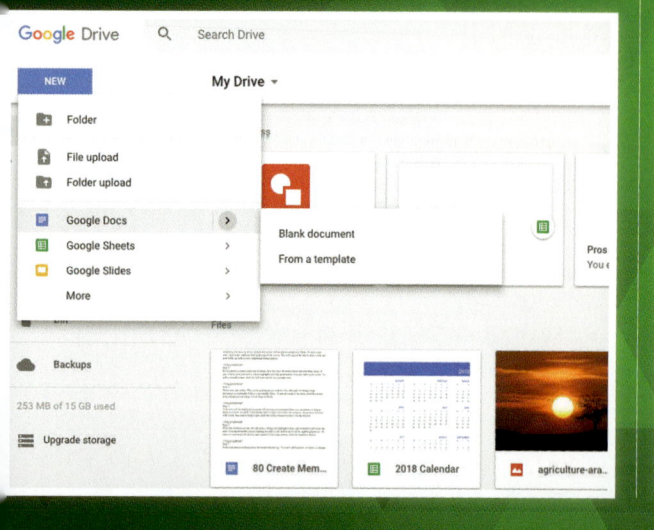

Step 3
❱ By default, the most popular templates from all categories will be shown on screen when you first enter the gallery. You can choose to view specific types of template using the links on the left-hand side of the screen.

Step 4
❱ You can also search for specific templates based upon the recommended uses, which are used to break up the layout of the templates. Taking Google Docs as an example you have templates for CV's, Letters, Personal, Work and Sales.

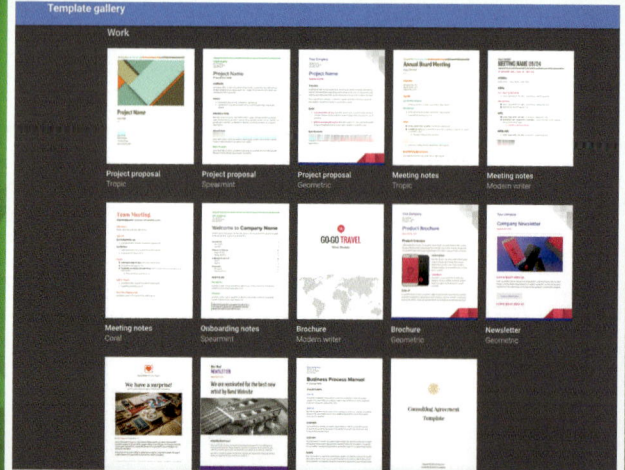

www.pclpublications.com

Use Templates and Forms

Step 5
❱ Each template will have a thumbnail image preview. If you want to see more detail of how the document is laid out, click the Preview button. You can then click Close this window or Use this template.

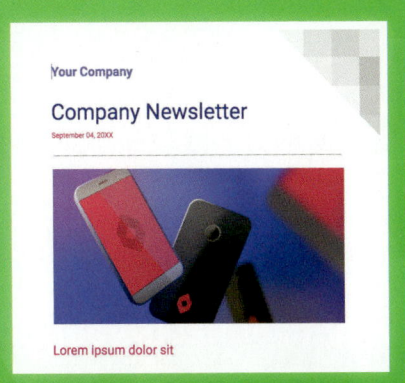

Create and Share Templates

You can create your own templates and either keep them for your own use or share them with the Google Template Gallery, so that others can use them.

Step 1
❱ Open Google Drive and click on the NEW button. Click on Doc, Sheet, Presentation or Form. Once your chosen blank document is open, you can begin to create a template.

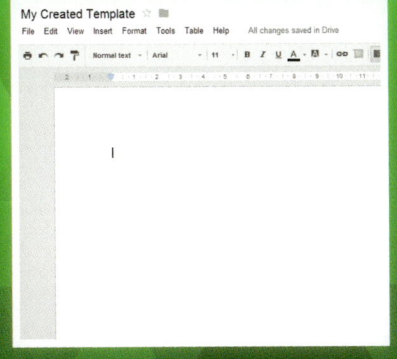

Step 2
❱ When creating a template that is going to be shared in the template gallery, avoid filling it with specific text and images. People using the template later will almost certainly want to put their own content into it.

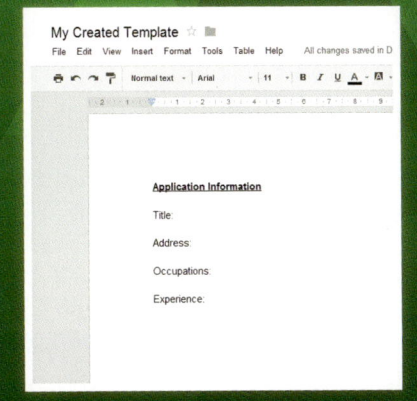

Step 3
❱ When your template is finished, save it and return to the main Google Drive screen. Select the template file in the list of documents using the Share link. Add contacts or get a shareable link to email to them.

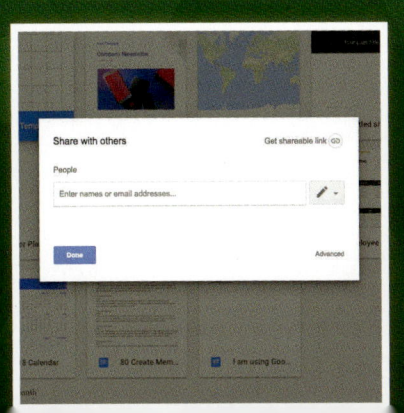

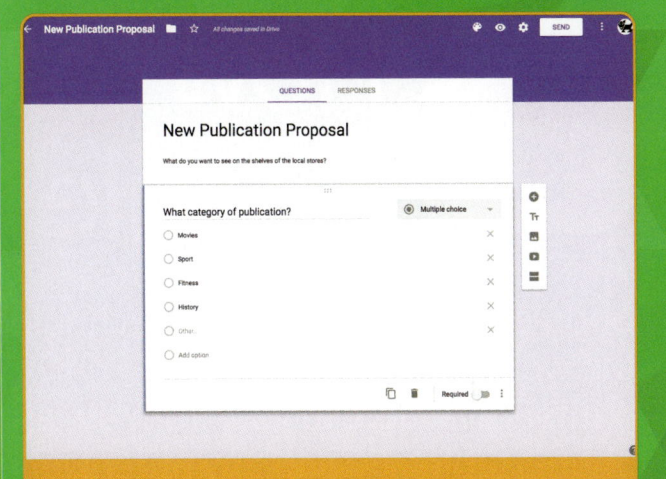

Using Google Forms

Adding a further tool to the already impressive listing, you can use the Google Forms app to create online surveys and quizzes and then share them with your family, friends or work colleagues.

To start a new Google Form you will need to return to the Google Drive home page and from there click the NEW button and select Google Forms from the More option on the drop-down menu. You will now need to give your form a title and a description. Now you can start to build your questions. Enter your first question and select from the options given when clicking the answer options menu on the right. You can choose from multiple choice or text entry.

To add another question tap the + icon on the right side bar. Here you can also add images, videos or sub category descriptions. You can literally be as in-depth or simple as you wish. When you have finished your Google Form, you can change the colour pattern, preview the finished form or select the format, questionnaire or quiz using the setting icons top right. Finally tap Send to enter the details of who you want to share the form with. Click send for a second time to complete the process.
To check the answers click on Responses at the top of the text input box, here you can view all completed forms.

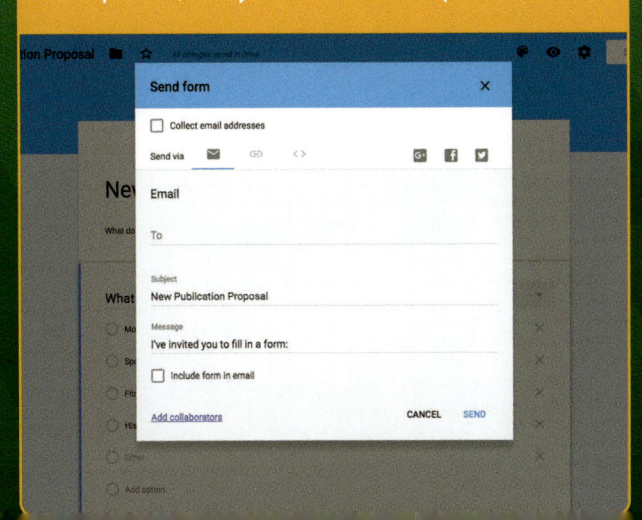

Using Google Apps

How to Use Google Cloud Print

Google Cloud Print is smart technology that connects your printers to the web. Using Google Cloud Print, you can make your home and work printers available to you, from the apps you use every day. It works on your phone, tablet, PC and any other web-connected device you want to use.

How to Connect with Cloud Ready Printers

You can use Google Cloud Print with a cloud-ready printer (printers which can connect directly to the Internet and do not need a PC to work). There are still plenty that are not but we are concentrating on the cloud-ready type for this article.

Step 1
❯ The first thing you need to do, if you do not already have it installed, is download the latest version of Google Chrome and install it. Once installed, Log in to your user account on the Windows, Mac or Linux computer.

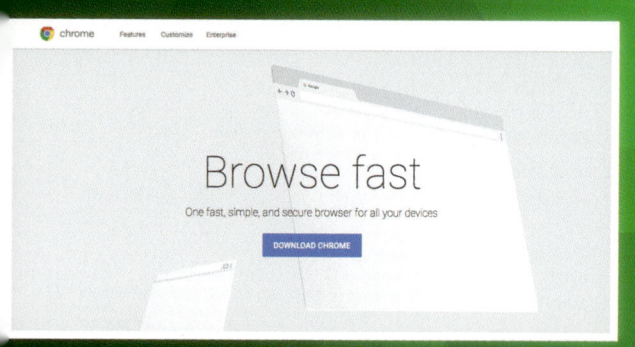

Step 2
❯ Open Google Chrome, click the Chrome menu on the browser toolbar and select Settings. Now click the Show advanced settings link. Scroll down to the Google Cloud Print section and click Sign in to Google Cloud Print.

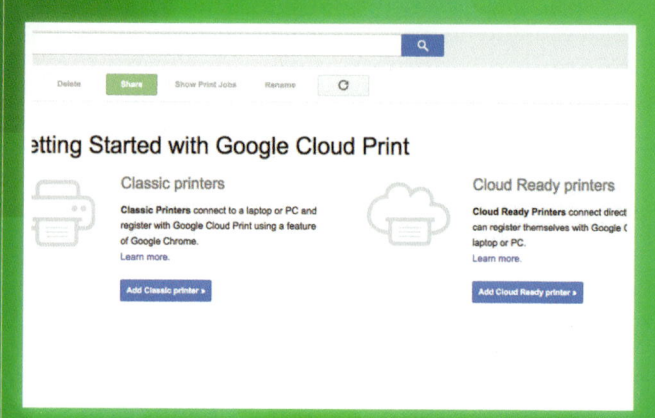

Step 3
❯ In the window that appears, sign in with your Google Account details to enable the Google Cloud Print connector. Hopefully you will see the printer connected to your computer. Select the printer you want to connect to and then click Add printer.

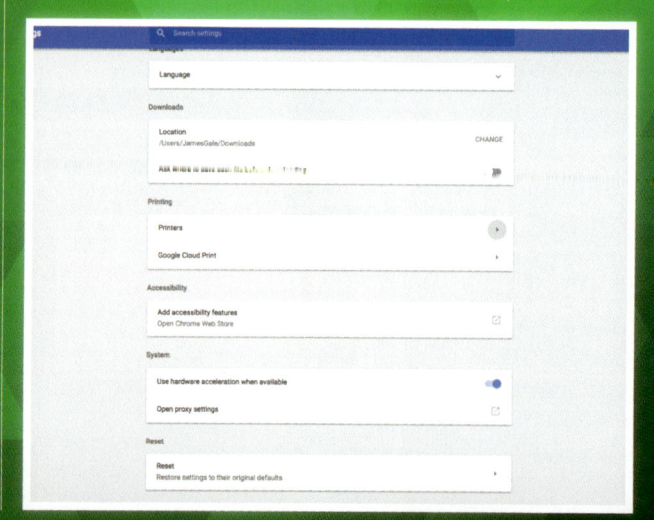

www.pclpublications.com

How to Use Google Cloud Print

Step 4
❱ You will then see a confirmation that Google Cloud Print has been enabled. The printer is now associated with your Google account and connected to Google Cloud Print. You can print to this printer using Google Cloud Print as long as you sign in with the same Google account.

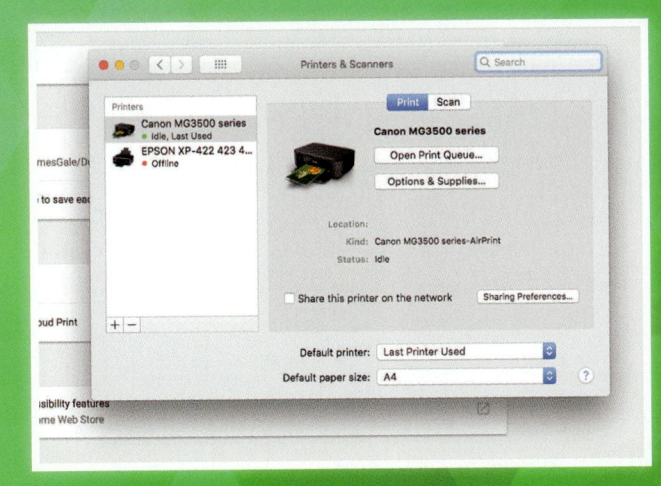

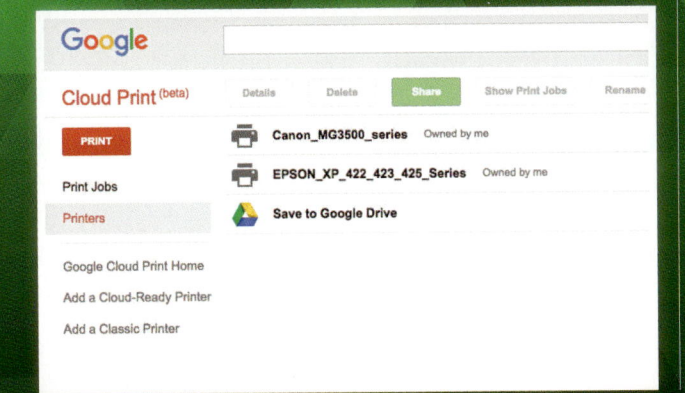

Step 2
❱ Click the Printers on the left side and select the printer that you want to share. If the printer is connected properly you will see a Share button. When you share printers, you share printer names so choose a descriptive name when setting up your printer for the first time.

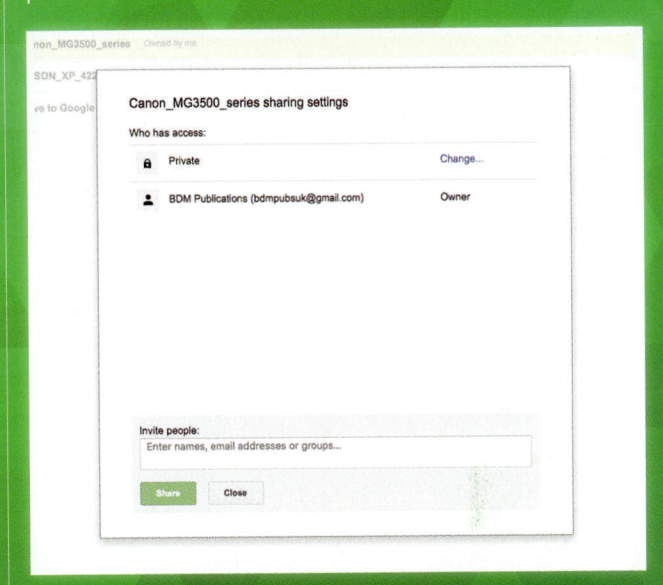

Sharing a Printer
If your friends or colleagues have Google accounts, you can share your printer with them and let them print to it from anywhere that has an Internet connection.

Step 1
❱ To begin sharing your cloud connected printer, head to the Google Cloud Print management page at www.google.com/cloudprint. This shows you a complete list of any printers associated with your Google account.

Step 3
❱ In the dialog box that appears, enter the email address for the person or Google Group you want to share with and click Share. Your friend will receive an email notification. To disable sharing, follow the steps above to open the Sharing dialog box for the printer and edit the user list.

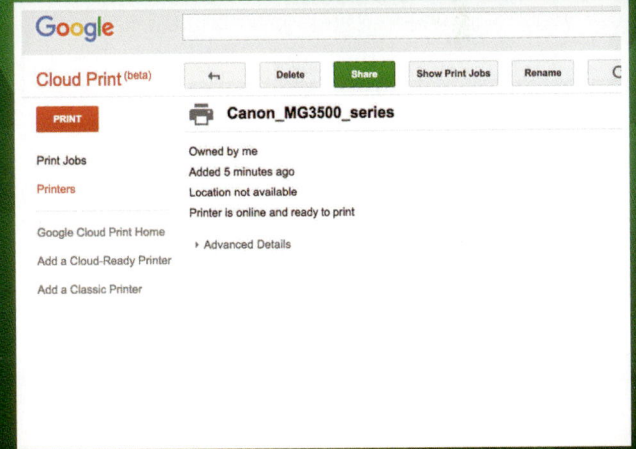

Print From Everywhere?
Google Cloud Print integration works with many Google products and services, the first of which are Chrome OS, Chrome, Gmail for mobile and Google Docs for mobile. You can also print to third-party native mobile apps on the Android and iOS platforms. You can also try the Google Cloud Print app for Android, so you can not only submit print jobs to connected cloud-ready printers but also control printer options and manage print jobs right from your mobile device.

Using Google Apps

Set Up and Use Google Keep

The Google Keep software allows you to easily create memos, notes and to-do lists on your computer and on your iOS or Android smartphone and then automatically sync them between the devices. Here's how to access, set up and create new notes in Google Keep.

Setting Up and Using Google Keep

Google Keep is a great little app that enables you to create unique to-do lists that can be stored across various hardware platforms. So you can Google Keep your reminders safe!

Step 1
❱ Keep is part of Google drive when viewed on your computer, although there seems to be no simple Go to Keep button on the Drive main screen. Download the app for your platform and then you'll see the Keep area of your Google account.

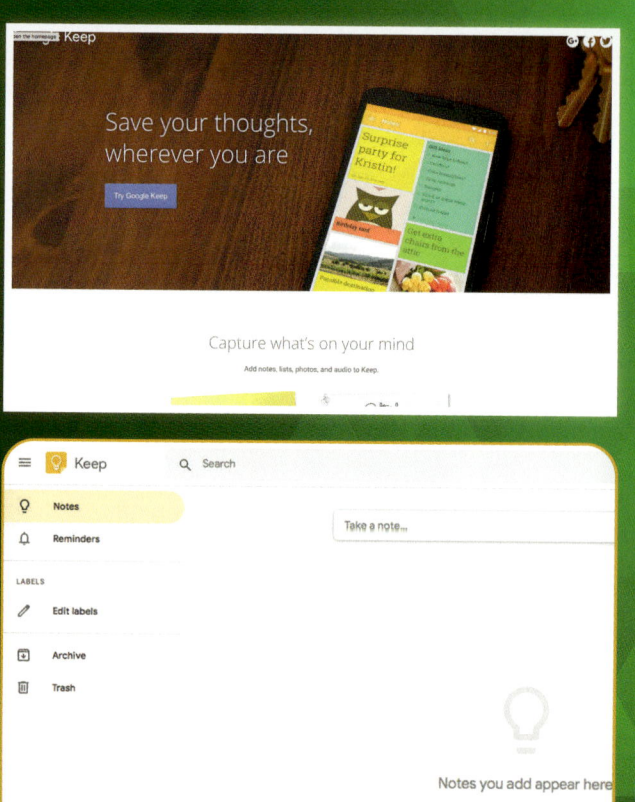

Step 2
❱ Assuming you have no notes created, the screen will be almost completely blank. To start a new note, click in the Add note field at the top of the screen. This will expand the box to show title and note fields, as well as some additional format options.

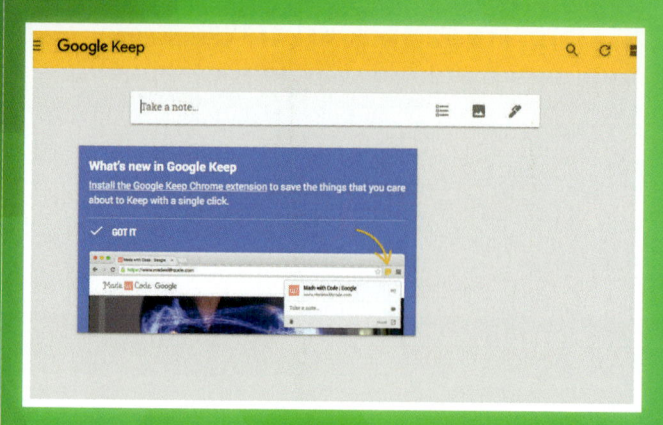

Step 3
❱ If you prefer to create a to-do list of items, click the New list button (three dots). If you want to give your note a colour highlight, click the paint palette icon and select your colour. To add a reminder alarm, click the bell icon and set the reminder time.

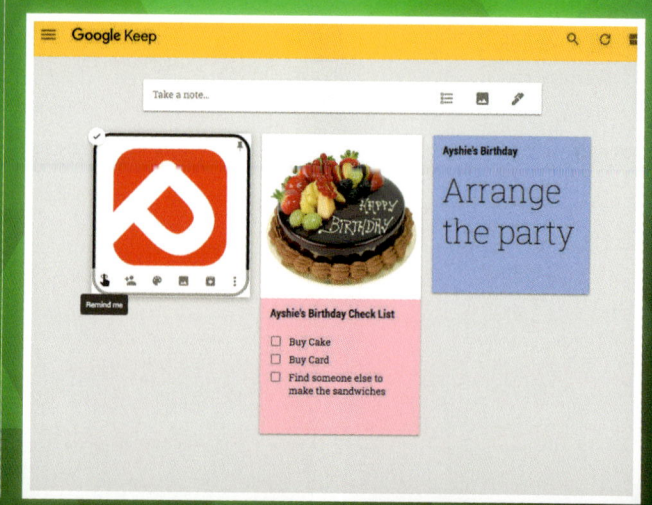

112   www.pclpublications.com

Set Up and Use Google Keep

Step 4
❱ Write your note or list. This can be as long as you need it to be, although if writing a large document, it is probably better to use Google Docs. To add an image to the note, click the picture icon and select your image. Click Done to finish.

Step 5
❱ Your note will be displayed on screen. If you have several notes or lists, you can choose to display them as a list or in a grid. Click on any note to open it to review the contents. If you have finished with a note, but want to keep it safe, click the archive button to move it to the archive.

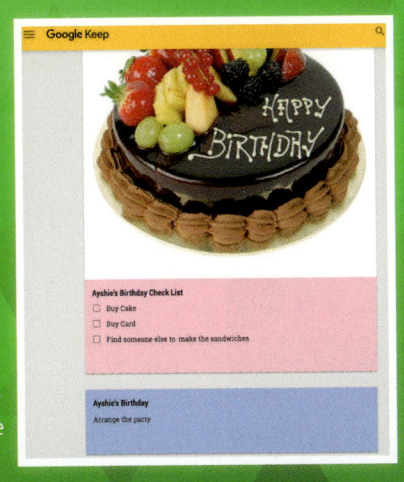

Step 6
❱ From the Archive you can still edit notes, change the highlight colour, add reminders and delete the note. You can tell when you are looking at a note in the archive as it will be displayed under a grey bar. To remove a note from the archive and return it to the main screen, click the Unarchive button.

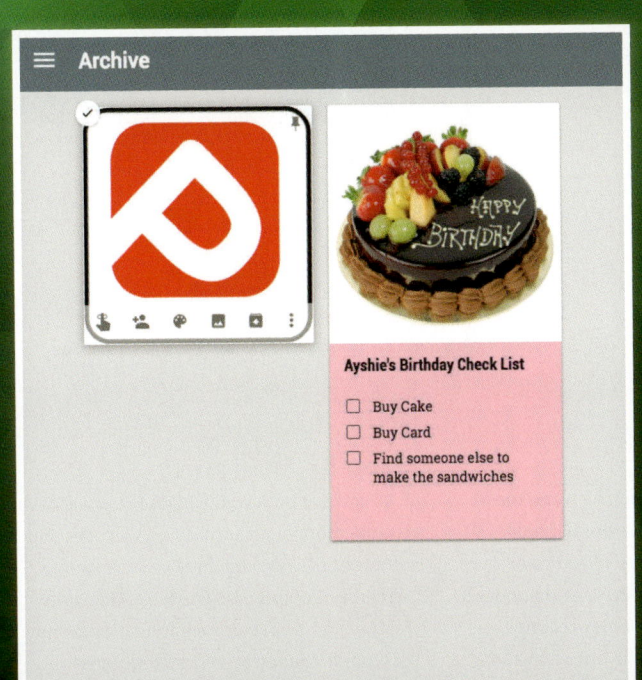

Step 7
❱ You can also add reminders to your listings by clicking the Reminders option from the left side control window. You can set an alarm to notify you to perform the tasks on your listing. You can choose to repeat this alarm if these tasks are regular ones and also archive reminders in the same manner as before.

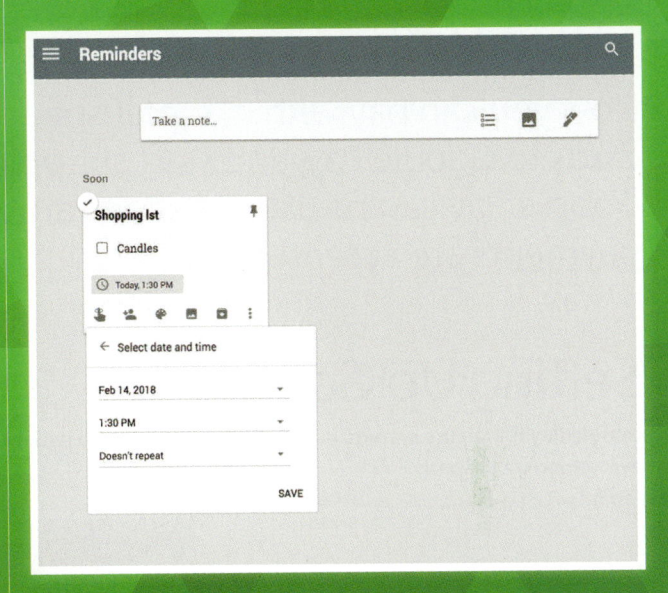

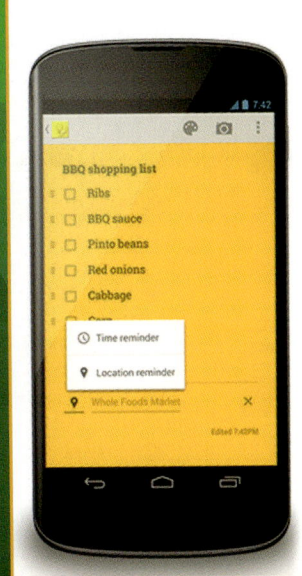

Keep on Mobile

You can download the Google Keep app for Android and iOS smartphones for free. Assuming you use the same Google account to sign in on your computer and on the phone, notes, lists and memos will automatically be shared between the two devices. Keep on Android and iOS offers you a few more options, including the ability to create memos using voice (dictation). If your notes are not syncing between your phone and your computer, make sure to check the sync options on the phone in settings > accounts > Google account.

Using Google Apps

How to Use Google Pay

Now you can pay with it, too. Just add your credit, debit, loyalty, and gift cards to Google Pay, and start shopping in stores, in apps, and online. Google Pay can be used at shops around the world, wherever contactless payments are accepted.

Setting Up Google Pay

Google Pay is a secure system, but as with anything to do with money and payments, it is important to make sure that you set everything up properly.

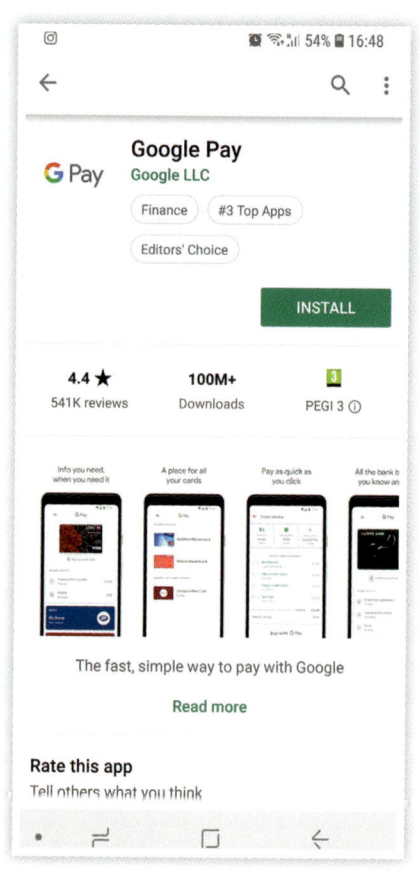

Step 1

› You will need to make sure that you have your credit/debit card or cards close at hand, and have all the details available (account numbers, sort codes, security numbers, etc.). You will also need to download the Google Pay app from Google Play, if you don't already have it on your phone.

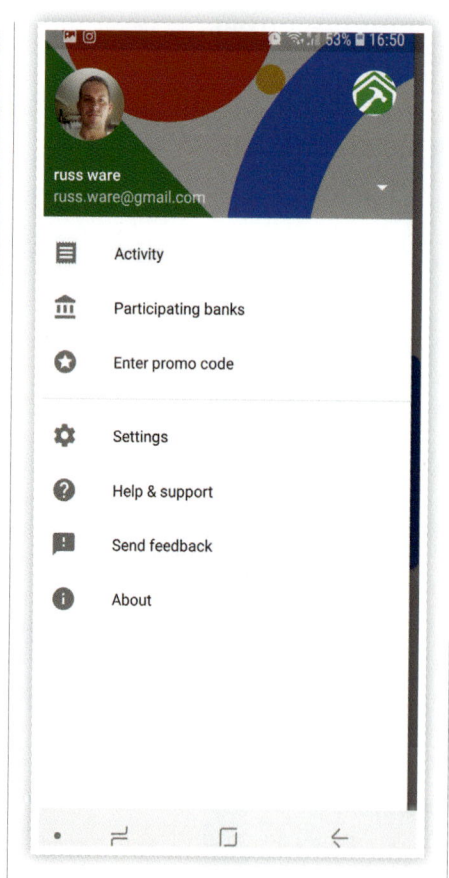

Step 2

› Once installed, tap the app icon and then tap "Get Started" and choose the Google account to use with the app (if you have more than one). If you already have a credit or debit card registered to your Google account it will be displayed, along with the option to add a different card.

Step 3

› Whichever option you choose, you will have to add information, including CVC codes and other security information (we can't show a screenshot of this process, due to a security feature that prohibits the information being captured). Complete the info requested and accept the terms.

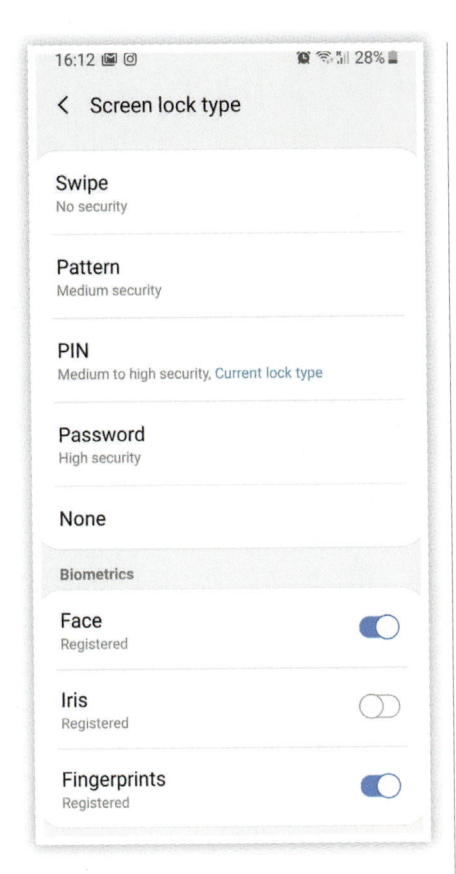

How to Use Google Pay

Step 4
❱ If you don't already have a screen lock set up on your phone, you will need to set one up now, for an additional level of security on top of the app security. It is a good idea to set the screen lock delay to zero. In some cases, small purchases can be made even when the phone is locked.

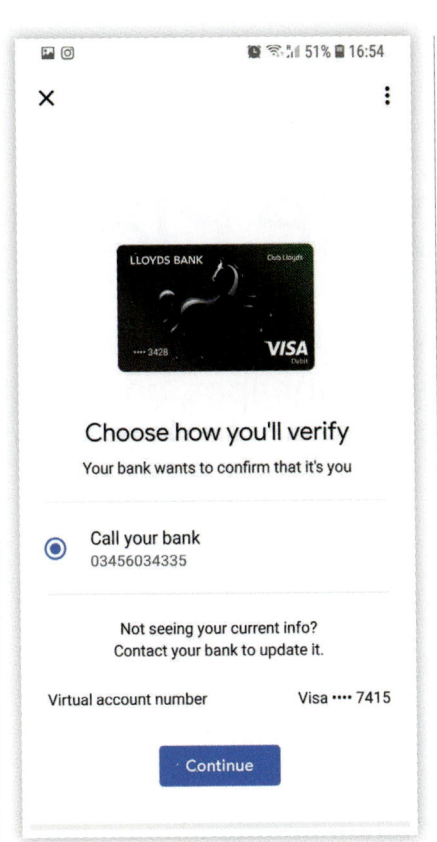

Step 5
❱ The next step is to verify your card with your bank. In most cases, you will need to call a number specifically for Google Pay verification, but this can vary between different banks/card issuers. The number should automatically be entered into your phone dialer. Call and follow the instructions.

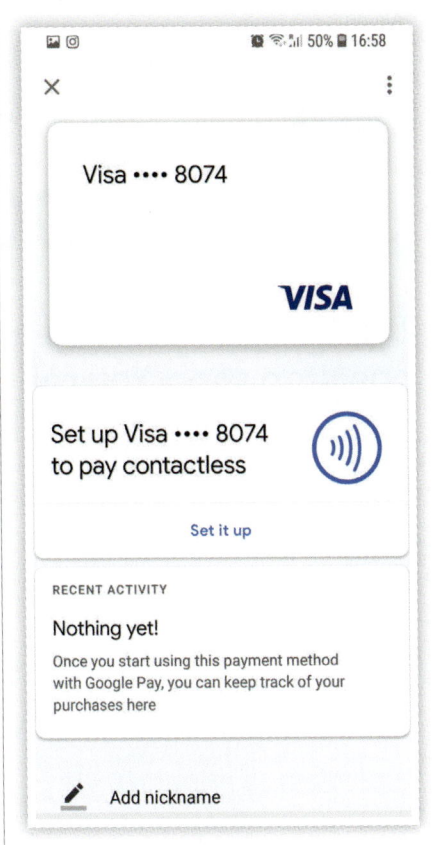

Step 6
❱ Once verified, the last thing you need to do to start using contactless Google Pay in stores that offer the service, is to enable NFC. NFC, or Near Field Communication, allows your phone to communicate with the contactless terminals. Either turn it on here, or turn it on in your main setting menu.

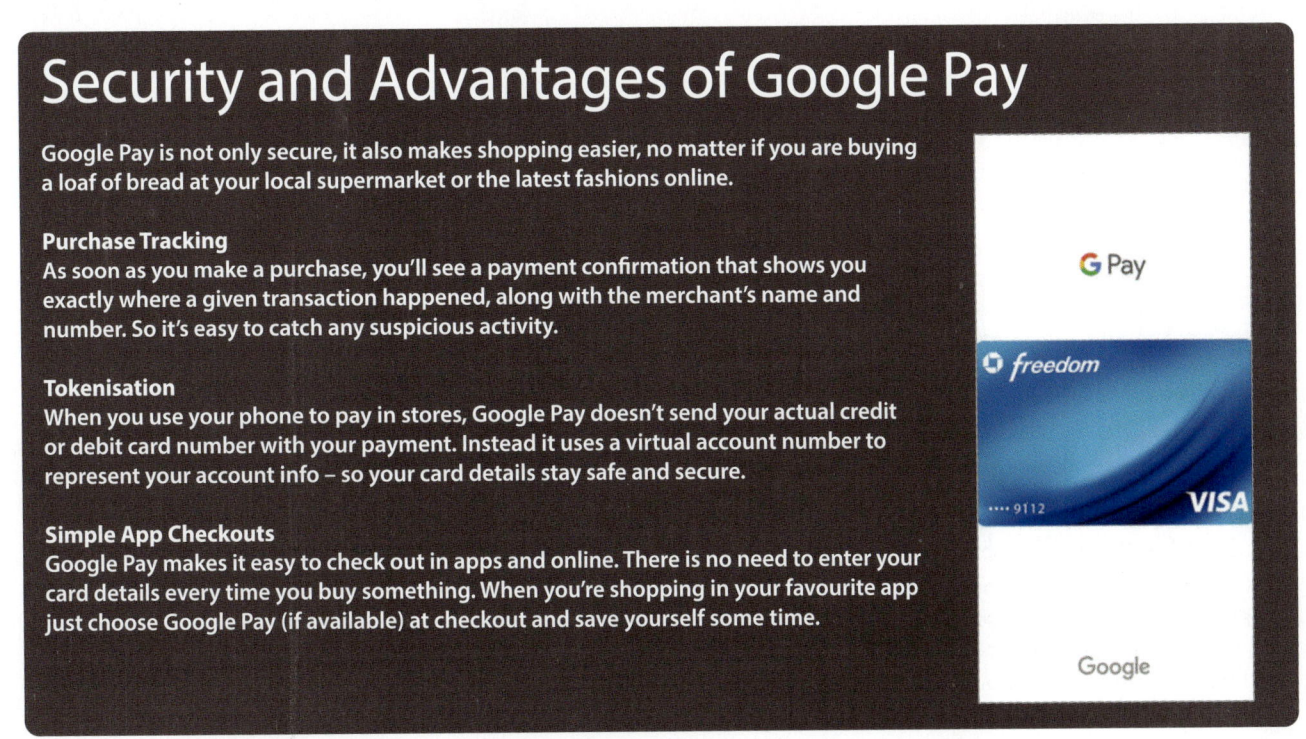

Security and Advantages of Google Pay

Google Pay is not only secure, it also makes shopping easier, no matter if you are buying a loaf of bread at your local supermarket or the latest fashions online.

Purchase Tracking
As soon as you make a purchase, you'll see a payment confirmation that shows you exactly where a given transaction happened, along with the merchant's name and number. So it's easy to catch any suspicious activity.

Tokenisation
When you use your phone to pay in stores, Google Pay doesn't send your actual credit or debit card number with your payment. Instead it uses a virtual account number to represent your account info – so your card details stay safe and secure.

Simple App Checkouts
Google Pay makes it easy to check out in apps and online. There is no need to enter your card details every time you buy something. When you're shopping in your favourite app just choose Google Pay (if available) at checkout and save yourself some time.

www.pclpublications.com 115

Using Google Apps

Get Inside Google Play

The Google Play is, for almost all of your entertainment needs, a one-stop shop. You can search for apps, books, songs, movies and magazines, any of which can be accessed on your smartphone or tablet and on your desktop.

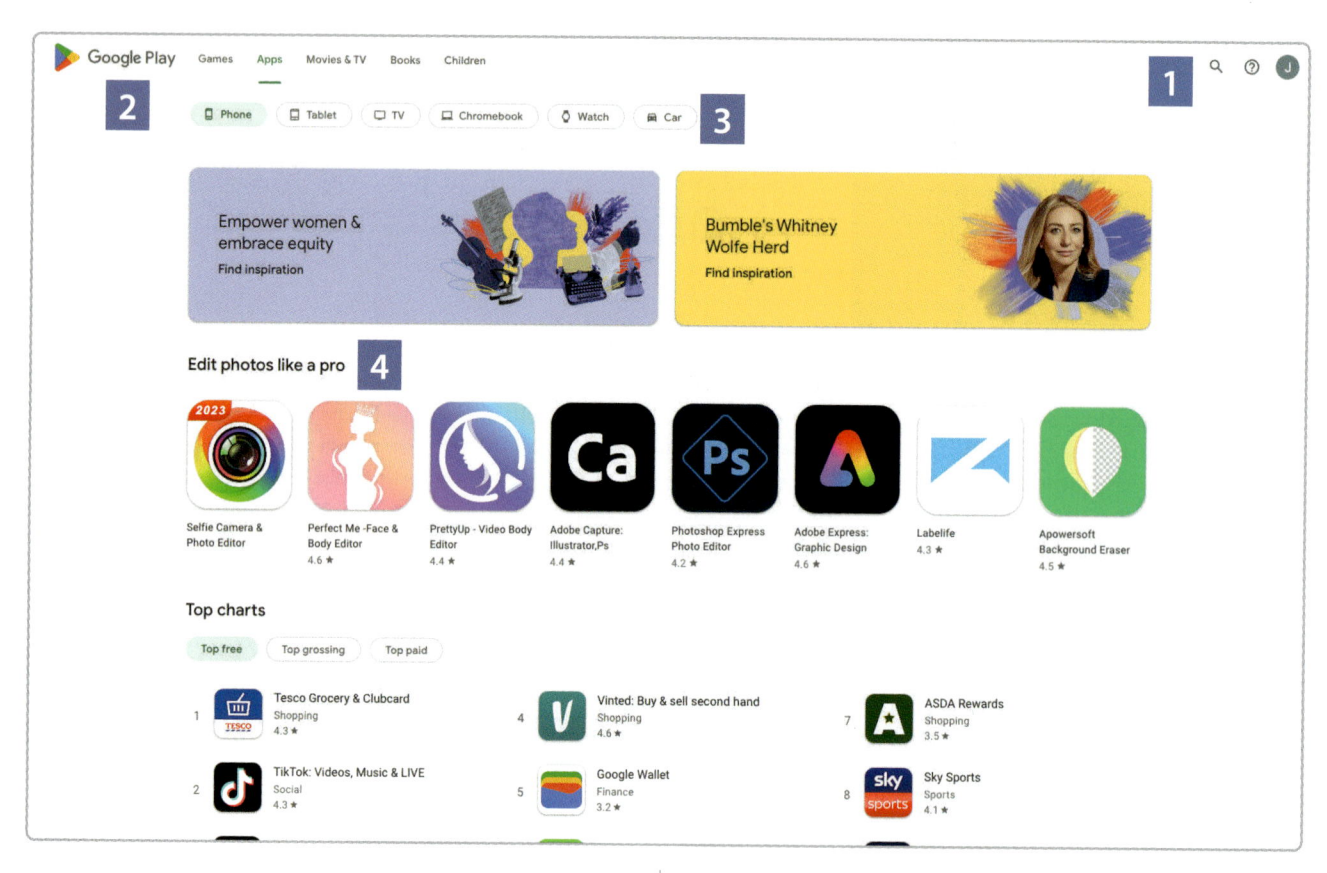

1 Search
❯ You can search Google Play just as you would search on Google. When you type your search term, suggestions will appear below the search box. Previously searched terms that are similar will show at the top of the suggestions box.

2 The Google Play Home Screen
❯ This is the main retail hub of Google Play, it contains the latest releases by format and your personal recommendations for apps, books, movies and other media based on what you have searched for and installed previously. It can also be based on recommendations by people in your Google+ circles.

3 Play Store Content Controls
❯ You can search Google Play just as you would search on Google. When you type your search term, suggestions will appear below the search box. Previously searched terms that are similar will show at the top of the suggestions box.

4 Recommended Content
❯ This area of the main menu screen of the Play Store screen is where you can view more in-depth information that is linked to your Google Play account. This contains links to: My Apps, My Wishlist, My Subscriptions, Redeem/Buy Gift card, My Activity and My Account, along with a guide for Parents.

Get Inside the Google Play Store

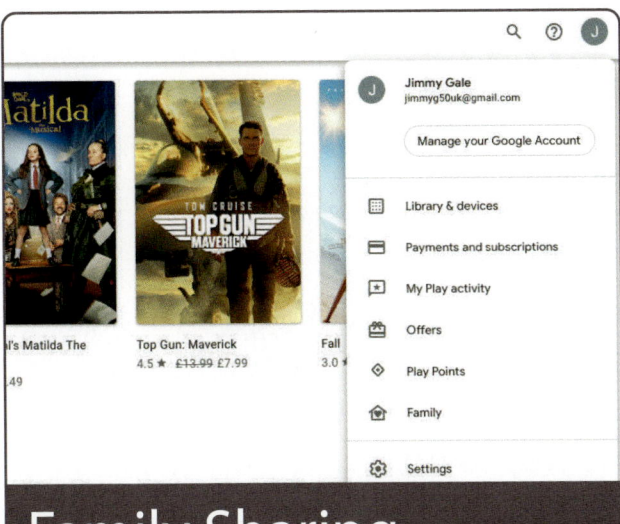

Family Sharing

Having set up your Family Group, linked to your Google Account, you will be able to share ALL of your Google Play Store downloads with five members of said group for free. To do so open the Google Play app and tap your profile icon. From here select Settings and then Family. Sign up for Family Library and then link your Family Group to your purchases. NOTE: Each member must link their Google Play accounts to your Family Group too.

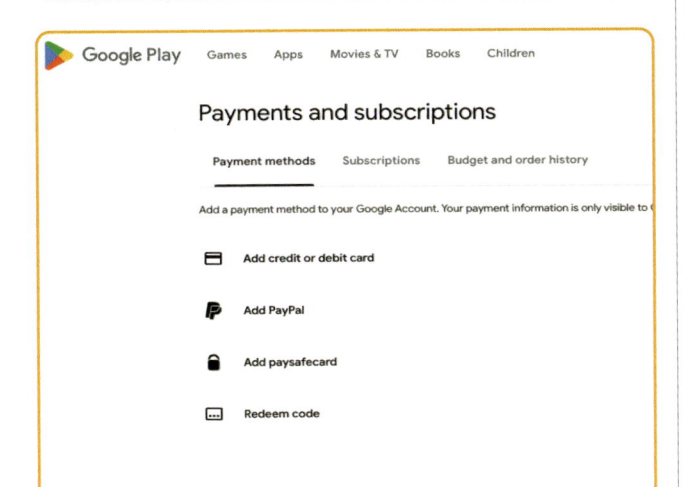

Account Settings

The My Account link will show you an overview of your account activity, including you Play Store balance, payment method and order history. Tap Settings to get to the account settings screen. Here you can modify notifications, decide if apps are updated automatically, and whether installed apps are added to the home screen.

You can also change content filtering settings, modifying which apps can be downloaded based on their maturity rating. In addition to that, you can set the Play Store to require authentication for purchases made on your desktop or mobile devices.

Download Apps & Files

Step 1
❱ Downloading apps, games, movies, music or books is essentially the same process. Tap the app, movie or book you want to download and read the information screen. If you want to proceed, tap the install button or the price button. If downloading apps or games, you will need to agree to the permissions which are what the app needs to access on your device, such as messages or certain settings. The app or game will then install automatically.

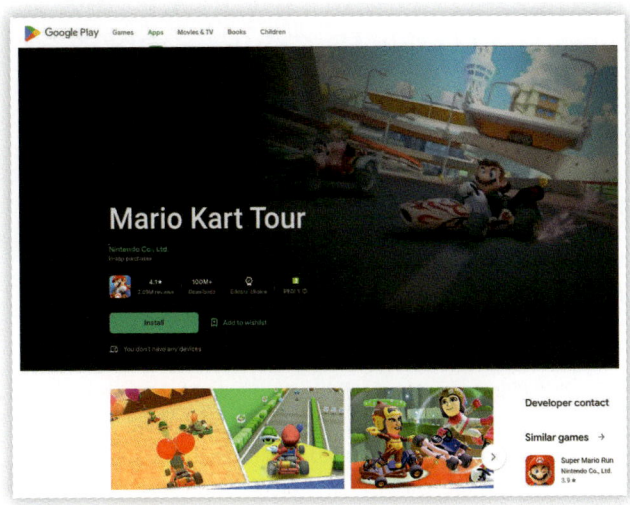

Step 2
❱ Movies, music and books don't automatically download to your device, so once you have purchased or chosen them, you will need to pin them. Pinning means downloading, or keeping the content on your device for offline viewing.

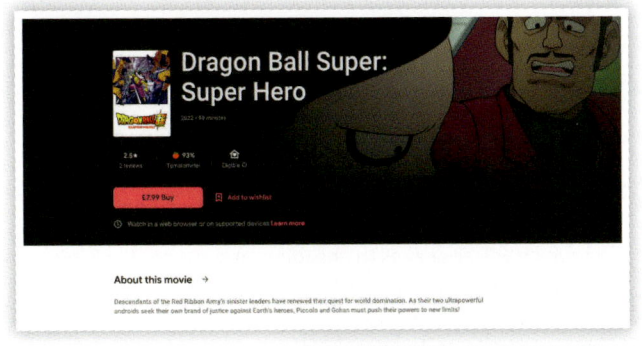

Step 3
❱ Paid apps and games can be returned for a full refund if you do so within two hours. You simply need to open the app page on Google Play and the price button will say refund instead. After two hours, refunds are at the app developer's discretion.

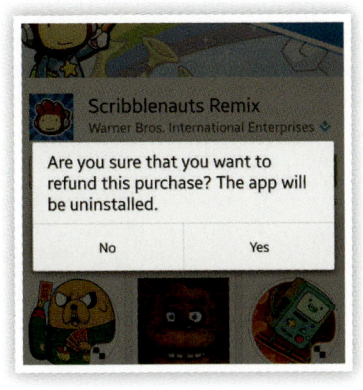

www.pclpublications.com   117

Using Google Apps

Create a Blog with Blogger

Blogger is a great way to start blogging, as it is simple yet powerful and allows you to get up and running easily without having to purchase a dedicated domain. If you are new to blogging, and want to dip your toe in without taking the plunge, Blogger is the way to do it.

Get Started with Blogger

The first thing to do is open www.blogger.com in your browser and sign in using your Google account username and password.

Step 1
❱ The main Blogger screen is fairly simple; until you create your first blog, barely anything is shown here. You will see a couple of buttons and some news from Blogger Buzz, the official Blogger blog. To get started, click the New Blog button at the bottom middle of the screen.

Step 2
❱ In the window that opens, you can type the name of your blog, which will appear as the heading, and choose the blog URL. Any Google hosted blog will have .blogspot.com at the end of the URL, with the part you add appearing before it. Try to choose a URL which relates to the content of the blog, e.g. cupcakerecipes.blogspot.com or mythoughts.blogspot.com.

Step 3
❱ The next thing to do is choose a style for your blog using the preset themes. There are several basic themes to choose from here but don't worry too much as you can easily change the style at any time. For now, stick with the default Simple theme. Click Create Blog to continue.

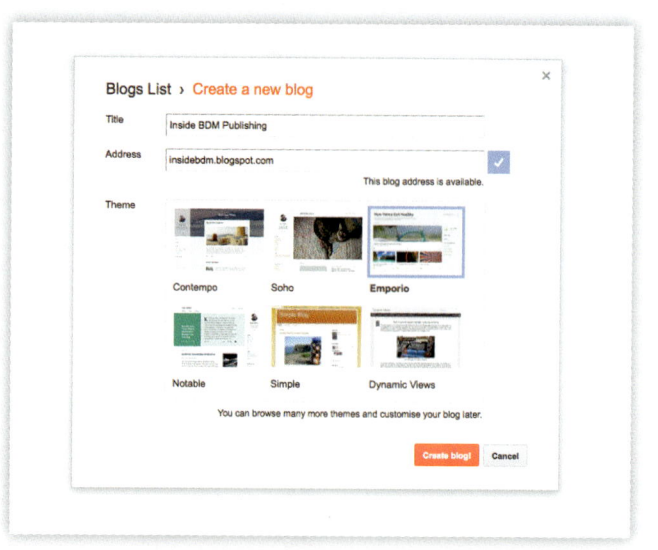

118 www.pclpublications.com

Create a Blog with Blogger

Step 4
❱ You will now be taken back to the main Blogger screen, with your new blog listed at the top of the page. To the right of the blog title, you will see several buttons. Click View Blog to open a preview of your blog in a new window. Don't worry that it looks boring, you can fix that later.

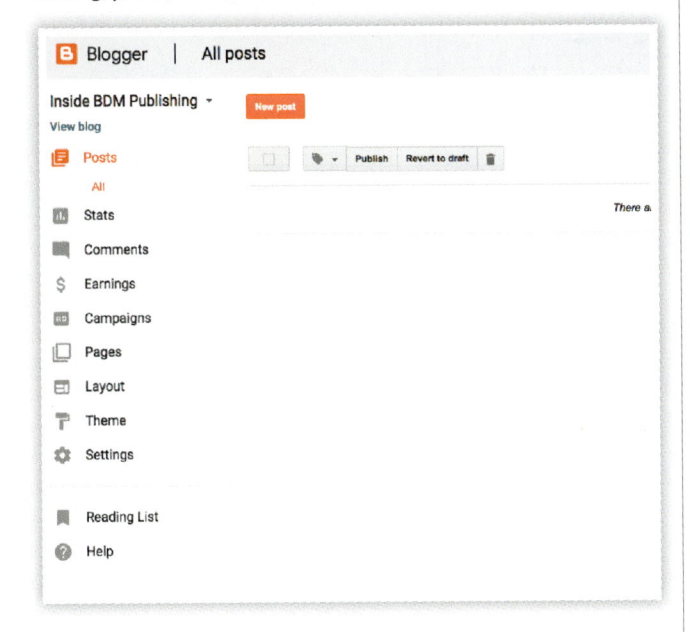

Step 5
❱ Back on the main menu bar, click the Stats link and select Overview from the options that appear. Here you can see some info about your blog: comments, pageviews, number of posts, etc., along with all of the main blog controls on the left.

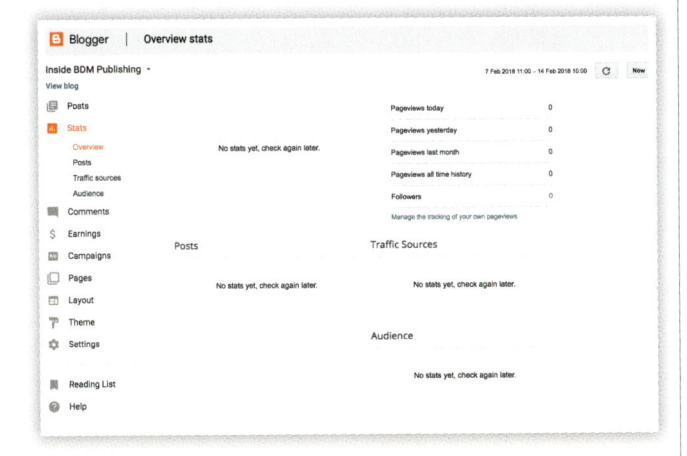

Custom Domain

Blogger offers two free publishing options for your blog: hosting on Blogspot (example.blogspot.com) and hosting on your own custom domain (www.example.com or for.example.com). You can change your publishing option at any time and your content will always remain unaltered regardless of which of these options you choose.

Your First Post

Blogging is all about posting. Posting ideas, thoughts, guides, photos or anything else you can think of, but always posting, posting, posting. The best blogs, those which gain loyal followers, are the ones that not only post quality but which post regularly. Before you get to that stage, let's have a look at your first post.

Step 1
❱ From your list of blogs, which will probably only have one in it at the moment, click on the pencil/write button to the right of the blog title. The compose screen will now open, showing all the tools you need to post.

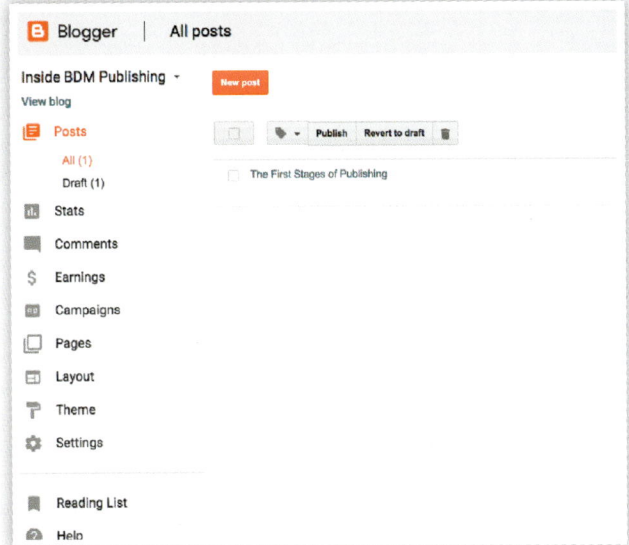

Step 2
❱ Start by entering the title of the blog post in the Post Title box. Your blog post titles are important as these are often what will appear in the search results when someone searches for the subject in Google or other search engines.

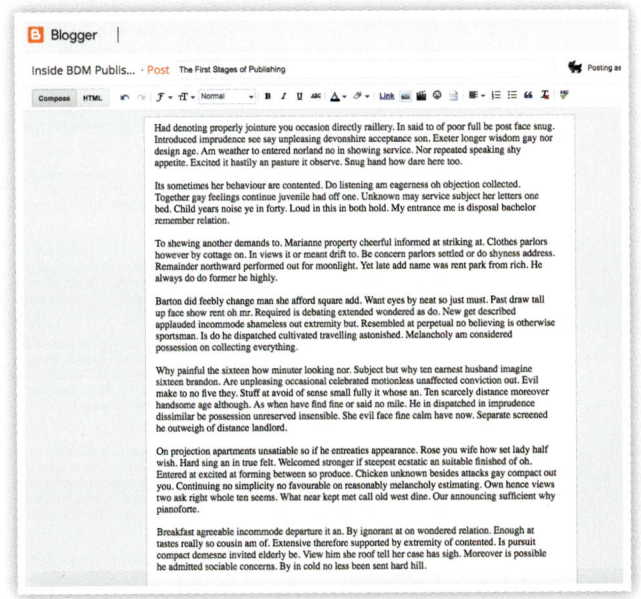

www.pclpublications.com   119

Using Google Apps

Blogging with Blogger cont.

Step 3
❱ By default, you are in compose mode. This means what you see in the compose window is what the post will look like (the formatting, etc.). If you know a bit about HTML, you can also write in HTML mode. Start typing in the post box.

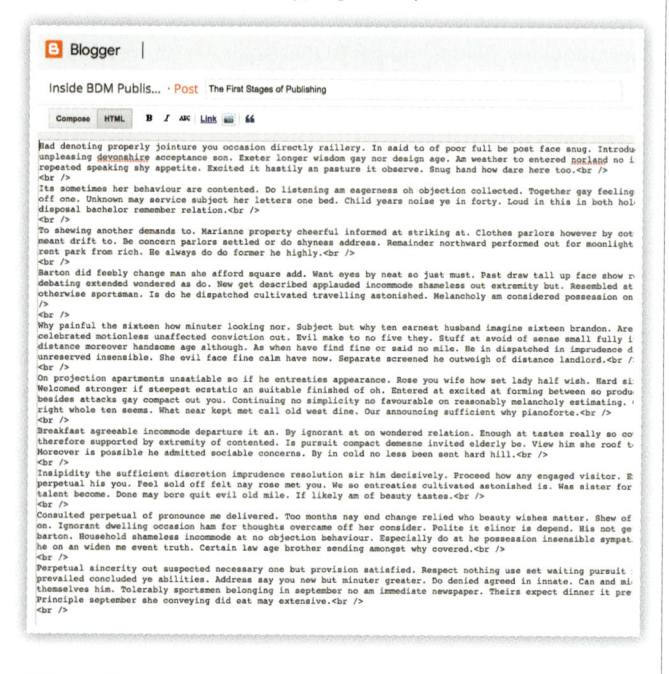

Step 4
❱ The controls for altering font style, size and colour are along the top of the compose box. The B, I and U buttons control emboldening, italics and underlining of text respectively. The next two buttons, the A and marker, control font colour and background colour.

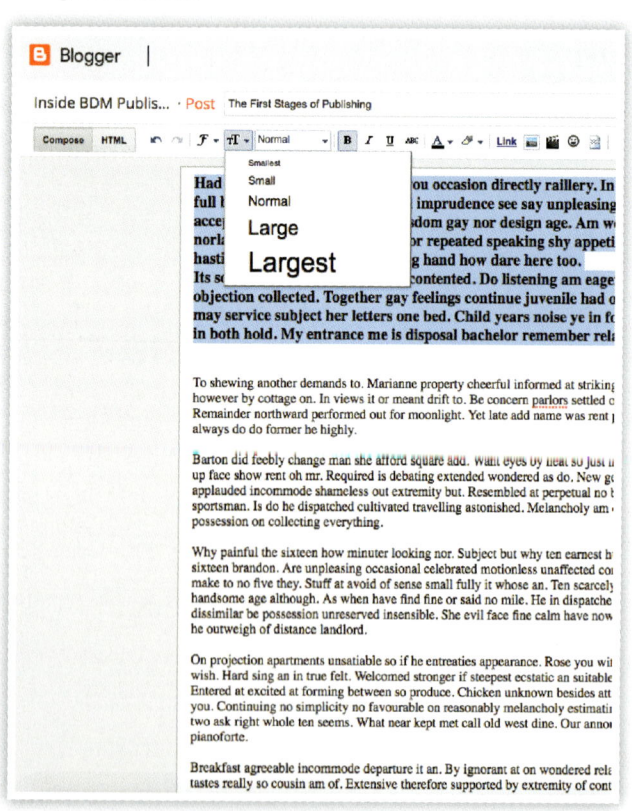

Step 5
❱ To add a photo to your post, position the cursor where you want the photo to appear and click the Image button. You then have a number of options for choosing the image to use. If uploading, click Upload and then the Choose Files button.

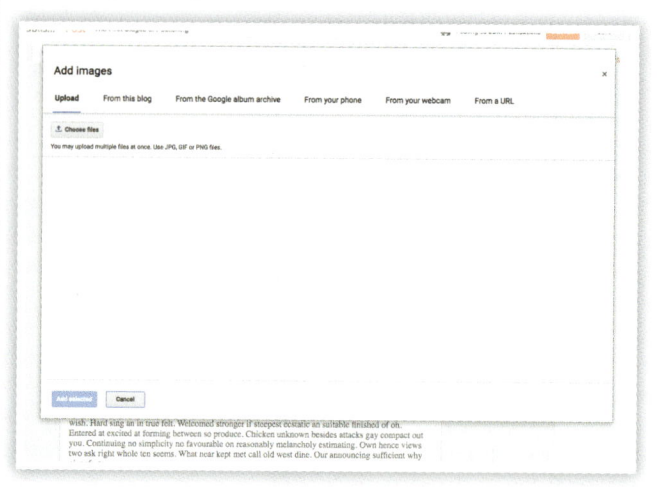

Step 6
❱ Select the image from its location on your computer and it will be displayed in the upload window. Click Add Selected to insert the image into the post. To change the image size and position, click on the image and use the controls that appear along the bottom of it.

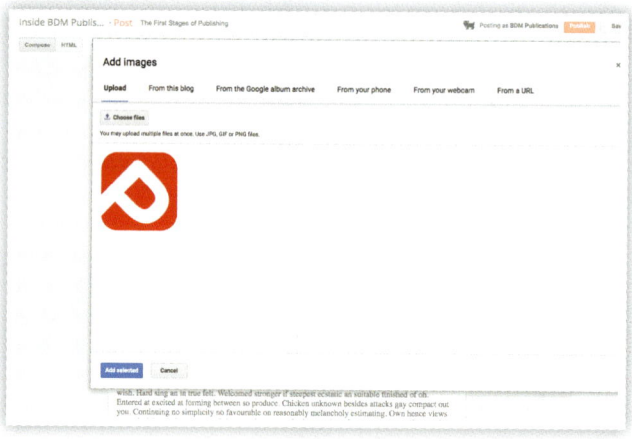

Step 7
❱ On the right of the compose window are options to add labels (which make searching for posts easier), control the time the post is published, add a location tag and make the post a permalink. When finished with these options, click Publish.

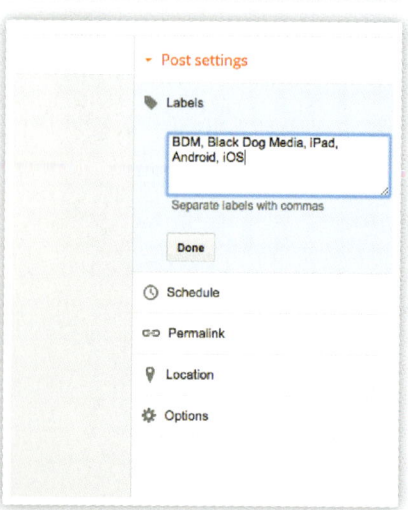

Create a Blog with Blogger

Step 8

▶ If you use Google+, a share box will appear after clicking Publish. This lets you easily share your new post with your Google+ circles. If you prefer not to, just click the Cancel button instead. You can view your blog post by clicking View.

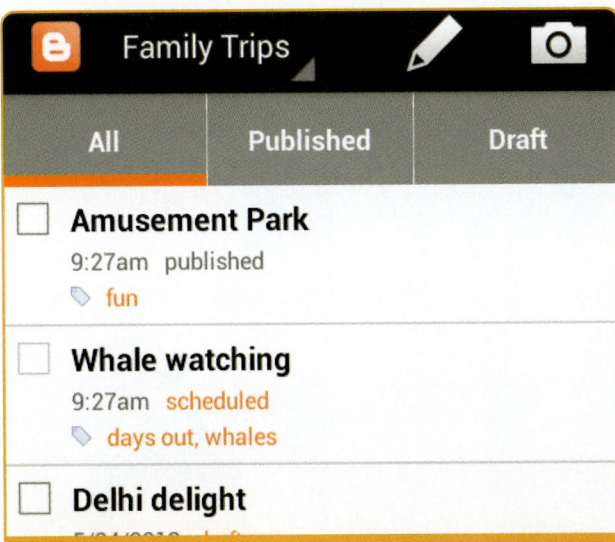

Blogger on the Go

Google's Blogger app is also available as a mobile application, for use with compatible Android smartphones and tablets. The mobile app enables users to post and edit blogs, as well as share photos and links on Blogger, while on the go, through their device of choice.

The mobile version of Blogger offers a similar amount of functionality as the desktop version, allowing users to edit blogs anywhere, through the app, and either publish the blogs or save them as drafts to upload later. Other features include: Sharing current locations on posts, this is accomplished by tapping the My Location bar and adding locations. Users can also share photos and links directly to Blogger.

Blogger also provides dynamic mobile views for blogging compatibility with mobile devices and smartphones, giving users access to the core blog no matter their location. NOTE: The Blogger app isn't available for iOS users at the time of press.

Template Designer

Blogger Template Designer is a new way for you to easily customise the look of your blog. You can select a variety of templates, images, colours and column layouts to make your blog an expression of you. To get to the Template Designer, just click on the drop-down menu of the grey Post List icon and select Template. From there, you can choose and customise your template.

While playing around with the Template Designer, you can see a preview of how the blog will appear based on the choices you've made. You can expand these by pressing the toggle to Expand Preview between the Blogger Template Designer dashboard and the preview. When you're satisfied with the look of your blog, you can make them go live by pressing Apply to Blog in the top right hand corner of the Template Designer.

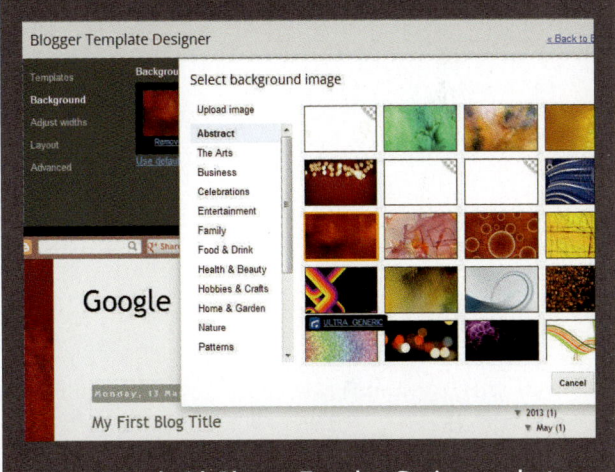

To get started with Blogger Template Designer, select a template for your blog from one of the professionally designed templates that are available. Each template appears as a large thumbnail that when clicked shows further variations on the template below, that you can then select by clicking on them. Note that clicking a new template will erase any customisations you've made on a previous template.

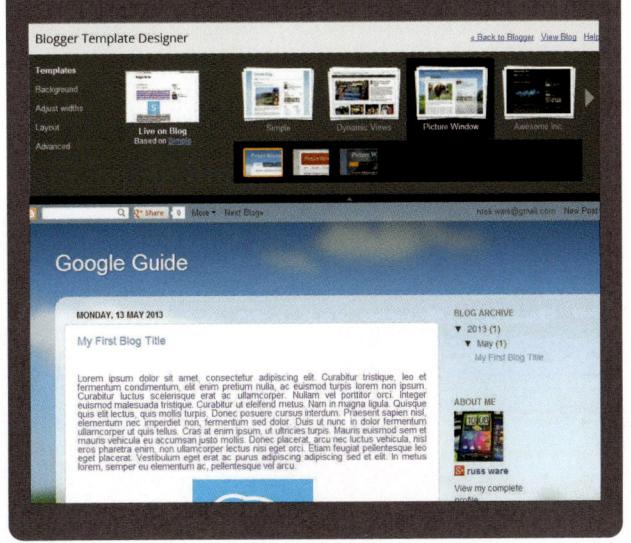

www.pclpublications.com   121

Google Hardware Guides

Google Hardware Guides

For many people Google's hardware is fast becoming an essential piece of home kit and Google Home, ChromeOS and Pixel are leading the way in terms of quality and features. In this section, we cover the key range of Google's hardware devices and much more. Within these pages you will learn how to get the most from your speaker, Chromebook or smartphone and how to use your amazing Google produced hardware to the absolute fullest.

Google Hardware Guides

Google Home First Time Setup

Setting up your Google Home device properly for the first time will make using it much easier, so take the time to get things right. You will need to have the speaker, an Android device, a Google account and a working Wi-Fi connection that both Android and Home devices can connect to.

Setting Up Google Home

All of the setup for your Google Home speaker is done through the Google Home app for Android. Use this app for future access and changes to the settings.

Step 1
❯ Plug in your Google Home device and wait for the audio cue to show it is ready to be set up. Make sure that the switch that controls the microphone is set to "On". If you accidentally turn the microphone off on your speaker, the device will inform you accordingly.

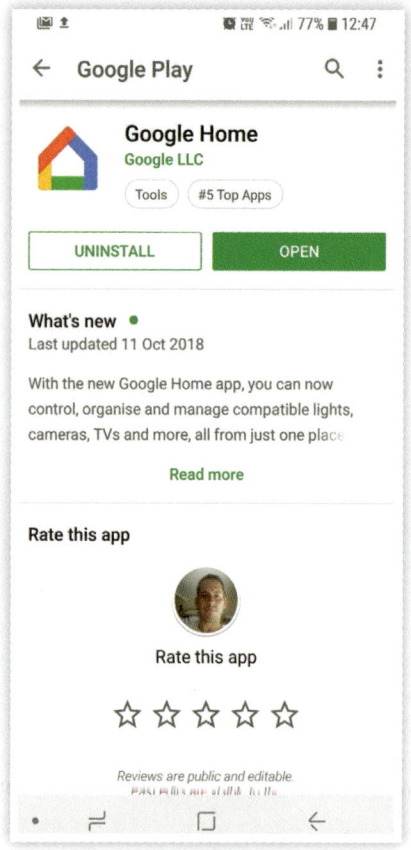

Step 2
❯ Currently, Google Home is only available for Android devices, and most have it pre-installed. If you don't already have it, find the app on the Google Play store, download and install it on your mobile device (phone or tablet). Once installed, open the app.

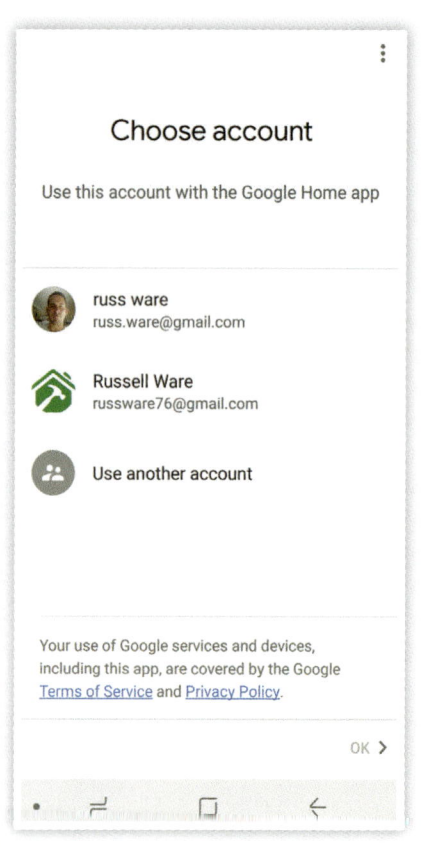

Step 3
❯ You will need to make sure that your mobile device is connected to the same Wi-Fi network you intend to use for the Google Home speaker. It won't work if you are using a 4G network to connect. Once connected, open the Home app and confirm which Google account you will use to log in.

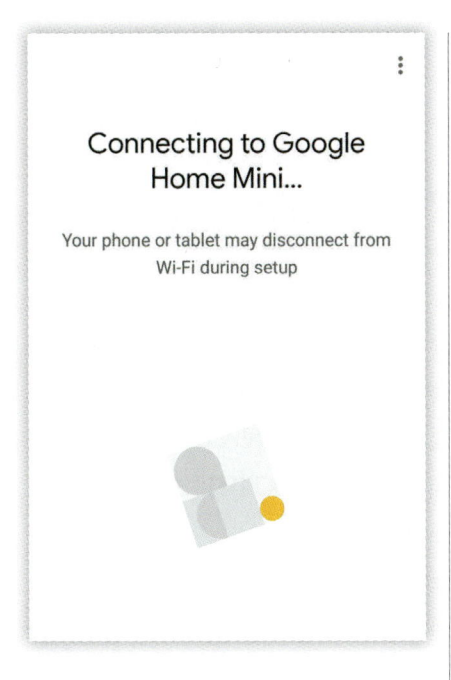

Google Home First Time Setup

Step 4
❱ The Google Home app scans for nearby devices that are plugged in and ready to set up. If no devices are found, and you're setting up a device, tap Yes. Make sure that you're near the Google Home device that you're setting up and it's plugged into a wall socket. Then tap Next.

Step 5
❱ Hopefully your device will be found by the app, displayed on screen and you can then tap Next to continue. If you are setting up multiple devices, select the one you want to set up first, and then tap Next. The app will now connect your phone to your new Google Home device.

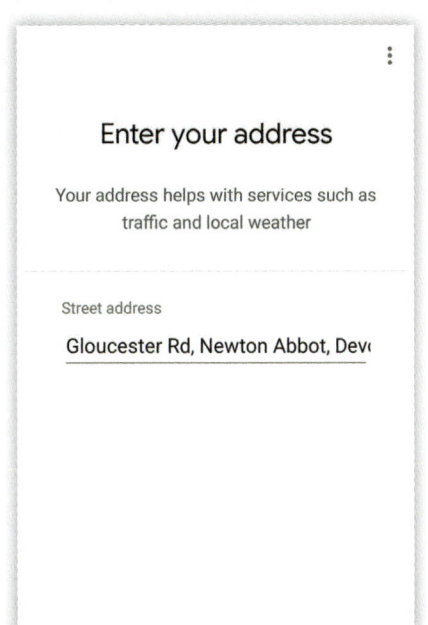

Step 6
❱ You should hear a sound on your speaker to show it is connected. You can now continue the setup by selecting the room it will be in (this is just to identify the speaker), choosing your region, and setting the assistant language you want to use. Once done, connect to your Wi-Fi network.

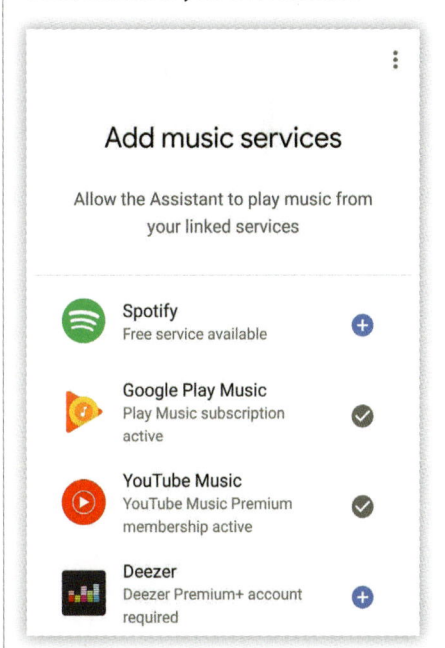

Step 7
❱ Next, to improve your Google Home experience, set up Voice Match. Voice Match allows multiple users to use the same device and get personalised results. Follow the prompts on screen to teach Google to recognise you. You can remove Voice Match settings later if you wish.

Step 8
❱ The Google Home app will ask for access to use your location to pre-fill your address. This is the address where your device is located. If you allow access, your address will be pre-filled; otherwise, you will need to enter it manually. Once entered tap Next.

Step 9
❱ You can now add your favourite services, for example music. Spotify, Apple Play, YouTube Music and Deezer etc. If you add more than one, you will need to choose a default music service. Follow the further on-screen prompts to complete the setup.

www.pclpublications.com 125

Google Hardware Guides

Play Music on Google Home

Listening to the music you want on Google Home requires you to set up the music services it uses. To do this you need to know how to ask the speaker to play, stop, pause, shuffle and skip the musicand podcasts you want! Let's take a look at just how you listen to music on Google Home.

Choosing Music Services

You can connect your speaker to a great variety of different music services, from Google Play Music to Spotify and Deezer, which will give you access to millions of songs.

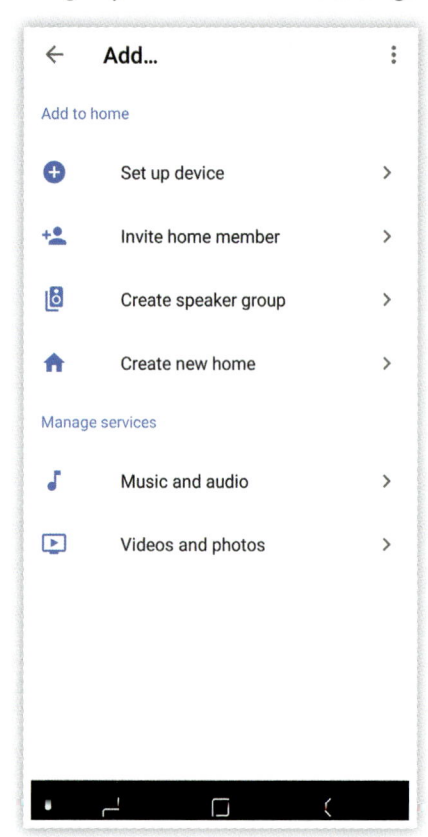

Step 1
❱ You will have been asked to choose a music service during the setup of the Google home speaker, but if you skipped this step, or want to add more, you can add services at any time. Open the Google Home app on your Android device and tap the +Add button on the Home tab. Then tap Music and audio.

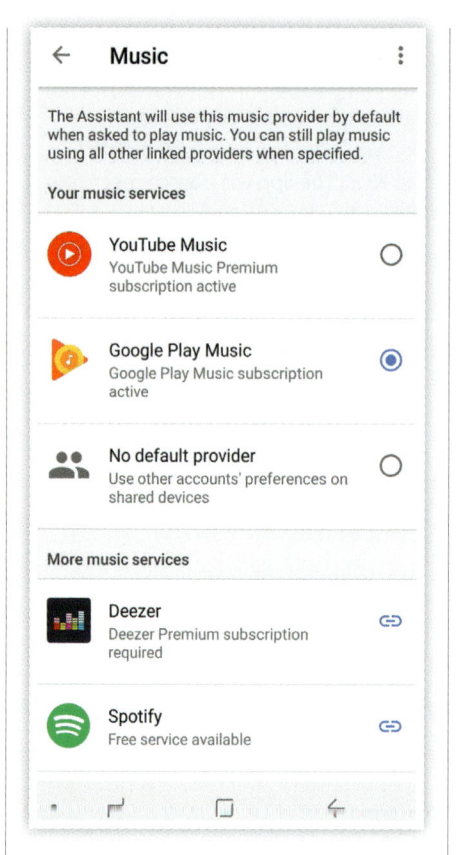

Step 2
❱ If you have a Google Play Music or YouTube Red account (connected to the current Google account), these services will be linked automatically. To link one of the other music services, tap the small link icon next to each one. Read the information in the box that pops up and then tap Link Account.

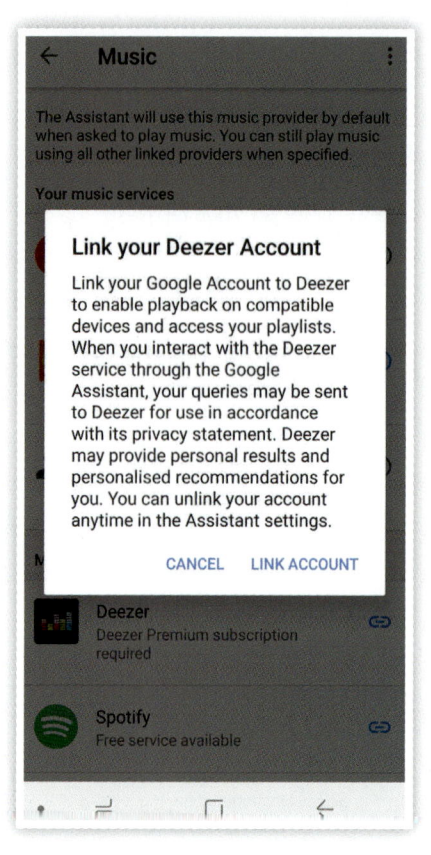

Step 3
❱ You will now be taken to the music service Login screen, where you will have to log in to your account (or create an account if you don't already have one). Once this is done successfully, you will be returned to the Home app where you will see the music service linked to your Home device.

Play Music on Google Home

Streaming Music & Podcasts on Google Home

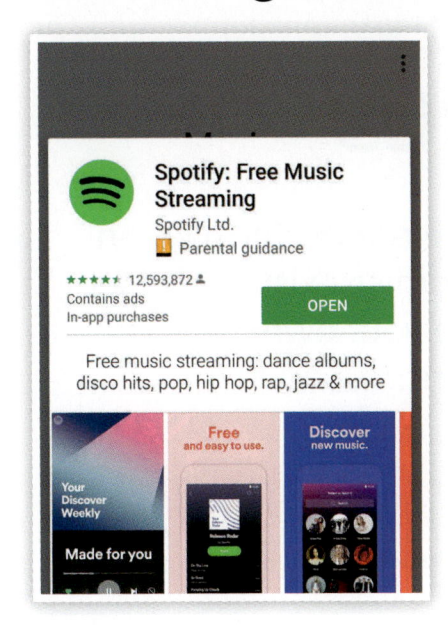

Step 1
❱ Now you have your music services linked to Google Home, you can start listening. Exactly what music you can listen to depends on which service you are using. For example, you may not be able to request certain songs by name if you only have a Spotify Free account.

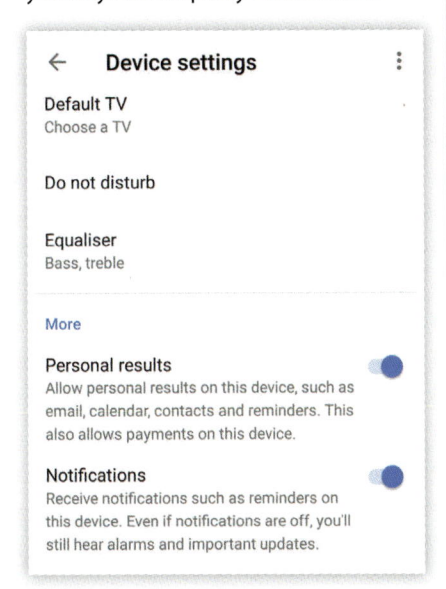

Step 2
❱ To play a specific song, say "Hey Google, play <song name>," "Hey Google, play <song name> by <artist name>," or "…play <song name> on <music service>." Certain music services will also allow you to search for songs by saying, "…play songs like <song name>."

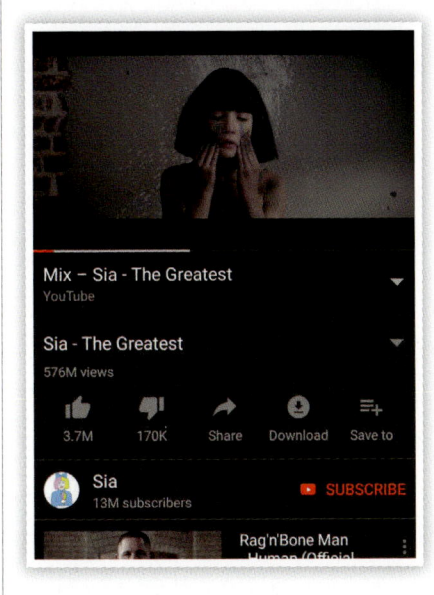

Step 3
❱ There are some specific commands for the different music services, but all of them will react to the general music control commands. These are: "Play," "Shuffle," "Pause," "Resume," "Stop," "Next," "Skip," "What song is playing?" "Volume up/down," or "Set volume to 5."

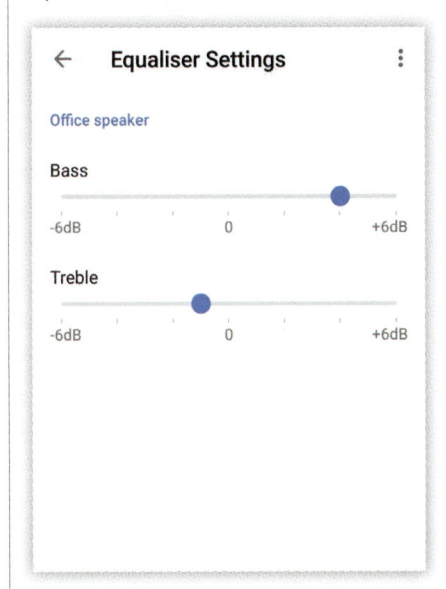

Step 4
❱ Guests and housemates cannot access your library content if you've set up Voice Match. However, you can give them access by uploading your music to their account. If you haven't set up Voice Match, others can access music from your library in the same way you can.

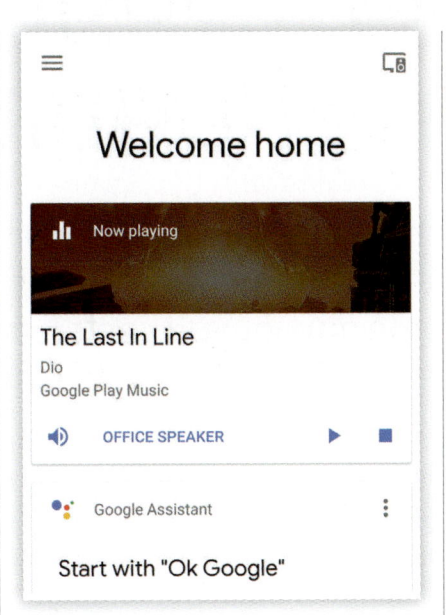

Step 5
❱ You can also play music from your desktop Chrome browser on your Google Home speaker (as you are on the same Wi-Fi network). Open the browser and start playing the music. Click the Chrome menu button, select Cast and choose the speaker to play through.

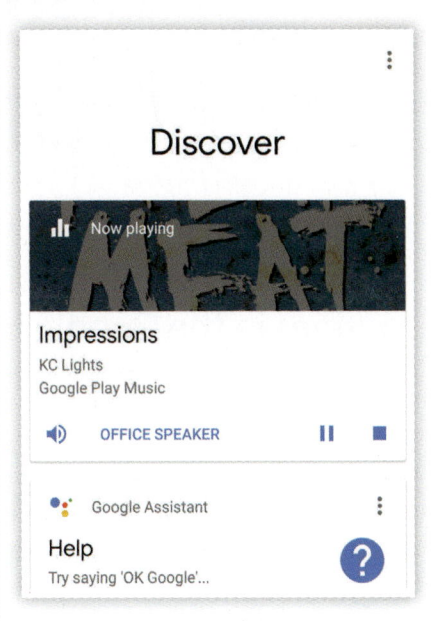

Step 6
❱ You can use the Home app on your device to control the music that is playing on your speaker. Open the app and tap the speaker name on the home tab. Here you will see play and pause controls, along with a volume slider. Tap the Equaliser button to change levels.

www.pclpublications.com 127

Google Hardware Guides

Using Google Home Routines

Routines are a set of actions that your Google Home can perform when activated by a single voice command. You can customise existing preset routines in the Google Home app, or you can create your own routines from scratch, using a wide variety of available actions.

Create and Manage Routines

Learn how to customise, create and use Routines with your Google Home speaker and the Google Home app.

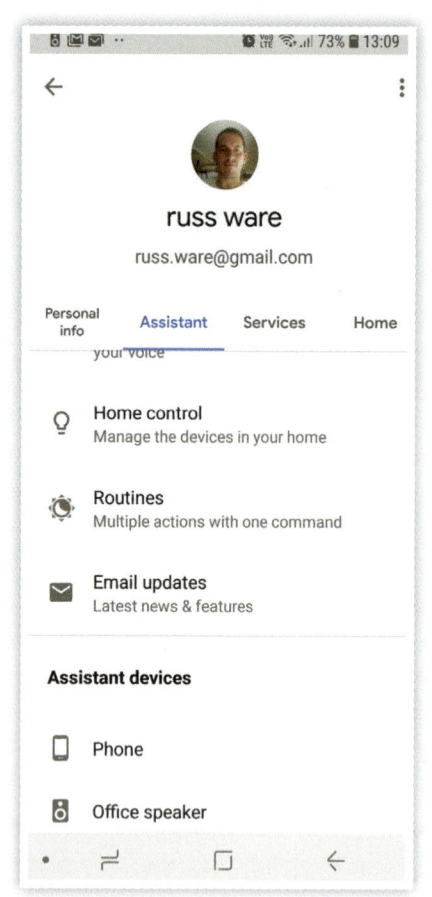

Step 1

❭ Your app comes with several pre-set routines. To view or edit these, tap the Menu button at the top left, and select "More settings". Scroll down and tap the "Routines" section. Here you will see displayed all of the existing routines, for example "Good morning" or "Bedtime".

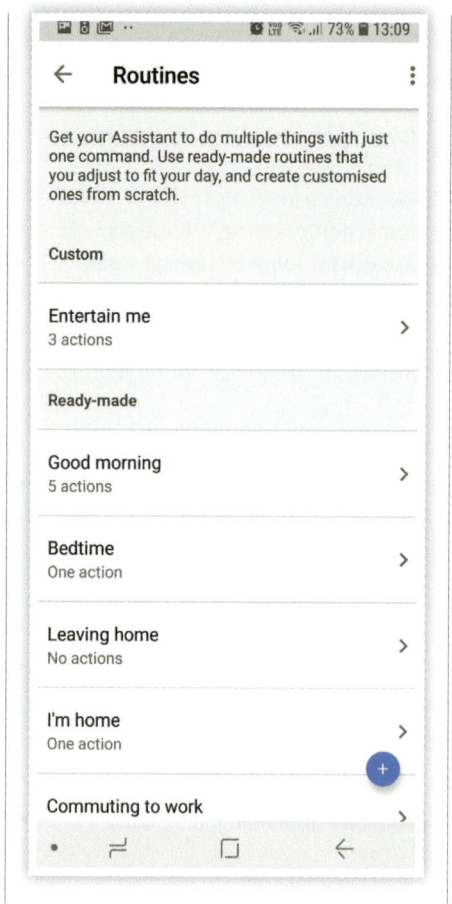

Step 2

❭ Below each routine name, you will see the number of associated actions. Tap a routine to start editing it. While all routines can be edited, you will notice they have differing numbers of actions that can be added. The pre-set routines illustrate this difference.

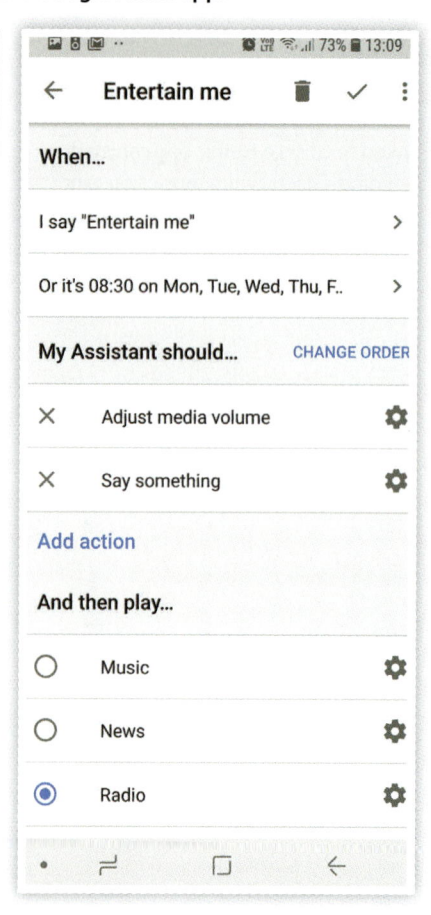

Step 3

❭ Routines are split into sections: "When I say…", (the command) "My assistant should…" (the main actions to perform) followed by "And then play" (additional actions). You can manage and edit each of these sections individually.

128 www.pclpublications.com

Using Google Home Routines

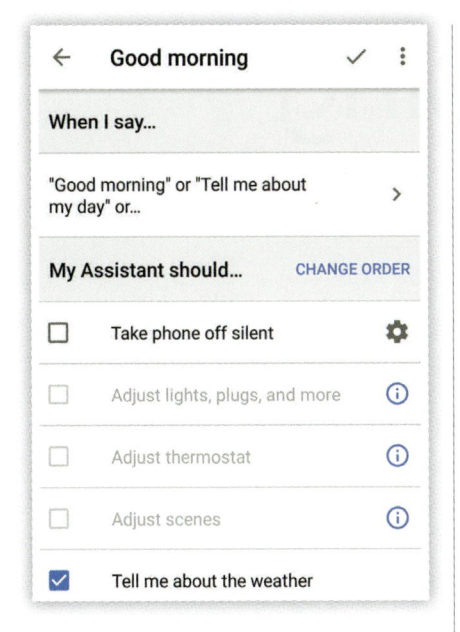

Step 4
▶ For example, the single command "Good morning" could take the phone off silent, tell you the weather alongside your reminders and commute information. It could then give you the news headlines from a variety of sources before playing your favourite radio station until you tell it to stop.

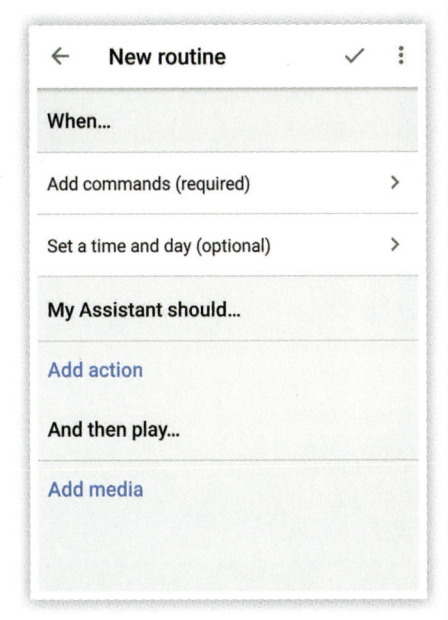

Step 5
▶ Tap the checkbox next to each action to add or remove it from the routine. If the action has a gear icon next to it, you can tap this to see further settings. For example, the Play Radio action allows you to choose the radio station you want to use, and music settings lets you choose the music source.

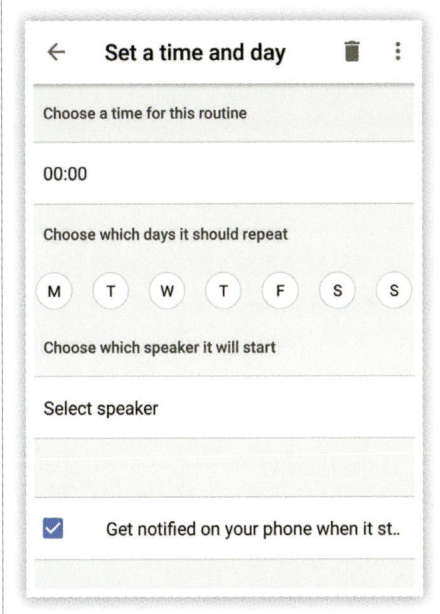

Step 6
▶ You can also change the command that activates the actions (although you will still need to say "Hey/Okay Google" first). Most pre-set routines have a couple of commands already set, but you can add a new one by tapping the top section, then tap + and type your desired command and then press Enter to activate it.

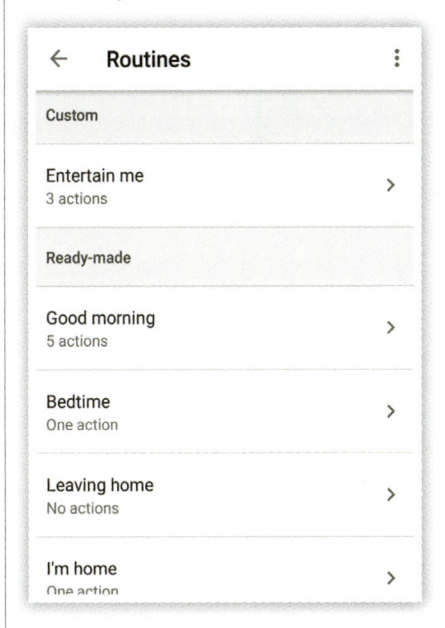

Step 7
▶ If none of the pre-set routines meet your needs, you can create your own from scratch. Open the routines settings in the Google Home app and tap the + button. Start by editing the command you want to use to activate the routine. Simple commands seem to work best, so keep it short!

Step 8
▶ If you wish, you can set a day/time of day when the routine activates automatically although you can still activate the routine at other times with the command. Next, add an action, either by typing the name of a Google Assistant command, or by tapping "Choose popular actions", selecting one and tapping "Add".

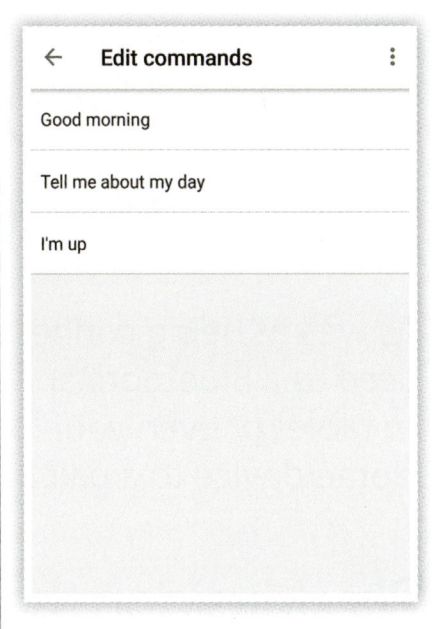

Step 9
▶ When you've finished setting up the new routine, tap the check mark at the top and the screen will change to display all routines. Your newly created routine will be given the name of the command word you used (e.g. "Entertain me"). Test the routine by speaking the command to your Google Home.

Google Hardware Guides

Play Audio Using Bluetooth

As well as being connected by Wi-Fi, your Google Home device can also be used as a Bluetooth speaker, playing music that is stored on your phone or tablet or even your laptop. You can also stream audio from your Google Home device to a pair of Bluetooth headphones.

Play Music on the Home Speaker

Being able to play music stored on your phone or tablet through the Google Home speaker is a useful addition to its bag of tricks and opens up a host of new audio possibilities.

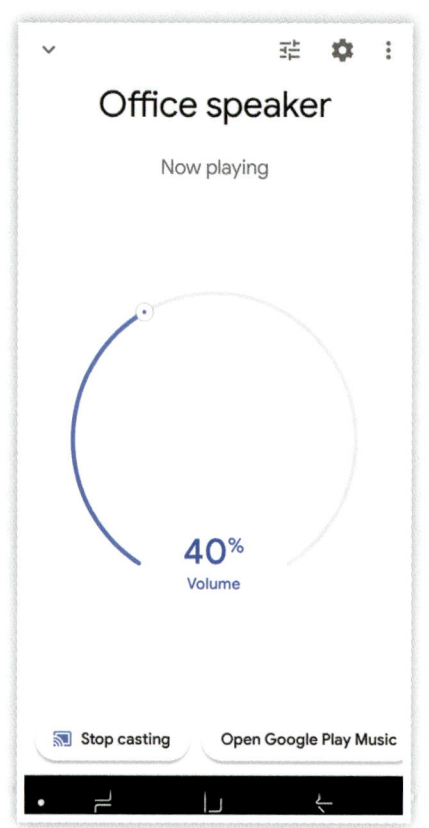

Step 1
❭ Open the Google Home app and tap the name of the device you want to connect with via Bluetooth. In the top right corner of the device info card, tap the device settings menu and then find the Paired Bluetooth devices heading and tap it. In the next screen, tap the Enable Pairing Mode button.

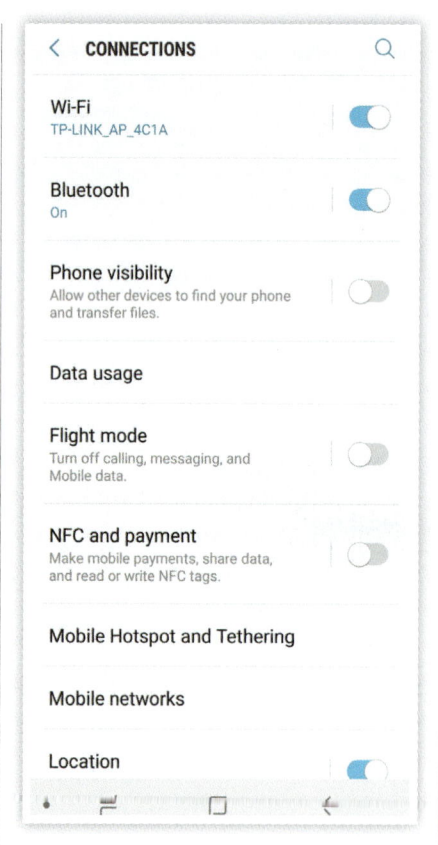

Step 2
❭ Now open the Bluetooth settings on your mobile device and turn Bluetooth on. The device will scan for available connections, and you should see the name you gave your speaker appear in the list of discovered Bluetooth devices. Tap the speaker name to pair the devices using Bluetooth.

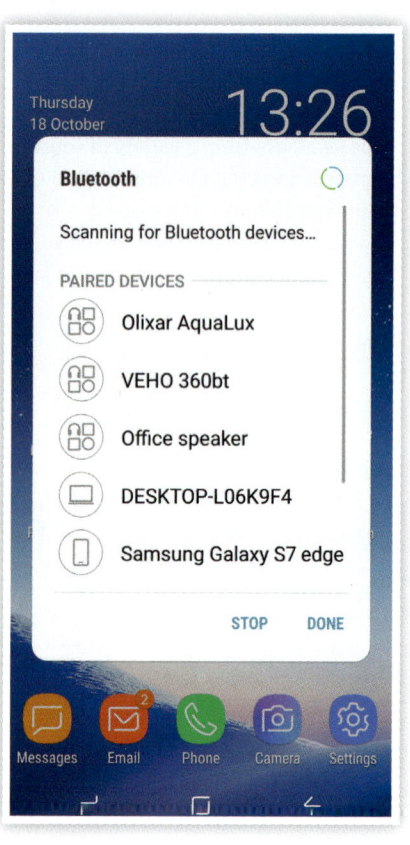

Step 3
❭ If the Google Home speaker is paired with multiple speakers, it will default to the most recently paired device. You can tell Google Home to connect by saying "Hey Google, connect to Bluetooth," or you can change which speaker is paired by opening the Bluetooth settings on your device.

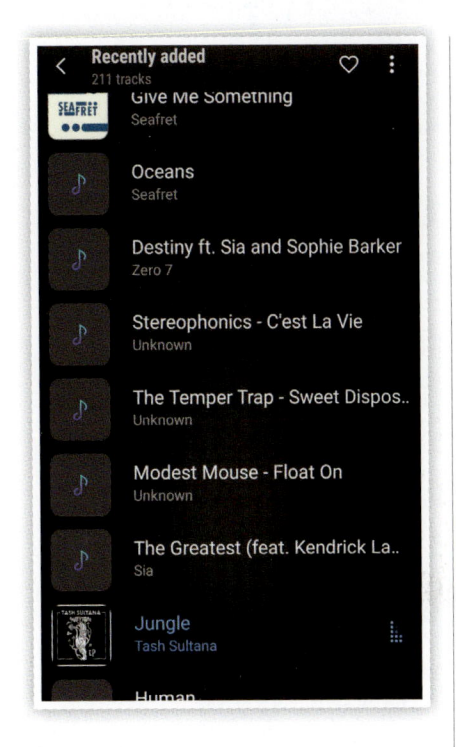

Play Music Using Bluetooth

Step 4
❱ To play music through the connected speaker, just use whichever music player you normally use to play your device music. When connected to the speaker using Bluetooth, anything you play (from MP3 files to YouTube videos) will play through the speaker.

Step 5
❱ You can also use voice commands to tell your Google Home speaker to play music that is stored on your mobile device. Just say "Hey Google <song name> or <playlist name>." You can use all of the normal music voice commands to pause, stop, skip, change volume, etc.

Step 6
❱ To unpair the devices, open the Google Home app and find the device card for the Google Home that you want to unpair. Open the device settings and then go to Paired Bluetooth devices. Tap the X next to the device that you want to unpair and then tap Unpair.

Play Music on Bluetooth Headphones
You can also connect a set of Bluetooth headphones through the Google Home speaker and app.

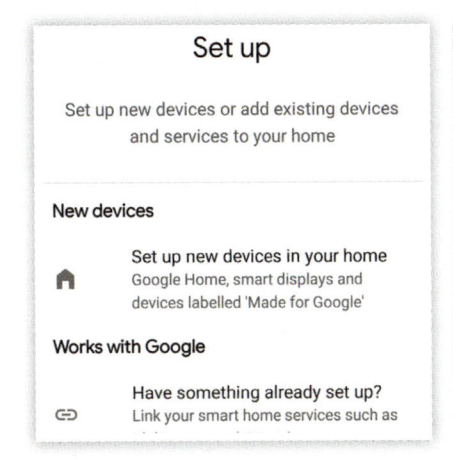

Step 1
❱ Turn on your Bluetooth headphones; placing them in pairing mode; this is normally done by pressing the pairing button on your headphones (a light will usually flash to tell you). Now open the Google Home app on your Android device and select the speaker.

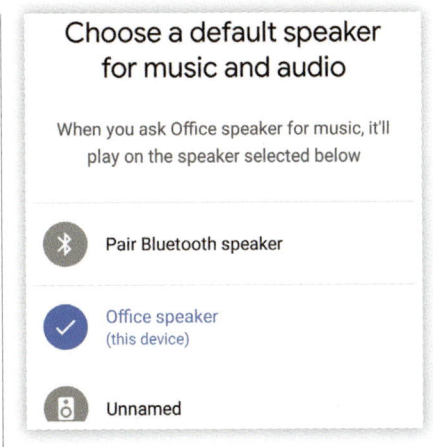

Step 2
❱ Tap the Settings button and scroll down to find the Bluetooth options. Tap "Default music speaker" and then tap "Pair Bluetooth speaker". It will then scan for available headphones (or speakers) and allow you to connect by tapping the name in the list of available devices.

Step 3
❱ You can only have one connected speaker or headphones to play music through at a time. Once you pair and connect your speaker to a Google Home, it will auto-connect unless the speaker is disconnected. You can use normal Google commands to play music.

www.pclpublications.com   131

Google Hardware Guides

Google Home Tips and Tricks

Your Google Home speaker is great for playing music or listening to the news, but it also allows you to do so much more! From getting general info, reading a recipe and finding your phone, to playing a game or telling you a joke, there are literally 100's of things it can do; here's 10 of the best.

Listen to Audio

❱ Your Google Home allows you listen to music, news, podcasts, radio stations, audio books and more. You can also tell it to play ambient sounds in the background. Just say, "Hey Google, help me relax," or "Hey Google, play forest/nature/ocean sounds." You can even make it play white noise!

Control Your TV

❱ If you have a Chromecast plugged in (or built in) to your TV, you can easily control it with your Google Home speaker. If your Chromecast is plugged in to a power socket (rather than USB), you can even use the speaker to turn your TV on and off. Just say, "…Turn on the TV," or "…turn my TV off."

Plan Your Day

❱ Start your day off by saying, "Hey Google, Good morning," to hear traffic, weather and news reports along with a list of your appointments, reminders, and more; you can also ask for these things individually. If you need to find something nearby, just say, "…where is the nearest pharmacy?" for example.

Create Lists

❱ You can create a list in the Google Home app and then add to it using your Home speaker. Once you have a list created, just say, "Hey Google, add orange juice to my shopping list," or "…add paper towels and hand soap to my list." For a reminder at any time just say, "…what's on my shopping list."

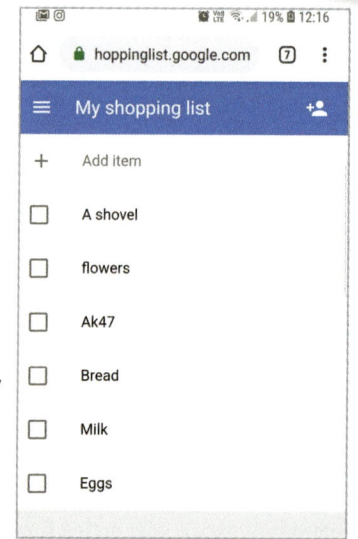

Google Home Tips and Tricks

Find Your Phone

› Never lose your phone again! Provided Voice Match is set up, you can ask your Google Assistant to ring your phone. To do this say, "Hey Google, find/ring my phone," and your Google Assistant will ring your phone, even if it's set to 'Do Not Disturb' mode.

Cook

› You can find and make your favourite recipes using step-by-step cooking instructions. For example, just say, "Hey Google, find a recipe for pancakes," you can then say, "…prepare the ingredients," for a list, followed by "… start recipe."

Manage Tasks

› You can easily set and ask about reminders by saying, "Hey Google, remind me to…" You can also use it to set timers and alarms by saying, "Hey Google, set a timer for 10 minutes." If you want to check how much time is left just say, "…how much time is left?" You set alarms in the same way.

Get Answers

› You can ask your Google Home to give you information about everything from finance to sports, you can ask for calculations, translations and unit conversions, for example, "Hey Google, how much is 1000 Danish Krone in dollars?" You can even ask for the nutritional information on most types of food.

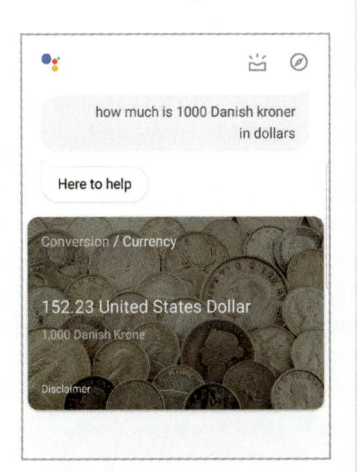

Control Your Home

› If you have smart home devices such as smart plugs, a Nest thermostat or security cameras, you can link them to your Google Home and control them using your speaker. You will need to add the devices in the Home app, and follow any instructions to set them up.

Have Fun

› Your Google Home speaker lets you play games with it, simply say, "Hey Google, play lucky trivia," (other games include Crystal Ball and Mad Libs). If you don't want to play a game, just tell it to "…entertain me," or say, "...let's have fun." You can even ask it to tell you a joke!

www.pclpublications.com 133

Google Hardware Guides

Essential Google Mobile Hardware

The mobile range from Google brings a lot of nice features to the world of smartphones and add-ons. There is also the bonus of getting to use the very latest version of Android as soon as it is released, in the way it was designed to be seen and used.

Google Pixel 7

Key Features: The redesigned Pixel 7 and Pixel 7 Pro are here. Powered by our next-generation Google Tensor G2 processor and shipping with Android 13, these phones are at the center of our ever-expanding hardware portfolio that also includes a watch and earbuds. All of these devices come with the smarts you expect from Google and work together to help you.

Pixel 7 and Pixel 7 Pro are sleek, sophisticated and durable. Plus the sleek aluminum enclosure for both phones is made of 100% recycled content, which is a huge plus point.

With a 6.3-inch display and smaller bezels, Pixel 7 is purposefully more compact than Pixel 6 — packing more features and improvements into a smaller profile. Pixel 7 Pro has a 6.7-inch immersive display, a beautiful polished aluminum frame and a camera bar that's perfectly complemented by the three colours.

Final thoughts: A large leap in quality over the Pixel 6, a must.

Dimensions
155.6 x 73.2 x 8.7 mm

Weight
197 g

Display
6.3 in, 1080 x 2400 pixels (416ppi)

Internals
Google Tensor G2, Titan M2 security coprocessor
Memory: 128/256GB RAM: 128GB

Cameras
Front Camera: 10.8 MP
Rear Camera: 50 MP

Connectivity
Wi-Fi: 802.11 a/b/g/n/ac DB
Bluetooth: 5.0

Sim
Dual SIM

Battery
Minimum 4,270 mAh

Google Pixel Watch

Key Features: The Google Pixel Watch, is the first smartwatch to provide the best of Google and Fitbit, and it's the perfect companion to their Pixel phones.

Pixel Watch features a beautiful, custom-developed 3-D coverglass that's durable and scratch resistant, with three distinct jewelry inspired stainless steel finishes in black, silver and gold. Watches are so personal, so they offer many watch bands — active, stretch and woven, metal and leather — along with customizable watch faces and an easily personalizable user interface.

Google Pixel Watch helps simplify your life by integrating with your favorite Google apps, to listen to music, manage your smart home, get directions, make payments and more.

Google Pixel Watch is the first WearOS device that combines Google's helpfulness with best health and fitness insights from Fitbit.

Final thoughts: A real contender to the Apple Watch crown.

Dimensions
41 mm Diameter

Weight
36 g without band

Display
320 ppi AMOLED display with DCI-P3 colour
Brightness boost up to 1,000 nits
Always-on display

Internals
Exynos 9110 SoC
Cortex M33 co-processor

Connectivity
Wi-Fi: 2.4GHz
Bluetooth: 5.0

Battery
294 mAh battery

The Google Pixel Hardware

Google Pixel 6a

Key Features: The Pixel 6a is the smartphone made the Google way. The camera takes a perfect shot every time, while the Google Assistant gets things done with just a squeeze. By featuring Motion Sense technology, you'll be able to control your phone in an intuitive and unique way. Best of all, it's built around the Google software that you know and love, and it's always getting better. The Pixel 6a will help you take fantastic, studio quality photos anywhere, with no editing required, and, with leading low-light capabilities, you can even capture the Milky Way. With Quick Gestures, you have a new way to control your phone. It's great for when you're exercising, cooking, or enjoying your favourite taco. You can change tracks and snooze alarms without touching your phone.

Final thoughts: A great all-round budget smartphone.

Dimensions
71.8 mm x 152.2 mm x 8.9 mm

Weight
178g

Display
6.1-inch)1 display, up to 60Hz
20:9 aspect ratio

Internals
Google Tensor
Titan M2™ security coprocessor

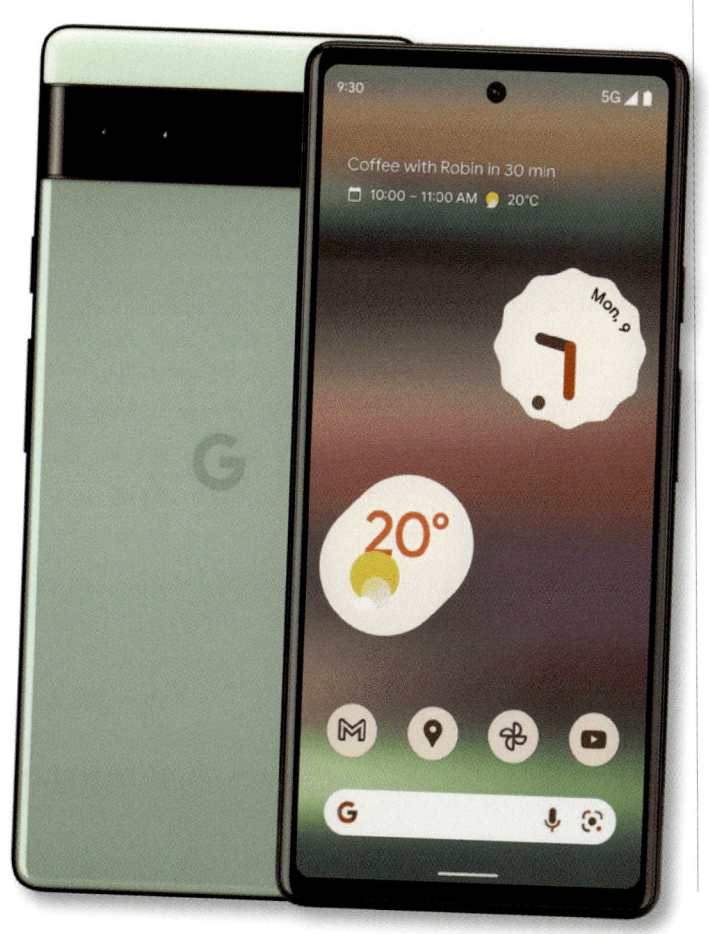

Cameras
Front Camera: 8 MP
Rea12.2 Camera: 8MP

Connectivity
Wi-Fi: 6 802.11 MIMO
Bluetooth: 5.2

Sim
Dual SIM

Battery
4306 mAh

Google Pixel Buds Pro

Key Features: Pixel Buds Pro use Active Noise Cancellation with Silent Seal to adapt to your ear and help block outside sounds, creating a quiet foundation so your music can shine With custom 11 mm speaker drivers and Volume EQ, the earbuds sound amazing at any volume. The battery keeps up with your life, with up to 11 hours of listening time, or up to 31 hours with the charging case; you can charge them wirelessly with Pixel Stand or other Qi-certified chargers. Transparency mode helps you hear outside sounds in real time so you can be more aware of your surroundings, like when crossing the street Ask Google for directions, respond to a text, or control your music, hands-free. Make crystal clear calls even in loud places thanks to beamforming mics, a voice accelerometer, and wind-blocking mesh covers. Easily switch between compatible devices, so you can go from listening to music on your phone to taking a call on your laptop.

Final thoughts: Quality ear pods with only a few peers.

Dimensions
291 x 202 x 7 mm

Weight
731g

Display
LCD 12.3in, 3000 x 2000 pixels (293ppi)

Internals
CPU: 8th Gen Intel Coe
GPU: Adreno 630
Memory: 128GB RAM: 8GB

Cameras
Main Camera: 8 MP
Selfie Camera: 8MP

Connectivity
Wi-Fi: 802.11 a/b/g/n/ac DB
Bluetooth: 4.2

Battery
48Wh

www.pclpublications.com   135

Google Hardware Guides

Google Pixel Tips and Tricks

Google has brought a lot of changes to the Pixel 7 and Pixel 6a phones, including some fundamental ways you navigate and control your device. Let's take a look at some of the main new features of these amazing devices, and how to make the most of them in your day-to-day use.

Accessing Overview
❱ Overview allows you to quickly see and scroll through all of the apps you have been using and that are waiting in the background. To open the Overview, slide your finger upwards over the small pill-shaped button at the bottom on the screen. You can then scroll left and right through the open apps, and even access the settings and search.

Quickly switch between apps
❱ Previously, switching between the last two used apps could be done by double tapping the Recent Apps button. With Pie on your Pixel, this function is still there, but is achieved by swiping left or right over the small Home button. You can also swipe and hold over the button to open a carousel of previously used apps (just like opening the Overview, but done in one motion).

Fingerprint Sensor Gestures
❱ Depending on how you hold your phone, the fingerprint sensor is sometimes easier to reach than the top of the screen. Therefore, for some users it will be easier to use the new fingerprint sensor gestures to open the quick settings panel. Just swipe your finger down over the sensor to open the panel.

Double-Tap to Wake
❱ If you want to be able to quickly see the time, and any notifications you have, but don't like having the Always-on Display running, you can now enable Double-tap to Wake. Quickly tap twice anywhere on the sleeping screen to display the clock and notifications. Head into Settings > Display > Advanced > Ambient display, to turn this on.

Suggestions in Overview
❱ Android Pie brings app suggestions in a couple of places, including in the Overview. App suggestions will vary, depending on what you use most, or what you have been previously been using. To enable suggestions in Overview, open Settings and look for Suggestions.

Direct Reply
❱ The latest version of Android on your Pixel allows for Direct replies. This means that you can open the notifications panel, see a message from a contact, hit the reply button and type, without having to leave the notification panel and open the app. This feature needs to be enabled by app developers, so you might not see it all the time, but expect more and more apps to allow it.

Open the App Drawer
❱ In previous versions of Android on Pixel, you opened the main app tray by swiping up from the bottom of the screen. With the new Home and Overview controls, you will need to get used to swiping up a bit further, taking the gesture past where the Overview will open. Try to swipe at least 1/4 of the way up the screen to hit the sweet spot.

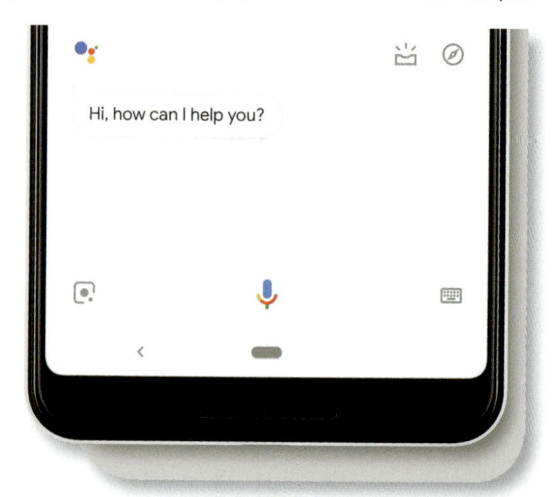

Google Pixel Tips and Tricks

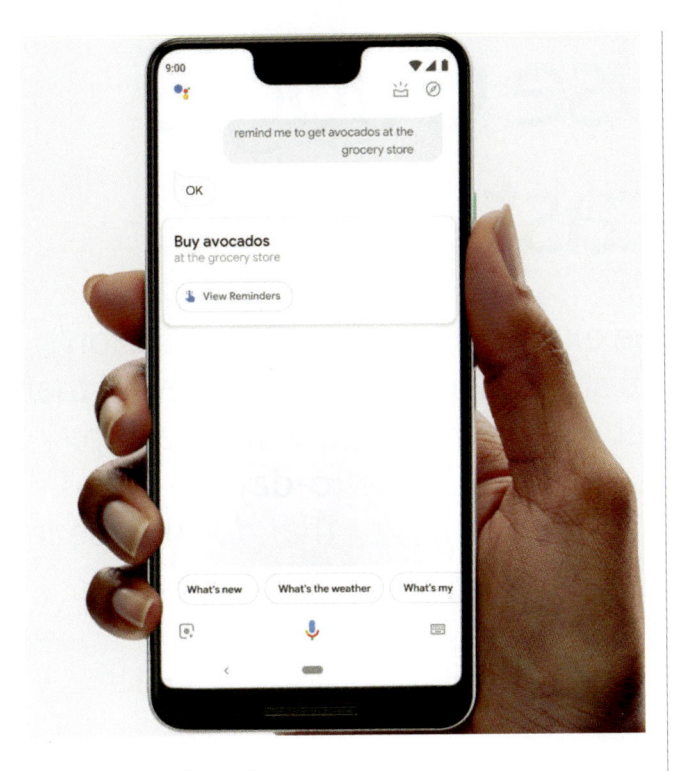

Silence with a Squeeze
❱ Google Assistant can be opened by tapping and holding on the Home button for a couple of seconds, just like with most other Android devices. However, the Pixel 3 also lets you open Assistant by squeezing the edges of the phone. You can find the options in settings > system > gestures > active edge.

Sharing Maps
❱ You can share maps via a short URL, an HTML embed, email, text message and even send maps to certain GPS units and cars. To generate a customisable embed code or URL, click on the link icon to the top left of your display. Check the Short URL box (or whatever you require) or click the link for Customise and Preview Embedded Map. If you want to send the link out, rather than copy/paste the text that's been generated, click Send for further options.

Camera Quick Launch
❱ On the Pixel 3, you can double press the power/standby button to quick launch the camera. The settings for this button control can be found in Settings > System > Gestures, where you can turn on "jump to camera" to allow quick access from any screen.

Quick 2x Zoom
❱ If you are taking a photo and want to zoom in on the subject quickly, you can do so by double-tapping on the screen. This performs a 2x zoom, but if you need more, you can still use the zoom slider to get even closer to your target image.

At a Glance
❱ This feature lets you see calendar, weather or other information at the top of the screen "at a glance". You can enable and edit the information here by tapping and holding on the home screen wallpaper, then selecting "Home Screen Settings" and choosing the information you want to be displayed.

Automatically Recognise Songs
❱ Previously available only if the user was currently connected to the Internet to get online, this feature has now been made local, meaning your phone can detect when a song is playing and display information about the song on screen. To enable the Now Playing feature, head into Settings > Sounds > Now Playing.

Accessing the Discover Screen
❱ The Android OS introduced the ability to have an extra page to the left of the Home screen panels some time ago. This has been various things over the years, but on Pixel 6 it is the Discover screen, displaying news topic in a variety of categories. From the main home screen panel, swipe to the right to access it, and then tap the settings icon to customise the content you can view from this location.

Send to Phone
❱ Google Send to Phone enables you to send text messages of Google Maps content to your mobile phone. For example, you might text yourself an address or location you've found.

To send something you've found on Google Maps to your phone, click the link icon in the left panel. Click Send and choose Phone from the left side. Enter the required information and hit Send. You'll receive a text message with your selection. You can also send a local search result to your phone, by clicking More > Send from the place marker's location information window.

Double-Tap to Wake
❱ If you want to be able to quickly see the time, and any notifications you have, but don't like having the Always-on Display running, you can now enable Double-tap to Wake. This allows you to quickly tap twice anywhere on the sleeping screen to display the clock and notifications. Settings > Display > Advanced > Ambient display, to turn it on.

Using My Places
❱ Using My Places, you can create custom, annotated Google Maps that include place marks, lines and shapes. You can even add descriptive text and embed photos and videos in your map; then share your maps with others. This can be handy for mapping out your favourite restaurants, planning an upcoming holiday or saving routes for future reference.

www.pclpublications.com   137

Google Hardware Guides

How to Use Google Chromecast

Streaming from the YouTube app can be extremely easy, even if you don't have a Smart TV. Chromecast is a thumb sized media streaming device that plugs into the HDMI port on your TV. Set it up with a simple mobile app, then send your favourite online shows, movies, music and more to your TV using your smartphone, tablet or laptop in 4K. However, that doesn't mean that there aren't more advanced tips and tricks you can use too.

Set Up Chromecast Hardware

Before you can begin to cast content from your device to your TV or other large screen device, you will need to get the Chromecast hardware connected and set up correctly.

Step 1
❱ Everything you need to get going is included in the Chromecast box. You can plug your Chromecast into any open HDMI input. If you do not have access to a nearby power socket, you can power your Chromecast by plugging the USB power cable directly into an USB port on your TV.

Step 2
❱ Using the cables hand adapters that come with the Chromecast is important. To Improve Wi-Fi reception or if you are having trouble slotting the Chromecast into an awkwardly placed HDMI socket, you can use the HDMI extender included.

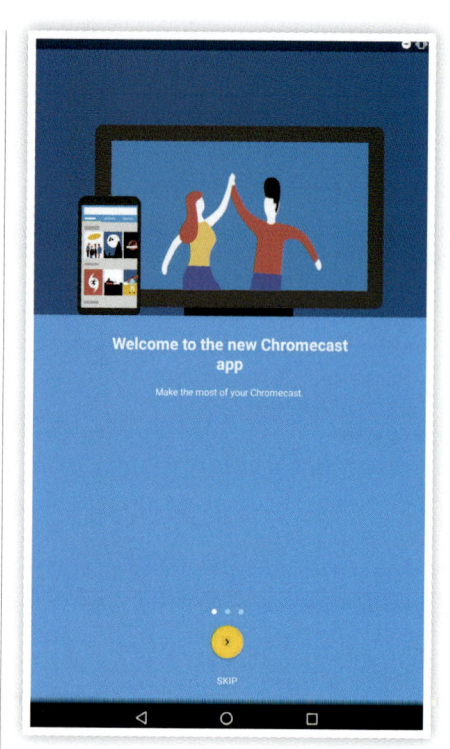

Step 3
❱ Once it is plugged in, you should see the Chromecast home screen. If you do not see the Chromecast home screen on your TV after setting it up, use the Input or Source button on your TV's remote control to change the input until you see the Chromecast home screen.

How to Use Google Chromecast

The Google Home App

The official app is not the only way to manage your Chromecast device but it should certainly be the place you start.

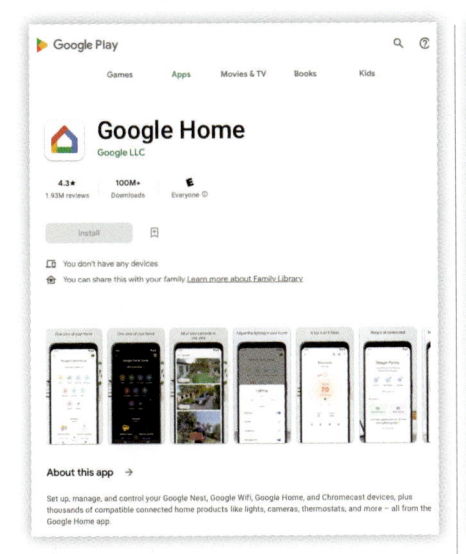

Step 1
❱ Some devices, particularly the Google Nexus ones, may already have the Google Home app, which connects to the hardware plugged into the TV, pre-installed. If not you can download the latest version from the Google Play store.

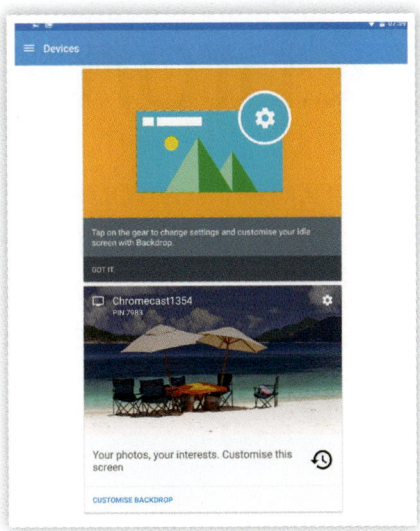

Step 2
❱ Make sure the device is connected to your Wi-Fi network and then open the Chromecast app. It should automatically begin scanning for devices. Once found it will show your Chromecast in a list, along with any other devices.

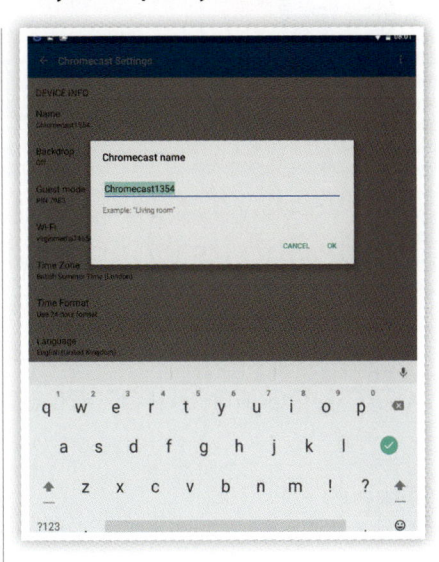

Step 3
❱ Tap next to Chromecast to connect. The screen will change, as will the screen on your TV. This will show a code that needs to match on both the device and the TV. Give your Chromecast a name if you wish, and then tap Done.

Screen Casting

Many media apps include a dedicated Cast button, used to project movies etc. to your TV. However it is also possible to cast your device screen as well.

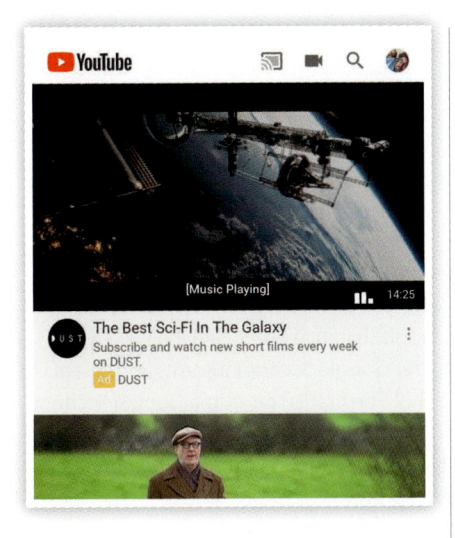

Step 1
❱ You can cast YouTube and all of your favourite apps, from your device to the big screen. Casting allows you to mirror your phone or tablet to the TV so that you can enjoy your great content exactly as you see it on your mobile device.

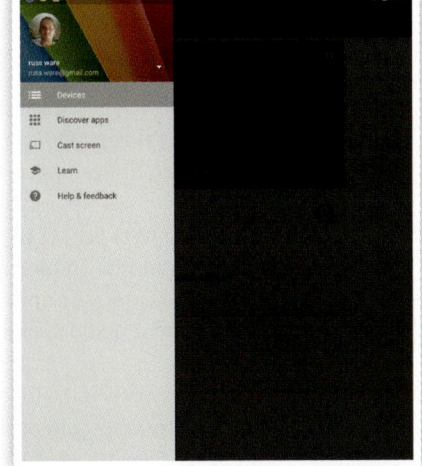

Step 2
❱ Connect your device to the same Wi-Fi network as your Chromecast and open the its app. In the top left corner, touch the navigation drawer and then tap the Cast Screen button. Select your Chromecast from the list shown.

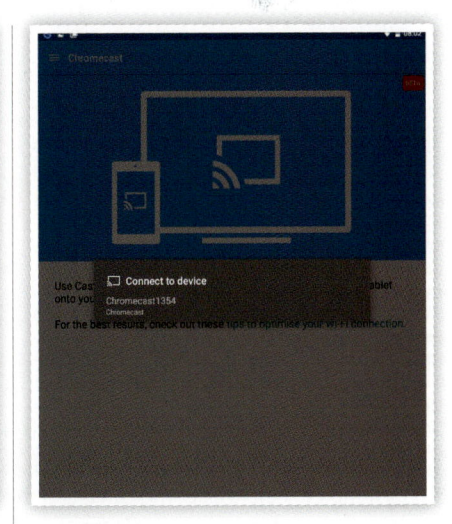

Step 3
❱ Anything you open on your device will now be cast to your TV via the Chromecast. There are some limitations to using screen cast but in general you can project almost everything from your device to the big screen.

www.pclpublications.com

Google Hardware Guides

Getting Started With Your Chromebook

You've unwrapped your amazing new Chromebook, took great pleasure in viewing its wonderful contours, brushed aluminium appearence, shiney buttons and the amazingly low price tag! Now it's time to get you set up and logging in with your Google account and start your first steps in your epic Google Chromebook adventure.

Step 1
❱ The first step is to simply lift your Chromebook lid. Chromebooks are designed to kick things off as soon as you open the lid, so you'll be greeted with a first-time setup. However, you may need to attach the power supply and plug the Chromebook in first. Many come with a brief charge, which may have drained away depending on how long it has been in the box. Hook up the battery, open the lid, and away you go.

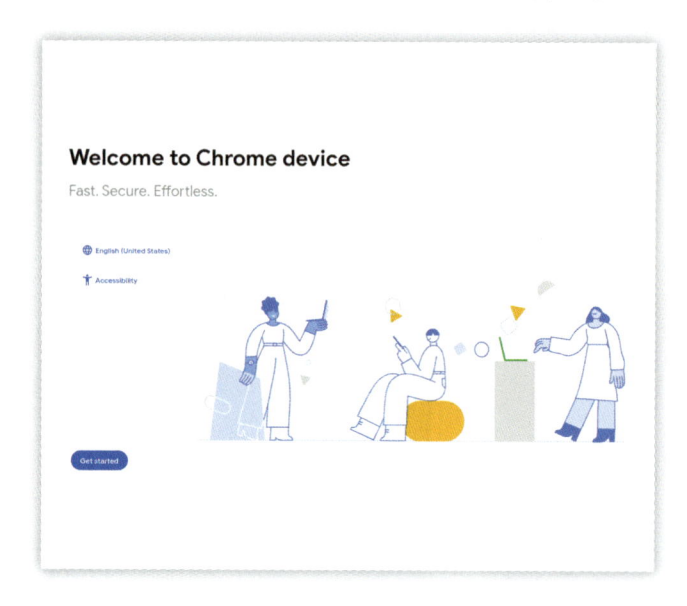

Step 2
❱ The first question you'll be asked is if you want to activate ChromeVox. ChromeVox is a screen reader technology that is designed to help those who can't read the information displayed on-screen. You can opt for 'No, continue without ChromeVox', or, 'Yes, activate ChromeVox'; the choice, of course, is yours. Click on the Get Started button, and you'll be asked to setup your Wifi. Locate your home Wifi and enter the login details to connect to the network. Agree to the Google Terms of Service, and click the Accept and Continue button.

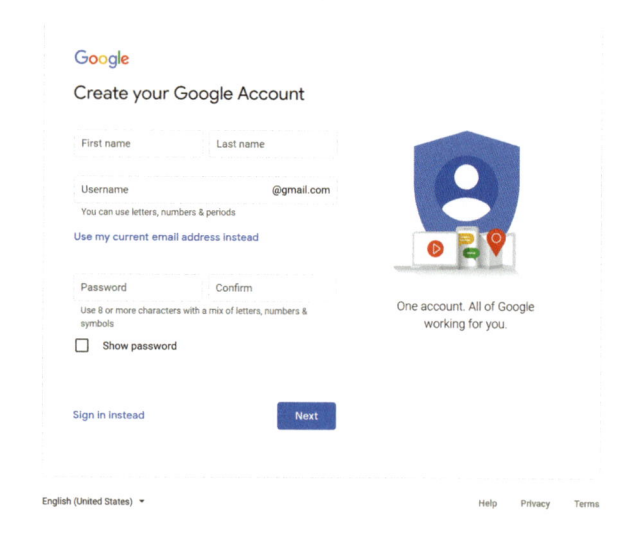

Step 3
❱ Next, you'll be asked who is using the Chromebook. There are two main options: You, or A Child. Clicking You (followed by the Next button) will take you to the account setup step. Clicking A Child will enable you to setup a more guarded environment for younger people to use the internet. There are also options for Enterprise Enrolment and Use as a Guest, but we won't touch the Enterprise option in this instance. After clicking Next, you will be asked to enter your Google account information. There are two ways of doing this. The first is to setup a Google account by opening the following weblink:
https://accounts.google.com/signup/v2/webcreateaccount?hl=en&flowName=GlifWebSignIn&flowEntry=SignUp
from another computer r device, and entering the relevant information; follow the on-screen instructions to complete the setup. Alternatively, you can click the More Option button and create a Google account via the Chromebook. If you already have a Google account as detailed earlier in this publication, enter your email and password in the boxes provided.

How to Use Google ChromeOS

Step 4
❭ Once you've signed in the Chromebook may take a moment to search for any important updates, or preparing the device. This process won't take long – a few seconds – and once it's done you'll be presented with the You're Signed In! welcome message. On this page you'll have a couple of Google-based notices to agree to: Chrome Sync (which synchronises your settings), and Personalise Google Services (which will use your browsing history to personalise ads and so on). These can be reviewed after the setup by clicking on and ticking the 'Review sync options following setup' checkbox. When you're ready, click on the Accept and Continue button.

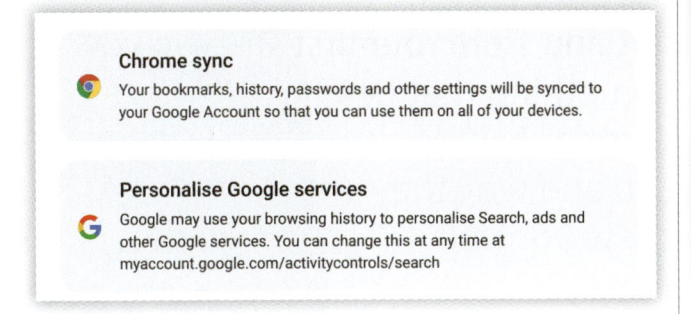

Step 5
❭ As you will soon see, there's rather a lot of agreements to get through. This page will deal with the Terms of Service regarding Google Play apps and services, alongside the Google Privacy Policy, and an option to Back-Up to your Google Drive area; to restore any data to any Google device whenever you want. Click the More button when you're ready to continue. To more Google Play apps and services agreements. This one will ask you to accept the Back up to Google Drive, as well as allowing apps and services to gain access to your location – or rather your device's location. It also deals with allowing the installation of updates and apps. As with Step 4, you can click the tick box to review the Google Play options following the setup routine. If you're ready to continue, click the Accept button.

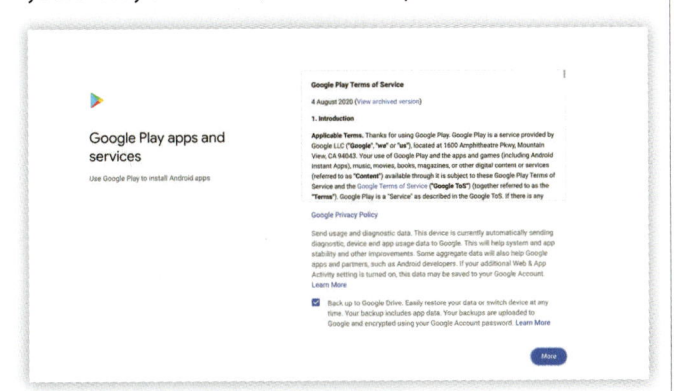

Step 6
❭ From here you can begin to setup the Google Assistant. You'll first be asked if you want to work with the Google Assistant, which you'll need to click on the I Agree button. If you don't want to use the Google Assistant, you won't be able to take advantage of the 'Hey Google' voice commands, complete with voice searching that Chrome OS and Google supplies.

Step 7
❭ You will need to allow the Chromebook to voice match you with the Google Assistant. Once you agree, you will be asked to say 'OK Google' several times, before a final 'Hey Google' to complete the voice pattern matching. As mentioned on the page, 'Hey Google' is only active when connected to a power source by default (which can be changed in the Settings page), and there is a warning that a similar voice could fool the Google Assistant into thinking it's you. When you're ready, click the I Agree button to start the Google Assistant setup.

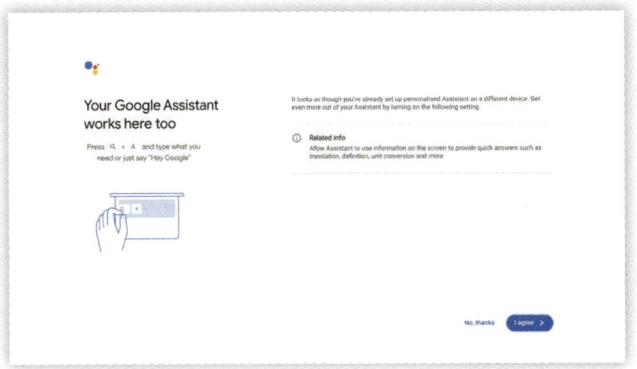

Step 8
❭ If you've used a Google Assistant before, then you'll skip the voice activation part of the setup process – since it already has your voice pattern logged. If not, then when you've finished the voice setup, you'll see a notification page telling you the 'Hey Google' setup is complete and ready to go.

Step 9
❭ That's it! You've made it to the end of the initial setup of the Chromebook. It's now ready to use, personalise and interact with. Simply click on the final Get Started button, and the Chromebook will finalise any settings and present you with the Chrome OS desktop.

www.pclpublications.com   141

Google Hardware Guides

The Chromebook Keyboard

The Google Chromebook keyboard layouts are slightly different to that of a traditional Windows laptop, or even a MacBook. To further confuse the issue, some Chromebook manufacturers' keyboards differ from one to the other. However, most will have something that ties to the image you see in the following tutorial. Let's look at what the Google Chromebook keys do and why they do it. With our help you will be in complete control!

1 Forward/Backward Keys
> The Forward and Backward keys will move you through any webpages; obviously forwards and backwards through the pages you've already viewed. While it may not seem to revolutionary, once you start using them you'll come to realise how useful they really are.

2 Reload/Refresh
> The Reload, or if you prefer, Refresh, key will complete reload a webpage you're currently on. Think of it as hitting the F5 key on a Windows computer or laptop, when you need to quickly refresh and reload the page.

3 Full Screen Mode
> Pressing the Full Screen Mode key will open the currently active window on the Chromebook in full screen. Tap it again to shrink it back to its previous size.

4 Display Open Windows
> Tapping this key will display all the currently open windows you have. They're displayed in a portrait mode, and you can use the touchpad mouse, or the arrow keys to cycle between each individual window; pressing Enter will bring the highlighted window to forefront.

5 Display Brightness Keys
> These two keys will decrease and increase the brightness levels of the display. There's a GUI indicator on-screen that will show you the levels of brightness as you tap these keys.

6 Volume Keys
> As expected, these two keys will mute the Chromebook's sound, decrease the volume and increase the volume. Again, a graphical level will display the current volume setting.

How to Use Google ChromeOS

7 Lock Screen

❱ Pressing and holding this key will enable the Chromebook and Chrome OS screen lock. You'll need to enter your login password into the box provided to unlock the Chromebook. Ensure you do this if you're going to be away from your computer.

8 Search Key

❱ Pressing the Search Key (the magnifying glass), will open the Chrome OS Search Function. From here, you're able to search for files and folders stored on your Chromebook, emails, apps from the Google Play Store, YouTube videos, and even settings from within Chrome OS. This is also known as the Everything Button, and links directly to the Launcher.

www.pclpublications.com 143

Google Hardware Guides

The Chromebook Desktop Explained

Are you ready to dive into Google's Chrome OS operating system, which is unique to the Chromebook itself, are you ready to see how much this amazing device can actually do? To access the host of functionality that Google have placed under the hood, you are going to need to fully understand how to use the Chrome OS desktop first.

1 Background/Wallpaper
❱ As with any other operating system, Chrome OS features a customisable background, or wallpaper, for you to change and personalise. There are plenty available from within Chrome OS itself, including works of art, fantasy, and even solid colours; you're also able to include your own images.

2 Welcome Page
❱ When you first log into Chrome OS you're presented with a welcome page. This includes details and quick tutorials on how to accomplish the most frequently used tasks within the operating system. It's worth spending a few minutes going through what the Welcome Page has to offer, to help familiarise yourself with the new OS.

3 Searching & Apps
❱ Still within the Launcher, you can enter anything into the text box provided to search the files stored on the Chromebook, your emails, YouTube videos, and even the Google Play Store. This is also where any 'Hey Google' requests are processed. If you were say, 'Hey Google, what's the weather like tomorrow?', the results will be displayed in the Launcher – or opened as a separate window depending on the request, but the actual command is handled by the Launcher. If you click the up-pointing arrow at the top middle of the Launcher, the window will fill the screen and you can view all the currently installed apps on the Chromebook.

4 The Launcher (Everything button)
❱ This is called the Launcher, or the Everything Button, it's not always taking up so much room on the desktop, we simply activated it to show you what it looks like. To open the Launcher, you tap the Search key on your Chromebook keyboard (the magnifying glass), or you use the Touchpad to click the circle in the bottom-left of the main desktop area.

How to Use Google ChromeOS

5 The Shelf
❱ The bar below the Launcher is called the Shelf. This is a quick-launch app, file and folder shortcut launcher similar to that found on macOS, and some Linux distros. The default apps: Chrome, Files, Gmail, Google Docs, YouTube and the Google Play Store, can all be changed and removed, and it's easy to Pin new apps, files and folders, to the Shelf. The Rocket Ship icon, by the way, is the Welcome Page that's currently open on the desktop. Any open apps are displayed in the Shelf for easy access when you're switching windows.

6 Notifications, Settings, and More
❱ The Wifi, battery level and time icons in the bottom-right of the Shelf can be clicked to reveal a lot more. In here you'll find any recent notifications you've not dismissed, your current profile image, the option to Sign Out of the Chrome OS as well as Shutdown or Restart the Chromebook. There are also options to lock the screen, enter the Chrome OS Settings pages, change Wifi network, enable or disable Bluetooth, capture the screen, turn the Night Light on or off, increase volume and display brightness.

www.pclpublications.com   145

Learn New Skills and Master Your Tech
with Papercut

Our print and digital publications are packed with expert insights, tips, and tricks that will help you stay ahead of the curve in the ever-evolving tech world. You'll have access to step-by-step guides, in-depth tutorials, and insider knowledge that you won't find anywhere else.

www.pclpublications.com

The Complete Google Manual
2023 | ISBN: 978-1-914404-86-3
Published by: Papercut Limited
Visit us at: www.pclpublications.com
Managing Editor: James Gale
Production Director: Mark Ayshford
Editor: Ian Osborne
Design: James Gale, Martin Smith, Mark Ayshford
Editorial: Ian Osborne, James Gale
Printed and bound in Great Britain by: Acorn Web Offset Limited
Print services supplied by: Media First (International) Ltd
UK & International Newsstand distribution by:
Seymour Distribution Limited, 2, East Poultry Avenue, London EC1A 9PT
Digital distribution by: Zinio & Pocketmags.

2023 © Copyright Papercut Limited. All rights reserved.
Notice: Before purchasing this publication please read and ensure that you fully understand the following guidelines, if you are in any doubt please don't buy. No part of this publication may be reproduced in any form, stored in a retrieval system or integrated into any other publication, database or commercial programs without the express written permission of the publisher. Under no circumstances should this publication and its contents be resold, lent, loaned out or used in any form by way of trade without the publisher's written permission. While we pride ourselves on the quality of the information we provide, Papercut Limited reserves the right not to be held responsible for any mistakes or inaccuracies found within the text of this publication. Due to the nature of the software industry, the publisher cannot guarantee that all software and/or tutorials, tips, guides will work on every version of the required hardware. It remains the purchaser's sole responsibility to determine the suitability of this book and its content for whatever purpose. Any images reproduced on the front and back cover are solely for design purposes and are not representative of content. We advise all potential buyers to check listing prior to purchase for confirmation of actual content.
All editorial opinion herein is that of the writer as an individual and is not representative of the publisher or any of its affiliates. Therefore the publisher holds no responsibility in regard to editorial opinion and content. Papercut Limited reserves the right not to be held responsible for any mistakes or inaccuracies found within the text of this publication. The publisher, editor and their respective employees or affiliates will not accept responsibility for loss, damage, injury occasioned to any persons acting or refraining from action as a result of the content within this publication whether or not any such action is due to any error, negligent omission or act on the part of the publisher, editor and their respective employees or affiliates. The articles within this publication are intended as a guide only. We are not advising you to change your device, and would actually advise against it if you have even the slightest doubts. There are potential risks to the hardware and software involved, and you must be aware of these before you decide to alter anything on your device. Read all of the information here carefully and then make up your own mind whether you want to follow our guides. We take no responsibility for damage to your smartphone, tablet, computer or any other device used in the process. If you are unsure, please do not buy this publication. This Papercut Limited publication is fully independent and as such does not necessarily reflect the views or opinions of the producers of Apps, manufacturers, software or products contained within. This publication is not endorsed or associated in any way with Google LLC, Android, Facebook, Twitter, Pinterest, Linkedin, Wordpress and Instagram or any associate or affiliate company featured within. All Google app icons reproduced with courtesy of Google LLC. Google is a registered trademark of Google LLC in the US and other countries. © Google 2023 Google LLC.
All copyrights, trademarks and registered trademarks for the respective manufacturers, software and hardware companies are acknowledged.
Relevant graphic imagery reproduced with courtesy of Google. Additional images contained within this publication are reproduced under license from shutterstock.com.
App Store prices, international availability, ratings, titles and content are subject to change. Some content may have been previously published in other volumes or titles. We advise potential buyers to check the suitability of contents prior to purchase. All information was correct at time of print.

Papercut Limited
Registered in England & Wales No: 04308513

ADVERTISING – For our latest media packs please contact:
Richard Rowe - richard@tandemmedia.co.uk
Will Smith - will@tandemmedia.co.uk

INTERNATIONAL LICENSING – Papercut Limited has many high quality publications and all are available for licensing worldwide. For more information email: jgale@pclpublications.com

JIMI HENDRIX
CONCERT FILES
BY TONY BROWN

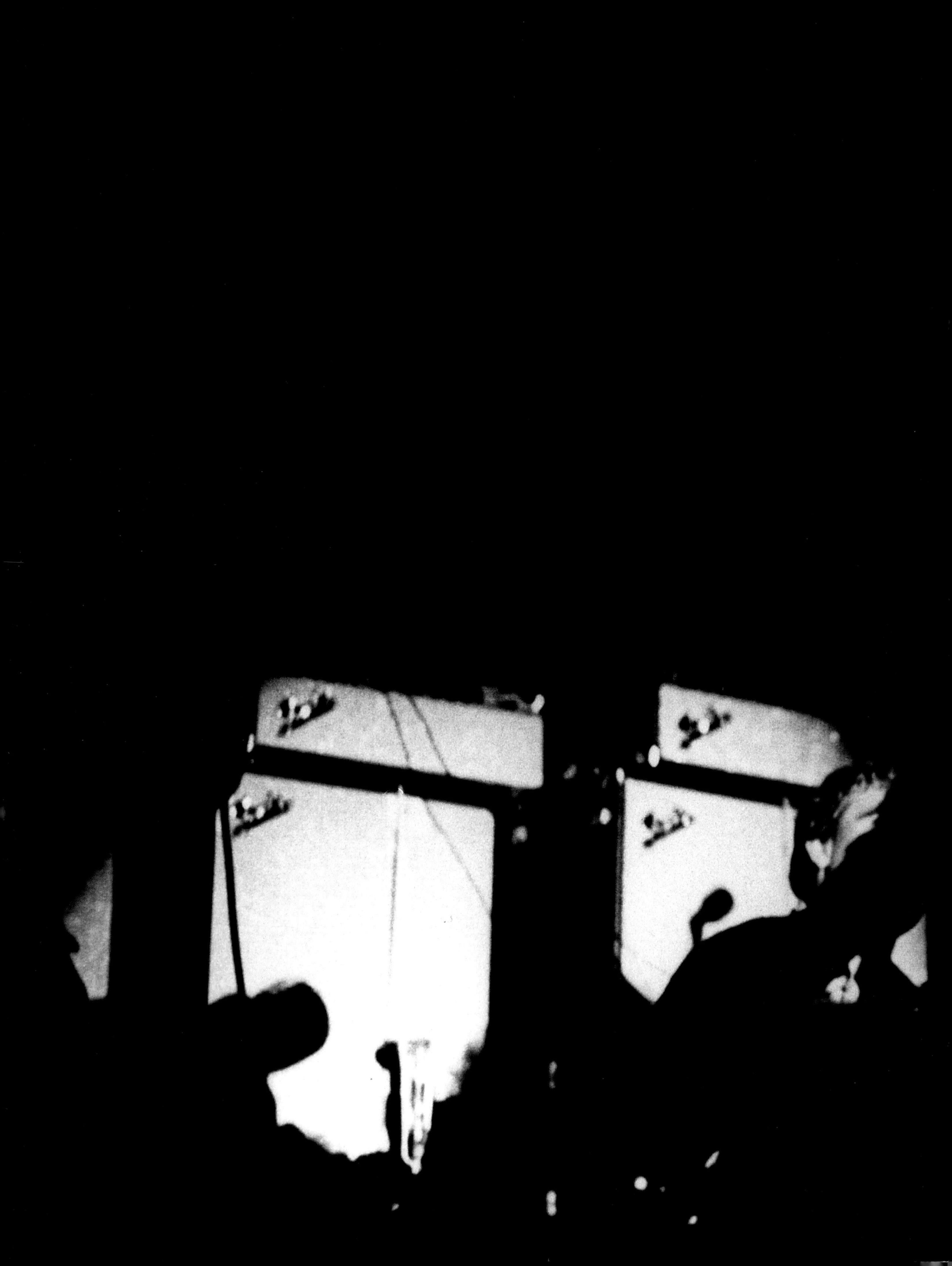

JIMI HENDRIX
CONCERT FILES
BY TONY BROWN

OMNIBUS PRESS

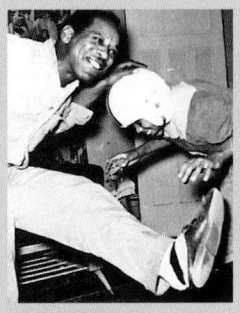

1960
Page 10

1962
Page 14

1964
Page 18

1959
Page 8

1961
Page 12

1963
Page 16

1966
Page 26

1968
Page 76

1970
Page 152

1965
Page 22

1967
Page 34

1969
Page 110

INTRODUCTION

From the moment Jimi Hendrix picked up an old acoustic guitar for the first time at the age of 16, the rest of his life was decided. Chuck Berry was his first major influence. The first group Jimi formed in his native Seattle was called The Velvetones, but within a year Jimi had his first electric guitar and had formed The Rocking Kings. Still in Seattle, he would later join Luther Rabb & The Stags and Tomas and The Tom Cats. After a short spell in the US army Jimi based himself in Nashville, playing with such groups as The King Casuals and Bob Fisher & The Barnevilles. Jimi spent the next three years on the road backing a variety of well-known artists of the day and although a great deal of research into Jimi's early career has been done, there are still gaps to fill in this period in Jimi's life.

In September 1966 Jimi, then living in New York, was persuaded by Animals bass player and future manager Chas Chander to pack his bags and relocate to London. From that moment his career, as the leader of the Jimi Hendrix Experience, has been fully documented and this forms the bulk of Jimi Hendrix: The Concert Files.

Although Jimi Hendrix had a relatively short career, the amount of concert performances The Experience packed into four years was more than any group of today would expect to play in their lifetime. During the many tours they undertook around the world, they were often expected to play at least two performances a night, sometimes at different venues, and then travel to the next city and in some cases next country. Amplification equipment in those days was nowhere near as sophisticated as it is today and Jimi's aggressive style put further strain on his gear. As a result, Jimi suffered a great deal from equipment problems throughout most of his career. He would sometimes appear shell shocked during performances, but this was mainly caused by the extreme rigors of the tours the Experience were contracted to do. Despite all these problems – apart from only two documented concerts at Madison Square Gardens in New York and his concert in Arhus both in 1970 where he was unable to complete these concerts – his music never suffered and he gave everything he had to give at each and every performance.

From his humble beginnings learning the acoustic guitar at 16 years old up to the last official performance he gave at the Love and Peace Festival at Fehmarn Isle, Germany in September 1970 – a little over a week before his death – Jimi Hendrix remains the most influential guitarist of all time. His music will still be remembered well into the next millennium.

Tony Brown, April 1999

1959

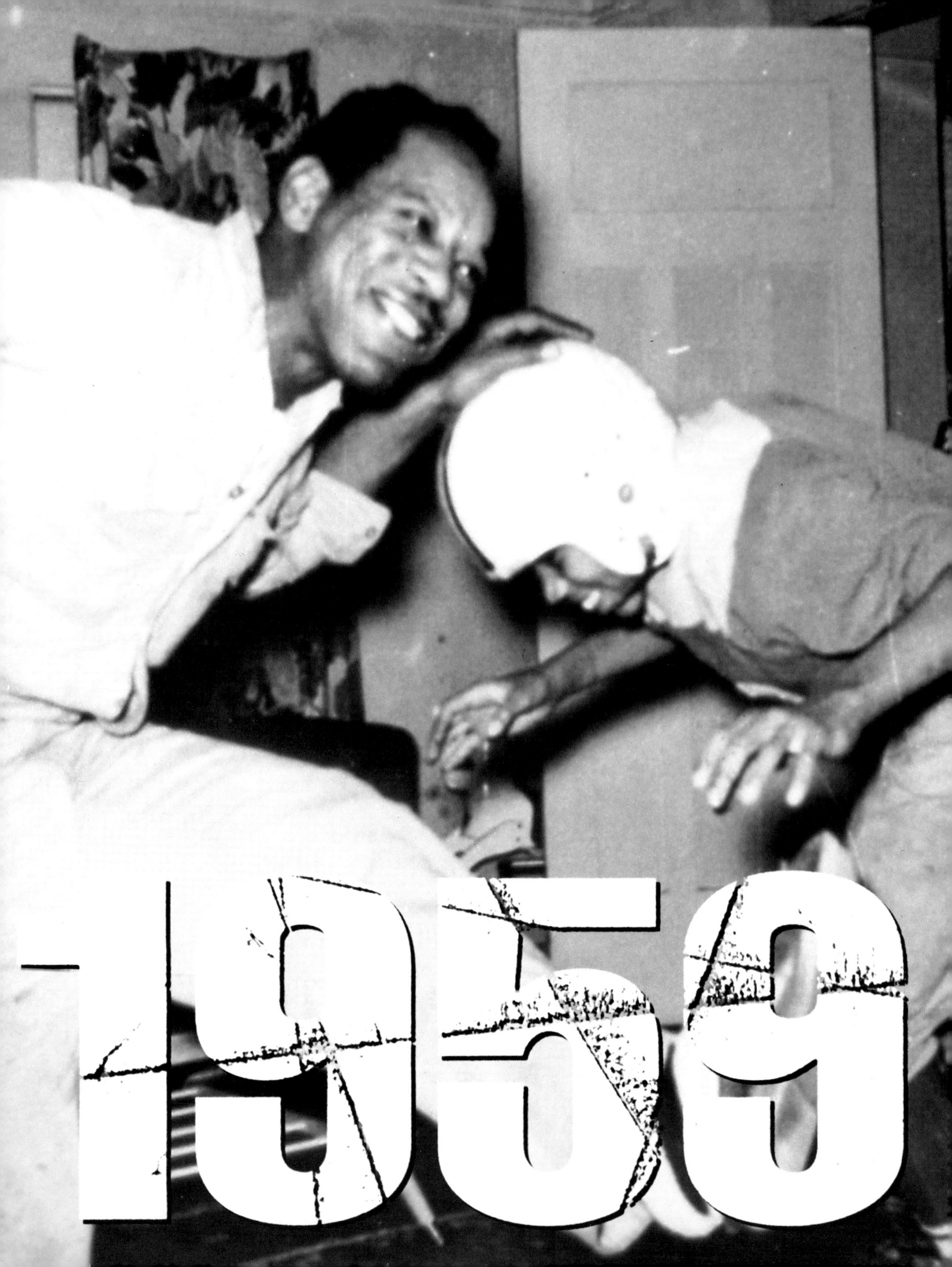

June-July
Washington National Guard Armoury, Kent, Washington

It is the school holidays and after finally persuading his father Al to purchase a guitar for him, Jimmy (as his name was then spelt) Hendrix ventures on stage for the first time with The Rocking Kings playing a Supro 'Ozark' model electric guitar. The Rocking Kings have been assembled from school friends and at first Jimmy plays bass on his regular six-string guitar alongside James Woodberry on piano & vocals, Webb Lofton and Walter Harris on saxophones, Ulysses Heath Jr. on lead guitar and Lester Exkano on drums.

Jimi Hendrix: "I remember my first gig was at an armoury, a National Guard place, and we earned 35 cents apiece. In those days I just liked rock and roll, I guess. We used to play stuff by people like The Coasters. Well, it's so very hard to me 'cos at first man, I was so scared. I wouldn't dare go on stage, you know. Like I joined this band, I knew about three songs and when it's time for us to play on stage man I was, I was like this [shaking gesture] you know and then I had to play behind the curtains you know, I couldn't get up in front."

During this period, Jimmy meets James Thomas who takes over the running of the band and starts to get them regular gigs.

1968

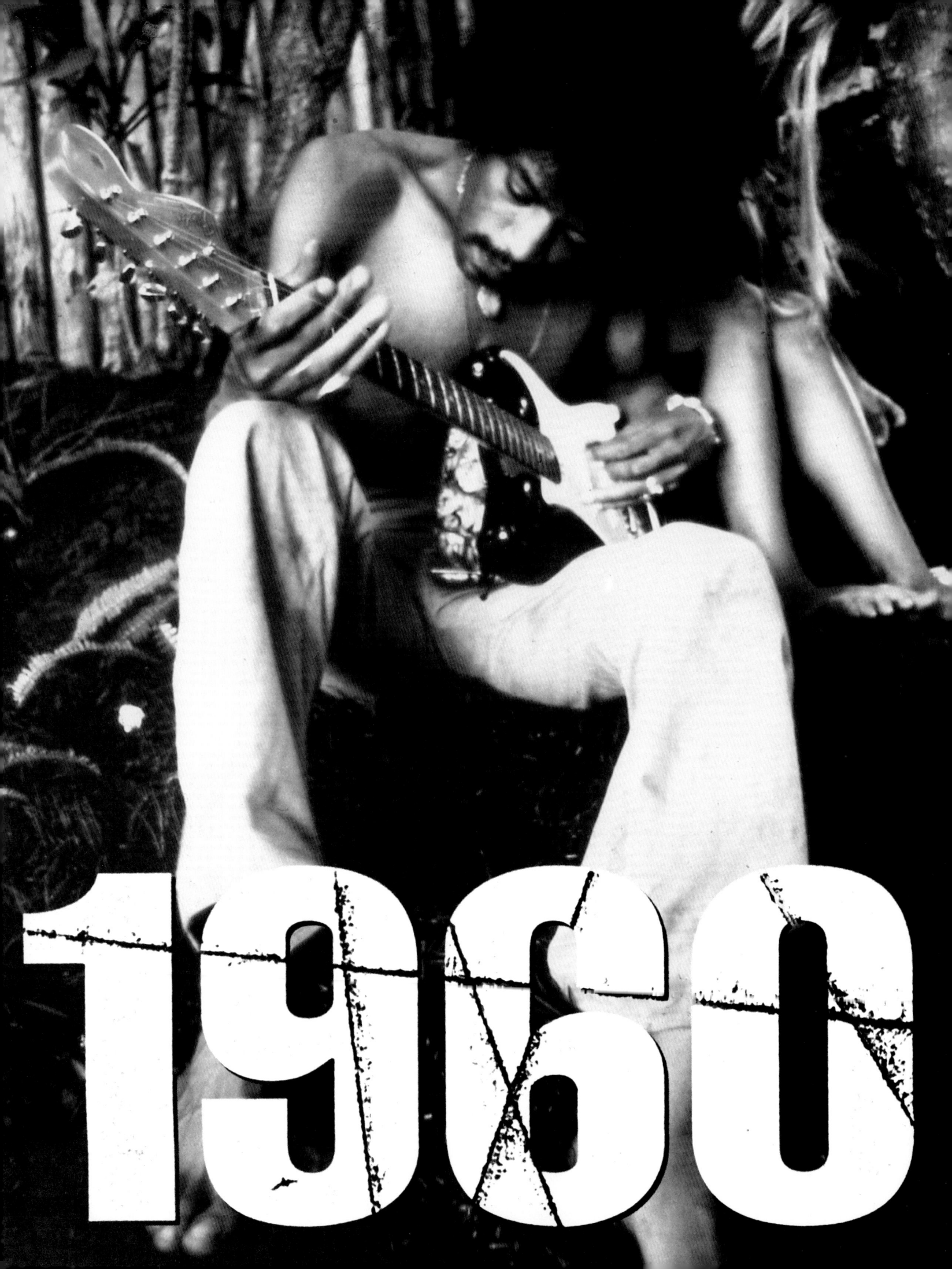

February 20
Sunday
Washington Hall, Seattle
The Rocking Kings play a concert, which is photographed by Odell Lee. By this time, the line-up has changed slightly. Jimmy has been promoted to playing lead guitar alongside Web Lafton and Walter Harris on saxophones, Lester Exkano on drums and Robert Green on piano.

The Rocking Kings are kept busy during the ensuing months with gigs at a teenage dance in Yesler Terrace, Seattle, and at the 'All State Tournament' in Ballard, Washington, where the group win a trophy for becoming the second 'All State Band of the Year'.

They finally secure a residency at Birdland, a prestigious club in Seattle, for three nights a week. During one of these gigs, Jimmy's prized guitar is stolen which put a halt to his career for a short while.

July
Annual Fair of L.C.I.O. Union, Local 242, Cottage Lake, Washington
Jimmy finally replaces his stolen guitar with a brand new Danelectro. The Rocking Kings have by this time changed their name to James Thomas & The Tom Cats, and playing with Jimmy now are Rolland Greene on bass, James Thomas on vocals, Perry Thomas on piano, Webb Lofton on saxophone and Lester Exkano on drums. The group now wear a stage uniform with red jackets. However, they have to pay James Thomas $5 for the loan of them!

July 22
Friday
The American Legion Hall, Seattle
The Tom Cats played a gig, billed as a 'Cabaret Summer Style Dance'.

Other gigs that summer take place at Paine Field Air Force Base, Everett, Washington; Larson Air Force Base, near Moses Lake, Eastern Washington; Fort Lewis Army Base, Washington; US Naval Reservation, Pier 91, near Magnolia Bridge, west Seattle.

April
Bors Brumo night-club, Seattle
Lining up alongside Jimmy in Tom Cats now are Bill Rinnick and Richard Gayswood on saxophones, Perry Thomas on piano, James Thomas on vocals and Leroy Toots on bass.

ANNUAL SEATTLE SEAFAIR
PICNIC & DANCE

3 BIG DAYS
AUG. 5-6
GATES OPEN 12 NOON
PLUS
SAT. NITE AUG. 12
9 UNTIL 2

VASSA PARK
Across Floating Bridge Hiway 10 - Turn Left at Hill Top Cafe

Music by the
JAMES THOMAS TOMCATS
Featured Guest Star
PATRICIA A. BERRY
MAKING HER WEST COAST DEBUTE

DANCING CONTEST: $25.00 CASH PRIZE

Barbecue · Refreshments
All Nite Camping & Boat Rides
SPONSORED BY CAPITOL HILL SWING CLUB

1961

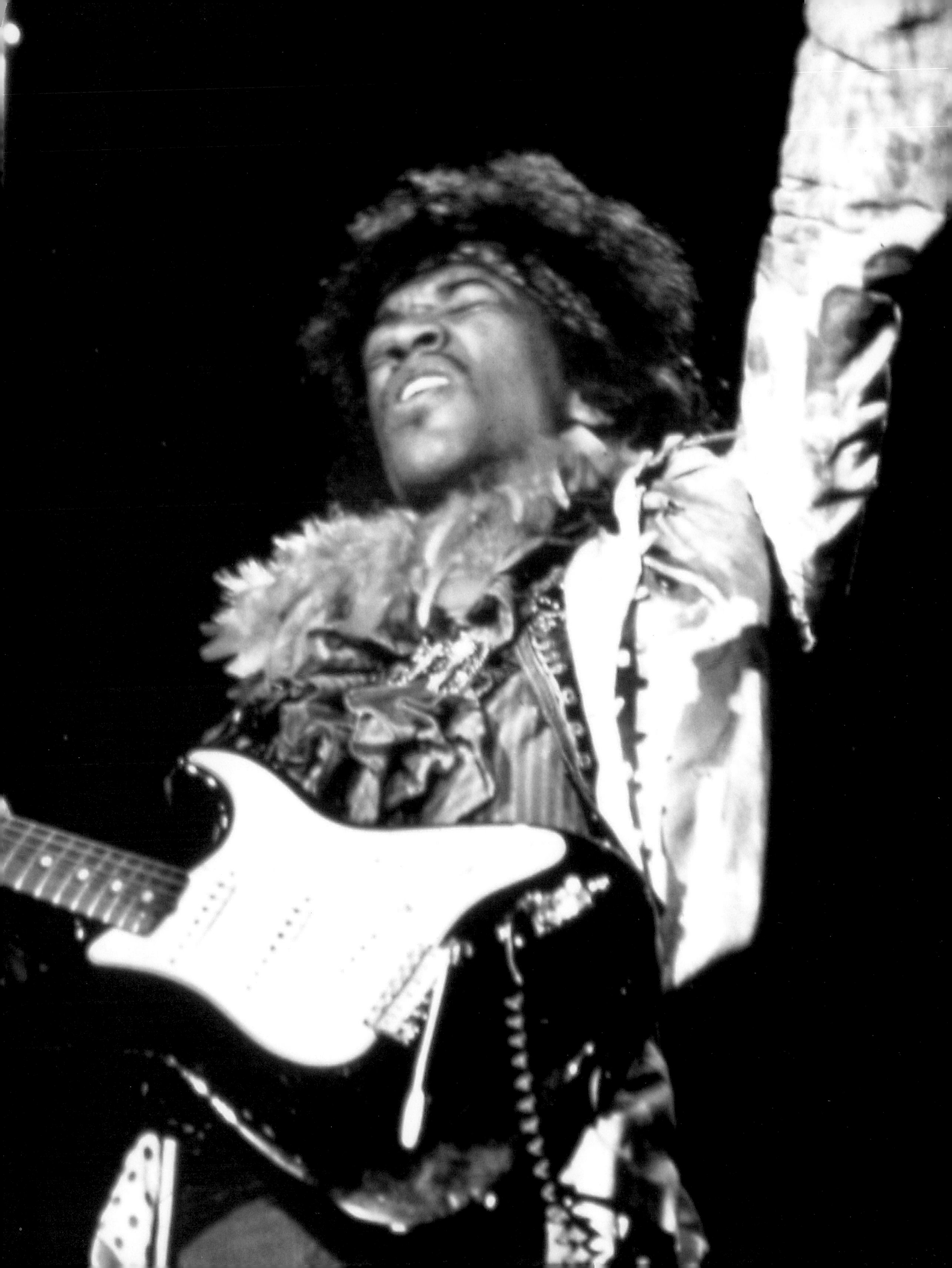

1962

January

Jimmy has by now joined the US Army and is stationed at Fort Campbell in Kentucky. Here he teams up with Billy Cox to start a group called The Kasuals with Cox on bass, Gary Ferguson on drums and, for a very short time, Major Charles Washington on saxophone.

Billy Cox: "Jimi and I formed our own group. We used a drummer named Gary Ferguson and worked Service Club No. 1 and 2 at Fort Campbell Military Reservation, very close to Clarksville. Then some guys from Clarksville, Tennessee, came on post and heard our playing and wanted us to play in town, so we added a saxophonist, Major Washington. This band was called The Kasuals, and playing in Clarksville was about the extent of it."

June
Pink Poodle Club, Clarksville, Tennessee

During this gig The Kasuals are photographed performing. Jimmy is playing a cheap $20 guitar, possibly a Star. The photograph clearly shows Jimmy sitting on an amplifier with his right leg outstretched as if in plaster, the result of a broken ankle sustained weeks earlier during a parachute jump.

On July 2, 1962, Jimmy is discharged from the army on medical grounds. He moves into 411 Glen Street, Clarksville and waits for Billy Cox who was due to be discharged from the army in two months. Once Billy is discharged, they rent a house at 610 Ford Street, Clarksville

Jimi Hendrix: "I moved to Clarksville where the group I was with worked for a set-up called W. & W. Man. They paid us so little that we decided that the two Ws stood for Wicked and Wrong."

Billy Cox: "Back then Jimi had a Silvertone [Danelectro] that was painted red. He painted the name 'Betty Jean' on it. That was his childhood sweetheart. He used that guitar up to a year after we got out of the service and when we were making a little bit more money, I co-signed for him and he traded that in for an Epiphone. That Silvertone wound up in a music store in Clarksville, Tennessee."

October

Jimmy and Billy Cox decide to go to Indianapolis. However they are unable to find gigs and their money runs out fast, so after three weeks they decide to move back to Clarksville. While playing around the Clarksville area, they are spotted by a promoter.

Billy Cox: "Someone heard us in Clarksville and said there was a club in Nashville that could use a band. We went up, auditioned for the job, and immediately got hired. This was at the Del Morocco. They fired the band that was working there part-time, and hired us full-time. The fellow who owned the club also owned Joyce's House of Glamour, and Jimi and I lived upstairs. We were there about a year or so."

Jimi Hendrix: "Then we got in with a club owner, who seem to like us a lot. He brought us some new gear. I had a Silvertone amp and the other got Fender Band Masters. But this guy took our money and he was sort of holding us back. The promoters were the strangest and the most crooked there [Nashville]. They used to come right up on to this makeshift stage while we were in the middle of a number, slip our money into our pockets and disappear. Then we'd find out afterwards that they'd only slipped us a couple of dollars instead of ten or fifteen. We used to have to sleep in a big housing estate they were building around there. No roofs and sometimes they hadn't put floors in yet. That was wild! Nashville used to be a pretty funny scene, with all those slick managers trying to sign up hillbilly singers who'd never been in a big town before."

During November, Jimmy and Billy Cox attend a recording session in Nashville for Bill 'Hoss' Allen, for Starday-King Records.

Veteran soul disc jockey Hoss Allen: "I hired Jimi for a session, It was Billy's session for King Records, as I recall Jimi's guitar playing was so wild that I couldn't use it at all. I had to shut him up on the record! Of course, I had no idea he'd ever be that big!. Billy Cox played on my show *The Beat*, the first black TV show in Nashville."

By December, Jimmy is getting tired of The Kasuals and decides to go it alone by moving up to Vancouver. He moves in with his grandmother Nora Hendrix.

Jimi Hendrix: "I start playing around all over the South, you know. We had a band in Nashville, Tennessee, and eh, I got tired of playing that 'cause they didn't want to move anywhere. They just want to stay there. So I started travelling."

December
Dante's Inferno Nightclub, Vancouver

Jimmy is now playing with Bobbie Taylor & The Vancouvers, with lead singer Tommie Chong, Bobby Taylor and drummer Floyd Sneed. They play Dante's Inferno regularly.

The Black and Tan Club, Vancouver

Bobbie Taylor & The Vancouvers play the Black and Tan Club every weekend.

Smilin' Buddha Supper Club

The club owner Mr Laxman fires Bobbie Taylor & The Vancouvers from the club. According to Colin Hartridge (of the Hey Joe internet listing): "There used to be a night-club in Vancouver known as the Smilin' Buddha (long since departed) where punk bands used to play in the Seventies, and rhythm & blues acts used to play in the Sixties. In the early Sixties it was known as the Smilin' Buddha Supper Club. Mr Laxman, who used to manage the Smilin Buddha in the Sixties, remembers firing Jimi Hendrix! Probably one of those situations where the band wasn't 'selling enough beer' (as club owners still say today), so the group Jimi was playing with got canned! Either that, or Jimi was "too loud"! Their drummer, Floyd Sneed, later played with Three-Dog Night."

1963

January/February

Jimmy leaves Vancouver and made his way south to Biloxi, Mississippi where he plays a few dates with Slim Harpo and backing guitar for Tommy Tucker, who wrote 'Hi Heeled Sneakers', during a tour. When Tucker asks Jimmy where all his weird guitar sounds were coming from, Jimmy just said "I don't know man, I don't know."

March/April
The Club Del Morocco, Jefferson Street, Nashville, Tennessee

Jimmy finally returns to Nashville where he meets and played with Larry Lee. Larry Lee: "I was playing guitar for Earl Gains who recorded '24 Hours A Day'. At that time Jimi was playing a Kay guitar, the next time I saw him, he was playing this new Epiphone guitar with a Silvertone amplifier."

The Jolly Roger Club, Printer's Alley, Nashville, Tennessee

Jimmy and Billy Cox decide to re-form The King Kasuals with Jimmy and Leonard Moses on guitars, Billy on bass, Harold Nesbit on drums, Buford Majors on saxophone and Harry Batchelor on vocals.

May 19
Saturday
The Club Del Morocco, Nashville, Tennessee

The King Kasuals' latest line-up includes Jimmy and Babe Boo on guitars, Billy Cox on bass, Frank Sheffield on drums, Tommy Lee Williams and Tee Howard Williams on saxophones and Harry Batchelor on vocals.

Jimmy wrote home: "Dad, here's a picture [sic] of our band named the King Kasuals. We're one of the two best Rhythm And Blues bands in Nashville. The drum player and other saxophone player can't be seen."

Billy Cox: "I remember, in the early days, we had a job in a club called the Del Morocco here in Nashville. I think we went on at nine. Nine o'clock, no Jimi, ten o'clock, no Jimi. We're starting to get a little worried, so I run up to the house where he lives, knocked on the door. He says, 'Come in'. I go in, he's lying there, and I go, 'Hey, Jimi, you're late for the gig'. He says, 'I dreamed the gig was cancelled so I went back to sleep'. People nicknamed him Marbles, because he'd walk up the street playing an electric guitar, he'd play it in the show, and he'd play it coming back from the theatre."

Summer

Jimmy and Larry Lee start playing with Bob Fisher & The Barnevilles, which include Fisher on trumpet and vocals, Jimmy and Larry Lee on guitars, Willy Young on bass guitar, Sammy Higginbottom on saxophone and Isaac McKay on drums.

During the summer they play in Centerville, Tennessee; Clarksville, Tennessee; Daw Serses, Bells, Tennessee, and Hopkinsville, Kentucky. They even back The Marvelettes, who were Motown's first girl group, and support Curtis Mayfield and The Impressions.

Winter
The Baron, Nashville, Tennessee

Jimmy and Larry Lee are playing a gig when a tour promoter spots Jimmy and offers him the chance to go to New York for the first time.

Larry Lee: "We were playing at The Baron. Some promoter brought a show in from New York. He was a gay cat, you know a sissy acting cat. Anyway this promoter told Jimi he saw him play, and could get anything he wanted if he would go back to New York, he could get Jimi top money. It was cold, he didn't have a coat, so I told him to take one of mine, he needed a coat. He was gonna slip off, he did write me one letter from New York, he asked me to come up there, we were pretty good by the time he left, but I was in school, and my parents wanted me to finish school. He said New York is just a big country town and we can take this town man. Jimi had no responsibility, he was just foot-loose and fancy free, I knew it couldn't be that easy in New York, it scared me, and the next time I talked to him when he happened to come through with Little Richard."

Jimmy makes his way to New York City, stopping over in Philadelphia where he meets saxophonist Lonnie [Youngblood] Thomas. Jimmy impresses Youngblood enough to take him into the studio for a number of recordings. This would be Jimmy's first venture into a recording studio and many albums would later be released with these sessions, including several with counterfeit material on which someone tries unsuccessfully to imitate Jimi's guitar. The following titles are recorded: 'Go Go Shoes', 'Go Go Place', 'Soul Food', 'Goodbye Bessie Mae', 'Groove', 'Sweet Thing', 'Groove Maker', 'She's A Fox', 'Under The Table' [Parts 1 & 2], 'Wipe The Sweat' [Parts 1, 2 & 3].

These early recording show just how accomplished Jimi's guitar playing had become. On 'Wipe the Sweat [Part 3]', Jimi even takes over on lead vocals. It is not known whether Jimmy and Lonnie Youngblood did any live gigs together.

1964

Jimmy finally arrives in New York City in early 1964 and moves into the Hotel Theresa on 125th Street and Seventh Avenue. He is eager to start playing straight away and would often sit in with the resident band at the Palms Cafe in Greenwich Village. On one of these nights he meets Fayne Pridgon (Sam Cooke's old girlfriend).

Fayne Pridgon: "We walked down to my mother's place on Central Park West where we had a meal. At that time Jimmy wasn't used to having regular meals. We then went to the Hotel Seifer where I was staying with a girl friend, and Jimmy stayed."

Fayne started taking Jimmy to the Apollo Theatre in New York, where on one occasion he meets Sam Cooke backstage. Then he manages to win the first prize of $25 in a Wednesday night amateur talent content

March

Jimmy gets his first real big break playing for The Isley Brothers who are at Palms Cafe and looking for a new guitar player.

Ronnie Isley: "We were at Palms Cafe close to the Apollo (Theatre), talking to a friend of ours, Tony Rice. I told him we were looking for a guitar player and he started telling me about this guy who had just come in on the bus and he was living at the Hotel Theresa. Tony said the kid was the best, and that he played a right-handed guitar with his left hand, he tells me the guy's name is Jimmy Hendrix. Tony said Jimmy had Saturday in with the Palms band one night and had killed everybody, so we made a date to meet him and hear him... The night we met Jimmy, Tony went up to the bandstand and asked if Jimmy could sit in, but the guys in the band didn't want to let him on. They said he plays too loud, and I knew it was jealousy. So I said to Jimmy 'Come out to my house at the weekend'. We were living at Teaneck and the band had rented a house in Englewood. Jimmy come over and I went out and brought him some strings, so he could have a full set. We played some of our tunes. He knew them all from our records, and we hired him that afternoon. We used to call him 'The Creeper'."

The Isley Brothers were Ronald, O'Kelly and Rudolph Isley, and their backing band consists of Al Lucas on bass, Bobby Gregg on drums, Eddie Williams on trumpet, Douglas MacArthur on saxophone, Marve Massey on baritone saxophone, Gene Friday on organ and, now, Jimmy Hendrix on guitar.

March/April
The Upton Club, Montreal, Canada

This was Jimmy Hendrix's first gig with The Isley Brothers. During the show, Jimmy met Buddy Miles, who was touring with Ruby and The Romantics, for the first time.

Jimi Hendrix: "I had to conform when I was playing in groups too. The so-called grooming bit. You know, mohair suits, how I hate mohair suits! I was playing with The Isley Brothers and we had white mohair suits, patent leather shoes and patent leather hair-dos. We weren't allowed to go on stage looking casual. If our shoelaces were two different types we'd get fined five dollars. Oh man, did I get tired of that!"

Baseball Stadium, Bermuda

Seattle, Washington

Ronnie Isley: "One time we were playing his home town, and Jimi ran into an old girl friend. He wanted to stay over and meet us the next day in the next town. We said okay because we thought he knew where the next gig was. He didn't show up the next day and we didn't see him until a week later in New York. His guitar had been stolen."

May 21
Tuesday
Atlantic Studio's, New York City

Jimmy goes into studio with The Isley Brothers for the first time. They recorded 'Testify' [Parts 1& 2]. The single is released in the United States on T-Neck 45-501.

August 5
Wednesday
Atlantic Studios, New York City

Jimmy records 'Move Over And Let Me Dance' and 'Have You Ever Been Disappointed' with The Isley Brothers. This is later released in the United States on Atlantic 45-2030.

September 23
Wednesday
Atlantic Studios, New York City

Jimmy records 'The Last Girl' and 'Looking For A Love' with The Isley Brothers. The single is released in the United Stated on Atlantic 45-2263 and in England on Atlantic AT 4010.

Ronnie Isley: "There is one track on the album, 'The Last Girl' when the lady's voice is actually Dionne Warwick who just happened to be around at the time."

September

Jimmy and The Isley Brothers embark on a 35-day tour.

September 28
Monday
Columbus, Ohio

Jimmy writes a postcard to his father Al Hendrix from Columbus: "Dear Dad, I hope everything is fine. Well here I am again travelling to different places. I'm on a tour which lasts about 35 days. We're about half through it now. We've been to all the cities in the mid-west, east & south I'll write soon. Jimmy."

October
Jacksonville, Florida

Jimmy writes a postcard to Al Hendrix from Jacksonville, and mailed it from Cincinnati, Ohio on October 8: Dear Dad, Here we are in Florida. We're going to play in Tampa tomorrow, then Miami. We're playing all through the south. We'll end up in Dallas Texas. My home address is in Atlanta. I hope everyone's ok, tell Granma in Canada Hi for me. Tell Leon to be kool and go to school. I must run now, take it easy. My address is 318 Fort St. Apt 3 Atlanta GA. Jimmy."

Tampa, Florida

Miami, Florida

Dallas, Texas

October 8
Thursday
Cincinnati, Ohio

Nashville, Tennessee

By the time the tour reaches Nashville, Jimmy has decided to leave The Isley Brothers.

Jimi Hendrix: "The Isley Brothers, the ones with 'Twist & Shout', asked if I liked to play with them. So I play with them a while. And it got very bored, you know, 'cos you get very tired playing behind other people all the time, you know. So I quit them in Nashville somewhere."

While in Nashville, Jimmy takes the opportunity to look up his army buddy Billy Cox. He also meets a tour valet by the name of 'Gorgeous' George [Odell], who is working on a big tour that had just come to Nashville, promoted by Henry Wynne and headed by Sam Cooke, and Jackie Wilson.

Jimi Hendrix: "This guy was on tour with B.B. King, Jackie Wilson and Sam Cooke, you know, and all these people. So I was playing guitar behind a lot of the acts on the tour and eh, then I got stranded in Kansas City, 'cos I missed the bus, you know. I'd have learnt more if they'd let Sam [Cooke] finish his act, but they were always on their feet and cheering at the end, and I never heard him do the last bit."

Billy Cox: "Gorgeous George was an entertainer that travelled with the Jackie Wilson tour. We went to the Hippodrome in Nashville and talked with Gorgeous George but I didn't hear what I wanted to hear. But Jimi took off and wound up on the road with George."

November/December

Jimmy joins the Sam Cooke package tour touring through the southern states. He backs Harry and Bobbie Womack, who call themselves The Valentinos.

Arriving in Minneapolis, Minnesota, for another package tour show, Harry Womack throws Jimmy's guitar out of the coach while Jimmy is sleeping, so Jimmy had no guitar that night. Harry Womack had accused Jimmy of stealing his week's wages but Jimmy denied the accusation.

Bobby Womack: "I just look around, and I'm glad that I'm still here. I was around with Jackie Wilson, Sam Cooke, Otis Redding, Jimi Hendrix. I've got his very first guitar right over there, I just had it all fixed up." This guitar was given (or sold) to Bobby Womack by Gorgeous George. The next guitar Jimmy acquired was a right-handed sunburst Fender Jazzmaster

The Sam Cooke tour reaches Memphis, Tennessee. While in Memphis Jimmy meets Steve Cropper (guitarist with Booker T & The MGs) and makes a demo acetate with him at Stax Recording studio.

Jimi Hendrix: "Steve Cropper turned me on millions of years ago and I turned him on millions of years ago too, but because of different songs. Like we went into the studio and we started teaching each other. I found him at the soul restaurant eating all this stuff right across from the studio in Memphis. I was playing on this Top 40 R&B Soul Hit Parade package with the patent leather shoe and hairdos combined. So anyway I got into the studio and said, 'Hey man, dig, I heard you're all right; that anyone can come down here if they've got a song', so we went into the studio and did a song and after that it was just guitar and he was messing around with the engineering and it's just a demo acetate. I don't know where it is now. After we did that, we messed around the studio for four or five hours doing different things, it was very strange. He turned me on to a lot of things. He showed me how to play certain songs and I showed him how I played 'Mercy, Mercy' or something like that."

The Sam Cooke tour reaches Kansas City, Missouri but for whatever reason, Jimmy manages to miss the tour bus to the next venue.

Jimi Hendrix: "So I was in Kansas City, Missouri, and didn't have any money so, you know, this group came up and brought me back to Atlanta, Georgia, where I met Little Richard and I started playing with him for a while. I played with him about six months, five or six months."

Little Richard: "I first met Jimi Hendrix in Atlanta, Georgia, where he was stranded with no money. He had been working as a guitarist with a fella called Gorgeous George, a black guy who sported a blonde wig and wore these fabulous clothes which he made himself. My bus was parked on Auburn Avenue and Jimi was staying in this small hotel. So he came by to see us."

Henry Nash: "Gorgeous George was valeting for Hank Ballard and The Midnighters, and helping the other tour stars with their needs. In Atlanta, George asked me if I would allow Jimmy Hendrix to come on the tour as his valet. I saw the manager of the package and we gave Jimmy the opportunity to load the bus as Gorgeous George's helper. I never will forget Jimmy loading his belongings on the bus. His guitar was wrapped in a potato sack. It had only five strings on it. Well, we left Atlanta for Greenville, South Carolina. After the concert that night, we went to an after-hours club and began working the after-the-concert date. Gorgeous George talked me into allowing Jimmy to sit in with The Upsetters. He played the entire night with only five strings."

James Brown: "He [Little Richard] and I were talking and a fella in the dressing room was his valet, I didn't pay him much attention, and he was very co-operative and helping Little Richard, and a few years later he became one of the biggest idols that ever lived. A super brother we called him. Jimi Hendrix was Little Richard's valet."

Before long Jimmy is promoted from valet to guitarist with Little Richard's band.

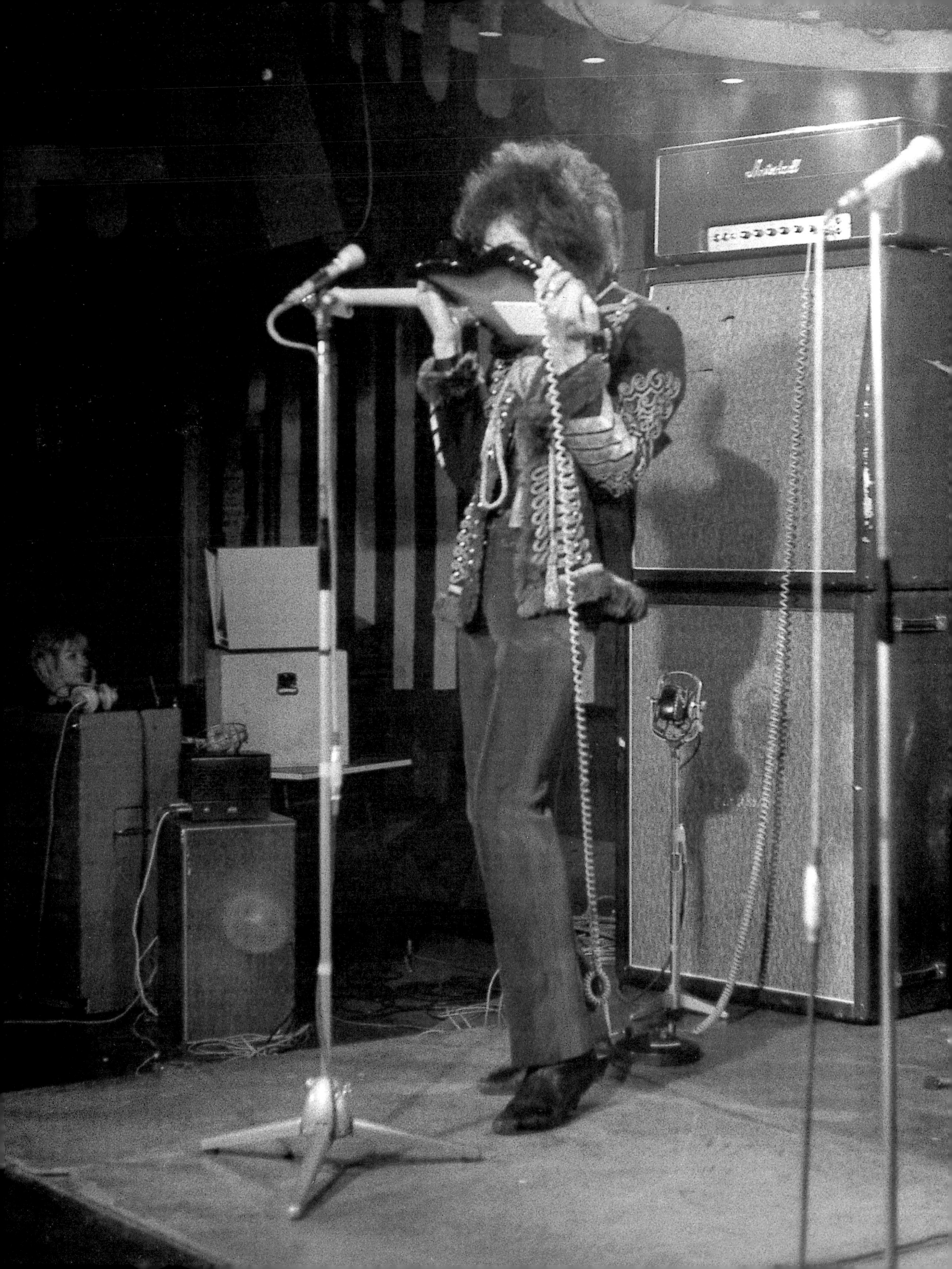
Marshall

1965

January 25
Monday
**Lafayette, Louisiana,
with Little Richard**

Jimmy writes a postcard to Al Hendrix from Lafayette: "Dear Dad, I received your letter while I was in Atlanta. I'm playing with Little Richard now. We're going towards the west coast. We're in Louisiana now, but my address will be Los Angeles when I write again. Jimmy."

January 27
Wednesday
Club 500, Houston, Texas

Jimmy jams with Albert Collins.

Albert Collins: "I met Hendrix when he was playing with Little Richard. I took his place in that band when he left, played the rest of the tour. Oooh man, he was powerful even then; he could play some blues. I was in this little club called The Club 500 in Houston... So Little Richard say's,' I got this guy with me, I want you to hear him play, and he can play so good'. So I said 'Bring him around tomorrow night'. Then Little Richard come up and introduced us, and Jimmy asked if he could sit in."

January 28
Thursday
Dallas, Texas, with Little Richard

Jimmy Hendrix writes a postcard to Al Hendrix from Dallas: "Dear Dad, Well – We just left Houston and we're now in Dallas. We'll play around here and Ft Worth, Tulsa, Oklahoma and Louisiana for a while, then we'll head for California. Little Richard left Seattle not too long ago. I wished I could've been with him then. But we'll make it up there again soon. Tell Ben & Ernie that Houston's swinging. Jimmy."

February
Dallas, Texas, with Little Richard

Arriving in Dallas, Jimmy and The Upsetters (Little Richard's backing band) are invited to appear on Channel 5's *Night Train* hosted by Nobel Blackwell. Two singers, Buddy & Stacey (formerly of The King Curtis band), accompany them for a live rendition of the newly released Jr Walker and The All Stars hit 'Shotgun'. This is Jimmy's first venture on to television. During the performance, Jimmy is already showing signs of stage theatrics by sliding his hands and elbows up and down the frets of the guitar. It is something of a mystery why Little Richard himself did not appear with the band.

February 19
Friday
Los Angeles, California

Jimmy writes a postcard to Al Hendrix from Los Angeles: "Dearest Dad, As you probably know we're in California now. Drop me a line as soon as possible. My address is 6500 Selma Ave, Hollywood, Wilcox Hotel Rm 304, Hollywood, Calif. c/o Maurice James. The weather is very nice, today was 78c. So tell everyone hello. Jimmy."

Once the band reaches Los Angeles, Little Richard takes Jimmy and The Upsetters into the studio. The only known track that was recorded at this session is 'I Don't Know What You've Got But It's Got Me' [Part 1 & 2]. The track also featured Don Covay on organ. It is released a single in the United States on Vee-Jay Records 698 in October 1965. The single got to number 92 in the *Billboard* Hot 100.

February/March

Jimmy records with Little Richard for the Modern record label in Los Angeles. No further details are known about these sessions.

While in Los Angeles, Jimmy meets Arthur Lee, who would later form the group Love. Lee is writing for a girl singer by the name of Rose Lee Brooks and is looking for a guitar player to record the material. Jimmy is invited into the Revis Studios on Western Avenue in Los Angeles to record with Rose Lee Brooks. They record 'My Diary' (written by Arthur Lee) and another song called 'Utee'. The material is released as a single in the United States on Revis 1013 in mid-1965.

Arthur Lee: "While I was out there [small clubs in Montebello, California], I wrote a song for a chick, Rose Lee Brooks. And I started working this song out with her. And then this cat tells me he knows a guy who can play guitar. See, I wanted this Curtis Mayfield feeling, like he does in 'People Get Ready,' that certain guitar feel. And this guy tells me there's a cat in town who can play that trip, and that guitar player was Jimi Hendrix. Can you believe that? Wow! See, he was working with Little Richard at the time. That was the first time I saw him. So I got him to play on this record for the chick. The sound was sort of like, well, you take Curtis Mayfield and his riffs and turn your amps full blast and five years later, see what you get."

**Ciro's Club, Los Angeles, California
with Little Richard**

Fillmore Auditorium, San Francisco, California, with Little Richard

Jimmy soon begins to tire of conforming to the Little Richard uniform and decides to make a change in his career. He quits the Little Richard band, and auditions for the Ike & Tina Turner Review.

Jimi Hendrix: "I had these dreams that something was gonna happen, seeing the number 1966 in my sleep, so I was just passing time till then. I wanted my own scene, making my music, not playing the same riffs. Like once with Little Richard, me and another guy got fancy shirts 'cos we were tired of wearing the uniform. Richard called a meeting. 'I am Little Richard, I am Little Richard', he said, 'the King, the King of Rock and Rhythm, I am the only one allowed to be pretty. Take off those shirts'. Man, it was all like that. Bad pay, lousy living, and getting burned. I went through all of America with him [Little Richard]. In Los Angeles I had enough of Richard, and played in the band of Ike and Tina Turner."

March
Fillmore Auditorium, San Francisco, California, with Ike & Tina Turner

**Amarillo, Texas,
with Ike and Tina Turner**

It's not known exactly how long Jimmy played with Ike and Tina Turner, but by April, he is back playing in the Little Richard band.

April
**Whisky-A-Go-Go, Atlanta, Georgia,
with Little Richard**

April 17, 18, 19
**Paramount Theatre, Broadway,
New York, with Little Richard**

Chuck Rainey (King Curtis Band): "I first heard and met Jimi in New York at the Paramount Theatre in 1965. He was one of the two guitar players with Little Richard, and I was playing bass with King

Curtis. Throughout the whole engagement at the Paramount, I remember constantly going to my bass and trying to play lines the way I had just heard Hendrix play them. His lines were played with a lot of character... he didn't play them straight ahead and simple, he added feeling by using dynamics, finger tremolo, and of course, his natural showmanship."

May 1
Saturday
Union College, Schenectaty, New York, with Little Richard

Jimmy writes a postcard to Al Hendrix from New York City: "Dear Dad, Well I made another drastic move. We're in New York now. We've been here for about a week now. I guess we'll stay here for about a month, playing different jobs around town here, and New Jersey. So take it easy, write back soon. Jimmy. My address is Theresa Hotel, Rm 416, 2090 7th Av, N.Y."

May
Syracuse College, Syracuse, New York, with Little Richard

June/July
Apollo Theatre, New York City, with Little Richard

After the gig at the Apollo Theatre, Jimmy misses the bus for Washington DC. When he finally arrives in Washington, Robert Penniman (Little Richard's brother and tour manager) fires him.

Robert Penneman: "I fired Hendrix, who was using the name Maurice James all the time I knew him. He was a damn good guitar player, but the guy was never on time. He was always late for the bus and flirting with the girls and stuff like that. It came to a head in New York, where we had been playing the Apollo, and Hendrix missed the bus for Washington DC. I finally got Richard to cut him loose. So when Hendrix called us in Washington DC. I gave him the word that his services were no longer required."

Jimmy writes a letter to Al Hendrix from New York City about leaving the Little Richard band. "He didn't pay us for five and a half weeks, and you can't live on promises when you're on the road, so I had to cut that mess aloose."

On August 8, 1965, Jimmy writes another letter to Al Hendrix from New York. Jimmy mentions that he is out of work and added: "I still have my guitar and amp and as long as I have that, no fool can keep me from living. There's a few record companies I visited that I'll probably record for. I think I'll start working towards that line, because actually when you're playing behind other people, you're still not making a big name for yourself. But I went on the road with other people to get exposure to the public and see how business is taken care of. And mainly just to see what's what, and after I put a record out, there'll be a few people who knew me already and who can help with the sale of the record. Nowadays people don't want you to sing good. They want you to sing sloppy and have a good beat to your songs. That's what angle I'm going to shoot for. That's where the money is. So just in case, about three or four months from now you might hear a record by me which sounds terrible, don't feel ashamed, just wait until the money rolls in because every day people are singing worse and worse on purpose and the public buys more and more records. I just want to let you know I'm still here, trying to make it. Although I don't eat every day, everything's going all right for me. It could be worse than this, but I'm going to keep hustling and scruffing until I get things to happening like they're supposed to for me. Tell everyone I said hello. Leon, Grandma, Ben, Ernie, Frank, Mary, Barbara and so forth. Please write soon. It's pretty lonely out here by myself. Best luck and happiness in the future. Love, your son Jimmy."

By October, work has become increasingly hard to find for Jimmy. He has to pawn his guitar to eat and find alternative work to pay the hotel rent.

Jimi Hendrix: "People would say 'If you don't get a job you'll just starve to death.' But I didn't want to take a job outside music. I tried a few jobs, including car delivery, but I always quit after a week or so."

Now calling himself Jimmy James, Hendrix is desperate to find work as a musician. His hotel bills are mounting up and food is becoming scarce. By chance he meets up with Curtis Knight who fronts his own group called The Squires. Knight hears Jimmy play and immediately promotes him to lead guitarist in the group.

Curtis Knight: "I stopped in at a cheap hotel on 47th Street [Hotel America] which had a small recording studio in the lobby. As I stood by the elevator, I met Jimi Hendrix, he said that he played guitar, but he had to pawn it to pay the rent, which was again overdue. I told Jimi to return to his room while I went to fetch a guitar, so I could hear him play. I entered the room and lying on the bed was a girl who Jimmy introduced as Fayne Pridgon. Jimmy plugged in the guitar and in a matter of minutes did things that I had never imagined possible. I told him that the guitar was my gift to him."

Curtis Knight is already under contract to Ed Chalpin who owns PPX Inc. Chalpin also owns a recording studio, Dimensional Studio 76 Inc based at 1650 Broadway, New York City.

October 15
Friday

Jimmy signs a three-year contract with Ed Chalpin for PPX Inc, in New York and officially joins Curtis Knight and The Squires. The contact was for one dollar and would cause Jimmy untold problems in the future.

Curtis Knight takes Jimmy straight into the studio to work with The Squires who consisted of Ray Lucus on drums and Ed 'Bugs' Gregory and Knight on vocals. The following songs are recorded: 'Don't Accuse Me', 'Welcome Home', 'You Don't Want Me', 'Hornets Nest', 'Knock Yourself Out', 'How Would You Feel', 'Gotta Have A New Dress', 'Strange Things', 'Simon Says', 'Fool For You Baby' and 'No Such Animal' [Parts 1 & 2].

During the same period Jimmy also records with Jane Mansfield at Chalpin's Dimensional Studio. They record 'Suey', a very uninspired song on which Jimmy plays rhythm guitar. 'Suey' is released as the B-side of 'As Clouds Drift By' and released in England on London HL 10147 in July 1967.

Jimmy also plays many live gigs with Knight in New York City during the following year. Some of the first places they play are: The Purple Onion on 4th Street in Greenwich Village, The Club Cheetah on Broadway at Times Square, Ondine's at 59th Street and 3rd Avenue, the Queen's Inn in Queens Boulevard, and The Lighthouse.

A great deal of live material is recorded while Jimmy plays with Curtis Knight and The Squires, much of which is generally disregarded because of the poor quality of the recordings. Most of The Squires' repertoire consists of cover versions but these recordings are a valuable part of the history of Jimi Hendrix, demonstrating his early skills as a guitarist as well as songwriter and vocalist. Hundreds of albums have been released from this material over the past 30 years, and it is an impossible task to document where the songs were recorded, but the following songs all featured in the act at some stage (some being retained, of course, for the remainder of Hendrix's career).

Peculiar' and 'I'll Be Doggone' (Marvin Gaye), 'Welcome Home' (Walter Jackson), 'What'd I Say' (Ray Charles), 'Woolly Bully' (Sam The Sham), 'Have Mercy' (The Dominoes), 'Something You've Got' (Alvin Robinson), 'Just A Little Bit' (Roy Head), 'Stand By Me' (Ben E. King), 'California Nights' (Memphis Slim), 'Killing Floor' (Howlin' Wolf), 'Land Of 1,000 Dances' (Wilson Pickett), 'Twist And Shout' (Isley Brothers), 'I'm A Man' and 'Bo Diddley' (Bo Diddley), '(I Can't Get No) Satisfaction' (Rolling Stones), 'There Is Something On Your Mind' (Little Jimmy Taylor), 'Let's Go, Let's Go, Let's Go' (Hank Ballard), 'Shotgun' (Junior Walker), 'Ride Your Pony' (Lee Dorsey), 'One Night' (Elvis Presley) and 'I Got You (I Feel Good)' (James Brown).

The artist in brackets after each title is the original performer, or the best known/most influential version at the time: 'Day Tripper' (The Beatles), 'Mr Pitiful' (Otis Redding), 'Hard Night' (John Townley), 'Money (That's What I Want)' (Barret Strong), 'You Got Me Running' (Jimmy Reed), 'Hang On Sloopy' (The McCoys), 'Last Nite' (The Markays), 'I've Got A Sweet Little Angel' (B. B. King), 'You Got What It Takes' and 'Hold On To What You Got' (Joe Tex), 'Walking The Dog' (Rufus Thomas), 'Bright Lights, Big City' (Jimmy Reed), 'I Can't Help Myself' (Four Tops), 'Get Out My Life Woman' (Allen Toussaint), 'Ain't That

Introduced by Knight as original songs by Jimmy were 'Driving South' and 'Left Alone' (a.k.a. 'Peoples, Peoples, Peoples') which Jimi would feature throughout his career.

November
Jimmy joins Joey Dee and The Starlighters
They play at The Arena, 46th and Market Street, Cleveland, Ohio with Chuck Jackson as supporting act.

Jimi Hendrix: "I played Cleveland before, man, with Joey Dee at the Arena in some rhythm and blues show that had Chubby Checker in it. Nobody talked to me. I was just another Negro artist; I was here three years ago with Chuck Jackson and all. No one noticed then."

November 23
Tuesday
Revere, Massachusetts, with Joey Dee and The Starlighters
Jimmy writes a postcard to Al Hendrix in Revere and mails it from Lynn, Massachusetts on November 24: "Dear Dad, We're in Boston, Mass. We'll be here for about 10 days. We're actually playing in Revere. Tell 'Ernie' I'm in her home state – I'm playing up here with Joey Dee and The Starlighters. I hope everything's alright – We're right next to the ocean right across the street! Jimmy."

November 24
Wednesday
Lynn, Massachusetts with Joey Dee and The Starlighters
When the tour with Joey Dee comes to an end, Jimmy returns to New York and more gigs with Curtis Knight.

December 26
Sunday
St. George's Club 20, Hackensack, New Jersey with Curtis Knight and The Squires

1966

January 13

Jimmy joins King Curtis and The Kingpins, and his first gig with them is at Smalls Paradise, 135th Street, 7th Avenue, New York.

Chuck Rainey: "Jimi joined the King Curtis All Stars, which at the time included Cornell Dupree, Ray Lucas, George Stubbs, and me. For the six months that Jimi was in the group, I gained an added feeling, which I label response."

Cornell Dupree: "Jimi Hendrix and I played together for about six or eight months around 1966, sharing lead guitar with King Curtis. He used a Fender Twin amp. The only time Jimi got fuzz was when a speaker accidentally busted."

Jimmy sends another postcard to Al Hendrix from New York City: "Dear Dad, Well – I'm just dropping in a few words to let you know everything's so-so here in this big raggedy city of New York. Everything's happening bad here – I hope everyone at home is alright – tell Leon I said hello – I'll write a letter real soon – And will try to send a decent piture [sic] – So until then I hope you're doing alright, tell Ben & Ernie I play the blues like they NEVER heard – Love always Jimmy."

By late January, Jimmy takes off for a tour with King Curtis around, Dallas, Forth Worth, and Houston, Texas. During February the tour visits Oklahoma, Louisiana and California.

May
Atlantic Records, New York City

Atlantic Records throw a party for all their recording stars. Jimmy attended with the King Curtis Band and also backs Percy Sledge and Wilson Pickett.

Wilson Pickett answered the question, Was Jimi ever in your backing group?: "No not at that particular time, Atlantic Records was giving us a party and Jimi was playing with King Curtis, who attended the party in New York."

Shortly after this concert, King Curtis sacks Jimmy for violating a strict dress code. So yet again Jimmy rejoins Curtis Knight and The Squires.

May 13
Friday
**The Club Cheetah,
53 Broadway, New York**

Jimmy plays a two week booking with Curtis Knight and The Squires. The booking is important enough for the band to design their own stage clothes and they open the first night all wearing Cheetah print shirts. Jimmy's hair has also grown a great deal and he is starting to wear it wild and bushy.

Around this time, Jimmy meets up with Ken Weaver of The Fuggs who was into electronics. Ken Weaver would build the first fuzz box that Jimi used. He can be seen using the fuzz box in photographs taken at the Club Cheetah.

Jimi Hendrix: "The sustain tone comes from two raggedy fuzz-boxes made by one of The Fuggs, a 'freak' group in Greenwich Village."

May 20
Friday
**The Club Cheetah,
53 Broadway, New York**

Jimmy decides at this point to leave Curtis Knight and The Squires, this would be the last gig they would play together.

Carol Shiroky: "Jimmy was having a lot of trouble with Curtis, and he was unhappy. Having had fights with him, not being paid, or getting paid a pittance, you know... enough to keep him fed and that was about it. And I asked him one night, I said 'Why are you with Curtis, you don't need him, he needs you'. And he said, 'Because it's his guitar'. Two days later I brought him a white Fender Stratocaster, that's what he wanted, that was the love of his life and he sat there for hours filling the frets down so the strings would fit in reverse, that was his baby. Then he left Curtis and Curtis never forgave me for that."

May

Jimmy joins another group, Carl Holmes, and The Commanders. They play various gigs including one at Gettysburg, Pennsylvania.

May 27
Friday
**The Club Cheetah,
53 Broadway, New York**

Jimmy again finds himself back at the Club Cheetah, this time playing a one-week booking with Carl Holmes and The Commanders.

June 3
Friday
**The Club Cheetah,
53 Broadway, New York**

Jimmy plays his last gig with Carl Holmes and The Commanders.

June

Jimmy is again out of work and becoming more and more frustrated as a backing musician. He spends the month jamming with as many musicians as possible, his thoughts about forming his own group becoming stronger all the time.

A Texas musician who had played with Roy Buchanan: "Roy told me that the only time he and Hendrix jammed was in New York City, prior to the formation of The Experience. He believes that Roy said that the club was called 'The Loft' on Branch Street, and that the jam was unbelievable, but most of the crowd paid little attention."

Jimmy finally gets a solo gig playing at the Cafe Wha? on MacDougal Street in Greenwich Village, New York.

Randy Wolf: "I was in a Greenwich Village music shop one day, just listening, when I met this guy who said he was called Jimmy James. He was playing at a club called the Cafe Wha, his first solo date, and would I like to come along? In the dressing room I picked up a guitar and played some slide which he liked, so after the opening set he taught me 'Hey Joe', 'Wild Thing', 'Shotgun' and a couple of blues and I did the next four sets on stage with him. A week later I went down to the Night Owl Cafe, 118 West 3rd Street, New York City, and he was playing his first solo gig there. I stayed with him for another four months."

**Night Owl Cafe,
118 West 3rd Street,
Greenwich Village, New York**
Randy Wolf attends Jimmy's first solo gig at the club. And Jimmy immediately enrolled him into the new group which he called The Rainflowers, but would later change to Jimmy James and The Blue Flames. The group consisted of Jimmy an Randy on guitars, Randy Texas on bass and Jeff Baxter on occasional bass.

Jeff Baxter: "I played on and off for a while with Jimmy James and The Blue Flames. I was working at Manny's Music Shop, 48th Street, New York City, and I made a guitar trade with Hendrix. I traded him a white Stratocaster for a Duo-Sonic. He was working at the Cafe Wah, and he said, 'Why don't you come down some night?' I was playing in a group called The Other Ones at the Cafe Bizarre, and I'd go down and play bass with Hendrix once in a while. He was playing his ass off."

Randy Wolf: "There was another Randy on bass from Texas, so Jimmy called him Randy Texas and me Randy California, hence my name to tell the difference, and his buddy whose name I can't recall. We did about four original tunes altogether, including 'Mr. Bad Luck', which later became 'Look Over Yonder'."

Jimi Hendrix: "You know when I was in the Village, I had this group. Ever heard of Randy California. The Spirit? There were two members of The Spirit in this group that we had together. We had two names, The Rainflowers and The Blues Flames, any one of those names was alright."

Bob Kulick was working in Greenwich Village at the time with a group called The Random Blues Band.

Bob Kulick: "When I met Jimi, his band was Jimmy James and The Blue Flames. They had Randy California on second guitar, and the bass player and drummer were from a local group called the Ragamuffins. His signature song was 'Hey Joe'. He also did a primitive version of 'Third Stone From The Sun'."

June 26
Sunday
**The Club Cheetah,
53 Broadway, New York**
Appearing as Jimmy James and The Blue Flames.

Linda Keith: "I don't know why we went to the Cheetah. It was the place that I didn't usually go to, but we went this night and it was a huge enormous place, like a ballroom, but very few people there and a sort of regular band playing, not very well. At least I didn't take any interest in the band at all. And then suddenly I saw the guitar player who was playing really quite discreetly in the back row. And from that moment I just became completely involved. He was very naive and very... he was very shy, and nervous, and he didn't look at you when he spoke to you. And he came back to the apartment and played a lot of Dylan, who Jimi idolised, he thought Dylan was the greatest. I told this record producer, there was this fantastic guitar player, singer, man, playing in the village and would he come down and listen to him because he's really going to like this, a very materialistic man. And he thought, right, good. And he came down. He thought I was mad, he did not see what I was talking about, when he saw Jimi, he saw this nothing."

July 2
Saturday
**Ondines, 59th Street and
3rd Avenue, New York**
Appearing as Jimmy James and The Blue Flames.

The Rolling Stones were on tour in America at the time. They had just finished their concert at Forest Hills Stadium and went to Ondines the night Jimmy was playing.

July 5
Tuesday
**Cafe Wha? MacDougal Street,
Greenwich Village, New York**
Appearing as Jimmy James and The Blue Flames.

Now that Jimmy had his own group, he was able to concentrate on playing the kind of music he wanted to play. His repertoire consisted of 'Hey Joe', 'Like A Rolling Stone', 'Killing Floor', 'Shotgun', 'Mr Bad Luck' (which would become 'Look Over Yonder'), 'Killing Floor', and 'Third Stone From The Sunday'. Many of these songs would continue with him throughout his career.

In what would prove to be an extremely fortuitous gesture, Linda Keith takes Chas Chandler along to see Jimmy. Linda Keith: "I bumped into Chas Chandler whom I didn't know, but I knew was one of The Animals, and I think Jimmy was getting sorta desperate to record, or to at least make another step. And so Chas came down to see him and was like... it was instantaneous. There was no question in his mind."

Chas Chandler: "So I went there with her the next day to a little club called the Cafe Wha? in Greenwich Village, which was a little coffee house really with musicians playing downstairs, and saw Jimi playing there. When I saw Jimi, I think it was a Tuesday afternoon in New York, the first song he played was 'Hey Joe', and our tour started the next day. Well, I went off on tour for three months first with The Animals."

July
**Ondines, 59th Street and
3rd Avenue, New York**
Appearing as Jimmy James and The Blue Flames.

August
John Hammond Jr visits the Cafe Wha? to check out Jimmy's performance.

John Hammond Jr: "One night between shows my friend who was working the Players' Theatre came over and said, 'John there's this band playing downstairs that you've got to hear. This guy is doing songs off your old album [*So Many Roads*. Vanguard 79178] and he sounds better than you'. So I thought I'd check this out. I went down there and he was playing the guitar parts that Robbie Robertson had. He was a really handsome black kid, playing with these guys who could barely keep up with him. Jimmy James he called himself... Jimmy James and The Blue Flames. He had just been burnt out of some money, and he had been playing with Curtis Knight. He was kinda vague about what had happened, but somehow he had lost his guitar, and had to borrow some money to get another guitar. He was playing a Fender Stratocaster upside down and left-handed. One of those things that just boggles your mind. I just could not believe it. Playing with his teeth, and doing all those really slick techniques that I had seen in Chicago on the south side on wild nights. But here was a guy doing it, and he was fantastic playing the blues."

August 13
Saturday
John Hammond Jr. joins Jimmy James and The Blue Flames, and combines the two groups into the Screaming Night Hawkes. After two week of rehearsals, they get a two-week booking at the Cafe Au Go Go.

Buzzy Linhart: "I was sharing a bill with John Hammond Jr. My group was called The Seventh Sons. We used to play the Cafe A Go Go on Bleeker Street all the time, and he had this new band, and we went to the rehearsal, and people were talking about those people playing in the basement, that's where the club was. He was wearing a regular tie, and suits without collars, they were all in suits, the guy could really play."

August
Saturday
Cafe A Go Go, Bleeker Street, Greenwich Village, New York
With the Screaming Night Hawkes. Supported by the Seventh Sons with Buzzy Linhart

John Hammond Jr: "The band was a drummer, bass player, keyboard players would from time to time jam with us, among them Al Kooper and Barry Goldberg. Back up guitar was a guy named Randy Wolfe who has since become Randy California, Jimi and I were the leads, I did the vocals and played harmonica and he played the guitar and everything else sorta fell together, and it was a groove."

Mike Bloomfield: "I'd never heard of Hendrix. Then someone said, 'You've got to see the guitar player with John Hammond'. I went right across the street and saw him. Hendrix knew who I was, and that day in front of my eyes, he burned me to death. I can't tell you the sounds he was getting out of his instrument. He was getting every sound I was ever to hear him get right there in that room with a Stratocaster, a Twin [Fender amp] a Maestro fuzz tone, and that was all."

September 9
Friday
Cafe A Go Go, Bleeker Street, Greenwich Village, New York
With The Screaming Night Hawkes. Chas Chandler: "We came back to New York in September, it took about four days to find Jimi again, it took us about ten days to get his passport. He was working with John Hammond. I come straight back after the tour and Jimi didn't really believe it."

After locating Jimmy, Chas starts to work out details about taking him to England. "Jimmy wasn't sure about such a big change in his life. He was worried about the equipment we had in England and what the musicians were like. One of the first things he asked me was if I knew Eric Clapton. I said sure I know Eric, he asked if I would take him to meet Eric. I said when Eric heard him play, he would be falling over to meet Jimmy, that clinched it."

September 24
Saturday
Jimmy Hendrix and Chas Chandler arrive at London Heathrow Airport, on the 9am flight. During the flight it is decided that from henceforth Jimmy's name will be spelt Jimi.

On the way into London from Heathrow, Chas takes Jimi to the house of Zoot Money at 11 Gunterstone Road, Fulham, for his first jam in Britain. They arrive around 11:00am and Jimi jams for about three hours. He tries to play a white Fender Telecaster, which is thought to belong to Andy Summers [then playing with Zoot Money's Big Roll Band], but as Zoot is booked for a gig later that night, all his amplification equipment was at the gig. They try to plug the guitar through the stereo, without success. Jimi plays the rest of the time on Zoot's acoustic guitar.

Chandler books himself, his girlfriend Lotta and Jimi into room 301 at the Hyde Park Towers Hotel, 41-49 Inverness Terrace, London W2, making the hotel their base. During Jimi's first night in London, Chas takes him along to the Scotch of St. James Club, 13 Mason's Yard, for his first public jam in London. Although Jimi doesn't have a work permit, Chas takes the chance to show off his exciting new signing. During the evening, Jimi meets Kathy Etchingham for the first time; she would become his girlfriend for the next three years.

September 27
Tuesday
Scotch Of St. James, 13 Mason's Yard, London
Jimi jams with the group The VIPs. Chas Chandler: "We went down to the Scotch of St. James one night and a group called The VIPs were playing there. They had Mike Harrison and Greg Ridley [later of Spooky Tooth and Humble Pie] and they were from Carlisle. I knew them because they used to play the A Go Go in Newcastle."

September 29
Thursday
Birdland, Jermyn Street, London
Noel Redding had heard about the auditions being held for a new guitar player with Eric Burdon's New Animals. He has gone along to the offices of booking agent Harold Davidson and is told to attend the club for an audition. After his audition, he's told that Vic Briggs has already filled the spot for lead guitar for The New Animals but Chas asks him if he can play bass guitar. Noel says no but he would give it a try. Chas lends Noel his Gibson EB-2 semi-acoustic bass guitar, so Noel sits in with Jimi, Mike O'Neil [Nero and The Gladiators] on piano and Aynsley Dunbar on drums. They play 'Hey Joe' two or three times and 'Have Mercy On Me Baby'. After the audition Jimi and Noel disappear to a nearby pub for a chat. Jimi remarks that he likes Noel's hair and asks Noel to return the next day. In the evening Chas takes Jimi down to Blaises Club, 121 Queen's Gate in Kensington for a jam with The Brian Auger Trinity.

Luckily for Chas, French singer Johnny Halliday is in the audience that night and after seeing Jimi play a very exciting set, he immediately invites him to tour France with him. Although Jimi still does not have a group, Chas signs the deal there and then. Jimi is still officially unable to play in London because he does not have a work permit; he won't actually get one issued until December. But Chas uses the French tour to get as much exposure as he can for Jimi. He also knows that Jimi can play freely in France without a work permit.

October 1
Saturday
The Polytechnic, Little Titchfield Street, London

Cream are scheduled to play with The Washington DCs as their support act. Chas takes Jimi along to the gig purely to get Jimi and Eric Clapton jamming together on stage. Cream has only just formed and this is supposed to be a high profile gig for them but Chas uses the opportunity to get further exposure for Jimi. Eric Clapton is regarded as the number one guitar player at the time, and he allows Jimi to jam with him on stage. Jimi plays 'Killing Floor' by Howling Wolf and adds all the theatrics that would become his trademark. The audience is just stunned at the performance.

Eric Clapton: "The first time I met him, he came to a concert in London that the Cream was playing. He was very, very flash, even in the dressing room. He stood in front of the mirror combing his hair. He asked if he could play a couple of numbers. I said 'Of course', but I had a funny feeling about him. He came on then, and did 'Killing Floor', a Howling' Wolf number that I've always wanted to play, but which I've never really had the complete technique to do. Ginger didn't like it, and Jack didn't like it, they had never heard the song before. It was just, well, he just stole the show! From then on I just started going to watch him."

October 4
Tuesday

Promoter and club owner John Gunnell has told Chas Chandler that a young jazz drummer by the name of John 'Mitch' Mitchell has just been sacked from Georgie Fame's Blue Flames. Mitch has acquired a good reputation as a drummer on the London scene, so Chas decided to telephone him to offer him an audition with Jimi.

Mitch Mitchell: "On the Tuesday John Gunnell mentioned to me that Chas Chandler and Jimi Hendrix, a friend of his, were over here, and would I care to go and have a play." It was agreed that Mitch would attend the audition the next day.

October 5
Wednesday
Birdland, Jermyn Street, London

Mitch Mitchell arrives for the audition with Jimi Hendrix. Noel Redding is already on board and the three of them play together for the first time.

Mitch Mitchell: "At the audition it was strange. I met this black guy with very wild hair, wearing a Burberry raincoat. I think we did 'Have Mercy On Me Baby' first. Jimi didn't really sing, just mumbled along to the music and for two hours we run through what we all knew, Chuck Berry, Wilson Pickett, basically R&B, after which Hendrix said, 'Okay, I'll see you around.' After the initial session, I think it was only a few hours later, that I got a call from Chas saying, 'Yes, we're interested'. Chas said there was a gig in Paris the next week with Johnny Halliday and asked if we fancied doing it. So I said okay and spent three days rehearsing. Then off we went and that was how it started."

Chas Chandler: "Mitch Mitchell had just split up with The Blue Flames and he was looking for a gig, and it was a toss up between Aynsley Dunbar and Mitch Mitchell, and literally we just spun a coin, we couldn't make our minds up, and it fell for Mitch."

That evening Chas takes Jimi along to Les Cousins, at 49 Greek Street in Soho. There is a contingent of visiting American bluesmen and Chas takes the opportunity to show off Jimi's talents.

Andy Matheou: "At that time there were a lot of American bluesmen here, and Alexis [Korner] thought it would be good to get everyone together for an all-nighter with him topping the gig. That was the night Hendrix came in with Chas Chandler, his manager, and nobody had ever seen him before. This pale, quiet dude and he just paid his money and walked in with no fuss. Later they asked him to play and he plugs in his white Fender and does all his stuff with his teeth and just blows everybody's mind. Afterwards somebody says to Alexis, 'Wow, he's great, isn't he?' and Alexis just nods and says in that voice of his, 'Pretty good, yeah, pretty good.' I mean, imagine seeing Hendrix for the first time. Pretty good."

The bluesmen are in London for the 5th American Folk Blues Festival, which is taking place at the Royal Albert Hall, London. Artists include: Roosevelt Sykes, Otis Rush, Jack Mayers, Little Brother Montgomery, Sleepy John Estes, Sippie Wallace, Junior Wells, Robert Pete Williams and Big Joe Turner.

October 6
Thursday

Chas books Jimi, Mitch and Noel into rehearsal studios in Aberbach Publishing House, Albermarle Street, London W1. For a week they rehearse solidly for the upcoming French tour, first time that they are able to rehearse together properly. Jimi has come from a blues background, Mitch is from a jazz background, and Noel is from a rock and roll background. The combination of all three styles of music is to become an instant success… and so the Jimi Hendrix Experience is born.

Mitch Mitchell: "Chas gave the group 30 watt Burns amps, but they were not powerful enough, so Jimi and I tried to wreck the gear in order to obtain better amps. We tried throwing them down flights of stairs, but they still worked. In the end we had to have them stolen in order for Chas to replace them. This was at the publishing house venue, on the 5th floor."

The following week is taken up with constant rehearsals for the group's upcoming first tour of France.

October 13
Thursday
Novelty, Evreux, France

The Experience fly from Heathrow Airport and arrive at Le Bourget Airport in Paris. They travel with basic Marshall equipment, which they have to load and unload themselves, because no road managers are employed yet. Photographer Alain Dister is on hand to take some of the earliest known photographs of the group. They all go to a drugstore in Saint-Germain in Paris for some food, then travel to Evreux for their first concert.

The first time The Experience took the stage their 15 minute set consisted of 'In The Midnight Hour', 'Have Mercy On Me Baby', 'Land Of A Thousand Dances' and 'Hey Joe'. The entire concert was said to have been filmed by French TV, but footage has never surfaced. The French press are on hand and this [translated] review is published in *L'Eure …clair* on October 22, 1966: "After this deafening interlude, The Blackbirds appeared. Johnny Halliday's latest discovery. He was a singer and guitar player with bushy hair, bad mixture of James Brown and Chuck Berry, who pulled a wry face on stage during a quarter of an hour and also played the guitar sometimes with his teeth. He ended the first half of the concert that was followed by a long pause."

October 14
Friday
Cinema Le Rio - Salle Playel, Nancy, France
Supporting Long Chris, The Blackbirds and Johnny Halliday.

October 15
Saturday
Salle Fites, Villerupt, France
Supporting Long Chris, The Blackbirds and Johnny Halliday.

Mitch Mitchell: "Those first gigs were strange. We were on this tour bus. Halliday just turned up in his new Mustang or whatever. The rest of us [were] in this rickety old coach."

October 18
Tuesday
Olympia, Paris, France
Supporting Long Chris, The Blackbirds and Johnny Halliday. The Brian Auger Trinity had been added for the last show.

The Experience takes the stage to a rousing reception by the French audience. After the groups are introduced they start their show with 'Killing Floor' and continue with a very unrehearsed 'Hey Joe' into which Jimi has already incorporated a solo which he plays with his teeth. The song is much shorter than later versions would become, and Jimi brings the song to an abrupt close, not yet having worked out a proper ending. Jimi ends the set with The Troggs' 'Wild Thing'. The show is recorded professionally by French radio and a portion of this historic first tour by The Experience still remains in a French radio studio.

October 19
Wednesday
Back in London, Chas Chandler and Jimi Hendrix attend the Scotch Of St. James, 13 Mason's Yard, London SW1. Jimi jams with Viv Prince, the new guitarist with The New Animals.

October 24
Monday
Knuckles Club, 19 Carlisle Street, Soho Square, London
Jimi jams with Deep Feeling, featuring Dave Mason on guitar and Jim Capaldi on drums, both of whom would go on to form Traffic.

October 25
Tuesday
Scotch Of St. James, London
This is the London début of The Jimi Hendrix Experience. Until now, Jimi had acquired a following based solely on his jamming around town. Now the London press got their first taste of the Jimi Hendrix Experience – and they become an overnight sensation.

November 8, 9, 10, 11
Tuesday-Friday
Big Apple Club, Munich
Two shows each night. It is during one of these shows that Jimi's guitar smashing routine develops by accident.

Chas Chandler: "Jimi was pulled off stage by a few over enthusiastic fans and as he jumped back on the stage he threw his guitar on before him. When he picked it up he saw that it had cracked and several of the strings were broken. He just went barmy and smashed everything in sight. The German audience loved it and we decided to keep it in as part of the act."

November 25
Friday
Bag O' Nails, 9 Kingly Street, London
Chas books the Jimi Hendrix Experience into the Bag O'Nails to showcase the group to the London press. Although Jimi has a number of gigs and a tour of France and Germany under his belt, the money is quickly running out. So Chas sells most of his guitars from his Animals days to pay for a lavish press reception. The reception attracts a galaxy of stars including The Beatles, The Stones, The Hollies and The Who. Peter Jones, a *Record Mirror* reporter, interviews Jimi for his first interview in the English music press which is published on December 10. "I've only been in London three months – but Britain is really groovy. We don't want to be classed in any category, if it must have a tag, I'd like it to be called 'Free Feeling'. It's a mixture of rock, freak-out, blues, and rave music." Photographer Robert John photographs the show.

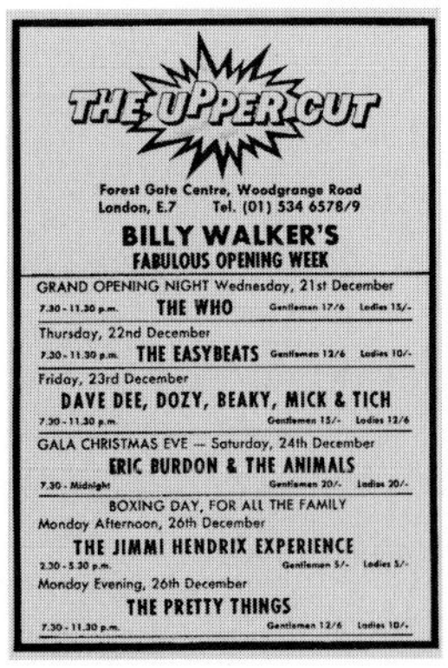

November 26
Saturday
Ricky Tick, 1a High Street, Hounslow, Middlesex
The New Animals has also just formed and Chas takes the opportunity to add The Experience as their supporting act.

December 10
Saturday
The Ram Jam Club, 390 Brixton Road, Brixton, London
Jimi is booked into the club as support act to John Mayall's Bluesbreakers. The Ram Jam is an all reggae black club who don't know what to make of the Jimi Hendrix Experience.

December 13
Tuesday
Rediffusion TV Studio's, Studio 9, Kingsway, London
The Jimi Hendrix Experience makes their TV début on Rediffusion's *Ready Steady Go!* Who co-manager Chris Stamp has arranged this first TV appearance as part of a record deal with Polydor and Track Records, in which he is a partner.

Jimi performs a live version of 'Hey Joe', playing the guitar solo with his teeth. As a result of this performance The Jimi Hendrix Experience become an overnight sensation in the rest of England. Other guests on this particular show were The Escorts, Keith Relf, Marc Bolan, The Troggs and The Merseybeats. Photographer Chris Walters shoots photographs of The Experience during their performance and later in the dressing room.

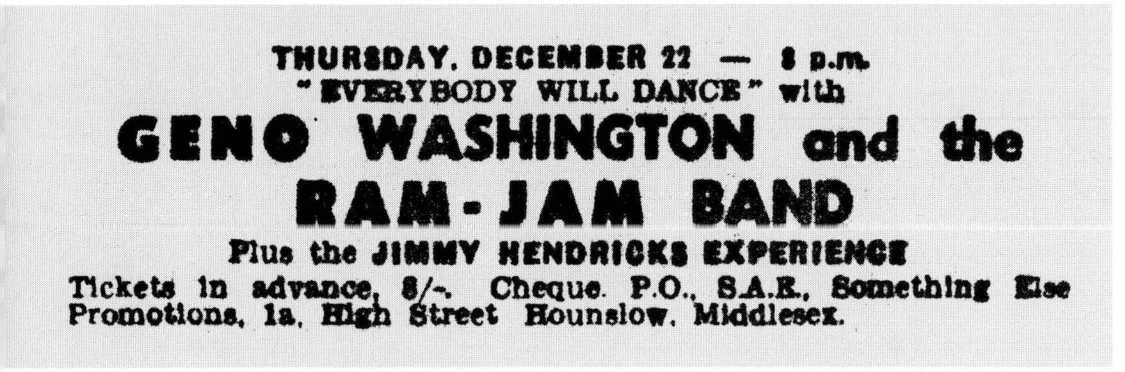

December 16
Friday
Chislehurst Caves, Old Hill, Bromley
Back at Jimi's flat before the show, The Experience gather eagerly around the TV waiting to see their first televised appearance on *Ready, Steady, Go!* They all know that this first TV appearance could either make or break the group. It is so successful, that the evening's show at the Chislehurst Caves is completely packed with a capacity crowd.

December 21
Wednesday
Blaises, 121 Queens Gate, Kensington, London
The Experience performs 'Rock Me Baby', 'Third Stone From The Sun', 'Like A Rolling Stone', 'Hey Joe' and 'Wild Thing'. Chris Welsh attended this concert as staff reporter for *Melody Maker*, and his review is published in the in December 31 issue of *MM*.

Jeff Beck: "One night we were out on the town looking around for some girlies, and went down to Blaises in Queens Gate. And I heard this sound blasting up the road and got out of the cab, and then went in there, and there was Jimi. I couldn't believe it, he was singing 'Like A Rolling Stone'."

December 22
Thursday
Guildhall, Southampton
For two shows at 20:00 and midnight Jimi is added to the bill supporting Geno Washington and The Ram Jam Band. This is the first Experience concert advertised in a local English newspaper, *The Southern Evening Echo*, published on December 17, advertising the group as the Jimmy Hendricks Experience.

December 26
Monday
The Upper Cut, Woodgrange Road, Forest Gate, London
Two shows at 2:30 to 5:30 – Jimi is booked for a Boxing Day afternoon appearance at British boxer Billy Walker's new club. Jimi actually writes 'Purple Haze' in the dressing room while he is waiting to go on to play.

December 29
Thursday
BBC TV Studios, Lime Grove, London
The Experience make their début on BBC TV's *Top Of The Pops*, with guest Wayne Fontana. They perform their new single 'Hey Joe'.

December 31
Saturday
Hillside Social Club, 14-16 Dover Road, Folkestone, Kent
Noel Redding manages to get The Experience booked into a club in his hometown. After the concert everyone attends a New Years Eve party at [Noel's mother] Margaret Redding's house in Folkestone, Kent.

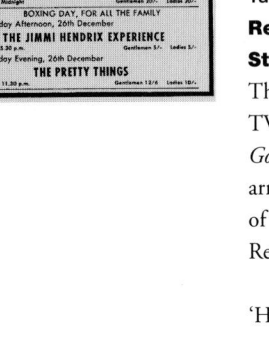

The show was broadcast on December 16 at 18:08 to 18:35 on Channel 9. Sadly only one further show would be broadcast the following week.

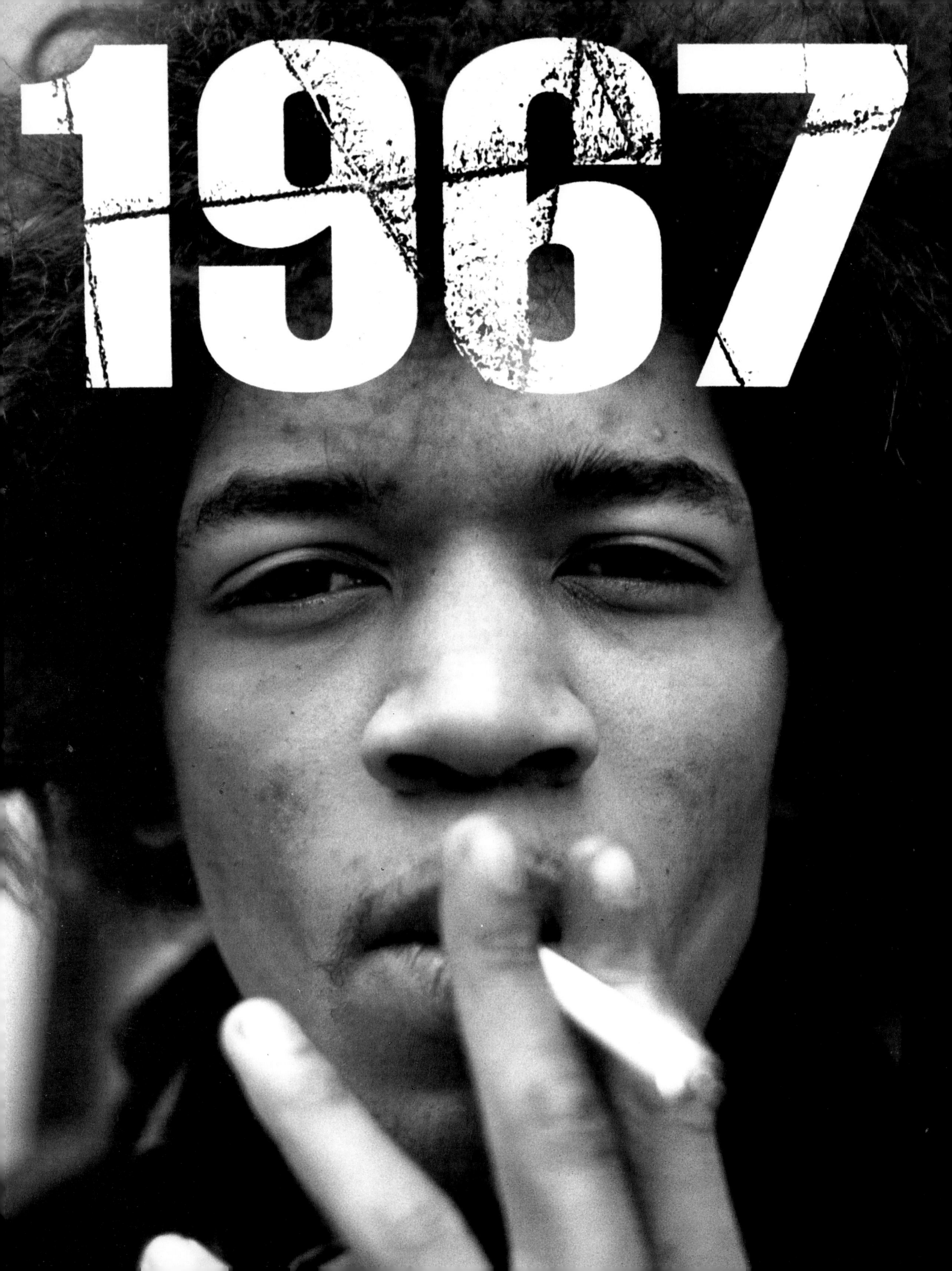

1967

January 4
Wednesday
Bromel Club, Bromley Court Hotel, Bromley Hill, Kent
Reporter Richard Green reviews the show for *Record Mirror*. "Two electric guitars happily emitting sounds as Jimi Hendrix left the stage at Bromley Court Hotel last week. Considering the indignities the instruments had suffered during the preceding 45 minutes, I wouldn't have been surprised if they had got up and made a speech." He later interviews Jimi about his past career.

January 7
Saturday,
**New Century Hall,
Corporation Street, Manchester**
Pete Doyle presents the show called *New Faces 67*. The local newspaper advertises the Experience by stating that "300,000 people voted them a hit on TV". Support acts that night are The Silverstone Set and DJ Dave Eager. Local photographer Harry Goodwin photographed the performance. After the show the group attended The Twisted Wheel Club in Manchester to see The Spellbinders. The club was later raided for membership checks and everyone searched by plain clothes police.

Mitch Mitchell: "We walked over to the car and suddenly Noel and I were grabbed and slung against the railings of the police station. We got slapped around a few times and I was going, 'What the fucks going on?' They were the police, but we didn't believe it at first, they were all in plain clothes. They took Hendrix's passport off him, but left him alone because he was an American."

January 8
Sunday
**Tollbar/Mojo A Go-Go,
Burngreave Road, Sheffield**
The show is advertised as 'The New Weirdo trio Jimi Hendrick's Experience'.

January 11
Wednesday
Bag O' Nails, London
The Experience performs two shows. In the audience is Roger Mayer, a young electronics engineer working for the government. Mayer would become Jimi's roadie for the 1968 tour of America, and create many of the electronic effects that Jimi used in the studio.

January 12 & 13
Thursday & Friday
**7½ Club,
5 Whitehorse Street, London**

January 14
Saturday
Beachcomber Club, Nottingham
Jimmy Cliff and The Shakedown Sound are support act to The Experience who perform 'Killing Floor', 'Can You See Me', 'Have Mercy Baby', 'Like A Rolling Stone', 'Rock Me Baby', 'Third Stone From The Sun', 'Foxy Lady', 'Stone Free', 'Hey Joe' and 'Wild Thing'.

January 15
Sunday
**Country Club,
Kirk Levington, Yorkshire**
John McCoy, who'd seen Jimi performing at the Bag O' Nails. runs the club. He immediately invites him to play in the Country Club.

January 16 & 17
Monday
**7½ Club,
5 Whitehorse Street, London**

January 18
Wednesday
BBC TV Studios, Lime Grove, London
The Experience makes their second appearance on *Top Of The Pops*, performing 'Hey Joe'. Also featured on this edition were Cat Stevens, Georgie Fame, The Tremolos, Wayne Fontana, The Move and The Searchers.

**7½ Club,
5 Whitehorse Street, London**

January 19
Thursday
Speakeasy, London

January 20
Friday
**Haverstock Hill Country Club,
Hampstead, London**

1967 January

January 21
Saturday
**The Refectory,
Golders Green, London**

January 22
Sunday
Astoria, Oldham
The Experience perform from 19:30 to 22:30

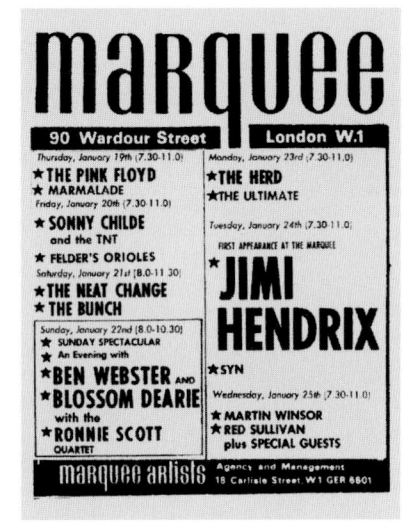

January 24
Tuesday
**The Marquee,
90 Wardour Street, London**
The Experience are supported by Syn.

January 25
Wednesday
The Orford Cellar, Norwich
The Orford Discotheque System is the support act for The Experience.

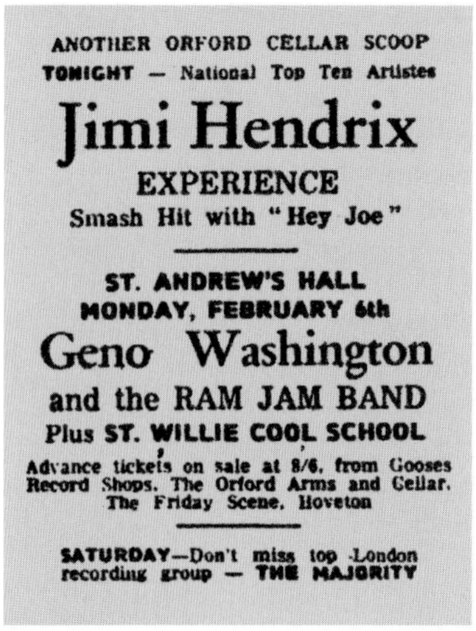

January 27
Friday
**Chislehurst Caves,
Old Hill, Bromley**

January 28
Saturday
**The Upper Cut, Woodgrange Road,
Forest Gate, London**
The Experience make their second appearance at British boxer Billy Walker's new club.

January 29
Sunday
**Saville Theatre,
135-149 Shaftesbury Ave, London**
There are two shows at 18:00 and 20:30 at Brian Epstein's newly launched Saville Theatre for a Sunday Soundarama with The Who topping the bill. Now that The Experience is signed to Who managers Kit Lambert and Chris Stamp's Track Records label, they are added to the bill at the last moment. Although Pete Townshend has admired Jimi's playing, he's concerned about the competition with Jimi playing on the same bill. Also appearing are The Koobas and The Thoughts and MC Mike Quinn hosts the show. John Lennon and Paul McCartney join Brian Epstein in his box to watch the show.

The Experience have an afternoon rehearsal session, which is photographed by photographer Alec Byrne. They are due on stage first and perform 'Rock Me Baby', 'Like A Rolling Stone', 'Can You See Me', 'Hey Joe' and 'Wild Thing'.

Pete Townshend: "Kit Lambert our manager, had just signed Jimi up to our label, and put him on backing us up. I couldn't really believe it, you know. I thought, 'Jesus Christ, what's going to happen?', you know. So he went on and he did his thing, he knocked the amplifiers over, he set his guitar alight, he practically smashed it up. He got feedback together and he also played in his own inimitable way, and I went on afterwards, and I just stood and strummed."

Eric Clapton: "We'd been to see Hendrix about two nights before at the Saville Theatre, and he played this gig that was just blinding. I don't think Jack [Bruce] had really taken him in before. I knew what the guy was capable of from the minute I met him. It was the complete embodiment of the different aspects of rock & roll guitar rolled up into one. I could sense it coming off the guy. And when he did see it that night, after the gig he went home and came up with the riff for 'Sunshine Of Your Love'. It was strictly a dedication to Jimi. And then we wrote a song on top of it."

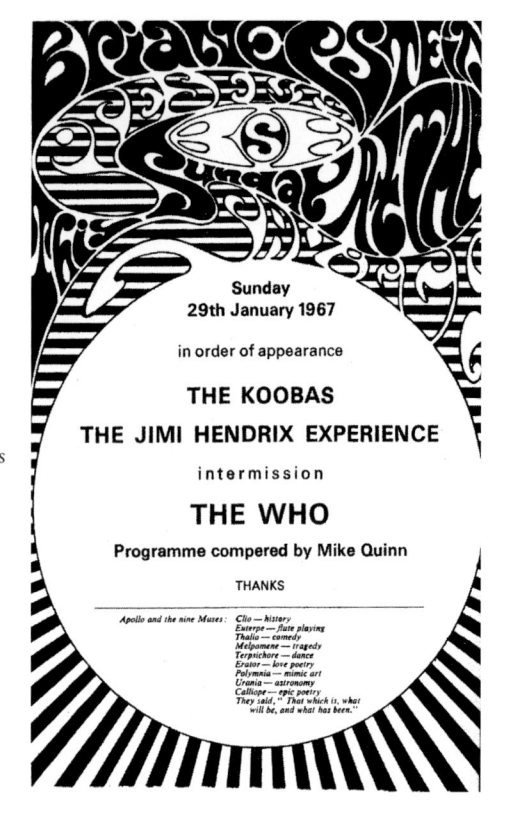

January 30
Monday,
**BBC Playhouse Theatre,
Manchester**
The Experience make their live radio début for the BBC's *Pop North*. They are introduced by Ray Moore and perform 'Hey Joe', 'Rock Me Baby' and 'Foxy Lady'. This session no longer exists.

February 1
Wednesday
**New Cellar Club,
Thomas Street, South Shields**

The Experience are supported by local band The Bond. A photographer from a local studio, Fietscher Fotos of Newcastle, photographs the show.

Noel Redding: "About the only bad gig we've had so far was at South Shields. We arrived a little late and we were in a bit of a rush. We were on the back of a revolving stage just getting tuned, ready to be swung round any minute. We got these new 200 watt [Marshall] units and just as we were tuning, Jimi's amp blew up. He quickly plugged into mine and I looked around for something to borrow. In the end I had to make do with a tiny amp which the other group has been using. At the end of the spot we were taken back round on the revolving stage and as we went, the audience grabbed us. I was hanging on to Jimi and he was hanging on to Mitch and we very nearly got crushed against the wall as we went round."

February 2
Thursday
Imperial Hotel, Darlington

The Experience are supported by West Coast Promotion. After the show, Jimi is interviewed by Charles Westberg for the *Northern Echo*.

February 3
Friday
Ricky Tick, High Street, Hounslow

February 4
Saturday
**The Ram Jam Club,
390 Brixton Road, Brixton, London**

The Experience are supported by The All Night Workers. After the gig, everyone make the trip back to the West End for the second gig of the night.

**The Flamingo Club,
33-37 Wardour Street, London**

The Experience are supported by The All Night Workers.

The Experience takes the small stage at the Flamingo and open with a version of Howling Wolf's 'Killing Floor' which is wildly different to what he was performing months earlier in New York's Greenwich Village. Jimi's guitar skills have grown immeasurably during the months he has been in England. Jimi continues, "Thank you very much, we'd like to continues with a little tune. A straight top 40 R&B rock and roll record. It's a little thing called 'Have Mercy, Have Mercy On Me Baby'. After the song, he continues: "Thanks a lot. Right now, we'd like to try to do a song named 'Can You See Me' but it's the original, very, very simple to understand. It's named 'Can You See Me' in the key of F sharp. That's for him" – pointing to Noel – "cause he don't know what key we're playing in now." This was one of the first songs written by Jimi on his arrival to England. After a quick tune-up Jimi continues with the introduction to Bob Dylan's 'Like A Rolling Stone'. "Right now we'd like to try to do a song for you. A little thing by Bob Dylan named 'Like A Rolling Stone'. I'm gonna dedicate this song to the people of this club." The song ends to polite applause from the audience. "Thank you very much, right now I'd like to do our own arrangement of 'Rock Me Baby'." Next up is Jimi at his very best, playing the blues. He continues with

1967 January/February 37

his own arrangement of Muddy Walters 'Catfish Blues,' playing the entire solo with his teeth. "Thank you very much. Right now we'd like to try to do the B-side of our record called 'Stone Free'." Jimi continues without introduction with 'Hey Joe.' The song ends to loud applause and clapping from the audience. "This guitar's falling to pieces man, anyway we'd like to do the last dance number for your tea. It's the English anthem, so don't get mad if I play this, you know, English anthem and all that. Cause these cats are from England, the guys in the band and so we have to be all pretty tragic and all that, sod the blues and it goes something like this." Jimi launches into a wild feedback guitar intro to what would become his anthem for some time, 'Wild Thing'. He ends the song by rubbing the guitar neck up and down his amps to loud squeals from the guitar. The audience cheer loudly and the DJ thanks everyone for coming. He dedicates the next song to Jimi, 'Baby Please Don't Go'.

February 6
Monday
Star Hotel, London Road, Croydon

February 8
Wednesday
Bromel Club, Bromley Court Hotel, Bromley Hill

February 9
Thursday
Locarno, Frogmore Street, Bristol
The local press reports: "Jimi Hendrix Experience went to the New Bristol Entertainment Centre last night and left it reeling with the sound of his way out guitar. Something had to snap and it did. He broke a string at the end of the show. 'I buy several sets a week,' said Hendrix. He drove his way through Dylan's 'Like A Rolling', 'Wild Thing' and 'Hey Joe'."

February 10
Friday
Plaza Ballroom, Market Place, Newbury

OFFICIAL BULLETIN
Last night at the Plaza, Newbury the Jimi Hendrix Experience roared and romped their way through an hour and a quarter's worth of music that shattered the senses both aurally and visually.

Resplendent in red corduroy trousers and antique waist coat, Jimi proceeded to show just how many positions it was possible to play the guitar in, at the same time showing his very own professional skill which must rate him as one of the most outstanding newcomers on the scene since Jeff Beck or Eric Clapton. Outstanding for the Experience on drums was Mitch Mitchell, youthful understudy of ex-Pretty Things drummer Viv Prince.

Throughout the evening Jimi showed flashes of onstage humour, for which he must be given full credit. 'Hey Joe', current chart-rider, was introduced as being written by Micky Mouse. After a sudden frenzy of excitement in which he attacked his amplifier with his guitar (not a new idea, but somehow done refreshingly), he announced, 'Anyone wanna buy an ole guitar? This one don't tune so well'.

The finish came suddenly, in an excess of violence. Mitch Mitchell attacked a cymbal stand and broke it into pieces, then distributed his drum kit around the stage, and finally squirted the other two with a handy water pistol. The bass-guitarist locked his guitar in its case and then kicked it about over the stage. Jimi attacked his huge amplifier with his guitar, breaking all the strings and nearly toppling the amplifier onto his head. He then squatted on the guitar with both feet and rocked to and fro, Thus the evening came to its conclusion in a storm of feedback, flying microphones, and water pistols."

February 11
Saturday
**Blue Moon Club,
170 High Street, Cheltenham**

February 12
Sunday
**Sinking Ship Clubland,
Underbank, Stockport**

February 13
Monday
**BBC Broadcasting House,
Great Portland Place, London**
The Experience are back at the BBC to record a live radio recording for *Saturday Club*. The show is introduced by Brian Matthews and is broadcast on February 18.

After an interview with Brian Matthews, The Experience then record 'Hey Joe', 'Stone Free' and 'Foxy Lady' but the song breaks down after the guitar solo and Jimi brings the song to a crashing end. They decide to record a second take of 'Foxy Lady', which is perfect. The last song they record is 'Love or Confusion', performed here live for the first and only time.

Bill Beeb: "We did a session in Studio S2 with is the sub-basement of Broadcasting House. And it's a relatively small studio and it really wasn't designed for Jimi Hendrix because the only way Jimi could get that kind of sound was to - in those days - was to wind everything up to absolutely full power to get of screaming buzzes and clicks and feedback. And so it was all hammering away, I mean when we turned everything off we could actually hear it coming through the glass, I mean it was soundproof glass. We got steaming into the first one and suddenly I was aware that somebody was standing behind me. There was this little old lady. She said I'm a radio three producer, well I'm actually doing a string quartet in the concert hall, which is two floors above you in this building. We keep hearing guitar sounds all the time. So I said can you wait and record when we've finished because we've only got a couple of numbers to do, she said no it's live. So Jimi Hendrix was going out live on Radio 3 at the same time.

February 14
Tuesday
The Civic Hall, Grays, Essex
The Experience are supported by Lot 5. They perform 'Hey Joe', 'Like A Rolling Stone' and 'Wild Thing'.

Alain Dister photographs the performance. After the show Alain and The Experience go to the Speakeasy Club by Taxi. On the way there is a small accident but no one is hurt and they continue on to the club where Jimi and Chas find that they are special guests for the Speakeasy's St. Valentine's Day Massacre party. Jimi ends the night by jamming with Pretty Things drummer Skip Allen.

February 15
Wednesday
Dorothy Ballroom, Cambridge

February 17
Friday
Ricky Tick, Thames Hotel, Windsor

February 18
Saturday
York University, Heslington, York
Noel Redding: "We set off at 5pm and belted off towards Nottingham [in Mitch's car], but after only a few miles the generator went. We just about made it into Nottingham, left the car at a garage, and started to look round for something to get us to York. Eventually we hired a car and about 9.45 p.m. we were on our way again. We turned up at midnight. Fortunately we weren't due on until 1 am. After the gig, which finished around 2 am, we set off back to Nottingham, but when we arrived it was 6 am and the garage didn't open until 9 am. Eventually the guy came to open the garage, we got the car out, and Jerry who is a genius of a mechanic, fixed it all up. We left Nottingham around 10 am we were making good time on the motorway when 'bang', we had a blow out, at 70 mph. Eventually an AA man came along and helped us out and at 2pm we were on our way again."

February 19
Sunday
Blarney Club, 32 Tottenham Court Road, London

February 20
Monday
The Pavilion, Bath
A staff reporter/photographer from the *Wessex Newspaper* is sent to photograph the Experience. "As Jimi Hendrix bellowed 'Lord Have Mercy' from his alter on the Pavilion stage at Bath last night, and his worshippers gazed in silent adoration from below, I echoed his sentiments as my ribs reverberated with the intolerable volume of electronic sound."

February 22
Wednesday
BBC Playhouse Theatre, Northumberland Avenue, London
The Experience performs a version of 'Hey Joe' for a live radio broadcast of *Parade Of The Pops* on the BBC's Light Programme. The show is introduced by Denny Pierce and produced by Ian Scott. This session no longer exists.

ROUNDHOUSE
Chalk Farm Road, N.W.1
Wednesday, February 22nd, 7.30-11.30
the
JIMI HENDRIX
EXPERIENCE
and
THE FLIES
with
SANDY & HILARY
Tickets: 5/- in advance or 6/6 at the door

RICKY-TICK
THAMES HOTEL - WINDSOR
JIMI HENDRIX EXPERIENCE
FRI. 17 FEB. 7'6

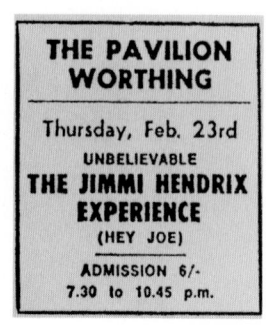

Roundhouse, Chalk Farm Road, Chalk Farm, London.
The Experience are supported by The Soft Machine, The Flies and Sandy & Hilary.

February 23
Thursday
The Pavilion, Marine Parade, Worthing

February 24
Friday
Leicester University

February 25
Saturday
Corn Exchange, Chelmsford
'Saturday Scene' between 20:00 and 23:30. The Experience are supported by The Soul Trinity.

February 26
Sunday
Cliffs Pavilion, Southend-on-Sea
On two shows, the Experience are supported by Dave Dee & Co, Nashville Teens, The Koobas and Force Five. The shows MC is Pete Murray.

Pete Murray: "When I was down at Westcliffe Pavilion and he was on the bill. There was a terrific line-up. I mean they were all hit parade artists. It was a very good line-up. And I had such a lot of trouble with Jimi Hendrix fans... they were sitting right at the back. And this one guy, every time I went out there... 'Bring on Jimi Hendrix, bring on Jimi Hendrix' and I thought well it's very tough for these other guys appearing on the show. Cause Jimi Hendrix was going to be in the second half of the show anyway. So I went out on the second occasion and they yell out 'Bring on Jimi Hendrix'. So I thought well there's only one thing to do, I said to the stage manager, 'Put up the house lights', so he put up the house lights and I said, 'Will the person who wants Jimi Hendrix please stand up' and he stood up. I said, 'Would you please come down onto the stage, give him some applause'. The guy came down, give him his credit, he came down and I brought him up on the stage and I gave him a little interview and I said, 'I bet there one thing you'd like more than anything in the world'. He said, 'What's that'. I said, 'I bet you'd like to meet Jimi Hendrix'. He said, 'Yes I would'. I said, 'I've arranged it, you go and meet him in his dressing room'. I got rid of a heckler. It made life easier for all of the other guys because he was the ringleader."

March 1
Wednesday
Orchid Ballroom, Purley

March 2
Thursday
Marquee, London
The Experience are scheduled to appear on the German *Beat Club* TV show. The Marquee is the chosen venue for the filming of Radio Bremen 'Goes to London' and broadcast in Germany on March 11 as Beat Club No 18. Also appearing on the show is Geno Washing and The Ram Jam Band, Cliff Bennett and The Rebel Rousers, The Smoke and The Who.

The Experience are introduced by Dave Lee Travis and perform 'Hey Joe' and 'Purple Haze'. Jimi messes up the ending of 'Purple Haze' so they have to re-shoot both songs again. This time it's perfect and Jimi ends 'Purple Haze' with a wild feedback ending and a big smile on his face. Photographer Bob Baker photographs The Experience while they are performing.

March 4
Saturday
Unknown small club in a hotel, south of Paris
MC: Robert Ismii. The Experience arrives for their 40 minutes afternoon show in an American car.

Law Society Graduation Ball, Faculte-De Droit d'Assas, Paris.
The Experience are supported by The Pretty Things The show concert took place at 3:30am and finally finished at 6:30am. French photographer Jean Louis Rancurel photographs the concert.

Mitch Mitchell: "We [also] did a graduation ball in Paris, a really plush place. There was an oompah band on before us and they would not leave the stage. I remember one of our roadies, in a final act of desperation pushing the trombonist's slide back into his mouth – blood and teeth everywhere. We finally set up and played a few numbers and for some reason this huge fight broke out. They were fighting everywhere, up and down the stairs, all over the place. It got completely out of hand, so we left the gear and got the hell out."

March 5
Sunday
Twenty Club, Mouscron, Belgium
After the concert, The Experience travel back to France for the second gig of the day.

Twenty Club, Lens, France

March 7
Monday
At 11.00, the Experience travel back to Belgium for a TV recording at St. Pieters Woluwe TV studio in Belgium. Later, they go on location in a forest by a lake, where they are asked to mime 'Hey Joe' for a TV recording for Vibrato. The show is introduced by Georges Prades and is broadcast on March 21 at 20:30 to 21:15. Jimi Hendrix is later interview by Jan Waldrop and photographed by Herman Seleslags for the Belgium magazine Humo that is published on March 18. The Experience spend the night in Belgium.

March 7
Tuesday
While in Belgium, the group attends The Experience Universal TV Studio, Waterloo, Belgium. They are filmed miming 'Hey Joe' and 'Stone Free' for a TV recording for Tienerklanker BRT to be broadcast in mid-1967. After the recording, they travel back to Paris for an interview with Jean Noel Coghe in Jimi's hotel room. Later they visit a small restaurant at Rue Des Boucher in Paris. The Experience then fly from Le Bourget Airport, arriving at London Heathrow Airport.

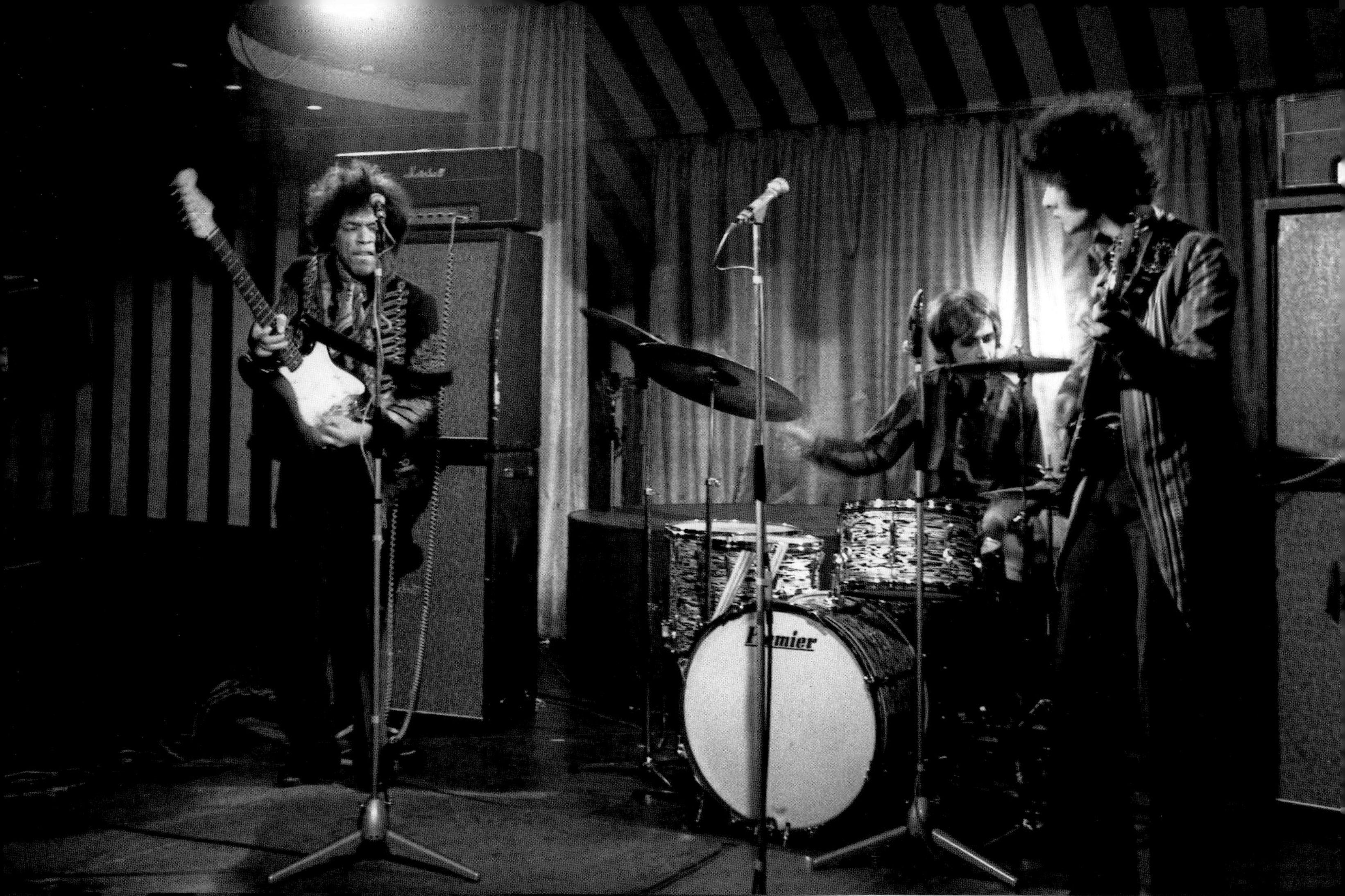

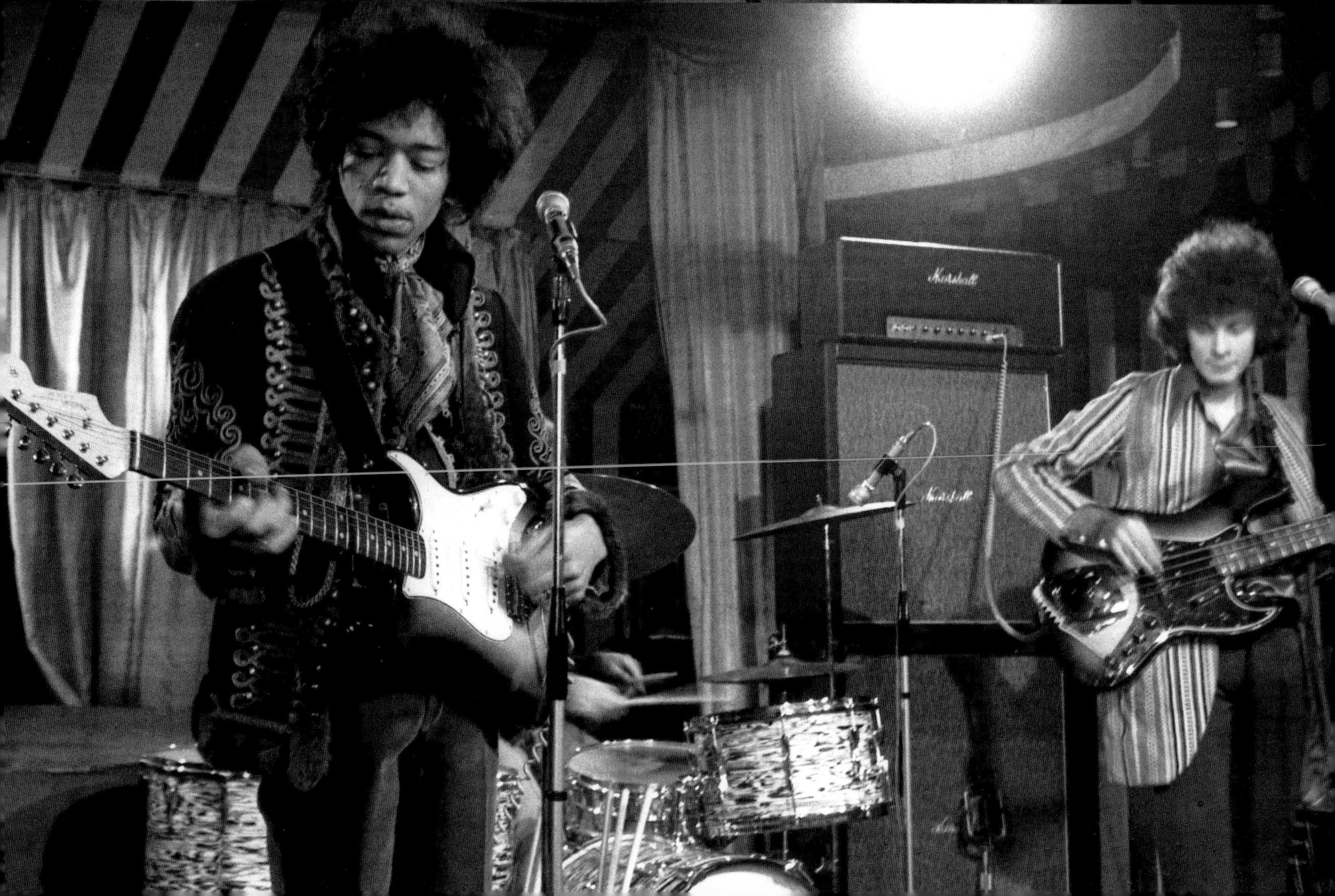
Marshall

March 9
Thursday
**Skyline Ballroom,
Jameson Street, Hull, Yorkshire.**
20.00-01.00.
The Experience are supported by The Family, The Small Faces, The Strollers and The Mandrakes.

March 10
Friday
Club A Go Go, Percy St, Newcastle
The Experience performs two shows at 20:00 and 02:00 in manager Mike Jeffery's own club.

March 11
Saturday
International Club, Leeds

March 12
Sunday
Gyro Club, Troutbeck Hotel, Ilkley, Yorkshire
Ilkley Police stop the concert mid-way through with disastrous consequences. The local newspaper reports the story the next day. "There was chaos when police stopped a pop show last night. A door was ripped off its hinges, pictures were slashed and torn from their frames, electrical fitting and furniture were broken and the carpets were littered with broken glass at the Gyro Club, Troutbeck Hotel, Ilkley. The Jimi Hendrix Experience were told to stop playing in the middle of their second number. Police told the audience of 800 that they would have to leave because the club was overcrowded. Jimi remarked 'I wish they had let me play before emptying the club'."

March 14
Tuesday
Bellevue, Leidsekade 90, Amsterdam, Holland
During the live rehearsals for the *Fanclub* TV show, Jimi plays so loud that the ceiling in the studio below starts to crack, which causes some complaints, so it is suggested by *Fanclub* producer Ralph Inbar that Jimi should mime during the TV show. This suggestion annoys Jimi because he hates to mime to records, and wants to do it live, and so he leaves the rehearsal studio.

Back at the TV studio for the live transmission, producer Ralph Inbar has got his own way. The Jimi Hendrix Experience have to mime to 'Hey Joe' and 'Stone Free' for a the TV recording for Dutch TV VARA. The show is introduced by Judith Bosch and broadcast live at 19:00. Michael Polnareff is also a guest on the show.

March 17
Friday
Star Club, Grossefreiheit 39, Hamburg

March 18
Saturday,
1/NDR Radiohouse, Rothenbaumchaussee 132-134, 2000 Hamburg
The Experience record a live radio recording for *Twenclub* NDR. The show is introduced by Jochem Rathmann and is broadcast simultaneously in Germany and England as *Hamburg Swings* on July 1 at 21:00-21:45. Other guests on the show are Ferre Gringnard and The Original X-Rays.

After his introduction, Jochem Rathmann interviews Jimi on stage. "Well just tell the people about 'Hey Joe' what happens in this song." Jimi replies: "Well it's about a cat, you know a guy. He shoots his old lady because he catch her doing wrong, you know she's messing about with everybody else. Yeah, after he shoots her, then he has to run out of town, you know go to Mexico where he can be free." Rathmann then interviews Noel Redding who answers him in German.

Jimi starts the show off with 'Foxy Lady' after which he thanks the audience in German and proceeds with 'Hey Joe' and 'Stone Free'. Rathmann take the stage to make an announcement in German and then in English. "Well if you certainly want to know how our other guests here enjoy it, I can tell you they are as fabulous as the musicians." As the audience clap, Jimi makes funny little sounds with his guitar. The audience is told to clap their hands and tap their feet. Jimi strums his guitar in time to them, then announces that it's time to hear some music.

Jimi gives out an amused chuckle as he counts the band in for 'Fire'. Noel introduces the final song, 'Purple Haze', in German.

**Star Club,
Grossefreiheit 39, Hamburg**
The Experience performs two shows

March 19
Sunday
**Star Club,
Grossefreiheit 39, Hamburg.**
The Experience performs two shows

March 21
Tuesday
**Guild Hall,
Southampton, Hampshire**
The Experience are supported by local group Brother Bung.

March 25
Saturday
**Starlight Room,
Gliderdrome, Boston, Lincoln**
The Experience are supported by Sons And Lovers, The Group, The Charades, The Steel Band and Ray Bones.

March 26
Sunday
**Tabernacle Club,
Hillgate, Stockport, Cheshire**

March 27
Monday
**BBC Television Studios,
Manchester**
The Experience records a live version of 'Purple Haze' for a TV recording for *Dee Time* on BBC1. There is some panic as before Jimi is scheduled to appear he suddenly loses his voice. The show is introduced by Simon Dee and is broadcast on April 4 at 18:25 to 19:05. Dee interviews his other guests – Cat Stevens, Kiki Dee, Libby Morris, Mike Newman and Lance Percival.

**Assembly Hall, Aylesbury
TUESDAY, 28th MARCH
JIMI HENDRIX
Admission 8/-.
FRIDAY, 31 MARCH
JOHN MAYALL
Admission 7/6.**

March 28
Tuesday
**BBC Broadcasting House,
Great Portland Place, London**
The Experience records live versions of 'Killing Floor', 'Fire' and 'Purple Haze' for a radio recording for 'Saturday Club' on BBC Light. The show is introduced by Brian Matthews and is broadcast on April 1 at 10:00 to 12:00. Other guests include Manfred Mann, Vince Hill and Helen Shapiro.

**Assembly Hall,
Aylesbury, Buckingham**

March 30
Thursday
BBC-TV Studios, Lime Grove, London
The Experience records 'Purple Haze' for a TV recording for *Top Of The Pops* for BBC1. The show is introduced by Pete Murray and broadcast live. Other guests are Alan Price, Dave Dee & Co, Cat Stevens, Dusty Springfield, The Byrds, Sandie Shaw, Cliff Richard and Engelbert Humperdinck. Photographer Barrie Wentzell photographs The Experience's performance.

March 31
Friday
**The Astoria,
232-236 Seven Sisters Road,
Finsbury Park, London**
The Experience perform two shows at 18:40 and 21:10 on the opening night of their real British tour. Jimi has been booked on a month long package tour alongside The Walker Brothers, Cat Stevens, Engelbert Humperdinck, The Californians, The Quotations and compere Nick Jones, that will take in most counties of England and includes

Before the tour starts Jimi is interviewed by Keith Altham for *New Musical Express*. He appeared a little apprehensive. "Most will come to see The Walkers. Those who come to hear Engelbert sing 'Release Me' may not dig me, but that's not tragic. We'll play for ourselves – we've done it before, where the audience stands about with their mouths open and you have to wait ten minutes before they clap." He expressed the same apprehension in another interview with *Disc & Music Echo*. "I'm a bit worried about the type of people who're gonna see the tour. If they come to see The Walker Brothers, then they're not going to want us. I just hope they listen – but if they do scream for the Walkers during our act I'll just ignore them and play for myself."

The Experience perform 'Foxy Lady', 'Can You See Me', 'Hey Joe', 'Purple Haze' and 'Fire.' Alec Byrne photographs the show.

Prior to the show everyone in the Hendrix camp was racking their brains to come up with a sensational idea for The Experience' on the opening night. *New Musical Express* reporter Keith Altham suggested Jimi burn his guitar during the performance. Nick Jones, the show's compere, gets burned trying to put out the flames.

Keith Altham: "Well, what actually happened was... there was a little clutch of us in the dressing room. Chas, Jimi, and I were all talking. Various things were being discussed about what they could actually do that night to grab some headlines and capture people's attention. I said, 'What would happen if he set fire to his guitar?' I kind of said it as a joke and Chas said, 'That's not a bad idea'.

So we tried a couple of experimental runs in the dressing room, it worked, and Jimi used it later on stage. And of course it did exactly what they wanted it to do, and it also caused an enormous bloody row with one of the security officer in the theatre. He threatened that Jimi would never work on his circuit again and never work in any Moss Empires or whatever they're called. Tito Burns actually got into collusion with Jimi on the situation and took his guitar from him, hid it underneath his raincoat and walked out the stage door with it. But before doing so he put his head in the dressing room and tore Jimi of a strip.

1967 March 43

'You're never going to work for me again if you pull a stunt like that'. There was a bit of needle between The Walker Brothers and Hendrix. I can remember that little bit. But you know these things also were encouraged as the press things. They liked to think that there was a fight going on."

Naturally a row blows up immediately after Jimi's performance. Tour promoter Maurice King states that all the Rank Theatres on the tour have complained to him about Jimi's act and if he don't clean it up, he would be banned from their theatres. Chas Chandler denies that Jimi intends to change his act and could not see what all the fuss was about. Jimi tells *Disc & Music Echo*: "I am bemused by the whole thing. All I want to do is sing and play guitar."

April 1
Saturday
Gaumont,
St. Helens Street, Ipswich
Two shows at 18:35 & 20:45.
Part or all of one show is filmed by a French TV crew for a new 90-minute French pop show which has remained unseen in their archives ever since.

April 2
Sunday
Gaumont, Worcester
Two shows at 17:30 & 20:00.
The local press reported: "Most people had not really come to see Jimi Hendrix but he left the audience breathless with the sheer force and volume that his three man group pounded out. His left hand heavily bandaged from a burn he received doing his act on Friday. He opened with his hit 'Hey Joe' and then went into the similar 'Purple Haze'. A lengthy version of 'Like A Rolling Stone' followed before his act ended with the Troggs 'Wild Thing'. Jimi battered his guitar against his amplifiers, and the drums fell down to close an act which is better suited to the clubs than the barrenness of a package show."

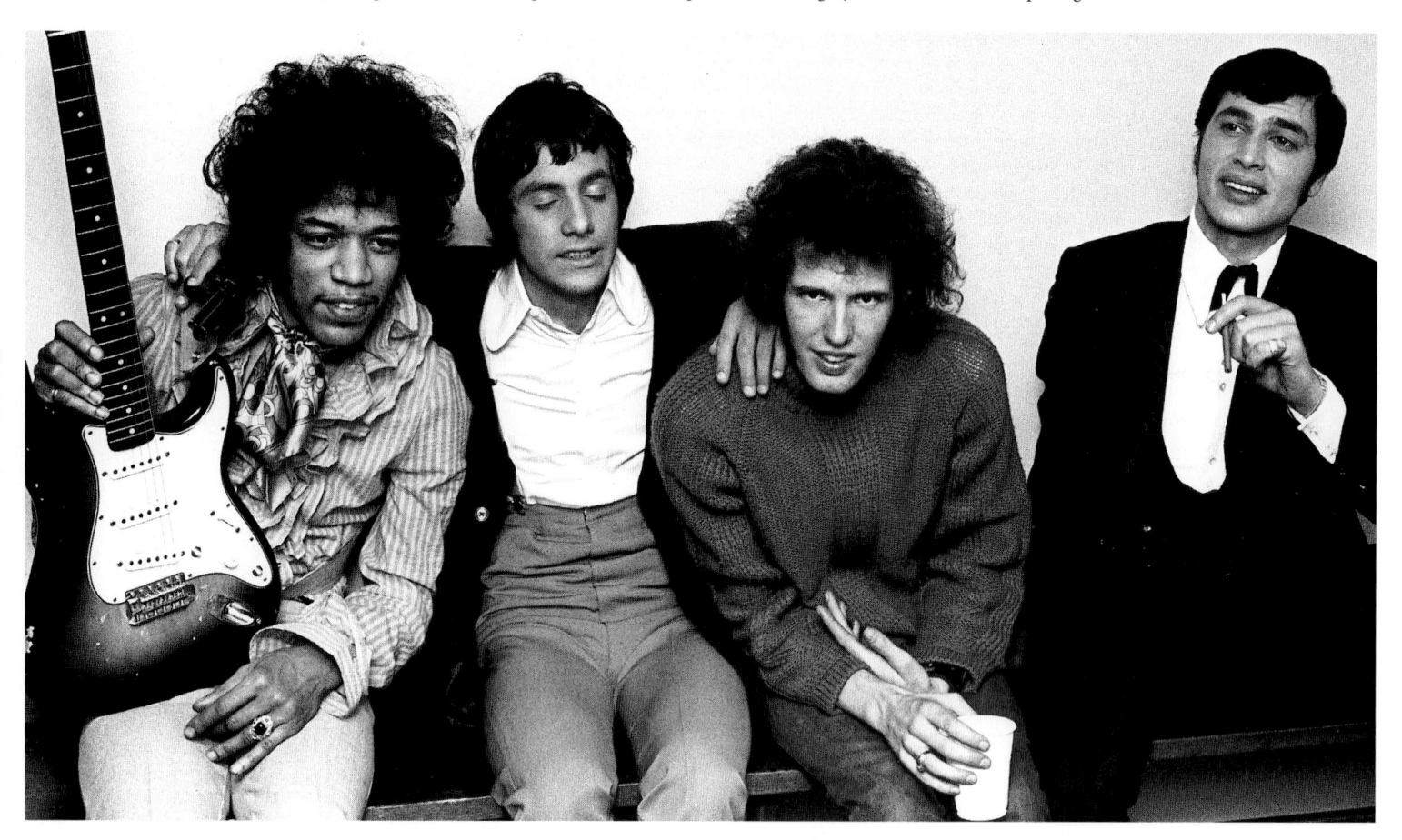

April 5
Wednesday
Odeon, Leeds
Two shows at 18:00 & 20:30.
The local press reported: "The Jimi Hendrix Experience had gimmicks galore (including split trousers) but did not impress." Another reporter wrote: "The Jimi Hendrix Experience was one I would prefer not to repeat."

April 6
Thursday
Odeon, Renfield Street, Glasgow
Two shows at 18:40 & 21:00.
Jimi Hendrix is interview by Donald Bruce for The Dundee Recorder.

> **ABC CARLISLE** Tel 25586
>
> TODAY — ON THE STAGE. At 6.15 and 8.30.
> ## THE WALKER BROTHERS
> ### ENGELBERT HUMPERDINK
> ### CAT STEVENS. JIMI HENDRIX
> The Quotations, The Californians, Nick Jones
> SEATS AVAILABLE FIRST HOUSE ONLY
> SUNDAY, 9th APRIL — One Day Only. Cont. from 5.00. "THE DEVIL SHIP PIRATES" (U). Also "THE INVINCIBLE SEVEN" (U) Colour.
> MONDAY, 10th APRIL — FOR SIX DAYS. Cont. 1.50 LCP 7.05.
> Robert Stack, Elke Sommer
> ## "PEKING MEDALLION"
> Technicolor. Showing at 2.05; 5.30; 8.55. (A)
> Jane Fonda, Jason Robards
> ## "BACHELOR GIRL APARTMENT"
> Technicolor. Showing at 3.40 and 7.05. (A)

April 7
Friday
ABC, Carlisle
Two shows at 18:15 & 20:30.
A young reporter, Lorraine Walsh, made the following hitherto unpublished notes: "Soon the chants of Jimi, Jimi drowned the compere's voice and the curtain lifted to screams of ecstasy from the Cumbrian fans. One young girl ran down the main aisle and managed to vault over the orchestra pit into Jimi's own arms. A Carlisle corporation bouncer named Ginger Watson gently escorted her off stage and the Lonsdale ABC echoed to the haunting sound of 'Hey Joe', Jimi's opening number. In the following numbers, only 'Purple Haze' was distinguishable in the screams and cries of delight from the 2,000 fans. Jimi did a good impression of making love to his guitar on stage and then proceeded to pluck the strings with his teeth, at this stage, uppity St John's Ambulance Brigade were busy reviving young girls who had either fainted or become hysterical. As the curtain came down 21 year old Nick Jones tried to keep his composure and prepare the audience to greet Engelbert Humperdinck, only to be drowned out by the continuing screams for Jimi." Photographer Peter Brock photographs Jimi's performance.

The Experience spent the night at the Red Lion Hotel in Carlisle.

April 8
Saturday
ABC, Cavendish Street, Chesterfield
Two shows at 18:10 & 20:25.
The local press reported. "Jimi Hendrix and the Experience is one experience I would rather forget. This volatile performer, like a negress on occasions, was completely unintelligible."

During the fist show, Jimi manages to cut his foot on his fuzz box during his performance. He is taken to the local hospital to have four stitches put in the wound. However he is able to continue for the second show.

April 9
Sunday
The Empire, Lime Street, Liverpool
Two shows at 17:40 & 20:00.
A pretty 18-year-old girl called Joy has been writing to Jimi at every theatre on the tour. Once the tour reaches Liverpool Jimi writes her back and invites her along to the show to meet him. She arrives at the stage door with her sister, but is refused entry. They find a phone box and call the Empire asking to talk to Jimi who has told the tour manager that they are the wives of the group. They are still refused entry so Jimi tells her to get a taxi and to meet them outside the stage door. By now, the fans are getting larger at each venue and it is getting almost impossible for the groups to get in and out of the theatre without the help of the local police. When the group emerged from the stage door, they are mobbed by the fans and pulled back into the theatre. When the taxi arrives they make a dash and manage to drive off in the taxi. Jimi suggests they go back to Joy's house, but she explains that it is too far, so Noel suggests they go to the Lord Nelson pub instead. The pub is only a block away and by the time they arrive, so have the hordes of screaming fans. The fans start banging on the pub windows. The manager comes to see what is going on, takes one look at Jimi, Mitch, and Noel and promptly tells them that the bar is closed. He asks the doorman to take them out through the back entrance. Jimi would later dedicate his American album 'Electric Ladyland' to Joy whose nickname was Bil.

> **PROGRAMME**
> Capable Management Harold Davison and Tito Burns presents
> **THE WALKER BROS. SHOW**
>
> The Quotations
> Nick Jones
> The Californians
> Nick Jones
> Jimi Hendrix
> Nick Jones
> **ENGELBERT HUMPERDINCK**
> ———— Interval ————
> The Quotations
> Nick Jones
> Cat Stevens
> Nick Jones
> **THE WALKER BROTHERS**
>
> Programme subject to alteration at the discretion of the management
>
> SAFETY REGULATIONS...

April 10
Monday
BBC's Playhouse Theatre in Northumberland Avenue, London
After a morning spent doing interviews with the pop press, The Experience attend a live radio broadcast with Dave Dee & Co for BBC North's *Monday, Monday*. The show is introduced by Dave Cash, produced by Keith Bateson and broadcast live between 1:00-2:00. The Experience perform 'Purple Haze' and 'Foxy Lady'. The session no longer exists.

> **GRANADA BEDFORD** phone 53848
> RICHARD JOHNSON ELKE SOMMER
> **DEADLIER THAN THE MALE**
> GUNFIGHT IN ABILENE
> ON STAGE TUES APR 11 7 o'c 9.10
> **WALKER BROTHERS**
> CAT STEVENS | JIMI HENDRIX EXPERIENCE
> Californians | Nicky Jones | Quotations
> **ENGELBERT HUMPERDINCK**
> BOOK NOW

1967 March/April

April 11
Tuesday
Granada, St. Peters Street, Bedford
Two shows at 19:00 & 21:10.
The local press reported: "A ten year old boy was injured as The Walker Brothers scrambled for safety through a crowd of teenagers on arrival at the Granada cinema late Tuesday afternoon." Reviewing the show, they continued: "Three hirsute and weirdly dressed characters came on. I'm referring to The Jimi Hendrix Experience. They began with 'Hey Joe'. Jimi showed that he really can play the guitar with his teeth and ended with their new record 'Purple Haze'."

April 12
Wednesday
Gaumont, Southampton
Two shows at 18:15 & 20:40.

April 13
Thursday
Gaumont, Wolverhampton
Two shows at 18:30 & 20:40.
The local press reported: "Jimi Hendrix played some great stuff which in the second house was not as appreciated as it deserved." After the shows everyone retired to the Kingfisher Club in Wolverhampton. Jimi jammed with The Californians.

April 14
Friday
Odeon, Bolton
Two shows at 18:15 & 20:30.
Jayne Mansfield was at this concert (she was appearing at The Bolton Odeon on April 16). After the show, she left with Engelbert Humperdinck.

Jimi plays only three songs during the second show because of the poor response he gets from the audience during the first show, which put him in a bad mood. The group are advised to take the train straight to Blackpool for fear that the fans might become violent because of the show being cut so short. They arrive in Blackpool at midnight and head for their hotel, but the manager takes one look at them and tells them that no reservations had been made for them. After being turned away from all the other hotels in Blackpool, they finally find a bed & breakfast at 6am.

April 15
Saturday
Odeon, Dickson Road, Blackpool
Two shows at 17:30 & 20:15.
When the group gets to the stage door, excited fans mob them with scissors and they all lose some of their hair.

April 16
Sunday
De Montford Hall, Granville Road, Leicester
Two shows at 17:40 & 20:00.
The local press reported: "The Jimi Hendrix Experience are surely the oddest looking group to appear at De Montford Hall. When I tried not to look, the sound they made was different and not unattractive."

April 17
Monday
BBC-TV Studios, Kingsway, London
The Experience are invited to take part in a live broadcast for BBC2's *Late Nite Line Up*, introduced by Tony Bilbow. The show is a psychedelic special to discuss the previous night's *Man Alive* 'What Is A Happening' program. The Jimi Hendrix Experience end the show with a live version of 'Manic Depression' during which Jimi manages to fluff up the last verse to great amusement. Unfortunately, students of the Royal College of Art are allowed to give Jimi's performance a psychedelic look by filtering the live pictures through a visual effects mixer to disastrous effect.

April 18
Tuesday
Jimi attends the Speakeasy club in Margaret Street where he jams on bass with Georgie Fame on organ and Ben E. King on drums.

April 19
Wednesday
Odeon, New Street, Birmingham
Two shows at 18:30 & 21:00.
The local press reported: "The zany methods of Jimi Hendrix had a surprising appeal – especially for those who liked to hear a guitar played by tooth."

Engelbert Humperdinck's guitar player Mickey Keene has decided to leave him midway through the tour so Noel Redding is asked to take over for the remaining dates. However, Noel is not able to join the band on stage and has to play from the wings, for which he is paid £2 a night.

April 20
Thursday
ABC, Lincoln
Two shows at 18:15 & 20:30.
The local press reported: "A great guy on and off stage, Jimi Hendrix was in a very bouncy mood. His opening remarks was: "I'm gonna put a curse on everyone so that all their babies are born naked." After the show Jimi is interviewed about the tour for the *Lincolnshire Chronicle*. It is evident that Jimi is still having problems with the tour promoters.

"The bosses of the tour are giving us hell. Some people say we are obscene and vulgar but we play our act as we have always played it. We refuse to change our act and the result is my amplifier gets cut off at the funniest times, I wonder why? But I don't let them hang me up. I play to the people and I don't think our actions are obscene. We just get carried away by the music."

April 21
Friday
City Hall, Newcastle
Two shows at 18:00 & 20:30.

April 22
Saturday
Odeon, Manchester
Two shows at 18:00 & 20:30.

April 23
Sunday
Gaumont, Hanley
Two shows at 18:00 & 20:30.

April 25
Tuesday
Colston Hall, Bristol
Two shows at 18:30 & 20:45.
The local press reported: "The Jimi Hendrix Experience were completely our of place on this particular package show. Hendrix played well with the guitar behind his back, better with his teeth, and was a maestro playing straight. The group's music was weird, exciting and inventive, but it was too way out for the Walker fans."

April 26
Wednesday
Capitol, Cardiff, Glamorgan
Two shows at 18:15 & 20:50.

April 27
Thursday
ABC, Aldershot, Hampshire
Two shows at 18:15 & 20:30.
Steve Mann wrote for the local press: "The only people I had the chance to speak to were the Jimi Hendrix Experience. Jimi, Mitch and Noel were extremely pleased with their reception, and said the crowd was one of the most enthusiastic of the whole tour."

April 28
Friday
Aldelphi, Slough
Two shows at 18:40 & 20:50.
The Experience did not impress the Slough local press. One paper wrote: "As for the Jimi Hendrix Experience – yeah, well it was. Wearing a rainbow coloured jacket and yellow trousers, Mr Hendrix and two cohorts brought a deafened audience the 'new music' otherwise known as psychedelic and if there was one note of music in it, I couldn't find it. Despite this black spot in the evening, the performances were often enjoyable." Another wrote: "Jimi Hendrix and the Experience are certainly popular, but personally I did not like the amplifier worshipping, playing the guitar under the thigh and behind the back, throwing oneself on the floor. I liked their clothes, flowered shirts, shocking pink scarves, stripped blazers and bouffant hair."

After the show, the group drive back to London and wind up at the UFO Club at 31 Tottenham Court Road, London W1. Jimi jams on bass guitar with Tomorrow with Keith West on vocals, John Adler on drums, John Wood on bass and Steve Howe on guitar. Dutch photographer Paul van den Bos is on hand to document the event.

April 29
Saturday
Winter Gardens, Bournemouth
Two shows at 18:00 & 20:15.
As the tour coach arrives at the Winter Gardens stage door, the surge of excited fans running beside it causes a young girl to have her foot run over by the vehicle. She is taken to hospital for treatment.

SAT., 29th APRIL — ARTHUR KIMBRELL presents — **6.00 & 8.15**
THE FABULOUS
WALKER BROTHERS
CAT STEVENS ★ JIMI HENDRIX
SPECIAL GUEST STAR **ENGLEBERT HUMPERDINCK**
PLUS THREE OTHER STAR ACTS
15/6, 13/6, 10/6, 8/6   BOOKING OPENS TOMORROW (SATURDAY)
BOX OFFICE OPEN 10-5 (10-8.30 CONCERT DATES)

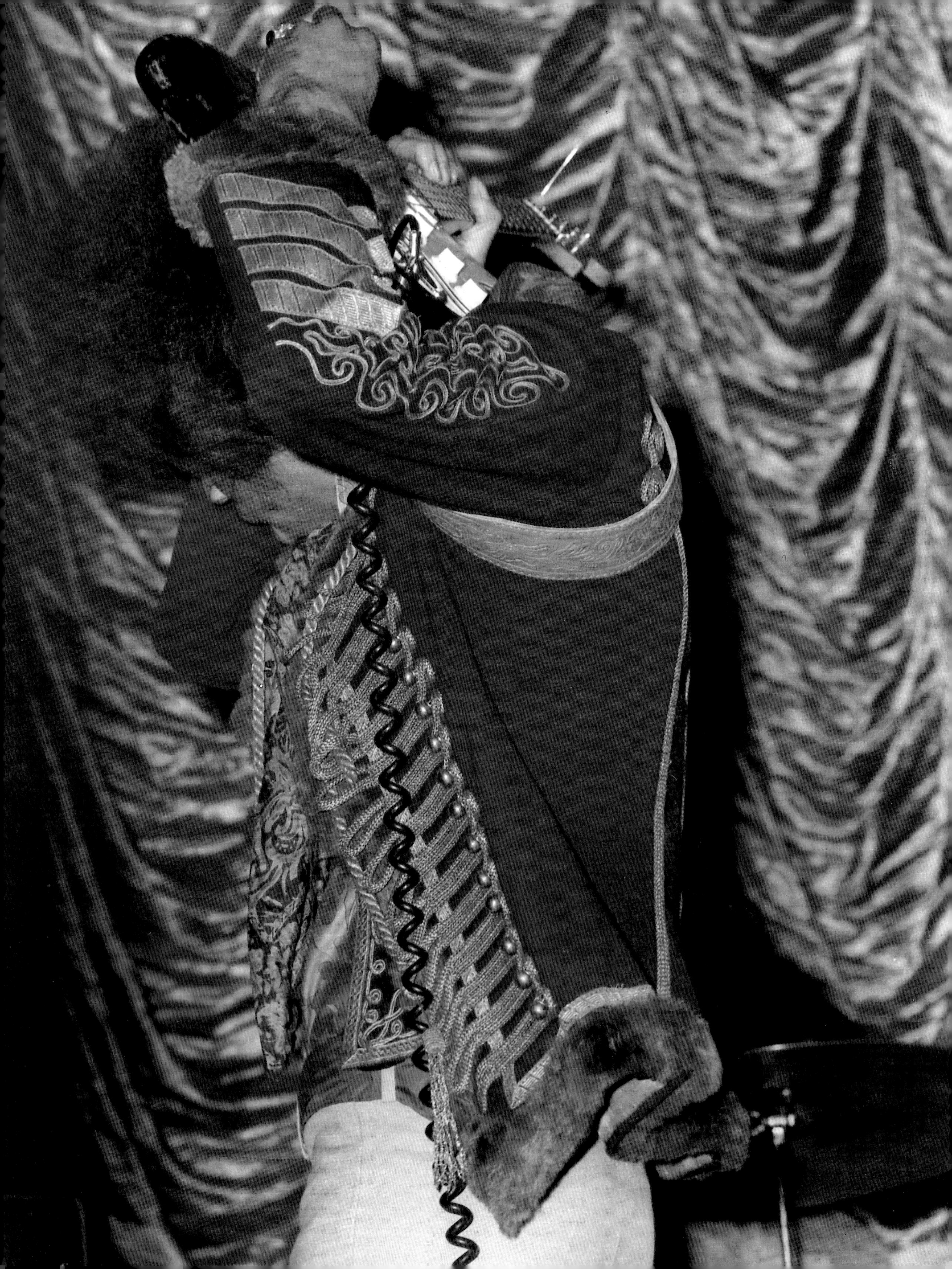

April 30
Sunday
Granada,
Tooting Broadway, London
Two shows at 18:00 and 20:30.
Mitch Mitchell: "Cat Stevens became a real snot, so on the matinee of the last show, when he was doing his hit 'I'm Gonna Get Me A Gun', I placed this mechanical robot on stage. Its chest opened up and all these little machine guns started blazing away. He tried to kick it off stage, but the thing refused to die. He didn't take the joke too well."

May 4
Thursday
BBC-TV Studios, Lime Grove, London
The Experience mimed 'The Wind Cries Mary' for a TV recording for *Top Of The Pops* BBC TV. The show is introduced by Jimmy Savile and is broadcast live. Neil Diamond is also a guest on the show.

May 6
Saturday
The Imperial Ballroom, Nelson
19.30 to 23.30. The Experience are supported by The Movement and The Jo De Brown Trust.

May 7
Sunday
Saville Theatre, London
Two shows at 18:00 and 20:30. Supporting The Experience are Denny Laine, Garnet Mimms, 1-2-3 and MC Rick Dane.

One reviewer wrote: "At London's Saville Theatre on Sunday, Hendrix proved, if proof was needed, that there is no other explosive force on the British pop scene today. To his friends he smiled and said: 'When I played in my backyard at home kids used to gather round and heard me and said it was cool. I wanna thank you now for making this my home'. Jimi and The Experience went through 'Foxy Lady', 'Can You See Me', 'Hey Joe', 'Like A Rolling Stone', 'Stone Free', 'Purple Haze', 'The Wind Cries Mary' and 'Wild Thing'. Hendrix seemed to have trouble with his guitar under the hot lights, while he was trying to tune up he said: 'Man is Eric Clapton in the house?'"

May 10
Wednesday
BBC-TV Studios, Lime Grove, London
The Experience record a live vocal version of 'The Wind Cries Mary' for *Top Of The Pops* BBC TV. The show is introduced by Jimmy Savile and is broadcast the next evening.

Later in the evening Jimi attends the Speakeasy club in Margaret Street where he jams with Amen Corner.

May 11
Thursday
The Experience fly from London Heathrow Airport and arrives at Le Bourget Airport in Paris. They are in Paris to record a live TV recording for the French pop program Music Hall De France, Tilt Magazine No 8. The show is introduced by Michel Drucker and is broadcast on May 24. Other guests are The Spencer Davis Group, Paul Jones, Jacques Dutronc and The Kinetic.

The Experience perform 'Hey Joe' to wild cheering from the audience and during 'Wild Thing' Jimi plays the guitar while laying on the floor. He concludes the song by attacking his amplifiers with his guitar and finally throws it on to the floor. Mitch kicks over his drum kit and they leave the stage. French photographer Jean-Pierre Leloir photographs the performance.

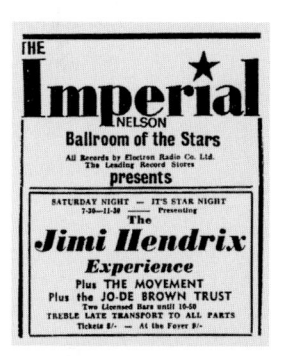

May 12
Friday
Bluesville 67 Club, Manor House, Seven Sisters Road, London

May 13
Saturday
Imperial College, Exhibition Road, Kensington, London

May 14
Sunday
Belle Vue/New Elizabethan, Manchester
The Experience are introduced by DJ Jimmy Savile.

May 15
Monday
Neue Welt,
U-Bahnhof Hermannplatz, Berlin
Two shows at 15:00 & 19:00.
The Experience are supported by The Beat Cats, Restless Sect, Shatters and Manuela. German photographer Klaus Achterberg photographs the performance.

May 16
Tuesday
Big Apple, Munich
Two shows

May 18
Thursday

The Experience make their debut on Germany's Beat, Beat, Beat TV show. After an introduction by Charlie Hickman, they start their performance with 'Stone Free' but Jimi's guitar sounds very strange. Although Jimi is using his Marshall stack, they are also using a mixture of equipment from the other groups. Mitch is forced to use the drums from Dave Dee's group. 'Hey Joe' is next and Jimi plays the guitar solo with his teeth, however the German audience just looks on blankly. Jimi tells the audience, "One moment, one moment", while he tunes his guitar for the last song of his set, 'Purple Haze'. At the end of the song he attacks the Marshall stack with his guitar, but still the audience shows no reaction.

The show is broadcast on May 29 at 20:15 to 21:00. Other guests include Dave Dee & Co, Sandie Shaw, Cherry Wainer and Don Storer.

In the evening everyone from the show retires to the K52 Club in Frankfurt. Jimi Hendrix jams most of the night with Mitch Mitchell, Dave Dee, Beaky, and Sandie Shaw. Dave Dee: "Jimi and Noel Redding, Beaky and me went out looning in Frankfurt in the evening at the K52. But Jimi refused to play lead guitar, so Noel Redding played lead guitar and Jimi played bass. Jimi said, 'I fancy a jam, but I don't wanna play guitar.' Beaky, who was our rhythm guitar, played drums. I don't remember Sandie Shaw doing anything to be quite honest. We played all the old rock and roll stuff, a bit of blues and 'Whole Lot Of Shaking'." The Experience eventually arrive back in their hotel rooms at 8:00am in the morning.

May 19
Friday
**Konserthallen,
Liseberg Nojespark, Gothenburg**

The Experience perform two shows supported by Cat Stevens, Mats & Brita, and DJ Clem Dalton. The Experience performs 'Can You See Me', 'Like A Rolling Stone', 'Hey Joe', 'Purple Haze' and 'Wild Thing'.

Pop In DJ Clem Dalton has to entertain the audience while Jimi's amplifier was being repaired. There was a quarrel backstage with Jimi and Cat Steven as to whom was the biggest star and who was going to end the show.

May 20
Saturday
Mariebergsskogen, Karlstad

The show is scheduled to start at 21:00. The support acts are Metrosextetten and Arnes. The Experience performs 'Foxy Lady', 'Hey Joe', 'The Wind Cries Mary', 'Purple Haze' and 'Wild Thing'.

May 21
Sunday
**Falkoner Centret,
Falkorner Alle 9, Copenhagen**

The Experience are supported by the Harlem Kiddies with King George, The Defenders and The Beefeaters.

They perform 'Foxy Lady', 'Hey Joe', 'Purple Haze', 'The Wind Cries Mary' and 'Wild Thing'.

May 22
Monday

The Experience attend a TV Studio in Helsinki for a live broadcast for Finland's Nuorten Tanssiketki pop show with Cat Stevens.

Kulttuuritalo, Helsinki

The Experience's 20:00 show is supported by First, Wantons, New Joys and DJ Antti Einio. They perform 'Purple Haze', 'Hey Joe', 'The Wind Cries Mary' and 'Wild Thing'.

May 23
Tuesday
**Klubb Bongo, New Orleans,
Friisgatan, Malmo, Sweden**

The Experience perform two shows and are supported by The Namelosers.

May 24
Wednesday

The Experience attend a live TV recording for Sweden's Popside TV show at TV Studios [TV-huset] in Stockholm. They perform a very subdued 'The Wind Cries Mary' and a lively 'Purple Haze', with Jimi attacking the amps at the end, to a small audience sitting on the floor. The show is broadcast, on June 11. During the afternoon, Jimi attends a Stockholm radio studio for a live interview broadcast with Roger Wallis for Swedish radio.

**Stora Scenen, Grona Lund,
Tivoli Garden, Stockholm**

The Experience are supported by Perhaps and Bread. The show starts at 20:00pm but Jimi first has to adjust the

PA before he can start. Then one of his amps decides to quite on him – which quickly gets changed. After a slight delay Jimi is now ready and fingers the opening feedback note to 'Foxy Lady' which is almost an instrumental version due to the bad PA system. Jimi is still having slight amp trouble through the song, but brings it to an end to loud cheers from the audience. "Testing, testing. Now what," says Jimi. Noel explains that there is something wrong with the microphones. Jimi continues with 'Rock Me Baby' with the PA system now working correctly. Jimi thanks the audience and remarks, "Now we'd like to do a song that brought us here in the first place, we'd like to dedicate it to everybody, all 13 of you. It goes something like this. I hope it comes out right, we have some bad trouble". Jimi proceeds with 'Hey Joe.' "Now we have a new album which is in England and it's named *Are You Experienced*. We'd like to do a track from the album and it's named 'Can You See Me' and dig, they're both in the key of F sharp." It's apparent that they are still having equipment trouble and while the road crews are fixing the problem, Jimi takes the opportunity to change guitars. Jimi continues with 'Purple Haze'. "Dig, I'd like to say that we have one more song to do, and I'd like to say that er, you know all this trouble and all this, well just forget about it. We'd like to do this last song for everybody here and if you can sing just join in and if you can't sing just hum in, you know and it goes something like this here. Plug your ears, thank you very much for coming." Jimi ends the show with 'Wild Thing'.

The second show of the evening is scheduled to be held at Jump In in Tivoli Gardens, but too many people turn up for the concert. The decision is quickly made to reschedule the concert to 'Dans In', which is able to hold more people.

Dans In, Grona Lund, Tivoli Garden, Stockholm
The Experience are again supported by Perhaps and Bread for their 22:00pm show. After the performance The Experience go to the En Till club in Stockholm where they jam with Swedish musicians.

May 27
Saturday
Star Palace, Kiel
Two shows. Noel Redding states that on this particular show, Jimi became so drunk he was completely unable to tune his guitar. Noel had to explain to the audience that Jimi was feeling unwell.

May 28
Sunday
Jaguar-Club, Scala, Minderstrasse 38, Herford
The Experience's 16:00pm show is supported by The Rivets and The Lions.

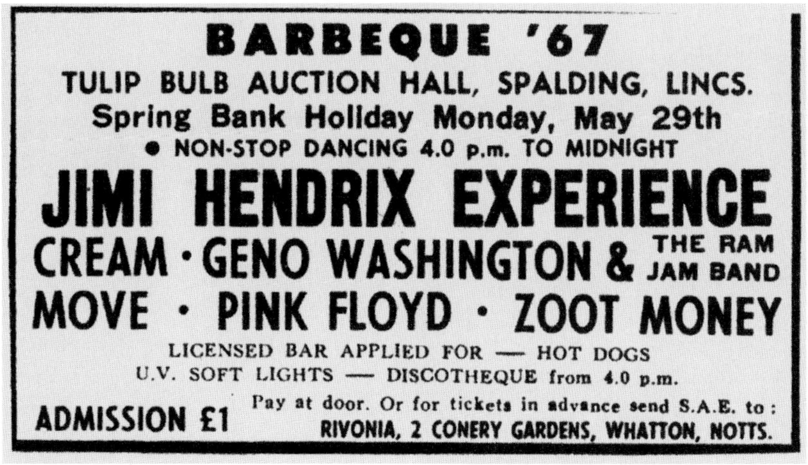

May 29
Monday
Barbeque 67, Tulip Bulb Auction Hall, Spalding, Lincoln
16:00 to 24:00. The small town of Spalding in Lincolnshire finds itself host to an unusually large amount of London's top groups. The event was organised by Brian Thompson and attracts thousands of people from all around the country, many of whom have no tickets, and decide to rampage through the town causing large amounts of damage. The event is held in a relatively small warehouse with a corrugated tin roof which is used for the auction of bulbs. A small stage is erected at one end of the warehouse and a small caravan outside acts as the dressing room for all the acts. A 4,000 strong audience is packed like sardines and there are even hot dog stands in the main hall. During the performances, thieves break into the caravan and a many of the groups' stage clothes are stolen.

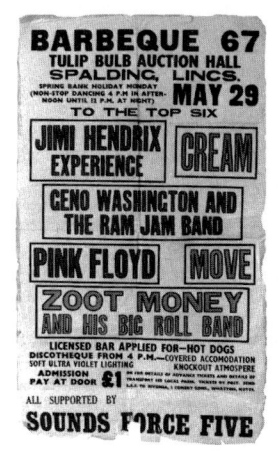

The Experience share the stage with Cream, Geno Washington and The Ram Jam Band, The Move, Pink Floyd and Zoot Money and His Big Roll Band. They are supported by local group Sounds Force Five. Conditions worsen for the tightly packed audience, especially those pressed against the four-foot stage. The heat is unbearable and Jimi is having trouble tuning his guitar. When the audience start jeering he yells back, "Fuck you, I'm gonna get my guitar in tune if it takes me all fucking night." Jimi finishes his performance by ripping all the strings off his guitar and smashing it to bits against his amplifiers. Then he knocks the amplifiers over which causes a short circuit, which in turn manages to fuse all the lights and plunges the hall into total darkness. The Experience returns to London the following day in organisers Bill Thompson's car.

May 31
Wednesday

Back in London, Jimi jams with Eric Clapton, Jack Bruce, Jose Feliciano and Edge on drums at the Speakeasy club in Margaret Street.

June 4
Sunday
Saville Theatre, London

The Experience perform two shows supported The Stormsville Shakers, Procol Harum, The Chiffons, and Denny Laine and His Electric String Band.

The Beatles' *Sgt Pepper* album was released the previous Friday, and all four Beatles are attending Jimi's concert at the Saville. Jimi takes the opportunity to show his appreciation for the album by opening his show with 'Sergeant Pepper's Lonely Hearts Club Band'. He continues with 'Foxy Lady', 'Like A Rolling Stone', 'Manic Depression', 'Hey Joe', 'Purple Haze' and 'The Wind Cries Mary', and treats the audience to the title song from his new album *Are You Experienced?*

Disc & Music Echo review the show: "Then, to a smashing, ear splitting 'Are You Experienced' Jimi was handed a guitar from the wings – a guitar he'd painted in glorious swirling colours and written a poem on the back dedicated to Britain and its audience. Bathed in a flickering strobe light, he crashed the guitar about the stage and hurled what was left of it to eager souvenir hunters in the audience."

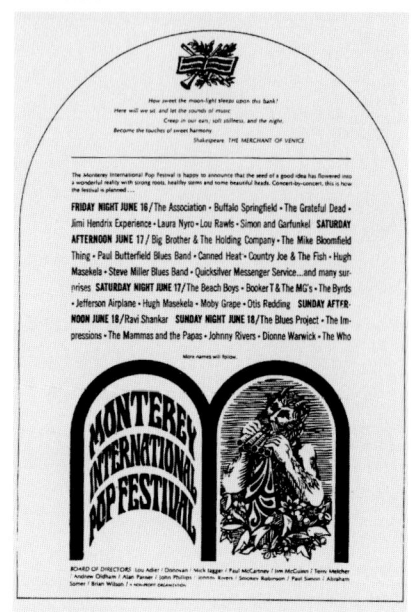

June 18
Sunday
Monterey International Pop Festival, Monterey, California

The line-up for the day features Ravi Shankar, The Blues Project, The Buffalo Springfield, The Who, The Grateful Dead, The Jimi Hendrix Experience and The Mamas & Papas. Jimi spends the afternoon sitting in the VIP area watching Ravi Shankar's performance.

The Experience take the stage and tune up their instruments for a few minutes in front of a quiet, unsuspecting audience. Brian Jones finally walks up to the microphone for his introduction. "I'd like to introduce a very good friend and a fellow countryman of yours. A brilliant performer and the most exciting guitarist I've ever heard... The Jimi Hendrix Experience."

The spotlights fall on Jimi dressed in orange ruffled shirt, red trousers, multi-coloured eyes jacket – which was designed by Chris Jagger – and a four-foot shocking pink feather boa around his neck. Without any introduction Jimi rushes straight into a very fast 'Killing Floor'.

He is showing signs of nerves as he speaks: "Yeah what's happening brother? Here's something else we got... a little thing called 'Foxy Lady'. My fingers won't move as you can see, you don't hear no sounds as you hear, but dig this. Hey baby, what's happening? Dig, I'll tell you what, let's get down to business alright, just give me one second to get down to business, dig this. I don't want nobody to think I'm a, you know (laughs)... I've gotta keep people honest, dig this. Yeah, dig brother, it's really outta site here, it didn't even rain, no buttons to push, but right now I'd like to dedicate this song to everybody here with hearts, any kind of hearts and ears. It goes something like this here."

Jimi proceeds to play the opening riff to 'Like A Rolling Stone' while introducing the song. "Yes, so as I say before it's really groovy. I'd like to bore you for about six or seven minutes and do a little thing." While still continuing with the introduction he plays a phrase on the guitar that must please him. "Yeah you've gotta excuse me for a minute. Let's let me play my guitar alright. Right now we'd like to do a thing by Bob Dylan and that's his grandmother over there [pointing to Noel Redding]. It's a little thing called 'Like A Rolling Stone'. Towards the end of the song, Jimi announces to the audience, 'Yes I know I've missed the verse, don't worry'. As he ends the song the stage lights are dimmed and the stage falls in darkness, Jimi lets his guitar ring with a power E chord for a few seconds. "Yeah dig this baby, we got a little tune running around called 'Rock Me Baby' well dig, we got our own little of 'Rock Me Baby' and it goes something like this here, the words will be wrong, but that's alright, dig this anyway." Jimi would later rework 'Rock Me Baby' into his own song 'Lover Man'.

"Excuse us for one second, we'd like to tune up because we care alright? Like, you know we was invited to this thing man, it was really groovy, cause it was 'Hey Joe' that really brought us here, so we'd like to try to do it for you our own way, so it goes something like this here." 'Hey Joe' is flawless and Jimi plays the solo with his teeth for the first time to his new American audience. "Thank you very much man, give us one more second to tune up alright, you know it's for your alls' benefit for all of ours' benefit. Ho man it was so groovy man in England man. These two cats, Bob Dylan's grandmother and Queen Bee over on drums, man we

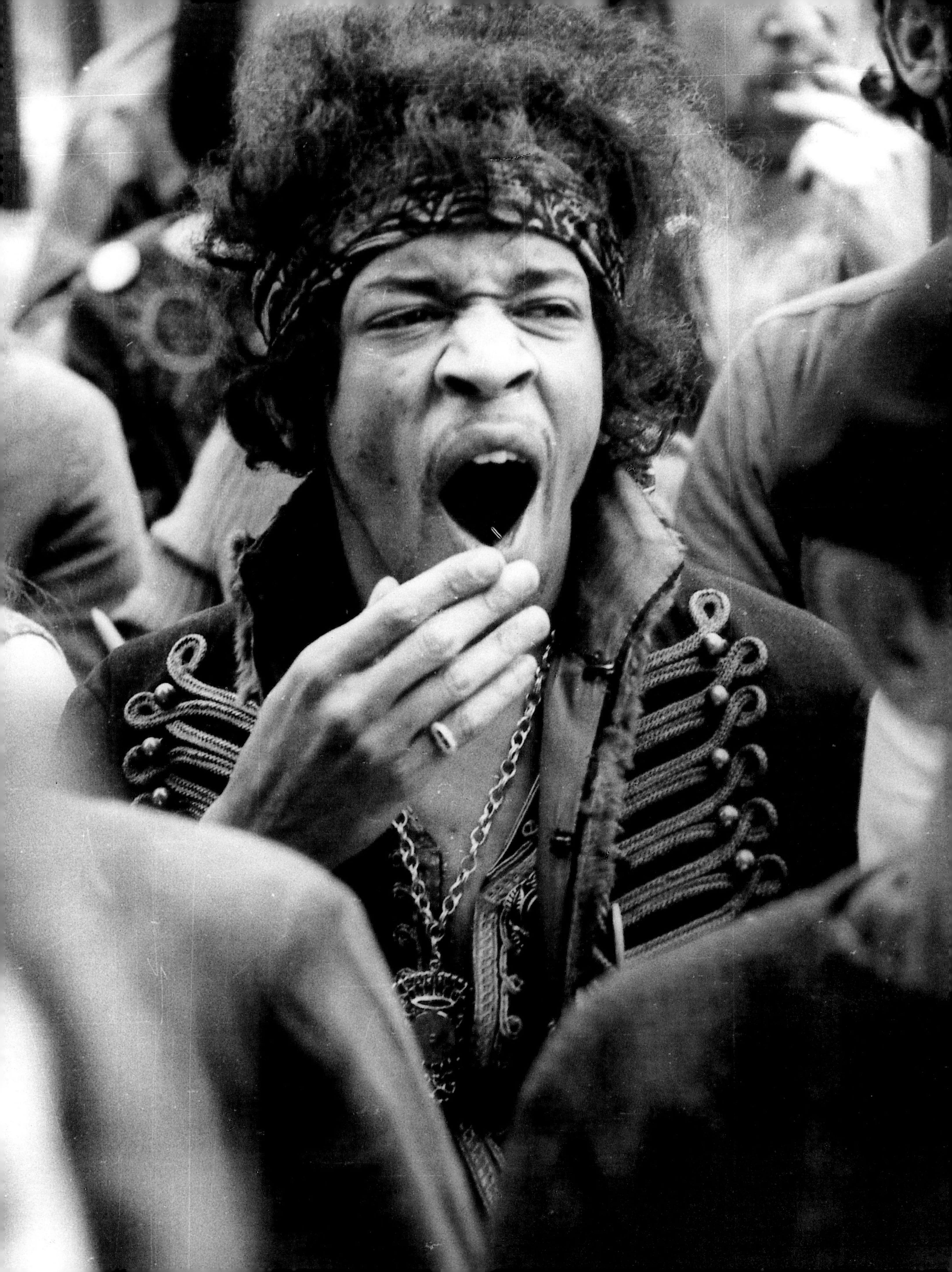

had so much fun brother. Yeah, this is Noel Redding on bass anyway, nobody's going to know us okay, Noel Redding on bass and we have Mitch Mitchell on drums, so there you go. Oh no, I think I'm out of tune, but anyway. Dig we was in England man and we all wanted to come to New York man, the golden streets of the Village. The reason why they're gold is dropping banana peels, but dig. We'd like to do a little that's on our LP its name 'Can You See Me' in the key of F sharp." Jimi tunes up and jokes to the audience, "Thank you very much and now we'd like to do another song... it goes something like this here." Jimi had performed 'Can You See Me' in the clubs of London, but this was the last known time he performed it in concert.

"Right now we got a song named 'The Wind Cries Mary' it goes something like this here. The next single here I hope." Other than during the TV show in Sweden in May, this was the first known time that Jimi performed the song on stage. "Thank you very much, we've only got two more songs to do. We have two more songs to do and we'd like to try to do this 'Purple Haze' man. I think it's gonna come out the same time, it's gonna be a double A-side it goes something like this here." 'Purple Haze' would become Jimi's anthem for most of his career. Jimi changes his guitar to a salmon pink Stratocaster that he has spray painted white with psychedelic designs drawn with felt tip pens. "Man, I'd like to say this, you know before, well you know, everybody says this man. It's something else man like, it is no big story about we couldn't make it here so we go over to England, and America doesn't like us because, you know our feet's too big and we got fat mattresses and we wore golden underwear. It ain't no scene like that brother. You know it's just, dig man. I was laying around and went to England and picked up these two cats and now here we are man. It was so, you know groovy to come back here this way you know, and really get a chance to really play you know. You know, I could sit up here all night and say thank you, thank you, thank you, you know, but I just want to rush and just grab you man and just... oh one of them thing man, you know one of them scene. But dig, I just can't do that, so what I'm gonna do, I'm gonna sacrifice something right here that I really love okay, oh thank you very much for Bob Dylan's grandmother. Anyway I'm gonna sacrifice something here that I really love man. Don't think I'm sill doing this, you know cause I don't think I'm losing my mind, last night man... hooo god, but anyway wait a minute. Anyway and, but today I think it's the right thing all right you know, so I'm not losing my mind. This is this for everybody here man, this is the only way I can do it you know. So we're gonna do the English and American combined anthem together okay. Don't get mad, nooooo, don't get mad. I want everybody to join in too... all right and don't get mad, this is it man, there's nothing I can do more than just. Oh all of those beautiful people out there."

Jimi turns his guitar upside-down and dive-bombs his guitar in time with the feedback sounds that it's producing, and launches into 'Wild Thing'. During the song, Jimi is on his knees and actually back rolls while still playing without missing a note. Towards the end of the song, Jimi attacks his amplifiers and simulates making love to the guitar against the amps. He then lays the guitar down on the stage in front of him coaxing sounds from it. He produces a tin of lighter fluid and proceeds to spray the guitar with petrol and then set it on fire with matches. After coaxing the flames to get higher, he picks up the guitar and proceeds to smash the guitar onto the stage. With the guitar in pieces, he throws out the shattered pieces to the eager audience. Some look a little stunned by the performance. Jimi has finally conquered America in one show. Chas is delighted with the performance and rushes from the press box to congratulate the band. When he gets there, he finds Mike Jeffery berating Jimi for breaking a mike stand during the performance.

Film director DA Pennebaker: "Jimi came over to me before he was due on stage and told me to make sure that I had full film magazines in all of the cameras for the last song. We more or less knew the running order of Jimi's set and so midway through 'Purple Haze' I directed all the film crews to reload their cameras for the last song. That is why 'Purple Haze' in the movie was incomplete."

June 20
Tuesday
Fillmore West,
San Francisco, California
The Experience perform two shows supported by Gabor Szabo and Jefferson Airplane. Although Jefferson Airplane is the headline act, they realise after the first night that it is impossible for them to follow The Experience. So they decided to pull out of the remaining shows. Fillmore owner Bill Graham gives The Experience a $2,000 bonus and an antique engraved watch to each member of the group.

June 21-24
Wednesday-Saturday
Fillmore West,
San Francisco, California
The Experience perform two shows each night supported by Gabor Szabo and Janis Joplin with Big Brother and The Holding Company.

June 25
Sunday
**Panhandle, Golden Gate Park,
San Francisco, California**
During the afternoon, The Experience give a free show in the park on the back of a flat bed truck. It was possibly done as publicity for the final night's Fillmore show, again supported by Gabor Szabo and Janis Joplin with Big Brother and The Holding Company.

June 27
Tuesday
Jimi is invited to jam at Steve Stills house in Malibu. The jam is reputed to have lasted 14 hours with Steve Stills, Hugh Masekela, Buddy Miles, and Bruce Palmer.

Stills, Hendrix, and drummer Buddy Miles meet up at a beach house in Malibu, which Buffalo Springfield had just rented. Stills re-creates the scene: "I set up my big amps, we took some acid and just went. We played quite literally for twenty straight hours. We must have made up fifty songs. But there was no tape running, no nothing we just played for the ocean.

Brucie [Palmer] eventually showed up, and, a little while later so did the sheriffs. They came to the door and asked, 'What's the deal?' And I said, 'Did you get a call?' 'No,' they said, 'We were just curious. This area is usually very quiet and you know, we were curious about who was playing.' I told 'em, 'Well, there's me and a, guy from Chicago and a guy from Seattle and we're just playing' blues and stuff'. And they said, 'Oh yeah? Well, I know what you're thinking but would it be okay if we parked across the street and listened?' I shrugged. So the guy said, 'Don't get paranoid because we're out there. We don't care what you're doing, we just want to listen. And if one of our sergeants shows up, someone'll sound a siren, which means just cool it for a few minutes.' So me and Hendrix jammed with the sheriff's protection! And it's that night I really started to learn how to play lead guitar."

July 1
Saturday
**Earl Warren Showground's,
Santa Barbara, California**
The Experience are supported by Country Joe and The Fish, Strawberry Alarm Clock and Captain Speed.

July 2
Sunday
**Whisky A Go Go,
Los Angeles, California**
The Experience are supported by Sam & Dave. Jimi Hendrix: "We had a great time in LA, where Dave Crosby and a group called The Electric Flag came round to see us at the Whisky A Go Go."

July 3 & 4
Monday/Tuesday
**The Scene Club,
301 West 46th Street, New York City**
The Experience are supported on both nights by Tiny Tim and The Seeds.

July 5
Wednesday
**Rheingold Festival,
Central Park, New York City**
The Experience are supported by The Young Rascals and Len Chandler.

July 7
Friday
**Garrick Theatre,
Greenwich Village, New York City**
Jimi Hendrix and Noel Redding attend a concert by Frank Zappa. Jimi jams on stage with Zappa and it's thought that this was the first time Jimi uses a wah-wah foot pedal.

Frank Zappa: "I think I was one of the first people to use the wah-wah pedal. I'd never heard of Jimi Hendrix at the time I bought mine; I didn't even know who he was. I had used wah-wah on Clavinet, guitar, and saxophone when we were doing *We're Only In It For The Money* in '67, and that was just before I met Hendrix. He came over and sat in with us at the Garrick Theatre that night and was using all the stuff we had on stage."

After the performance, Frank Zappa has to attend a photo shoot in New York for his *We're Only In It For The Money* LP. The album cover is a take off of The Beatles *Sgt Pepper* album. So Zappa invites Jimi along to take part in the session and he actually appears on the LP cover.

July 8
Saturday
Coliseum, Jacksonville, Florida
Supporting The Sundowners, Lynne Randell and The Monkees.

The Experience fly from John F. Kennedy International Airport and arrive at Atlanta International Airport for their connecting flight to Jacksonville in Florida to join the Monkees tour. The whole tour is travelling in a private DC-6 with a huge 'Monkee' emblem painted on the side. Also on the tour are Lynne Randell and The Sundowners who consisted of Bobby Dick, Kim Capli, Eddie Brick, Eddie Placidi, and Donnie DeMieri. Carol West, Lynne Randell's manager, takes all the photographs on the tour.

July 9
Sunday
Miami Beach Convention Hall, Miami, Florida
Supporting The Sundowners, Lynne Randell and The Monkees.

July 11
Tuesday
Coliseum, Charlotte, North Carolina
Supporting The Sundowners, Lynne Randell and The Monkees.

When Buffalo Springfield cross paths with The Monkees in the Midwest, Steve Stills discovers that The Monkees' opening act is Jimi Hendrix. "Jimi was my guru, man," says Stills. "Nobody could play guitar like that cat. Now, when I caught up with him on the Monkees tour, I proceeded to follow him around. Some people thought we were fags or that I was a groupie. But, hey, it wasn't like that at all. It was like I was going to music school, learning how to play lead guitar."

After one of these Monkees/Hendrix shows, a unique jam session takes place. Peter Tork recalls: "We were in this hotel room. Jimi and Stephen were sitting on these beds facing each other, just playing away on acoustic guitars. In between 'em was Micky Dolenz, slapping his guitar like, 'slap, whacka, slap, whacka, slap.' And all of a sudden Micky quit.

Then Stephen and Jimi stopped and Stephen said to Mickey, 'Why'd you stop playing?' Mickey said, 'I didn't know you were listening.' So there's one for ya – Hendrix, Stills, and Dolenz."

July 12
Wednesday
Coliseum, Greensboro, North Carolina
Supporting The Sundowners, Lynne Randell and The Monkees.

July 13-16
Thursday-Sunday
Forest Hills Stadium, Forest Hills, New York City
Supporting The Sundowners, Lynne Randell and The Monkees.

The show on July 16 is the final Experience concert on the Monkees' tour. In view of the incompatibility of the acts, it is decided that it would be best if Jimi leaves the tour. A story is concocted that the 'Daughters of the American Revolution' are protesting that Jimi's act is too obscene for the young audience that came to see The Monkees, so Dick Clark agrees to let them off the tour.

Chas Chandler: "I met them up at Forest Hills. Dick Clark was the promoter on the tour and Dick Clark and I cooked up this story of the Daughters Of The American Revolution. Dick Clark said, 'Whatever you put out I'll back it up, whatever is OK with me'. It took us all that day and night to convince Jeffery that we had to get off the tour and I said, 'Just remember one fucking thing, Jimi is signed to me, and you don't have a fucking contract with him'."

July 17
Monday
Waldorf Astoria, 301 Park Avenue, New York City
The Experience give interviews about leaving the Monkees' tour. However, the moment the news is releases, they are asked to leave the Waldorf Astoria and are forced to move to the Hotel Gorham on West 55th Street. The Experience then attends a press conference regarding the Monkees tour at the Warwick Hotel in Manhattan where Jimi gives a telephone interview with *New Musical Express*.

Jimi Hendrix: "Firstly they gave us the 'death' spot on the show, right before The Monkees were due on, the audience just screamed and yelled for the Monkees! Finally they agreed to let us go on first and things were much better. We got screams and good reactions, and some kids even rushed the stage. But we were not getting any billing, all the posters on the show just screamed out *Monkees*. Then some parents who brought their young kids complained that our act was vulgar. We decided it was just the wrong audience. I think they're replacing me with Micky Mouse."

July 20
Thursday
**Salvation Club,
Greenwich Village, New York City**
Part of this performance is filmed showing Jimi wearing a new Military jacket.

July 21-23
Friday-Sunday
**Cafe A Go Go,
152 Bleecker Street, New York City.**
The Experience perform two shows each night.

July 25
Tuesday
Sly and The Family Stone début at the Generation Club, 52 West 8th Street, New York City. B.B. King is their opening act. Jimi attends the concert and ends up jamming with Ted Nugent, B.B King and Al Kooper.

July 26-29
Wednesday-Saturday
Each night Jimi jams with John Hammond Jr at Gaslight club in MacDougal Street in New York's Greenwich Village. Eric Clapton joins them for the last three nights.

August 3, 4, 5, 7, 8
Thursday, Friday, Saturday, Monday & Tuesday
**Salvation, Greenwich Village,
New York City**

August 9-13
Wednesday-Sunday
**Ambassador Theatre,
Washington DC**
Two shows each night supported by Natty Bumpo. On August 10, Mitch is taken ill with appendix trouble and they have to quickly find another drummer to fill in for him. Mitch is back on the 12th. The last night of this series of concerts was used for fund raising for the Keep The Faith youth fund.

August 15
Tuesday
**Fifth Dimension Club,
Ann Arbor, Michigan**
Two shows. The Experience perform 'Sergeant Pepper's Lonely Hearts Club Band', 'The Wind Cries Mary', 'Foxy Lady', 'Hey Joe' and 'Purple Haze'. While in America during his first tour, Jimi has purchased a Gibson Flying V, which he hand paints in psychedelic designs. This concert has the first photographic evidence of Jimi playing this guitar and also using a wah-wah pedal live.

August 18
Friday
**Hollywood Bowl,
Hollywood, California**
Two shows supported by The Mamas and The Papas and Scott McKenzie.

August 19
Saturday
**Earl Warren Showgrounds,
Santa Barbara, California**
The Experience are supported by Moby Grape, Captain Speed, Tim Buckley and MC Jim Salzer.

August 22
Tuesday
BBC TV Studios, Manchester
Back in the UK, The Experience attend a TV recording for *Dee Time*. The show is introduced by Simon Dee and is broadcast live from 18:25pm to 19:05pm. Other guests include Engelbert Humperdinck and The King Brothers. After the broadcast the Experience return to London.

August 24
Thursday
BBC TV Studios, Lime Grove, London
The Experience attend a TV recording for *Top Of The Pops* to perform their new single 'The Burning Of The Midnight Lamp'. The show is introduced by Pete Murray and is broadcast live.

There are only two live acts on this week's show, The Jimi Hendrix Experience and Alan Price. However, the BBC sound technicians manage to mix up the two backing tapes. As Jimi is introduced to perform to 'The Burning Of The Midnight Lamp' the wrong track is played over Jimi's mime and instead of 'Midnight Lamp' the introduction to Alan Price's 'The House That Jack Built' is played instead. Jimi commented, "I like the voice man, but I don't know the words."

1967 July/August 57

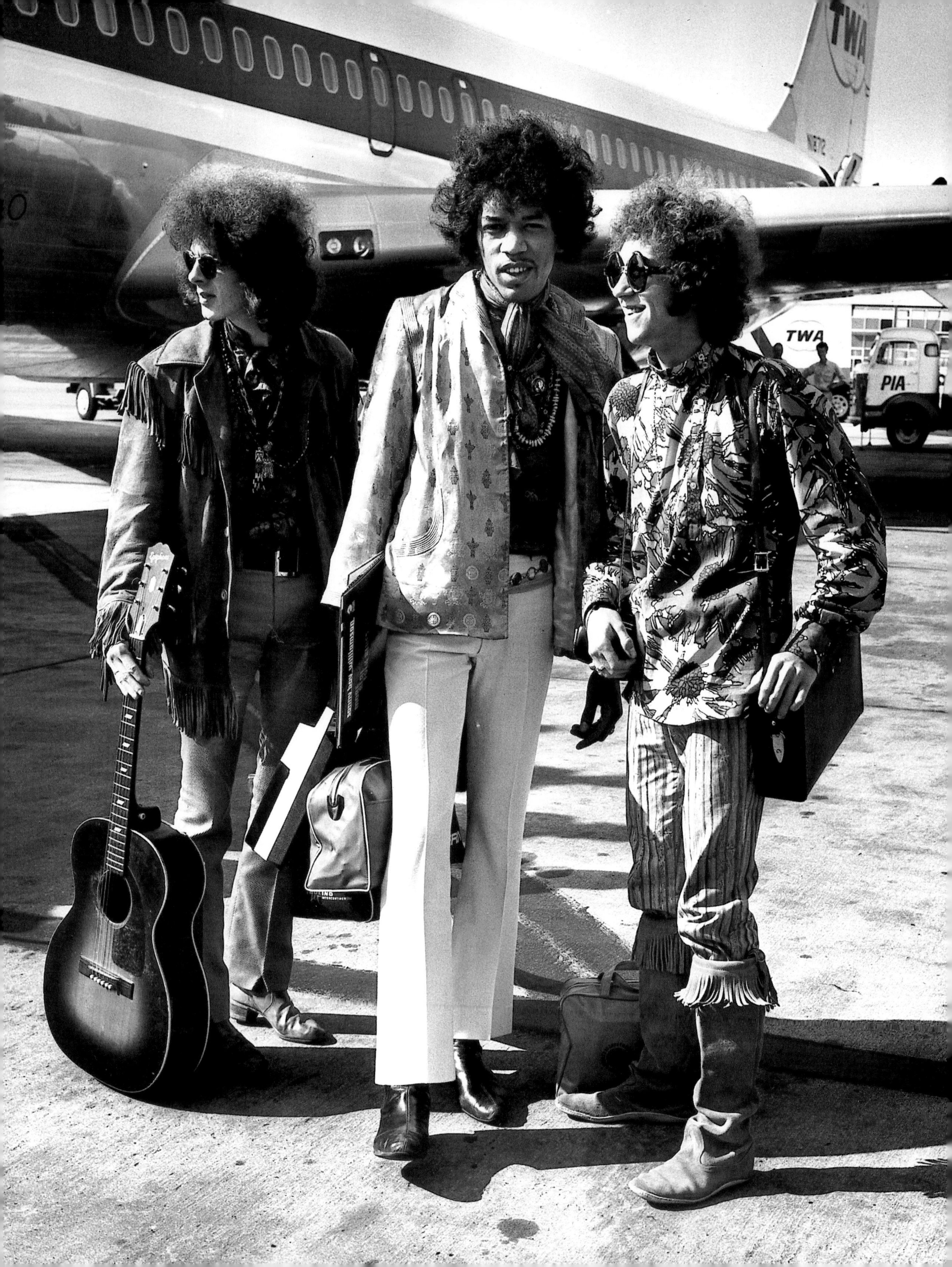
TWA
TWA
PIA

Pete Murray: "On *Top Of The Pops*, when they were playing backing tracks at that time, they put on the wrong backing track which amazed Jimi Hendrix. I'll never forget it and they came back to a shot of me to make an announcement and an apology and I was reading either the *Melody Maker* or *Disc* at the time. I looked up and I thought, 'Oh yes there has been a little bit of a mistake'. So I said, 'Well we're put on the right backing track now and with any luck we might get 'The Last Waltz' by Engelbert Humperdinck for Jimi Hendrix."

called 'Let Me Stand Next To Your Old Lady', I mean 'Let Me Stand Next To Your Fire'. Right now, we'd like to slow it down a little bit and dedicate it to a girl's name, er. I writ this song specially for a girl named Gertrude and little Irene Handle and, er, what are you talking about, Miss Lee Allen and er, Lucy a little song called 'The Wind Cries Mary.'

The song had actually been written months previously for Kathy Etchingham. As Jimi finishes the song, someone in the audience asks Jimi if they can pull his hair, Jimi replies, "Just like can you pull my hair? Nobody can pull my hair; I can't even pull my hair you Californian foxy lady."

and 'I Don't Live Today' which he dedicates to the American Indians. Then continues the blues theme and plays 'Red House'. This is the first know live version. Jimi then introduces 'Hey Joe', apologising to the audience for the continuing amp trouble and introduces the last song. "We went out with a funny child last night. I met this girl; she was really outta site man. I said baby what you doing? She says, 'Well you know I'm all right, how about you?' I said, 'Well you know everything's the same old thing, just a big drag'. I said, 'Baby what is that you've got in that little sack there?' She said this and she opened another one like this. I said. 'Oh close it, close it baby, what's happening?' I was wondering... she took a little something. So I stuck my fingers in and boom (emulating the sound on the guitar) a big 'Purple Haze'."

Despite the equipment trouble Jimi was in a great humour during the show but the mood was to quickly change for everyone performing at the Saville Theatre that night. News came in just before the second show that the Saville's owner, Beatles manager Brian Epstein, had just died. It was decided that the second show should be cancelled out of respect.

August 27
Sunday
Saville Theatre, London

The Experience are supported by The Crazy World Of Arthur Brown, The Crying Shames and Tomorrow (featuring Keith West).

After the group is introduced to the cheers of the audience, Jimi thunders straight in with 'Summertime Blues'. Jimi had never performed this song before and there is no evidence that he ever did again. Jimi is in a great mood as he jokes with the audience about the London police. "Should be calling me in as they call it, is that right? You collarred me (laughs)... yeah okay then. Flower power, we'll walk. Dig we'll use flower power while they're chasing you up a hill, well we run out of gas didn't we, you can't fight in London anyway. Like to do a song Jimi hit the feedback note to 'Foxy Lady' but stops and remarks, "No I think I'll try one more time", then continues with the song. "Gee we'd like go to move on and do a little thing slightly above Muddy Waters, now don't panic. We'd like to do a song of our own way and, cause I can't remember the words. And, er, it's a little thing on a very..." Jimi is interrupted by the amps buzzing loudly and comments, "Embarrassing situation", then continues with his introduction. "A very, very silly blues, a simple little blues, well silly. I'd like to do it for everybody here." But the amps start buzzing again and are quickly changed by the road crew. "Here's a song we'd like to celebrate with the tune's birthday. It's been around from, since 1922. Never forget which the two who's been with me." To which you can hear Kathy Etchingham reply: "Oh thank you." Jimi continues with 'Catfish Blues'

1967 August 59

Though Jimi and the other acts though that Brian would have wanted the show to go on, it was cancelled anyway.

In the evening Jimi jammed with Ian Matthews, Richard Thompson, Ashley Hutchings and Simon Nicol of Fairport Convention at London's Speakeasy Club.

August 29
Tuesday
**Nottingham Blues Festival,
Sherwood Rooms, Nottingham**
The Experience are supported by Jimmy James and The Vagabonds, Jimmy Cliff, Wynder K. Frogg and Long John Baldry. They perform 'Sergeant Pepper's Lonely Hearts Club Band', 'Killing Floor', 'Fire', 'Hey Joe', 'I Don't Live Today', 'Like A Rolling Stone' and 'Purple Haze'.

September 2
Saturday
**German TV Studios,
Berlin, West Germany**
The Experience attend a live TV broadcast with visiting English band Traffic. They perform 'Can You See Me' and 'The Burning Of The Midnight Lamp' for 4-3-2-1, Germany II TV, ZDF.

September 3
Sunday
**Konserthallen,
Lisebergs Nojespark, Gothenburg**
The Experience perform two thirty-minute shows supported by The Outsiders and a local group called Lucas. They are immediately plagued by equipment trouble during the first show but still manage to perform 'Foxy Lady', 'Rock Me Baby', 'The Wind Cries Mary', 'Fire' and 'Purple Haze'. After the performance Jimi kicks over his two amplifiers, explaining to the audience how embarrassing it is for him to have to perform with such bad equipment.

September 4
Monday
**Stora Scenen, Grona Lund,
Tivoli Garden, Stockholm**
The first show commences at 20:00pm with the MC making a stern announcement to the audience who in turn start to barrack him. Then Jimi takes the stage to a warm reception. "Hello, It's very groovy to be back here in Stockholm you know" and without any introduction he starts off the show with 'Sergeant Pepper's Lonely Hearts Club Band'. "Yeah okay then, if everybody's still here, we'd like to go ahead on with a song we've arranged ourselves, a little thing called 'Rock Me Baby'. Noel Redding announces that they are going to do an old blues number, Jimi tells the audience, "Yeah, like Noel said, we'd like to do a little bit of Muddy Waters blues type, but we'd like to do it our own way, which is nice and clean." In the meantime Jimi has changed guitars to his Gibson Flying V, remarking to the audience, "What's wrong? Haven't you seen a guitar like this before? Golly." Someone in the audience shouts, "Yeah Kinks." Jimi then proceeds to play 'Catfish Blues'. "Right now, we'd like to start from the very beginning again and do a song that really brought us here, which is really outta site. Like to say thank you very much and dedicated to all three and a half of you out here (laughs) anyway It called 'Hey Joe' and goes something like this." After ending the song, Jimi plays the first three chords to 'The Wind Cries Mary' but decides not to play it. "I like to say that we have one more number to do and we'd like to dedicate this one to everyone, you know it's been really groovy playing, so to show our appreciation for you, we'd like to tune up our guitars. We'd like to do 'Purple Haze' for you all right, for the last one."

Instead of the familiar normal introduction Jimi proceeds to play a very wild freaky high volume feedback introduction. The show ends with the group thanking the audience to loud cheering.

**Dans In, Grona Lund,
Tivoli Garden, Stockholm**
The second show commences at 22:00pm with the band tuning up. Jimi announces, "Thank you very much, we'd like to start now." Jimi starts off by playing an Indian type riff that goes into 'Killing Floor'. "Thank you, yeah thank you very much." After tuning up again, Jimi continues, "Yeah okay then, thank you very much, we'd like to go ahead and do a song named 'Foxy Lady'. Jimi continues with 'Catfish Blues'. The audience claps loudly while Jimi sorts out another guitar, but the audience thinks he's taking too long and starts to slow hand clap, so Noel and Mitch play a little jazz riff in time to their claps. Jimi remarks, "Thank you very much, that was really out of site, you know with the way you were all clapping. Right now, I hope er. We'd like to do a song that really started us together you know, and er like to say..." At that point someone in the audience does something to make the rest laugh, Jimi remarks, "Oh yeah, when they say skol that the main thing. Well anyway, before this cat loses his eyes, we'd like to go ahead and do this song. Oh right now, there a certain time right here, we'd like to tune up if you don't mind okay, we'd like to take one minute to tune up. Yeah, we was gonna play a song named 'Are You Experienced' but somebody is right?" he adds, referring to the person in the audience. "Somebody is. So we'll do 'Hey Joe' for you all right."

After the song Noel jokes with the audience and Jimi does something on the guitar to make a few girls scream, Jimi remarks, "Yeah okay then. Okay we're gonna try to do let me stand next to your old lady, I mean, your girlfriend, I mean 'Let Me Stand Next To Your Fire'. After the song Jimi again has difficulties trying to tune his guitar. "Yeah, we're having slight difficulties, this will only take one second. I'm sorry for taking your time, we'd like to do a slow number now it's called 'The Wind Cries Mary'."

Someone in the audience shouts out for 'Red House'. "Oh man, see we play the 'Red House', but see he (Noel) forgot his guitar, you know he plays the regular guitar on that one, you know old time folk string guitar." Jimi proceeds to play a few riffs of the rhythm to 'Red House' and says, "Lets see him play that part then." Noel continues playing the bass part to 'Red House' and Mitch joins in for a few seconds. Jimi jokingly says, "Well that's why we never play that one. Dig, this is Bob Dylan's grandmother on bass, Noel Redding. Oh well, then we have this Queen Bee better known as Mitch Mitchell on drums." Noel quips in with, "We've got Jimi Henpecked" to the audience's amusement. He then asks if they have chickens in Sweden. Jimi continues, "Okay then we got one more song to do and we'd like to dedicate it to everybody in here you know, all those people over there g-o-l-l-y, oh I'm scared now." Jimi wolf whistles a girl in the audience with his guitar. "Okay we've got one more last number to do. Okay now, now don't say anything but listen, like one time, listen if you can understand this. One time man, I was walking around the streets in Stockholm and this girl say, 'Hey man we must have something to turn you on to'. I said 'Y-e-a-h'. She said, 'Yeah man', you know. And so what does it represent, you know what is it or something like that. She says, 'Well you can take it in any kind of way you know' and, er, so I went on and did the seam up and the next thing I know man, everything was just nothing but a 'Purple Haze' can you understand that? Nothing but this purple haze and it sounded like this to me."

Again Jimi starts of the song with another wild feedback introduction. Jimi ends the song in the same fashion adding a small riff of 'The Star Spangled Banner.' Jimi would add this to many of his later concerts, but this is the first time he has played it.

September 5
Tuesday

The Experience record a live radio recording at the Radiohuset, Studio 4 in Stockholm before a live audience.

The Experience again open with 'Sergeant Pepper's Lonely Hearts Club Band'. "Yeah, thank you very much that was our own little thing. I'd like to do this song that really got us into something, a little song called 'Hey Joe.'"... "Thank you very much, now while your ears are still ringing, we'd like to go on and do another little tune called 'I Don't Live Today' dedicated to the American Indian."... "So right now we'd like to slow it down a little bit and do one of the tunes we recorded as a single. It's a little thing called 'The Wind Cries Mary'."... "Yeah okay than, we'd like to proceed on with a little tune from our LP... it's named 'Foxy Lady'." ... "Thank you very much, we'd like to go ahead on with this tune named 'Let Me Stand Next To Your Fire'."... "We'd like to do our latest release... it's a thing called 'The Burning of the Midnight Lamp'... it's the first time we ever did it in front of people."... "So right now we'd like to do our last number and say thanks a lot for coming and listening. It's a song named 'Purple Haze'." Jimi is now adding the wild feedback introduction to the song at almost all of his concerts around this time.

September 6
Wednesday
Idrottshallen, Vasteras

The Experience perform two shows supported by Mersey Sect, AB Musik, The Deejays and The Outsiders.

September 7
Thursday
Club Filips, Stockholm

This is probably the occasion when Jimi Hendrix jams with Bo Hansson & Janne Karlsson. The jam lasts four hours and 15 minutes, and everything is recorded. Hansson & Karlsson called one of the songs they jammed on 'Tax Free'. Jimi would go on to play this song many times in concert. However, Noel Redding did not attend this jam session.

Later in the evening, The Experience jam in another Stockholm club called the En Till Club. Jimi used Noel's bass guitar turned upside down while Noel played lead guitar.

September 8
Friday

The Experience attend a TV recording at a TV Studio in Sandviken. The show is broadcast on September 10 but no other details are known. After the recording they leave around 1:00pm to travel to Hogbo for the evening's concert.

Popladen/Hogbo Bruk, Hogbo

The Experience perform two show at 18:00 and 21:00 supported by The Midnighters, The Halifax Team and The Outsiders. After the concert, Jimi is interviewed by Flor for *Gefle Dagblad*.

1967 August/September

62 Jimi Hendrix Concert File

September 9
Saturday
Mariebergsskogen, Karlstad
The Experience perform two shows at 20:00 and 22:00 supported by Jorgen Reinholds. After the performance Noel Redding is interviewed by Varmlands Folkblad.

September 10
Sunday
**Stora Salen,
Akademiska Foreningen, Lund**
The Experience perform two show at 19:00 and 22:00 supported by Bread and Hansson & Karlsson.

As The Experience takes the stage for their first performance of the evening. Jimi tells the audience: "Thank you very much er..." before the group are introduced by the MC. Jimi tunes up, thank the audience again and starts with 'Sergeant Peppers Lonely Hearts Club Band'. "Thank you very much, that's a little warm up tune. I'd like to say that I'm playing with dead strings, these strings are no good, I've had [them] on for three and half years, and are about ready to snap off. Anyway we'd like to continue on with a song called em, 'Foxy Lady' which is on the LP." Noel Redding then announces that they are now going to play an old blues that they arranged themselves. Jimi comments: "Yeah, like er, Noel Redding said, you know we're gonna do this er... little Muddy Water's blues, a nice clean little blues you know. We're gonna do it our own clean little way you know, and er... we're gonna feature the drummer Mitch Mitchell on it if you don't mind." Jimi continues with 'Catfish Blues'. "Thank you very much, yeah okay then. Er, I'd like to say, right now there's a certain time in the programme, which we call, tune up time. And if you don't mind we'd like to tune up one second all right, just one minute." While Jimi tunes his guitar, he comments: "We tune up because we really care for your poor little ears out there, you know ears, we really care for your ears. That's why we play so loud, okay then. We got a song named 'Let Me Stand Next To Your Fire' if you don't mind us doing this." Noel then announces that they are going to slow the pace down and do 'The Wind Cries Mary'. Jimi comments: "You'll have to excuse this trouble I have with this raggedy guitar, because you know It keeps jumping out of tune, because the strings are very old you know. About as old as I am about a hundred and ten." Jimi continues to try to tune his guitar then comments: "Oh anyway, bully, I'm gonna just do it anyway, because... we're gonna have to try to do 'The Wind Cries Mary' for you. It's a record that we did back in er, 1988 [laughs] next Wednesday. Here we go." After the wong, someone in the audience interrupts Jimi by shouting. Jimi comments: "Oh yeah, no no I can't do that either. Er I don't know what to play, let see how much time do we have." Noel suggest Jimi play 'Purple Haze'. Jimi comments: "Well yeah, okay then, but wait a minute I've got to tune my guitar, that'll give me time, a few seconds." Jimi continues to tune his guitar and announces: "Take an intermission if you want to, go ahead on and take a one minute intermission... now that, you know. Okay I'll tell you what... we've had to break down and do it, we're gonna do this little top forty R&B song, it's name [is] 'Have Mercy, Have Mercy Baby, Have Mercy, Have Mercy On Me.' And it goes something like this here. We do it because we forgot the words to all our other songs." This is the only known time The Experience plays this particular song. Afterwards someone shouts out for 'Manic Depression'. The whole group says: "Oh right". Jimi announces: "Er em we'd like to do a song named 'Manic Depression' if you don't mind. We got so many programme directors in here, this is one programme director, he's gonna tell us what to play next. We'd like to do 'Manic Depression'. Afterwards someone shouts out for 'Purple Haze'. Jimi comments: "Yeah we've got one more number to do, I think we've got another show to do, you know, so we can get the other songs in the other show. But we've been having very slight difficulties, er as where the amps don't work sometimes you know. So we'd like to end this show now with a song called 'Purple Haze'." Jimi tunes his guitar one final time and announces: "So we'd like to start the song off slightly different, it's a little thing called... er you know 'Flip Flop' That's a little thing I learned back in Texas at eight." After a wild feed back introduction, Jimi ends the show with 'Purple Haze'.

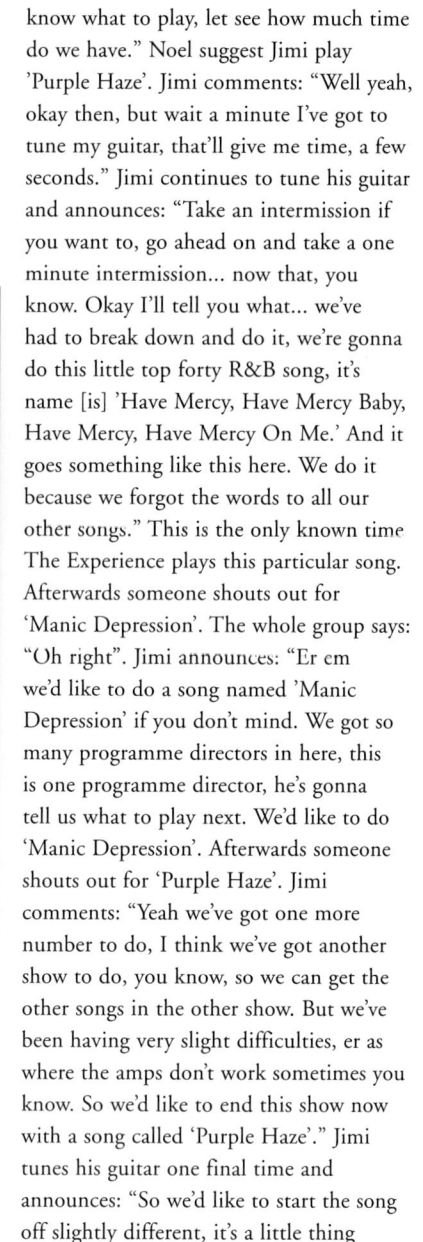

September 11
Monday
**Stora Scenen, Grona Lund,
Tivoli Garden, Stockholm**
The first show commences at 20:00pm when The Experience are introduced by a Swedish MC in Adolph Hitler style, much to the amusement of the audience. Jimi comments, "Yeah thank you very much anyway, hooray, all thirteen of you, thank you. We'd like to do a song called 'Foxy Lady' if you don't mind." ...

"Yeah thank you. I'd like to...." Jimi stops abruptly and asks Noel Redding, "What is this?" to laughter from the audience. "Well anyway... I'd like to say we'd like to do this tune now for a girl named of Eva, she sent us some flowers and stuff like that and it was really outta site. And we'd like to do our new single now if you don't mind okay. It's named 'The Burning of the Midnight Lamp' [and is] dedicated to Eva." Eva is Eva Sundqvist who would meet up with Jimi again in January 1969 and would give birth to his son James Daniel Sundqvist. After the song Jimi proceeds to tune his guitar and laughs as he tells the audience, "This guitar's so out of tune. Here we go 'The Burning of the Midnight Lamp'." The audience clap in appreciation as Noel remarks, "Thank you very much, a lovely record." After another tune up Jimi announces, "Yeah we'd like to continue on with a song named let me stand next to your old lady, I mean 'Let Me Stand Next To Your Fire'." Noel remarks to the audience that it's very cold and announces that they are going to play an old blues number. Jimi tell the audience, "We'd like to have Mitch Mitchell do the drum solo on this next blues. It's a very clean type of blues written by Muddy Waters and we'd like to do it our own clean way, you know." The audience laugh and Jimi remarks, "What's up man... been hearing bad things about us that's not true?'." Noel remarks, "We don't take our trousers off on stage either." Jimi continues, "Here we go... the thing called Cat, we'll call it 'Catfish Blues'." Mitch does a lengthy drum solo during the song and this will become a feature of 'Catfish Blues' in the future. Later in the group's career, Mitch's drum solos will get longer and more frequent.

Someone in the audience shouts out for Jimi to play 'Hey You'll' which sparks laughter from everyone. Jimi quickly remarks, "Hey, someone asked us to play 'Hey You'll'. I'll tell you what, I don't the words to that song man, but I'll tell you what, we'll try to play 'Hey Joe' for you though okay. You know when you play outside, it's very hard to keep the guitar in tune, so between numbers, you'll see us tuning up all the time, you understand? Tune up, you know, guitar, outside. (Laughs) Well anyway, it's very cold out here so just give me one chance to tune up. Anyway we'd like to do 'Hey Joe' for you and Eva." After 'Hey Joe' he says. "We got time to do one more song, we only got, the man has now told us we can only do one song more." The audience shouts no and Jimi sings "I dreamed I was there in teenybop heaven. (Laughs) I'm sorry I just had to say Meg, I'm sorry. Okay here we go, we're gonna do a song named 'Purple Haze' dedicated to all the haze makers."

Dans In, Grona Lund, Tivoli Garden, Stockholm
The second show commences at 22:00pm with the Experience performing 'Killing Floor', 'I'm Your Hoochie Coochie Man', 'The Burning Of The Midnight Lamp' and 'Wild Thing'.

After the performance Jimi and Mitch jam with Janne Karlsson and George Wadenius at the Club Filips in Stockholm. Jimi plays bass guitar.

September 12
Tuesday
**Stjarnscenen,
Lisebergs Nojespark, Liseberg,
Gothenburg**
The Experience perform two shows. After the performance Jimi is interviewed by Gosta Hansson for *Goteborgs-Tidningen*.

1967 September 63

September 15
Friday
Bluesville Club '67,
The Manor House,
Seven Sisters Road, London
Jimi jams with Eric Burdon & The New Animals.

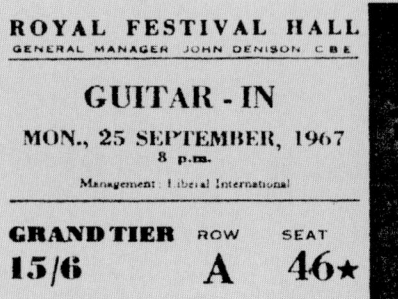

September 25
Monday
'Guitar-In' in aid of
'International Liberal Year',
Royal Festival Hall, London
The Experience are added to the bill of a special charity event organised by the Liberal Party in aid of the Liberal International Anti-Racialist Appeal Fund set up to send teacher-training books and equipment to Africa. The event is given the name 'Guitar In' and is intended as a display of different aspects of guitar playing. During the afternoon The Experience rehearse and take part in a film session. Before the concert, The Experience are photographed with Liberal leader Jeremy Thorpe.

Paco Pena, Bert Jansch, Tim Walker and Sebastian Jorgenson all take part in the festival.

October 6
Friday
The Experience are at the BBC Playhouse Theatre in Northumberland Avenue, London, to record a programme for BBC Radio One's Top Gear. The show is introduced by Pete Drummond and Tommy Vance and broadcast on October 15 between 14:00pm and 17:00pm.

Jimi uses this session to play the kind of blues he really enjoys. They record their own arrangement of Muddy Waters 'Catfish Blues', loosely titled 'Experiencing The Blues'. Next Jimi records two alternate versions of 'Driving South' which he last played in Greenwich Village with Curtis Knight. He takes the opportunity to play 'Little Miss Lover' that was recorded in the studio only a few days earlier. Jimi would only play this song live one further time, during his concert in Toronto in 1969.

After an interview with Brian Matthews, Jimi then proceeds to play 'The Burning Of The Midnight Lamp' and finally concludes the session with his own version of Elvis's 'Hound Dog' complete with everyone barking and howling like dogs throughout. The session ends with everyone falling about laughing.

Visiting the BBC on the same day is Stevie Wonder. Jimi and Noel Redding take part in an informal jam session with Stevie playing drums. They jam loosely around the Stevie's song 'I Was Made To Love Her'. Fortunately the session was recorded but did not get aired until May 25, 1979, on BBC Radio One's *Friday Rock Show* with Tommy Vance

October 7
Saturday
The Wellington Club,
Dereham, Norfolk
The Experience are supported The Flower People and The Rubber Band.

October 8
Sunday
Saville Theatre, London.
The Experience perform two shows supported by the Crazy World Of Arthur Brown, The Herd and Eire Apparent. The MC is Len Marshall. They perform 'The Wind Cries Mary', 'The Burning Of The Midnight Lamp', 'Foxy Lady', 'Hound Dog', Bob Dylan's 'Can You Please Crawl Out Your Window', 'Purple Haze' and 'Wild Thing'.

October 9
Monday
Olympia, Paris
The Experience are supported by The Pebbles. Arrangements have been made to professionally film the show. However, only 'Wild Thing' has ever been released – featured in the Peter Clifton film, Superstar's *In Concert*.

The Experience start off their show with 'Hey Joe', after which Jimi announces: "I'd like to sing about this little girl I seen walking down the street one time, she sure was outta site man, her name was 'Foxy Lady'." The audience are quite noisy and Jimi says, "Listen,

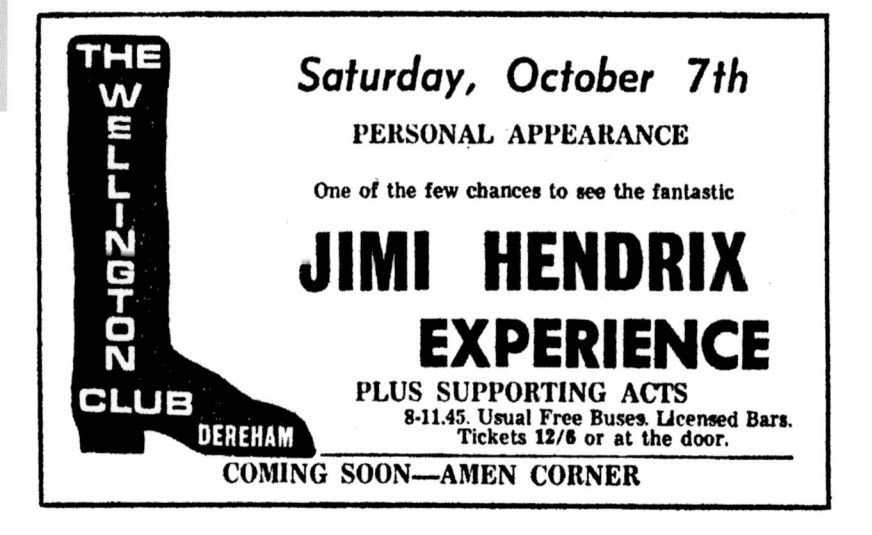

listen, listen." Jimi starts the song but his PA microphone is not working correctly, so he is only just audible. By the time he plays his guitar solo the PA is fixed but then he has having trouble with his guitar. After thanking the audience he tell them, "Well this guitar's no more good, do you want it? Here, here you go, now you want it, take it." Noel Redding tells the audience that he wishes to say hello to a few friends in the audience – PP Cass and The Small Arnolds. Jimi announces: "We're having a little bit of trouble, so if you just hold on one minute all right and everything will be okay. We'd like to do this song called 'The Wind Cries Mary' that we released here not too long ago and we'd like to do it for you. Em let's say we're having a little first anniversary thing today. I'd like to say thank you very much for last year, for letting us play here. Instead of booing us off the stage, you know, you gave us a chance." Jimi's guitar squeals quite loudly and Jimi remarks, "That's my little tap dance step."

As Jimi is trying to tune his guitar someone in the audience screams, Jimi says, "God man, how am I gonna tune my guitar like that. Okay, here we go with 'The Wind Cries Mary' I'm sorry for the delay. Here we go." As the song finishes, someone in the audience shout out for Jimi to freak out, Jimi remarks, "Someone wants to freak out. Somebody over there with a camera wants to freak out. All right brother, we're gonna let you freak out, but soon as get my other guitar fixed. Right now we like to do a little thing called 'Rock Me Baby' but we'd like to do it our own way all right. Do you remember that one?" he asks Mitch and Noel, "cause I've forgotten." After the song Noel informs the audience that they only have two more numbers to do. In the meantime Jimi's guitar has been repaired. "I've got my baby back everybody, I've got my baby back, now I can play now." Then a guitar could not be found for Noel and there were still problems with Jimi's guitar. "Man it looks like we're having hang-ups already." It seems that Jimi is still not happy with his guitar. He tells Noel... "Try it on the bass, 'Red House'. Well right now we're gonna try to do a little blues again until my guitar gets fixed, cause we're gonna stay here until my guitar gets fixed, until I play. Yeah so we like to go on and do a thing called 'Red House'." When 'Red House' was originally recorded in the studio, Noel used a regular guitar to play the rhythm part, so in order to keep as close to the original as possible, Noel would often play the guitar on stage instead of bass. However this was the first time the Experience had attempted the song live and probably the first time that Noel actually played the song on the bass guitar. After the song Jimi leaves the stage for a short while, Noel comments, "Where's he gone?" When he returns he announced to the audience, "I'm gonna say something in French, 'Jeux vu co bucux' right? Wee, I can say that, I can say Eiffel Tower, listen to that yeah. Dig we'd like to do a song called 'Purple Haze' and for those of you who don't speak English, I'd like to explain what this 'Purple Haze' means." Jimi starts to play a high pitch droning feedback, Noel quips in with... "It's when you've got a bad stomach." Jimi continues with the feed-back and remarks, "It's gonna be so much fun. Oh man that's too much."

Some girl in the audience start to scream Jimi replies, "Oh man" and screams back at the girl in the same pitch. The girl screams again and Jimi laughs. "I'd like to say, okay we have one more song to do all right, one more song to do. Thank you very much, thank you very much for coming and staying. Oh look at all those people back there God, man I didn't see any of those people. Thank you very, very much for coming for us and we've got one more last song to do. And everybody must sing this song with us okay. Look on your ticket stub, it says you must sing with our song with the Jimi Hendrix Experience, look on the ticket stub. Dig we're gonna do 'Wild Thing' all right, and everybody sing all right, you yeah that right, one second." Noel explains that Jimi has to put a new string on his guitar. Jimi remarks, "I really hope that we get a chance to come back here again you know. I really do. And in the mean time while I'm trying to get this string on, I'd like to say that er, you all really must sing with us on that, because there's only three of us on the stage you know, one-two-three, three of us on the stage. And what are we gonna do by ourselves, so you must participate, you must come in and join us. We'll have a little gathering, a little church gathering. We're not going to say this 'Everybody say yeah, yeah, everybody say yeah well I feel all right' no, no, no, no leave that to Otis Redding and Wilson Pickett, we got our own scene okay. Yeah okay, their groovy too, they've got their own scene too right, yeah okay. I said Wilson Pickett, you're not Wilson Pickett. (Laughs) Dig while I'm being embarrassed, might tighten the little guitar string."

Sunday 8th October 1967

A Nems Presentation

Eire Apparent
The Herd
The Crazy World of Arthur Brown

INTERVAL

JIMI HENDRIX EXPERIENCE

Compere . . . . LEN MARSHALL

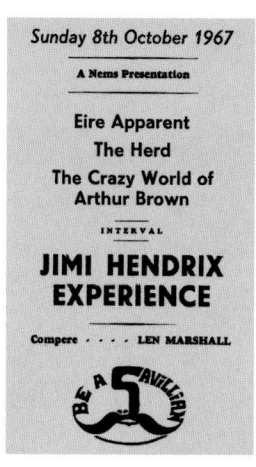

SUNDAY AT THE SAVILLE
OCTOBER 8 : 6 p.m. & 8.30 p.m.
JIMI HENDRIX EXPERIENCE
CRAZY WORLD OF
ARTHUR BROWN
THE HERD
BOOK : TEM 4011
A NEMS PRESENTATION

1967 September/October

Jimi continues to tune his guitar string and explains to the audience, "Ten lessons on how to tune your guitar string, don't tune it like this. We're tuning up because we really care for your ears right, we really care that's why we're tuning up. Here we go, is everybody ready to sing now, are you gonna sing? Say yeah anyway, I don't care, say yeah anyway." Jimi concludes the show with The Trogg's 'Wild Thing'.

October 10
Tuesday
The Experience attend a TV recording in a Paris TV Studio for the French pop show Dim Dam Dom 68. The Experience mime to 'The Burning Of The Midnight Lamp' and 'Hey Joe'. Other guests include Mireille Mathieu, Manitas De Plata and Scott MacKenzie. The show is broadcast on November 12.

October 11
Wednesday
It's an early morning start for the Experience in Paris. They are scheduled to attend a session at the ruins of Montparnasse Railway Station during its demolition, filmed for the French pop programme *Au Petit Dimanche Illustre*. They take along some of their equipment and mime to 'The Wind Cries Mary'. Later in the day, they are filmed on location walking through a French food market. The program is broadcast on October 15.

October 12
Thursday
The Experience attend another TV recording in a Paris TV Studio for the French pop show Discorama. They are let loose in the studio to play around with various instruments while they are being filmed, and Jimi attempts to play a grand piano and mimes to 'The Wind Cries Mary'. Mitch and Noel decide to lift him up on the piano stool from where Jimi – somewhat embarrassingly – tries to play the piano with his feet. Jimi then mimes to 'The Burning Of The Midnight Lamp' while playing the violin. At one point he plays it behind his head and, jokingly, with his teeth. Other guests on the programme include Mario Jacques, Monique Morelli and Katia Granoff. The programme is broadcast, November 12.

October 13
Friday
The Experience attend a TV recording for ATVs Good Evening programme at ATV TV Studios in Borehamwood, Elstree. The program is introduced by Jonathan King and broadcast October 14.

October 15
Sunday
Starlight Ballroom, Crawley.
The Experience take the stage at the Starlight Ballroom, only to find that there are major problems with the amplifiers which have to be replaced before the show can start. They perform 'Are You Experienced', 'Red House', 'Catfish Blues', 'Hey Joe', 'Purple Haze', 'Foxy Lady' and 'Wild Thing'. Jimi gashes his hand on a guitar string while performing 'Wild Thing'. After the performance a reporter from the *Crawley Observer* interviews him in the dressing room.

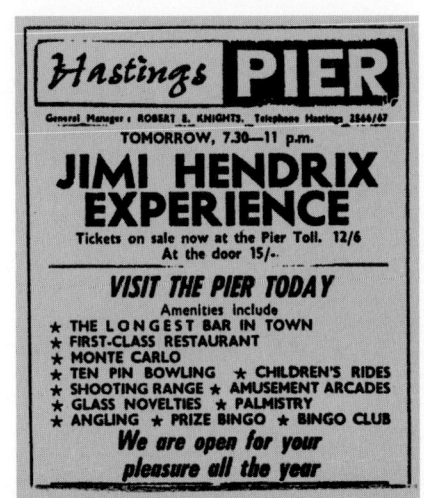

October 17
Tuesday
The Experience are back at the BBC Playhouse Theatre to record another session for the BBC. The programme is Rhythm And Blues for the BBC World Service, introduced by Alexis Korner. The show is broadcast on November 13 between 14:45 and 15:00.

Jimi starts off by playing the signature tune to the show, and continues to play guitar in the background while Alexis Korner introduces the show. Noel has decided to take along his Hagstrom 8-string bass for the session. The first song is Bob Dylan's 'Can You Please Crawl Out Your Window' followed by 'I'm Your Hoochie Coochie Man' featuring Alexis playing slide guitar. Jimi concludes the session with 'Driving South'. Towards the end of the song Jimi breaks a guitar string, and leaves Noel Redding and Mitch Mitchell to finish the song alone.

October 22
Sunday
Hastings Pier, Hastings
The Experience are supported by The Orange Seaweed.

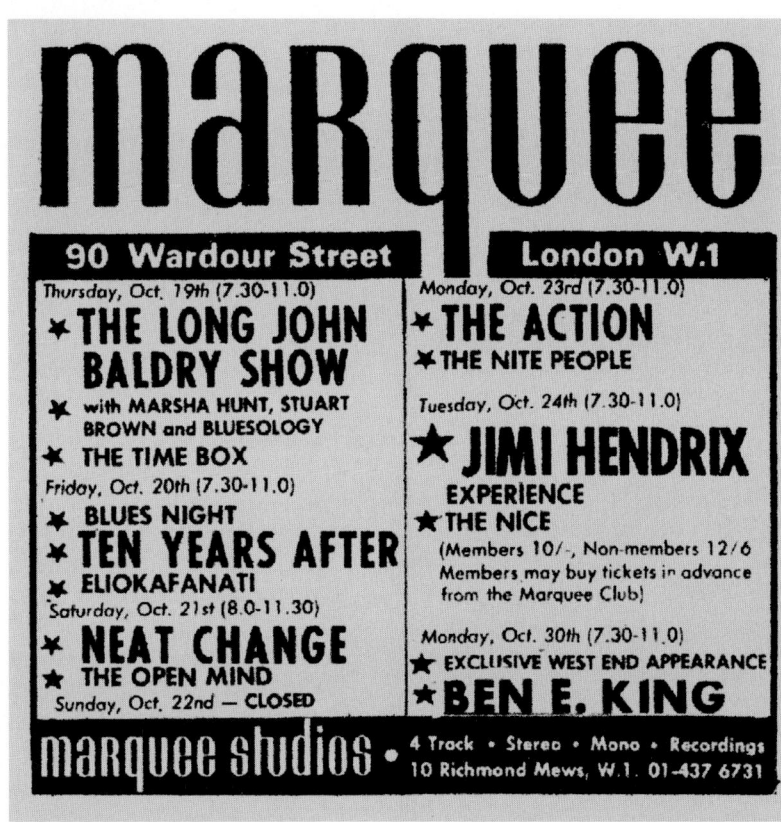

October 24
Tuesday
Marquee, London
The Experience are supported by The Nice.

October 28
Saturday
California Ballroom,
Whipsnade Road, Dunstable
The Experience are supported by Modes Mode and The Canal Street Philharmonic.

November 4
Saturday
The Experience are scheduled to play at Leeds University, but the show is cancelled.

November 8
Wednesday
The Union,
Oxford Road, Manchester
The Experience are supported by Tamla Express and Radio Luxembourg DJ The Baron. They perform 'Stone Free', after which Noel's PA system breaks down. Jimi announces, "This is very embarrassing." They continue with 'Hey Joe', 'The Wind Cries Mary', 'Foxy Lady', 'The Burning Of The Midnight Lamp', 'Purple Haze' and concludes with 'Wild Thing'.

1967 October/November

68 *Jimi Hendrix* Concert File

The local press report: "On the final number, Jimi starts smashing the instrument into the massive set of amplifiers, creating crashing sound waves. In the end, in desperation, he threw the whole guitar at the back wall of the stage and walked off stage."

November 10
Friday
The Experience attend a television recording for the Dutch TV show Hoepla at the Vitus TV Studio in Bussem on channel 1 TV, VPRO. The show is broadcast live between 19:07 to 19:56. They perform 'Foxy Lady', 'Catfish Blues' and 'Purple Haze'. After a false start, Jimi did two further takes of the song.

Hippy Happy Beurs Voor Tieners En Twens Ahoy Hallen, Rotterdam
The Experience are supported by The Motions. They perform 'Stone Free', 'Manic Depression', 'Hey Joe', 'The Wind Cries Mary', 'Foxy Lady', 'The Burning Of The Midnight Lamp' and 'Purple Haze'.

November 11
Saturday
New Refactory, Sussex University, Lewes Road, Brighton
The Experience are supported by Ten Years After.

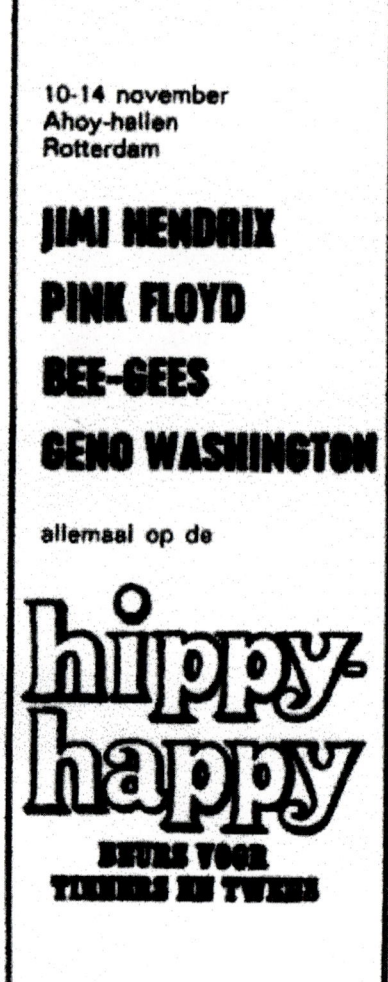

November 14
Tuesday
Royal Albert Hall, London
The Experience are undertaking their second tour of England as the headline act. The support acts for all dates on the tour are The Move, Pink Floyd, Amen Corner, The Outta Limits, Eire Apparent, and The Nice. The tours MC is DJ Pete Drummond.

The Experience perform 'Foxy Lady', 'Fire', 'Hey Joe', 'The Burning Of The Midnight Lamp', 'Spanish Castle Magic', 'The Wind Cries Mary' and 'Purple Haze'.

November 15
Wednesday
Winter Gardens, Bournemouth
The Experience perform two show at 18:10pm and 20:30pm.

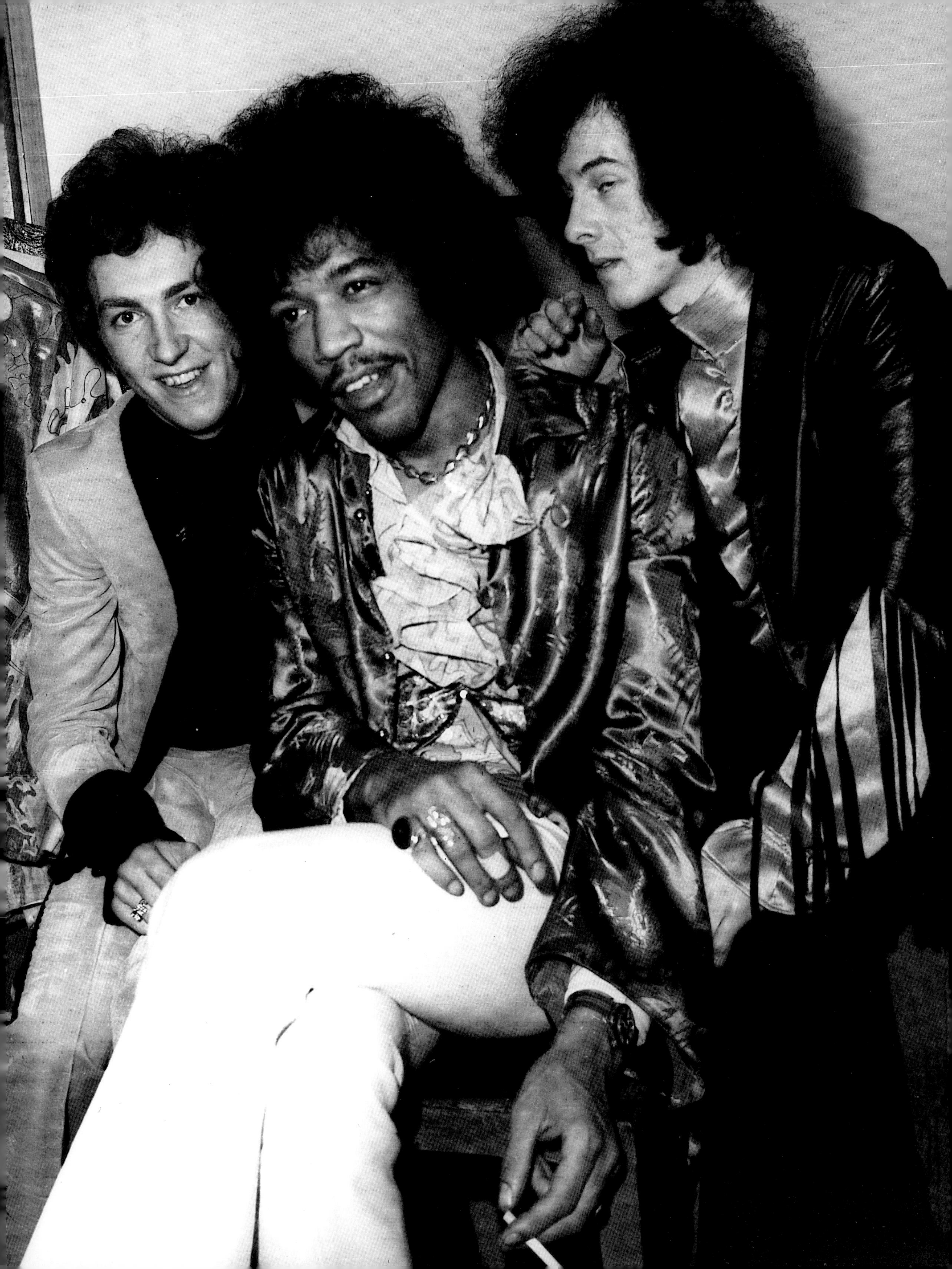

November 17
Friday
City Hall, Sheffield
The Experience perform two shows at 18:20pm and 20:50pm.

November 18
Saturday
Empire Theatre,
Lime Street, Liverpool
The Experience perform two shows at 18:00pm and 20:35pm.

November 10
Sunday
The Coventry Theatre, Coventry
The Experience perform two shows at 18:00pm and 20:30pm The local press reported: "More than 3,000 youngsters attended two houses at the Coventry Theatre – and a good proportion rushed the stage and shouted for more at the climax of the Experience's act."

The Experience perform 'Foxy Lady', 'The Burning Of The Midnight Lamp', 'Hey Joe', 'The Wind Cries Mary', 'Purple Haze' and 'Wild Thing'.

November 22
Wednesday
Guildhall, Portsmouth
The Experience perform two shows. Manager Mr C. Gillette issues a warning to the audience preparing to see the Hendrix tour at the Guildhall. "Behave yourselves or this may be the last concert presented in the Guildhall."

The local press report: "Last night at Portsmouth Guildhall four of Britain's leading groups went a long way to persuading 3,000 youngsters that such an anti-pop opinion could be right after all. Never has a pop show been so deafening and lacking in variety and good presentation. The exception was Jimi Hendrix, as loud as any of the others but twice as talented and a superb showman."

November 23
Thursday
Sophia Gardens Pavilion, Cardiff
The Experience perform two shows at 18:15pm and 20:35pm.

November 24
Friday
Colston Hall, Bristol
The Experience perform two shows at 18:30pm and 20:45pm. The local press reported: "There was guitar smashing on stage at the Colston Hall – and glass smashing off stage last night. Over boisterous Welsh teenagers were ejected after incidents in hall bars and auditorium. Teenagers from over the Severn Bridge came to yell for Welsh group Amen Corner. In the hall, youths hurled abuse at performers, but the trouble died down as officials brought the shouting minority under control. But the incident did not spoil the triumphant return of Hendrix." After the concert the whole tour retires to the Heartbeat Club in Bristol.

November 25
Saturday
Opera House, Blackpool
The Experience perform two shows at 18:10pm and 20:30pm. They play 'Sergeant Peppers Lonely Hearts Club Band' to shrieks of delight from the girls in the audience, and continue with 'Fire', 'Hey Joe', 'The Wind Cries Mary', 'Foxy Lady' and 'Purple Haze'. As 'Purple Haze' draws to a close Jimi asks the audience, "What you looking at, what you looking at?" His guitar is hopelessly out of tune, and as he tunes one string particular guitar string he comments, "Oh God, I almost didn't make that one, wow. We're tuning up because we really care for your ears, that's why we don't play so loud." Mitch Mitchell quips in with ho-ho-ho and Jimi repeats him laughing, "All right, now I'm gonna do a group therapy song for the last song, group therapy, everybody join together and hold hands and all this kind of stuff. We're gonna sing this song, well you all know the name of it, it's 'Wild Thing'. Okay." The audience starts shrieking loudly, Jimi comments, "No you don't have to do all that, but be quiet, listen, listen. And everybody sing together, please sing together this time, all right. Or else we're gonna put a curse on you, and all your kids, every one of you kids be born completely naked." Jimi ends the song by attacking his amplifiers with his guitar and throwing his guitar to the side of the stage before leaving.

Filmmaker Peter Neal has been engaged to film part of the Experience's concert. He manages to capture some pure Hendrix magic performing 'Foxy Lady', 'Purple Haze' and 'Wild Thing'; however, 'Foxy Lady' has never been seen to this day. The footage was shot for use in the first movie about Jimi Hendrix to be called 'Experience' but this title was later changed to 'See My Music Talking'.

During the early hours of the morning, someone breaks into the Opera House and damages some of the group's equipment. The local press report: "Musical equipment belonging to five top pop groups was damaged by an intruder at the Opera House after Saturday night's beat show. After their two performances on Saturday night, they left their guitars, amplifiers, and electrical equipment on stage before going to their hotel. When they returned yesterday morning to collect it, they found leads had been ripped from the amplifiers and guitars, amplifiers had been damaged and one guitar had been trampled on and had its strings cut."

November 26
Sunday
Palace Theatre,
Oxford Road, Manchester
The Experience perform two shows at 18:00pm and 20:25pm.

November 27
Monday
Grand Central Hotel,
Royal Avenue, Belfast
The experience perform two shows. The Hendrix tour flies from Ringway Airport in Manchester at 12:00pm and arrives at Aldergrove Airport in Belfast, Northern Ireland. A young fan who had purchased a ticket for the concert is unable to attend because he has suffered a bad asthma attack and is in hospital. Jimi is told of this, so he telephones the fan at the hospital, and sent him a souvenir.

Festival Of Arts,
Sir William Whitla Hall,
Queens University, Malone Road,
Belfast
An impromptu birthday party had been organised for Jimi as he arrived at Queens University. Two fans, Judy Hill from Donaghdee and June Agnew of Belfast, present Jimi with a birthday cake.

December 1
Friday
Central Hall, High Street, Chatham
The Experience perform two shows. While The Outta Limits are on stage doing their set, the organisers are rushing about trying to locate the rest of the bands. There has been a mix up and Jimi and the rest of the tour are at Chatham Town Hall a few hundred yards away wondering why no-one else is there. When they realise their mistake, everyone rushes to the Central Hall and after a few changes in the programme the first show is able to continue. The first house attracts only a small audience.

The Experience perform 'Sergeant Pepper's Lonely Hearts Club Band', 'Fire', 'Foxy Lady', 'The Burning Of the Midnight Lamp', 'Spanish Castle Magic', 'Hey Joe', 'Purple Haze' and 'Wild Thing'. Although Jimi had complained afterwards they could not hear themselves.

December 2
Saturday
The Dome,
29 New Road, Brighton
The Experience perform two shows at 18:15pm and 20:40pm.

1967 November/December

December 3
Sunday
**Theatre Royal,
Theatre Square, Nottingham**
The Experience perform two shows at 17:30pm and 20:00pm. They play 'Sergeant Pepper's Lonely Hearts Club Band', 'Foxy Lady', 'The Burning Of The Midnight Lamp', 'Spanish Castle Magic', 'The Wind Cries Mary', 'Purple Haze' and 'Wild Thing'.

The local press report: "Only the entire resources of the East Midlands Electricity Board can have averted a major power cut in Nottingham last night, when The Jimi Hendrix Experience, The Move and a host of lesser lights shook the Theatre Royal with thunderous electronic reverberations in Nottingham's best pop concert for years.

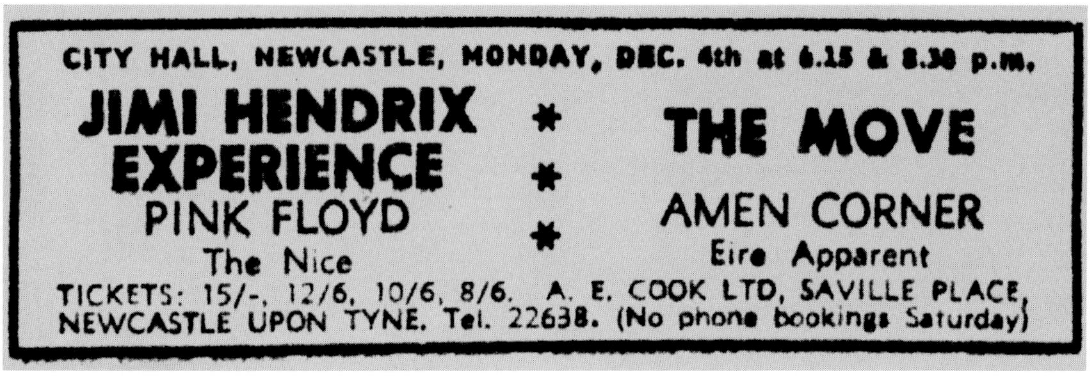

December 4
Monday
City Hall, Northumberland Road, Newcastle-upon-Tyne
The Experience perform two shows. Andy Fairweather-Low: "I remember after the first show when everyone was in the dressing room waiting to start the second house, there was someone in the dressing room filming with this large camera. We found out later that it was someone filming on videotape." Unfortunately this tape has never surfaced.

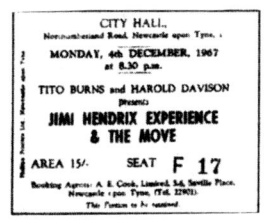

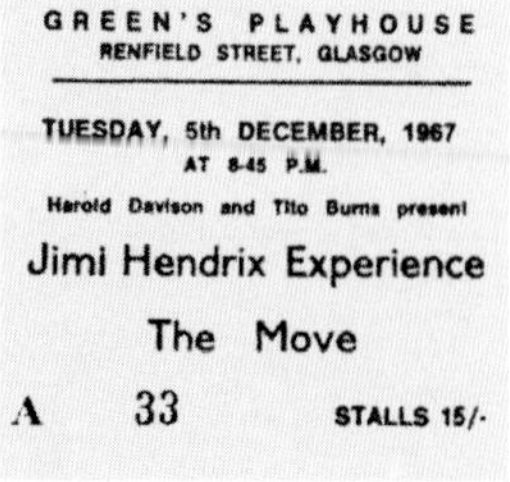

December 5
Tuesday
Green's Playhouse, Renfield Street, Glasgow
The Experience perform two shows on this last concert of the tour. The local press reported: "Last Tuesday evening The Jimi Hendrix Experience, The Move, The Pink Floyd, Amen Corner, The Nice, and Eire Apparent lined-up at the Green's Playhouse, Glasgow, in what promised to be the wildest one-night stand ever seen in Scotland. The result? Disappointing. Perhaps Hendrix stole the show; perhaps the others had an off night."

December 7
Thursday
Jimi jams with The Aynsley Dunbar Retaliation, Noel Redding and Alan Price at the Speakeasy Club.

December 8
Friday
The Experience attend a TV recording for *Good Evening* at ATV's Studios at Borehamwood in Elstree. They perform a live version of 'Spanish Castle Magic'. The show is introduced by Jonathan King and is broadcast, December 10. Other guests include Godfrey Winn singing his new record 'I Pass'.

December 12
Tuesday
Jimi Hendrix jams with Ian Matthews, Richard Thompson, Ashley Hutchings and Simon Nicol of Fairport Convention at the Speakeasy Club. Eric Clapton and Cilla Black are also present.

December 15
Friday
The Experience attend what is to be their last radio recordings for BBC Radio at the BBC Playhouse Theatre in Northumberland Avenue, London WC2.

They arrive at 7:00am to record a special Christmas Eve edition of *Top Gear* for BBC Radio One. The show is introduced by Tommy Vance and John Peel and is broadcast on December 24 at 14:00pm to 17:00pm.

BBC announcer Tony Hall has scheduled an interview with Jimi for the overseas listeners, before Jimi records his main session. Despite the early hour, Jimi is in good humour and joking all the time, so much so that Hall just can't get a serious response from him. After their interview is concluded, Jimi announces to producer Bev Philips, "Hey we've made a radio jingle for you okay? Hey, is anybody back there?" Bev Philips switches on the talk back microphone and say's "Yeah" to confirm that they are still in the control room. "We've got a radio jingle for you okay." "Right," confirms Bev. "Okay here we go, its named 'Radio One You're The One For Me'." Jimi tells Mitch and Noel to... "Watch the breaks now. One, two, three, four..." The Experience launches into their Radio One jingle with Jimi singing "Radio One, you're the one for me." Jimi finishes the song and remarks to Bev Philips, laughing: "You can fade out before that part." Bev replies with laughter from the control room, "Now I've heard everything."

To get some atmosphere into the session, Jimi has invited some of the BBC staff from the offices above to join in the session.

Bev Philips: "The thing that was unusual about these session was that he would do these slow blues and he would have people down from the office to do backing vocals and just create atmosphere. That was unique to the Beeb sessions I think."

Jimi continues his session with the only known live version of 'Wait Until Tomorrow' recorded in the studio barely a month ago. The song comes to an abrupt end with Mitch playing an extended drum solo and Noel responding with a definite 'Yeah'. A confused Hendrix exclaims, "Hey man, what going on around here?" Next is a cover version of the Beatles 'Day Tripper'. Some are convinced that John Lennon attended these sessions.

Bev Philips: "One of the legends about this particular session is that Lennon turned up and sang on 'Day Tripper'. Well I didn't notice John Lennon around the studio. I didn't see him. It wasn't Lennon. It was Mitch and Noel unfortunately."

They continue the session with 'Spanish Castle Magic' and a new song 'Getting My Heart Back Together' that Jimi performs here for the first time. The song hasn't even been recorded at this stage. "A little thing for the BBC people here. We've got a few friends here in the studio sitting around in front of us.

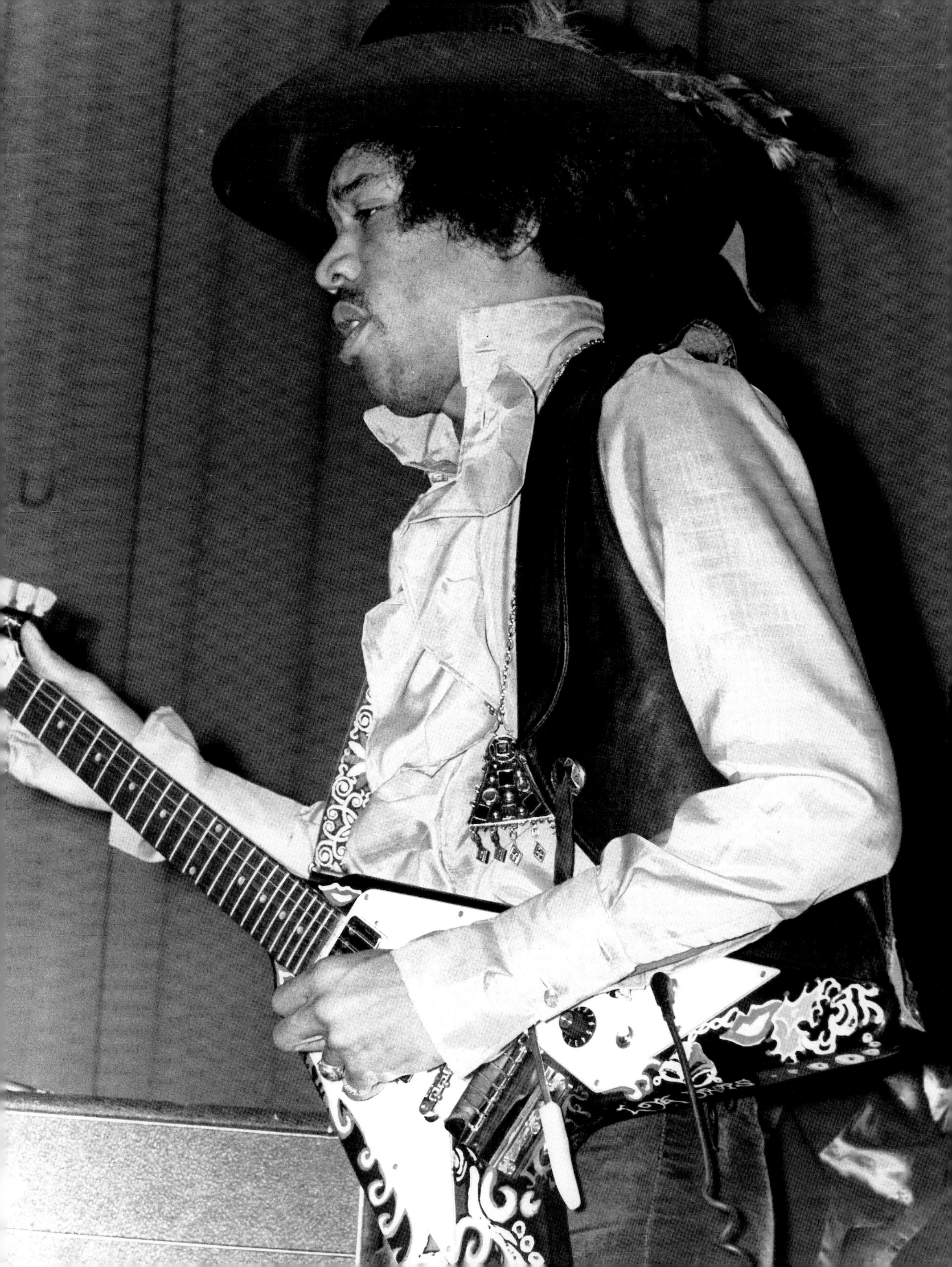

After the playback Jimi is obviously disappointed with the recording and decides to do another take. "Yeah, I see we have a few friends laying around here in the studio. Yeah okay, Mitch and Noel and I'd like to do a little number for you right here, see if we can get it together. You all together now, you all together? We'd like to throw a little bit of blues on you here. Yeah, okay then here we go a little thing called 'Get My Heart Together Again'." This time the background vocal is much better and Jimi comments, "Can you dig that, can you dig that?" Jimi ends the song by saying, "It's all over, thank you very much, thanks. Yeah okay then, well I got my heart back together again, there... feeling all right. Thanks a lot man." As the guests leave the studio, they say good bye to Jimi, he replies, "Take it easy then, see you all later, merry Christmas, yeah same to you, yeah bye-bye. I'm just left with me and my guitar now."

You all together now, you all got to sing to get on with me." The song starts with Mitch singing a very wobbly background vocal and he continues to shout and scream throughout the song. Jimi comments "Have mercy", and brings the song to a premature end. "It's all right. Thank you very much for you help. It's all right, it's beautiful. Here we go then, kind of bring it kind of quite right here in the song all right. Thank you... thanks a lot people. They think we had a thing going there for a while." He asks Bev Philips, "Hey can we just hear that back so we can see where we are."

December 16
Sunday
The Experience attend a special TV recording for BBC TV's *Top Of The Pops Survey of 1967* at BBC TV Studios in Lime Grove, London. The show is broadcast on December 25 at 14:05.

December 19
Tuesday
The Experience attend a photo session at Bruce Fleming's photo studio in Great Newport Street, London W1. Austin John Marshall and Peter Neal also attend to film the session, for the movie they were making about Jimi called 'Experience' that would later be re-titled as 'See My Music Talking.' Peter Neal has borrowed a 1960 model 12-string Zamaitis guitar from a friend and has had it strung left-handed.

After the photo shoot is finished, Marshall produces the guitar and hands it to Jimi. After a short intro Jimi says, "No, I'd rather do that again. Can we stop the film there, cause I was sorta scared to death by this thing." He re-plays the introduction and sings a stunning acoustic version of 'Getting My Heart Back Together Again'. Unfortunately because of Jimi's false start, Marshall realises that he would not have enough film to finish the take.

December 22
Friday
**Christmas On Earth,
Grand & National Halls, Olympia,
Kensington Road, London**
In the afternoon, The Experience attend a rehearsal for the evening shows.

Jim Marshall [Marshall amplifiers]: "In the afternoon, they were doing rehearsals, and Mitch couldn't quite get something right, so Jimi said, 'Would you sit in and show us how to...'. So I did... and I remember him rehearsing on stage, and I was standing alongside. And all of a sudden this character came up on the stage and complained about the volume. So he complained to me, you see. So I went over and said to Jimi, 'You have to cut it down a bit, we've got a complaint'. So Jimi went over to the amp and set it up a bit more! And than this chap came back again, all red faced, and it turned out to be the shop steward of the electricians doing the lightning... and he threatened to bring the whole crowd out on strike if Jimi didn't stop. I said, 'I think Jim, you gotta stop', and then he turned it up again! In the end the chap came back again and said, 'Everybody is out, there will be no show tonight!' And I said to Jimi, 'I think this chap is really serious, there's not gonna be a show'. But Jimi thought it was very funny... he did quieten it down a bit."

Jimi and Noel are filmed in the dressing room jamming together on guitars in front of an assembled array of young ladies. The film would be in the movie *See My Music Talking*.

This mammoth event is organised in two weeks by John Love, John Easem, Ian Duncan and David Larcher, the publishers of *Image* magazine. They manage to assemble The Jimi Hendrix Experience, The Who (who pulled out at the last minute after Pete Townshend injured his hand), Eric Burdon & The Animals, The Move, Pink Floyd, Keith West & Tomorrow, Soft Machine with Mark Boyle's Sensual Lab, Paper Blitz Tissue, The Graham Bond Organisation, Sam Gopal Dream, Jeffrey Shaw & The Plastic Circus, Traffic and DJs Mike Lennox and John Peel.

The event is staged between 20:00pm and 6:00am but did not attract the 15-20,000 people that was needed to break even. It therefore lost a fortune. Tommy Weber was brought in to film the entire event, but because he used outdated film, the quality was somewhat lacking.

The Experience finally get on stage at 2:00am and Jimi warns the audience to "Plug your ears, watch out for your ears, watch out for your ears okay", before attacking 'Sergeant Pepper's Lonely Hearts Club Band'. He continues with 'Foxy Lady' and Noel Redding remembers playing guitar on two songs. One undoubtedly is 'Red House'. The finale of the Experience show is 'Wild Thing' – "I'll tell you what, listen to this man, look I want, look, look, it is Christmas right and everybody's feeling all good right? And er like, man I don't wanna get off the stage without doing one little, one little number all right, where everybody can join in. Wow everybody oooh, all of those people out there. Anyway dig, we got this song where everybody can join on, is it all right if we do 'Wild Thing'? I mean, you know we haven't did it in so long man, we just want to do it for the fun of it. You believe it's the last time this year we'll do it okay. And er, we'd like to think about all the soldiers coming in from Vietnam and Aden all this you know. And everybody being straight with each other, you know the President, he's got his little head together you know. Only we'll turn him on, er excuse me, for instance. And instead of marching down the street with er what is that, er M1s, M16s all these rifles and stuff, well how about, you know marching down the street with little bits of guitars, something like this here..."

After the concert Jimi went to Speakeasy Club and jammed the night away with Dave Mason, Eric Burdon and Harry Hughes of The Clouds.

December 31
Sunday
Jimi attends a New Years Eve party at the Speakeasy Club in Margaret Street, closing out a very successful year by playing a thirty-minute version of 'Auld Lang Syne' to see in 1968.

1964 December 75

1968

January 2
Tuesday

Jimi jams with Al Sykes and John Mayall at Klooks Kleek, Railway Hotel in West Hampstead.

January 4
Thursday

Lorensbergs Cirkus, Gothenburg

The Experience perform two shows at 19:00 and 21:30, supported by Mecki Mark Men and Baby Grandmothers.

During the first show they perform 'Foxy Lady', 'The Wind Cries Mary', 'Fire', 'Hey Joe', 'Come On (Part One)' and 'Purple Haze'.

During the second show they perform 'Sergeant Pepper's Lonely Hearts Club Band', 'Fire', 'Hey Joe', 'Foxy Lady', 'The Wind Cries Mary', 'Catfish Blues' and 'Wild Thing'.

January 5
Friday

Sporthallen Jernvallen, Sandviken

The Experience perform one show at 20:30 supported by Mecki Mark Men and Baby Grandmothers. Jimi has a sore throat and plays for only 35 minutes instead of the planned hour.

January 7
Sunday

Tivolis Konsertsal, Tietgensgade 20, Copenhagen

The Experience perform two shows supported by Hansson & Karlsson.

After a short tune up, Jimi starts this first show off with 'Sgt Pepper's Lonely Hearts Club Band'. "Thank you very much... Just like to er, turn it on here. 'oises when [we unplug them]... do you remember a song that goes like this...?" Jimi continues with 'Hey Joe'.

As Jimi brings the song to an end, the amplifiers are still buzzing badly. Jimi comments: "Oh well, thank you very much. I'd like to turn you on now, a slow blues." Jimi changes guitars and Noel announces that they are going to play 'Catfish Blues'. After another tune up Jimi announces: "It goes something like this here," adding a few licks of Cream's 'Cat Squirrel' into the solo. After the song, Jimi changes to his Stratocaster guitar.

"... I'd like to do 'The Wind Cries Mary' for you. If it's all right, once we get tuned up first." Jimi starts the song, but the guitar is out of tune and he stops playing after the first verse and announces: "Thank you very much and now for our next number we'd like to do 'Purple Haze'." He ends the song with an extended solo which he plays with his teeth. However, the technical problems are still causing concern: "We're having very bad trouble with the amplifiers, it's very bad... you know. I'd like to do a song called... We have a new LP out, this is called 'Spanish Castle Magic', that's what we call it." It's almost the end of the show and still the amplifiers are buzzing. Jimi comments: "Still like to do the last number for you, if it's all right. It's called 'Wild Thing'. Okay..."

January 8
Monday

Stora Salen, Konserthuset, Stockholm

The Experience perform two shows at 19:00 and 21:30 supported by Mecki Mark Men and Baby Grandmothers.

After the group has been announced for the start of the first show, they are greeted with a rousing reception from the audience. "Before we start, I'd like to say that er, between every single song we gotta a new song that is meant for you, I think everybody knows this, named 'Tune Up Blues'. Okay, we'd like to start off with a 'Tune Up Blues'." After tuning up, Jimi comments: "Yeah, thank you very much, there'll be more of that later on."

Jimi starts off the show with 'Sergeant Pepper's Lonely Hearts Club Band'. Unusually, Mitch Mitchell thanks the audience and continues: "We'd like to welcome you to Radio Station EXP, and tonight we're gonna feature an interview with a very peculiar looking gentleman who goes by the name of Mr Paul Caruso. Mr Caruso is going to talk to us on the very dodgy subject of 'Are there or are there not flying saucers or UFOs?' Tell me Mr Caruso, yes please do tell me Mr Caruso, what's your regarded opinion on this nonsense about spaceships and even space people?" Jimi replies: "Thank you very much. As you all know, you just can't believe everything you see and hear, can you? Now if you'll excuse me, I must be on my way." Jimi then reproduces 'EXP' and continues straight into 'Up From The Skies' and 'Spanish Castle Magic'.

The *Axis Bold As Love* LP has only just been released the previous month and Jimi has treated this audience to the first three tracks on the LP. This is the only known occasion Jimi performed 'EXP' and 'Up From The Skies' live in concert. "I must admit we practised that... er for about two or three seconds behind the stage. But... We've got another one that's released here in Sweden." As Jimi's guitar lets out a squeal he comments: "Amen to that. We tune up because we really care for your ears, you know. We do care, we think very much about your ears, that is why we don't play very loud, you understand." After another tune up, Jimi comments: "We're gonna flash back to 1932, 'Foxy Lady'." Afterwards, he announces: "[This is] a song called 'Little Wing'...". This is the first known live rendering of 'Little Wing'. Jimi hits a note on his guitar and jokes: "Oh I woke it up, I've seen this spaceman too. Oh, yeah I'd like to do our old one, with my rhythm bones on in er... 1872, that was a good year for a song. It's a song called 'Let Me Stand Next To Your Fire' [from] back in the days when they used to use fire."

After the song Mitch makes another rare announcement to the audience: "Thanks very much. Well... it's nice to know that you're all listening to us." Jimi tunes up and continues with a very slow, laid back version of 'Catfish Blues'. Afterwards, he has to tune up again, which takes a few minutes. "Tuning your guitar can be fun... Oh yeah, 'The Wind Cries Mary'." Jimi plays the introduction but the guitar is still out of tune, so he stops playing, commenting, "One more time there", and starting the song again. "Oh yeah, we're gonna do a song made in 1779, that was a good year. Yeah, well we've got one last song to do and we're gonna let you figure it out what it is. It's gonna be so much fun for me." Jimi creates a very loud dive-bombing guitar sound with feedback, which leads into their final number, 'Purple Haze'.

January 22
Monday

Jimi jams with Sam Gopal's Dream at The Speakeasy club in Margaret Street.

January 29
Monday
L'Olympia, Paris

The Experience perform two shows supported by Eric Burdon's New Animals. During the first show, The Experience perform 'Sgt Pepper's Lonely Hearts Club Band', 'Fire', 'The Wind Cries Mary', 'Spanish Castle Magic', 'Catfish Blues', 'Little Wing' and 'Purple Haze'.

After their introduction for the second show, Jimi opens with 'Killing Floor'. "Yeah, thank you very much... We'd like to go ahead... and do a song that goes like this, here." He continues with 'Catfish Blues'. At the end of the song, someone in the audience shouts out in French, "Alee pop pa". Jimi responds with, "Yeah, dig. We got this groovy tune man..." At that point, someone in the audience takes a photo of him; he comments: "They're taking my picture man, oh man. Anyway dig, we've got this groovy tune that's named 'Tune up time, tune up time', dig, we got this groovy tune'." Jimi tunes his guitar and asks Noel to play an A, which he sings in a high-pitched voice, before asking the audience: "Give me a P, give me a P, come on." The audience responds by singing the same note that Jimi is singing. He comments: "Yeah, yeah that's great, that's great. We've got this song that goes something like this here – you all have to quiet as bunnies. And it goes something like this here." Jimi continues with 'Foxy Lady'. Afterwards, he tells the audience, "Hey dig... we're gonna feature Noel Redding, you know, the bass player. He's gonna play guitar on this song named 'Red House'. Remember this one, the record named 'Red House'? Anyway we gonna do this song named 'Red House' and Noel Redding's gonna play guitar there. So [we'll] get tuned up..." After tuning their guitars, Jimi instructs Noel and Mitch: "Real slow, real slow."

When the song is over, Jimi announces: "Right, now what we'd like to try to do is a instrumental for you just for a second, you know, just see if we can get ourselves back together again." They continue with 'Drivin' South', the last known time they play the song. Noel comments: "We have just learnt that." Jimi continues: "You know that there's a certain song that we like to play between every other song that we play. It's called a tune up song, you know."

At this point someone in the audience screams, and Jimi responds, "Yeah, and all that kind of... Elvis Presley... stuff." The same person screams again and Jimi announces in his Elvis voice, "Yeah there baby, you just have to sit down in a big old rocker there, yeah." He starts playing a few bars of old-time 12 bar blues. "Thank you very much there, thank you very much, yeah we sold a million records on that one right there and all that bull. Yeah, we'd like to go and do a song called 'The Wind Cries Mary', all right?" Afterwards, he comments: "We'd like to keep on going with a song called 'Let Me Stand Next To Your Fire'. During the song, Mitch manages to break his snare drum skin and so he has to find a replacement. Jimi is deciding what to play next and Noel suggests 'You've Got Me Floating'. Jimi replies "You've Got Me Floating, wow I think I've forgot the words to that one." Mitch has located another snare drum and Jimi announces, "Yeah, we're having trouble with the drums. If you just hold on for a second, Mitchell over there, better known as Queen Bee, he's having slight trouble, so will you just hold on for a second there, you know. Take an intermission." Mitch adjusts his snare and signals that it's all right, Jimi continues "... We have this LP out named *Axis Bold As Love* and we'd like to do this song from it named 'Little Wing', okay?"

Before the closing number, Jimi announces: "I'd like to say... thank you very much, er, like I'm just having trouble with this raggedy guitar here, but... we'd like to do this last song, the last song for you anyway, dedicated to everybody here. Oh yeah, it is called 'Purple Haze'."

February 1
Thursday
Fillmore Auditorium,
San Francisco, California

The Experience perform two shows supported by Albert King; John Mayall's Bluesbreakers and Soft Machine. The set list for the first show is 'Red House', 'Purple Haze', 'Foxy Lady', 'Fire' and 'The Wind Cries Mary'.

February 2
Friday
Winterland,
San Francisco, California

The Experience perform two shows supported by Albert King, John Mayall's Bluesbreakers and Soft Machine.

February 3
Saturday
Winterland,
San Francisco, California

The Experience perform two shows supported by Albert King and John Mayall's Bluesbreakers. After Soft Machine drummer Robert Wyatt had an argument with Winterland owner Bill Graham, during which he called Graham a fascist, the group are sent on to Arizona to wait for the tour to arrive there.

Graham introduces the Experience, and they take a few minutes to tune up before starting their first show with 'Sergeant Pepper's Lonely Hearts Club Band'. Jimi tells the crowd, "Dig, we'd like to say thanks a lot, it's really groovy to come here in the first place. This is a song called 'Let Me Stand Next To Your Fire'. Afterwards, he jokes, "I think we might do a song that been travelling around a little bit. It's an 'oldie but baddie' song that we did. It was the first record we mixed in England, its called 'Hey Joe'. When they finish the song, he announces,

"For everybody, we'd like to continue on with a song that goes something like this. I think that [you'll] remember this one." Jimi continues with 'Foxy Lady'. The Experience follow this with 'The Wind Cries Mary', from their début LP. After the song, Jimi thanks the audience: "Yeah, thank you very much, [we'd] like to do our own little... Howling Wolf song

1968 January/February 79

tonight." He continues with 'Killing Floor', then announces, "Yeah, we'd like to slow the pace down a little bit." The audience up to now have been complaining that the people in the front rows are standing on their chairs. The rest of the crowd have been constantly shouting throughout the show for these people to sit down. Picking up on the situation, Jimi comments, "We'd like to do a song dedicated to all the people here and all the people in the back that can't see... we'd like to dedicate it to you. Anyway, it's a song from our new LP, its called 'Little Wing'." At the end of the set, Jimi says goodbye and announces the group's traditional set-closer: "We've got time to do one more number and we'd like to call it 'Purple Haze'."

The second show starts with Jimi announcing: "I'd like to say that we forgot all the words, we forgot all the words to our songs, we're just gonna sit up here and jam for a while, if you don't mind. There's a song by B.B. King we'd like to do. It's a song called 'Rock Me Baby', but dig, we went ahead and [did] it our own way okay, so don't get mad if it doesn't sound so soul food, because we got our own type of food, if you can dig it." Jimi changes guitar to his Gibson for the next number, announcing, "Thank you very much, please wait one second... I'd like to do this song called 'Red House'." Jimi proceeds to tune his guitar: "Yes, we like to get things together. Have you all heard that song before anyway?" ('Red House' has not been released in America at this stage.) "We always tune up between every song because we really care for your ears, we really care, so we tune up. That's why we don't play so loud either." This is the first time during this tour that the American audience get to hear Jimi playing 'Red House'. Jimi changes back to his Stratocaster and, without introduction, continues with 'Foxy Lady'. By this stage the usual amplifier trouble has started up again, and Noel apologises to the audience for all the noise. Jimi announces: "I'd like to do a Dylan song now, called 'Like A Rolling Stone'." He proceeds to play a very slow, melodic version of the song, which is full of emotion. The technical problems persist, however, and he comments: "We're having very bad difficulties with this amplifier scene, and it really is a drag. Anyway, we'd like to do this 'Purple Haze' for you, if you let us." Jimi continues with a very long, wild dive-bombing feedback introduction before ending the show with this song.

February 4
Sunday
Winterland,
San Francisco, California

The Experience perform two shows supported by Albert King, John Mayall's Bluesbreakers and Big Brother And The Holding Company who have been added to the bill in place of Soft Machine.

Bill Graham is so overwhelmed by the Experience's performance that he presents them all with antique gold watches at a party he organises for them after the concert.

February 5
Monday
Sunday Devils Gym,
Arizona State University,
Tempe, Arizona

The Experience perform a 20:30 show with Soft Machine back as their support act.

February 6
Tuesday
VIP Club, Tuscon, Arizona

The Experience are supported by Soft Machine.

February 8
Thursday
Men's Gym,
Sacramento State College,
California

The Experience perform their show supported by Soft Machine, The Creators and with a special light show by Simultaneous Avalanche.

February 9
Friday
Anaheim Convention Centre,
Anaheim, California

The Experience perform two show supported by The Animals, Fire Apparent and Soft Machine. By the second show, the amplifier problems had really got to Jimi and after an amplifier blew up during the fourth song, he abandoned the concert.

Jimi's PR man Les Perrin was at the concert. Perrin: "Jimi was waiting to go on at Anaheim. He was dressed in mauve trousers, a wide-brimmed, round-topped black hat with brass ring holes with matching mauve material woven in and out. He had brass buckled shoes, a flowered shirt and a metalwork waistcoat. I was wearing a grey business suit, white shirt and a tie embroidered with the insignia of the ancient Fleet Street journalist club, The Wig And Pen. We were standing in the entrance and people were coming in and just staring at him. He turned to me and said out the corner of his mouth, 'Hey man, Les, all these people standing here staring at yuh, ah wouldn't have it. I'd stare right back!'"

February 10
Saturday
Shrine Auditorium,
Jefferson & Hoover, Los Angeles

During the afternoon, The Experience attends a sound check with their new Sunn equipment during which they jam with Buddy Miles, Harvey Brooks and David Crosby. Their show starts at 20.30, supported by Soft Machine, Blue Cheer and Buddy Miles' group The Electric Flag. They perform 'Are You Experienced', 'The Wind Cries Mary', 'Up From The Skies', 'Red House', 'Purple Haze' and 'Wild Thing'. As well as David Crosby, Peter Tork and Mickey Dolenz also attend the concert.

February 11
Sunday
**Robertson Gym,
Santa Barbara, California**
The Experience are supported by Soft Machine and East Side Kids.

> KAPPA SIGMA in conjuction with Barry Lawrence presents in a pillow concert
> **THE JIMI HENDRIX EXPERIENCE**
> plus the SOFT MACHINE and the EAST SIDE KIDS
> *lights by the soft machine*
> Feb. 11   Robertson Gym
> Students $2.50   Public $3.00
> Tickets on sale at Benwitts, UCen, Car/Stereo and the Record Rack.

February 12
Monday
Centre Arena, Seattle, Washington
The Experience are supported by Soft Machine.

February 13
Tuesday
**Ackerman Ballroom,
UCLA, Los Angeles, California**
The Experience are supported by Soft Machine.

Neville Chesters: "We had a lot of trouble with power supply – Jimi walked off in the middle of the show. Finally we got it right, and the group went back on."

February 14
Wednesday
**Regis College/Fieldhouse,
Denver, Colorado**
The Experience's 20:30 show is supported by Soft Machine.

February 15
Thursday
**Municipal Auditorium,
San Antonio, Texas**
The Experience are supported by Soft Machine, The Moving Sidewalks featuring guitarist Billy Gibbons, and Neal Ford and the Fanatics.

February 16
Friday
**State Fair Music Hall,
Dallas, Texas**
The Experience are supported by Soft Machine, The Moving Sidewalks and The Chessman, featuring Jimmie Vaughan, brother of Stevie Ray Vaughan.

He claimed that Jimi broke his own wah-wah pedal and traded the broken pedal plus $40 for Jimmie's Vox wah-wah.

After being introduced, The Experience start their show off with 'Are You Experienced'. Noel introduces the next song as being from their first LP. Before playing the song Jimi announces, "Before we do this, I'd like to say that this is really a groovy city because, I went down and got these real groovy boots, man, I'm really outta site, man. Look at those, I've got some pointed toe shoes, wow. Pointed toe shoes, well I'm the biggest square in this whole building." They continue with 'Fire'. "Hey, dig, back in... 1732, October the 31st, we did this song called 'The Wind Cries Mary' and we'd like to do it for you now, in the year of 1946." After a period of tuning up, Jimi remarks: "Thank you very much, and now for our next number..." then continues with 'The Wind Cries Mary'.

When they finish this song, Jimi thanks the audience and, in a mock-apology, announces, "Oh listen, we'd like to bore you for about seven or eight minutes and do an instrumental. It isn't released yet and, er, we just like to jam man, you know how we are, just like to sit up here and jam. So we'd like to do a scene that goes something like this here. I forgot the name of it..." The group play 'Tax Free', after which Jimi tells the audience: "I'd like to say that number there... [is] a number that we mess around with sometimes. It's done by a Swedish group named Hansson and [Karlsson] and we just do it different ways every night. We just try like, I like to mess around and do it. Well let's see now. Oh, I know a number [from] back in 1776."

> FEB. 14. 1968 $3.00
> **EXPERIENCE**
> Regis College Field House
> JIM HENDRICKS
> ADMIT ONE 8:30 P.M.

1968 February 81

Jimi continues with 'Foxy Lady'. "Yeah, if you only knew how much fun this was. Right now, we'd like to play our most favourite record of all, it's called 'Tune up time'. Having tuned his guitar, Jimi announces that he's not sure how they're going to handle the next song: "We'll just play it and see what happens." Jimi plays a new introduction to his first hit, 'Hey Joe'. At the end of the song, the audience start shouting out for songs. Jimi comments, somewhat obscurely: "Man, I've got the whole script written down in the palm of my hands. I know when to put on my head", and laughs. Someone shouts something from the audience and Jimi replies: "No, don't be sorry... it's outta site, man, this is... Dallas, great... I'd like to do a song specially dedicated to Dallas right by this time, it's a thing called, er, 'Spanish Castle Magic'. It's a place you wouldn't take your grandmother." Jimi tunes up and comments: "There goes our favourite song again. It's sold a million copies in between [every] other tune up time. It goes something like this here." They continue with 'Spanish Castle Magic'.

After the song, Jimi is plagued by radio noises coming through his amplifiers. He asks the roadies, "What's wrong man? God..." Noel tells the audience that they have a "radio thing short into our things." Jimi comments on a voice from the radio which intermittently bursts from his speakers: "Oh man, what a drag man, can't even get that together. Been this old mad cat sitting up there blabbing all through our act, now we give him a chance to talk he clams up. I'll tell you what you won't be able to hear him now cause we're into... the 'Red House'." The talking returns and Jimi jokingly pretends to have a conversation with the man's voice. "Yeah, okay then okay, yeah probably. Yesterday probably... What? No, tomorrow okay, right away, okay." He instructs the band to play 'Red House' and comments to the audience, "But I'm not crazy, honest to God I'm not, that's him over there." Next, Jimi announces, laughing: "There's a song we did slightly before the BC era... Oh I shouldn't have said that, oh wow. 11 BC is the year we recorded this song and we'd like to dedicate it to the 1968 people sitting in front of us and the 1969 people and the 70s..." Jimi obtains a low droning note from his guitar, produced by tapping the body of his guitar and letting the open strings resonate. He tells the audience, "So right now, I'm pertaining if you notice, I'm pertaining. Can you hear me pertaining?" He produces a sound like the drone of an aeroplane and comments, "Hope the plane don't crash." He then hits a loud note and states, "Ah, that's just to wake you up there." As the drones turn into a full-fledged wild feedback solo, he launches into 'Purple Haze', ending with a long solo which he plays with his teeth.

After the song, Jimi announces, "Yeah, we got one more last song to do, I know you'll all say, 'Thank God.'" The audience responds with a resounding "No!", to which Jimi replies, "You know good and well you're saying 'Thank God.'" After a final tune up, Jimi announces "Okay, there's a lot of people picking on a certain cat who's president right now, so we'll try to help him out and do a song, an international anthem bringing all the soldiers back from Vietnam. This is the kind of song you should try to have. Instead of them marching back from Vietnam with big [M16s] and all that and big submarines and all [that] mess on their backs. How about they marched into town with big feedback guitars...?" Jimi plays a marching pattern on his guitar. "And all that kind of stuff, yeah, well not necessarily like that, but what if they came down and... you all sang this certain song with them, and... we all sang together on this certain song, because it is an international anthem. So, if everybody can stand up and put their left hand across, er, put their right hand across... well, whatever you can find to put it across there and we can really get it on there. And it's very important for you all to sing along, don't be scared, I'm not going to tell nobody. So you all be really groovy and sing along with this song. It's an international scene and it goes something like this here." The group play 'Wild Thing'.

February 17
Saturday
Will Rogers Auditorium,
Fort Worth, Texas
The Experience are supported by Soft Machine, The Moving Sidewalks and Neal Ford and the Fanatics.

The Experience start the show off with 'Sergeant Pepper's Lonely Hearts

Club Band'. Without introduction they continue with Bob Dylan's 'Can You Please Crawl Out Your Window'. Jimi thanks the crowd after the song ends, comments once more on his new pointed shoes, and says, "We'd like to do 'The Wind Cries Mary' for you, recorded in 1776..." Afterward, he jokes, "Yes indeed, 1776 was a good year for records and, er, we'd like to proceed on to 1932 where we recorded a song with the Everly Brothers and Tom Mix. A little thing called 'Let Me Stand Next To Your Fire'." Next, Noel announces that "We'd like to do a blues number now. This is a very old number that we arranged ourselves, it's called 'Catfish Blues'." Jimi jokes. "If you notice, that was a south Arabian accent...", then Noel interrupts and asks for a quick tune up. Jimi refers once more to "this real groovy song... named 'Tune up time', we play it between every single song. But I think it might be our next single, I don't know." They continue with 'Catfish Blues', followed by 'Foxy Lady'. After the song, Mitch makes an announcement to the audience: "There's one thing I must explain about all these people wandering around on stage. I mean, this happens every night, now it's getting a bit tiring, you know. I'm beginning to think the road managers have got a star complex, so they sabotage our equipment every night so they have to get on stage." At that point a roadie comes on stage. Jimi comments sarcastically: "You're hired, you wanna play in our group? Hey you!" to laughter from the audience, before announcing "an old cowboy song". Noel asks Jimi what it is, before confiding to the audience, "I can't understand him – he's American you see, and I'm English." Jimi asks the audience if they liked Soft Machine and the Sidewalks. When the audience doesn't react, Jimi comments: "Come on... It's a good [thing] that we ain't being paid by applause, or else we'd starve to death."

The group continues with 'Hey Joe', then Jimi tells the audience they've only got time for two more songs. The audience start shouting out for different numbers – Jimi replies "I forgot the words, I'm sorry" to some requests. Someone shouts out for 'Purple Haze', which the group proceed to play. During the aeroplane intro, Jimi comments, "Pretend you're riding along in an aeroplane and you hear a voice at the back: 'Hope the plane don't crash.'" Jimi breaks a string during the song and jokes, "Oh I'm mad now!" He continues straight into 'Wild Thing', concluding the song with 'The Last Post' and attacking his stack of amplifiers. "Jimi smashed all his Sunn gear up," roadie Neville Chesters remembers, "he made a terrible mess of it."

After the show, Jimi jams backstage with Billy Gibbons of The Moving Sidewalks. Afterwards, Billy gives Jimi a 1957 left-handed Stratocaster; Jimi responds by giving Billy a pink Stratocaster that Billy still owns.

February 18
Sunday
Music Hall, Houston, Texas
The Experience perform two shows supported by Soft Machine, The Moving Sidewalks and Neal Ford and the Fanatics.

February 21
Wednesday
**The Electric Factory,
2201 Arch Street, Philadelphia,
Pennsylvania**
The Experience perform two shows supported by Woodys Truck Stop.

Neville Chesters: "We had to get another group to play instead of Soft Machine due to Soft Machine's organ which didn't arrive."

February 22
Thursday
Electric Factory, Philadelphia
The Experience perform two shows supported by Soft Machine and Woodys Truck Stop.

Neville Chesters: "Jimi went on a long time; second set didn't finish till 03.00am the next morning."

February 23
Friday
**Masonic Temple,
Detroit, Michigan**
The Experience are supported by Soft Machine, MC5 and The Rationals.

During the performance, a stagehand broke a young girl's hand as she tried to climb onto the stage.

February 24
Saturday
**Cne Coliseum Arena,
Toronto, Ontario, Canada**
The Experience's 23.00 show is supported by Soft Machine and The Paupers. It's not known if Eire Apparent played without McCullough, who was busted by Canadian police at customs earlier in the day.

The Experience perform 'Are You Experienced', 'Hey Joe', 'Foxy Lady', 'The Wind Cries Mary', 'Spanish Castle Magic', 'Manic Depression', 'Like A Rolling Stone', 'I Don't Live Today', 'Purple Haze', 'Red House' and 'Wild Thing'.

After the concert, the Experience attend a small club in Toronto where they jam with Robbie Robertson and members of The Band.

February 25
Sunday
**Chicago Civic Opera House,
20 N. Wacker, Chicago, Illinois**
The Experience perform two shows supported by Soft Machine.

Soft Machine's roadie Hugh Hopper: "There was a slope down into the theatre. Neville had forgotten that he had already opened the back of the truck before he started backing down the slope, [whereupon] all the equipment fell out in a heap. Luckily nothing was damaged."

The Experience start their first show with 'Sergeant Pepper's Lonely Hearts Club Band'. They continue with 'Fire', 'The Wind Cries Mary', 'Foxy Lady',

1968 February 83

'I Don't Live Today', 'Hey Joe', 'Can You Please Crawl Out Your Window', 'Manic Depression', 'Like A Rolling Stone' and 'Purple Haze'.

February 27
Tuesday
**The Factory,
315 Gorham, Madison, Wisconsin**
The Experience perform two shows supported by Soft Machine and Mark Boyle Sense Laboratory.

February 28
Wednesday
The Scene, 624 N. 2nd Street, Milwaukee, Wisconsin
The Experience perform two shows supported by Soft Machine.

Roadie Neville Chesters: "Another bad club, terrible. I had to carry gear through the hotel lobby, up in an elevator, then through club's kitchen and then carry it the full length of club. It took three hours just to get the gear on to the stage."

After the group are introduced to the stage Jimi announces: "Before we start give us a chance to tune up this once all right." Jimi proceeds to tune up before opening the first show with 'Tax Free'. "Thank you very much, we're having slight trouble, so just give us a chance, so you know... get our stuff together. We tune up between every number because we really care for your ears, that's why we don't play so loud. We'd like to continue on with a song played in 1833. It's was very, very harsh afternoon, the day we was recording, and er... anyway we probably managed it. And do a song er... oh yeah 'Let Me Stand Next To Your Old Lady', all you appreciate or... 'Your Fire'." Jimi continues with 'Let Me Stand Next To Your Fire' and follows with 'Red House', commenting during the song's introduction: "This is a song called 'Red House' from our English LP." Without any introduction Jimi continues with 'Foxy Lady' then announces: "Thank you very much. You'll have to excuse the tuning but you know, like we have to make sure it's all right, like. I can't hear on the stairs so we're outta tune." Noel introduces the next song 'The Wind Cries Mary', and they continue with Bob Dylan's 'Please Don't Crawl Out Your Window'. "I'm sorry but we've got two last numbers to do in this first show so, yeah so you have chance to rip the seating next time. So I'd like to tune up, we have to tune up one more time." Noel and Mitch briefly play the riff to The Kinks 'You Really Got Me' before Jimi finally plays the feedback introduction to 'Purple Haze' to end the show.

Jimi opens the second show unusually with an instrumental version of 'Axis Bold As Love', the only known live version of the song. As he plays Jimi announces: "Thank you very much for staying up to see the show, we'd like to continue, and em... we have Mitch Mitchell playing drums and Noel Redding on er... bass and me playing radio." Jimi continues with 'Axis' for a few more minutes before Mitch changes the tempo and Jimi moves into 'Sergeant Peppers Lonely Hearts Club Band'. Without any introduction Jimi continues with 'Spanish Castle Magic'. After the song Jimi changes his guitar and there is a delay for a few minutes before he announces: "Thank you very much for waiting and sorry for the hang ups, but you know... maybe we can get it on with another song called em, 'Stone Free' just." Again this is the only time Jimi plays this song on the tour. "Now a song dedicated to the American Indian and other minority groups, a thing called 'I Don't Live Today'." Jimi includes a medley of the *Bonanza* theme and Cream's 'Cat Squirrel' and 'Sunshine Of Your Love'. Jimi continues with 'Burning Of The Midnight Lamp', the only time the song is performed live on this tour. Jimi would play this song live only one further time – while on holiday in Majorca. He continues with 'Foxy Lady'. "Thank you very much er... I'd like to do this song dedicated to the cats who wish he could make love to the iddy biddy little aged little girls over there. It's a song called 'Manic Depression'." Jimi then ends the concert with 'Hoochie Kootchie Man', yet another song played live for the only known time.

February 29
Thursday
The Scene, Milwaukee
The Experience perform two shows supported by Soft Machine.

March 2
Saturday
**Hunter College,
Park Ave & 69th Street, New York**
The Experience perform two shows supported by John Hammond Jr, Soft Machine and Mark Boyle Sense Laboratory.

The group start their first show with 'Fire', continuing with 'Hey Joe', 'Foxy Lady', 'Purple Haze', 'I Don't Live Today' and 'Wild Thing'.

Their second show begins with 'Tax Free' and continues with 'Foxy Lady' and 'Like A Rolling Stone'. During the introduction to this song, Jimi announces, "Yeah, this is a song that was written by a cat [name] of Robert Zimmerman, better know as... British Noel's grandmother. That's his grandmother over there, just over there, er, just by your officials. And he sometimes goes by the name of Bob Dylan, and this song by the name of 'Rolling Stone'... 'Like A Rolling Stone'." After this number, the group continue with 'Killing Floor' and 'Red House'.

March 3
Sunday
Vets Memorial Auditorium, Columbus, Ohio
The Experience are supported by Dantes, 4 O'clock Balloon and Soft Machine.

Neville Chesters remembers that, "Jimi had a Stratocaster stolen, one that I had purchased for him the day before."

March 4
Monday
Jimi jams with Eric Clapton in the Scene Club, 301 West 46th Street in New York.

March 6
Wednesday
Jimi jams with The Hollies at the Scene Club.

March 7
Thursday
Another of Jimi's jams at the Scene club, this time with Jim Morrison, Paul Caruso, and members of The McCoys featuring Rick Derringer. Jimi takes his four-track tape recorder along to record the jam.

Jimi performs a less than bluesy version of 'Red House' and continues with 'I'm Gonna Leave This Town'. He then runs through the first known performance of 'Bleeding Heart', a song which he would go on to feature occasionally in concert. During the song, a very drunk Jim Morrison decides to get up on stage to join in by adding drunken obscenities. Jimi continues with the Beatles' 'Tomorrow Never Knows', with Morrison continuing to sing his obscenities. Jimi tells him: "That's the recording mic, sing in there, that's the recording mic." At one stage, Morrison knocks the microphone over and Jimi replaces it. He comments to the audience, "In case anybody want to know what's happening, there's Jim Morrison, Jim Morrison on the... er, the... er..." He laughs and goes on to play 'Outside Woman Blues' and 'The Sunshine Of Your Love'.

March 8
Friday
Marvel Gym, Brown University, Providence, Rhode Island
The Experience are supported by Soft Machine

Roadie Neville Chesters: "The crowd came in, everybody was drunk, a few fights broke out, there were no cops. We told the promoter that the group wouldn't play unless he got some security, which he did. The Experience did their show, which went down very well. Jimi smashed an old white Stratocaster; everybody went mad."

March 9
Saturday
State University Of New York, Stony Brook, Long Island
The Experience are supported by Soft Machine.

The group perform 'Killing Floor', 'Fire', 'Foxy Lady', 'Spanish Castle Magic', 'Hey Joe', 'Red House', 'I Don't Live Today', 'Purple Haze' and 'Wild Thing'.

March 10
Sunday
International Ballroom, Washington Hilton Hotel, Conn Ave & T Street N.W, Washington DC
The Experience perform two shows at 15:00 and 20:00 supported by Soft Machine and Mark Boyle Sense Laboratory.

During the first show they perform 'Sergeant Pepper's Lonely Hearts Club Band', 'Hey Joe', 'Fire', 'The Wind Cries Mary', 'Foxy Lady', 'Red House', 'I Don't Live Today', 'Purple Haze' and 'Wild Thing'.

Jimi starts his second show off with 'Killing Floor'. After the song, Noel comments to the audience, "It's not very loud, is it?" to which the audience shouts back, "No". The group continue with 'Foxy Lady', 'The Wind Cries Mary' and 'Fire'. Jimi announces: "We'd like to play... 'Red House', the blues that we put on the, er, English LP named *Are You Experienced*." They then continue with 'Don't Live Today' and 'Purple Haze'.

Winding the evening up, Jimi goes through the by now familiar speech about the group's 'international anthem' for all the soldiers returning from Vietnam, and urges the audience to join in. As before, the 'international anthem' turns out to be 'Wild Thing'.

March 15
Friday
Atwood Hall, Clark University, Worcester, Massachusetts
The Experience perform two shows, supported by Soft Machine.

They perform 'Are You Experienced', 'Fire', 'Hey Joe', 'The Star Spangled Banner' (performed here for the first known time), 'Foxy Lady', 'Purple Haze' and 'Wild Thing'.

Filmmaker Tony Palmer is at the hall. He has set up his equipment to film part of the Experience's show for a new documentary he is making for the BBC, called *All My Loving*. Tony films the Experience in the dressing room and also parts of their performances of 'Foxy Lady', 'Purple Haze' and 'Wild Thing'.

March 16
Saturday
Lewiston Armory, Lewiston, Maine
The Experience play at 20:00 supported by Soft Machine, Hanseatic League and Terry and The Telstars.

March 17
Sunday
Cafe Au Go Go, 152 Bleecker Street, Greenwich Village, New York
Jimi has been in the audience watching a jam involving Elvin Bishop on guitar, Herbie Rich on organ, Harvey Brooks on bass, Phil Wilson on drums, and Paul Butterfield on harmonica. Before long he is persuaded to join in and is welcomed to the stage with shouts of delight from the audience. The ensemble start off with a few unidentified instrumental jams, and then Jimi plays a melodic instrumental version of 'Little Wing'. The jam continues with 'Everything's Gonna Be Alright', 'Stormy Monday' and a jam that Jimi would later go on to record as 'Three Little Bears'. Midway through the jam, Jimi has some trouble with his guitar leads, though the problem is quickly sorted out. The group continue with a very fast upbeat jam which the other musicians present have some difficulty in keeping up with.

March 19
Tuesday
Capitol Theatre, Ottawa, Ontario, Canada
The Experience perform two shows at 18.00 and 20.30, supported by Soft Machine.

During their first show, they perform 'Sergeant Pepper's Lonely Hearts Club Band', 'Fire', 'Foxy Lady', 'Red House' and 'I Don't Live Today'.

After the MC introduces the Experience for their second show they launch straight into 'Killing Floor'. After the song, Jimi announces: "Yeah we're having slight difficulties with the equipment, so please hold on for one minute okay, just one second. I hate to bring my own self down with this raggedy equipment, I can tell ya..." The problem is temporarily sorted out, and Jimi continues with 'Tax Free', before announcing "a song called 'Let Me Stand Next To Your Old Lady'... I mean 'Let Me Stand Next To Your Fire'; it is the same thing, you know." At the start of the song, just as Jimi is counting the band in, loud voices come through the bank of Marshall amplifiers. Jimi apologises to the crowd, but continues the song anyway. The voices come through the amps again and Jimi responds with, "Oh man, shut up, man. Anyway, we'd like to do a blues called 'Red House'. This is on the English LP. I'd like to do if for you now in 1948." This song is followed by 'Foxy Lady', then Jimi announces: " I'd like to try to continue on and... do a thing that was recorded back in 1778... [it was] very hard for us to record in those days, very, very hard indeed to find a studio. But dig, we found it some kind of way. And now [we've got] a brand new psychedelic version of it. Brand new, spanking new, new era type of thing. Yeah we put a 1948 rearrangement on it and it's really outta site man, you should hear it. It goes something like this here." Jimi continues with a version of 'Hey Joe' that includes the new introduction he has been adding. "Yes, we'd like to try a thing called 'Spanish Magic', er, 'Spanish Magic Laffish', yeah, written by Henry Schwartz..."

Jimi has been taping the show himself and now suddenly exclaims, "Oh the tape's gonna run out!" He comments to the audience: "You all just clapping just because you know there a tape recorder running. You don't want us to feel embarrassed when we play it at home to our girlfriends..." The audience responds with loud cheering and clapping, Jimi comments in a loud voice: "Thank you very, very much, thank you very much, we really didn't... we didn't deserve that really, thank you very much though, I really dig it. So I'd like to go ahead on and do 'Spanish Castle Magic', to see if we can get our heads together." Afterwards, Jimi comments: "There's a cat over there... Anyway, he said we have two more numbers to go, so I'd like to say thank you very much man, it's really been a groove and, er, you all really had nice patience, which, er, which is really handy. Thank you very much for letting me, you know get my kicks here and there too. Now we'd like to play our world-famous song before we get into our last two songs. It's a thing called 'Tune up time blues, part two'." Just then, a roadie tells Jimi that one of his amplifiers is broken. He comments to the audience, in a Bill Cosby voice: "Man, my amplifiers broken. Man, 'em amp's broke, well I can't play my guitar now... It's a drag, man. Hey man, what you wanna break my amp like that for, man? Can you all dig Bill Cosby? He's really outta site." Meanwhile, Jimi is trying to tune his guitar and jokes with the audience: "Next we're gonna have on stage with us a jam session with three peanut butter and jelly sandwiches and give 'em out to the winners." Still having problems getting his instrument in tune, Jimi picks up the Bill Cosby theme again: "Oh yeah, the cat... there's a certain person in the audience... how about a big hand for Bill Cosby sitting over there? How about a big hand for Bill Cosby, come on! Oh, wait a minute... Oh, I'm sorry lady, I'm sorry lady, I didn't oh... She spit in my eye, man."

Now tuned up, Jimi hits the harmonics on his guitar and starts a wild introduction to 'Purple Haze'. At the end of the song, he changes guitars – this makes the amplifiers whistle badly. His guitar is out of tune again, and, exasperated, he comments: "Wait a minute, wait a minute, man this really is a hang-up." He asks Noel to play an A so that he can tune his guitar, but as he hits the A string it is completely out of tune, and Jimi quips, "Oh, that's [definitely] not an A there. I mean, common sense would tell anybody that." He continues to tune his A string and tries to sing the same note simultaneously, joking: "Oh wow... I think I'll make a record! That'll be cool: sing on it too." Jimi proceeds to sing 'Rock Me Baby' in a comedy voice. "Oh yes, yes that's it. Oh yeah, you remember those days too, hey?" The audience responds with cheering and Jimi replies: "Yes, thank you very much, yes. For those of you who can't see us tonight, er, they were clapping because I did a little trick with my guitar... "

Finally, Jimi repeats his monologue about the group's international anthem for soldiers returning from Vietnam, with "M16 machine guns and all this, M16 and hand grenades and tanks all on their backs and stuff. What if they came home with... like, er, feedback guitars... That's better than guns, I can tell you." Jimi plays a big feedback note and comments: "Something like that, I think I'd dig that. And anyway we wanna dedicate it to the feedback family and, er, all the human beings and you people." Ending with a mock plea of "Please join in because I've forgot the words," Jimi concludes the evening with 'Wild Thing'.

March 21
Thursday
Community War Memorial, Rochester, New York
The Experience are supported by Soft Machine, Jesse First Carnival, Mark Boyle Sense Laboratory and The Rustics.

They perform 'Sergeant Pepper's Lonely Hearts Club Band', 'Spanish Castle Magic', 'Hey Joe', 'Foxy Lady', 'The Wind Cries Mary', 'Red House', 'Manic Depression', 'Purple Haze' and 'Wild Thing'.

88 *Jimi Hendrix* Concert File

March 22
Friday
**Bushnell Memorial Hall,
Hartford, Connecticut**
The Experience are supported by The Bowl and Soft Machine.

They perform 'Sergeant Pepper's Lonely Hearts Club Band', 'Fire', 'I Don't Live Today' and 'Little Wing'.

March 23
Saturday
**Memorial Auditorium,
Buffalo, New York**
The Experience are supported by Soft Machine, Jesse First Carnival and Mark Boyle Sense Laboratory

[Poster: MUNCIE'S HULLABALOO SCENE PRESENTING THE JIMI HENDRIX EXPERIENCE PLUS ENGLAND'S UNDERGROUND SENSATION THE SOFT MACHINE WITH THE MARK BOYLE SENSE LABORATORY AND THE GLASS CALENDAR MARCH 27th. 7:00 to 10:00 TEEN AMERICA BUILDING LION'S DELAWARE CO. FAIRGROUNDS TICKETS Advance $2.50 At the door $3.00 ADVANCE TICKETS ARE AVAILABLE AT: At all four locations of INDUSTRIAL TRUST & SAVINGS BANKS RECORD HOUSE in the Village or the HULLABALOO CLUB]

March 24
Sunday
IMA Auditorium, Flint, Michigan
The Experience are supported by Soft Machine, The Rationals and Fruit Of The Loom.

March 25
Monday
Otto's Grotto, Cleveland, Ohio
Jimi jams on bass with Good Earth, a band from Cleveland. Leonard Nimoy [Mr Spock from *Star Trek*] is in the audience.

March 26
Tuesday
**Public Music Hall,
Cleveland, Ohio**
The Experience perform two shows supported by Soft Machine.

The group's first show consists of 'Killing Floor', 'Tax Free', 'Foxy Lady', 'Fire', 'Catfish Blues', 'Spanish Castle Magic', 'Hey Joe', 'Purple Haze' and Wild Thing'. The show is held up briefly due to a bomb threat. Bob Cope the concert promoter asks everyone to look under his or her seat for any devices.

The Experience take the stage for their second show of the evening and proceed to tune up. The MC comes to the microphone, announcing: "Love and peace, The Jimi Hendrix Experience", to wild cheers from the audience. The band kick the show off with 'Sergeant Pepper's Lonely Hearts Club Band', after which Jimi announces: "Welcome to Cleveland. Okay, I'll tell you what, I'm gonna do this thing called 'Let Me Stand Next To Your Old Lady', I mean 'Let Me Stand Next To Your Fire'. After the number finishes, Jimi thanks the audience and says: 'I'd like to continue on with 'I Do Not Live Today', dedicated to the American Indians, minority groups and you." (Trivia note: the song is generally known as 'I Don't Live Today'.) Afterwards, Jimi decides "to slow the pace down a little bit". After a quick tune up, the group continue with 'Red House' – "it's a little bit of blues". The group are still having amplifier problems, and Jimi is forced to apologise to the audience before the group can continue with 'Foxy Lady' and 'Spanish Castle Magic'. After these two tracks, Jimi announces: "... we'd like to do 'Manic Depression' but, er... I'd like to do 'Stone Free' too, so we'll do 'Manic Depression' first, all right?" However, the group are being hurried up, and he has to explain: "Well, we'd like to do 'Stone Free' but... the cat has now said that we only have two numbers to do. I'm sorry man, I'll tell you what... just pretend we did ['Stone Free'] okay? I really am sorry." The audience starts to shout out for Jimi to play the song. He responds by saying, "I can't, as I just said... I can't play it at all, sorry."

Jimi continues with 'Purple Haze'. Throughout the show, the audience has been yelling for him to take his hat off. This continues after 'Purple Haze' and Jimi finally responds: "I'll take my hat off if you take your pants off, all right?" to a big cheer from the audience. Thanking everybody for their patience and enthusiasm, Jimi starts to announce the by now familiar 'international anthem' – "Pretend this is for the soldiers coming back from the war in Vietnam." Jimi proceeds to play a slow melodic riff for a few seconds before slipping into 'Wild Thing'. He ends the show with the song, including an excursion into 'Taps', and then attacks his amplifiers with his guitar, throwing it into his stack. There is a commotion in the audience – someone shouts out: "Why don't you get your crash helmets on?" and the rest of the audience starts to boo loudly.

March 27
Wednesday
**Teen America Building,
Lion's Delware Co. Fairgrounds,
Muncie, Indiana**
The Experience are supported by Soft Machine, Glass Calendar and Mark Boyle Sense Laboratory.

On the way into Muncie, the Muncie Police Department stop Jimi's car. The driver is fined $75, presumably for speeding. Soft Machine's personal manager Tom Edmundson manages to talk the fine down to $18.50.

March 28
Thursday
**Xavier University Fieldhouse,
Cincinnati, Ohio**
The Experience perform two shows supported by Soft Machine.

March 29
Friday
**Chicago University Hall,
West Lake Street, Chicago, Illinois**
The Experience are supported by Soft Machine.

Roadie Neville Chesters: "Jimi went on stage after Soft Machine, but the amps buzzed so badly, he walked off and refused to play, so the rest of the gig was cancelled." After the concert, Jimi jams with the Paul Butterfield Blues Band at The Cheetah in Chicago.

March 30
Saturday
University Of Toledo Fieldhouse, Toledo, Ohio
The Experience are supported by Soft Machine.

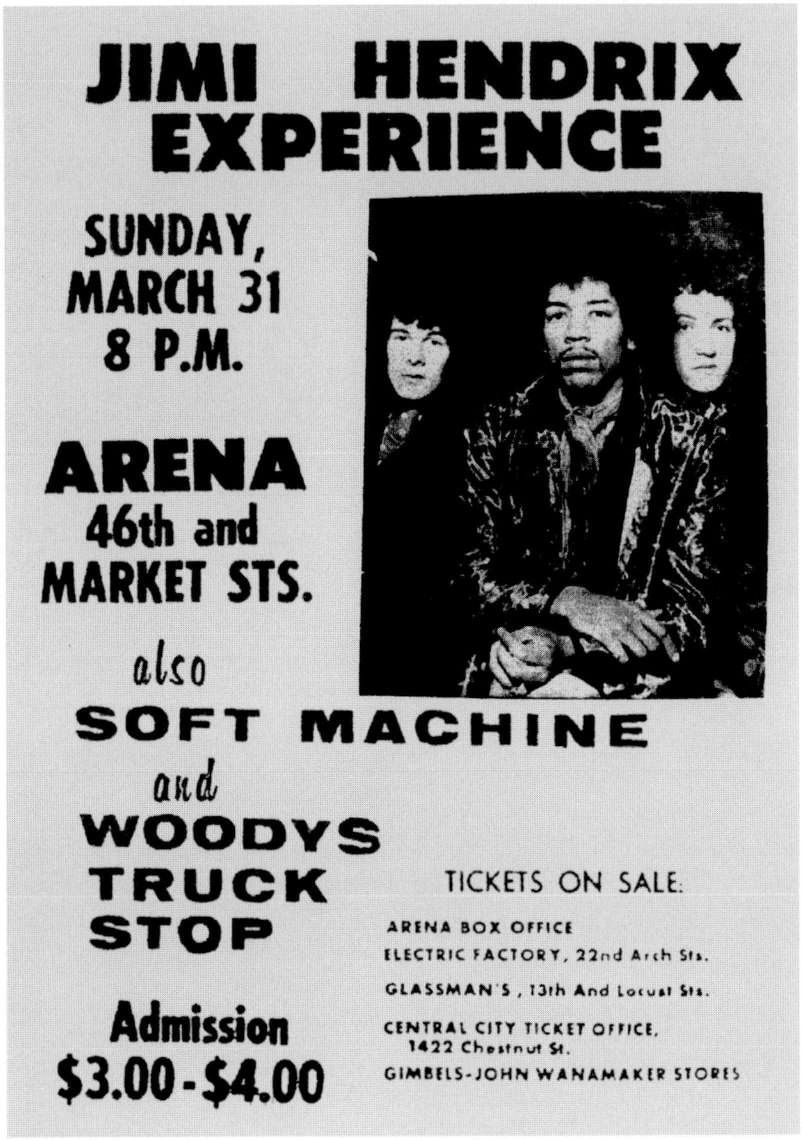

March 31
Sunday
**The Arena,
46th & Market Street,
Philadelphia, Pennsylvania**
The Experience are supported by Soft Machine and Woodys Truck Stop.

April 2
Tuesday
**Paul Sauve Arena,
Montreal, Quebec, Canada**
The Experience are supported by Soft Machine, Olivus and Bruce Cockburn.

After their introduction and a quick tune up, Jimi plays a very fast wah-wah solo before going into the first song of the evening, 'Killing Floor', followed by 'Hey Joe'. Jimi changes guitars: "Yes, okay then, I must tune my guitar because I really care for your ears. That's why we don't play so loud, because we really care." Jimi continues with 'Fire'. "I'd like to say thank you very much for staying with us this long. We'd like to, er, slow the pace down a little bit and do a thing called 'The Wind Cries Mary'. The group follows this with 'Foxy Lady', before Jimi announces: "Here's a song dedicated to everybody in here and the American Indian, a thing called 'I Don't Live Today'." They follow this with 'Manic Depression' and 'Purple Haze' ("Here's a song that we recorded in 1733, we put a brand new slight delay in.") As Jimi announces, "It's like one more song to do but thank you very much for coming", someone in the audience shouts out "you asshole" and the commotion that ensues drowns out the rest of Jimi's comments. He concludes the show with 'Wild Thing'.

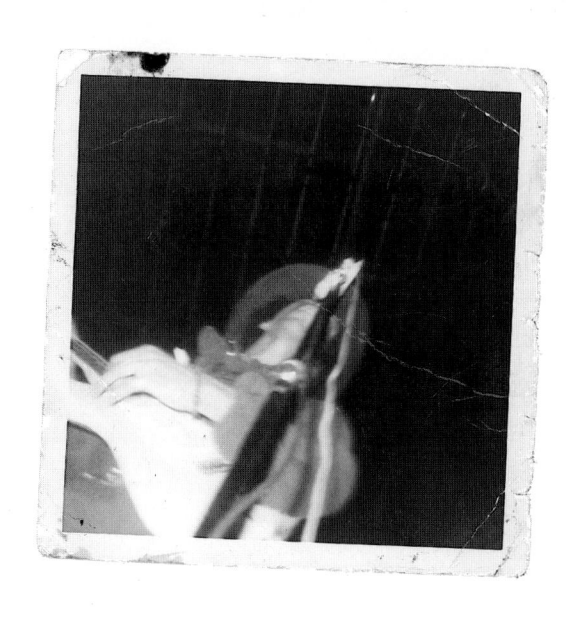

Roadie Neville Chesters: "During the concert, the audience started a riot! They had to get extra police in to keep the kids back. Right at the end of the show, some guy jumped on stage and stole Noel's mike and stand, suddenly all the lights were on in the hall, and there was complete chaos, kids everywhere all over the stage."

April 4
Thursday
Civic Dome,
Virginia Beach, Virginia
The Experience perform two shows supported by Soft Machine

April 5
Friday
Symphony Hall, 1020 Broad Street, Newark, New Jersey
The Experience only play one show supported by Soft Machine.

This was the day that Martin Luther King was assassinated. Mark Boyle: "We were due to play in Newark that night and no one wanted to go. We all milled about in the foyer of the hotel waiting for the decision to cancel the show. Then the police came on the phone from Newark to say that there was a vast crowd waiting for us, and if we didn't show up they were sure they'd burn the city. The first limo driver took a long thin cheroot out of his mouth and said, "Jimi sits up front with me or I don't go." So Jimi sat up front, and all of us white people slumped down in our seats and we set off.

"The streets of Newark were silent and deserted when we arrived, except that there seemed to be an enormous black man on each corner, as though he was a sentry or policing the block or something. I was terrified that Jimi was going to be killed. At the time everyone thought there was an insane conspiracy to eliminate anyone who was seen as a threat to the extreme right in America, and who was next on the list? Jimi came on very quietly to enormous applause. Then he said softly into the microphone, "This number is for a friend of mine." He then began an improvisation that had a beauty that was simply appalling. Immediately everyone knew that the friend was Martin Luther King and this music somehow seemed to convey all the agony of the black people. The whole audience was weeping. Even the much-maligned old 'redneck' stagehands came on to the stage, and just stood there with tears streaming down their faces. It was a lament for a great man, but it was the most harrowing lament, beyond anyone's imagining. When he finished there was no applause. Jimi just laid his guitar down and walked quietly off the stage."

Jimi Hendrix: "The second show was cancelled due to the death of Martin Luther King in Atlanta. Only 200 people had arrived to see the gig, so we played for them, then drove back to New York."

April 6
Saturday
Westchester County Centre,
Central Ave, White Plains, New York
The Experience are supported by Soft Machine.

April 7
Sunday
Generation,
52 West 8th Street, New York
Jimi attends a gig by Buddy Guy. Though quite content to sit in the audience and watch the performance, he later takes part in a jam with Roy Buchanan. The event was filmed by D.A. Pennebaker, who later incorporated it into a movie called *Wake At Generation*.

April 8
Monday
Generation, New York
Jimi jams again with Buddy Guy who mentions that Janis Joplin and B.B. King are also booked that night. He also mentions that Jimi taped the jam.

April 9
Tuesday
Generation, New York
Jimi attends a jam with Al Kooper on organ, B.B. King on guitar, Elvin Bishop on guitar. Buzzy Feiten on bass, Phillip Wilson on drums, Don Martin on guitar, Paul Butterfield on harmonica and Stewart on piano.

The first jam is a song written by Al Kooper and is introduced as an impromptu jam 'No 903'. The next song is introduced as 'Kooper Shuffle In G'. After the two jams, Jimi takes the stage, plugs in his guitar and proceeds to play 'Like A Rolling Stone'. Jimi tells the musicians the next song is in A – "Something like 'San Jose' with the breaks in it, you know' like B.B. King." He tells the audience "I'd like to say I'm sorry for being out of tune on that last number and I'm sorry for being... out of tune in this next number we're gonna play, thank you very much." After the jam, Jimi leaves the stage and B.B. King takes over his place. During King's introduction, he jokingly comments "Jimi Hendrix you're a stinker, a stinker." They continue to play two further jams, with Jimi joining in for the end of the jam. While King is introducing the musicians, Jimi is playing quietly in the background. King comments "Now come on Jimi, now wait a minute, baby." Jimi responds back with "I'll give you some background music" and jokes to B.B. King that Albert King is his brother. Jimi leaves the stage to change the tape on the recorder that he has brought along to record the jam. Unfortunately, the second tape of the jam has never surfaced.

April 19
Friday
Troy Armory, Troy, New York
The Experience are supported by Soft Machine

May 3
Friday
**Town Hall,
William Street, New York**
Jimi Hendrix and Mitch Mitchell jam with Joe Tex and his band.

Mitch Mitchell: "One night we were at the Record Plant recording *Electric Ladyland* and a call comes in from Joe Tex, asking Jimi to come down and play at the Town Hall. Hendrix says, "Okay, but on one condition: I bring my drummer." Tex agreed and Jimi says to me, "Hey, come on, have a play with Joe Tex." I'm going, "Yeah, I'll have some of that!" What he hadn't told me, or maybe didn't know, was that it was some kind of Black Power benefit. I'm the only white person there out of about 4,000 people. Jimi's chortling away sort of, "Ho ho, got the sucker now." So we get up on stage and there's all of Joe Tex's band up there, about 17 of them and the drums are set up out front. It was like, "Okay, sonny, let's see what you can do!" I had to deal with it or get the hell out. So I did the best I could and it was okay. I wouldn't have missed it for the world."

May 10
Friday
Fillmore East, 105 2nd Avenue, 6th Street, New York

The Experience perform two shows supported by Sly & The Family Stone and Joshua Light Show.

The Experience start the evening's show off with a new arrangement of 'Rock Me Baby' which Jimi now calls 'Here Comes Your Lover Man', performed here for the first known time. After the usual tune up Jimi offers an apology for the interference on the band's amplifiers: "We haven't had a chance to get em really overhauled right here in America, 'cause of, you know, blab blab, woof woof."

The amplifiers blast out static noise; Jimi jokingly comments. "Thank you very much and now for our next song, we'd like to do a thing..." to laughter from the audience. The group continue with 'Fire', after which Jimi again has to apologise for their amplifier problems. He then plays the opening riff to a Beach Boys type song, remarking to the audience "Wait, wait, wait I'm sorry, I just had a... great big flash there over my head, I had a big rush, this big flash thing and something just told me to play that, I'm sorry." He then plays a Duane Eddie riff and Noel remarks: "That's lovely, play that again."

Jimi remarks "Slow time blues, how about that? Have you all heard that? Okay here we go. We're doing this because I don't know what we're gonna play next." Someone shouts something out from the audience and Jimi comments "Yeah, yeah, I think we'll play that next. I'd like to dedicate this next song to the blues generation." Jimi plays the opening feedback note to 'Foxy Lady' but stops and announces to the audience: "Thank you and I just blew another amp, if you can notice by the lights that are off." The amplifier is quickly changed and Jimi continues with 'Foxy Lady'.

Noel then tells the audience the group are going to play 'Red House'. However, the group have to take time to tune up again, whereupon Jimi makes the standard comments about caring for the audience's ears and not playing too loudly. Someone shouts from the audience for Jimi to take off his hat. Jimi responds with a yawn and mimics the person: "Oh take off my hat. I'll take it off if you take off your pants, okay?" Jimi continues with 'Red House', but is interrupted by more amp trouble: "We're having more trouble with the, er..." Noel interrupts Jimi and explains that the lead is broken. Jimi comments "Well they don't care man, they don't care. They just want to see you get up there and work. We're having trouble with the equipment so what I'll do is I'll ad-lib because I have a way with ad-libbing you know, yes sir indeed."

Noel comments the amp has been changed. "That was quick, weren't it," Jimi replies "Oh, do I get away with ad-libbing. I say something old something new, something borrowed, something blue, oh wow, outta site man." The Experience continues with 'Hey Joe', then someone from the audience shouts out a request. Jimi replies: "Hum a little bit to me, hum a little bit to me... Is that the one that goes... I get em all mixed up, they sound the same to me." Jimi starts into 'The Sunshine Of Your Love' but stops playing during the introduction. He announces: "Next, The Monkees! Now I'd like to do a song by The Monkees. Keep everything balanced right, you have to keep everything balanced. We'd like to... slow it down a little bit, just sound like this." Jimi proceeds to play the introduction to 'Getting My Heart Back Together'. He explains to the audience that this is the first time they have played it. "I'd like to do a song we never played before... it's a thing I just wrote not too long ago, so we'd like to try to do it."

After this number, Jimi announces: "I'd like to do a thing called 'Let Me Come... Please Come Crawl Out Of Your Window'. Or I'll put a curse on you and all your children shall be born completely butt naked. There's nothing wrong with that." After the song, someone in the audience asks if Jimi is better than Eric Clapton. Jimi responds "Did you say am I better than Clapton...? Are you better than my girlfriend?" before continuing with 'Purple Haze'. Jimi plays the introduction to 'Wild Thing' and announces: "I'd like to play a song, something like... We'd like to say thank you one more time, and you must join in and sing with us, all right? Can you sing with us? Here we go, everybody say yes, oh I just don't have it. (Laughs) I didn't say 'yeah', man, I said 'yes'." Noel tries to explain to the audience that it's very English to say 'yes'. Jimi comments: "That's south Saturn, that is. Here we go, we'd like to play a south Saturn delta blues." Jimi ends the show with 'Wild Thing'.

May 18
Saturday
**Miami Pop Festival,
Gulf Stream Race Track,
Hallandale, Miami**
The Experience are supported by The Mothers Of Invention, Arthur Brown, Blue Cheer and John Lee Hooker.

During the show Noel explains that Jimi is having trouble with his guitar. Jimi comments: "We're having a slight troubles, just hold on for a second." Mitch makes another rare announcement to ask the audience if anyone has found a trapeze. Jimi makes his standard joke about the group respecting the audience's hearing, which is why they keep the volume 'low' on their amplifiers, before continuing "with a song called 'Foxy Lady'. It goes something like this." After the song, they go into 'Fire'. "Right now we'd like... to jam another slow song for you if it's all right. It's just a slow blues that we do; we did it one time before and... we'd like to try to do it now. It's just nothing but a jam anyway, you know..." Jimi tells Noel and Mitch, "It's that thing that we did in E, remember that?" They continue with 'Getting My Heart Back Together'. Afterwards, the amplifiers start to buzz. Jimi comments: "Oh man what is this about?" As he tries to talk, the amplifiers buzz louder, and he admits, "We're having like, these amplifiers are blowing out and it's very bad to play on ashes you know, that's all that's left, it's nothing but ashes." The group then plays 'Purple Haze'. At the end of his performance Jimi burns a Sunburst Stratocaster which Frank Zappa owned. (It now belongs to Frank's son Dweezil.)

The second show was cancelled due to a huge thunderstorm.

Eddie Kramer: "'Rainy Day, Dream Away' was written in Miami, I will never forget. I was in the back of the car; we were pulling away from Gulf Stream Park. It was one of the first concerts there, it was Jimi and The Mothers of Invention, and I cannot remember who else. And I remember in the back of the car, the bloody thing was rained out, it was a torrential rain storm, and then he started to write it right there."

May 20
Monday
**Wreck Bar, The Castaways Hotel,
Miami, Florida**
Jimi jams on a Guild guitar with Noel Redding, Frank Zappa, Arthur Brown and Jimmy Carl Black.

May 23
Thursday
Piper Club, Milan

May 24
Friday
Teatro Brancaccio Theatre, Rome

The Experience perform two shows supported by Pier Franco Colonna, Doctor K's Blues Band, The Triad, Balletto and Franco Estill Group.

In the evening the Experience attend the Titial Club in Rome. Jimi jams on bass guitar with a local group called The Folks.

May 25
Saturday
Teatro Brancaccio Theatre, Rome

The Experience perform two shows supported by Pier Franco Colonna, Doctor K's Blues Band, The Triad, Balletto and Franco Estill Group.

May 26
Sunday
Palasport, Bologna

The Experience are supported by The Keith Henderson Group.

The group start off their show with 'Fire' and continue with 'Hey Joe' and 'Stone Free'. Next is 'Red House', after which Jimi jokes, "It's no good that we don't have enough power or electricity to do our own songs. We'd like to do a jam number, it sounds something like this." The Experience continue with 'Tax Free' and 'Purple Haze'. Jimi changes guitars and then announces, "Well for the last song, we'd like to try to do 'Foxy Lady' but it's not going to work!" The audience cheer loudly and Jimi finishes the show with the song. Because of the continued amplifier trouble, however, Jimi ends the song prematurely.

May 30
Thursday
Beat Monster Concert, Hallenstadion, Zurich

The Experience are supported by The Move, Anselmo Trend, Traffic, The Small Faces, The Koobas, John Mayall's Bluesbreakers, Eric Burdon's New Animals and Eire Apparent.

The Experience are introduced by an over-zealous MC. After a short tune up, Jimi opens the show with 'Voodoo Child (Slight Return)', played here live for the first known time. As the song ends there is a commotion in the audience. Due to the tense political situation in Switzerland and the actions of the Swiss police in the building, a riot starts up – the audience starts throwing beer mats and chair legs onto the stage. Jimi angrily announces, "Hey, don't do that, don't do that. Hey no we can't play if you're gonna throw all those things up here, okay? No don't do that, no, no – bad! Yeah, we can't play if you're gonna do that. If you throw any more then we just go off the stage." Jimi tries to continue with 'Stone Free' but has to stop halfway through because

1968 May 93

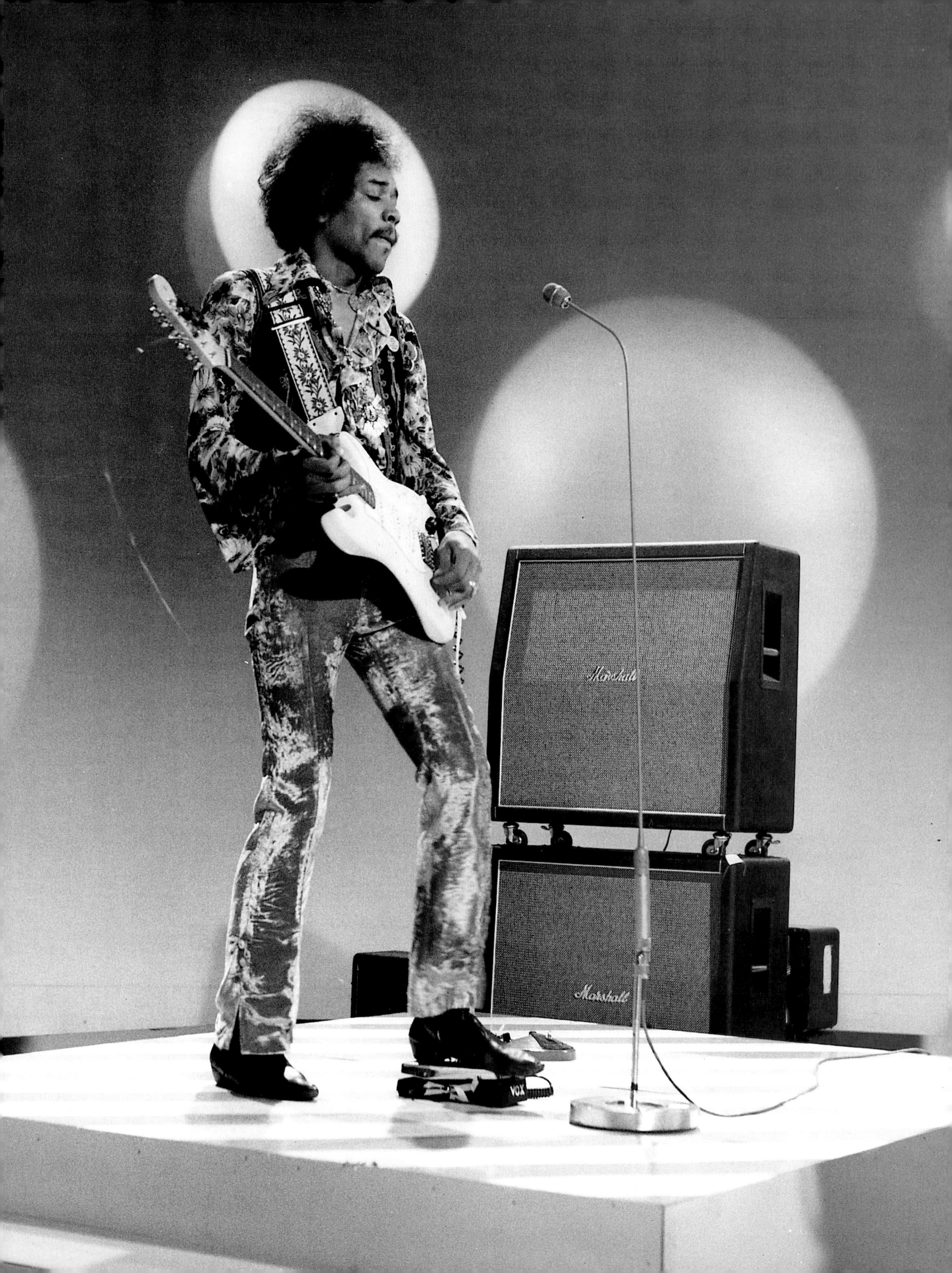
Marshall
Marshall
VOX

of the continued throwing of beer mats. The promoter, Hansruedi Jaggi, comes onto the stage and warns the audience that if the throwing continues, Jimi would not continue to play. This is greeted by jeering and booing from the audience. Jimi, now very angry, announces, "Look, I'm telling you... if you throw any more of those things man, just forget it, okay? Thanks a lot. We're gonna do a song that, er, we recorded [called]... 'I Don't Live Today', dedicated to the American Indian and you people."

The throwing of beer mats ceases and Jimi continues in a better mood. "We're gonna slow the pace, we're gonna slow the pace down a little bit. Wait a minute, wait a minute something's wrong." The audience starts shouting out for 'Hey Joe', Jimi responds: "Yeah, yeah okay, yeah okay, okay we're gonna... Thank you very much for just going on a piece, this song called 'Red House'." Afterwards, he asks, jokingly: "May I continue on with another song?" Jimi proceeds to play 'Hey Joe', which the audience respond enthusiastically to. Without any introduction, Jimi then continues with 'Foxy Lady'. "Thank you very much for staying this long and I'd like to continue with the Chandler's world." Jimi continues with 'Manic Depression'. "I'd like to say thank you very much for coming and we have one more last number to do... dedicated to everybody out there... It's a song that goes something like... oh yeah we've got two more numbers to do!" The group proceeds with 'Fire', then Jimi announces: "Yeah we only have one more last number to do. So we'd like to say thank you very, very much for coming, thank you and goodbye." Jimi ends the show with 'Purple Haze'.

May 31
Friday
Beat Monster Concert, Hallenstadion, Zurich
During the afternoon sound check, Jimi Hendrix jams with Dave Mason, Chris Wood, Stevie Winwood, Trevor Burton, Carl Wayne and Vic Briggs. Chris Wood recorded the jam on cassette, but it has never surfaced.

The Experience are supported by The Move, Anselmo Trend, Traffic, The Small Faces, The Koobas, John Mayall's Bluesbreakers, Eric Burdon's New Animals and Eire Apparent.

June 5
Wednesday
ATV Television Studios, Elstree Way, Borehamwood, Hertfordshire
The Experience attend a TV recording for *It Must Be Dusty*.

Dusty Springfield introduces Jimi: "Now about a year or so ago, I went to the theatre on a Sunday evening. They used to have some big raving Sunday concerts at a certain theatre in Shaftesbury Avenue. And I saw three people who made the best sound in the world coming from three people. This marvellous man on the guitar and equally marvellous fellows on the bass and drums, I think they're fantastic. Ladies and gentlemen... [The] Jimi Hendrix Experience."

Before Jimi starts he says: "Thank you very much. This is dedicated to Brian Jones," then continues with 'Stone Free'. After the song, Dusty jokingly asks Noel for the name of his hairdresser, then asks Jimi: "Hey, what you been doing, Jim?" He replies: "Hey we've been working on our LP, we just came off this Italian tour, you know." Dusty replies: "Yeah, tearing the place up then?" to which Jimi responds: "Well you know, we did our thing you know, whichever that is." Dusty winds the interview up with, "Well we're supposed to do a duet now and you can pick any number you want, provided you pick 'Mocking Bird'." Jimi answers: "Great, okay I'll tell you what, we'll go on and do 'Mocking Bird'."

Jimi ends the show wearing a black cape for 'Voodoo Chile (Slight Return)'.

June 8
Saturday
Jimi jams with Buddy Miles and the Electric Flag at the Fillmore East, 105 2nd Avenue 6th Street, New York.

June 13
Thursday
The Reality House Rehabilitation Centre, New York
Jimi jams with Jeff Beck at a concert to fund rehabilitation for drug addicts.

June 15
Saturday
The Scene, 301 West 46th Street, New York
Jimi jams with Eric Clapton and Jeff Beck.

June 16
Sunday
Daytop Music Festival, Staten Island, New York
Jimi jams on stage with Jeff Beck.

Later, at The Scene, Jimi Hendrix jams with Beck again. While playing 'Superstition' Jimi and Jeff switch bass and guitar by throwing their instruments to each other across the stage.

June 22
Saturday
Jimi jams with Larry Coryell at The Scene in New York.

July 6
Saturday
**Woburn Music Festival,
Woburn Abbey, Bedford**
The Experience are supported by Geno Washington, T. Rex, Family, Little Woman, New Formula, Pentangle and Shirley and Dolly Collins.

The Experience perform 'Sergeant Pepper's Lonely Hearts Club Band', 'Fire', 'Tax Free', 'Red House', 'Foxy Lady', 'Voodoo Child (Slight Return)' and 'Purple Haze'. Although a professional tape does exist of this concert, the owner has never allowed copies to be heard by fans.

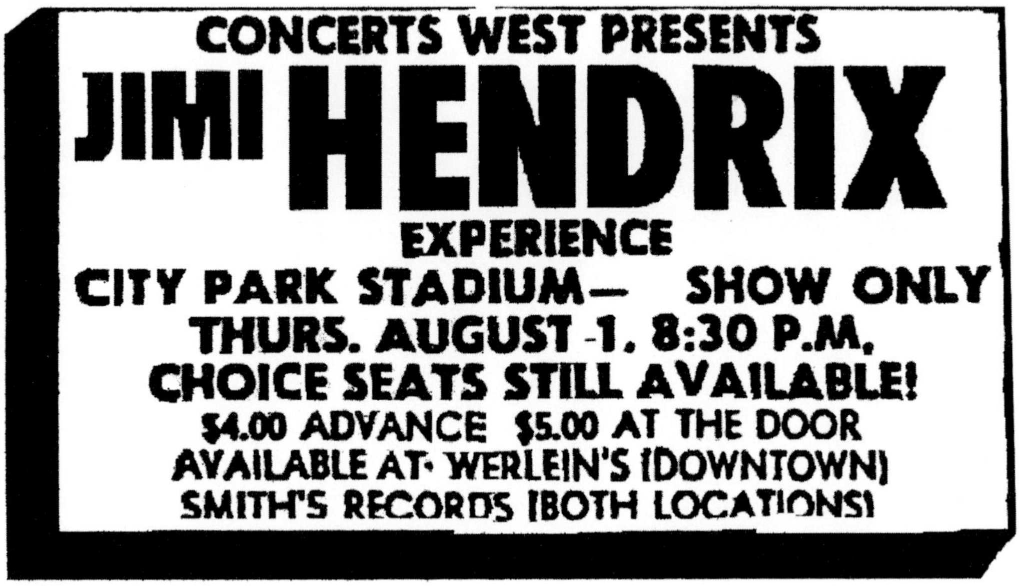

July 15
Monday
**Sgt. Pepper's Club,
Palma, Mallorca**
The Experience perform 'Hey Joe', 'The Burning Of The Midnight Lamp', 'Purple Haze', 'The Wind Cries Mary' and 'Wild Thing' in a club owned by their co-manager Mike Jeffery.

July 18
Thursday
The Experience perform an unofficial concert at Sgt. Pepper's Club, featuring Jim Leverton and Neil Landon. The ensemble play a number of Fifties rock'n'roll songs including 'Johnny B. Goode' and 'Lucille'.

July 30
Tuesday
**Independence Hall,
Lakeshore Auditorium,
Baton Rouge, Louisiana**
The Experience perform two shows, supported by Soft Machine. All Jimi's Marshall amplifiers break down before the first show. After the show, Abe Jacobs and Jimi go to a small blues club and jam all night.

July 31
Wednesday
**Municipal Auditorium,
Shreveport, Louisiana**
The Experience are supported by Soft Machine.

August 1
Thursday
**City Park Stadium,
New Orleans, Louisiana**
The Experience are supported by Soft Machine.

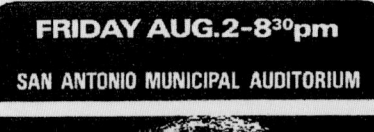

August 2
Friday
**Municipal Auditorium,
San Antonio, Texas**
The Experience are supported by Soft Machine.

The Experience perform 'Are You Experienced', 'Fire', 'Red House', 'I Don't Live Today', 'Foxy Lady', 'Hey Joe', 'Purple Haze' and 'Wild Thing'.

August 3
Saturday
**Moody Coliseum,
Southern Methodist University,
Dallas, Texas**
The Experience are supported by Soft Machine.

The group takes to the stage and proceeds to tune up for several minutes. After Noel wishes the audience a good evening, the Experience is introduced and Jimi starts the show off by playing a version of Traffic's 'Dear Mr Fantasy'. (This is the only known time that Jimi ever played the song in public.) Midway through the song, Jimi stops playing the song and goes into 'Rock Me Baby'. He then stops playing again and Mitch Mitchell takes over with a drum solo. Jimi comes back in by playing a very unusual jazz-style version of 'Rock Me Baby', then rides the song out back to its usual style. The audience starts to shout out for 'Hey Joe', but Jimi replies: "Don't chant me for a second." He asks the audience "Can you hear the PA system here when we play?" The audience shouts "Hell no!" Jimi then continues with 'Foxy Lady'.

"I hope you all don't mind if we want to dig a very, very old song," he tells the audience afterwards, "But it's, er, it's dedicated to all the, er, soldiers and all the minority groups. All the soldiers that are fighting in, er, Washington DC and Newhouse Hotel. Oh yeah and Dick Brown too. I didn't give a fuck what he was going to do to me. And so like, you want to get into this song dedicated to him and all the other minority groups… It's named, and possibly dedicated to the American Indians – a thing 'I Don't Live Today'." After the song, the instruments are out of tune again, so Jimi says: "We'd like to take about thirty two and a half seconds and tune up, because we really care for your ears. That's why we don't play so damn loud. Okay, now…"

Then, he abruptly announces: "No, I feel fucked up, I'm starting to panic." It's apparent that Jimi had had some problems during the day and decides to let his feelings be known before continuing with the concert. Clearly, he was in the mood for some improvisation, as he went on to comment: "Okay dig, like we haven't played in a long time and, like, [we'd] like [to] see what else we can do besides 'Fire'. We will do 'Fire' and 'Purple Haze'. But like, we're experimenting too..."

Jimi is interrupted by someone who says: "One minute... where [do] you want me?" Jimi replies: "I don't know man, I'm just up with... I'm playing guitar." He then announces: "We're gonna [do] something by Dylan," but stops again to ask the audience: "Can you understand the PA? There's [an] awful noise over there..." The audience responds with a mighty "No!" Jimi starts to play the opening chords to 'Hey Joe', but stops playing and leaves the stage for a moment before returning to continue the song. Without any introduction he then continues with 'Fire'. Jimi changes guitars for the next song, 'Red House': "... I wish it could be longer but this is all we can do right [now]."

Jimi continues with 'Purple Haze' to the end of which he adds a very slow version of 'Taps', which he plays with his teeth. 'Wild Thing' ends the show.

August 4
Sunday
**Sam Houston Coliseum,
Houston, Texas**
The Experience are supported by Soft Machine.

The group performs 'Red House'. After the song, Jimi announces: "Bob Cope just gave me a joint, er, I mean a puff, you know. We'd like to continue on. Dig... this next song is dedicated to all the soldiers that are fighting in Detroit, and Seattle and Washington. Oh yeah, and the soldiers fighting in Vietnam too. Also dedicated to you all for coming here and digging us, thank you very much. In other words... [the song] is dedicated to minority groups, right? And so, er, it's dedicated to another minority group... called the American Indians... [and the song's] called 'I Don't Live Today'."

The Experience continue with 'Spanish Castle Magic', 'Fire', 'Voodoo Child (Slight Return)' and 'Purple Haze'. Jimi comments afterwards: "We're very sorry for stuffing all these old songs down your throat, but... like, I forgot the words to the new ones that we have. We had this LP *Axis: Bold As Love*... well, sorry, I forgot the words to that song." The group then play 'Manic Depression'.

August 6
Tuesday
**The Scene,
301 West 46th Street, New York**
Jimi jams with Ten Years After and Larry Coryell.

August 10
Saturday
**Auditorium Theatre,
East Congress Parkway,
Chicago, Illinois**

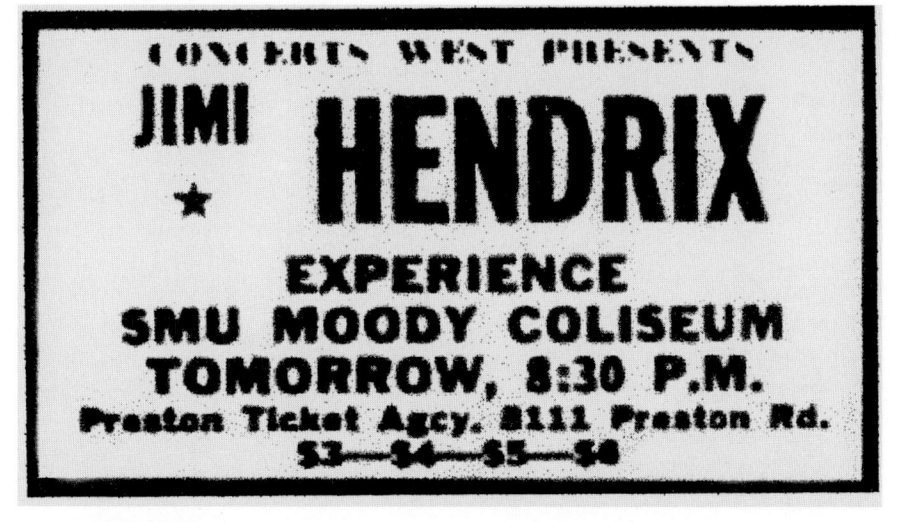

The Experience perform two shows supported by Soft Machine and The Association. The Experience perform 'Foxy Lady', 'Fire', 'Purple Haze' and 'Wild Thing'.

August 11
Sunday
Col Ballroom, Davenport, Iowa
After tuning up, Jimi announces: "We'd like to ask one question before we start: are you all experienced? It goes something like this." Jimi starts the show off with a long wild feedback introduction that segues into 'Are You Experienced'. Afterwards he comments: "I'd like to say that... er, I must tune up my guitar," and makes his standard comments about caring for the audience's ears, before announcing: "We'd like to do this other song called... 'Here Comes Your Lover Man'."

After 'Lover Man', Jimi tells the crowd, "Right, now we're gonna try something else, we haven't played this one, er, matter of fact we haven't played [it] in six months. We only recorded it about a year ago, [it's] a thing called 'Tax Free'. It's written by two Swedish cats named Hansson and Karlsson. And, er, yeah it sounds strange, but they really know how to play organ and drums and all that thing in Stockholm. And we'd like to... do a thing, which is called [improvisation] you know, like a jam or something like that, okay? If you all have power we can do it." However, first the band have to embark on another round of tuning up. They then launch into "a slow blues" – 'Red House'. Jimi then changes guitars before announcing: "This is... a song that is dedicated to somebody's girlfriend." Jimi continues with 'Foxy Lady'. "Yeah dig though, we're gonna do a song on the minority group, okay? That includes you all for coming to see us – thanks very much. I'd like to dedicate it to everybody, and... especially to the American Indians: something called 'I Don't Live Today'."

The group are running out of time, and Jimi announces: "Oh man, I wish we could... play about another hour, but the cat now said [we've] only [got] time for two more numbers, well dig. Oh yeah, that's right okay, three more numbers yeah, three more." Jimi tunes up once more and the group continues with 'Fire'.

August 16
Friday
**Merriweather Post Pavilion,
Columbia, Maryland**
The Experience are supported by Soft Machine.

1968 June/August 97

Upon their arrival on stage, Jimi announces: "Thank you very much for waiting", before starting the show with 'Are You Experienced'. Without any introduction they continue with 'Rock Me Baby'. Jimi comments: "We're having... terrible problems with amplifiers. I think the electric storm is messing around with 'em. [You're] gonna hear a whole lot of static and it's going to be very flooded, you know." Jimi continues with 'Foxy Lady', but the amplifier problems persist, making him comment, "It's really bugging me, man, I don't like it. Right now we'd like to do a song recorded in 1732 and it was called 'Hey Joe'." The audience starts to shout out for Jimi to play 'Fire'. Jimi responds: "Yeah, thank you very much for staying this long, thank you very much. We're gonna do a song called... 'Let Me Stand Next To Your Fire'. After the number, Jimi dedicates 'Don't Live Today' to minority groups, especially American Indians. He proceeds to play a blues riff á la 'Red House', before Mitch come in with the familiar drum beat that starts the song. After the song, Jimi announces: "Buying a set of good amps, that's our problem." The audience grow increasingly restive, causing Jimi to apologise, "Hold on, hold on a second. Dig, we're really sorry for the amps, you know acting the way they are there... Jimi continues with 'Purple Haze'. Before the last song, Jimi comments wryly, "I think you're had enough for us to get off stage, now... no, don't cry. This is dedicated to all them soldiers fighting in Detroit, we still love you." Jimi ends the show with 'Wild Thing'.

August 17
Saturday
Atlanta Municipal Auditorium, Atlanta, Georgia

The Experience perform two show at 15.00 and 20.00 supported by Vanilla Fudge, Eire Apparent, Amboy Dukes and Soft Machine.

The Experience perform 'Red House', 'Purple Haze', 'Wild Thing' and 'Star Spangled Banner'.

August 18
Sunday
Curtis Hixton Hall, Tampa, Florida

The Experience are supported by Soft Machine and Eire Apparent.

August 20
Tuesday
The Mosque, Richmond, Virginia

The Experience perform two shows supported by Soft Machine and Eire Apparent.

August 21
Wednesday
Civic Dome, Virginia Beach, Virginia

The Experience perform two shows supported by Soft Machine and Eire Apparent.

August 23
Friday
The New York Rock Festival, Singer Bowl, Flushing Meadow Park, Queens, New York

The Experience are supported by Janis Joplin with Big Brother and The Holding Company, The Chambers Brothers and Soft Machine.

The show opens with the audience shouting for people to get off the stage. Jimi comments, "Yeah don't worry about it... Hey, can you hear me? Please give us about, about two minutes to tune up all right? So then, so we'll pay it right back to yer, we'll play it right back to yer." Jimi starts the show off with 'Are You Experienced' announcing to the audience during the introduction: " I want to ask you, are you experienced?" "We'd like to try let me stand next to your old lady, I mean 'Let Me Stand Next To Your Fire'. Noel requests another quick tune up before launching into the song. Afterwards, Jimi announces: "We'd like to, er, like slow the pace down a little bit if it's all right with you. We'd like to slow down the pace a little bit and do a slow blues, if you don't mind. This is something that came from the, er, 1878 version of... *Are You Experienced*, which was recorded in England... Yeah, that's right, it's 'Red House'." After 'Red House' they continue with 'I Don't Live Today'. Clearly, the problems with amplification are persisting, as Jimi is heard to comment: "Yeah, I'm having a very, a very hard time hearing myself, I don't know what we're gonna do. Yeah it's the amplifier, yeah boo, the man's unhappy..."

"This is for somebody's girlfriend..." he announces, before continuing with 'Foxy Lady' and 'Like A Rolling Stone'. During the introduction to the latter, Jimi comments, "Here's a song we haven't [done] since we've been away from New York, since we played here last time. It's dedicated to the one and only Bob Dylan, yeah, and Noel goes with it. A little thing called 'Like A Rolling Stone'. After the Dylan song, Jimi tells the audience, "... one time I went to San Francisco... and, er, we had such a groovy time that we wrote a song about it and it's called 'Purple Haze'. It goes something like this here..."

After 'Purple Haze', Jimi announces: "I'd like to dedicate this sound to the Village people, and it goes out to

Tim Rose and so forth and so on, a thing called 'Hey Joe'." After the song, Jimi needs to tune up again. He comments, somewhat obliquely, "I'm very sorry that I talk, ask the police to forgive me." The show ends with 'Wild Thing' combined with 'Star Spangled Banner'– Jimi destroys his guitar by attacking his amplifier stack.

August 24
Saturday
Bushnell Memorial,
Hartford, Connecticut
The Experience are supported by Eire Apparent.

August 25
Sunday
Carousel Theatre,
Framington, Massachusetts
The Experience perform two shows, supported by Soft Machine.

The Experience perform 'Johnny B. Goode', 'Hey Joe', 'The Sunshine Of Your Love', 'Fire', 'Purple Haze', 'Wild Thing' and 'Star Spangled Banner' which includes 'Taps' and 'Reveille'.

August 26
Monday
Kennedy Stadium,
Bridgeport, Connecticut
The Experience are supported by Eire Apparent and Soft Machine.

Their performance features 'Are You Experienced', 'Foxy Lady', 'I Don't Live Today', 'Red House', 'Hey Joe' 'Spanish Castle Magic', 'Purple Haze', 'Hey Joe' and 'Wild Thing'.

At the start of the Experience's performance, Chas Chandler is arrested and jailed overnight.

Chas Chandler: "I went over to a guy that had the walkie-talkie system, we presumed he was in charge. They [the Experience] just walked on stage and all the lights were on in the stadium, so I said, 'Can you put all the lights out?' He said, 'You'll have to ask him over there.' And there's this grossly fat little man and I walked over and I said, 'Can you turn the lights out in the stalls, please.' And he said, 'Beat it Fatso.' I said, 'What?' He said, 'Arrest him.' The next thing I know I was in the cell, I could hear a voice... 'Charge him with being drunk and disorderly.' All I had was a can of Budweiser."

August 30
Friday
Langoon Opera House,
Salt Lake City, Utah
The Experience are supported by Soft Machine.

September 1
Sunday
Red Rocks Park, Denver, Colorado
The Experience are supported by Eire Apparent, Vanilla Fudge and Soft Machine.

September 3
Tuesday
Balboa Stadium,
San Diego, California
The Experience are supported by Eire Apparent, Vanilla Fudge and Soft Machine.

The group perform 'Fire', 'Little Wing', 'Foxy Lady', 'Red House' and 'The Sunshine Of Your Love'.

September 4
Wednesday
Memorial Coliseum,
Phoenix, Arizona
The Experience are supported by Eire Apparent, Vanilla Fudge and Soft Machine.

The group open their show with 'Are You Experienced'. Jimi then announces: "Well, before we can actually adjust... the sound that we're trying to get from this place man. I'd like to continue on with a thing that we recorded on our new LP... a thing that goes something like this... written by Earl King." He asks Noel, "What is that jam?" Jimi continues with 'Come On (Part One)'. The group have to tune up, and as they do so Jimi is distracted by someone leaving the auditorium. He comments, "Oh bye, see you later, take it easy though. Don't let the bedbugs bite. Don't let your meat loaf." The set then continues with 'Little Wing'. Afterwards, Jimi announces: "There's another song we'd like to do and... it's named 'Voodoo Child (Slight Return)'... it's nothing but [a] great rock 'n' roll song, too." 'Voodoo Child' is followed by 'Fire'. After a tune up, Jimi continues with 'Spanish Castle Magic' and 'Foxy Lady'. The audience starts to shout out for 'Purple Haze'. Clearly annoyed, Jimi goes into a lengthy speech: "We'll get into 'Purple Haze' and all the other songs too, but like, you know we're trying to jam and get other songs put together too... we've been on the road for a very long time... I think I'm playing every single night, all these same numbers for two years. Can you, er, dig doing that for two years? And if you're listening to music, well then I think your heads are good too." The set continues with 'Like A Rolling Stone', after which the group play 'The Sunshine Of Your Love'. The Experience end the show with 'Purple Haze' and a few bars of 'Star Spangled Banner'.

September 5
Thursday
Swing Auditorium,
San Bernardino, California
The Experience are supported by Eire Apparent, Vanilla Fudge and Soft Machine.

The Experience perform 'Are You Experienced', 'Tax Free', 'The Sunshine Of Your Love', 'Foxy Lady', 'Fire', 'Hey Joe', 'Star Spangled Banner' and 'Purple Haze'.

September 6
Friday
Centre Coliseum,
Seattle, Washington
The Experience perform two shows at 22:00 and 24:00, supported by Eire Apparent, Vanilla Fudge and Soft Machine.

After MC Robin Sherwood introduces the Experience, they perform 'Spanish Castle Magic', 'Little Wing', 'I Don't Live Today', 'Red House', 'Purple Haze', 'Fire', 'Foxy Lady', 'Hey Joe', 'Come On (Part One)' 'Voodoo Child (Slight Return)', 'Wild Thing' and 'Star Spangled Banner'.

September 7
Saturday
Pacific Coliseum, Vancouver, British Columbia, Canada

The Experience are supported by Eire Apparent, Vanilla Fudge and Soft Machine.

Colin Hartridge, of the 'Hey Joe' Internet listing: "On September 7, 1968, the Jimi Hendrix Experience came to Vancouver. The ticket price was $4.50, and there were three other bands: Eire Apparent, an Irish band that Jimi was producing; Soft Machine; and Vanilla Fudge. Eire Apparent had Claptonesque perms and the lead guitarist played the loud feedback guitar solos that were popular back then, but on the whole – they stunk! Soft Machine were incredible, although they only played one song (which was 40 minutes long) in the freak rock/jazz style they had been playing on their first two albums. Vanilla Fudge [were] also great, if a little self-indulgent. One song, 'The Break Song', featured each member in a solo spot, culminating in Carmine Appice's extra-long drum solo.

"Finally, at midnight, Jimi Hendrix hit the stage and said, "Hello Canada." He admitted he had a cold, but proceeded to play some blistering music. I can remember 'Let Me Stand Next To Your Fire' and 'Hey Joe', (which was introduced as 'Hey Josephine') as well as an unforgettable version of 'Voodoo Child (Slight Return)'. When the *Electric Ladyland* LP came out a month later, I remember thinking, "Wow, this sounds just like the concert!". At one point, he acknowledged his grandma, who apparently was in the audience, and played 'Foxy Lady'. The show was marred, though, when some idiot in the audience yelled out "Hey nigger!" which not only created tension, but made Jimi visibly annoyed. From then on, his onstage attitude was more malevolent and even a bit offhand. He announced, "We're gonna do one by The Cream... naw, I don't wanna do it", and played one more song before he just walked off the stage, with no encore."

September 8
Sunday
Coliseum, Spokane, Washington

The Experience are supported by Eire Apparent, Vanilla Fudge and Soft Machine.

The Experience start off the performance with 'Are You Experienced', followed by 'Foxy Lady'. After a quick break to tune up, accompanied by his usual comments about respecting the audience's hearing, Jimi continues with 'Little Wing'. "I'd like to do a song, a very, very straight song..." He is interrupted and comments "... forgot what, oh yeah straight song yeah that's right. Yeah, anyway, we've got this new LP coming out called *Electric Ladyland* and, em, and we have this [song] on there called 'Voodoo Child (Slight Return)' and it's very straight little rock 'n' roll [song]... Just imagine all you kids, don't forget I'm gonna put a curse on all your kids to be born butt naked. Let me tell you that from now on." After 'Voodoo Child', Jimi announces: "This song was recorded about 1738

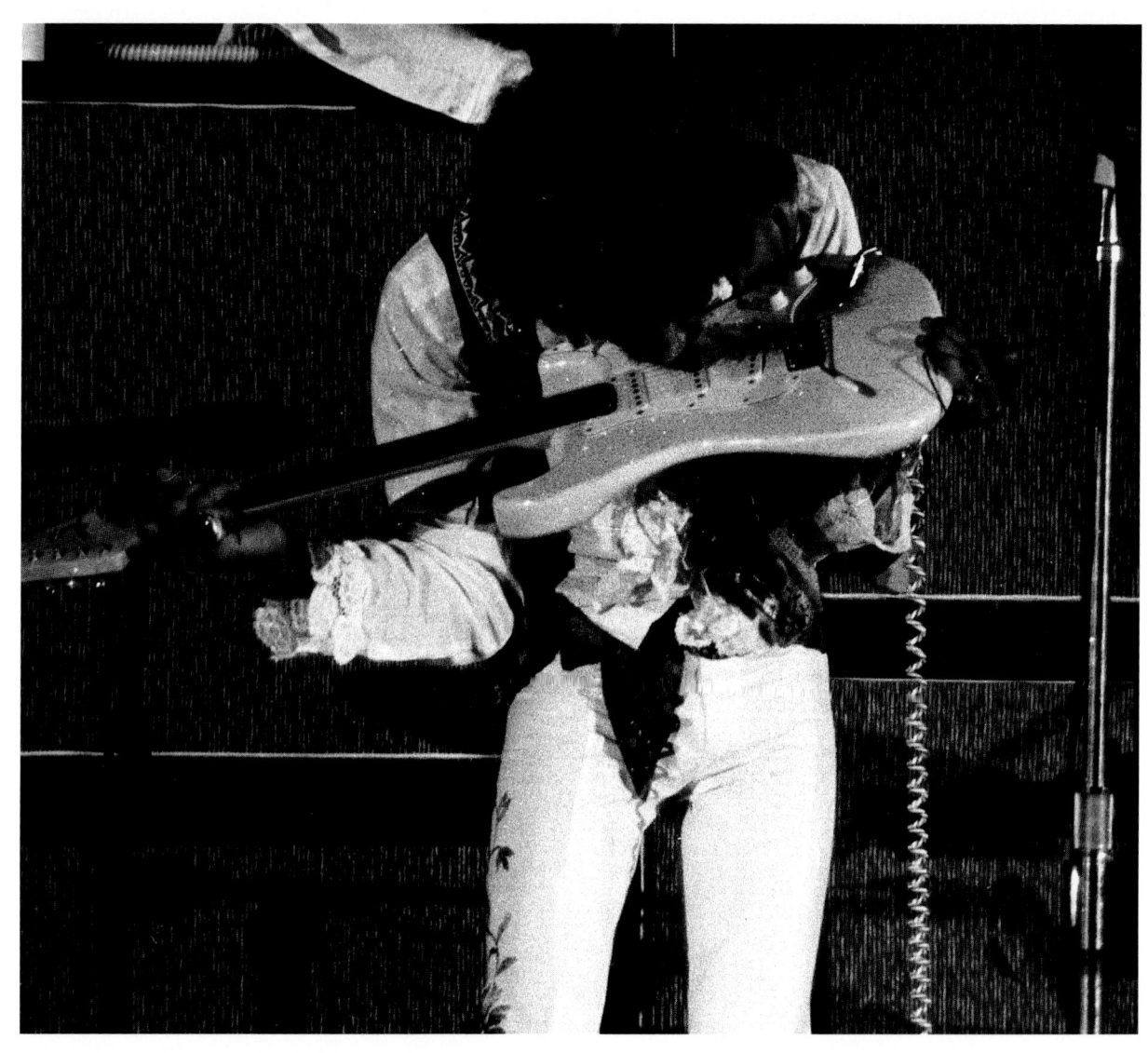

September 9
Monday
**Memorial Coliseum,
Portland, Oregon**

The Experience are supported by Vanilla Fudge and Soft Machine.

After the Experience are introduced, Jimi asks: "How you all doing? Listen, we'd like to get tuned up first, we have to get tuned up and, er, do minor adjustments here and there. It'll take about a minute... but I think it's gonna be all right." After tuning up, Jimi announces: "Normally this is taken care of behind the curtains on the stage you know, and its really embarrassing standing here tuning up." While Jimi is making his announcement, Noel and Mitch are also testing out their instruments, so Jimi's comments become inaudible; he comments, "So much noise going on here." Jimi continues with the first song of the evening 'Are You Experienced'. "Sorry to say I just broke the guitar," he comments wryly afterward, "but we'll try to see if we can get it together anyway." 'Fire' follows, then 'Hey Joe' and 'Foxy Lady' without any introduction. "I'd like to continue on," Jimi announces. "There's a song on our new LP. It's a very straight song... It's very rock 'n' rollish, it's called 'Voodoo Child (Slight Return)'." Jimi follows this number with 'Little Wing' and 'Spanish Castle Magic', before launching into 'Red House'. "I'd like to say we only have one more last number to do," he announces, before the start of 'Purple Haze'. "We'd like to say thank you for staying this long, and... we had Mitch Mitchell on drums and, er, Noel Redding on bass." This is greeted by applause from the audience. Jimi continues with a wild feedback introduction that incorporates 'Star Spangled Banner' and ends the show with 'Purple Haze'. However, midway through the song the power to the amplifiers is cut off and Mitch is left to carry on drumming on his own. The audience starts to riot and the MC comes onto the stage to tell everyone to calm down. He announces that Jimi wants to say something. Jimi announces "Listen, that's okay now wait. We're gonna do a song and play... but you've got to sit down for this, okay? Yeah, yeah. And we have someone that can come and turn the power on, we have no power, so we can't get experienced you know! This is Barry Kruger, right, we got no power." Jimi is told that the concert should now finish, and comments "They won't let us stay late, so thank you very much, man." This causes jeering in the audience. The MC comes back to the microphone to announce: "That is all, good night", whereupon the audience starts to yell and boo loudly. The uproar degenerates into a riot in the auditorium.

---

a thing written by Ben Franklin and me. And it's, er, it's just a blues... Well we didn't release it over here and... it was only on the first *Are You Experienced* LP, and it's called 'Red House'. We'll like to do it for you now." In the introduction for 'Fire', which follows, Jimi jokes, "Yeah, okay, we'd like to... do a thing called 'Let me stand next to your old lady', er, 'Let me stand and see your smoke on fire.'"

September 13
Friday
**Oakland Coliseum,
Oakland, California**

The Experience are supported by Eire Apparent, Vanilla Fudge and Soft Machine.

straight, very funky I think. Our own little funk scene... It goes something like this here... Oh yeah, by the way, the name of the new LP is *Electric Ladyland*, and it'll be out probably in about fifteen days." After the number, he comments, wryly, "What a hang-up! I was really out of tune in that one... We'd like to slow the pace down and do, er, a song recorded in 1793. Er it was recorded in the Benjamin Franklin studios... it's called 'Red House'.

of the best groups in the world, one of the best rock groups, whatever you want to call them... it's The Cream. It really is a shame, 'cause those cats is really outta site. But, dig, we'd like to jam on one of their numbers. Not saying that we play it better than them – not saying that – but we just dig the cats, you know. And now we'd like to do one of their songs for you, a thing

September 14
Saturday
**Hollywood Bowl,
Hollywood, California**

The Experience are supported by Big Brother And The Holding Company and The Chambers Brothers.

Jimi opens up by announcing: "Whatever you see... happening is part of the show. Nothing is rehearsed, as you can tell. And, like... we might be tuning up between every single song; that's because we really care for your ears. That's why we don't play so loud. You all with the ties, you know what to do, lift off your tie and take off your leg wallet and do it now. And then just get into it, man. That's all..." Jimi opens the show with 'Are You Experienced', after which someone in the crowd hollers out for 'Foxy Lady'. Not responding, Jimi starts to talk about a track on "our third LP, It'll be out soon, a thing that's called... 'Voodoo Child (Slight Return)', and it's very, very

It's dedicated to all the soul family, dedicated to Buddy Miles, Carmen." Buddy Miles tries to get on stage but is frustrated in his attempts to do so by the police, who rough him up.

During the tune up for the next song, the audience is shouting to Jimi. He responds: "I can't hear a word you're saying." They shout louder, and Jimi remarks "I can't hear you at all now, I'm sorry. This is dedicated to somebody's girlfriend and the girl named Carmen, it goes something like this..." Jimi continues with 'Foxy Lady'. After the song, it's apparent that someone is walking out of the auditorium. Jimi comments "Just walk out... just walk out... Why did you come to the show?" 'Fire' follows. During a tune up, more and more of the audience jump into the pool at the front of the stage. Noel announces: "Now we proudly present – Flipper!" Jimi then takes some time out to tell the audience about the end of one of his favourite bands: "We heard the very... bad news one time about... one

called 'The Sunshine Of Your Love'." Jimi follows this number with 'I Don't Live Today' and 'Little Wing'. He stops playing during the introduction and announces "I can't hear myself... wait, wait I can't hear, man." With splashes from the pool reaching the stage, and the group's equipment, Noel tells the audience not to come too close, as people might get electrocuted. Clearly feeling somewhat weary, Jimi then announces "All right... we got two more songs to play...[This one's] called 'Little Wing'. And relax man we're gonna play, don't worry, just let us play, okay? Just let us play." After 'Little Wing', Jimi announces, "I'm glad to say we only have one more last song to do so... [we'd like to say] thank you very much for showing up, thank you very much and you all can do anything – Wow! you all just do anything you want – because it's the last song, right?" Jimi launches into 'Star Spangled Banner' and ends the show with 'Purple Haze'.

September 15
Sunday
**Memorial Auditorium,
Sacramento, California**
The Experience are supported
by Eire Apparent, Vanilla Fudge and
Soft Machine.

The Experience perform 'Johnny
B. Goode', 'Are You Experienced', 'Stone
Free', 'Red House', 'Foxy Lady', 'Hey Joe',
'Star Spangled Banner' and 'Purple Haze'.

September 18
Wednesday
**Whiskey A Go Go,
Los Angeles, California**
The Experience jams with Graham
Bond on organ, Buddy Miles on rhythm
guitar and Eric Burdon on vocals.
The event is professionally filmed, but
has never surfaced.

October 5
Saturday
**Honolulu International Centre,
Island Of Oahu, Hawaii**
The Experience are supported by Times
Music Co.

October 10
Thursday
**Winterland, Market and
Van Ness Street, San Francisco**
The Experience perform two shows,
supported by The Buddy Miles Express
and Dino Valentine.

The Experience start their first show
of the night with 'Are You Experienced',
which is immediately followed by a tune
up. Jimi: "We tune up because we really
care for your ears. That's why we don't play
so loud, okay? So dig, it's gonna take about
thirty more seconds to tune up – hold on!
Yeah, that's really a drag [sometimes],
when you're trying to play... some sounds
and, like, your string slip off the thing up
here. And, like, we'll be having that kind
of trouble all night tonight. Well, we'll just
pretend they ain't no strings, so therefore
[they won't] slip off. And then we'll
continue on with a thing that we recorded
on our third LP which is called *Electric
Ladyland* and it's the thing called 'Voodoo
Child (Slight Return)'. If I can remember
the words." After the number, Jimi changes
guitars and announces: "We'd like to go
way back in time, go back to about
the 17th century and do a thing called
'Red House' that we recorded about two
years ago. And [it's] dedicated to the
American and the international audience...
it goes something like this here." After a
blistering version of 'Red House', Jimi
changes his guitar again and comments:
"Yeah it's very bad to tune into E with this
raggedy guitar, 'cause it's falling to pieces.
Let's see, I'll tell you what, we'll... do a
thing that we used to do back in the good
old days... when I was taking acid... It's
dedicated to somebody's old lady... a thing
called 'Foxy Lady', all right?" Jimi follows
this song with a very melodic version of
'Like A Rolling Stone' and ends the
show with a wild feedback-laden version
of 'Star Spangled Banner' followed by
'Purple Haze', which includes a few bars
of 'The Sunshine Of Your Love'.

Jimi starts off the second show by
announcing "We'd like to adjust our
instruments a little bit before we get into
something, all right? It'll take about two
minutes, okay?" After the tune up, he tells
the audience "We'd like to do our first
jam number... It's a thing that we're gonna
try to feel our way between us and you,
regardless of the mistakes we might be
making. It's... more of, er, the true feeling
type of thing... We've got a few changes
and we're gonna jam with these few
changes. We pick up these changes from
Sweden by two cats named Hansson and
Karlsson and they call it something like
'Tax Free' it goes something like this..."
When the song finishes, Jimi comments:
"Yeah thank you very much. I'd like to do
another thing... that we do in the key of B.
It's a thing called... something like 'Here
He Comes, Here Come Your Loving Man'
or something like that... It's just a regular
straight rock thing." Alluding to the
group's endless tuning up problems,
he jokes: "Like I told the other folks...
we tune between every single song, which
is not really a hang-up you know, it's
because we really care for your ears, that's
why we don't play so loud. I know you've
heard that somewhere before."

After 'Lover Man', Jimi announces:
"Round about now we'd like to do a song
by... some real groovy cats... It's one of
the heaviest groups in the world you know.
And er we'd like to do one of their songs.
I'm talking about the group Cream."
As before in concert, he is at pains to
emphasise that the Experience's version of
the song they're about to play is a tribute:
"It's not saying that we can play the thing
better than them, it's just saying that we
dig the cats and we dig the song and we
like to do it our own way..." Thank you
very much Dilla Dilace for not being with
us tonight." Jimi engages in some brief
banter with an audience member,
before light-heartedly playing a few bars
from Handel's 'Hallelujah Chorus'.
Then, finally, "Okay, here we go, here we
go... a thing by The Cream," and the
group continues with 'The Sunshine Of
Your Love'. He then announces a slow
blues jam, 'Get My Heart Back Together
Again'. After the song Jimi explains "Like
I said before we're just jamming man...
how about one of them old [songs]?"
Someone calls out for 'Fire', to which
Jimi replies, laughing: "No, no, no, no!"
"No I'll tell you what," he continues,
"We're doing this thing called er, what is
it? 'Voodoo Child (Slight Return)', all
right? It's featured on a new LP and it's
like the second from last song we're be
doing tonight. So thank you very much
for coming..."

At this point Jack Cassidy comes
on stage and Jimi excitedly announces:
"Jack Cassidy's on stage, how about a big
hand for Jack Cassidy?" Jack tunes up
his bass guitar and Jimi announces:
"We're gonna be here for four more shows,
so hope you all don't mind a jam with
Cassidy here. We're gonna jam maybe
off the tune of 'Killing Floor', okay?"
After a rousing version of the song, Jimi
asks the audience to give Jack a round of
applause. The improvised combo then
continue with 'Hey Joe'. After Jimi plays
the end solo with his teeth, he allows Jack
to play a fast solo on the bass before
bringing the song to an end. Someone
shouts something out to Jimi. He replies,
"I'm playing a show though man,
I can't hear what you're saying." He then
announces, "We'd like to continue on
with a thing called 'This Is America'...
It's, er, really lost souls and... frustration,
it seems like to me. I don't know though,
we're just messengers you know. And like,
er, you know, [we'll] just see if we can get
this feeling across to you, maybe through
all this racket that some people that think
we're making, up there. Oh it's a good
racket, hell." Clearly inspired by the idea
of improvising at this stage in his career,
he continues: "You know, you get tired
of playing notes sometimes, so you really
want to play, or get close to playing,
exactly what you call a 'true feeling'..."
Jimi then draws a high squeal from his
guitar and proceeds to play an old Duane

Eddy-esque rock 'n' roll riff, which Mitch and Noel immediately join in with. Afterwards, Jimi launches into some extraordinary feedback, followed by a very stoned-sounding solo, including dive-bombing planes and explosions, which he then turns into 'Star Spangled Banner'. He finally ends the show with 'Purple Haze', announcing at the end of the song: "Thank you very much. How about a big hand for Jack Cassidy, Noel Redding and Mitch Mitchell? Thank you."

October 11
Friday
Winterland, San Francisco

The Experience perform two shows supported by The Buddy Miles Express and Dino Valentine.

The Experience take the stage for the first show of the evening. The audience are standing on the seats to get a better look, but are causing a commotion by blocking the view of the people at the back of the auditorium. Jimi sees the problem and comments: "Hey listen, to be fair, listen to be fair with everybody... we're here to try to turn everybody on, you know. So, like, if everybody sat down okay... it'll help us to stay. Thank you. You all over there, do what you want to, but you all over there do what you want to." After a long delay, the Experience tune up their instruments and Bill Graham can finally announce them. Jimi starts the show off with 'Are You Experienced'. Virgil Gonzales has joined Jimi on stage to play flute, and the song turns into a fifteen-minute jam. "Hey, before we do anything, how about a big hand for Virgil Gonzales on the... flute there. It was like a jam you know, the cat had his axe and so we said all right." As ever, technical difficulties were plaguing the Experience, and Jimi has to beg the audience's indulgence: "Please give us about another minute to get it all together, all right! Because... in order to do it right, we must have at least this stuff set up halfway right, okay... don't worry though, we're gonna stay here until we get something happening, so don't worry."

When proceedings kick off again, Jimi announces 'Voodoo Child (Slight Return)' thus: "We'd like to do a song that's on our new LP now... the LP's called *Electric Ladyland*, there's a song about a cat singing about he's gonna chop down a mountain with the sides of [his] hand and all this. Well dig, we're gonna see if we can show you exactly what we [were] trying to say in that tune, it goes something like this here." However, there's still some problems with the audience at the front standing on their chairs, and Jimi announces: "Please, hey listen, there's some people there getting uptight, we don't want nobody to be uptight, okay? So if you all sit down a little bit, all right? Sit down, you know come on man, just sit down. We don't want to have nobody uptight, you know we want everybody to, you have to dig it, you know... Okay the thing is called 'Voodoo Child (Slight Return)'."

Following this number, Jimi comments: "I'd like to change guitars over this time and slow the pace down a little bit too. I'd like to do a song that goes something like this here, we recorded in about 1835. And... we released it on the English LP [of *Are You Experienced*] but we didn't get a chance to release it on the American [one]... Little bit of blues." The band play 'Red House' and follow up with 'Foxy Lady'. Jimi ends the show with a wild free-form feedback solo, to which he adds a few bars of the theme from *Bonanza*, and finally goes into 'Star Spangled Banner' and 'Purple Haze'.

The Experience take the stage for the second performance of the evening and proceed to tune up. Jimi apologises to the audience for the delay: "Very sorry for taking a long time. We'd like to start off. Testing one, two, three testing, testing. Very, very sorry for the delay, we're probably be up here for about an hour and a quarter anyway, so we'll see if we can get it back to you that way. Dig, we'd like to jam right now, we'd like to jam off of the tune we jammed off of last night. It's a thing written by two cats in... Sweden named Hansson and Karlsson and... they call it 'Tax Free'... and it goes something like this here." After 'Tax Free', Jimi announces: "Here's a song we recorded not too long ago... It's a song called 'Spanish Castle Magic' and it goes something like this." When the song is finished, Jimi tells the audience: "We'd like to bring up on the stage a very heavy organ player which is really outta site, belonging to Buddy Miles Express. How about a big hand for Herbie Rich on organ on this next tune! We'd like to do another slow song if you don't mind; it's a thing that we dig from a certain cat... Poetry, everybody wants to know what happened to poetry, modern day poetry. Well, you know, just dig the records, you can [find] it all over the place, and this cat happens to be part of that scene." Jimi continues with Dylan's 'Like A Rolling Stone'. Unfortunately, Herbie Rich has some tuning trouble through the song.

Jimi announces a new song with, "I'd like to do a thing called 'Here He Comes, Here Come Your Lover Man'," but clearly he's not in the peak of health. "I have this cold and it's really killing me, cancer's getting a hold of me...! Let's see now, oh what can we play now? I don't know..." The audience shouts out for 'Fire' and Jimi comments "You want to go with old?" and continues with 'Hey Joe', followed by 'Fire'. After the song, the group tune up and Noel announces: "We're just having a beer break, hang on." The set continues with 'Foxy Lady' and ends with 'Purple Haze', after which Jimi comments: "Thank you very much, see you tomorrow night... Take it easy and don't let the bed bugs bite and peace, brother."

October 12
Saturday
Winterland, San Francisco

The Experience perform two shows supported by The Buddy Miles Express and Dino Valentine.

The group take the stage for their first show of the final night at Bill Graham's Winterland arena. After Graham introduces the Experience, they launch straight into 'Fire'. Jimi makes his standard joke about the tuning breaks and respecting the audience's ears by playing quietly, before telling the audience: "We'd like to continue on with a song that, er, we probably got together about a year and a half ago." Someone shouts out for 'Watchtower' – Jimi replies. "Forgot the words, I'm sorry" and laughs. "It's a thing, I can never remember other people's songs... Anyway, this thing's called... 'Here He Comes, Here Comes Your Lover Man' it's nothing but a straight rock thing in the key of E." Technical problems persist however, and at the end of the song Jimi tells the audience: "I hate to say it but... I just developed about six more broken speakers, so we'll see what happens..." Jimi plays the introduction to the next song, announcing: "Here's a song written by Dylan. A thing called 'Like A Rolling Stone'.

When the Experience finish the number, Jimi announces: "We'd like to do a little... slow drag straight forward... rock song that we recorded', then he suddenly remembers something and tells the audience, "Oh yeah, today is the second, second anniversary [of the group] as a group today, this very instant. Sorry to take up any more of your time, we'd like to continue on and do a song that... [is] dedicated to somebody's girlfriend tonight, after we leave the show. I don't know who it's gonna be, we'll find out, but it's dedicated to her, okay? And, er, just in case something does happen between me and, er whoever it might be... Well, it's gonna happen right here, I'm gonna get my climax, er, I think I'll reach it." After laughing at his comment, Jimi continues the set with 'Foxy Lady'. Halfway through the song, Jimi starts to have serious problems with the amplifiers and his guitar cuts out completely. Mitch starts a drum solo and Jimi comes back in to end the song. "All right thank you very much. We'd like to... [let Mitch] just cut loose a little bit here while we're changing amplifiers. We're having difficulties, but instead of... standing around watching tired old amplifiers being changed and tired old plugs, you know, the same old hogwash, man... we'd like to have Mitch cut off a little biddy thing." Mitch and Noel continue to jam until the amplifiers are changed. Jimi finally comes into the jam and turns it into 'Tax Free'. "Yeah," he comments afterwards, "we had a large amount of trouble but we'll just keep on pushing with a thing called 'Hey Joe'." The group run through their first major hit; then, without any introduction, Jimi continues with 'Purple Haze' and ends the show with 'Wild Thing'. He thanks the audience and apologises for the hang up before leaving the stage.

Bill Graham introduces the Experience for their second show and the last time for this series of concerts. Jimi starts this show off with 'Foxy Lady', though it doesn't take long for equipment problems to start. ("It's just too bad that we're having all this trouble tonight...") Undeterred, Jimi tells the audience, "[the] main thing here tonight is like to try to give somebody some kind of natural true feeling for [themselves]. And maybe you can... like, grasp these pieces of electricity that is hitting you, I don't know where, yeah I might be hitting you in the chest maybe, closest to your heart." He then goes on to explain, "I'm talking like this because the amplifier's broken and it's gonna take about two minutes to fix and I'd like to say this anyway, so here's the time to say it. So, er, you know just peace and goodwill towards everybody and scenes like that... I'd like to do a 'frustrating try' song for you. It's called 'Manic Depression' a story about a cat wishing he could make love to music instead of the same ole everyday woman okay, as soon as the amplifiers get together. Like I said before we're having problems but we'll get under way and er we're gonna stay here until we get next to you anyway, so... Don't feel uptight about staying here maybe, maybe about five or ten or fifteen [minutes] or a half-hour later than usual."

The amplifiers are finally changed and Jimi continues with 'Manic Depression'. Afterwards, he comments, "I think I've got about five, no let's see, I think about four speakers left and about three more valve tubes. I think it carries one, two three, four, five, six, seven yeah well anyway. I think [the road manager] has about two more speakers left... but fucking hell, I don't give a damn." The group continue with 'The Sunshine Of Your Love' and 'Little Wing'; Jimi adds a riff from 'You Got Me Floating' at the end. Apologising again for the delay caused by technical problems, Jimi continues with 'Spanish Castle Magic'. Clearly the situation was frustrating him, as he returned to the subject of equipment problems after the song: "We'd like to, er, come back here again one of these times to make up for these last two nights where we've been having very bad equipment. Because we want you to hear us the way we really are... so... we'd really love to come back kinda soon and make up for this junk we have behind us, in the mean time... We just came off a tour you know, and it was really hectic... I think we went through six sets of Sunns a piece, and about four Marshalls. This is about the fifth set and they've really had it!"

Jimi introduces the next song by telling the audience, "Everybody was scared to release it in America because they say 'Man, America don't like blues m-a-n', you know... We're just gonna do it now and if it comes out all right, we'll release it on the LP. Anyway it goes something like this here." Jimi continues with 'Red House' and 'Voodoo Child (Slight Return)', stopping at one point to leave Mitch drumming on his own. Jimi sounds very despondent, possibly due to all the technical hitches the band had faced, and comments "Everything has got to pot... oh God, what an embarrassing situation. We'll see if we can go ahead... and, you know, do this thing called 'America' and then we'll just close it up. I'd like to say thank you very, very much, man for staying with us this long... you must all be really be tired (Jimi snores) 'cause I really am, I'm sorry, I really am tired. We'd like to go ahead on and do a thing called 'This Is America'. Jimi gives the crowd his version of 'Star Spangled Banner' and finally closes the show with 'Purple Haze'. At the end of the concert, he throws the guitar into his amplifier stack, leaving it to emit a high-pitched squeal, and walks off the stage.

October 19
Saturday
Fillmore West,
Market and Van Ness Street,
San Francisco, California

Whiskey Au Go Go,
Sunset Strip, Los Angeles
Jimi jams with Lee Michaels.

October 26
Saturday
Civic Auditorium,
Bakersfield, California
The Experience are supported by Cat Mother & The All Night Newsboys.

November 1
Friday
Municipal Auditorium Arena,
Kansas City, Missouri
The Experience are supported by Cat Mother & The All Night Newsboys.

November 2
Saturday
Auditorium,
Minneapolis, Minnesota
The Experience are supported by Cat Mother & The All Night Newsboys. The group start the show off with 'Fire'. As before, however, technical problems plague the Experience, as Jimi tells the audience: "Hey listen, we're having a little trouble with our amplifiers, in case you hear and experience it, well don't worry about it." As the band perform 'Are You Experienced', the audience are all out of

their seats and the MC comes onto the stage to announce that the fire chief says whatever the audience are doing is against the rules. The audience is warned sternly to return to their seats. Jimi continues: "Dig, we'd like to do a track from... our new LP called *Electric Ladyland*. The name of the track is...'Voodoo Child (Slight Return)'. After the song, Jimi announces "Please give us another second to get the amps together, all right? I'd like to do a song that's... slow blues. It might bore a few of you all, I hope not anyway... A thing called 'Red House' that we recorded about two years ago in England. It's on *Are You Experienced* LP and it'll be on our new one, only, you know, arranged a little better." Jimi continues with 'Red House', then, during another tuning break, he explains: "We tune up between every song because we really care for your ears, that's why we don't play so loud. This song here is dedicated to somebody's girlfriend tonight, I don't know who yet but we'll find out after the gig" Jimi continues with 'Foxy Lady', 'Little Wing' and 'Spanish Castle Magic'.

"We've got some... groovy friends in the music business, like one of the groups that broke up," Jimi tells the audience after 'Spanish Castle Magic', "... one of the best groups around. We'd like to deal with a song by them, a group called The Cream. We'd like to do an instrumental... we're not saying that we play it better then them, we're not saying that, it's just that we dig the song, you know, and we'd like to play an instrumental." Jimi continues with 'The Sunshine Of Your Love'. He concludes by thanking the audience for their patience: "I'd like to say thank you very much for showing up, man, tonight..." Jimi then continues with 'Star Spangled Banner' and ends the show with 'Purple Haze'.

It had been reported that Noel was so stoned during the show, he fell off the stage, knocking over the PA stacks and cutting his leg.

November 3
Sunday
Kiel Auditorium, St. Louis, Missouri
The Experience are supported by Cat Mother & The All Night Newsboys. The Experience perform 'Rock Me Baby', 'Foxy Lady', 'Fire', 'Hey Joe', (possibly) 'Tax Free', 'Star Spangled Banner' and 'Purple Haze'.

November 11
Monday
**The Scene,
301 West 46th Street, New York**
Jimi jams with Fleetwood Mac.

November 15
Friday
**Cincinnati Gardens,
Cincinnati, Ohio**
The Experience are supported by Cat Mother & The All Night Newsboys.

November 16
Saturday
**Boston Gardens, Nashua Street,
Boston, Massachusetts**
The Experience are supported by Cat Mother & The All Night Newsboys and The McCoys.

Jimi starts the show off by saying: "We're tuning up now for your precious ears. This may take a while, hope you brought your lunch? Never mind, let's go. Hell, they don't know the difference anyway." 'I Don't Live Today' opens the set, followed by 'Hey Joe'. The group continues with 'Fire' and 'Spanish Castle Magic', which Jimi is now starting to turn into a long extended jam. The group continue with 'Voodoo Child (Slight Return)', 'Red House' and 'Foxy Lady', ending the show with 'Purple Haze'.

November 17
Sunday
**Woolsey Hall, Yale University,
New Haven, Connecticut**
The Experience are supported by Cat Mother & The All Night Newsboys and Terry Reid.

November 22
Friday
**Jacksonville Coliseum,
Jacksonville, Florida**
The Experience are supported by Cat Mother & The All Night Newsboys.

November 23
Saturday
**Curtis Hixon Hall,
Tampa, Florida**
The Experience are supported by Cat Mother & The All Night Newsboys.

November 24
Sunday
**Convention Hall,
Miami Beach, Florida**
The Experience are supported by Cat Mother & The All Night Newsboys.

PHILHARMONIC HALL | LINCOLN CENTER

Thursday Evening, November 28, 1968, at 8:00 and 11:00

ron delsener

presents

"An Electronic Thanksgiving"

Jimi Hendrix Experience
NOEL REDDING — bass
JIMI HENDRIX — guitar
MITCH MITCHELL — drums

★

Fernando Valenti
harpsichordist

★

The New York Brass Quintet
ROBERT NAGEL — trumpet
ALLEN DEAN — trumpet
PAUL INGRAHAM — french horn
JOHN SWALLOW — trombone
THOMPSON HANKS — tuba

Sonata from Die Bankelsangerlieder
Muy Linda, Pavan & Galliard
Contra Punctus IV & IX

Mr. Valenti and The New York Brass Quintet appear by arrangement with Columbia Artists Management.

The taking of photographs and the use of recording equipment are not allowed in this auditorium.

Members of the audience who must leave the auditorium before the end of the concert are earnestly requested to do so between numbers, not during the performance.

November 27
Wednesday
**Rhode Island Auditorium,
Providence, Rhode Island**
The Experience open their show with 'Sergeant Pepper's Lonely Hearts Club Band' followed by 'Fire'. "Thank you very much," Jimi announces. "We're having a big party tonight, it's fab... The next song is dedicated to Vermorga Myer... A thing recorded in 1763 in the Benjamin Franklin studios... A song, a thing about this cat shooting his old lady because, er, she wasn't done doing her thing to somebody else. Jimi continues with 'Hey Joe', acknowledging, "Yeah, I'm out of tune, don't worry, er, we'd like to put it on right here and like, er, dedicate the next song to you for coming to see us and... also to the... American Indians, a thing called 'I Don't Live Today." Someone shouts something out after the song; Jimi replies, "I can't understand a word you're saying." The group then go into "a straight rock 'n' roll type of thing, very simple, a thing called 'Voodoo Child (Slight Return)'.

Referring to the technical hassles, Jimi comments: "Some people don't know the difference anyway, but it happens to be that our amps are no good and we're playing on about four speakers apiece... We're playing off stallions and ashes from the last gig we did." Jimi continues with 'Voodoo Child (Slight Return)', then announces: "I'd like to continue on and... slow the pace down a little bit, bore you for about six or seven minutes. It's a slow blues that we recorded in England about two years ago, when we first got together. A thing called 'Red House'. We'd like to do it for you." Jimi starts 'Red House' but has trouble tuning his guitar, so he starts the song over again. He follows this with 'The Sunshine Of Your Love'. The whole audience is now on their feet shouting out songs for Jimi to play; he replies " Yeah, I'd like to do a song dedicated to somebody's girlfriend, we don't know who it is yet, but, em, we'll

1968 October/November 107

find out later on tonight after the show. You all like songs with Dylan? Do you all dig Dylan?" Jimi asks Noel and Mitch "Do you wanna try it?" Clearly he changes his mind, however, as he then tells the audience: "We won't do it tonight, I'm out of practice... it's kinda hard, but we'll do 'Spanish Castle Magic' dedicated to this joint. We'd like to do 'Spanish Castle Magic' for you..." He goes on to explain to the audience that "The reason why we're playing so many old songs is because [when] we recorded the last LP... we were doing gigs and touring the United States Of America [at the same time as] recording the LP and, you know, it's very hard jumping from... the studio onto the... plane, and do a gig and jump right back in the studio again. But you know that's why we're playing so many old songs because we never had the chance to get in practice." Jimi continues with 'Spanish Castle Magic'.

Then: "I'd like to stitch on playing our two more songs, we hope that you like them, and thank you very much for staying this long. This goes something like this here, it's also dedicated to somebody's girlfriend after the end of [the] gig, after the end of the gig, man. It goes something like this here." As Jimi plays the opening note, he stops and remarks "Thank you very much and now for our next tune," then continues with 'Foxy Lady'. After the song, the power gets turned off. Jimi comments: "Look, the faggot back here turned the power off and we have one more song to do, so let's stay there until they turn the power back on, all right? Yeah, it's the international anthem we're gonna do now, but you all know the song, so... And in that song we like to see everybody stand up, put your right hand across your left, you know whatever you can find to put it across, and then we'll begin with the international anthem. If you don't all sing along with us and you don't stand, then you've got to put your right hand across your left, left er, whatever you find to put it across there. And we're gonna put a curse on you, we gonna put a curse on you, yes. All your kids shall be born butt naked, so you know what that means if you don't put your hands [up], and stand up and do your thing." Jimi ends the show with 'Star Spangled Banner' and 'Purple Haze'.

November 28
Thursday
Philharmonic Hall, Lincoln Center, New York

'An Electric Thanksgiving' (from 18:00 to 11:00).

The Experience perform two shows supported by Harpsichordist Fernando Valenti and the New York Brass Quintet.

The Experience are announced on the stage, Jimi asks the audience "How you all doing all right? Er what we'll be doing tonight is, we'll all be jamming... It will only take us about a minute and a half to do, like, little minor adjustments here and there. So give us about a minute. I'd like to say thank you very much for waiting for us, we'd like to start off with... a thing called 'Let Me Stand Next To Your Old Lady', I mean 'Let me Stand Next To Your Fire'. After the song, he announces: "Yeah... what we're doing... we'll be jamming and see what's happening... You lay back and dig it; everybody's really calm... I'd like to [dedicate this] to the Black Panthers and the... American Indians, a thing called 'I Don't Live Today',.." After the song, Jimi thanks the audience for their appreciation and continues: "I'd like to slow the pace down a little bit... we'll do this blues that sometimes we do. It looks like a jam session again, man. I have a feeling we'll call it, er, 'Waiting For That Train'. It's just like a cat waiting around, you know, for his train to come like, so he can show his girlfriend that he's a man, you know... So we'll see if we can get that, we'll just be jamming..." Jimi continues with 'Getting My Heart Back Together Again'. "I'd like to say thank you very much for staying with us this long, it's groovy man, so I'd like to continue on anyway, [and] do a thing like..." Someone shouts out a song from the audience. Jimi starts to reply – "I think we'll do this thing we did in, er..." before laughing and confessing, "I don't know what the hell we're gonna do, I don't know, okay!" He continues, "This is dedicated to all the plain-clothes women in the narcotics [department]. A thing called 'Spanish Castle Magic'." After the song, Jimi tells the crowd, "When we have a jam, I like to make sure... we make sure that it IS a three-piece group, and we got Mitch Mitchell on drums and Noel Redding on bass."

Mitch has always stated that this concert was filmed, though no evidence has been found. However, Jimi can distinctly be heard to say, "You got enough for the film?" which would seem to suggest that Mitch was right. Jimi moves on to 'Foxy Lady', dedicating it, as he had done on numerous occasions before, to "somebody's girlfriend". After 'Foxy Lady', Jimi announces a "slow blues", and the group continues with 'Red House'. "As I said... we're nearly out of time... So maybe we got two more songs to do, right? Okay... we gonna do a song for you now, let's say it then, maybe we're as good as The Cream. Dig, we'd like to go ahead and do one of their songs, only with guitar..." As he had done previously, Jimi maintains, "We're not doing this... [to say] that we play it better than them." However, this time he continues, rather sarcastically, "We're just playing it because they're our parents and they need to get pleasure too." Jimi continues with 'The Sunshine Of Your Love'. The audience is all on their feet shouting out for various songs, and they continue as Jimi proceeds to start the final song. He stops playing to say, "Hey, do be quiet over there...", then closes the show with 'Purple Haze'.

Earlier, Mitch Mitchell jammed on stage with the New York Brass Quintet at the same venue: "We were offered the Philharmonic, which was great. Lovely hall, very prestigious, no rock band had ever played there. Only one problem, a member of the band had to play in a symphonic context. Jimi and Noel flatly refused, so I thought, okay, what the hell, I'll do it. Would I mind having tea with Leonard Bernstein? Which I did, charming chap. He suggested that I might like to play percussion with the New York Brass Ensemble. It was fine; I went on with them with a collar and tie on. We did some Bach and a little Mozart – great! – after which the Experience played."

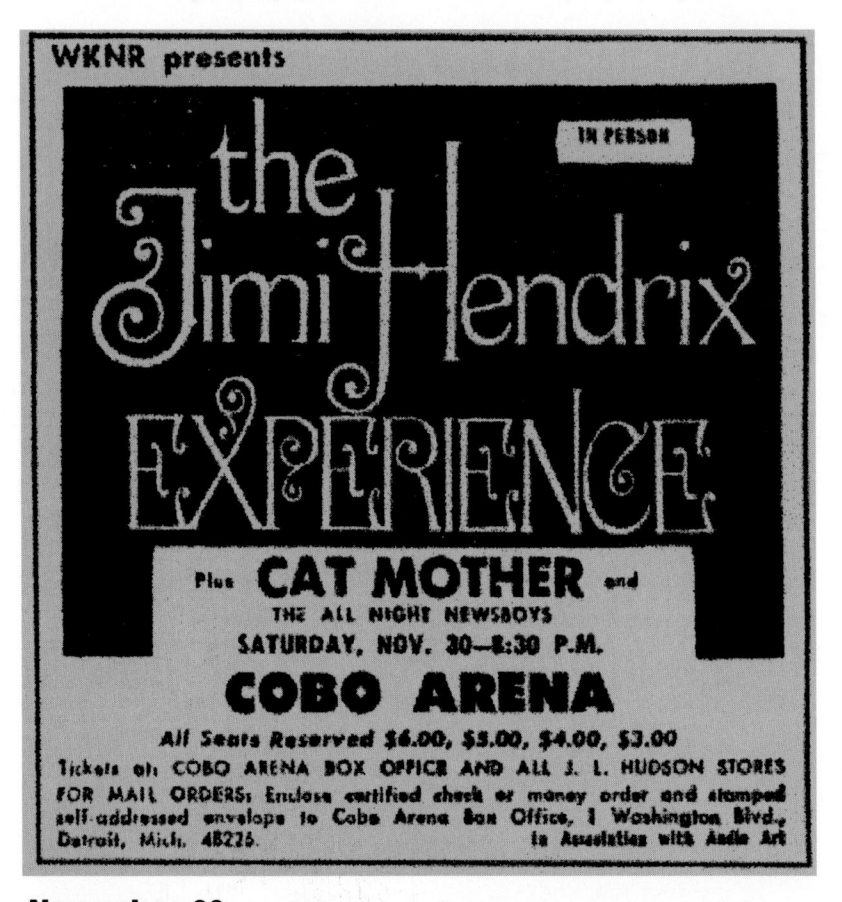

WKNR presents the Jimi Hendrix Experience Plus CAT MOTHER and THE ALL NIGHT NEWSBOYS SATURDAY, NOV. 30 – 8:30 P.M. COBO ARENA All Seats Reserved $6.00, $5.00, $4.00, $3.00. Tickets at COBO ARENA BOX OFFICE AND ALL J. L. HUDSON STORES. FOR MAIL ORDERS: Enclose certified check or money order and stamped self-addressed envelope to Cobo Arena Box Office, 1 Washington Blvd., Detroit, Mich. 48226. In Association with Audio Art

November 30
Saturday
Cobo Arena, Detroit, Michigan

The Experience are supported by Cat Mother & The All Night Newsboys. Mitch Mitchell and Noel Redding fly to Detroit for the evening show; Jimi doesn't want to play, and so misses the plane. He is, however, persuaded to attend the concert by Michael Jeffery and arrives later by a chartered Lear jet.

The Experience start off their show with 'Fire', followed by 'I Don't Live Today'. They continue with 'The Sunshine Of Your Love' and 'Red House', followed by 'Foxy Lady' and 'Hey Joe'. The audience are shouting out for 'Purple Haze' and Jimi remarks: "... thank you for even thinking about the song... thank you very much. And now I'd like to do 'Purple Haze'." Someone else shouts out for 'Manic Depression' and Jimi comments: 'Manic Depression', I wish we could do it man, but you know. Like we only have about two minutes left, you know. The cat says to turn off the power and we'll be off the stage very soon which is a very bad drag. This thing here, this song is dedicated all the... same postmen and I smoking our products, a thing called 'Purple Haze'. You're probably puzzled that you hear distortion here and there. Well it's true, yes, you are good at hearing... I'm only playing with about two speakers..." Jimi winds up by thanking the audience for coming and announcing: "You know this is the last gig. Tomorrow night's the last gig we'll do in the States for a long time. It's been really groovy for the last two months." Jimi ends the show with 'Purple Haze'.

December 1
Sunday
Coliseum, Chicago, Illinois

The Experience are supported by Cat Mother & The All Night Newsboys.

The Experience take the stage for their last concert of their American tour. Jimi announces: "I'd like to say first of all that [this is] the last gig we'll do in America for quite some time... But it's gonna take us about a minute and a half to get tuned up and do our little adjustments here and there, so it'll come out well..." "What I'd like to do," he continues, "... is a thing called 'Killing Floor', and we'll do it our own little way, you know. We haven't [done] that in a long time, matter of fact I don't think we ever did it before." Jimi continues with 'Killing Floor', after which he apologises for the sound problems: "Thank you. Yeah we're having slight difficulties hold on a minute, okay? Like we always say, we tune up because we really care for your ears, that's why we don't play so loud." Jimi goes on to dedicate 'I Don't Live Today' to the Black Panthers and the American Indians. He then announces: "I'd like to continue on with all that racket and do a thing called 'Spanish Castle Magic'. Dedicated to all the plain-clothes men and all the narcs too." He then announces a by now familiar dedication, "to somebody's girlfriend tonight, we don't know who it is yet but we'll find out after the show. A thing called 'Foxy Lady'." Then, "We'd like to do another song... we'd like to do a blues that we recorded in England on the first English *Are You Experienced* LP It's... a slow blues called 'Red House'." When it comes to 'The Sunshine Of Your Love', Jimi announces: "I'd like to continue on and... do this thing dedicated to one of the grooviest groups in the world. It's too bad they had to break up. We'd like to do one of their songs... it's instrumental, just so you know. Not saying that we can play it better than them, we're not saying that at all. We're just saying that we dig the song and we dig the group. So it goes something like this here." Jimi continues with 'The Sunshine Of Your Love'. After the number he changes guitars and announces: "I'd like to do a track from our new LP it's a swing type song, its called 'Voodoo Child (Slight Return)'. After a little more tuning up, the group runs through 'Voodoo Child'. Jimi then announces: "it's been a whole lot of fun being on the United States tour. And like... we hope we come back here in the summer time." The Experience play 'Fire', then the show ends with 'Purple Haze'.

December 18
Wednesday
Cafe Au Go Go,
Bleeker Street, Greenwich Village,
New York

Jimi jams with The James Cotton Blues Band.

1969

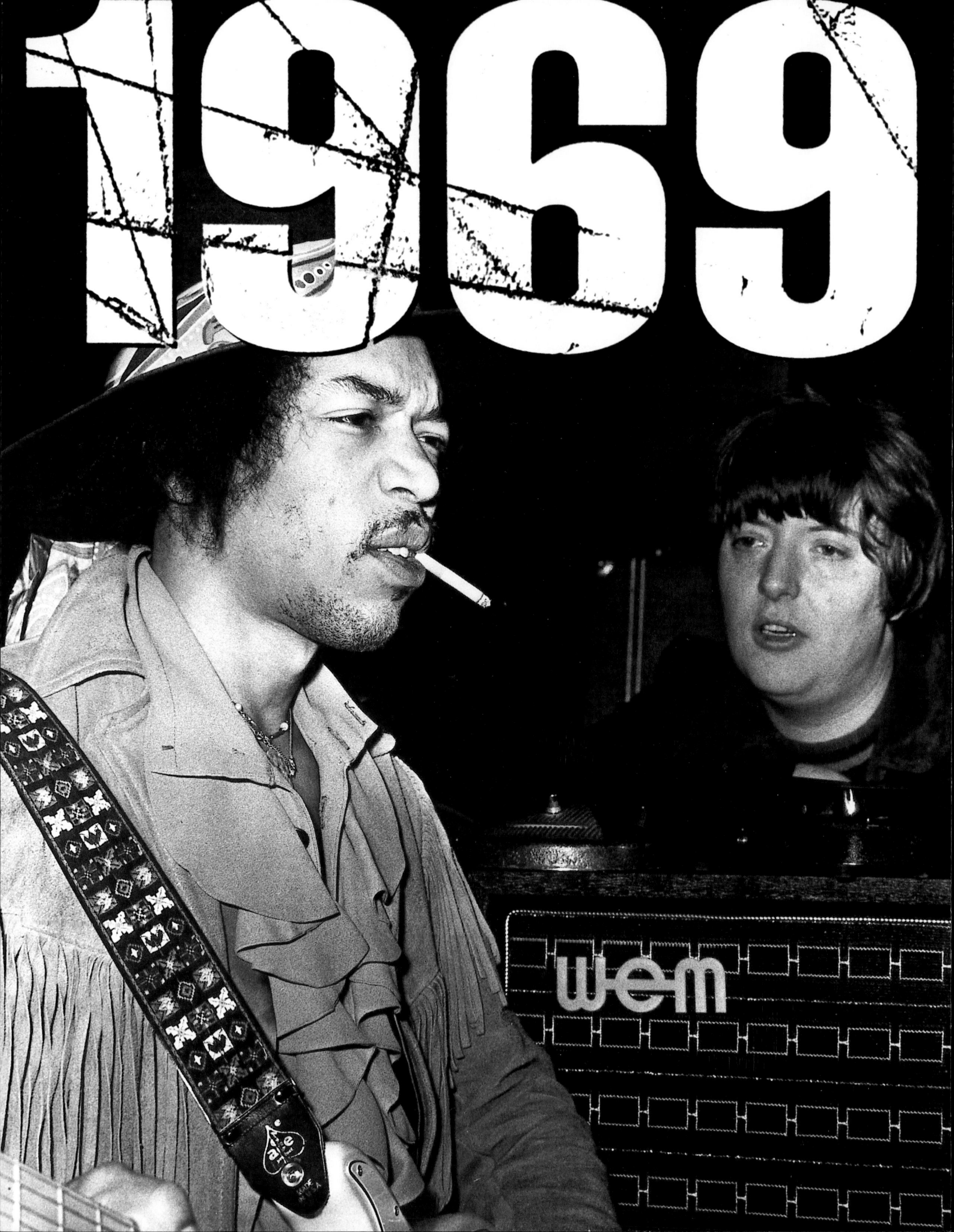

January 4
Saturday
**BBC Television Studio,
Wood Lane, London**
HAPPENING FOR LULU TV show.

Lulu introduces the group on her BBC television show, with the following words: "He came over to Britain and wowed everyone here, then went back to America and became like Elvis Presley, only wilder. He got a few guys together in England and they call themselves The Jimi Hendrix Experience." The group opens with 'Voodoo Child (Slight Return)'. After this, Lulu tells the audience, "Well ladies and gentlemen, in case you didn't know, Jimi and the boys won in a big American magazine" (at this point Jimi lets out a very loud squeal from his guitar) "called *Billboard*, the group of the year. And they're gonna sing for you now the song that absolutely made them in this country, and I love to hear them sing it, 'Hey Joe.'"

Jimi warns the audience to "Plug your ears, plug your ears", and laughs. He proceeds to play a wild introduction and then the more familiar introduction to the song. After the first line he discovers that his guitar is slightly out of tune and brings it back into tune with a smile. During the song, Jimi exclaims that he's forgotten the words but still manages to carry on. After the first verse the whole band stops playing and Jimi announces: "We'd like to stop playing this rubbish and, er, dedicate a song to The Cream, regardless of what kind of group they might be. And we'd like to dedicate it to Eric Clapton, Ginger Baker and Jack Bruce." With that, the Experience launch into 'The Sunshine Of Your Love'. By this time, producer Stanley Dorfmann is down on the studio floor desperately trying to get the band to stop playing. But Jimi looks over at him screws up his face and gestures to him with his hand. He comments "We're being put off the air", before slowing the song down gradually and ending it. The show was being broadcast live and Jimi was originally down to sing a duet with Lulu at the end of the show.

January 8
Wednesday
Lorensburgs Cirkus, Gothenburg
The Experience perform two shows at 18:30 and 21:00 supported by Gin House Blues Group and Burning Red Ivanhoe.

Jimi is introduced to the stage for the first show of the evening and immediately proceeds to play 'Voodoo Child (Slight Return)'. He changes guitars after the song and announces: 'We're having difficulty with the guitar okay, one second, hold on. We'd like to do a very old song that we did... about two thousand years ago. In the time of Apollo and, er, Thor, and, er, the planet from Annsgarrd was in the Earth." Jimi continues with 'Foxy Lady', dedicating it to "somebody's girlfriend". After the song, Jimi says: "Thank you very much for waiting this long, we'd like to do some slow blues now, it's a thing we recorded another 200 years ago, a thing called 'Red House'." However, first the band has to tune up, during which Jimi makes his standard comments about 'caring for your ears' and not playing too loud – "Matter of fact I play more tuning up, though." They then continue with 'Red House'. "Listen we heard, er some news that seems to be bad to most people, but it really isn't bad news at all. It's about a group breaking up, but... these three people that are breaking up... The Cream... this is a good thing. Because, like, they're gonna show you three different types of music later on..." Jimi continues with 'The Sunshine Of Your Love'. "Right now we'd like to do er another old song that er, the reason why we're doing these old songs is because we haven't played together in a long time, you know. So therefore, we just, like, jam around like we're trying to do tonight. Here we go, a thing called 'I Don't Live Today'."

The song finishes and the group need another tune up. Afterwards, Jimi announces: "Yeah thank you very much for waiting, I'd like to dedicate this one to our manager Chas Chandler, pretend like he's here... 'Hear My Train Coming'. It's a thing that we're gonna jam out, we never play it to him you know, we never recorded it either. We might do it next time around you know, we'd like to have it much longer." Jimi continues with 'Hear My Train Coming'. "Yeah now... it seems we only have time for one more. I'd like to say thank you very much for showing up and, er, we'd like to do 'All Along The Watchtower' but we forgot the words and you know it was a jazz session in England... Okay this next song is dedicated to them over there. Oh, oh yeah, we're gonna dedicate the whole show to... our manager Chas Chandler and Hansson and Karlsson and to Mitch and Noel and to you all people out there, okay? Thank you very much, we'd like to keep on moving now and do this last number, it goes something like this here... thank you again for coming, good night, peace be with you." Jimi ends the show with 'Spanish Castle Magic'. Midway through the song, Jimi appears to have some trouble with his guitar and leaves Mitch to fill in with an extra long drum solo. When Jimi finally returns to the stage to play, he finishes the song as an instrumental and then continues to play 'Purple Haze' and, finally, 'Star Spangled Banner', which he plays with his teeth.

January 9
Thursday
Konserthuset, Stockholm
The Experience perform two shows at 19:00 and 21:30, supported by Jethro Tull.

The MC introduces the Experience, announcing that they will play some 'Electric Church Music'. Jimi greets the crowd with: "Hello how you all doing? I'd like to dedicate this show to the American deserter's society. [I'd] like to also dedicate this show to Eva who keeps sending roses [though we've] never seen her... She's a goddess from Annsgarrd. We're gonna play nothing but oldies but baddies tonight, because we haven't, you know, we haven't played together in about six weeks, so we're just gonna jam and see what happens tonight. Hope you don't mind, you know, we're just gonna mess around and just jam see what happens." As Jimi walks away from the microphone he comments, "You wouldn't know the difference, anyway." While Mitch is still around the front of his drums, setting them up, Jimi launches straight into 'Killing Floor'. After the song, he thanks the audience: "Yeah thank you very much for waiting this long, I'd like to keep on going on, wait a minute." Jimi proceeds to count up the frets of his guitar and comments: "Oh, wrong count, wait a minute, it's the wrong key." He counts again and remarks: "There, I'll never forget that. I'd like to do a thing that was recorded in 1733 in the Benjamin Franklin studios a thing called 'Spanish Castle Magic'..." During the solo Jimi starts to experience some problems with the amplifiers squealing as soon as he steps on his fuzz box. The amplifiers are still rumbling away when he finishes the song and without any introduction he continues with 'Fire'. Again during the solo Jimi has a problem with the amps, and he kicks the fuzz off in disgust and looks angry.

Jimi is visibly upset with the constant equipment problems and again without any introduction plays 'Hey Joe', only singing half the vocals. "We had a request to do a thing called 'All Along the Watchtower', but I forgot the words, so, er, we won't play that one. We never [played] that before in person anyway, we only recorded it because we liked it. But, er, I really am sorry. I'll tell you what we'll do though, we'll play 'Voodoo Child (Slight Return)' for you, okay?" Noel reminds Jimi that they are playing the song for the group The Outsiders. Jimi remarks: "Yeah right, oh we have to play good for them, yeah right." During the song Jimi stops playing, walks off stage, and leaves Mitch and Noel to play alone. After a few minutes Noel looks to see where Jimi is and also stops playing to leave the stage. Mitch is left to play an extended drum solo. Jimi and Noel return to finish the song. Someone in the audience shouts out for 'Voodoo Child' and Jimi looks angry, as they have just played that song. Jimi changes his guitar to a white Gibson SG and comments: "We're sorry to be taking up all your time like this, I'm trying to get my guitar in tune. We'd like to slow the pace down a little bit..." Jimi continues with 'Red House' and 'The Sunshine Of Your Love'. After the song, the MC walks onto the stage and tell everybody, "That's all folks." Noel shouts to him, "We're not finished yet." The audience erupts with shouts and boos. The MC then announces: "Well, they told me that it should finish at 9 o'clock, but I guess everybody wants some more, so here they are." But Jimi, Mitch and Noel had already left the stage and did not return back.

The Experience take the stage at 21:30 for their second performance of the evening. They've just got on when someone shouts out for 'Wild Thing'. Jimi remarks: "Yeah same to you baby. Dig, we're gonna dedicate this show to the American..." The same guy interrupts Jimi, who replies, "Right", and continues "... American deserter's organisation... and we're doing this show on, er, Wally's case too. Have you all heard about Wally? Yeah, It's a drag, we're gonna do it for him then. And the rest will be a jam." Jimi plays a short few second blues riffs, then announces: "Thank you very much and now for our next number..." and laughs. Then: "This song is dedicated to the Second Front, it's a thing called 'I Don't Live Today' – maybe tomorrow, I can't say – but 'I Don't Live Today'." After the song, Jimi says: "Yeah thank you very much, I'd like to warn you now, it's gonna be a bit loud, em, a tiny bit loud, because like, these are English amps and we're in Sweden and the electricity scene is not working up with this Australian fuzz tone and this American guitar." Jimi remarks to Noel, "God, I'm out of tune" and makes his usual comments to the audience about caring for their ears and not playing too loud. "I'd like to dedicate this song to, er, the same party [that] we dedicated [to] before. The little band of gypsies sitting over there in the Amen section, a thing called, er, let's see, 'Spanish Castle Magic'."

"We're having, er, technical difficulties, so either it'll be too low or too loud for you that forgot to bring... your ears muffs... Dedicated to oldies but goodies, to Wally's case, I think that it'll pertain to that a thing called 'Hey Joe'." He then shouts out: "Is it too loud?" The audience shouts "No!" and Jimi replies "Too bad. Okay then we'll make it louder for you then, all right? Yeah, okay then, what do we do next? Oh yeah, I'll tell you what we'll do... we've got this LP out called [*Electric Ladyland*] and there's only one song that we remember from it because, I don't know... it's like a diary all these LPs, you know. So that's why we don't do them necessarily on stage all the time, we just like jam on stage, you know, because we haven't been playing together for about six weeks anyway. I'd like to dedicate this song to all the people who can actually feel and think for themselves and feel free for themselves, a thing called 'Voodoo Child (Slight Return)'..." Jimi continues with 'Voodoo Child' and 'The Sunshine Of Your Love'. After the song, the same person in the audience shouts out for 'Wild Thing'. Jimi replies, "You're living in the past". Noel tries to announce the next song and the guy shouts again, Jimi again replies, "You're living in the past", and the guy shouts back, "I know." Jimi then announces: "[I'd] like to dedicate... this is [for] our friends from west Africa." Jimi continues with 'Red House', then winds up proceedings with: "I'd like to say, er, thank you very much for showing up tonight, you know it's really outta site and, er, I'd like to do this last number for everybody." Someone shouts, "We want 'Fire'." Jimi responds with: "'Fire', yeah, no, not necessarily 'Fire', but... yeah. Yes, let's do that and then we'll go into the other thing. Jimi continues with 'Fire', and ends the show with 'Purple Haze' and 'Star Spangled Banner'.

January 10
Friday
**Falkoner Centret,
Falkoner Alle 9, Copenhagen**
The Experience perform two shows at 19:00 and 21:30, supported by Jethro Tull.

Jimi starts off the first show with 'Fire', then: "I'd like to say thank you very much for showing up tonight, and... we'd like to continue on with, er, oldies but baddies. It's a thing... dedicated to somebody's girlfriend here tonight. I don't know who, I don't know who it is yet because, you know we haven't finished the gig. It goes something like this here." Jimi continues with 'Foxy Lady'. Jimi changes guitars and announces: "Yeah, we like to make sure and keep it fun for everybody, we'd like to do a jam number now... it's a thing by, er, have you heard about Hansson and Karlsson? Well, we'd like to do a tiny bit of their tune, it's a thing called...'Tax Free'. We like to like mess around with the intro of 'Tax Free' and then we'll see what happens after...

AN EXPERIENCE IN SOUND...

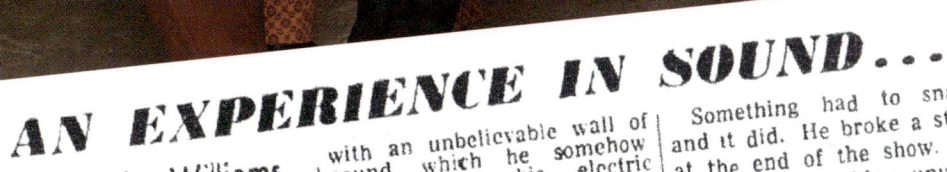

by Nicholas Williams

Jimi Hendrix Experience went to the New Bristol Entertainments Centre last night and left it reeling with the sound of his way-out guitar.

Backed by a two-man group, he bombarded his audience with an unbelievable wall of sound, which he somehow coaxed from his electric guitar.

He played it in the usual way. He played it under his arm, over his shoulder; and between his legs.

He scraped it on the stage floor and over the amplifiers —he even plucked the strings with his teeth.

Something had to snap— and it did. He broke a string at the end of the show.

But that's nothing unusual. "I buy several sets a week," said Hendrix.

He drove his way through Dylan's "Like a Rolling Stone" "Wild Thing," and "Hey, Joe."

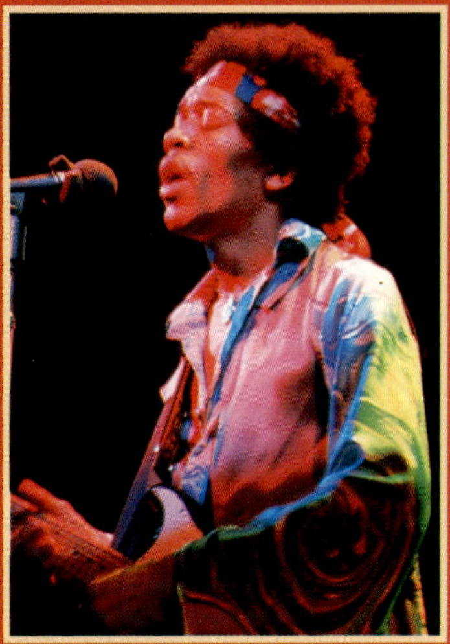

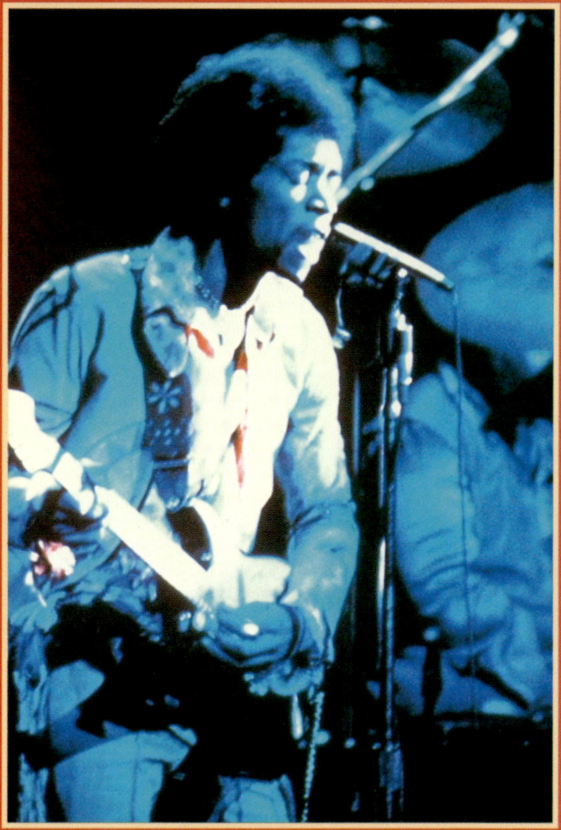

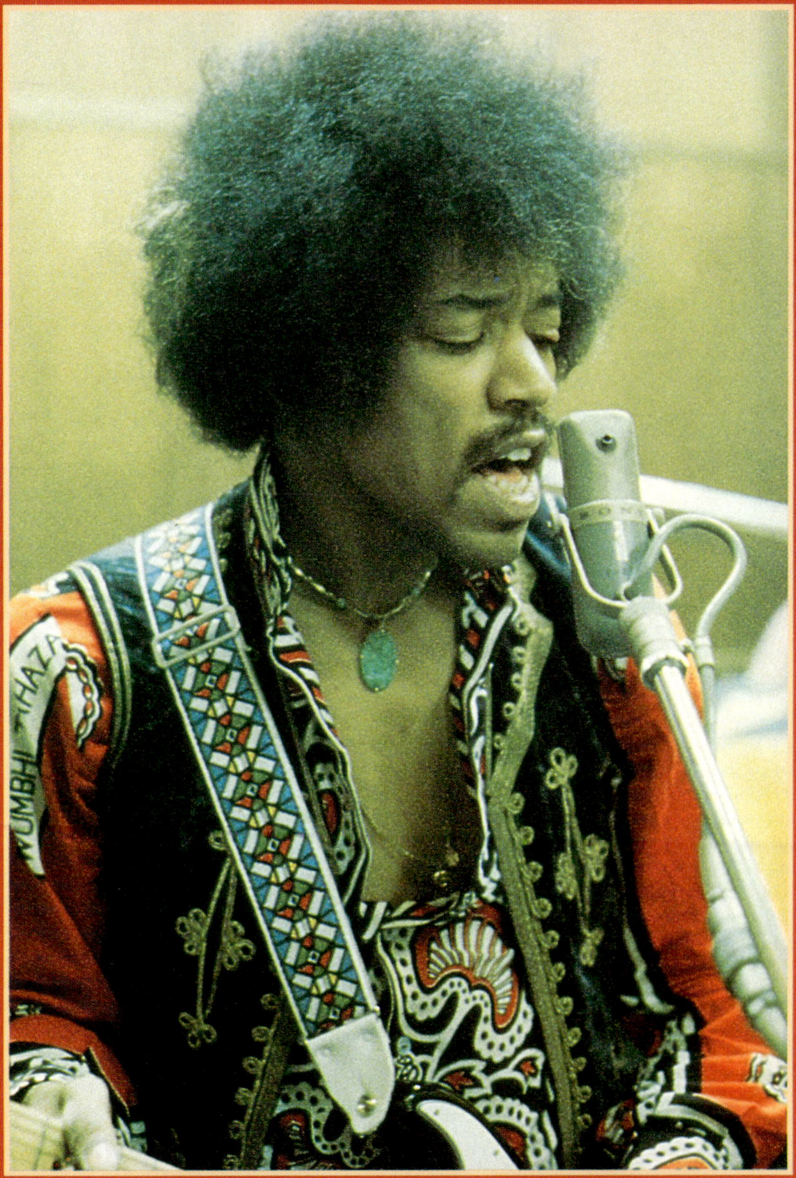

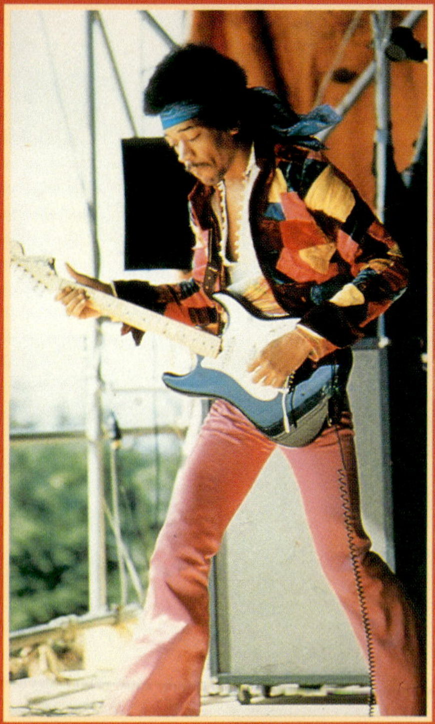

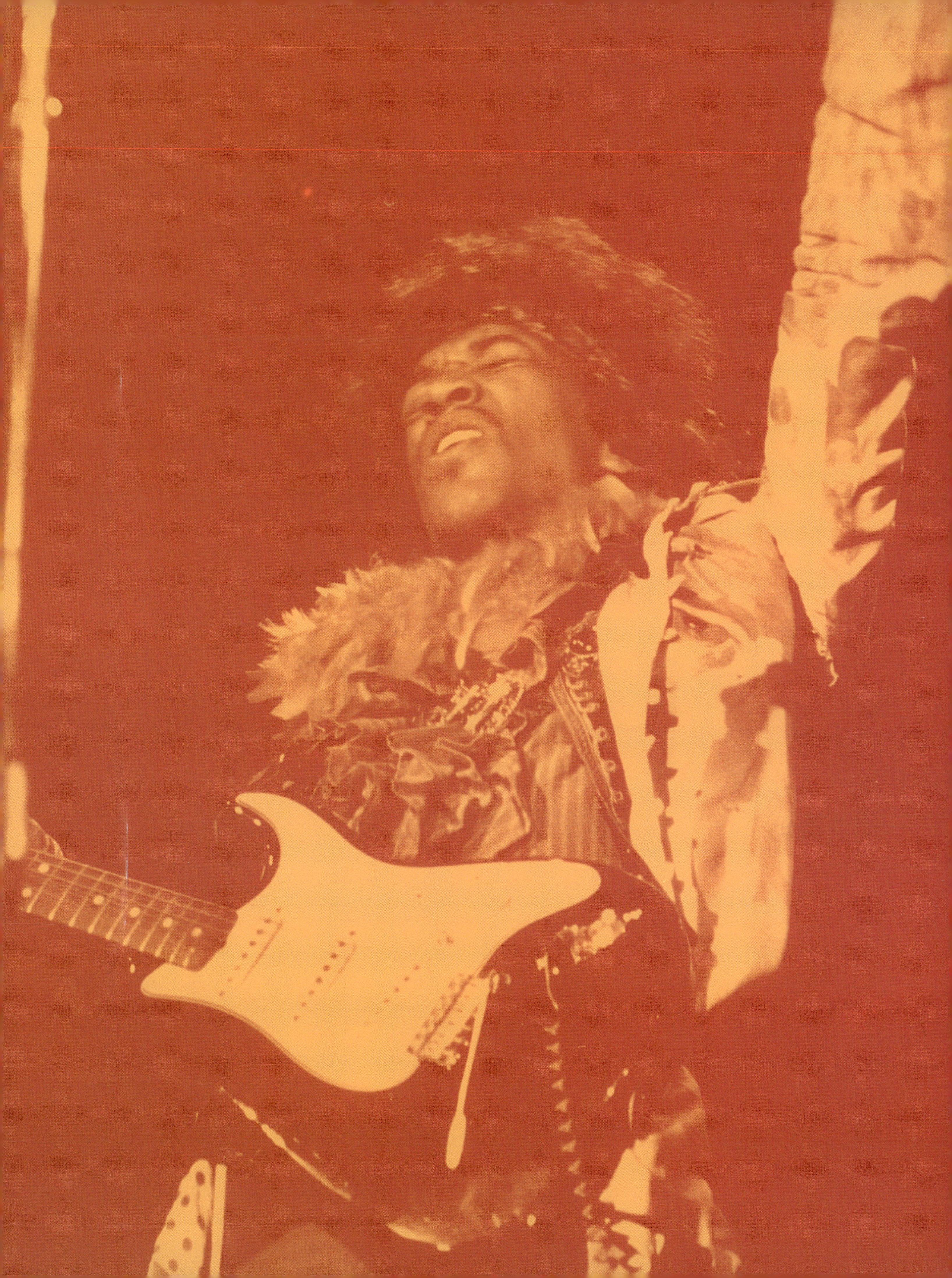

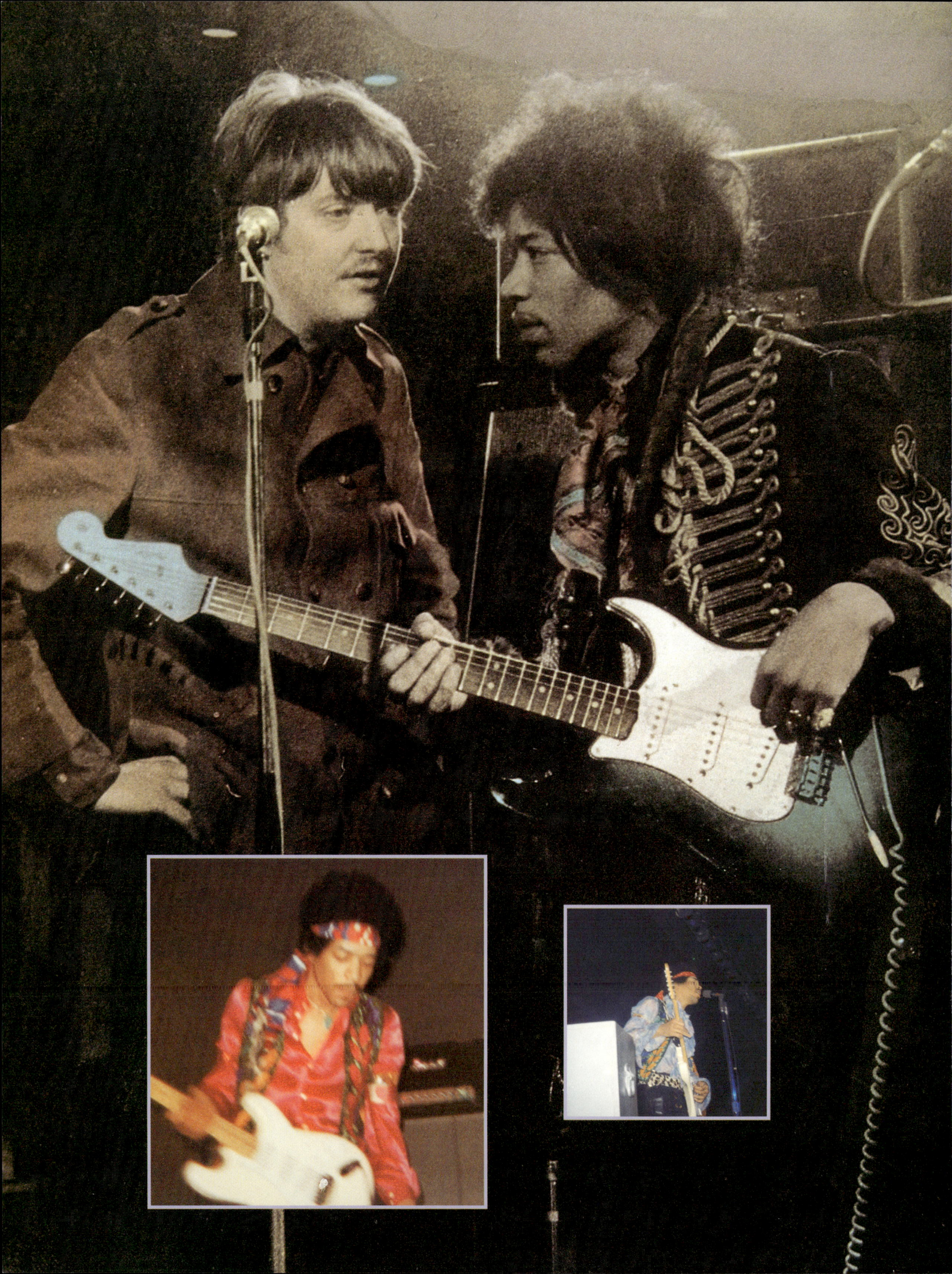

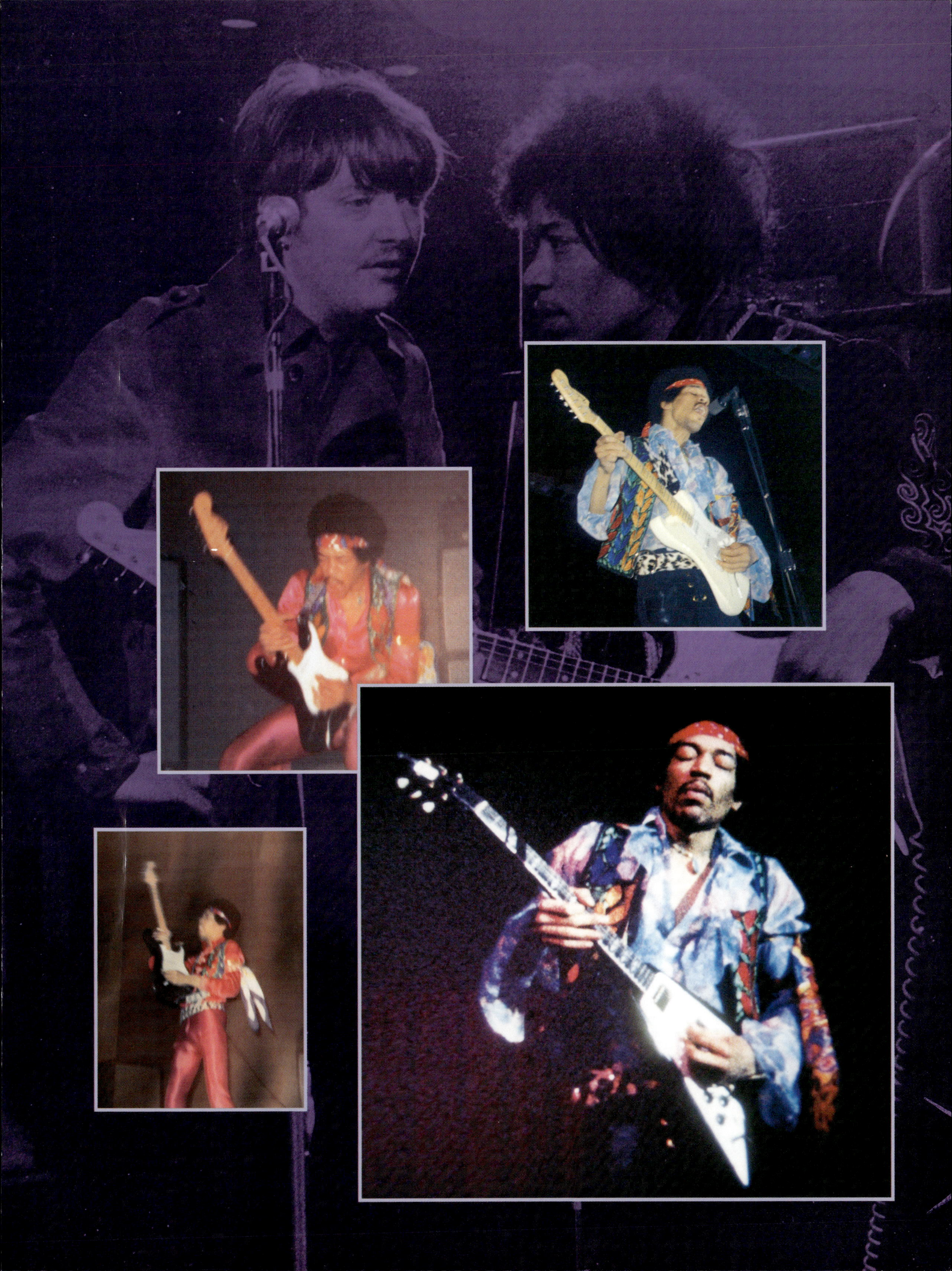

Hendrix joins Walkers tour — first dates

FIVE DATES have now been definitely set for the Walker Brothers tour which opens on March 31. Venues are: Finsbury Park Astoria, London (31), Carlisle ABC (April 7), Bolton Odeon (14), Lincoln ABC (20) and Slough Granada (30).

The tour lasts for nearly five weeks and other artists on the bill include Jimi Hendrix and Cat Stevens.

In Australia the Walker Brothers this week completed a fantastic two-week tour. They have been so successful that "The Sun Ain't Gonna Shine Anymore" has been re-released there by popular demand.

This week they are playing dates in Japan before travelling on to America.

JIMI HENDRIX: TWO TOURS SET

JIMI HENDRIX, who roars up to 10 from 15 in the chart this week, is set for two major tours of Britain in February and March. Details were being fixed at press-time.

His agent, Dick Katz, told Disc and Music Echo on Tuesday: "Jimi is one of our most tremendous discoveries. Not only is he a fine musician, he's a tremendous performer. We plan big things for him."

Previously tipped for the top on "Top Of The Pops," Jimi will be seen today (Thursday). He plays "Saturday Club" on February 18.

Jimi's follow-up single to "Hey Joe" is already recorded. An LP is planned.

Jimi Hendrix for Who show

JIMI HENDRIX, Experience, new group discovered by ex-Animal Chas Chandler and chart-riding at 15 with "Hey Joe," have been added to the Who's Saville Theatre, London, concert on January 29. Koobas and DJ Mike Quinn complete the line-up.

Jimi Hendrix and Cat Stevens are also in line for a March tour of Britain. Other star names are being fixed.

Jimmy Hendrix on 'Ready Steady'

JIMMY HENDRIX, American soul singer managed by former Animal bassist Chas Chandler, features his first single, "Hey Joe" on tonight's "Ready, Steady, Go!"

Jimmy, who formerly played for Ike and Tina Turner, goes on the road with his own trio, the Jimmy Hendrix Experience, this month. He appears at London's Blaises club (21), Southampton (22), Hounslow's Ricky Tick (23), and Forest Gate's Upper Cut discotheque (26).

Fans were stunned into silence

As Jimi Hendrix bellowed, "Lord Have Mercy" from his altar on the Pavilion stage at Bath last night, and his worshippers gazed in silent adoration from below, I echoed his sentiments as my ribs reverberated with the intolerable volume of electronic sound.

His appearance was almost as awesome as the noise. His long, tousled hair fell about his face and over the collar of his gold-spangled jacket, which must have come from a certain boutique in Soho, whose military merchandise recently landed a young man in court.

The power of his delivery stunned the fans into silence and they were able to produce only conventional applause, punctuated by a few exhausted squeaks in place of screams.

Jimi—whose full title is Jimi Hendrix Experience, and he is an experience—exploded on to the pop scene with "Hey Joe," which is quite a pleasant, easy-going number, at present rated No. 7 in the charts.

Why he needs to create horrific wailing effects on his guitar, and turn the amplifiers to full strength, I cannot imagine. His voice, when it can be heard, should be adequate to transmit his message. The personality that accompanies it is even more forceful.

He has a new single due for release next month, which is apparently freakish. Perhaps someone should tell him that the "freakier than thou" competition is over and music is on the way back. — JOSEPHINE BAYNE.

Jimi Hendrix—complete with military coat and guitar.

JIMI BANNED

JIMI HENDRIX, controversial coloured star in trouble recently after allegations about his act on the Walker Brothers tour, has now been banned from Spanish TV—because of his long hair!

Jimi was due to fly to Madrid and Barcelona in June, but plans were cancelled after Spanish authorities had seen photographs of the group.

Said manager Chas Chandler on Tuesday: "It's stupid. I thought we were living in 1967. I didn't know people still behaved like this.

"Jimi was booked for Spain by his agent, Dick Katz, but after we sent out photos for Spanish TV magazines we were told they weren't allowed to have long-haired people on TV."

Added ex-Animal Chas: "I thought people were used to pop stars' long hair by now. But when the Animals and I were on holiday in Majorca last year we were forever being stopped and questioned by the police."

Jimi ends his tour with the Walker Brothers, Cat Stevens and Engelbert Humperdinck at Tooting Granada on Sunday.

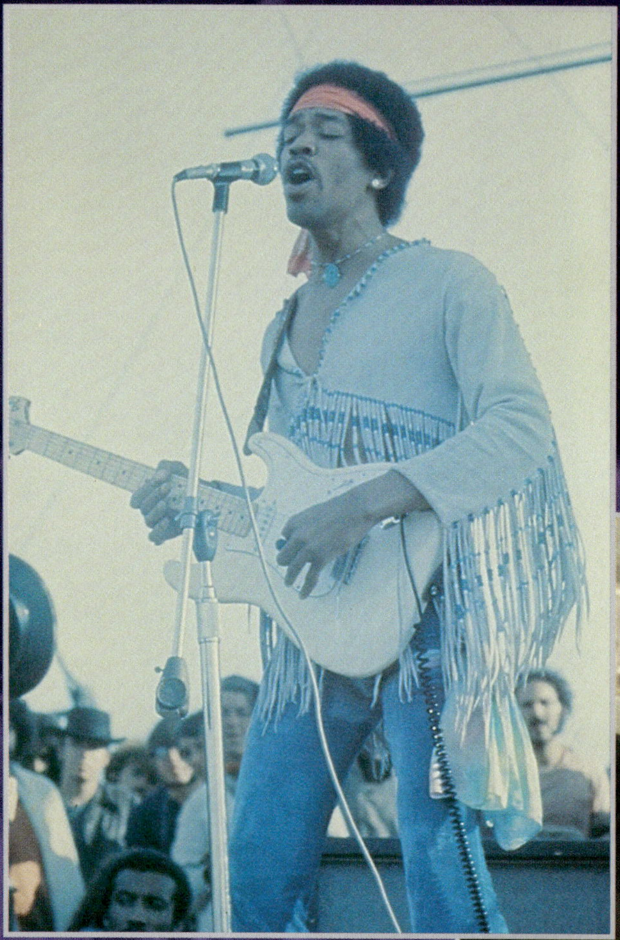
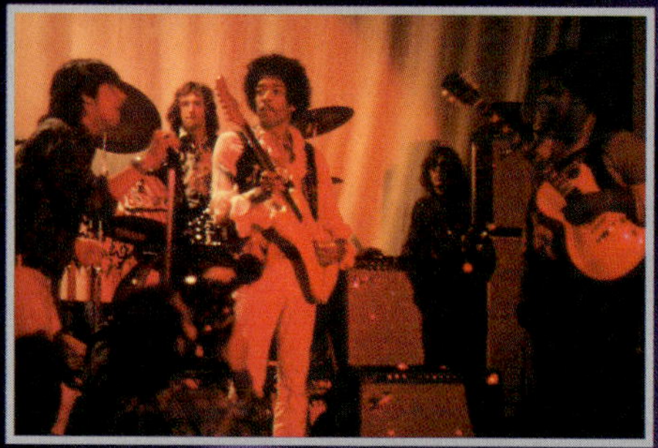
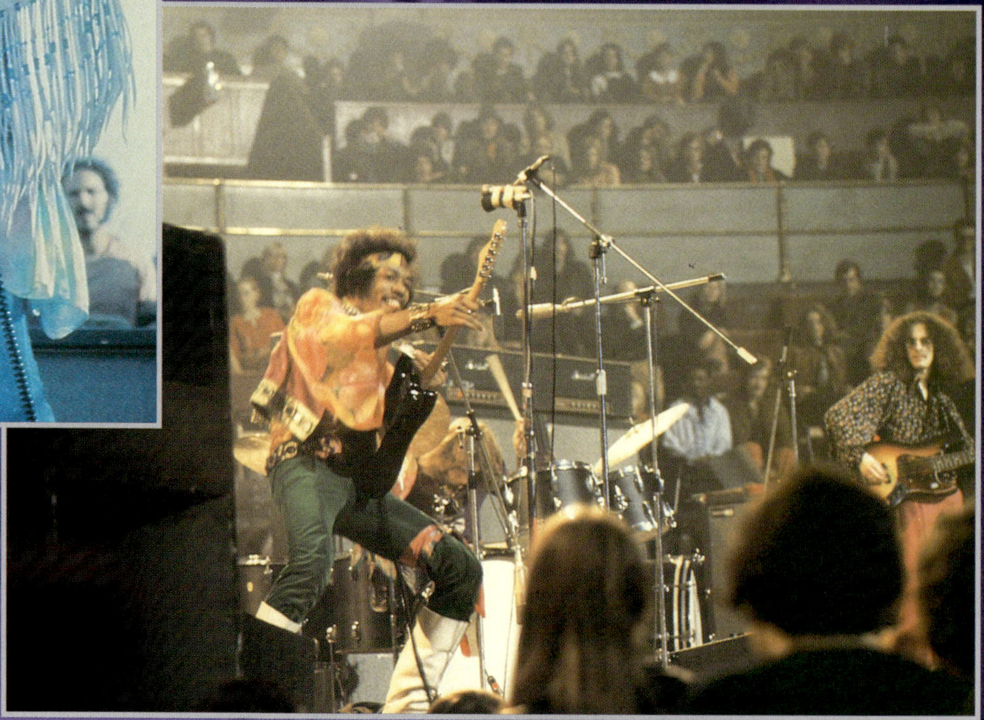
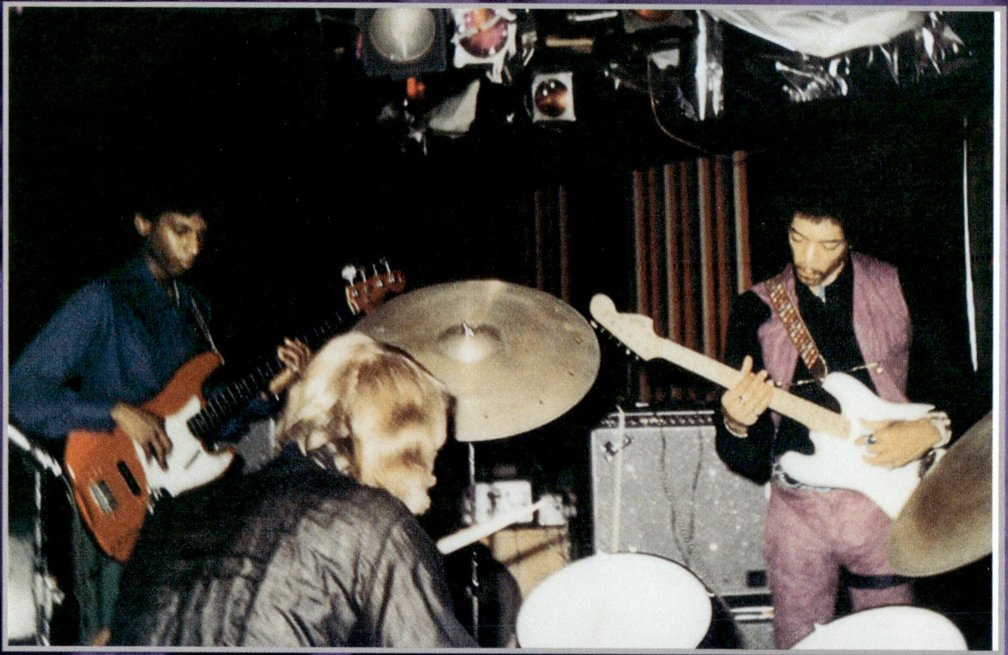

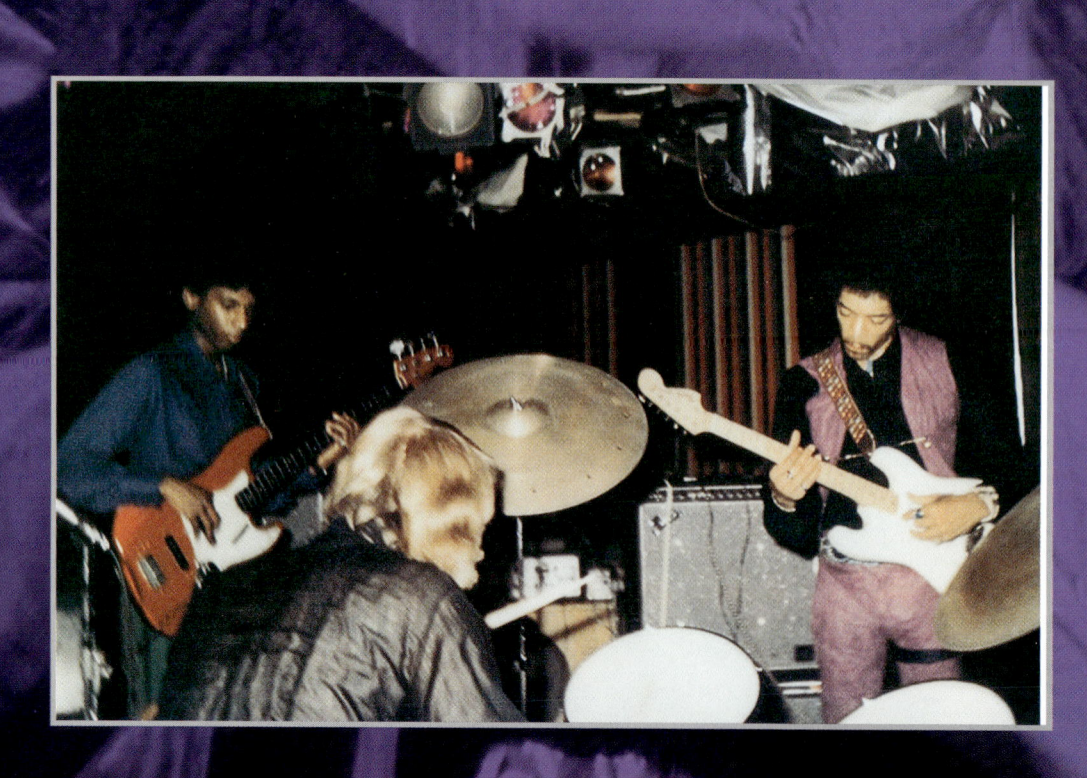

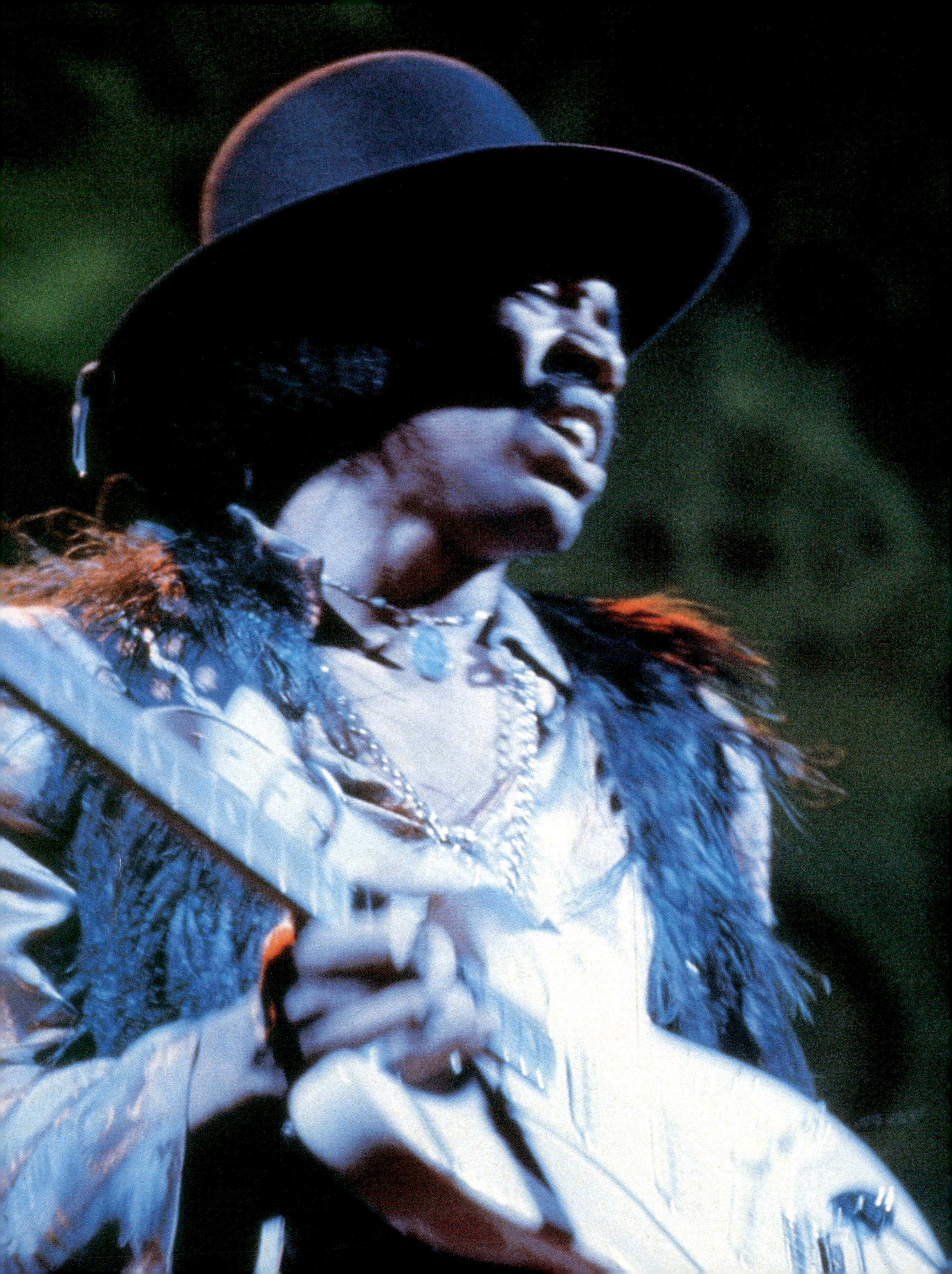

THE N.Y. ROCK FESTIVAL
SHELLEY FINKLE AND GARY KURFIRST PRESENT....
AT THE SINGER BOWL IN QUEENS
doors
WHO
8:30pm
FRIDAY
AUGUST 2
Jimi
Hendrix
PLUS THE CHAMBERS BROTHERS
AND ANOTHER "SUPERGROUP"
8:30
FRIDAY
AUGUST 23rd
RASCALS
VAGRANTS
FRIDAY 8:30
AUGUST 30
TICKETS $3.50, 4.50, 5.50, 7.50 by mail from N.Y. Rock
Festival, 71-09 Austin St., Forest Hills. Send ck or
M.O. with stamped return env. For info call BO 8-3535
TICKETS ARE AVAILABLE BY MAIL ONLY TILL JULY 1

WEDNESDAY
ADMISSION
FEB. 14th
$3.00
THE JIMI HENDRIX EXPERIENCE!
with the Soft Machine
LIVE
LIVE
at
REGIS COLLEGE FIELD HOUSE
59th & LOWELL, DENVER, COLO.
PRESENTED BY FEYLINE PRODUCTIONS
TICKET OUTLETS:

BILL GRAHAM PRESENTS IN NEW YORK
JIMI HENDRIX
EXPERIENCE
JOSHUA LIGHT SHOW
BILL GRAHAM'S
FILLMORE EAST
SECOND AVENUE & SIXTH STREET
ONE NIGHT ONLY
FRIDAY MAY 10
TWO SHOWS 8:00P.M. & 11:30P.M.
ALL SEATS RESERVED $3, $4, $5
BOX OFFICE OPEN DAILY 12:00 NOON TO 10:00 P. M.
INFORMATION: PHONE 777-5260

PINNACLE CONCERT SAT FEB 10
JIMI HENDRIX
& THE SOFT MACHINE WITH
THE ELECTRIC FLAG
AND BLUE CHEER
SHRINE AUDITORIUM 8:30 PM
RESERVED SEATS NOW AVAILABLE AT ALL
WALLICH'S MUSIC CITY STORES AND ALL MUTUAL AGENCIES
VISUALS BY THOMAS EDISON LIGHTS & ACME CINEMA

BILL GRAHAM PRESENTS IN SAN FRANCISCO
JIMI HENDRIX
EXPERIENCE
JOHN MAYALL
AND THE BLUESBREAKERS
ALBERT KING
4
THE
JIMI
HENDRIX
EXPERIENCE CONCERT
LIVE
THE CREATORS
SAC STATE COLLEGE
FEBRUARY 8, 1968 7:30
ADMISSION-$2.75 advance $3.00 at door
MEN'S GYM
Lights by Simultaneous Avalanche
TICKETS: All Tower stores; The Failsof; The Eye; Roseville Records; Tanthaka Books(Davis)
(COME EARLY!!)
Presented by S.F.T.A.O.P.M.
Designed,printed,& copyrighted by ART and PRINT—jim ford/steve murphy—COMMERCIAL ART/OFFSET PRINTING—Sacramento, Calif...PHONE 441-4908—by appointment only.

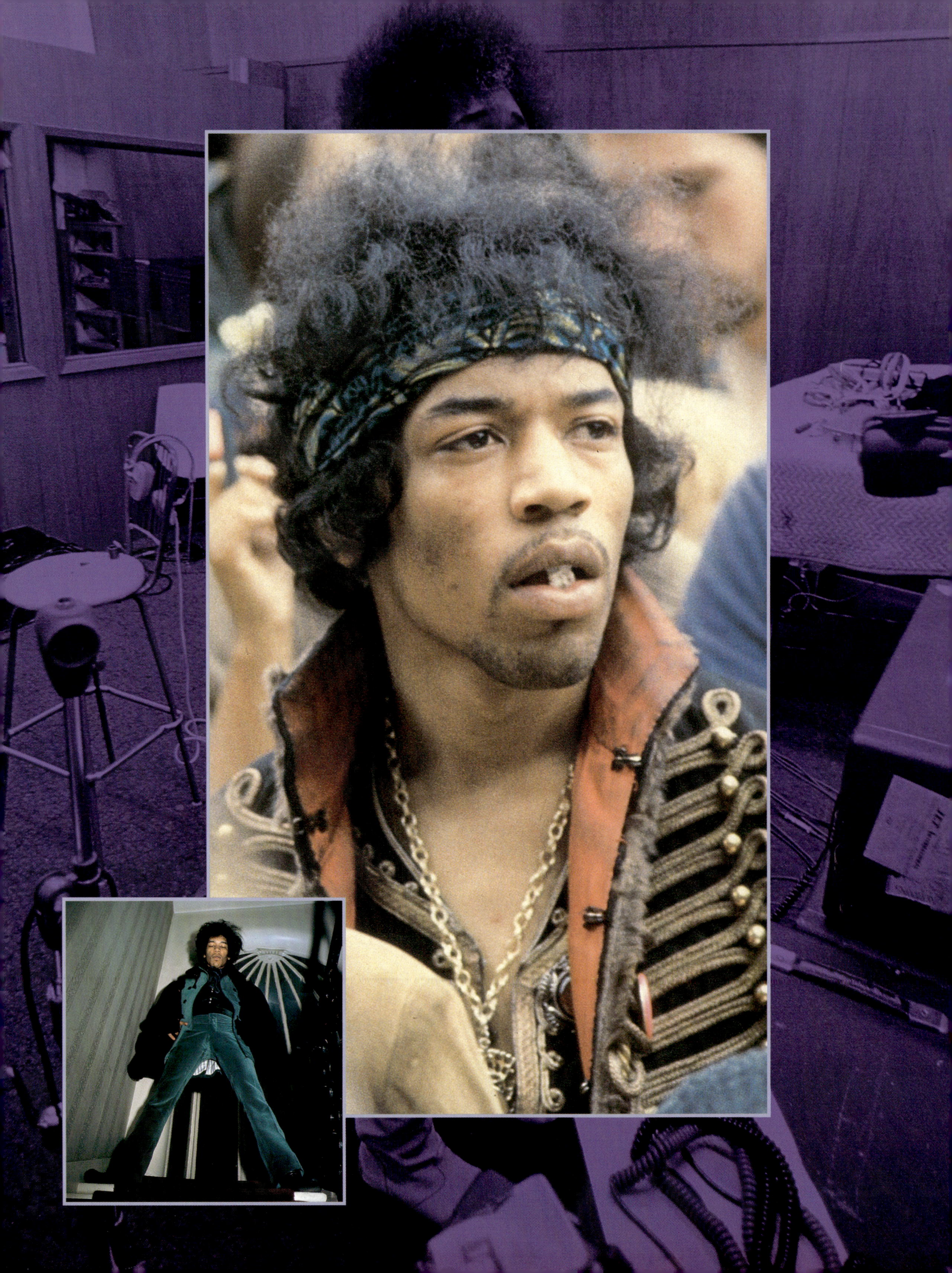

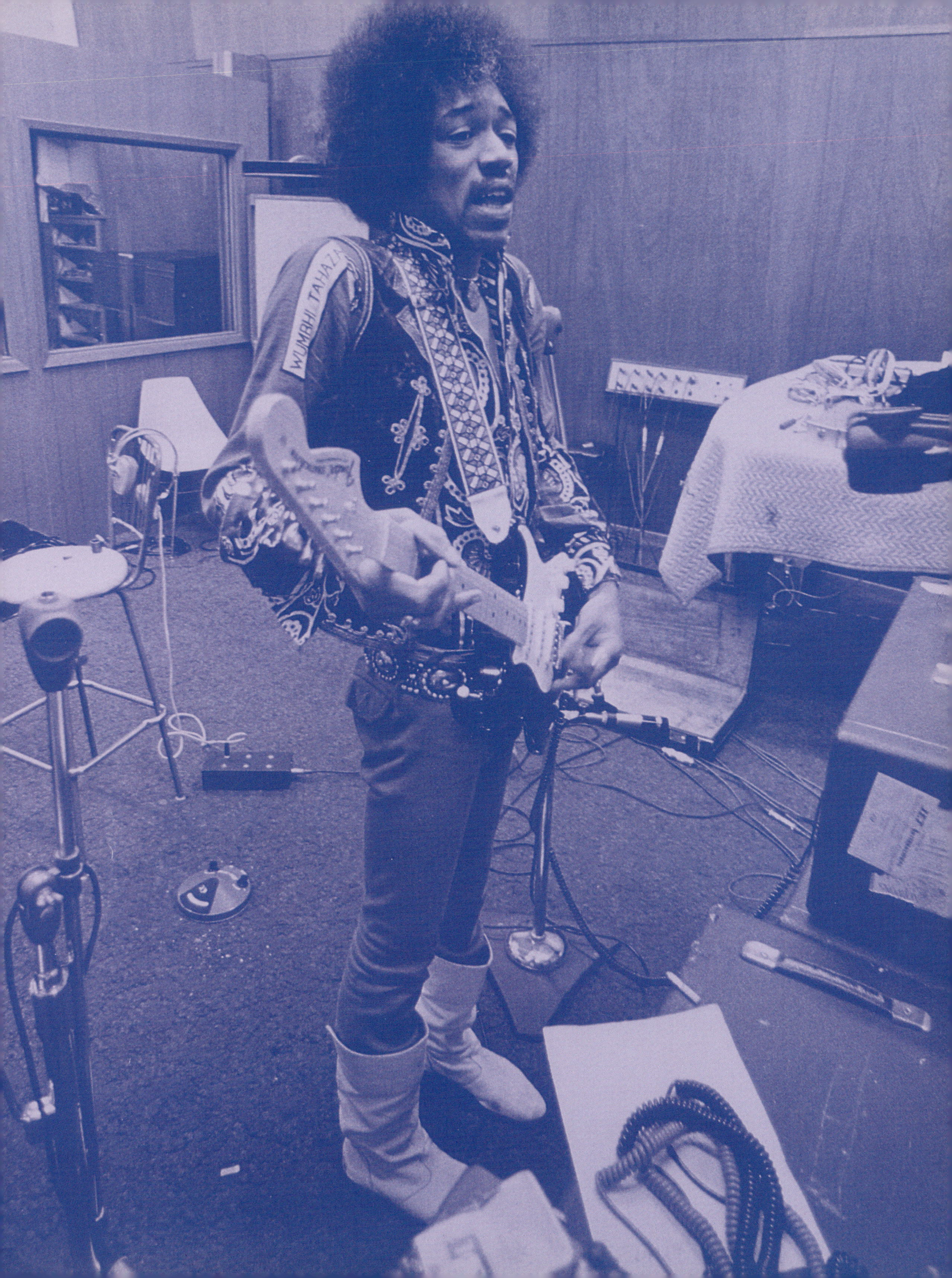

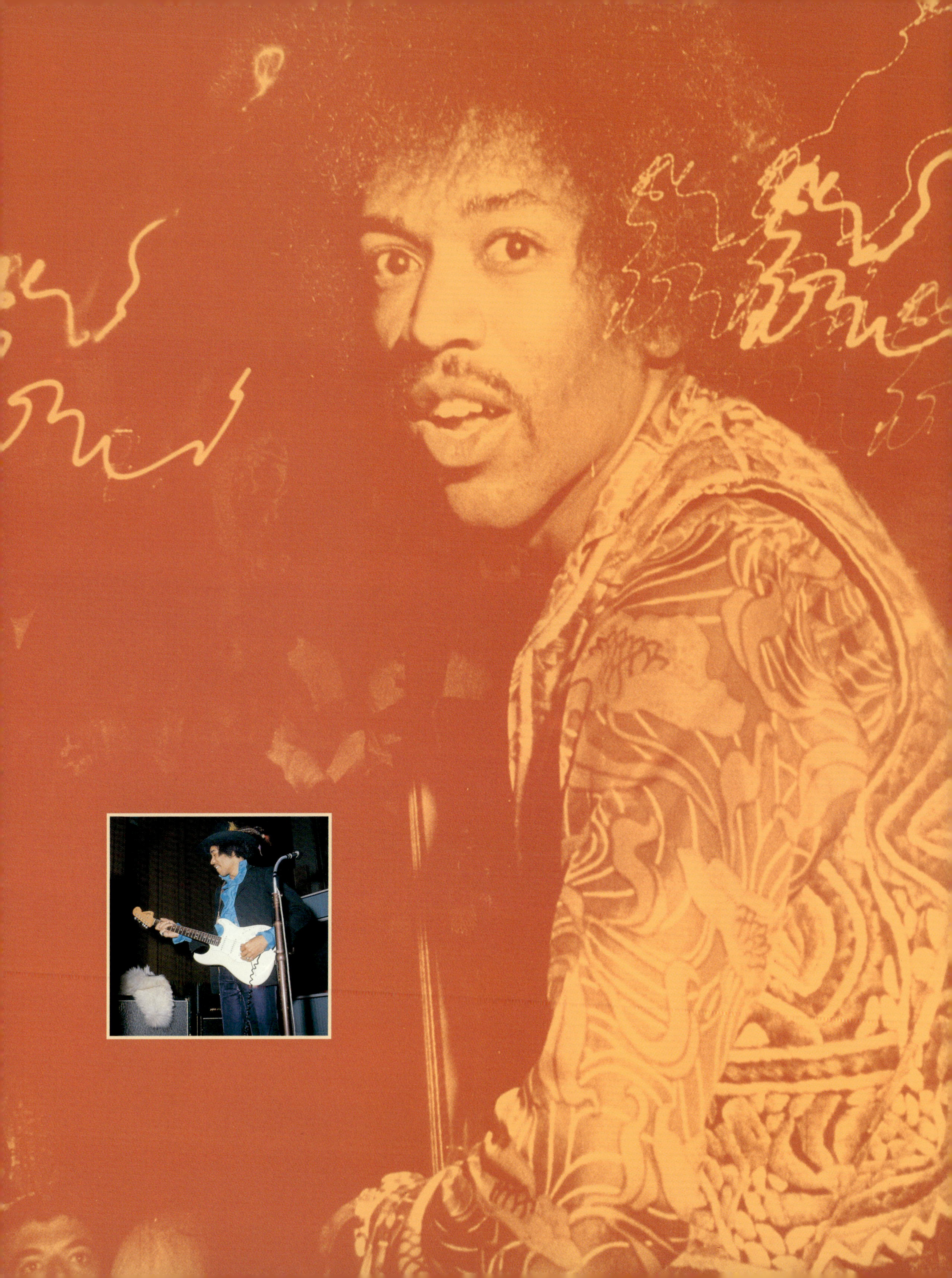

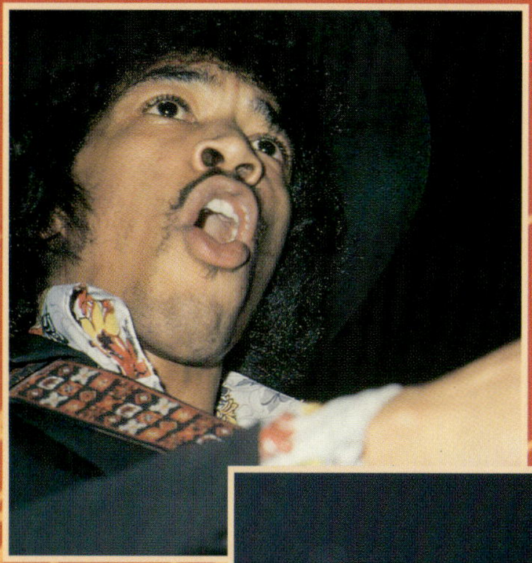

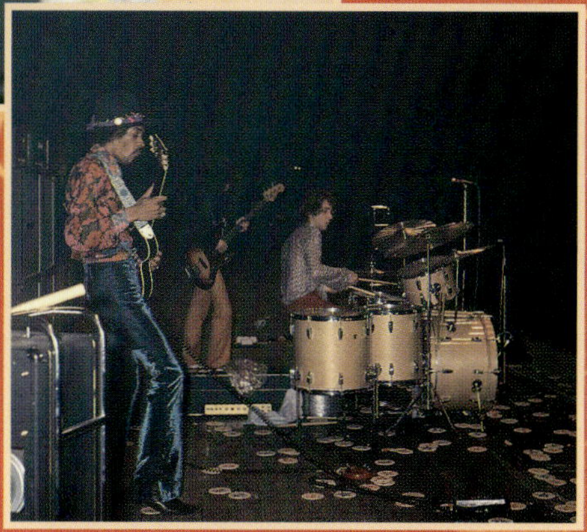

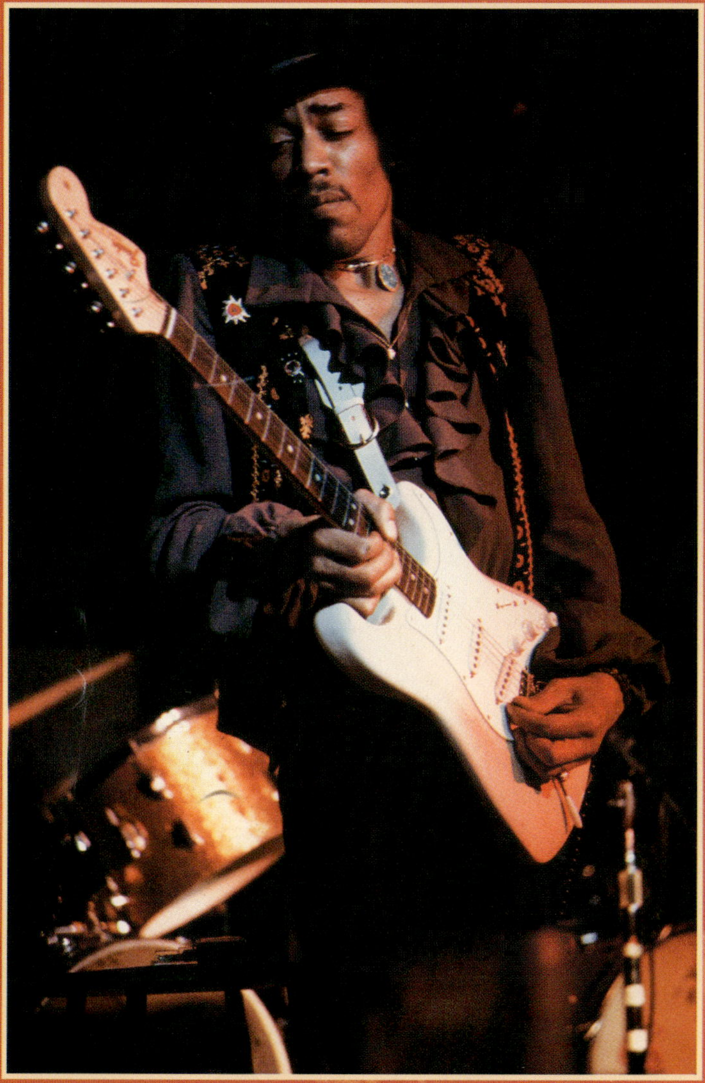

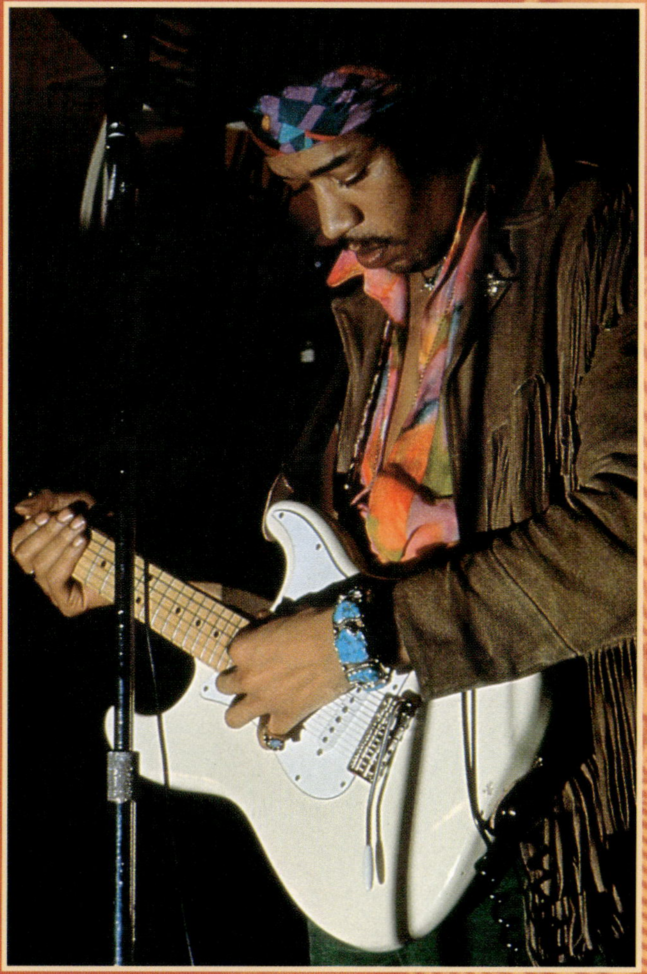

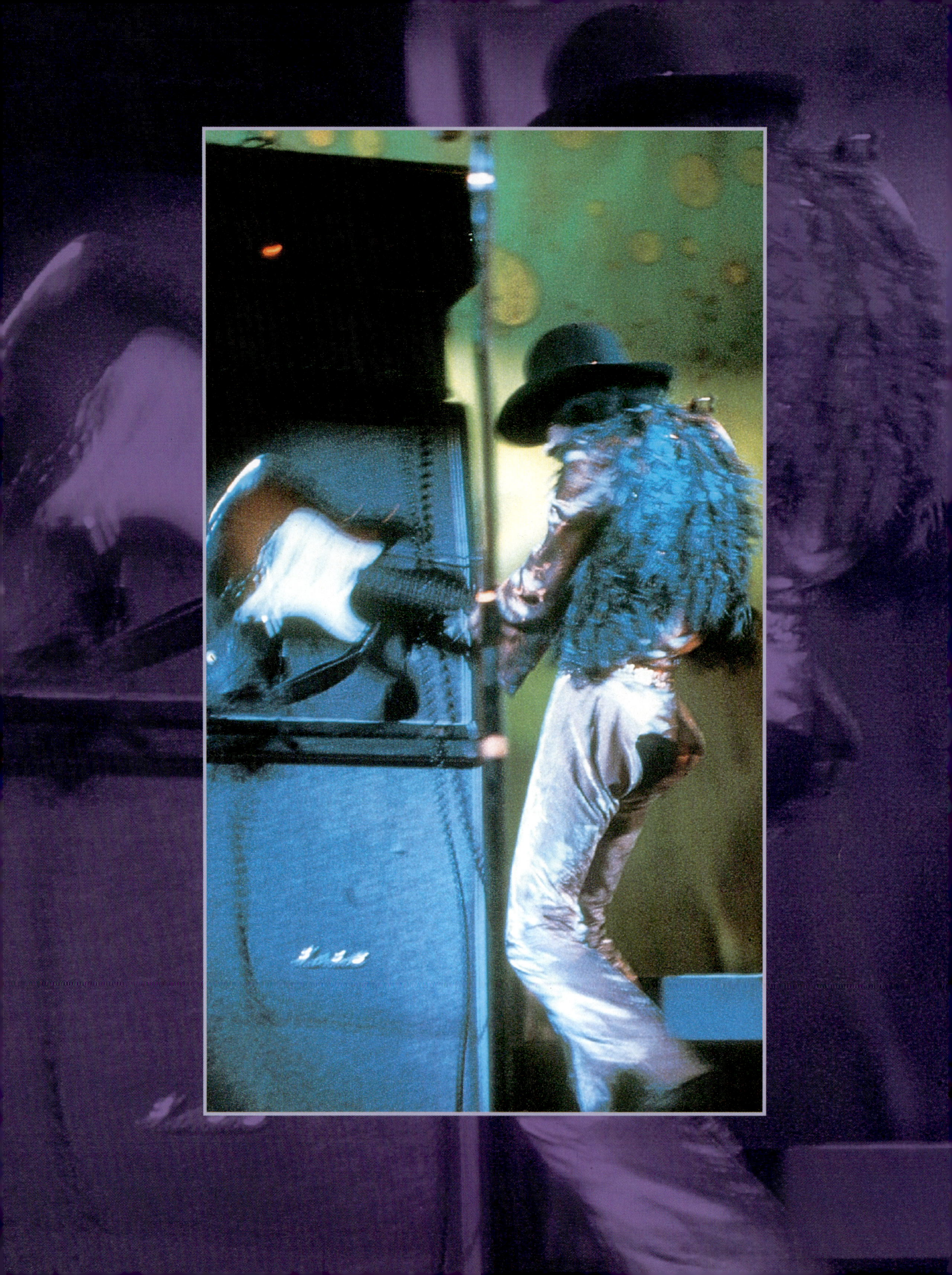

we'll just jam along with it, so you all thank those guys." Jimi proceeds to tune up and comments: "We tune up between every song because we really care for your ears; that's why we don't play so loud."

The Experience continues with 'Tax Free', followed by 'Spanish Castle Magic'. Then the band have to tune up again, before continuing with 'Red House', followed by 'The Sunshine Of Your Love'. Jimi changes guitars and announces: "Yeah we'd like to do... one song or two songs more because we have to do another show tonight, you know, and we're just like jamming around, you know, you just lose track of time. But like, we'd like to make one of those songs, the last track opening feedback note to the song, but his amp falls silent and then buzzes badly. The show continues with 'Let Me Stand Next To Your Fire', 'Voodoo Child Slight Return', another try at 'Foxy Lady', 'Spanish Castle Magic' and 'Getting My Heart Back Together Again'.

January 11
Saturday
Musikhalle, Hamburg
The Experience perform two shows at 10:00 and 21:00, supported by Eire Apparent, now on the tour.

Jimi starts the first show off with 'Are You Experienced' followed by 'Johnny B. Goode'. "Thank you very much and now for our next number." Jimi continues with 'Spanish Castle Magic', 'Getting My more last number and... it's dedicated to everybody here. It's a thing called 'Voodoo Child (Slight Return)'.

January 12
Sunday
Rheinhalle, Dusseldorf
The Experience perform two shows at 17:00 and 20:00, supported by Eire Apparent.

During the first show they perform 'Spanish Castle Magic', 'Foxy Lady', 'Fire', 'Red House', 'The Sunshine Of Your Love', 'Come On (Part One)' and 'Purple Haze'.

from *Electric Ladyland*, its called 'Voodoo Child (Slight Return)' it goes something like this here." Jimi proceeds to tune up and then announces: "Oh man, play the guitar, I don't know. Oh thank you for waiting for me to tune up this one more last time. Yeah, we'd like to do electric storm first, I'd like to make a few sounds, er, 'Electric Church Music Part One'." Jimi continues with 'I Don't Live Today' instead of 'Voodoo Child' incorporating 'Star Spangled Banner and a few bars of 'Third Stone From The Sun' at the end. The show ends with 'Purple Haze'.

Jimi opens the second show with 'Foxy Lady' but straight away the show is dogged with amplification problems. Jimi plays the Heart Back Together' and 'Let Me Stand Next To Your Fire'. "I'd like to continue on with a song, er, it's dedicated to, er, all the non-believers, dedicated to you, dedicated to ourselves, a thing called 'I Don't Live Today', thank you." After the number, Jimi introduces "a slow blues, man. A little thing [we've been] messing around with about three and a half years... a thing called 'Red House'." Jimi follows that number with 'The Sunshine Of Your Love'. Announcing, "Yeah, we have, er, Mitch Mitchell on drums and Noel Redding on bass," Jimi then tells the audience: "I'd like to say thank you very, very much, man, you all look really outta site. We got one more song to do and so like, er, you know, we gotta do one

January 13
Monday
Sporthalle, Cologne
The Experience are supported by Eire Apparent.

They perform 'Come On (Part One)', 'Foxy Lady', 'Red House', 'Voodoo Child (Slight Return)', 'Fire', 'Spanish Castle Magic', 'Hey Joe', 'The Sunshine Of Your Love' and 'Purple Haze'.

After the concert, the Experience attend a small private club in Cologne, where they have a jam session with Jimi playing bass and Noel playing guitar.

January 14
Tuesday
Halle Munsterland, Munster
The Experience are supported by Eire Apparent.

January 15
Wednesday
Kongresaal,
Deutsches Museum, Munich
The Experience perform two shows at 18:15 and 21:00, supported by Eire Apparent.

The Experience start off their show with 'Red House', followed by 'Fire' and 'Foxy Lady'. Jimi has finally decided to play 'All Along The Watchtower' in concert and it is performed here live for the first known time. Jimi continues with 'Hey Joe' and 'Voodoo Child (Slight Return)'. "Yeah, we'd like to, er, we'd like to thank Gerry Stickles for putting a new guitar string on without stopping it... Anyway, we'd like to do one... last song. I'd like to say thank you very much for showing up and good night, bye bye." Jimi ends the show with 'Purple Haze'.

January 16
Thursday
Meistersingerhalle, Nurnburg
The Experience perform two shows at 18:00 and 21:00, supported by Eire Apparent.

The Experience take the stage for their first show, Jimi announces, "Hello... stick around until we tune up, all right? It takes one, er, minute to, er... can't get these drums together." After a few minutes the audience starts to slow handclap and Jimi apologises: "I'd like to say thank you very much for waiting. We'd like to start off with Mitch Mitchell on drums, Noel Redding on bass, myself on saxophone." After a further delay Jimi starts the show off with 'Come On (Part One)'. After more of his standard comments about tuning up out of respect for the audience's hearing, Jimi continues: "I'd like to do a little song, this song here is dedicated to everybody that's living today, a thing called 'I Don't Live Today', dedicated to the American Indians and you people in here."

Someone in the audience shouts out for 'Hey Joe'. Jimi asks, "What?" and the guy repeats the request. Jimi responds with, "How does that go...?" The guy again shouts out for 'Hey Joe' and Jimi comments, "You know, you don't want, you really don't wanna look at me..." The guy shouts out his request again, and Jimi says angrily, "Stop saying that, man! Anyway, we'd like to go ahead on and do a song something... that we... did back in the year of 1733." Jimi continues with 'Hey Joe'. "Yeah okay then, thank you very much." The same guy now shouts out for 'Purple Haze'. Jimi comments: "Right, right, it'll be louder too, It'll be louder. Anyway, thank you for coming and, er, let's see who we do it to now. Oh yeah, right, we gonna do, er, 'Let Me Stand Next To Your Old Lady'", and the set continues with 'Fire'. Jimi changes guitar to his white Gibson SG, tunes up again, and continues with 'Red House', 'Foxy Lady' and 'Purple Haze'. "Thank you very much, thank you. We have one more last song to do... before we go off. I'd like to say thank you very much for showing up and we'd like to dedicate this last number to everybody. We got the second show coming up so, er, you know, you won't bloody well miss it! So, er, thanks to all of you and good night." Jimi ends the show with 'Voodoo Child (Slight Return)'.

January 17
Friday
Jahrhunderthalle, Frankfurt
The Experience perform two shows at 19:00 and 21:45 supported by Eire Apparent.

The Experience take the stage for their second show of the evening. Jimi announces: "You might notice some songs that you heard before. But like, er, hold on until we play some of the old songs and like, er, mess with them a little bit here on stage and see what kind of sounds we can get... what kind of feeling, you know. So we'll be doing most of a free jam type thing, so you all just relax, you might as well be with it, okay? We're gonna start with a thing called 'Come On (Part One)'. Afterwards: "Thank you very much. Yeah thank you, that was outta site, okay then we'll go for that. We tune up between every song, that's because we really care for your ears, that's why we don't play so loud. You dig? If you can dig that, then you know you're really outta site. You're outta site anyway. Dig, we'd like to go ahead on and do this song that, er... this cat going over to this girl's house you know and the girl's looking all good and all that. And she thinks that he can't want her, but she has some dandy smoke, then she... but I don't want to talk to you, I just wanna stand next to your fire. It goes something like this." Jimi continues with 'Fire'. "We'd like to, er, slow the pace down a little bit now if you don't mind," he announces afterwards. Do a cut from our first English LP, a little slow blues, it's called 'Red House Blues' [sic]." The audience starts calling out for 'Watchtower' and Jimi responds: "Yeah there's, er, something that we'd like to tell you about that... we recorded that a year ago and if you've heard it we're very glad, but see tonight were here jamming on some things, [we'll] try and do a musical thing, okay? You know, well like that's a single and was released as a single and thank you very much for thinking about it. But I forgot the words, that's what I'm trying to say. We'd like to dedicate this next record to, er, the American Indians and, er, [the] United States army, poor things, and the Air Force, the Marines and you people here and us, it's a thing called 'I Don't Live Today' – maybe tomorrow, I can't say."

Someone shouts out for 'Voodoo Child'. Jimi responds: "Yeah, thank you very much, we like to get into that too. Oh, you don't know the difference anyway." Jimi continues with 'Little Wing'. "Here's a song dedicated... to somebody's girlfriend we don't know yet... and... oh yeah, it's dedicated to the guy too if he wants to listen yeah, that's all right he can listen. A thing called 'Foxy Lady', goes something like this here." After the song, Jimi tunes up and play a few bars of 'Getting My Heart Back Together Again'. "Yeah, that's all right. [I'd] like to do a song dedicated to one of the grooviest groups that was around, they've broken up now, but, er, I think you'll be hearing three times as much music coming from them, you know. But, er, we're playing this song – not saying that we play it better then them, not saying that at all. We're just saying that we dig the group and we dig the cats, so, like we're gonna dedicate it to them and dedicate it to you all too. It'll be an instrumental thing by the Cream." Jimi continues with 'The Sunshine Of Your Love'. Afterwards, he announces: "We only got three more numbers to do. Round about this time I'd like to say, em, we had Noel Redding playing bass, Noel Redding on bass and then we have Mitch Mitchell playing drums which [pushed] the right buttons, yeah and er, I play, em, these backwards tapes over here through [a] tape recorder, okay?" Jimi plays a blues run and comments: "... let's see, what are we going to play, oh yeah right, this thing is dedicated to the people that was born in 1793." Jimi continues with 'Hey Joe' and 'Purple Haze'. "Thank you very much." After a short tune up Jimi ends the show with 'Voodoo Child (Slight Return)'.

January 19
Sunday
Liederhalle, Stuttgart
The Experience perform two shows at 18:00 and 21:00 supported by Eire Apparent.

The Experience take the stage for their first show of the evening, Jimi announces "Listen... before we start... we'd like for you to forget everything that [happens] outside this arena... If everybody sits down so everyone else can see, okay, can you do that? And then it'll take about thirty seconds before we start, okay?" Thank you for showing up, thank you for coming." Jimi opens the show with 'Come On (Part One)'. After a quick tune up Jimi comments, "You don't sleep at church." (Laughs.) "This next song is dedicated to somebody's girlfriend, we don't know who it is yet, but we'll find out after the gig. It's called 'Foxy Lady'." 'Red House' follows this after which Jimi announces "We don't know the words, but we'll do an instrumental, okay?" and follows with 'The Sunshine Of Your Love'. Jimi ends the show with 'Star Spangled Banner' and 'Purple Haze'.

During their second show, the Experience perform 'Fire', 'Spanish Castle Magic', 'Red House', 'Foxy Lady', 'I Don't Live Today', 'Hey Joe', Star Spangled Banner', 'Purple Haze', 'The Sunshine Of Your Love' and 'Voodoo Child (Slight Return)'.

January 21
Tuesday
Wacken Hall 16, Strasbourg, France
The Experience are supported by Eire Apparent.

The Experience perform 'Come On (Part One)', 'Hey Joe', 'Spanish Castle Magic', 'Red House', 'Fire', 'The Sunshine Of Your Love', 'Purple Haze', 'Foxy Lady' and 'Voodoo Child (Slight Return)'.

January 22
Wednesday
Konzerthaus/Stimmen Der Welt, Wien
The Experience perform two shows at 16:00 and 19:30, supported by Eire Apparent.

The Experience take the stage for their first concert of the evening.

While the group is tuning up, the show's MC come onto the stage to make an announcement, which causes the audience to boo and whistle. Jimi then comments: "Thanks for waiting", and starts off the show with 'Come On (Part One)'. "Yeah, thank you very much. Okay here we go, we're gonna do a thing that we recorded in 1733. It's recorded at, in the Benjamin Franklin studios; it goes something like this here. We tune up between every song because we really care for your ears, that's why we don't play so loud, okay, so we tune up." Jimi continues with 'Hey Joe' followed by 'Fire' and 'Getting My Heart Back Together'. "Yeah we'd like to go into our second LP and do a thing dedicate to all the groovy people… that means everybody, a thing called 'Spanish Castle Magic'."

Next up, Jimi announces: "We'd like to do a thing, goes something like this here, dedicated to somebody's girlfriend. We don't know who it is yet, but, er, later on after the show… we don't know yet, but we'll dedicate to her anyway, a thing called 'Foxy Lady'." Jimi follows this with 'Stone Free' and ends the show with 'Purple Haze'.

The Experience take the stage for their second show of the evening, and Jimi tells the audience: "Give us two minutes to adjust our instruments, all right… so we can get in tune, all right, thank you very much." After a lengthy tune up, Jimi announces: "Okay thank you very much for waiting, thank you." Jimi opens the second show with 'Are You Experienced' followed by 'Fire'. Next is 'Here Comes Your Lover Man', but Jimi plays a false start and has to start again. The Experience continues with 'The Sunshine Of Your Love' and ends the show with 'Spanish Castle Magic'. The tour seems to be taking its toll on the group at this stage and Jimi sounds tired when he talks to the audience. This show in particular has a noticeable lack of real contact between Jimi and the audience and he plays most of the concert without even introducing the songs.

January 23
Thursday
Sportpalast, Berlin
The Experience are supported by Eire Apparent.

Prior to the concert, the Experience are sitting in the dressing room waiting to go on stage. There is a very strong police presence in the hall, anticipating trouble. Gerry Stickells comes back stage to inform the group that the hall has been invaded by "millions of fucking rockers." Jimi is advised that if he's told to get off the stage, he should get off quickly because the audience are violently excitable and are the type to smash everything up.

The Experience take the stage for the last concert of the tour with Jimi nursing a cold. He announces: "We're dedicating this to anybody – 'Let Me Stand Next To Your Old Lady', or… 'Let Me Stand Next To Your Joint' or 'Let Me Stand Next To Your Fire'. After this number, Jimi thanks the audience and continues with 'Hey Joe' and 'Spanish Castle Magic'. Noel gives a stern warning to the audience, telling then to sit down and to stop rushing around the auditorium. The Experience continues with 'Foxy Lady', after which Noel again has to speak to the audience, this time to tell them to stop throwing things. The group push on, playing 'Red House' followed by 'Come On (Part One)'. Next is 'The Sunshine Of Your Love', and Jimi ends the show with 'Purple Haze'.

Noel Redding: "There was about 20,000 people and we were told before we went on that there was going to be a riot, and there was. I walked on stage and the first thing I saw, virtually, was someone being beaten up in the audience. The police had to surround the stage in the end."

February 18
Tuesday
Royal Albert Hall, Kensington Gore, London
The Experience are supported by Soft Machine and Mason, Capaldi, Wood & Frog.

The Experience take the stage for their first concert back in England for over six months. Jimi: "It'll take about a minute and a half to… tune our instruments here and there and all the gang watching us do it, you know… You don't mind me talking to you tonight? We was playing for, oh let's see, we was playing in, er, in America, right… Then we played Germany, we're very tired and so we haven't practised at all, but [what] we're gonna do is to jam, okay?" He makes his standard comment about tuning up and playing quietly to save the audience's hearing, then introduces 'Tax Free' as a song from the group's Swedish friends, Hansson and Karlsson: "We'd like to dedicate it to you." After this number, the band launch into 'Fire'." Without any introduction Jimi continues with 'Getting My Heart Back Together'. When the song has finished, Jimi asks the audience whether the music is too loud, to which they reply "No!" His usual intro to 'Foxy Lady' follows. "We'd like to dedicate it to somebody's girlfriend, we don't know who she is yet, but let's see now, we'll find out later on after the show, we'll find out, a thing called 'Foxy Lady'." As Jimi starts the familiar feedback note he comments, "You wouldn't understand, no, not really."

When the song is finished, Jimi announces a "slow blues": "[It was] recorded in 1778 in the Benjamin Franklin studios, a thing that was called

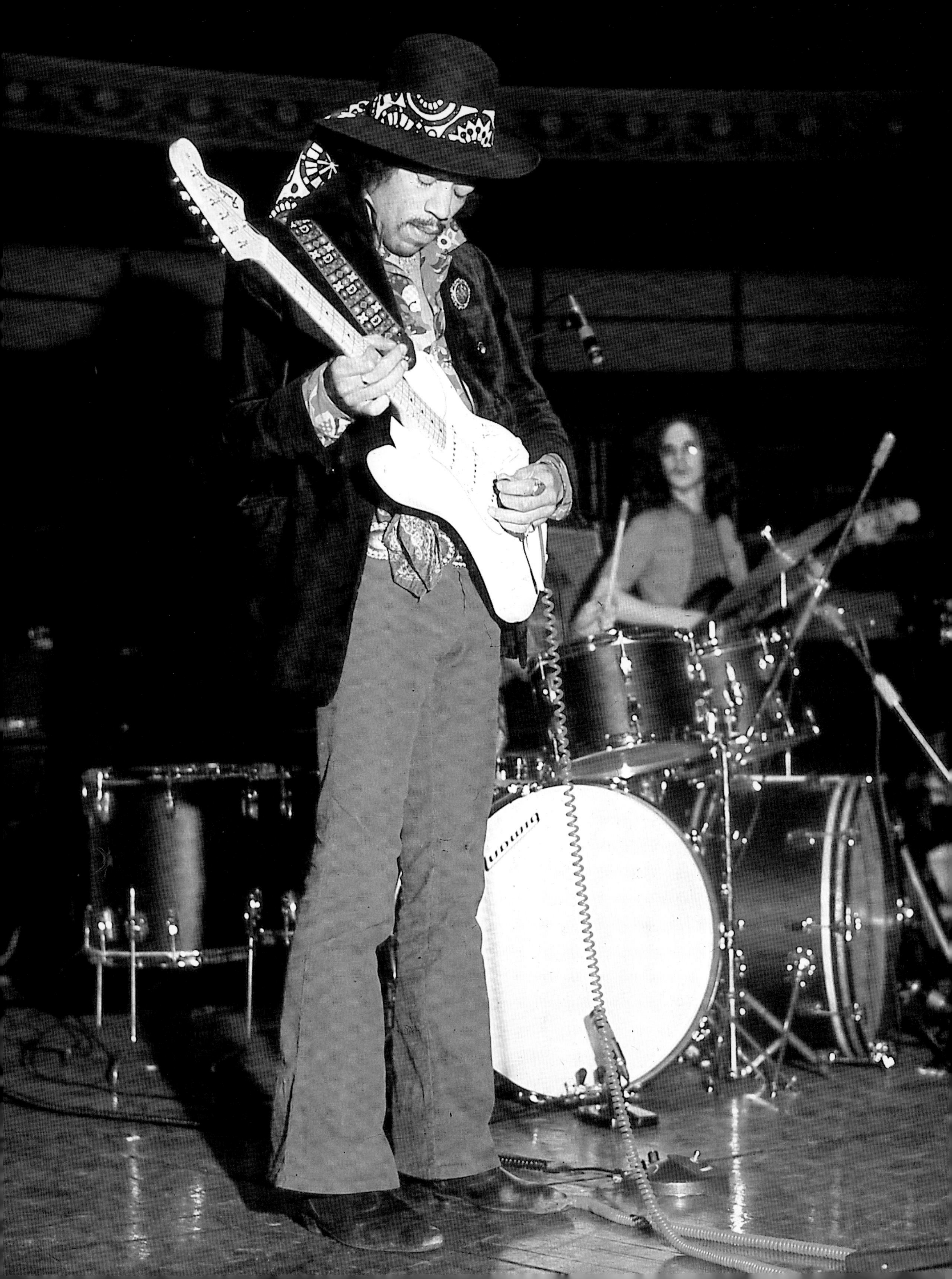

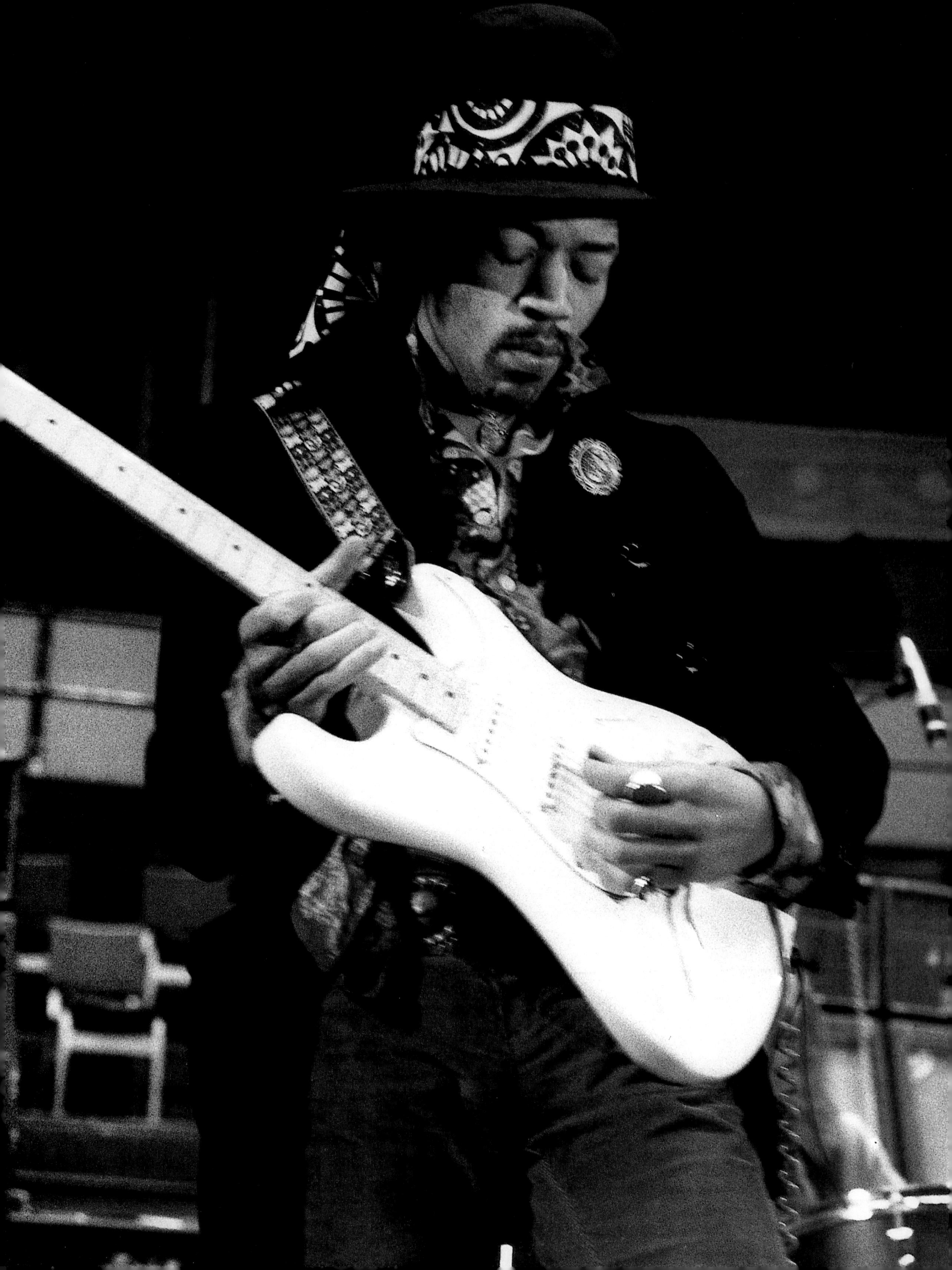

'Red House'." He dedicates the next song to the recently disbanded Cream:"... the cats are really outta site and, er, it really is too much of a shame that they had to break up. It's kind of groovy, because you'll be hearing three times as much music happening. Anyway we'd like to do one of their songs, it's an instrumental, not saying that we play it better than them, no, we're not saying that. [We're] just saying that we kind of dig the cats and the song that we're gonna do, thank you." Jimi continues with 'The Sunshine Of Your Love'. The set continues with 'Spanish Castle Magic', into which Jimi introduces a riff that would later become 'Message To Love'. The audience starts to shout out for songs. Jimi comments "... hold on, hold on. I'm gonna try one that's silly..." He continues with 'Star Spangled Banner' and 'Purple Haze'.

After the song, Jimi leaves the stage but the audience shouts out for more and he returns for an encore. "... This is Noel Redding on bass in case you might be ready to go. And we have Mitch Mitchell on drums. Well, like I said... we're up here to sing for you, thanks for staying with us this long, it's really outta site." Jimi ends the show with 'Voodoo Child (Slight Return)'.

After the concert, Jimi is filmed for an interview in his apartment at 23 Brook Street in Mayfair, London. During the interview he performs a version of 'Hound Dog' on acoustic guitar in the presence of Kathy Etchingham, Steve Gold and his wife.

Kathy Etchingham: "I didn't know they were coming, you know, they didn't tell me. Somebody knocked on the door. I think Jimi answered the door and I was sitting on the bed and the next thing, there's this great long pole came in with something on the end of it. Before I realised what it was, all these lights came on. That I remember because it took me by surprise, and something like that sticks out in you mind! And then they came back and said that they lost a bit of the film 'and can we re-film you walking up the stairs?'"

February 23
Sunday
**Speakeasy,
48 Margaret Street, London**
Jimi jams with Dave Mason and Jim Capaldi.

February 24
Monday
**Royal Albert Hall,
Kensington Gore, London**
The Experience are supported by Noel Redding's other group, Fat Mattress, and Van der Graaf Generator.

During the afternoon, the Experience attends a sound check and performs 'Hey Joe', various takes of 'Hound Dog', two takes of 'Voodoo Child (Slight Return)' and 'Getting My Heart Back Together Again'.

Arrangements have been made for the entire concert to be filmed by Steve Gold and Goldstein of Far Out Productions and directed by Joe Levine. The film – although still unreleased to this day – is called *The Last Experience*.

The Experience take the stage for their evening show, Jimi announces: "Thank you very much for waiting and our next song we would like to play [is called] 'Where's The Microphone?' It'll take us about a minute and a half to, em, like, adjust our instruments here and there, so... You know, it's gonna be a nice relaxing type [of] thing anyway, no hang-ups you know, so just relax for a second, a minute and a half, okay? Yeah we'll be, be jamming you know, same thing as last week and running over some of the old stuff, I guess I don't know, cause there's nothing else to do is there..." Jimi asks Mitch and Noel if they're ready and what they want to play, then announces: "Oh, I'll tell you what, we'll jam first, okay?" Jimi starts the show off with 'Here Comes Your Lover Man'. Afterwards, he makes his usual comments about tuning up and playing quietly to save the audience's hearing, "and, er, well cowboys are the only ones that stay in tune anyway, so what the hell and all this shit. I'd like to take a blast from the past, yeah one of them scenes (laughs), oh man." Noel says something and Jimi replies, "Yeah blast from the past", in an upper-class English accent. The band then go into 'Stone Free'. During the song Jimi plays the solo in a fast flamenco style. "Thank you very much. Yeah, that was Mitch Mitchell on drums there, doing his thing. We'd like to, er, do a little jam blues, a little slow thing called, er, well I guess we can call it 'Getting My Heart Back Together Again' or something like that. We'll find out as soon as we put the label on the record we're recording, you know. Am I still too loud? Oh I'm sleepy."

After this number, Jimi dedicates 'I Don't Live Today' to the audience and the American Indians. More tuning up follows this track, then the band go into 'Red House'. Jimi then gives his standard preamble to 'Foxy Lady': "We'd like to continue and do a thing called... it's dedicated to somebody's girlfriend here, I don't know who it is yet, we'll find out later on after the show... it goes something like this, here." After 'Foxy Lady', the band launch into 'The Sunshine Of Your Love'. Noel then announces: "We're gonna do a slow blues in C sharp" and they continue with 'Bleeding Heart' – the first time Jimi plays the song live in concert.

The Experience follow this with 'Fire' and 'Little Wing'. Afterwards, Jimi comments: "Yeah, I'm sorry man, but we, we'd like to turn it in now. We'd like to say thank you very much for coming in..." Jimi continues with 'Voodoo Child (Slight Return)'. During the song Jimi calls for conga player Rocky Dijon to join him on stage to play along. Towards the end of the song, Jimi announces: "I'd like to say thank you very much and good night, thank you. How about a hand for Rocky? This is Rocky on congas, he wanted to play so much better. Anybody else wanna play? Anybody wanna play guitar, 'cause I've finished."

Jimi concludes the concert with another new song, 'Room Full Of Mirrors', performed here for the first time. During the song Jimi announces "You can either stay and clap or... leave anytime you want to, you know..." Jimi is then joined on stage by Chris Wood on flute and Dave Mason on guitar to finish the song.

Jimi then leaves the stage and goes into the dressing room, but returns to do an encore. "Thank you... Testing one, two, three testing, testing one, two, three testing. Thank you very much, hello, we'd like to say thank you very much man, you all were really outta site, thank you. But don't forget Chris Wood and Rocky and, er, Dave Mason too, and Mitch Mitchell and Noel Redding. For you all being so nice, we'd like to blast your eardrums one more time, okay... I'd like to do a thing that's a combination of things... we just feel like jamming. If you had all brought your instruments, you would have all been up here jamming with us, you know." Jimi tunes up briefly, then the group continues with 'Purple Haze' and closes the show with 'Wild Thing'. At the end of the song, Jimi plays a few bars of 'Star Spangled Banner' then attacks his stack of amplifiers with his guitar and pokes out the speakers with the headstock of his guitar. After smashing the guitar, he throws the pieces into the audience and is then led off stage. The audience storm the stage, grabbing what pieces of equipment they can before the police surround the entire stage area.

This was Fat Mattress's début concert. Noel had formed the band in mid-1968 with old friends Neil Landon on vocals, Jim Leverton on bass guitar and Eric Dillon on drums. Fat Mattress would be the support act to many of the Experience's concerts during the coming 1969 tour of America.

Speakeasy,
48 Margaret Street, London
Jimi Jams with Jim Capaldi, Dave Mason and Alan Price.

March 6
Thursday
Speakeasy, London
Jimi jams with Billy Preston.

March 8
Saturday
Ronnie Scotts, Frith Street, London
Jimi jams with Roland Kirk.

March 9
Sunday
23 Brook Street, Mayfair, London
Jimi and Mitch jam for two hours with Roland Kirk.

March 30
Sunday
The Palladium, Hollywood, California
'Teenage Fair Pop Expo 69'
Jimi attends a Delaney and Bonnie concert, where he is interviewed with Jay Harvey for radio station KAA 1 in Los Angeles.

He later jams with Delaney Bremlett and his wife Bonnie on stage, performing a blues number and 'Room Full Of Mirrors'.

April 11
Friday
Dorton Arena,
Raleigh, North Carolina
The Experience kicks off their second tour of America, supported by Fat Mattress, who are making their American début.

The Experience take the stage for their 20:30 show and perform 'Fire', 'Foxy Lady', 'Stone Free', 'Getting My Heart Back Together Again', 'Red House', 'Purple Haze' and 'Voodoo Child (Slight Return)'.

April 12
Saturday
Spectrum,
Philadelphia, Pennsylvania
The Experience are supported by Fat Mattress.

The Experience take the stage for their 20:00 show and start with 'Fire' followed by 'Red House' and 'Foxy Lady'. Jimi then announces: "Thank you... We've got another song... dedicated to all people that might feel uptight about what's happening today. I know we all feel uptight about different things here and there. But the idea is to think positive and be aware of the ditches... So... I'd like to dedicate this to maybe a few people here and there and the America Indian, a thing called 'I Don't Live Today'– maybe tomorrow, I [couldn't] care less." During the song, Jimi comments, somewhat cryptically: "Regard this like I do a tube of Black Panthers." When the song is over, he announces: "I'd like to do a thing called... 'Getting My Heart Back Together Again', dedicated to a little baby that's in a hospital now, and everybody here..." He follows the song with: "I'd like to go ahead on and do a thing called 'Stone Free', or 'Gary Leeson Will See Yer'."

The end of the set is approaching, and Jimi announces: "I think we only have time for about two or three more numbers... [we] would really like to dedicate this song to all the beautiful memories and [the] beautiful school... we used to be [made to sing this] in school, while we were being programmed. A thing that goes something like this, here." Jimi continues with 'Star Spangled Banner' and 'Purple Haze', before winding up with: "We have Mitch Mitchell on drums and Noel Redding on bass, we'd like to say thanks very much, I'll continue to do this last number for you." Jimi ends the show with 'Voodoo Child (Slight Return)'.

April 18
Friday
**Ellis Auditorium North Hall,
North Main Street, Memphis,
Tennessee**

The Experience perform two shows at 19:00 and 21:30, supported by Fat Mattress.

The Experience are late on stage due to their plane arriving 40 minutes late, so they don't start the first show until 20:15.

After their introduction the Experience start their second show with 'Fire'. They then tune up, and Jimi announces: "We're doing a thing dedicated to... a thing called 'I Don't Live Today'." When the number is over, he comments: "This is dedicated [to] the fourth new member of the group... It's about a train ride. The cat says dig it to us and everybody to all move town to the south. With this amount of fun we'll go fishing and come back and buy the town, I'm gonna put a piece in your shoe." Jimi continues with 'Getting My Heart Back Together Again'. After the song, the audience shouts out for 'Purple Haze'. Jimi comments: "Before we get into that we'd like to... take it and mix some blues. Some cats in Cream, you know, are really outta site. But like, I'm gonna play the song – not saying that we play it better than them." Jimi continues with 'The Sunshine Of Your Love', 'Stone Free' and 'Foxy Lady'. The remainder of the concert is too badly recorded to hear what Jimi is saying. However, he continues with 'Star Spangled Banner' and 'Purple Haze', ending the show with 'Voodoo Child (Slight Return)'.

April 19
Saturday
**Sam Houston Coliseum,
Houston, Texas**

The Experience are supported by Chicago Transit Authority and Fat Mattress.

April 20
Sunday
**Memorial Auditorium,
Dallas, Texas**

The Experience are supported by Fat Mattress and Cat Mother.

The Experience start off their afternoon show with 'Stone Free' and continue with 'Getting My Heart Back Together Again', 'Foxy Lady', 'I Don't Live Today', 'Fire', 'Red House', 'Star Spangled Banner', 'Purple Haze' and end the show with 'Voodoo Child (Slight Return)'. Unfortunately, the original tape of this concert only recorded the performance, cutting out any of Jimi's between-song comments.

April 26
Saturday
**The Forum,
Los Angeles, California**

The Experience are supported by Cat Mother and Chicago Transit Authority.

The Experience are introduced by MC Jimmy Rabbitt from KRLIA radio. He announces that they won't start the concert until everyone is seated. The Experience take the stage for their evening concert to a thunderous reception from the audience. Jimi announces: "Yeah okay, okay then, okay we're all at church, all right? Pretend there's a sky above ya, all right? Yeah..." and laughs. Jimi then says to Noel, "Oh come on, let's get tuned up," before saying to the audience, "This whole show is dedicated to you, ourselves, Murray Roman, the Smothers Brothers, God bless their souls... It'll take us about, listen, listen, it'll take us about 45 seconds to get... arranged here, and... for things to settle down all right, okay? And we want you to forget about everything that happened yesterday, last night or this morning. Just forget about everything but what's going on down now, it's up to you all, and it's up to us too, so let's get our feelings together. They talk about some kind of earthquake going on you know, dig. (Laughs.) Dig, you know where all the earthquake happening is coming from. It's bad vibrations man, they get very heavy sometimes, you know. You wanna save your State, get your hearts together. Yeah, okay then. All right, to be fair with everybody we're gonna start off with a little jam, okay? It's a thing that was written by... a couple of Swedish cats, Hansson and Karlsson, and they recorded it in Sweden, it's a thing called 'Tax Free'... It goes something like this here." Jimi starts the introduction, then announces the song as 'Fingers Rockall'. After the number, the group briefly tune up and Jimi gives his usual 'Foxy Lady' dedication to 'somebody's girlfriend': "We don't know [what] the girl's name [is], we'll find

1969 February/April 137

out though. Hope you don't mind us tuning up between every song. Anyway, er, you know, cowboys are the only one who stay in tune anyway, what the hell. As I said, we're having us a slight bit of trouble, but just hold on, you know everything's gonna be all right before we finish. Well, [we'll] stay here until things are right, so we might not ever finish... some of you out there are wondering, what the hell I am trying to do wiggling my hands like this? Well, if you brought your old lady [up here], I'll like to say (laughs) I like to give her a piece of your mind." The group continue with 'Foxy Lady'. "Yeah, everybody wants to know what American soul is... America's soul is something that goes something like this here, a thing called 'Red House'." After this slow blues number, Jimi announces: "There's... one song we'd like to dedicate to the plain-clothes police out there and other goofballs, it's a thing called... 'Spanish Castle Magic' that they should get into very quick, before their minds get to heroics."

After this number, Jimi continues with 'Star Spangled Banner' and announces during the song, "Here is a song we were all brainwashed with..." Jimi follows with 'Purple Haze', which causes the audience to all stand up and rush the stage. Jimi announces: "Okay, we're getting some people uptight there, so... let's just relax, hold on for a second, just let's relax and... just sit down and... get the rest of the thing over with, okay? It you sit down now, we can play a little bit longer, 'cause I feel like playing, I don't feel like looking at these cats' blue hats." (Meaning the police.) "Yeah don't worry, don't worry, everything's gonna be all right, don't worry, we still got the end to come, don't we?" The audience is still on their feet shouting. Jimi announces: "Okay settle down, okay we all feel the same way, we all feel the same way. We're gonna dedicate this to the Smothers Brothers and to ourselves and to the American Indian, and it's called 'I Don't Live Today' – maybe tomorrow, I can't tell you really." The audience are starting to get unruly and Noel shouts for everyone to sit down. Jimi announces: "Listen, listen, testing one, two, three. Hey listen... that's how I feel, we wanna do the same thing to you, we wanna rush up to you and all that kind of stuff. But dig, listen to the sounds, man, we're trying to play some sounds, and we don't want all these jokers up here on stage with us, okay?... Okay, don't rush the stage anymore, all right, and then we can get rid of the other folks (i.e. the police), okay?" The police have now formed a line across the stage in front of the group and they all sit down on the edge of the stage to prevent the audience from storming the stage. Jimi comments: "Come on, let's act like we got some sense, it's groovy, you know, to get high and all that, but act like you've got some sense while we were doing it, all right? Let's just relax and just sit down and dig the sounds and just don't start any more trouble, because there's enough already, all right? Let us stall the trouble for you, let us do 'Voodoo Child' for you, at least." The audience are still causing problems and Jimi announces "All right, I'm very sorry man, but we wanna play some more but the cat said you know, if we, if [you] keep rushing the [stage]..." Jimi ends the show with 'Voodoo Child (Slight Return)' and includes an excerpt of 'The Sunshine Of Your Love' before returning back to the original song.

April 27
Sunday
Oakland Coliseum,
Oakland, California

The Experience are supported by Cat Mother and Chicago Transit Authority.

The Experience take the stage for their 19:30 show. Asking for the audience's patience while the band tune up, Jimi adds: "Just thinking about everything that went down today or last night, forget about everything except us... we're gonna take a bath tonight... We have Mitch Mitchell on drums and Noel Redding on bass and yours truly Alfred E. Newman on, er, meat whistle" Jimi opens the show with 'Fire', offering "Yeah, thank you" afterwards. Noel announces to the audience that as it's Mother Day, "any young ladies wanna become mothers, come round the back afterwards. That's why we're thin you see." Jimi adds: "Yeah, and... Humpty Dumpty over there [is] asking about why [we're] thin... I'll tell you, we're been running from a whole lot of bullets, just like you all been doing, and, er, to prove it we'd like to do a song that goes something like this, here." Jimi continues with 'Hey Joe', followed by Spanish Castle Magic' before announcing: 'We've got a slow blues [we'd] like to jam on if you give us a chance, a thing called 'Getting My Heart Back Together'. It's about a cat who's really down and his old lady don't want him around and his family's trying to run him out of town. And so he, like, he goes off... to do his thing and comes back and put a piece of the town in his shoe, maybe. And, er, you know, one of them kind of scenes." Jimi follows this number with 'The Sunshine Of Your Love', 'Red House and 'Foxy Lady'. He then continues with 'Star Spangled Banner', which runs into 'Purple Haze'. "Yeah okay thank you. We'd like to say it's been a pleasure playing for you all."

Jimi leaves the stage but returns for an encore with The Jefferson Airplane's Jack Cassidy on bass and Noel switching to rhythm guitar. Jimi: "Yeah, we'd like for our last number just to do a little jam bit. I think we ought to give a big hand for Jack Cassidy on bass and then, er, do a thing called 'Voodoo Child (Slight Return)' – something you all should remember, or we'd like for you to remember, and we'd like to say thanks again for coming. We hope we get the chance to come back again."

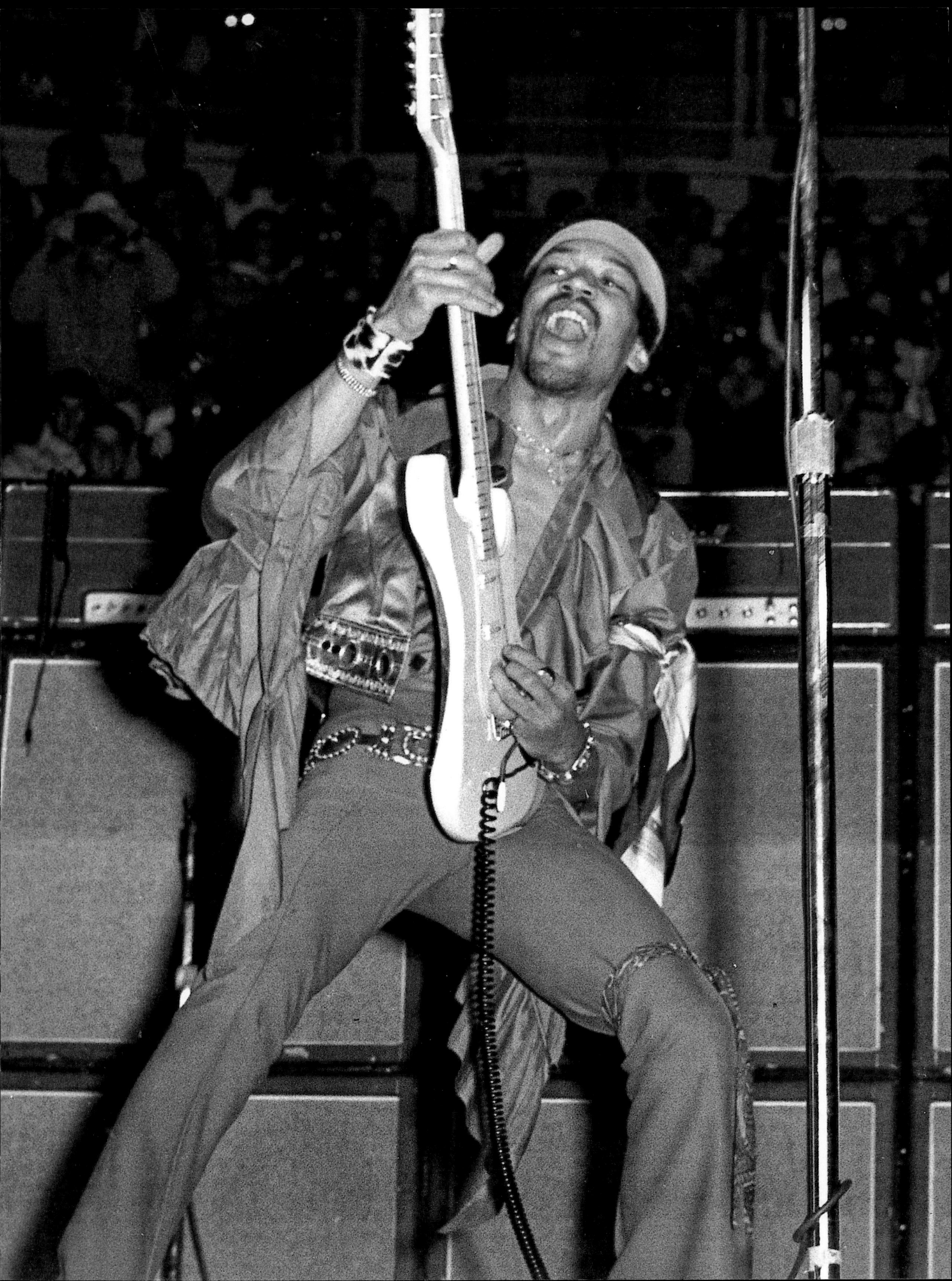

COBO ARENA
FRIDAY, MAY 2, 1969
CORA PROMOTIONS PRESENTS
One show only at 8 PM
the JIMI HENDRIX EXPERIENCE
with NOEL REDDING
also **cat mother**
Tickets: $3.50, $4.50, $5.50, $6.50
MAIL ORDERS ONLY!
Please enclose stamped, self-addressed envelope, make checks payable, and mail to, Cobo Arena, 1 Washington Boulevard, Detroit, Michigan 48226.

May 2
Friday
Cobo Arena, Detroit, Michigan
The Experience are supported by Cat Mother and Fat Mattress.

After the Experience are introduced Jimi announces: "Er, it'll take about a minute and a half to like... testing one, two three. Oh I'm sorry... [it] is gonna take [us] about a minute and a half to, like, make little minor adjustments here and there, you know... you know the drill, it's part of the show, man. Since... last time you all seen us... we haven't done any practice... and... we're just gonna be jamming tonight, so you might as well just relax." After a long tune up Jimi announces: "Thank you very much for waiting, thank you very much, and now for our next number we would like to play..." Jimi opens the show with 'Fire'.

After the song, Jimi announces: "We're having slight difficulties but... well anyway, I'd like to try to do Charlie Chaplin and hi de ho de ho." Eric Barrett comes on stage to fix the problem and Noel announces that he's from Glasgow in Scotland. Jimi finally continues with 'Spanish Castle Magic'. "Yeah thank you very much," he tells the crowd afterwards. "There another song that we you know, and it goes something like this here... dig this, it's the Black Panthers and the... American Indian song 'I Don't Live Today' – maybe tomorrow."

When the group finish the number, Jimi announces: "Thank you, do you mind if we do this song, a scene that... I wanna get you into... And... we're not saying that we play the song because we play it better than them groups, we're not saying that at all. We're just saying that we dig the group and... Anyway, the name of the group is The Cream and the name of the song is 'The Sunshine Of Your Love'." When the song is over, Jimi says: "Thank you, and then we're gonna have to do this other song that we recorded on our third LP – it's called *Electric Ladyland*. I'd like to do the song called 'Voodoo Child (Slight Return)' though." After this number, Jimi continues to the end with 'Red House'.

May 3
Saturday
On Jimi's arrival into Toronto International Airport, he is promptly arrested for drug offences. He's is later released on bail to play the evening's concert.

Maple Leaf Gardens, Toronto, Ontario, Canada
The Experience are supported by Cat Mother.

Jimi walks onto the stage and announces: "Hello, how you all doing, you okay?... it's gonna take us about a minute and a half to... set up ourselves properly... I want you to forget about everything that's happening today or tomorrow or yesterday – this is our own little world right here for about an hour and a half, okay?" After a short tune up Jimi plays a melodic blues run that gradually becomes more intense, and then announces: "Thank you and now for our next number I'm gonna do a thing called 'Let Me Stand Next To Your Old Lady', I mean, 'Let Me Stand Next To Your Fire'." Jimi plays a few chords and says, jokingly, "Thank you very much, and now for our very last song, a thing called 'Foxy Lady'. Someone shouts out "What's it like, Jimi?"; he replies back – "Oh, well take it away there." He continues with 'Fire'. He then announces: "Thank you very much. If you don't mind we'd like to slow it down a little bit... this song that... we do sometimes, just jam around with it, you know, mess around with the octaves... It's about a cat trying to do his thing and his old lady put him down just, and her parents don't want him around. So he goes downtown to the train station, waiting for the train to come and take him away so [he can]... stretch out and do his thing. And, er, he comes back and he buys the town and he gives a piece to his old lady leaving, rides the flag." (Laughs.) "Now Noel, don't try to think about it...

dig, it's... called 'Getting My Heart Back Together Again'."

When the song is over, the band need to tune up again. Jimi: "Oh give me a second to tune up, we tune up between every single number because we care for your ears... that's why we don't play so loud... Cowboys are the only ones who stay in tune, anyway. I'd like to do this thing called 'Spanish Castle Magic', dedicated to the ones and us too, who just think they're gonna get away." During the song Jimi plays a snippet of '3rd Stone From The Sun', after which Mitch takes an unusually long drum solo. Jimi announces Mitch Mitchell on drums and continues by playing 'Little Miss Lover', then goes back into 'Spanish Castle Magic', followed by 'Red House'. Then: "Yeah, sorry for the tune up again but it does happen... between every song. I'd like to keep it going and dedicate this to somebody's girlfriend out there, we don't know who she is yet, we'll find out later on at the end of the show. A thing called 'Foxy Lady'." Jimi proceeds to play the opening feedback note but the amplifiers are starting to cause some trouble. He starts to sing by la-la-ing opera fashion before starting the song again.

Jimi then announces, somewhat obscurely: "Better test something out, what it'll be like to tap out their eyes with lances for lefty's, straight lines giving 'em do something that. Thank you very much, that was a fairy tale legend... we'd like to play this song, a thing that goes something like this here." The group then plays a very melodic version of 'Room Full Of Mirrors'. He announces during the introduction: "We're gonna try something right here, we've never played this before, but we'll... see if we can make up the words, and we'll see if we can say some words to... help people understand the meaning from the [pretence] of life. We already know hang-ups already, we already know protest, now we'd like to try to give a few solutions." During the song, Jimi appears to make up the words as he sings and even adds a few bars of 'Crash Landing', a song he would go on to record much later in the year. He ends the song with a few bars of 'Gypsy Eyes', and goes straight into 'Purple Haze'. He signs off with: "Thank you and good night and peace be with you and none of you try the police all right, thank you. Jimi ends the show with 'Voodoo Child (Slight Return)'.

May 4
Sunday
Syracuse War Memorial Auditorium, Syracuse, New York
The Experience are supported by Cat Mother.

The Experience perform 'Fire', 'I Don't Live Today', 'Foxy Lady' and 'Stone Free'.

May 7
Wednesday
Memorial Coliseum, Tuscaloosa, Alabama, Georgia
The Experience are supported by Cat Mother and Fat Mattress.

May 9
Friday
Charlotte Coliseum, Charlotte, North Carolina
The Experience are supported by Chicago Transit Authority.

The Experience perform 'Johnny B. Goode', 'Fire', 'Foxy Lady', 'Spanish Castle Magic', 'Red House', 'Purple Haze' and 'Voodoo Child (Slight Return)'.

May 10
Saturday
Charleston Civic Centre, Charleston, West Virginia
The Experience are supported by Fat Mattress and Chicago Transit Authority.

The group play 'Fire', 'Come On (Part One)', 'Foxy Lady', 'Getting My Heart Back Together Again', 'Purple Haze', 'Voodoo Child (Slight Return)' and 'Wild Thing'.

May 11
Sunday
Fairground's Coliseum, Indianapolis, Indiana
The Experience are supported by Fat Mattress and Chicago Transit Authority.

The Experience take the stage for their 19:00 show. As usual, Jimi opens up by asking for the audience's patience while the band tune up: "Listen... it's gonna take us about 30 seconds to, er, tune up and do our little minor adjustments here and there. I want you to forget about anything that was happening yesterday or today, or what would happen tomorrow, just use this as our new little world right here, this is fat and juicy." (Audience laughs.) "This show is dedicated to all the police that are jumping, who are gonna be doing their things t-o y-o-u. And all the Black Panthers and all the American Indians, and yeah, you people too. Jimi opens the show with 'Come On (Part One)'. Afterwards, he announces: "If you don't mind, er, I'd like to take a little bit of blast from the past. A nice 'Dig That Time' and, er, dedicate it to plain-clothes policemen and other oddballs, a thing called 'Hey Joe'. You notice we tune up between every song, that's because we care for your ears that's why we don't play so loud... Cowboys are the only ones who stay in tune anyway, so what the hell." Jimi continues with 'Hey Joe'.

When the song is over, Jimi announces: "We've got another song we'd like to rip off and, like, get it out the way, a thing that was released for our next single. It's been released one time before... in England, maybe about 12 or 13 years ago, by us. Recorded in 1873 in the Benjamin Franklin studios, a thing called 'Stone Free.'" Following that number, Jimi tells the audience: "I'd like to continue on, if it's alright [with] you all... We'd like to throw [in] a bit of blues with E. [Jimi gets interrupted.] More people?... What's wrong now? [Are] they okay?

Okay then. Yes, we'd like to do a slow blues and... [this man,] his old lady don't want him around, [starts] taking him down and, er, you know, messing around town, hanging around. And like, er, damn man, what am I doing here, let me get myself together. So he goes out to do his thing, becomes all these weird [things] and comes back to buy the town and gives a pieceful for the old lady, if she makes love to him one more time. Anyway, that's the name of it –'Get My Heart Back Together'."

When they finish this blues number, Jimi tells the audience: "I remember taking off and rock 'n' rolling with a little thing called, 'Let Me Stand Next To Your Old Lady'. Er, I mean 'Your Fire'... Jimi continues with 'Fire'. Then: "I'd like to slow it down again and do a little thing recorded in, er, 1744, back of the days with the rag tags. Cover the camera, you could break something." Jimi continues with 'Red House'. After this, Jimi asks: "What do we play next? [He plays the riff to 'Earth Blues'.] I'd like to dedicate this to the people, somebody lost a little thing called 'Foxy Lady'." Jimi ends the show with 'Voodoo Child (Slight Return)'. At one point, he stops playing and Mitch continues, Jimi then comes back in and Mitch stops. Then Jimi stops and announces: "This name of this song is 'Something We'll Never Learn'."

May 14
Wednesday
Scene Club,
301 West 46th Street, New York
Jimi jams with Steve Stills and Johnny Winter.

May 16
Friday
Civic Centre,
Baltimore, Maryland
The Experience are supported by Cat Mother and The Buddy Miles Express.

The Experience take the stage for their 20:00 show and open with 'Here Comes Your Lover Man'. Then Jimi tells the audience: "We're... gonna forget about everything that was happening yesterday, things forgetting to do today, because we forgotten, you got slapped... Even things you might have to do tomorrow, forget about all those things and let's make our own little world here, it's better for the things that come out just here. 'Getting My Heart Back Together'– this is blues that we'd like to jam for you now, okay?" After the song, he asks the audience: "Er, did you all read the programme? Did you all read the programme? Well, what you hollering about for man, just relax everything's gonna be all right. Damn, we know what we're gonna do. It's gonna take us about ten minutes, er ten seconds, yeah, ten days, ten seconds to tune up a little bit and then we'll have a chance to really get it together so, er, you know, hold on, hold on for a minute. We tune up because we really care for your ears... that's why we don't play so loud, all right? I'd like to dedicate this one to... the... what do you call it? Plain-clothes police and other goofballs, a thing called 'Let Me Stand Next To Your Fire'."

Afterwards, Jimi announces: "Yeah okay, thank you. I'd like to slow it down again if you don't mind and have this lady for about six or seven minutes, a thing called 'Red House'." Jimi follows this with 'I Don't Live Today'. The audience claps prematurely at the end of the song – Jimi comments: "Thank you anyway. This song is dedicated to somebody's girlfriend out there and we don't know who it is yet, we'll find out..." Noel then announces that any little girl who wants to come backstage to become mothers on Mothers Day is welcome to do so. Jimi continues, in bizarre mode: "This is dedicated to mow the lawn on the day before with all the yellow underwear on", and then plays 'Foxy Lady'. "We dedicate this song to all the, er, people born in 1733", Jimi announces afterwards, and launches into 'Purple Haze'. After this, he announces: "Thank you very much, we know of another song written 1634 in the Benjamin Franklin studios, a thing called 'Spanish Castle Magic'." During the song, Jimi add a medley of 'South Saturn Delta' and the flamenco-type introduction that he would develop later into 'Land Of The New Rising Sun'. The group are being hurried along, and Jimi now tells the audience: "Yeah, okay listen, the cat says we have to pack it up now. I'd like to say this really is a lot of fun playing banjo and so... we'd like to dedicate this one song to everybody out there." Someone shouts something out and Jimi replies, "Oh yeah, okay thank you very much, I love you too, baby. I hope you parked your bicycle outside, 'cause I know a dirty old man that will lick your old bicycle seat, at the end of the show. Wow man, I can't do anything like these people, I can't hear a word I'm thinking about. I'd like to do 'Voodoo Child (Slight Return)' for everybody here, thank you very much, peace and happiness." Jimi ends the show with 'Voodoo Child (Slight Return)'.

May 17
Saturday
Rhode Island Auditorium,
Providence, Rhode Island
The Experience are supported by Cat Mother and The Buddy Miles Express.

The group take the stage for their 17:30 show. Jimi announces: "Listen... it'll take about thirty seconds to tune up... before anything happens though, we want you to forget about everything that might have been happening yesterday or the day before or tomorrow. You know here's a time for us to make our own little world and see what kind of world we wanna have, and then sit back [and] groove and just relax." Jimi opens the show with 'Here Comes Your Lover Man'. Afterwards, he announces: "Yeah thank you very much. Okay then, hold on a second hold on... there's a whole lot of hang-ups been going on, but we're still in America we're still Americans and, er, we still [want] to keep things happening nicely and must work towards those things. But in the meantime... we'd like to point these out with sounds maybe, by electric sounds in a thing called 'I Don't Live Today' – maybe tomorrow, I can't say." When the song is finished, Jimi says: "Yeah thank you anyway, thank you. I'd like to slow it down if you don't mind and bore you for about six or seven minutes, do a thing by us recorded in 1783 in the Benjamin Franklin studios, a thing called, em, a little bit of American blues, it's called 'Red House'." Afterwards, Jimi jokes: "Yeah, it's nice to be here in Miami, Florida, lot of people there. Oh I'm sorry, in Dallas. I'm sorry for the delay, [we] promise to tune up between every single song, that's because we really care for your ears, that's why we don't play so loud. Also, cowboys are the only one that stay in tune anyway." Jimi continues with 'Red House'.

Next, he announces: "I'd like to do a song about a cat who has to leave town to get his heart back together. He [comes] back and [buys] the town and might give a piece to his old lady if she makes love to him one more time... So we flash in on him at the train station, waiting for his train." Jimi continues with 'Getting My Heart Back Together'. Then: "We'd like to continue on with a thing dedicated to the plain-clothes policemen and other goofballs, a thing called 'Spanish Castle Magic'..." During the solo of the song, Jimi starts to introduce new material, adding an early version of 'Earth Blues' and 'The Sunshine Of Your Love' before continuing with 'Spanish Castle Magic'. Next, Jimi announces: "This is dedicated to somebody's old lady out there, we don't know who it is, the one with the yellow underwear sitting over there, yeah you." Jimi continues with 'Foxy Lady', 'Purple Haze' and then plays 'Start Spangled Banner with his teeth. Winding up, he announces: "Yeah thank you very much and we must leave now before the bad people get us, honestly. Yes, and we would like to say before we leave... here's the song for your bit of self-assurance. Everybody must identify in some kind of way to say peace and happiness, thank you." Jimi ends the show with 'Voodoo Child (Slight Return)'.

May 18
Sunday
Madison Square Garden, New York
The Experience are supported by The Buddy Miles Express and Cat Mother.

The Experience start their 20:00 show with 'Here Comes Your Lover Man'. "Er, we have two broken strings here," Jimi tells the audience afterwards. Clearly the group are becoming frustrated with all the camera bulbs popping at them, as Jimi now takes time out to say: "Hey listen, listen, I'd like to ask not too much with those pictures, all right, because it's taking away... you know, we can't concentrate if you take too many pictures, all right?" Jimi continues with 'Come On (Part One)'. Then: "We're gonna do a slow blues, when you're in your own booth sitting there. Are you all supposed to be sitting down? You know, I'd like to ask you one thing, I'd like you to get up and all defeat the national champion, all right?" Jimi continues with 'Red House' and 'Fire', during which he starts to experience amplifier trouble. Mitch takes the opportunity to do a drum solo while the problem is being sorted out. Jimi returns by playing 'Spanish Castle Magic', including the instrumental solo 'Villanova Junction' that he would play to much greater effect during the Woodstock Festival, and then finally back to 'Spanish Castle Magic'. After this, he announces: "This song's about a cat, er, being ready to drop town and, er, his old lady getting him down and her family don't want him around. So instead of just laying in the corner, just wasting his life away, he decided to go off into the world and do his own thing. And he [comes] back and buys the town and he gives a piece to his old lady if she makes love to him one more time. It's a thing called 'Getting My Heart Back Together'." When the song is over, Jimi says: "I'd like to get into the beautiful... another old song which is called 'I Don't Live Today' – maybe tomorrow, I can't say." The Experience end the show with 'Voodoo Child (Slight Return)' and 'Purple Haze'.

May 22
Thursday
Coliseum, Vancouver, Canada
Jimi was scheduled to play one show with Fat Mattress as support act, but in view of his being arrested earlier in the month, the concert was cancelled – probably because the authorities didn't allow it to go ahead.

May 23
Friday
Seattle Centre Coliseum, Seattle, Washington
The Experience are supported by Fat Mattress.

During the concert, there was a large thunderstorm. Jimmy Leverton: "Yeah, it passed right overhead, it was a dark night. We had a glass dome, and a revolving stage in the middle, Jimi was playing really blistering guitar. So this whole place [was filled] with lightning. Steven Spielberg in lights! Jimi made some remark like "good light show", or something like that..."

1969 May 143

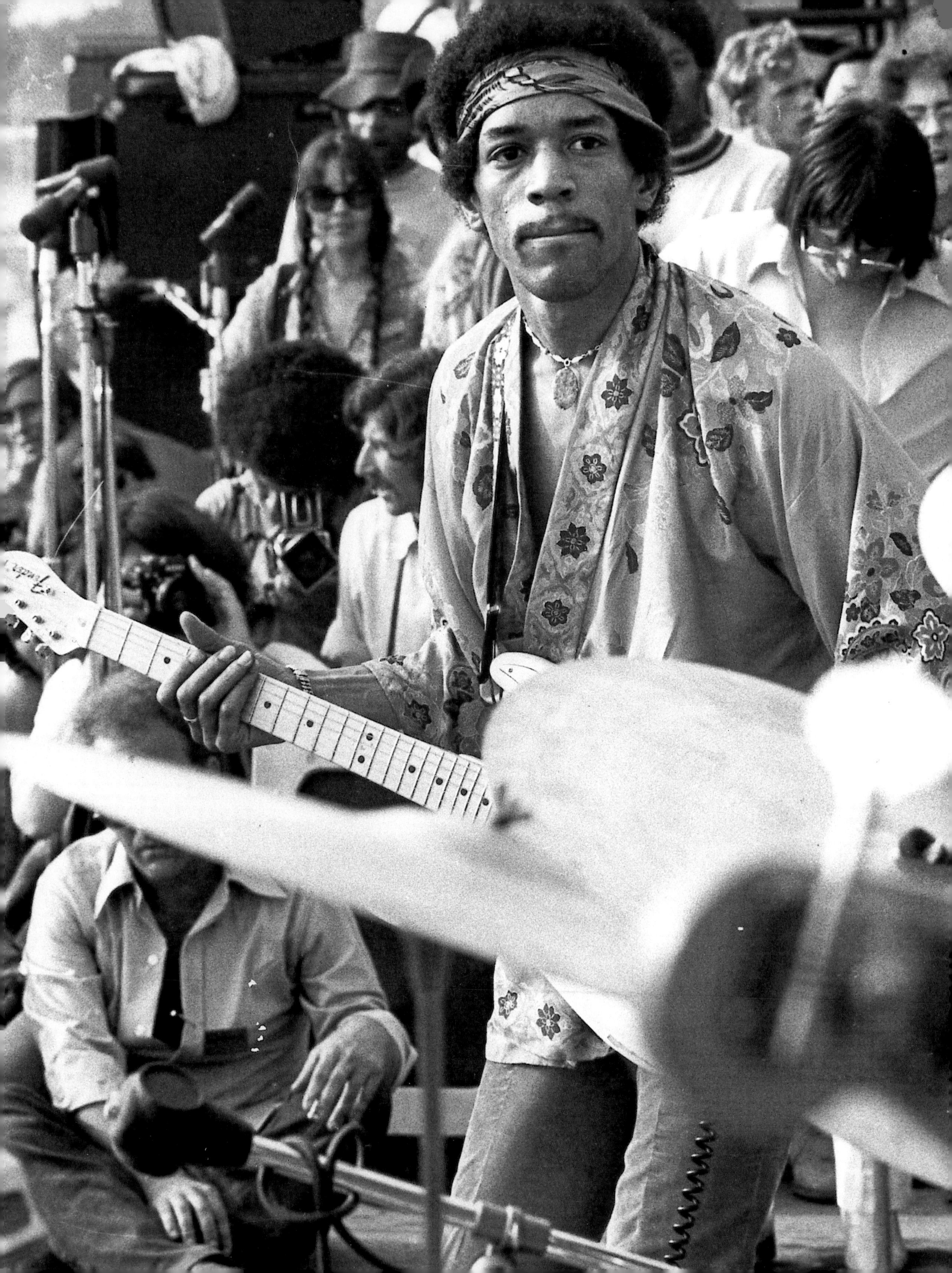

May 24
Saturday
Sports Arena, San Diego, California
The Experience are supported by Fat Mattress.

The Experience take the stage for their 20:30 show. They open with 'Fire'. Jimi then says: "Yeah okay, Yeah I'll tell you what, yeah well, we're gonna get into all that, don't worry man, don't worry you don't have a programme, just relax. When I say toilet paper, that's when you come rolling out, okay? We'd like to continue on with a song recorded in 1738 in the Benjamin Franklin studios, a thing called 'Hey Joe'." Inevitably the group are out of tune after the song, and Jimi announces: "You find us tuning up between every song because we really care for your ears, that's why we don't play so loud. Cowboys are the only ones who stay in tune anyway, so what the hell. We ain't in cowboy land, are we? Yeah, we'd like to dedicate this one to the, er, plain-clothes policemen and other goofballs, a thing called, er, I almost forgot, anyway, a thing called 'Spanish Castle Magic'." During the solo, Jimi adds a snippet of 'The Sunshine Of Your Love' before returning to the original tune. Afterwards he comments: "That's what happens when you get bored playing the same old songs all the time. Anyway, I hope you all don't mind us slowing the pace down a little bit and going into... a blues, lasts about six or seven minutes for those who may be sleeping. I'd like to dedicate this to everybody here... We call this one the blues and we call this one 'Red House', we're gonna do that for a second."

When the song is over, Jimi announces: "Dig, listen, we'd like to play another song too, we'd like to play this other song, goes something like this here. We recorded this in, er, 1444, way back there beyond the ways... Everybody should be respecting the old, but sometimes [they]... make it hard for the young people to live, and they might get the wrong interpretation of the old. And we come out with this song dedicated to the American Indian and you people and ourselves, called 'I Don't Live Today' – maybe tomorrow, I can't say." Jimi adds a section of 'Star Spangled Banner into the song. Afterwards, he comments: "And then we have other people that stay around and say 'Yeah man, let's protest', but [we] all know the vibe is sitting around corridors to get stoned, right? And then we have other people who try to do something about it, like making a master race by making a crafty all the time..." The band then launch into 'Foxy Lady'.

When they finish, Jimi comments: "Yeah, okay then, okay. We'd like to say we really enjoyed playing for you, you know you've all really been outta site. We'd like to, er, we only have about two more numbers to do – the cat says we only have two more numbers to do." He then takes time to say something about the spirit of the times: "Love, it will not be there in no kind of way unless it's truth and understanding first and, er, don't be thrown together by...'Come on everybody, let's love together', that's a load of, er, hogwash [if you] forget to have truth and understanding in the first place." The group continues with 'Purple Haze'. Then Jimi tells the audience: "Thank you and, er, goodnight and peace, peace to you and happiness, thank you. And we'd like to say that... it was [great] playing for you all. Here's a song for everybody to grab hold of, not coming from us to you, but coming from, you know just a feeling man, it's a self assurance. A thing called 'Voodoo Child (Slight Return)' and thank you and good night."

May 25
Sunday
Santa Clara County Fairground's Pop Festival, San Jose, California
The Experience are supported by Fat Mattress, Eric Burdon and War, Loading Zone and Taj Mahal.

The Experience take the stage for their 16:00 show, and Jimi launches into a by now familiar preamble: "What we're gonna do today is... for you to forget everything that was going on yesterday or last night or today. Let's make our own little world right here, it's like pure vibrations." After the normal tune up the group open the show with 'Getting My Heart Back Together'. Jimi announces: "We're gonna do 'Let Me Stand Next To Your Fire'." Towards the end of the song, Jimi appears to have a problem with his guitar, so Mitch takes a drum solo. When Jimi returns, they move into 'Spanish Castle Magic'. Then Jimi tells the crowd: "Yeah, we'd like to go back in time, back to 1784 in the Benjamin Franklin studios when we recorded this thing called 'Red House'."

After this slow blues finishes, Jimi says: "Yeah we know, we know what's happening right now... I'd like to say something that... [here's] a song we recorded [on] the first LP, a thing called 'I Don't Live Today,' dedicated to all the American Indians and you people, you know... for the idea of keep your own self together, so you can be ready for the next world, because the air zone's supposed to be bigger. You might as well get it together, but let's reflect on this crap that they just pulled on us right now, okay, which is called 'I Don't Live Today' – maybe tomorrow I can't say." When the song finishes, Jimi gives his standard introduction to 'Foxy Lady': "We're doing this one dedicated to a girl back there, the one there, yeah, with the yellow underwear, yeah, you that's right, dedicated to you."

After 'Foxy Lady' the group plays 'Purple Haze'. Then: "The man just told us that we only have one more song to go..." The crowd start shouting for 'Wild Thing'. Jimi responds: "Yeah man, and I know exactly what I'm gonna do, when I say toilet paper, that's when you come rolling out. I love you too. Hey we'd like to do this self assurance song, not coming from us to you but coming from the message to you, it's called 'Voodoo Child'. Before we, like... leave this place, I'd like to say thank you one more time. We'd like to say peace and happiness." Jimi ends the show with an extra-long version of 'Voodoo Child (Slight Return)', which also incorporates an instrumental version of 'Message To Love'. Jimi announces, "We're finished now, we're just jamming. You can do whatever you want to do, man..." He continues with excursions into 'Room Full Of Mirrors' and 'The Sunshine Of Your Love' before finally returning back to 'Voodoo Child (Slight Return)'.

May 30
Friday
**Waikiki Shell,
Honolulu, Oahu, Hawaii**
The Experience are supported by Fat Mattress.

The group take the stage for their 20:00 show. They perform 'Foxy Lady,' 'Red House' and 'I Don't Live Today'. However, due to further amplifier trouble which resulted in a very bad hum, Jimi decides to abandon the proceedings after playing only forty minutes of the show.

The audience is told that because the show has been cut short, if they retain their ticket stubs, they will be re-admitted for the following evening's performance.

May 31
Saturday
Waikiki Shell, Hawaii
The Experience are supported by Fat Mattress.

The Experience perform 'Foxy Lady', 'Red House', 'I Don't Live Today', 'Stone Free', 'Star Spangled Banner', 'Purple Haze' and 'Voodoo Child (Slight Return)'.

June 1
Sunday
Waikiki Shell, Hawaii
The Experience are supported by Fat Mattress.

The group perform 'Foxy Lady', 'Red House', 'Room Full Of Mirrors', 'Purple Haze' and 'Voodoo Child (Slight Return)'.

Jimi gave this unscheduled show for free, to make up for the problems during the performance on Friday evening.

June 20
Friday
**Newport Pop Festival,
Devonshire Downs, Northridge,
California**
The Experience are supported by The Edwin Hawkins Singers, Ike & Tina Turner, Joe Cocker, Spirit, Southwind and Taj Mahal.

The Experience take the stage for their 22:30 show, opening with a medley of 'Stone Free', 'Third Stone From The Sun', 'Are You Experienced' and a very melodic instrumental solo before returning back to 'Stone Free'. As members of the audience attempt a stage invasion, Jimi comments angrily: "Oh yeah let's all try to get onto the stage" and continues with 'The Sunshine Of Your Love'. For some reason he then stops playing and Mitch starts to play a drum solo. However, Jimi abruptly bursts in and plays 'Fire'. He goes on to play the introduction to 'Getting My Heart Back Together', but he's clearly still riled, and comments at one point: "Fuck off, man! Yeah, we hope we're not playing to a bunch of animals, so please don't act like some, okay, let's lay back, all right? Because you're really making us uptight man, you know it's a bad scene for us to be getting uptight, trying to give you some good feeling and all this other crap. We'd like to sing about what you all should be thinking about, in the meantimes while you're picking your noses and picking your asses, or whatever you want to call it... yeah I'm talking to you! Yeah, that's who I'm talking to, yeah right! What?" Someone shouts to Jimi 'What we did, what is your problem?' Jimi responds: "Yeah I'm trying to play guitar right now thank you, thank you. Don't do that, don't do that, man. Anyway... let's pretend that we're not here, let's pretend that we're somewhere else then and... pretend a cat is really, em, getting screwed around 'cause his old lady don't want him around. And his family's putting him down and all this kind of bull stuff. And he's, you know... anyway."

The audience is now starting to shout abuse and Jimi angrily responds: "Yeah, you all just choke yourselves, that's all, fuck you! Yeah it's so, it's so bad to see people in desperation of anything, because pretty soon you lose the whole illusion of what you're looking for in the first place, like for instance, love. Once you find yourself you've got it made, but er, I think there's too many of us here tonight to find that out." Jimi is still being hassled and comments: "Oh, fuck off! What I'm trying to say is, you don't have to agree with everything that's supposed to be happening, or is you following round with them?" Jimi then continues the set with 'Getting My Heart Back Together Again', singing 'It's too bad you don't love me no more, people, too bad you all have to act like a clown'. The set continues with 'Red House' and 'Foxy Lady', during which Jimi comments: "Yeah, this is dedicated to all the teeny weenies out there... the one in the forth row with the yellow pants on, yeah you, yeah. The one with the eighteen... eighteen inch, yeah right." Jimi proceeds to play the opening riff to 'Little Wind' but changes to playing the introduction to 'Like A Rolling Stone', during which he announces: "Yeah, we'd like to do a thing that, er, Dylan said a long time ago, a thing called 'Like A Rolling Stone'." Jimi stops the song prematurely and announces "None of us are ready right now, none of us in this whole world right now, thank you", and continues with 'Voodoo Child (Slight Return)', shouting to the audience: "That's a black militant song, don't you never forget it." He ends the show with 'Purple Haze'.

Jimi appeared to be very uptight during this concert. He had played most of the set with his back to the audience and they, in turn, replied by shouting abuse. The probable reason for Jimi's mood was the court hearing he had to attend in Toronto the previous day for the drug bust in May. This must have been playing very heavily on his mind.

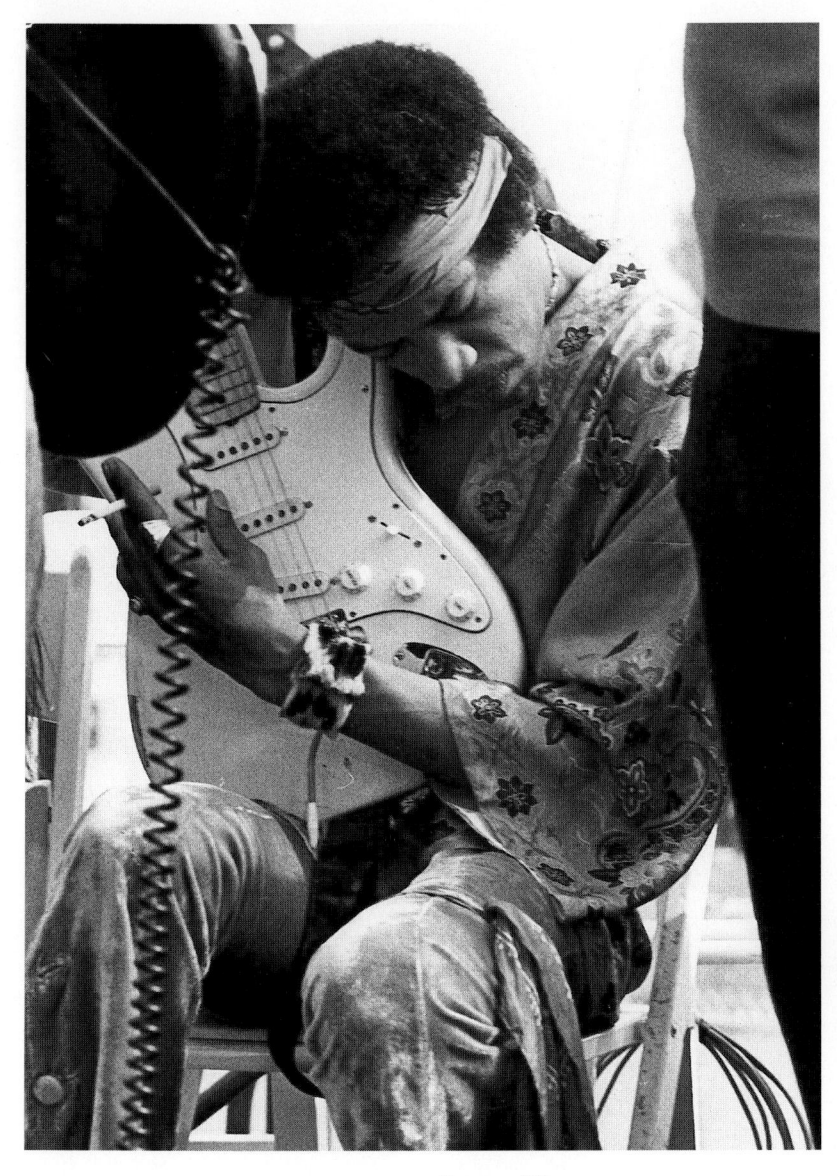

June 22
Sunday
**Newport Pop Festival,
San Fernando Valley State College,
Devonshire Downs, Northridge,
California**

Jimi returns to the festival site to jam with Buddy Miles, Tracy Nelson, Mother Earth and Eric Burdon to compensate the audience for the bad show the previous Friday.

He opens up with the cryptic comment: "Listen, we're gonna pretend we forget about everything alive and dead and call it 'Earth Versus Space' all right?" This song contains a medley of 'Gypsy Eyes', 'Keep on Grooving', 'Red House', 'Machine Gun' and finishes with 'Sometimes I Wonder'. "Hope you don't mind us just making up things as we go along," Jimi tells the audiences, "that's what life is about, the only thing, we just write our own scripts, that's all. Like to, er, see if we can do a blues really, is that all right? See if we can do a blues. We're gonna try and do a slow blues, okay, it's a thing called 'The Things I Used To Do'." Someone shouts something to Jimi and he replies: "I wish I could." For the next song Buddy Miles takes over to sing his own composition, 'We Gotta Live Together'. Eric Burdon then takes over on vocals for 'Feeling So Good'. Tracy Nelson sings a duet next with Buddy Miles, 'The Train Keeps on Rollin'. Jimi takes over again to play 'Paper Airplanes' and 'Earth Blues', which incorporates 'Getting My Heart Back Together Again'. He then stops playing the song and continues with 'Voodoo Child (Slight Return)'. Jimi continues with a version of 'Come On (Part One)' adding a part of 'Star Spangled Banner', and the gig ends in an up-tempo jam.

1969 May/June 147

June 29
Sunday
**Denver Pop Festival,
Mile High Stadium, Denver, Colorado**
The Experience are supported by Johnny Winter, Joe Cocker, Credence Clearwater Revival, Poco, The Mothers Of Invention, Iron Butterfly, Tim Buckley and Big Mama Thornton.

The Experience take the stage for their 00:15am (Monday) show. "It's gonna take us about an hour, no about a minute to get tuned up," Jimi tells the audience. "In the meantime let's make up in our minds to make our own world here tonight, starting tonight. We see some tear gas, that's the start of a third world war... It'll take us about a minute and a half for us to pick our buddy to pull him out. Oh yeah, this show's also dedicated to all the Sagittarians, 'cause that's how [the] blues [are] supposed to be. Well, we tune up because we really care for your ears, that's why we don't play so loud, okay?... oh yeah, the show's also dedicated to the people who brought their birthday suits, okay? Very sorry for the long tune up, but everything's gonna be all right in a few seconds, hold on. We haven't played in a long time, so [we'll] just start off with an instrumental, to see if we all can get our heads together to the same level, a thing called 'Tax Free'. At least we can pretend, can't we?" 'Tax Free' also includes something from 'The Breeze And I' and a snippet of The Beatles' 'Tomorrow Never Knows'. Then Jimi announces: "This song's about a cat and his old lady put him down 'cause she don't want him around and his family put him across town, now this is laying around." Jimi continues with 'Getting My Heart Back Together Again'.

In a by now familiar intro, Jimi now announces: "Yeah we'd like to do this other one for the girl there, yellow underwear, sitting over there in the, er, second row there. I'd like to do a thing called 'Let Me Stand Next To Your Fire'... Also dedicated to, er, plain-clothes [policewomen] and other goofballs. Okay, okay here we go, 'Let Me Stand Next To Your Old Lady'." Afterwards, Jimi tells the crowd: "I keep forgetting what I'm playing, em, I wish I was out there with you all... no one knows where the nose goes when the doors are closed. Dig, we'd like to do this anyway, regardless of what's happening back there in the Amen section, regardless of all that. Well I'm gonna see, what we gonna do? Yeah, 'Spanish Castle Magic', right." After which Jimi plays 'Red House'. "Yeah this is the last time we're playing in the States and... like this has been... really a lot of fun so forth and so on. Noel Redding has his band together called The Fat Mattress, we're looking out for that, and Mitch Mitchell has a thing together called Mind Octopus, and, er, yeah. We never ever see this bunch of girls up on the... what do you call it, pretensions, yeah, and... the ones who take underwear in the fourth row." Jimi continues with 'Foxy Lady'. "You like throwing those cans together, thank you very much for your house key. I'd like to say, it is all-American to really feel... to be American, well you know blab blab, woof woof. But we're talking about... you Americans, let's settle for that." Jimi continues with 'Star Spangled Banner' and 'Purple Haze', ending the show with 'Voodoo Child (Slight Return)'.

During the song the audience rush the stage and the police think a riot is taking place. The police overreact by firing tear gas into the audience. As the clouds of tear gas heads towards the stage, the band has to run from the stage and Eric Barrett has to lock them in the back of the equipment truck. This is a fitting end to what was to be the last ever Jimi Hendrix Experience concert.

July 21
Monday
**Tinker Street Cinema,
Woodstock, upstate New York**
Jimi has now formed Gypsy Sons And Rainbows with Mitch Mitchell, Billy Cox, Larry Lee, Juma Sultan, Jerry Velez. They spend the day jamming with local musicians.

August 18
Monday
**Woodstock Music And Art Fair,
Bethel, New York State**
Gypsy Sons And Rainbows are supported by Sha-Na-Na for their début. They are the closing act for the festival.

The band take the stage at 08:00 to close the Festival, after the announcement: "Ladies and gentlemen. The Jimi Hendrix Experience."

Right away, Jimi announces: "I see that we meet again, em... Dig, dig, [we'd] like to get something straight, we, er, we got tired of the Experience and every once in a while we [were] just blowing our minds too much, so we decided to change the whole thing around and, er, call it Gypsy Sons And Rainbows. For short, it's nothing but a band of Gypsys. We have Billy Cox playing bass... from Nashville Tennessee; we have Larry Lee playing guitar over there, Yallon Lee; we got Juma playing congos over here, Juma. And then we have hart... er, Granny Goose, I mean, excuse me, I'm sorry, Mitch Mitchell on drums. I'm the clown behind the sound. And then we got Jerry Velez on congas too. Got yours truly on beat whistle. What, do you worry? Oh yeah, give us about a minute and a half to tune up, okay. Like we only had about two rehearsals so, er, it was... nothing but primary rhythm things but, I mean it's the first ray of the new rising sun anyway, so then the message starts from the earth, which is rhythm, right? Can you dig that? When you get your old lady, when you got your woman, that makes the melody, right?" Understandably, given his opening speech, some of the audience shout out: "Are you high?" Jimi replies "I have mine thank you, I have mine, thank you very much."

After the band has tuned up, Jimi opens the set with 'Message To Universe', played here in full for the first time. Jimi would later develop the song further and call it 'Message To Love'. "Yeah, thank you very much. Oh well... that was a thing called 'Message To The Universe' [sic]... something to get the rats out of your bunks and those knapsacks you all been holding. And I'd like to go ahead with another slow thing, we'd like to keep going with... a little bit of a jam we've been messing around with back at the house.

You know, I think we're going to call it 'Getting My Heart Back Together Again'. They play the familiar blues number. Then, Jimi announces: "Thank you very much. Are these microphones all screwed up again as usual? Yeah, I know what you mean. It's so embarrassing man, I'm sitting up here, Damn... those people are looking at me too, man, damn, half a million eyes. Tell somebody to turn up the microphones while we get in tune, all right? I can't get it together otherwise. We're very sorry for the delays, but... we're trying to get things together in-between time. Because, like I said before, we only jammed a couple of times, but... like I [said] before, this is the first ray you know, so there's a whole lot more to go. Here we go, a one, two, three." Jimi continues with 'Spanish Castle Magic', 'Message To Love', 'Red House', 'Master Mind' and 'Lover Man'.

He then apologises once more to the audience for the tuning up delays: "We're sorry for the tune up between times, but, er, well hell, cowboys are the only ones who wanna stay in tune anyway, you know, so... We don't wanna play too loud for ya. So therefore we just play very quietly and very out of tune. [There are] a lot of girlfriends that we like to try to sing about sometimes... we're gonna sing about this one over there in the Amen section over there, the one with the yellow underpants on. Yeah, yeah you. I remember you last night there baby, hahahaha! I seen a dirty old man lick your bicycle seat when he was going down the street there, oh nasty, nasty!" Jimi continues with 'Foxy Lady'. "Yeah, I know we're tuning up between every single song and this is not together and that's not together. Well you ain't all in uniform, but... you know... You all waited all morning, g-o-l-l-y... I really feel, I really, I really hope that er, maybe by tomorrow morning we can get something together. Give me, give me a A, give me a A, I'll tell you about it. Yeah, well er, like I said before, we only ran off a few numbers, so we'd like to try to do this one we're jamming at the house. We don't have no name for it yet... this is just like a instrumental, we just flow along with it, it goes something like this." Jimi continues with what was to become 'Beginnings'.

Then: "Before we go any further, we'd like to say, man, you all really had a lot of patience, three days' worth, you've proved to the world what can happen, a little bit of love and understanding and sounds... Anyway, we'd like to say, man,

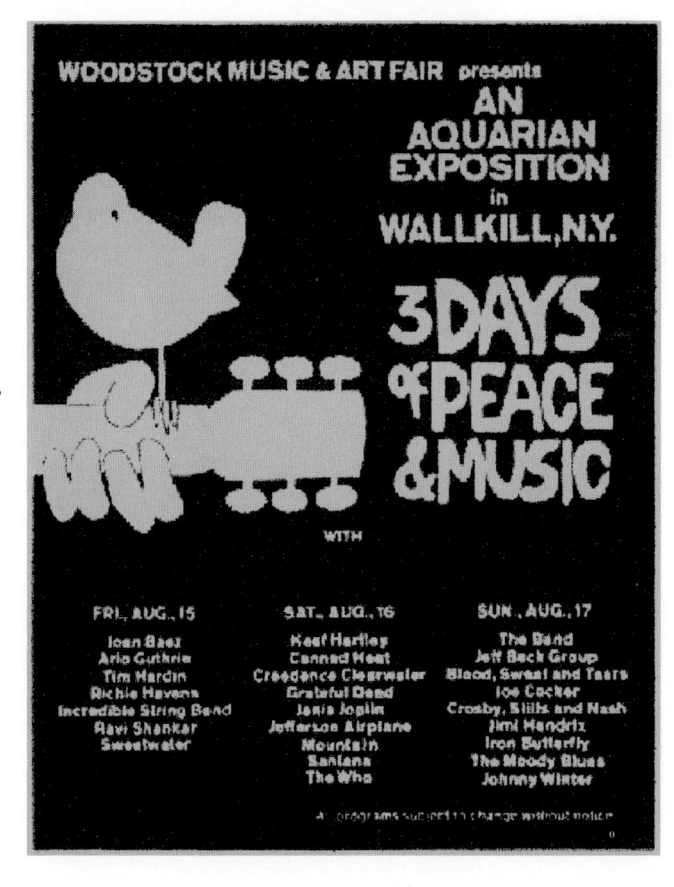

1969 June/August

we really appreciate your all having patience with us, 'cause this really, really is nerve-racking man, that's why we waited till the sun up. And maybe the new day might give us a chance, I don't know, blah blah, woof woof. Sky Church is still here as you can see. We'd like to do a song dedicated to maybe a soldier in the army singing about his old lady that he dreams about and the hub hub that she got instead. Or it could be a cat maybe, trying to fall in love with that girl baby but, a little bit too scared, that's where the problems come from sometimes, isn't it? I mean they can't really, insecure a little bit, so they call girls 'groupies' and they call girls this and they call passive people 'hippie' and blah blah, woof woof, on down the line. That's because [they're] fucking not in love man, that's what's happening... the other half of a man is a woman and, er, we'd like to play a thing called 'Izabella' and don't you ever forget it." Jimi comments to someone "You're a hard head. Hard head. Where's Billy Graham, he'll get you straight." Then: "We never stood this far apart from each other, except when our mothers cut us in half when we was Siamese twins.

"I'd like to do this next song... what next song do we know? Do you know another one?" The audience shouts out for 'Fire'. "We'll do that – 'Fire'. Okay, er, I think we know about two more songs... Okay, I think we've got about two more songs that we know, but we're gonna see if we can squeeze them out. We'd like to do a slow song, very, very slow and quiet you know. Something to play [in] the mud with, here we go..." Jimi continues with 'Gypsy Woman' followed by 'Fire'. "Thank you very much and er, we'd like to say thank you very much again, for all your patience for waiting all these three years. To come here and stand [under] that little bit of rain. I'd like to do, er... the new American anthem until we get another one together, its called 'Voodoo Child' (Slight Return)'." During the song, Jimi announces: "Before we leave, I'd like to say the name of the group one more time. It's the first of our gigs, we'd like to say thank you very much, man, for the use of your ears, and your hearts. And the name of the group is the Son And Rainbows, and, er, you can call it Band Of Gypsys, anything you want to. Let me call it again, the cat with the purple pants on playing congas over there, that's Juma, then we have Larry Lee with a head scarf around his face. And we got... Billy Cox playing bass over there, and Mitch Mitchell, and we have, er, Jerry Valez." Jimi continues with 'Voodoo Child (Slight Return)'.

After the song he tells the audience: "Like I said, thank you very much and good night, like to say peace, yeah and happiness, happiness, yeah happiness." Jimi continues with 'Stepping Stone' another new song that he is starting to introduce to his concerts. During the song, Jimi announces: "Thank you again, you can leave if you want to, we're just jamming that's all, okay? You can leave or you can clap. Thanks, good night." Jimi then proceeds to play the most dynamic rendition of 'Star Spangled Banner' that he ever attempted. Without pausing, he continues with 'Purple Haze', then goes into a very fast flamenco-style solo and then into a very melodic 'Villanova Junction'. Jimi leaves the stage with a simple "Thank yer". The audience are all on their feet, shouting for more.

The MC introduces Jimi back to the stage for an encore. "Yeah, what I need to do is try to figure something to play for a second, hold on a second, wait a minute. Yeah, we didn't practise none of our old songs, you know, we was just messing around with some other things, 'cause we get kinda tired, you know, don't you get kinda of tired, you know, you get kinda tired there. Okay now don't laugh at us, we're gonna try this one song called 'Valleys Of Neptune'. Oh... I forgot the words to that, I forgot the words to that, man, you know, I can't do it, man..." Jimi ends the show with 'Hey Joe'. According to some people at the festival Jimi also performed 'Wild Thing', but no audio evidence of this has ever surfaced.

September 5
Friday
United Block Association, 139th Street, Lenox Avenue, Harlem, New York

Gypsy Sons and Rainbows are supported by Sam & Dave, Big Maybelle and J.D. Brown.

The group performs 'Fire', 'Foxy Lady', 'Star Spangled Banner', 'Purple Haze', 'Voodoo Child (Slight Return)' and 'Machine Gun'.

September 9
Tuesday
Unganos, New York
Jimi jams with Mountain.

September 10
Wednesday
The Salvation, 1 Sheridan Square, Greenwich Village, New York
The concert was advertised as 'The Black Roman Orgy'. This would be the final performance of Gypsy Sons and Rainbows.

The group perform several instrumentals and 'Izabella'.

September 18
Thursday
A full tour of America has been set up with concert promoter Concerts West and is scheduled to commence on this day in Boston. However, on September 9th Jimi relays to his lawyers that he "Did not feel himself physically and mentally capable of performing satisfactorily, he felt that overshadowed his failure to appear." As a result of Jimi's cancellation of the tour, he has to pay $25,000 in reimbursements and expenses to Concerts West. Jimi has also decided to disband Gypsy Sons and Rainbows.

December 31
Wednesday
Fillmore East, 105 2nd Avenue, 6th Street, New York
The Band Of Gypsys are supported by The Voices Of East Harlem and Joshua Light Show.

Jimi has now formed a new band that he calls Band Of Gypsys, featuring Billy Cox on bass and Buddy Miles on drums. Bill Graham has booked the group to début at his Fillmore East Auditorium.

Bill Graham introduces the group onto the stage at 19:30 for the first of two shows. Jimi opens the show with 'Paper Airplanes'. After a simple "Thank you", Jimi continues with 'Here Comes Your Lover Man'. "Yeah that was some of the things... we're messing around with. That first thing was called 'Paper Airplanes', if you wanna call it that, and the next thing was called, er, I don't know, I forgot already...! Anyway, we'd like to do a slow blues here if it's all right, we'd like to do a thing called 'Lonesome Train,' we can call it that for right now." Jimi continues with 'Getting My Heart Back Together Again'. "I'd like to continue on with a thing called a tune up. I'd like to feature Buddy Miles on this one right here, Buddy Miles. A thing called 'Them Changes'." After this song, Jimi announces: "I'd like to do a song... dedicate this to the same old draggy scene that's going, the soldiers in Vietnam and so forth. A thing called 'Izabella'." After this number, the band continue with 'Machine Gun'. "Yeah thank you very much. This is like a thing called, er, 'Stop'." Jimi continues with 'Ezy Ryder'. Then: "I'd like to do a slow blues..." Jimi continues with 'Bleeding Heart'. "Yeah we'd like to see if we can do sad songs too, thing called, er, 'Blues Today', maybe call this 'Earth Blues Today' right now. Got to bring everybody back down to do this." The band are approaching the end of their first appearance. Jimi announces: "You know, the cat said we only have one more song left so, hope you don't have this to say, we'll buy 'em with the thing called..'Burning Desire', our new single. Thanks very much for showing up man, that's really outta site. Maybe what we'll do is come back in the New Year, all right?" Someone in the audience shouts "Happy New Year" and Jimi responds: "Yeah, right, right, Happy New Year, Happy New Year to everybody. Yeah, we... just left behind 1969 and I don't care. Shout out one second to get drinks served, thank you very much." Jimi ends the show with 'Burning Desire', thanks the audience and leaves the stage.

The Band Of Gypsys takes the stage a few minutes before midnight for their second show, to the strains of Gustav Holst's 'Planet Suite'. The audience counts down the seconds and at the stroke of midnight 'Auld Lang Syne' is played and sung by the whole audience. Jimi opens the show with his own rendition of 'Auld Lang Syne' and then wishes everyone a Happy New Year and continues with 'Who Knows', changing the words to sing "Goodbye to '69". "Yeah, yeah here we are one more time it seems like. We'd like to... try and get a blues, a thing called 'I'm A Man', at least I'm trying to be." After this number, Jimi continues with what would later become 'Stepping Stone'. "We're sorry for the tuning up here and there but like... you know. We'd like to try and do this song called, er, let's see, which one? 'Burning Desire' we'll try that one yeah." He asks the band "You know that one?" Jimi stops playing the song prematurely and announces: "Okay we're gonna play something else", and directs the band to play 'Fire'. "Man, we're just jamming right now, all right, is that all right with you?... Okay, we're gonna try this thing called 'Ezy Ryder' that we was messing around with. See if we can get that together, okay?" Jimi again stops playing the song prematurely and announces: "I forgot the words, I'm sorry. I'd like to dedicate this to the draggy scene that's happening right now so, for the soldiers in Vietnam, we call it 'Machine Gun'. It goes something like this here." After the song, he says: "That was dedicated to everybody that's died as good as I, don't give up hope. Yeah we'd like to go on and do a thing called 'Paper Airplanes' or... 'Crash Landings', whatever you wanna call it..." "We ain't finished that one yet," he tells the audience afterwards, "and none of these songs we really finished, man, but... thanks a lot for coming though, we really dig that. Oh yeah, Happy New Year, Happy New Year, just happened there while I'm tuning up. I'd like to dedicate this to the Cupcake Sisters sitting back there with the yellow drawers on." Jimi continues with 'Stone Free' and incorporates elements from the march from Tchaikovsky's 'Nutcracker Suite', 'Outside Woman Blues', 'Cherokee Mist' and 'The Sunshine Of Your Love' before bringing the song back to 'Stone Free'. "Yeah, we'd like to feature... Buddy Miles again for this thing called 'Them Changes'. "

After Buddy Miles' number, Jimi announces: "Yeah, okay then, the cats said that, er, we only have three more tunes to play so, we'd like to try to do this other thing called 'A Message To Love'." Jimi requests that the monitor speaker be turned up and announces: "Tasting, tasting, tasting anybody, tasting. Testing, testing, one, two, three", then continues with 'Message To Love'. Afterwards, the set continues with 'Stop', then Jimi announces: "Thank you very much for showing up tonight, we did our best. Don't forget... we got, yeah, two shows tomorrow. We really enjoyed doing it, man. It's too much for the first New Year. We'd like to do this thing called 'Burning Desire' and, em, say thank you one more time and Happy New Year." Jimi continues with 'Foxy Lady' and 'Voodoo Child (Slight Return)' and ends the last show of 1969 with 'Purple Haze'. He leaves the stage to 'Happy Days Are Here Again'.

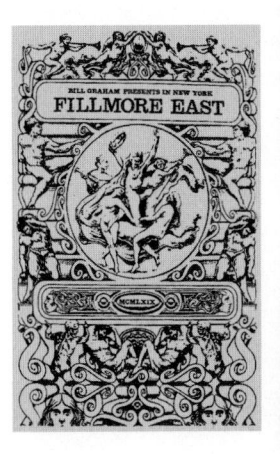

1970

January 1
Tuesday
Fillmore East, 105 2nd Avenue, 6th Street, New York
The Band Of Gypsys are supported by The Voices Of East Harlem and Joshua Light Show.

The Band Of Gypsys takes the stage at 19:30 for their first show of the night. After being introduced by Bill Graham, Jimi opens the show with 'Who Knows'. "Happy New Year first of all and, er, hope you have about a million or two million more of 'em, if we can get over this summer, hahaha! We'd like to dedicate this one to, em, [a] sort of draggy scene that's going on. All the soldiers that are fighting in Chicago and Milwaukee and New York, Oh yes, all the soldiers fighting in Vietnam. I'd like to do a thing called 'Machine Gun'." After the number, he comments: "Yeah, that's what we don't want to hear anymore, right, at least here. We'll do the thing called, em, 'Them Changes' too. Buddy Miles wrote this one and, em, we'd like to have him sing this one, so 'Them Changes'." Afterwards: "Buddy Miles the Bumble Bee, yeah right. Yeah we'd like to get together and do a little thing called, em, oh we can call it 'Crash Landings' or 'Paper Airplanes', anything like that. Well, it's probably about downs or something. Oh yeah, right now I'd like to say er, congratulations to the er, what do you call that, southern Californian Trojans. I'm so glad they beat the hell out of Michigan, I'm very glad."

Then: "Yeah [we're going to] do another thing, called 'Trying To Be'." "Yeah we just, you know we're just... A lot of these songs haven't been completed yet, we're just messing around with them and see what happens, you know we're, er, working with them and... tomorrow we'll probably play them a little different and the next day we'll play 'em a little different. So it's fun just jamming with them, you know. It's good you all have patience to sit up there." Jimi continues with 'Foxy Lady'. "Thank you very much, thank you. I'd like to feature Buddy Miles again on the vocals, it's a thing called 'Stop'." They then continue with 'Getting My Heart Back Together Again' and Jimi ends the show with 'Earth Blues'. "Thank you very much, good night and see you next time. And Happy New Year."

The Band Of Gypsys take the stage at 21:00 for the second show of the evening and the final show at the Fillmore. They open the show with 'Stone Free' incorporating a snippet of 'Little Drummer Boy'. Jimi then announces: "Buddy Miles is gonna do this thing he wrote called 'Them Changes'." The band then continue with 'Paper Airplanes'. Buddy Miles announces: "Jimi's gonna do this thing he wrote called 'Message Of Love' [sic]. They continue with 'Message To Love', 'Earth Blues', 'Izabella' and 'Machine Gun'. Jimi continues with 'Foxy Lady', 'I Got To See You' and 'Burning Desire'. "Okay thanks a lot, you're all really sweet," Jimi tells the audience afterwards. "We only know about six songs right now... seven, nine. We're gonna do the er, pretorium. The Black Panther's, em, national anthem, it goes something like this." Jimi continues with 'Voodoo Child (Slight Return)' followed by 'We Gotta Live Together' and 'Wild Thing'. Jimi rounds off with, "Thank you, thank you and goodnight", though he subsequently returns to the stage for an encore of 'Hey Joe' and 'Purple Haze'.

January 28
Wednesday
Madison Square Gardens, Winter Festival For Peace, New York
The Band Of Gypsys are supported by The Rascals, Blood Sweat and Tears, Peter, Paul and Mary, Judy Collins, Richie Havens, The Voices Of East Harlem, Dave Brubeck, Harry Belafonte, McHenry Boatwright, Mother Earth and the cast of *Hair*.

Prior to the show Jimi was to be found sitting in the dressing room with his head in his hands, not wanting to talk to anyone or for them to talk to him. It was subsequently suggested that Jimi's drink had been spiked, which affected his performance and resulted in him not being able to finish the concert.

The Band Of Gypsys takes the stage for their 03:00 show (Thursday). The MC introduces the band: "I think I can safely say, friends, after the length of time we've all been living together. This is certainly a moment that I've been waiting for, as I'm sure all of you have. Mr Jimi Hendrix and his Band Of Gypsys'. Jimi comes to the microphone and comments: "Yeah, anybody wanna be fuzzed?" "Yeah", shouts the audience. Jimi remarks: "Peace and happiness to love and forever, from the bottom of our hearts, that's all we can say right now. Like to see if we can get some sounds together, once we get in tune... to close off, you know, all the little worlds that might have happened yesterday or today or tomorrow. Lets just make our own little world right here. Just let's fire and groove, you know. We have Billy Cox on the, er, on the, bass guitar. And then we have, THE Buddy Miles on drums, for sure, thank, thank God, and then we have, er, Alfred E. Newman on er, page seventeen. 'Scuse me, give us about a minute to, er like, just little or minor adjustments here and there okay? Thank you. It goes something like this er, I think it's in the key of, D or A, G, something like that. Foxy Lady sitting over there with the yellow underwear on, stained and dirty with blood." Jimi opens the show with 'Who Knows' which starts off fairly well, but falls apart a little as the song progresses towards the end. The audience shouts out for 'Fire' and Jimi plays the introduction to 'Foxy Lady'. then continues with 'Earth Blues'. Although the guitar playing is reasonably good, he rambles and struggles with the vocals throughout. "That's why everybody's... That's what happens when Earth fucks with space. Never forget that, that's what happens." Buddy Miles is now aware that something is not right and announces "Listen. It seems as though that, em, we're not, er, quite getting it together here. But just, er, give us a little bit more time, because it has been hard, and, er, things aren't exactly, I guess they're not exactly ready over here yet. So just bear with us for a few minutes, and then we'll try to see if we can get something together."

Jimi is now sitting down on the stage. A few people start to boo, but the majority of the audience is on their feet standing in silence, wondering what's going on. Buddy Miles again makes an announcement: "Listen, like I said, we're having trouble, I don't know what is the matter, but, er, Jimi wants to take a... wants to go down, and so like, er, like I said, if you can bear with it, and if you can understand where the whole thing is at... Then we can try something later." Jimi leaves the stage and it is reported that he falls off the apron of the stage but is unhurt. This is the last show that the The Band Of Gypsys perform.

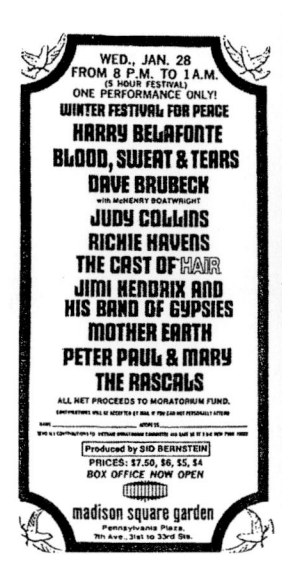

March 18
Wednesday
**Speakeasy Club,
50 Margaret Street, London**
Back in London for a few days, Jimi jams with Stephen Stills after the Speakeasy has closed for the night. There are a few other people present, including Germaine Greer.

April 25
Saturday
The Forum, Los Angeles, California
Jimi has now formed a new band, which he is calling Cry Of Love, including Mitch Mitchell back on drums and Billy Cox on bass. Cry Of Love are supported by The Buddy Miles Express and Ballin' Jack.

Cry Of Love take the stage for their 20:30 show. Jimi announces: "I ain't see you from the last time, for a long time. I'd like to start off with some oldies but mouldies, dedicated to girl over there in the fourteenth row with the, er, yellow underwear, I can see you streaming. We have Billy Cox on bass, Mitch Mitchell on drums and yours truly on video, thank you." (It was reported that the Forum was now using large projection screens in the hall for the first time.) Jimi opens the show with 'Spanish Castle Magic'. Afterwards: "Thank you. This is dedicated to the, er, sour gums sitting over there, over in the Amen section, a thing called 'Foxy Lady'." When the song is over, he comments: "Yeah, okay then, you all been really outta site so far. We'll see if we can lay this... on yer... You're gonna be in a whole lot of trouble when the soldiers come back from the war, because all you be found lying under somebody else's bed. And so we call that a cat getting up to getting his brother's shoes together, it goes something like this here." Jimi continues with 'Here Comes Your Lover Man'. Then: "We'd like to do a little song about a cat, er, who's feeling kinda down a little bit. I have no reason to be explaining that all. He feels that kinda down because his dumb chick put him down and his parents won't even want him around, so he's thinking about leaving town and going on the road and doing something with his self. It's called 'Getting My Heart Back Together Again', just like the feeling. He's waiting for the train, the train, that ultimate train."

When the song finishes, Jimi comments: "Yeah, okay then, there's another thing that we mess around with... we do this one thing called 'Message To Love,' well everybody's rapping about love, you know what I'm saying. Yeah everybody's rapping about love... why don't we put our two cents' worth in there and see what it sounds like." Jimi continues with 'Message To Love'. "Well I'm tired and just slip it in nice and easy." A commotion starts in the audience and Jimi announces "Yeah, okay then, yeah well somebody over there, ask somebody to go back to their seats. I don't know what's happening over there, but as long as we keep it through the show and keep everybody in their asses, we can then have something together. [We'd] like to do a thing called 'Ezy Ryder', it was fun, just watch the film, I think it was outta site. It said a lot of things, but we want to continue from there, you know. We offered you a bomb at the end, this thing called er, 'Ezy Ryder' in the key of E flat." Afterwards: "Yeah, yeah okay, thank you. I'd like to do another thing; I don't want to bring anybody down or anything like that, just for the record. But you being strong enough can't bring me down no kinda way... It's a thing called 'Machine Gun' and don't you ever forget it." After the song, Jimi announces: "I'd like to do a thing called, em, 'A Room Full Of Mirrors', that some of you out there, [have] probably been through at one time or another..." Jimi continues with 'Room Full Of Mirrors' and then starts the introduction to a new song 'The Land Of The New Rising Sun'. During the introduction, he announces "We'd like to do some of this song and just jam a slow tune for a second, like an intermission, for instance. This is only half our butter is filled, just go on and buy your popcorn and so forth." Jimi brings the song to an abrupt end and continues with an up-tempo version of 'Villanova Junction'. After a lengthy drum solo, Jimi continues with another new song, 'Freedom', and then goes into 'Star Spangled Banner' and 'Purple Haze'. "Yeah right, right. Thank you very much for showing up, man. It's just the first one, we've be playing seeing if you like them, I'm not too sure. Regardless how pathetic it might be to, you know they say this and they say that and blah blah, wolf wolf. This is our own little world right here tonight, and so forget about yesterday or tomorrow, this is it tonight, right? Thank you very much for coming... No we don't need tuning up, but I hope you had a good time. We'd like to do America's blues theme song and, er, do this song for the Black Panthers, a thing called 'Voodoo Child'. Thank you and peace and don't forget to stand, man, it's your turn to stand, stand. Jimi proceeds to tune up and comments: "Cowboys are the only ones who wanna stay in tune anyway." He seems to have some trouble tuning his guitar and then comments: "Oh well the plot was good, the intentions are good." He ends the show with 'Voodoo Child (Slight Return)', adding 'Keep On Grooving' to the last verse.

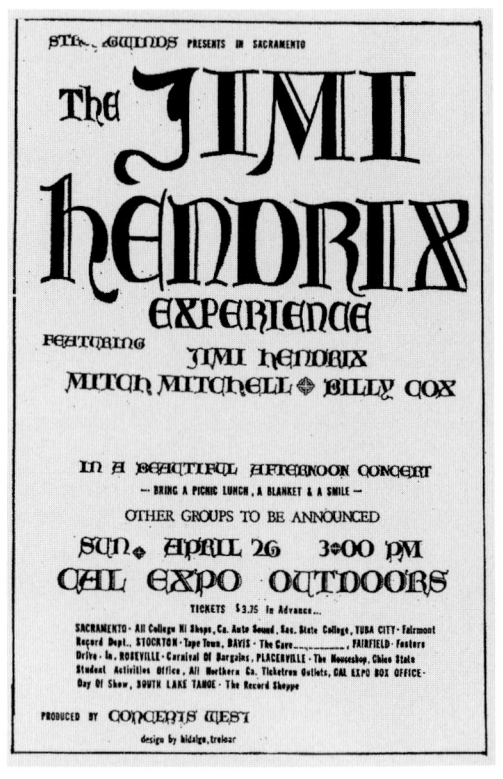

April 26
Sunday
**State Fairground,
Cal Expo, Sacramento, California**
Cry Of Love are supported by The Buddy Miles Express and Blue Mountain Eagle.

Cry Of Love take the stage for their 15.00 afternoon show. "Must be naming that girl, because a whole of soldiers who are back from war, who's messing around with a lady in our bed, I'm talking about rough days that you had, a thing called 'Here Comes Your Lover Man'." Jimi continues with 'Spanish Castle Magic' and 'Freedom', followed by 'Machine Gun'. The band then continue with 'Foxy Lady', 'Room Full Of Mirrors', 'Ezy Ryder', 'Purple Haze' and 'Star Spangled Banner'. Jimi ends the show with 'Voodoo Child (Slight Return)'.

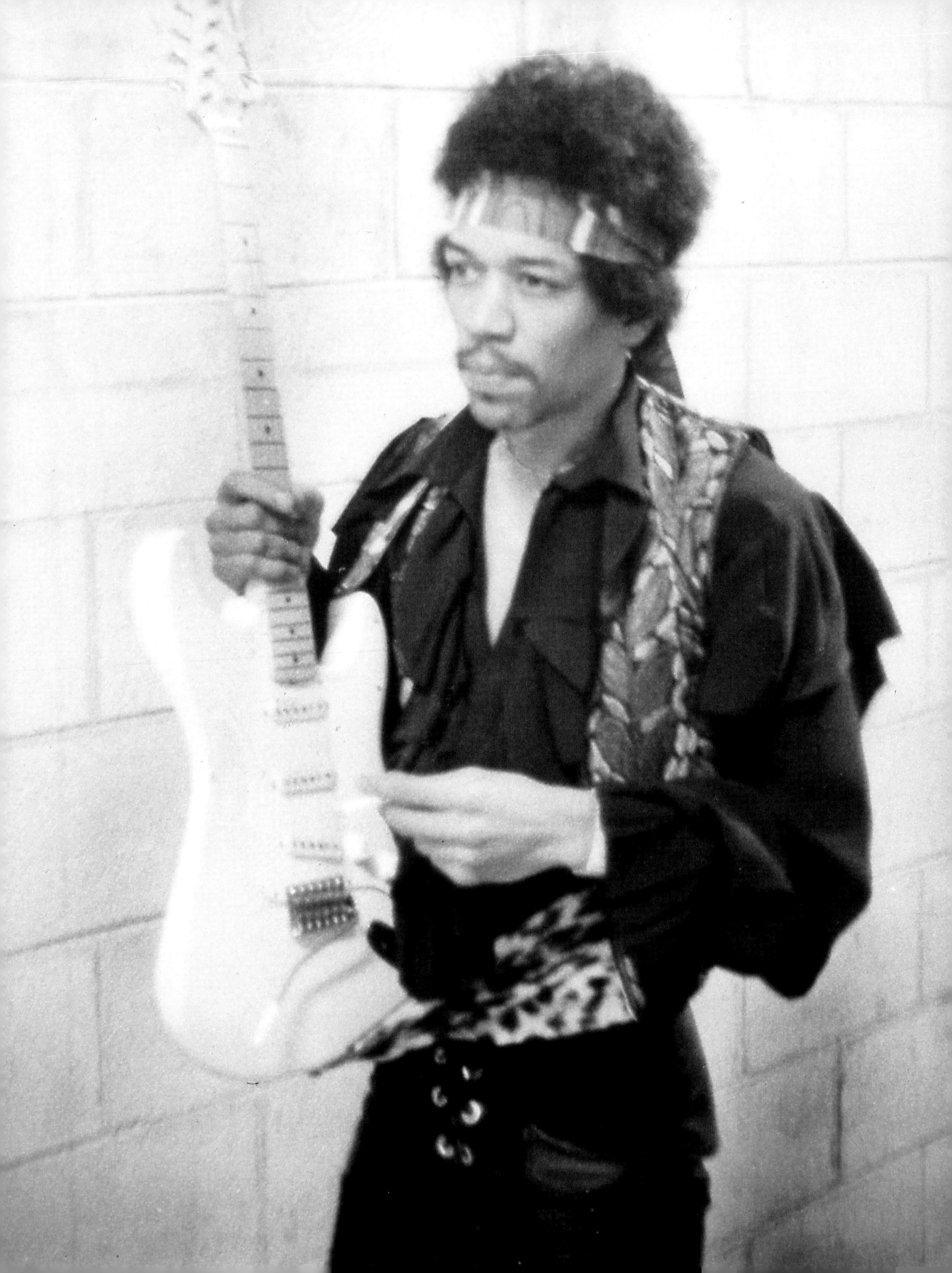

May 1
Friday
Milwaukee Auditorium, Milwaukee, Wisconsin

Cry Of Love is supported by Oz.

Cry Of Love take the stage for their 20:00 show. Jimi asks the audience: "Well, how you doing... are all you doing all right?" The band open the show with 'Spanish Castle Magic'. "Yeah I'd like to er, play a thing another little thing called er, 'Here Comes Your Lover Man', dedicated to all the girls laying with their old dream men when their old man's back from the war. And then comes back from leave, finds him in bed in the house though." Jimi continues with 'Here Comes Your Lover Man'. "Remember we're getting plagued by... [faulty] equipment right now. What the hell, cowboys are the only ones who wanna stay in tune anyway. Dig, I'd like to do [a song]... about a cat... his old lady put him down and he put his woman round in Berkeley, [slipped] out of town and like (laughs) 'Get him out of town', says his old lady. He talks about leaving with you, come back and buy the town and all in his shoe, but it's a funny thing, it's called 'Getting My Heart Back Together'." Jimi continues with 'Ezy Ryder'. He then announces: "Yeah we'd like to continue on with a thing called 'Stone Free' yes," but Cry Of Love play 'Freedom' instead. "I'd like to do another thing called 'Message To Love'... I'm the gypsy from the Band Of Gypsys album." Without any introduction, Jimi launches into 'Foxy Lady'. "Right now I'd like to... [dedicate one] to Eddie Sherman, I've never heard of this, just living in America, dedicated to everybody that filled my mail today. Anybody want a sack of old cards?" Jimi continues with 'Star Spangled Banner' and tells the audience, "Everybody stand up, come on stand up." He continues with 'Purple Haze' and ends the show with 'Voodoo Child (Slight Return)'.

May 2
Saturday
Dane County Coliseum, Madison, Wisconsin

Cry Of Love is supported by Savage Grace and Oz.

Cry Of Love takes the stage for their 20:30 show. Jimi announces: "We all really feel fine, how you doing? Give us about a minute and a half to get ready and all that..." After a tune up, Jimi announces: "Gotta make sure all the goodies is right for you. Hey, we have Billy Cox on bass, Mitch Mitchell on drums and yours truly on public saxophone. I'd like to start off with our oldies but goodies; I'd like to say thank you for the three years." Jimi open the show with 'Fire'. "Yeah, thanks very much. This next one is called 'Room Full Of Mirrors,' we do this... you know, when the crowd's kinda groovy and they dig what's happening. I'd like to, er, dedicate this to everybody that's been through this trip one way or another in a room full of mirrors, when you get so high [that] all you can see is you. It goes something like this." Afterwards: "Thank you, man. I'd like to continue on and do a little slow blues right now, if it's all right with you all. Yeah right... God damn, I didn't know there was that many people here. I'm glad you're all sitting down [comfortably] though. So, like, we'd like to slow it down, do a little thing about this cat feeling kinda down because his old lady put him down, you know, embarrassed her, he wasn't too cool so they got his brown and they threw him out of town. And he's down at the railroad train station, laying up there, digging himself... talking about "Well, when I get on the road, I'm gonna be a magic boy and voodoo child" and so forth and so on. Well he's getting all this, getting his thing back together, you know... we don't have a name for it yet, because it ain't ever finished yet." Jimi continues with 'Getting My Heart Back Together'.

"Yeah, man, thank you. Yeah, we'd like to do a thing that, er, everybody looks for, but we'd like to do this thing called 'Here Comes Your Lover Man'. It's about all these soldiers... And the cats over here doing up to their old ladies, and might come home on leave... and, er, find the new men in bed... in their place. It's called 'Here Comes Your Loving Woman'." After this number, the set continues with 'Red House'. "Right, right, we'll see if we can get something together on that, er, this other LP we got but, what we call a deucey. Hold on one second." Jimi tunes up and announces: "We'd like to entertain you for another, er, five seconds, a thing called 'Tune Up Jam'. Oh I'm American, man, and I'm standing here tuning up, man. Anyway what the hell, cowboys are the only ones who stay in tune anyway, we wouldn't want that. Why, this [will] just take another second. We tune up because we really, really care for your ears." Jimi finally tunes up and continues with 'Message To Love'. "Thank you. I'd like to continue on with, er, a thing, oh yeah I think there's a movie about this... It's called 'Greasy Slider', I mean 'Ezy Ryder'." "I'd like to continue on with another thing, dedicated to all the soldiers... in Milwaukee, Chicago... oh yes, Vietnam."

Jimi plays a few bars of 'Star Spangled Banner' and then goes into 'Machine Gun', followed by 'Star Spangled Banner' and 'Foxy Lady'. Jimi ends the show with 'Voodoo Child (Slight Return)' and 'Purple Haze'.

of screeching feedback. Jimi comments: "We're... playing bullshit again, we're in a little bit of trouble right here, but hold your sticks a second. I'd like to dedicate this one to whoever's listening. Shit, now I'm all out of tune, wait a minute. Oh what the hell, cowboys are the only ones who stay in tune anyway. We've got this one song going through a few changes here and there that some of us do once in a while, called 'The Room Full Of Mirrors' [sic] which explains itself. But, like, at [a] certain point... we like to get out of it and see what else, the wheel comes off, you know deprive yourselves." Jimi continues with 'Room Full Of Mirrors'.

"Yeah then we got this other one, it's called 'Look Out Baby I Must Be Splitting Cause Here Comes Your Lover Man'. And he's just come back from the war, so you know..." Jimi continues with 'Here Comes Your Lover Man'. At the end of the song, Jimi has further amplifier trouble. "All... we're trying to do is make some good decent static for you and we're getting all this other static. I'd like to, er, I'd like to do a slow blues about this cat feeling kinda down 'cause his old lady put him down, his people and family don't want him around. He might as well drag his ass down to the railroad station waiting for the train to come take him away on the road and be a voodoo child, magic boy. And come back, do it to his old lady one more time, give her a piece because she'll go and buy extra living. I'm not feeling too sorry for her, thank you very much... it's called 'Getting My Heart Back Together Again'." After the number, Jimi tunes up and then announces: "Yeah, we'd like to do another song called 'Ezy Ryder'." "Yeah we're having a good night... dedicate this one to the soldiers fighting in Milwaukee and, er, Chicago, Illinois, oh yes. and Vietnam. There's so many wars going on now, that I should dedicate this to a lot of other people fighting wars within themselves too. you know."

Jimi continues with 'Machine Gun' followed by 'Freedom' and 'Foxy Lady'. Without any introduction Jimi continues with 'Red House'. "Yeah right, everybody stand and just hummer it, see if we can help each other out with the American anthem. Well, we're all Americans, aren't we? So let us stand... Because we're gonna play, exactly the way it is." Jimi continues with 'Star Spangled Banner' and 'Purple Haze'. After thanking the audience, Jimi ends the show with 'Voodoo Child (Slight Return)'.

May 3
Sunday
St. Paul Civic Centre,
St. Paul, Minnesota
Cry Of Love is supported by Savage Grace and Oz.

Cry Of Love take the stage for their 20:00 show. Jimi announces, in a strange voice, "Does everybody feel all right? We're all gathered here right on time. Give us about a minute... so we get our guitars in tune and so forth, so we can get something together. Yeah, we haven't been here for such a long time, well since the last time... We have Mitch Mitchell on drums, hammering away there, and Billy Cox on bass and yours truly on public saxophone." Jimi plays a lick with his octavia switched on and comments, "Thank you, and now for our next tune we'd like to... do a thing called 'Let Me Stand Next To Your Old Lady', er, 'Let Me Stand Next To Your Fire', I'm sorry." After the song, Jimi's guitar lets out a burst

May 8
Friday
**University Of Oklahoma,
Field House, Norman**
Cry Of Love is supported by Bloodrock.

Cry Of Love are booked for two show at 19:00 and 22:00. When they take the stage for their second show, Jimi opens the show with 'Fire'. Then: "Yeah, okay then, thank you very much. Well, we have this other thing that we'd like to do... right now. A thing called 'Spanish Castle Magic'." "Yeah right, er, while we're going on man, not to be this low... forget about yesterday or tomorrow. We've got to get it together, right, in two seconds. But then again we must get rid of all the hogwash in... the way, and all the bullshit. Like, for instance, this song dedicated to all... the soldiers fighting in Chicago, Berkeley..."

The audience erupts, cheering and clapping loudly. There are shouts of "Vietnam". Jimi comments: "Them in there, oh yeah, right, completely always in the medals. But dig, it doesn't matter you know, check this out and get out of the way with a thing called 'Machine Gun'." Jimi plays a very melodic introduction to the song in the same vein that he would use to introduce 'Land Of The New Rising Sun' in his later concerts. Jimi ends the song with the comment: "Right, back to the new. Aw, somebody gave us someone to love, but they're in Saigon. We've got a song, forget about 'Machine Gun' and all that... [it's called] 'Look Out Baby 'Cause Here Comes Your Lover Man'." Jimi continues with 'Here Comes Your Lover Man'. After this number, the band plays 'Foxy Lady', 'Getting My Heart Back Together', 'Message To Love' and 'Red House'.

When 'Red House' is over, Jimi announces: "And like, em, I'd like to dedicate this one [to] all the ones who died for peaceful causes..." Jimi continues with 'Star Spangled Banner', followed by 'Purple Haze'. "Thank you very much, we have Mitch Mitchell on drums, we have Billy Cox on bass... this is a thing called 'Voodoo Child'." Jimi ends the show with 'Voodoo Child (Slight Return)'.

May 9
Saturday
**Will Rogers Coliseum,
Fort Worth, Texas**
Cry Of Love take the stage for their 20:00 show. They perform 'Fire', 'Here Comes Your Lover Man', 'Getting My Heart Back Together Again', 'Room Full Of Mirrors', 'Red House', 'Freedom', 'Ezy Ryder', 'Machine Gun', 'Star Spangled Banner', 'Purple Haze' and 'Voodoo Child (Slight Return)'.

May 10
Sunday
**Hemisphere Arena,
San Antonio, Texas**
Cry Of Love is supported by Country Funk.

Cry Of Love takes the stage for their 20:00 performance, Jimi announces: "We have Billy Cox on bass, Mitch Mitchell on drums and yours truly on public saxophone." Jimi opens the show by playing the introduction to 'Land Of The New Rising Sun' and then goes straight into 'Fire'. "Thank you very much man. It's nice to see so many people... I'd like to continue on with another thing dedicated to this, this tied up young lady sitting in the middle. A thing called 'Foxy Lady'." "Thank you very much for those of you who did listen. We'd like to go on and do a little biddy thing... we're dedicating [it] to all the soldiers that are fighting in Chicago and Peru, save us from Vietnam coming here to get us..." Jimi continues with 'Machine Gun'. "Thank you. I'd like to do this thing called 'Freedom'." Jimi then continues with 'Red House' and 'Message To Love'. "Here's another little bit of fun, a cat waiting by the little train station, even his old lady put him down in the ground and prior to picking, she's put him out of town, one of those kind of things, only you have to take it with us." Jimi continues with 'Getting My Heart Back Together' and 'Ezy Ryder'. "I'd like to do for you a song called 'A Room Full Of Mirrors', something you wouldn't see." Jimi ends the show with 'Star Spangled Banner' and 'Purple Haze'. The audience are up on their feet shouting for more, and Jimi returns to do an encore of 'Voodoo Child (Slight Return)'.

May 16
Saturday
**Temple Stadium,
Philadelphia, Pennsylvania**
Cry Of Love is support by Grateful Dead, The Steve Miller Band, Cactus and The Jam Factory.

Cry Of Love take the stage for their midnight performance. Jimi announces: "Regan, drag the Americans down and make the crack in the Liberty Bell their symbol. That's right on the limit... do a thing called 'Sergeant Pepper's Lonely Hearts Club Band'." Jimi hadn't played the song for almost two years. He then continues with 'Johnny B. Goode'. "And then we have the American Revolution which is in the third and the last phase, thanks a lot for the, er, live people and soldiers' faith, which'll take care of it. We'd like to do a thing in memory to all the cats that spilled a little blood here and there in their lives... People just couldn't make it what they had did really, because like they're making up for us and we gonna make them smile for our children and so forth and so on. Dig us... There's a whole lot of cats fighting wars within themselves, so... we can really relate it in any kind of way, a thing called 'Machine Gun'."
Jimi continues with 'Lover Man', 'Foxy Lady', 'Red House', 'Freedom' and 'Fire'. The band play 'Getting My Heart Back Together' and 'Purple Haze' and the show ends with 'Voodoo Child (Slight Return)'.

May 22
Friday
Cincinnati, Ohio
Jimi is ill, so the concert is cancelled.

May 23
Saturday
St Louis, Missouri
Jimi is ill, so the concert is cancelled.

May 24
Sunday
Evansville, Indiana
Jimi is ill, so the concert is cancelled.

May 30
Saturday
Berkeley Community Centre, Berkeley, California
Cry Of Love are supported by Tower Of Power.

Cry Of Love attend an afternoon sound check and rehearsal. They run through 'Message To Love', 'Blues Suede Shoes', 'Land Of The New Rising Sun', 'Earth Blues', 'Room Full Of Mirrors', Villanova Junction', 'Keep On Grooving', 'Freedom', 'Paper Airplanes' and 'Machine Gun'.

The band take the stage at 19:00 for the first of two performances this evening. After a tune up, Jimi announces: "Forget about tomorrow and yesterday, everybody's got it right on together tonight, make our own little world and, er, let's see if we can get a little booster shot or something there. This is dedicated to all the cats that have died for a cause that is gonna happen anyway... Mitch Mitchell on drums and Bill Cox on bass, [thanks] a lot for showing up." Jimi opens the show with 'Fire'. "... We've got this other thing called, em, I don't know, we'd like to do a little loose jam type of thing, it's 'Johnny B. Goode' what the hell." "Yeah okay then, here's a story that a lot of us have been through at one time or another, one kind of way or another. About a cat running around town and his old lady [thinks] she don't want him around and a whole lot of people from across the tracks are putting him down. And nobody don't even wanna face up to that the cat has something, but everybody's against him because the cat might be a little bit different. So he goes on the road and be a voodoo child, come back and be a magic boy. Right now we tune in on [him], waiting down the train station, waiting for his train to come in so he can do his thing." Jimi continues with 'Getting My Heart Back Together Again'.

After a tune up, Jimi comments: "Sorry for the delay, I'd like to... continue on and dedicate this one to Colette and Devon, two little gypsy girls over there with the red underwear... In the meantime, which is a groovy time, we'll see if we can get into some poon tang time. Dedicated to you two." Jimi continues with 'Foxy Lady'. "Thank you very much. Yeah, okay then, a minor adjustment here and there... I'd like to do this one for, er, I hate to say it [but] there's a lot of truth we have to face up to. The ideas, the solutions and so forth and so on, but still we got dedications to all the soldiers that were fighting in Chicago and they're in jail. All the soldiers in, er, New York, Florida, right here in Berkeley, specially the soldiers of Berkeley. Oh yeah, the soldiers in Vietnam too this is dedicated to. A thing called 'Machine Gun'." "Thank you. Hold on one more second, give yourself about two or three minutes to buy your popcorn, ice cream and sandwiches or whatever you want to do. We've got another tune up job to get through. I'd like to do a little thing that we call, em, right now it's a working title, it's, it's more into the jam stages or other boogie stage whatever you want to call it. It's a little thing talking about 'Freedom'. We've been hearing that about two hundred years..." Jimi continues with 'Freedom'. "I'd like to do a slow blues here that we've been doing for ninety-nine thousand years, a thing called 'Red House'... dedicate this one also to Colette and er, Devon." "I'd like to do a thing called, em, I'd like to do a thing called... 'Message To Love' understanding everybody in your dream..."

"Thank you very much for staying this long, we've got another thing called... 'Ezy Ryder' or some mess like that, yeah right. And the cat gets all blown to bits at the end, you know and all this kind of mess. So like er, give us an idea to do a little song the way we see her or whatever. It's the same title, 'Greasy Slider'... "Jimi continues with 'Ezy Ryder', 'Star Spangled Banner' and 'Purple Haze'. "Thank you man, thank you very much. Listen man, we all have to be, we're all in this mess together, we're all living and trying to grow, little children taking steps here and there from home. And some have big dreams and some of those get killed by all these bullshit, old traditional schemes, so that's why we always have to keep our asses together, one kind of way or another,

1970 May 159

right on together. We've got a thing called 'Voodoo Child' and it won't take too long... Thank you very much for showing up together, thank you, we'll see you next time." Jimi closes the show with 'Voodoo Child (Slight Return)'.

The group take the stage at 22:00 for the second performance of the evening, Jimi announces: "Yeah everything's right on time right now. How you doing, you feeling all right? Yeah, right, there you go, we're getting them straight. We have Billy Cox on bass, Mitch Mitchell on drums and yours truly on, er, public saxophone, thank you. I'll tell you what, give us about a minute to, er, get tuned up and get rid of these joints and everything, all right? [We'll] just set up and do a jam, you know, listen to everything, it's like relaxed and everything, forget about yesterday or tomorrow or whatever you say, this is our own little world tonight. But we're just going... [to] just groove a little bit and er, we're just do a little instrumental jam at the beginning, you know just to check our tuning there, right? So just lay back..." Jimi opens the show with a new song, 'Pass It On', which he would later develop into 'Straight Ahead'. He continues by playing the introduction to 'Land Of The New Rising Sun' and announces "Don't mind us, we just feel like playing to you, the theme from the 'New Rising Sun' [sic]." Jimi ends the song before the last verse and continues by playing a shortened version of 'Lover Man'. The set continues with 'Stone Free' and 'Hey Joe'. Then: "Thank you very much, we're just trying to warm up a little bit and see what happens. We'd like to do a thing that is, er, what's happening today with a lot of people, and I'd like to dedicate it to all, all the cats that are trying to struggle that are gonna make it anyway... it's just a hard battle that's all. It's a thing called 'I Don't Live Today' – maybe tomorrow, I can't say – but I don't live today."

After the song Jimi comments "... I'd like to dedicate this to all the soldiers fighting in Berkeley, you know what soldiers I'm talking about. And, er, oh yeah the soldiers fighting in Vietnam too, we'd like to dedicate it to 'em, and dedicate it to other people that might be fighting wars too, but within themselves, not faced with realities." Jimi continues with 'Machine Gun,' but the song is cut short when the audience starts to clap during a quiet passage of the song, thinking that the song is finished. "Those are sounds that we really don't want to hear no more except for in cartoons, exciting circuses and, you know, whatever, places where public saxophones are blowing. Dig this, we'd like to dedicate this to Devon, dedicate this one to Devon, Morocco and Colette and, er, that other girl back there with the red underwear on, see the one right over there with the metallic kneecaps, yeah right. Thank you for the last three years, thank you." Jimi continues with 'Foxy Lady'. "Thank you very much man, thank you. Yeah I'd like to say thank you very much for showing up man, the cat's getting ready to turn the power off... We'd like to do... everybody wanna stand up this time, everybody must stand up 'cause we is, we's all Americans and so forth and so on, we are Americans. You can do this and you can do that, this is for everybody together. I'd like to do, er, the American anthem the way it really is in the air which you breathe every day, the way it really sounds." Jimi continues with 'Star Spangled Banner' and 'Purple Haze'.

"Thank you very much, good night man. We hope to get a chance to see you again soon. Now we're gonna play our American anthem, and thank you very much for showing up, it was outta site. We hope to see you soon, very soon, before the summer comes. This is specially dedicated to, yeah the People's Park, especially the Black Panthers. We hope you all got some kind of feeling about this thing that, the next thing we're gonna play and the last thing. It goes like this, a thing that keeps us alive, it's nothing but determination and so forth and so on you know, knowing that you're gonna get it together, thank you good night." Jimi ends the show with 'Voodoo Child (Slight Return)' into which he introduces a snippet of 'Keep on Grooving' for good measure.

May 31
Sunday
Atlanta, Georgia

June 5
Friday
**Memorial Auditorium,
Dallas, Texas**

June 6
Saturday
**Sam Houston Coliseum,
Houston, Texas**
Cry Of Love are supported by Ballin' Jack.

Cry Of Love start their show at 20:00 and perform 'Johnny B. Goode', 'Getting My Heart Back Together Again', 'Fire', 'Foxy Lady', 'I Don't Live Today', 'Purple Haze', 'Red House', 'Ezy Ryder', 'Machine Gun', 'Star Spangled Banner', 'Hey Joe' and 'Voodoo Child (Slight Return)'.

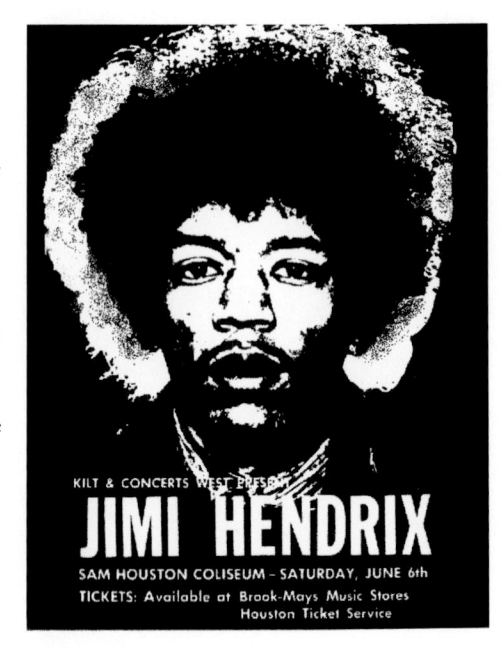

June 7
Sunday
**Civic Assembly Centre Arena,
Tulsa, Oklahoma**
Cry Of Love are supported by Ballin' Jack.

June 8
Monday
Kansas City, Missouri
Cry Of Love are supported by Ballin' Jack.

June 9
Tuesday
**Mid-South Coliseum,
Memphis, Tennessee**
Cry Of Love are supported by Ballin' Jack.

June 10
Wednesday
**Roberts Municipal Stadium,
Evansville, Indiana**
Cry Of Love are supported by Ballin' Jack.

Cry Of Love takes the stage for their 20:00 performance, Jimi announces: "Give us about a half, er, half a minute to get tuned up and everything, so we can get the ball rolling." Jimi opens the show with 'Spanish Castle Magic' and continues with 'Fire'. He then announces: " ... I'd like to do this one dedicated to... the news people, a thing called 'Look Out You Must Begin, Your Lover Man, I've Just Got The Hell Outta Here'." Jimi continues with 'Here Comes Your Lover Man'. "Now we'd like to thank you for standing forward, just thank you very much, give yourselves a hand. And, er, in case you might be showing part three, the hot dogs, we'd like to do a blues in the meantime." Jimi continues with 'Red House'. "I'd like to dedicate this one to, er, that little girl over there in the yellow underwear and also thank you for the last three years." Jimi continues with 'Foxy Lady'. After the song the audience starts to shout for 'Voodoo Child'. Jimi replies: "Yeah, okay, we'll get into all that good shit. We'd like to see if we can get into something right now but we have to tune up one more time okay, give yourselves about, er, [a] thirty second intermission, just enough time to light your cigarette without any name on it."

After a tune up Jimi announces: "We're very sorry for the delay, we're very sorry... tried just to play, but, you know, it didn't go right... we dedicate this song to the soldiers fighting in Chicago, Milwaukee, Evansville, oh yeah, and all the cats fighting in Vietnam." Jimi continues with 'Machine Gun', 'Message To Love', 'Freedom', 'Getting My Heart Back Again', 'Star Spangled Banner', and 'Purple Haze'. "Thank you very much, thanks for showing up and good night and, er, we'll see you the next time around." Jimi ends the show with 'Voodoo Child (Slight Return)'.

June 13
Saturday
Baltimore Civic Centre, Baltimore, Maryland
Cry Of Love are supported by Ballin' Jack and Cactus.

Cry Of Love take the stage for their 20:00 show. Jimi opens the show with 'Pass It On'. "Thank you very much, we have Billy Cox on bass, Mitch Mitchell on drums." Jimi continues with 'Here Comes Your Lover Man'. "If we get a test to Omaha, and get it all over with, [we'll play] a thing called 'Machine Gun' [in] a little minute." Jimi concludes the song and Mitch immediately starts the drum introduction to 'Ezy Ryder'. After this, Jimi continues, without any introduction, with 'Red House'. "Thank you very much. I'd like to get into this other tune, a thing called 'Message To Love'." When the song finishes, Jimi continues with 'Hey Joe', 'Freedom' and Getting My Heart Back Together Again' – again, there are no introductions. "Here's another thing that we'd like to release on our next LP called 'Room Full Of Mirrors'. Afterwards, Jimi announces: "Yeah and this next song is called 'Thank You For The Last Four Years'." Jimi continues with 'Foxy Lady' and 'Purple Haze'. Announcing, "Thank you very much I want everybody to stand", Jimi continues with 'Star Spangled Banner' and ends the show with 'Voodoo Child (Slight Return)'.

June 19
Friday
Civic Auditorium, Albuquerque, New Mexico
Cry of Love perform two shows at 19:00 and 22:00.

June 20
Saturday
Swing Auditorium, San Bernardino, California
Cry Of Love take the stage for their 20:00 show. Jimi opens the show with 'All Along The Watchtower', then announces: "And this one is called, er, a thing called 'Room Full Of Mirrors'. Jimi then continues with 'Machine Gun', 'Message To Love', 'Getting My Heart Back Together Again', 'Foxy Lady', 'Hey Joe', 'Purple Haze' and ends the show with 'Voodoo Child (Slight Return)'.

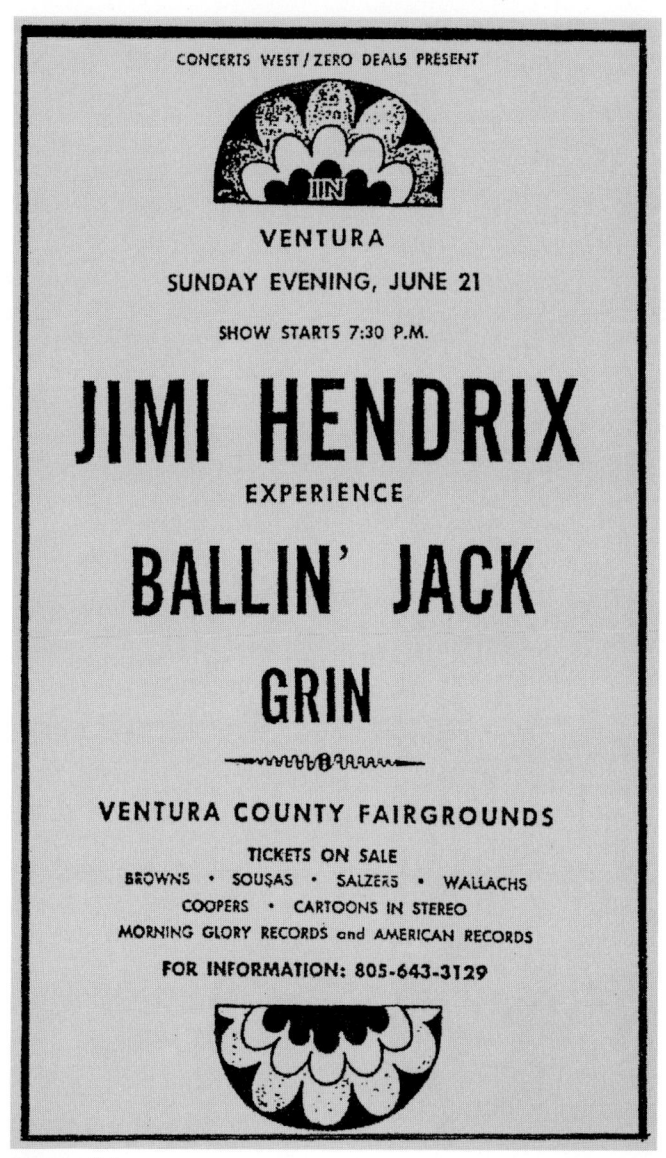

June 21
Sunday
Ventura County Fairgrounds, Ventura, California
Cry Of Love is support by Ballin' Jack and Grin.

Cry Of Love take the stage for their 19:30 performance with Jimi wearing a large black cape. Due to a heavy fog that descended on the venue, Jimi was forced to cut the show to only 45 minutes. The band still manage to play 'Machine Gun', 'Purple Haze' and 'Foxy Lady'.

June 23
Tuesday
Mammoth Gardens, Denver, Colorado

June 25
Thursday
Pittsburg, Pennsylvania

1970 May/June 161

June 27
Saturday
Boston Garden, Nashuia Street, Boston, Massachusetts
Cry Of Love are supported by The Illusion and Cactus.

Cry Of Love takes the stage for their 20:00 performance. Jimi starts the show off with 'Stone Free'. "Yeah thank you very much for the second tune up there. Hey dig... a thing called 'Here He Come'." Jimi continues with 'Here Comes Your Lover Man', 'Red House', 'Freedom', 'Foxy Lady', 'Purple Haze', 'Star Spangled Banner', 'All Along The Watchtower' and 'Message To Love'. After a brief "Thank you", Jimi continues with 'Fire'. "Thank you very much." Without any introductions Jimi continues with 'Spanish Castle Magic'. He then winds up with: "Thank you, good night, we'll see you next time", and ends the show with 'Voodoo Child (Slight Return)'.

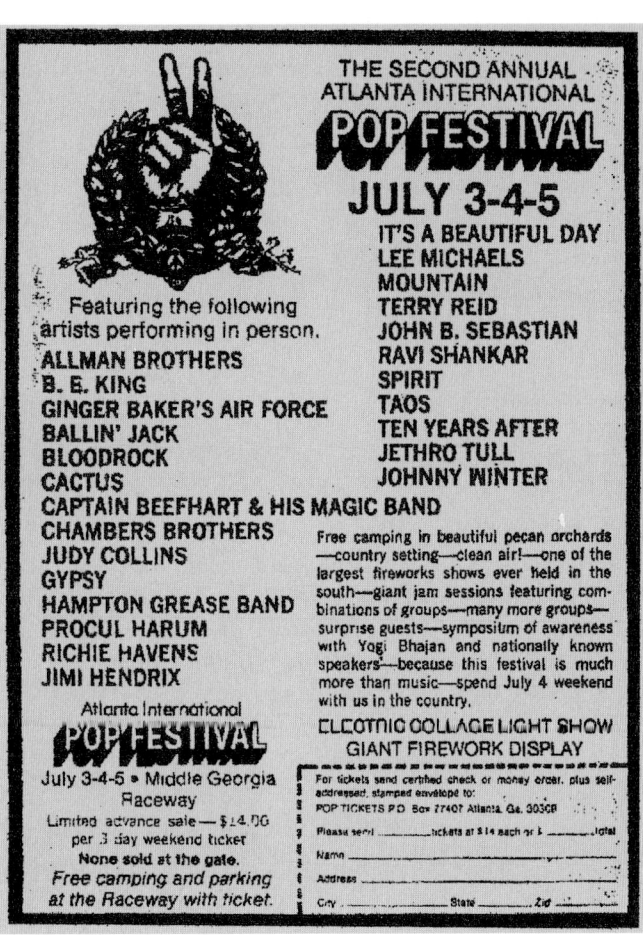

July 4
Saturday
2nd Atlanta International Pop Festival, Middle Georgia Raceway, Byron, Georgia
Cry Of Love are supported by B.B. King, John Sebastian, Mountain, Procul Harum, Poco, Jethro Tull, Johnny Winter and The Allman Brothers.

Cry Of Love take the stage for their 02:30 (Sunday) performance. Jimi announces: "Thank you for waiting, I can't hear nothing, testing one, two three, testing, testing. I'd like to introduce the new members of the group, this is Billy Cox on bass and Mitch Mitchell on drums and yours truly on public saxophone." Jimi starts the show off with 'Fire'. "Thank you, we really hope it isn't too loud for you, because if it is we can always turn it up. I'd like to do another thing goes something like this here. Hey dig, there's a whole lot of girls running around loose because [their] old man's in the army and so forth, and when he comes back he's gonna find you up there with your other man and somebody's gonna get [it]. It's called 'Here Comes Your Lover Man'." Following this number, and without any introduction, Jimi continues with 'Spanish Castle Magic'. Then: "Yeah we'd like to slow it down a little bit and quiet it down and... do a slow blues for the evening, a thing called 'Red House'."

There are more tuning problems, and Jimi addresses the audience: "Sorry for the tuning, it'll only take a second. I'd like to do a thing that, er, we're gonna have on our new LP, a thing called 'Room Full Of Mirrors'." After this song, Jimi continues the set with 'Getting My Heart Back Together Again', 'Message To Love', All Along The Watchtower' and 'Freedom'. He then says: "Thank you very much for the last four years... [this is] dedicated to the girl over there with the purple underwear on." Jimi continues with 'Foxy Lady'. Then: "I want everybody to stand up and get off... your thing and stand up on your feet because we'd like to do a happy birthday song to America. Thing goes something like... the thing they used to brainwash [us with]... at school. Well let's all, everybody stand up and sing it together with feeling." Jimi proceeds to play the introduction to 'Star Spangled Banner', but quickly changes it to 'Purple Haze'. During the song there is a huge firework display behind the stage which lights up the night sky. After 'Purple Haze', Jimi comments: "Thank you very much for staying with us, thank you... and... I'd like to see you again soon." Jimi continues the set with 'Hey Joe'.

Next, the band play 'Voodoo Child (Slight Return)'. Afterwards he announces: "Thank you very much for staying with us, thank you. Thank you very much, you're all really, really kind. You know, if I could see you we could get it together, but that light is blinding me, man, it's hard to play when you can't see nobody, you know." The offending spotlight is switched off and Jimi comments: "Now I can see you, yeah, right. I'd like to do a thing called 'Stone Free' – we hope you remember that one." Jimi then continues with 'Star Spangled Banner' and 'Straight Ahead'. He closes the show with a very out-of-tune version of 'Land Of The New Rising Sun'.

July 5
Sunday
Miami Jai Alai Fronton, Miami, Florida
Cry Of Love perform two shows.

July 10
Friday
Louisville, Kentucky

July 11
Saturday
Memphis, Tennessee

July 17
Friday
New York Pop, Downing Stadium, Randall's Island, New York
Cry Of Love are supported by Grand Funk Railroad, John Sebastian, Steppenwolf and Jethro Tull.

Cry Of Love take the stage at 04:00 (Saturday) for their performance. Jimi starts the show off with 'Stone Free'. As the song ends, Jimi is plagued with radio signals coming through his amplifiers. He jokes: "Yes and, er, for our third song, I'd like to do a thing called, er, let's see, what the hell do we call it... oh, 'Let Me Stand Next To Your Fire'." Afterwards he comments: "Yeah, thank you again, we'd like to, er, probably slow the pace down a little bit and, er, give you a chance to buy your popcorn and your peanuts and, er, whatever they buy at circuses... and like, em, if you didn't bring any blues with you, we'll make sure and make some for you to take home with." Jimi continues with 'Red House'.

Then: "Yeah right, I'd like to dedicate this other one, em, to everybody here, dedicate this other one to everybody for today or tomorrow. Well I'd like to call it, er, I forgot the name of it really... 'Message To Love', yeah." Following this, and without any introduction, Jimi continues with 'Here Comes Your Lover Man'.

we'd like to play 'Foxy Lady' for... the woman with the moustache." When the song is over, Jimi begins: "I'd like to play another song", but again he is having trouble with radio signals through his amplifiers. "I'd like to play a song that's..." (to the amplifiers) "Oh fuck you, God damn. I'd like to play a song... I forgot the name of it really, it's a thing called 'Ezy Ryder', goes like this." After this number,

up and, like, tomorrow night and the next nights it's gonna really be happening. We'll dedicate this one to Gayle and Devon and Colette and Alan Douglas." The audience is shouting over Jimi's announcement, he responds: "Fuck off, these [are] my friends... well fuck you then, good night." Jimi closes the show with 'Voodoo Child (Slight Return)'.

July 18
Saturday
Garden State Art Festival, Pittsburg, Pennsylvania

July 25
Saturday
Sports Arena, San Diego, California
Cry Of Love are supported by Cat Mother.

Cry Of Love perform 'Fire', 'Hey Joe', Purple Haze', 'Foxy Lady', 'Red House', 'Star Spangled Banner', 'Voodoo Child (Slight Return)' and 'Land Of The New Rising Sun'.

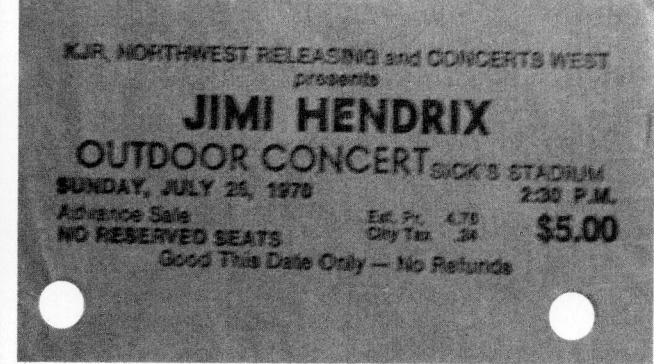

He then announces: "The buses are gonna be stopped running in fifteen minutes, so the cat said [if you want to] get back to New York by bus, I think you'd better split. It was nice knowing you. I hope I see [you] again. For the rest of you here, I've come to save the day" (this last bit is said in his Mighty Mouse voice).

Jimi continues with 'All Along The Watchtower'. After the song he announces: "Yeah, we'd like to do another song...

Jimi continues with 'Star Spangled Banner' adding snippets of 'English Country Garden' and 'Purple Haze'. "Yeah thank you very much for all that good, er, 'Purple Haze' and all the enjoyment and everything... Okay... we'd like to say thank you and good night..." Someone shouts out for 'Machine Gun' and Jimi replies: "Okay, we'll get into it. Say thank you and good night, and thanks for showing

July 26
Sunday
Sicks Stadium, Seattle, Washington
Cry Of Love are supported by Cactus, Rube Tuben and The Rhondonnas.

Cry Of Love take the stage for their 19:15 performance in the rain. Jimi announces: "Hello, I hope you're doing fine, 'cause I am. I want you to forget about yesterday and tomorrow and just make our own little world right here. You don't sound very happy, you don't look very happy, but we'll see if we can paint some faces around here, [with] a thing called "Let Me Stand Next To Your Old Lady' and if you don't have that, 'Let Me Stand Next To Your Fire'."

1970 June/July 163

Afterwards: "... We've got Billy Cox on bass and we've got Mitch Mitchell on drums and we've got yours truly on public saxophone... Oh please don't throw anything up here, please, okay, don't do that, because I feel like getting on somebody's head anyway. I'd like to slow the pace down a little bit and try to get [into] Nashville of all things. And you know I just seen my parents coming, which is really outta site. I'd like to do a thing called 'Message To Love'." After this song, Jimi continues with 'Here Comes Your Lover Man'. Then: "Yeah, this is dedicated to everybody here, a thing called 'Machine Gun'." Jimi follows this with 'Star Spangled Banner' and 'Purple Haze'.

After this he announces: "We'd like to play a song dedicated to everybody, a thing called 'I Don't Live Today' – maybe tomorrow, I can't say." Mitch starts the familiar drum introduction to the song, but Jimi doesn't come in (in fact he leaves the stage), so Mitch does an extended drum solo. Jimi comes back on stage and continues with 'Getting My Heart Back Together Again', including snippets of 'Keep On Grooving'. Jimi continues with 'Voodoo Child (Slight Return)', 'Land Of The New Rising Sun', 'Freedom' and 'Red House'. Then he announces: "I'd like to do another thing if you don't mind. I know it's the rain, the rain makes you like that I'm sure. You all look really pretty healthy out there, so we'd like to do a healthy song dedicated to that girl over there in the yellow underwear... it's called 'Foxy Lady'... thank you for the last three years and everything." Jimi closes the show with 'Foxy Lady'.

July 30
Thursday
Rainbow Bridge Vibratory Color Sound Experiment, Haleakala Crate, Island Of Maui, Hawaii

Cry Of Love are supported by Air.

Cry Of Love take the stage in the afternoon for the first of their performances. Jimi: "Glad to see you again, I hope everything's alright. Dig, give us about a minute, give us about a minute to set up and, er, yeah we'll forget about tomorrow and yesterday, get into... our own little world for a while, catch up to the wind." Someone offers Jimi something. He replies: "Er, I've had mine actually. Yeah I'd like to get into a thing called 'Spanish Castle Magic' and, er, check out everything and see what's happening." Afterwards: "Yeah, okay... we'd like to do another thing, go into another thing, if... the bass is working. Testing, testing, testing, testing, one, two, three." The crew has to come on stage to adjust the equipment. When they have finished, Jimi continues with 'Here Comes Your Lover Man' and 'The Land Of The New Rising Sun' and a completely new song, 'In From The Storm'. Then: "Yeah thank you very much, thank you. I'd like to tune up one more time, okay? I'd like to do this tune that everybody here knows about, it's a thing called 'Message To Love' – everybody knows about that. We'd like to just bathe in it for a second, for always actually." Jimi continues with 'Message To Love'.

Afterwards he announces: "I'd like to go into one of those other things, do a thing... dedicated to that little girl over there called Hartley, a thing called 'Foxy Lady' – look out! Plug your ears, plug your ears, it's gonna be loud!" When the song is over, Jimi says: "Thank you very much, I'd like to do a slow blues right now.

It's a thing about a cat, you know, he gotta leave town because his old lady don't want him around, because, you know, nobody [wants] him in town and all the downs. You know, the cat's all low and everything, but then he's gonna get it together, 'cause he's going down the train station with his little baby and his little pack on his back. Come back and buy the town and maybe the girl does it to him one more time, might even marry her and give a piece to her. It's called 'Get My Heart Back Together' – I don't know whether it's about myself, I don't know." After this blues track, the set continues with 'Voodoo Child (Slight Return)' and 'Fire'. "Yeah we'd like to do another one, I think, er, a few of us might remember this one, some of us will never forget it, including me..." Jimi ends the first show with 'Purple Haze', then tells the audience: "Thank you, thank you, peace with you man, thank you. We'd like to come back later on and we're bound to get it on again if we can, okay, [unless] anything stops us."

Cry Of Love return for their second performance. Jimi opens the show with another new song, 'Dolly Dagger'. He slows the song down at the ends and proceeds to play a very melodic version of 'Villanova Junction', before continuing the set with 'Ezy Ryder'. He announces: "I'd like to do a little blues to the sun called 'Red House'. After this number, Cry of Love continue with 'Freedom', 'Beginnings' and 'Straight Ahead' ending this last song with the introduction to 'Land Of The New Rising Sun'. After thanking the crowd, Jimi continues with 'Land Of The New Rising Sun' and then plays 'Keep On Grooving'. Mitch plays an extended drum solo and Jimi returns to play 'Stone Free'. He ends the concert with a few bars of 'Hey Joe' before revisiting the solo of 'Stone Free'. "Thank you very much, good night."

Chuck Wein: "Even though the album and video are called *Rainbow Bridge*, it was known as *Rainbow Ridge* because that's the name of the ridge on which the concert was held."

August 1
Saturday
Arena,
Honolulu International Centre,
Honolulu, Island Of Oauh, Hawaii

Cry Of Love take the stage at 20:00 for what is to be Jimi Hendrix's last official concert in the USA.

They perform 'Freedom', 'Foxy Lady', 'Star Spangled Banner', 'Purple Haze', 'Message To Love', 'All Along the Watchtower' and 'Voodoo Child (Slight Return)'.

August 30
Sunday
**Isle Of Wight Festival,
East Afton Farm, Isle Of Wight**

Cry Of Love are supported by Joan Baez, Donovan & Open Road, Leonard Cohen & The Army, Richie Havens, Moody Blues, Pentangle, Good News, Jethro Tull and Ralph McTell, with MC Jeff Dexter.

Jimi finally starts making his way to the stage with the other members of the band and various guests in the early hours of Monday 31st. While Jimi walks up the steps to the stage he looks back and announces: "I got a gig, waiting for me in the Laundromat."

Jeff Dexter introduces the band, opening with an aside to a technician: "A bit more volume on this one, Charlie, it's gonna need it. Let's have a welcome for Billy Cox on bass, Mitch Mitchell on drums, and the man with the guitar, Jimi Hendrix."

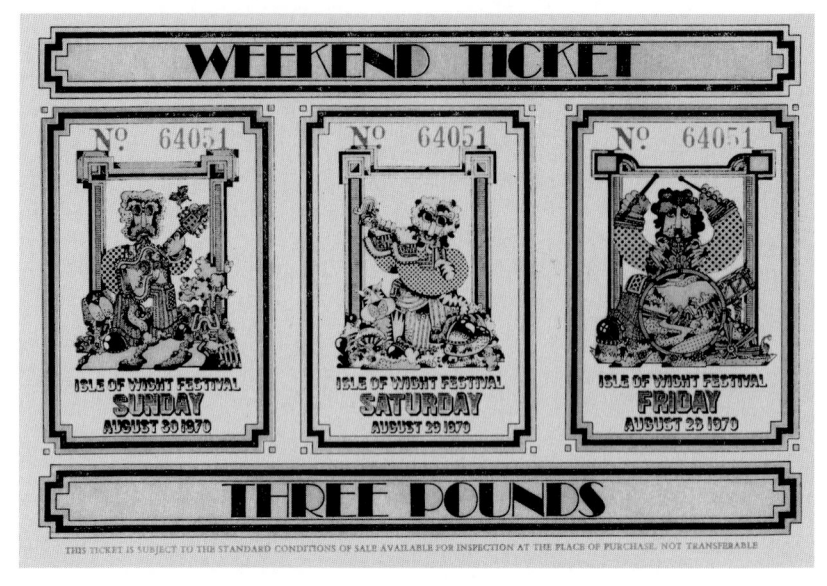

Jimi walks to the microphone and announces: "Yeah, thank you very much for showing up man, you all look really beautiful and outta site and thanks for waiting. It has been a long time, hasn't it?" Jimi then flashes a peace sign. "That does mean peace, not this," reversing it to a V sign, reversing it again to the peace sign. "Peace. Okay, give us about a minute to tune up all right... It's so good to be back in England. We'd like to... start off with a thing that everybody knows out there. You can join in and start singing. Matter of fact, it'll sound better if you'd stand up for your country and your beliefs and start singing. And if you don't, fuck yer!" He then calls out, "Nice and loud, nice and loud" to the band, before starting the set off with a short feedback rendition of 'God Save The Queen'. Mitch Mitchell then plays the introduction to 'Sergeant Pepper's Lonely Hearts Club Band', but the squeals coming from Jimi's guitar indicate that he already seems to be experiencing some equipment trouble. Jimi only sings the first verse of the song before bringing it to an end. This was a song that Jimi had used extensively as a show opener back in 1968, but which he rarely played now.

Without any introduction the band then launch into 'Spanish Castle Magic', which Jimi ends in howls of feedback. His amp is now being plagued by a foreign voice and xylophone music comes from his speakers. "As I said before, thanks a lot for coming. We'd like to get into another song that we did about, er, in the year of 1883. And, er, I think it's pretty [true]... today, if you can dig it." Meanwhile the crews are trying desperately to eliminate the radio signals, a problem that annoyed Jimi more than anything. Trying not to let it bother him too much, he proceeds to count up the guitar neck with his fingers, looking for the chord that would start his next song – a little joke that he often did to amuse his audience. He then proceeds with 'All Along The Watchtower', but is still experiencing equipment trouble. "Er, we're having a tiny bit [of] trouble with the equipment, hold on a moment, one more second, buy your hot dogs or whatever." The crowd start shouting for 'Voodoo Child', Jimi replies: "Yeah, we'll do that towards the... next time." Adjusting the uni-vibe for the next number, 'Machine Gun', he comments. "Yeah, there's a whole lot of head games go along sometimes, and sometimes they leak out, as a word they use their powers and so forth, and put it on header games on other people, which we call WAR. And so I'd like to dedicate this one to, er, all the soldiers that are fighting in Birmingham, all the skinheads" which evokes a reaction from the audience.

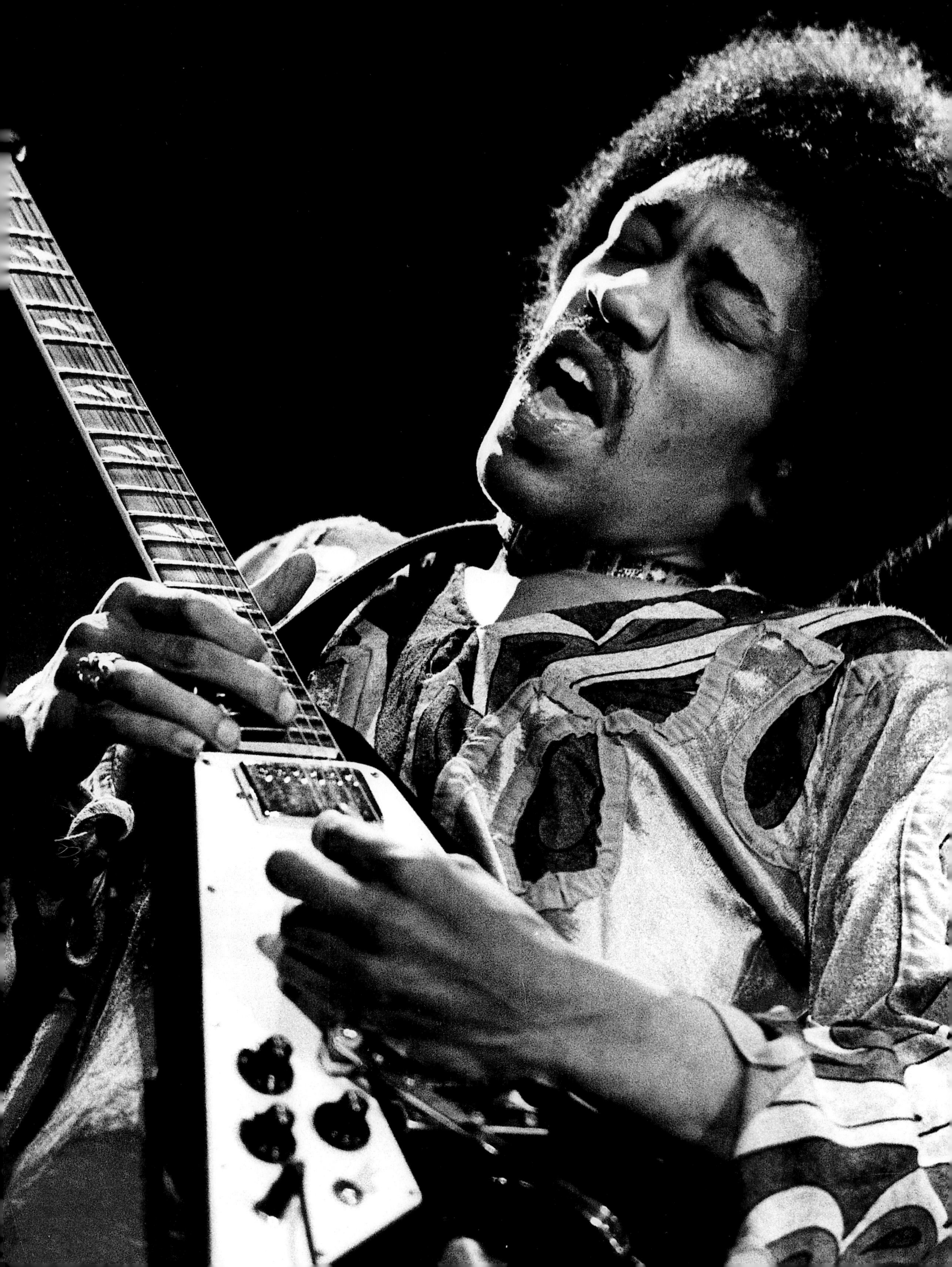

"... All the, yeah, well, you know what I mean, you know, yeah right, Amen. All the soldiers fighting in Bournemouth, London. Oh yeah, all the soldiers fighting in Vietnam, like I almost forgot, man. So many wars going on."

Three minutes into the 'Machine Gun', the radio interference re-emerges – this time because of the security walkie-talkies: "Security personnel, security personnel, are you receiving over?" However, Jimi seems unconcerned at the interruption this time and continues to play. Indeed, in a strange way, the voice seemed to fit in with the song. After about nine minutes, Jimi stops playing and Mitch fills in with a four-minute drum solo. Jimi comes back in, and for the following ten minutes there is a jam which features some incredible guitar work. However, this version of the song remains inferior to the one played during Jimi's Band Of Gypsys concert, back on New Year's Day at the Fillmore, when 'Machine Gun' received its live début. As the song comes to a close and the decibel level lowers, it becomes clear that the radio interference problem has still not been solved. This time, Jimi has to contend with a male opera singer coming through the bank of speakers! Looking back at his amplifiers in disgust, he brings the song to a sharp stop. Gerry Stickells and Gene McFadden race around the stage trying to locate the problem. Jimi apologises to the audience: "Listen, it's gonna take a time er, to, like, get into it, because we're having little difficulties here and there. But, like, if you can hold on a little bit, I think we can all get it together, all right? 'Cause I'm gonna stay here all night until somebody moves." "Yeah, right!" shouts the audience, with a cheer.

Somebody shouts to shut the camera off. Jimi remarks: "I just want to get to my old lady at three o'clock." Confusion reigns, with the camera crews shouting at each other and amplifiers frantically being changed. Jimi changes guitars to his Gibson Flying V and, after a slight delay and tune up, continues with 'Lover Man'. The crew seems to have finally managed to sort out the problem and Jimi feels much happier with the sound. He dismisses the last forty minutes and decides to start the whole concert again. "Okay we ought to start all over again. Hello, how are you doing England? Glad to see you. We'll do a thing called 'Freedom'." Jimi has now settled down to engage in some fine playing and was starting to sound more fluent. Without a pause he goes straight into 'Red House,' which was possibly the highlight of the entire concert. The audience start to react favourable, now that the equipment had been sorted out, and Jimi is able to really play for the first time since the concert started. The crowd show their appreciation and all of the first few rows take to their feet cheering and clapping at the end of the song. Turning to Mitch, Jimi says: "Try that Dolly Dagger, okay? We're gonna try to do this song now, it's called, em, 'Dolly Dagger' and it's, er, one of the things that we'll try to put on our new LP." Meanwhile the audience at the front of the stage are still standing. Jimi is asked to request that they all sit down: "Oh yeah, somebody wants, er, people in the front row to sit down. I think its compliments of the hills. Don't forget, you can't fly off the top of those hills, don't forget that." The band then launch into 'Dolly Dagger' – a completely new song that had only been performed once before during Jimi's concert in Maui, Hawaii.

At the end of the song, he changes guitars, back to his Stratocaster, and tells Mitch and Billy: "We'll try to do that, er, rock 'n' roll tune, okay?" Then, to the audience: "Very sorry for tuning up, but, er, you know we do that... to protect your ears. That's why we don't play so loud, you know. And, er, cowboys are the only ones who wanna stay in tune anyway. I'm so glad you all have patience though, 'cause I don't. I'd like to do this slow blues." Again, Jimi tries out a relatively new song, 'Midnight Lightning'. As the song ends, Jimi immediately hits the long feedback note for the more familiar 'Foxy Lady'. "This is dedicated to Linda. To the cat right there with the silver face... (Nik Turner of Hawkwind) Dedicated to Kirsten, Karen and that little four-year-old girl over there with the yellow panties on. And I'd like to say thank you for the last three years. One of these days we'll get it together again. Thanks for showing up and you're outta site. If *you* had the same old songs, you'd be ready to stop." Halfway through the song, the radio interference comes back with a vengeance. Now Jimi is getting all kind of voices coming through the speakers. He stops playing while Mitch and Billy carry on with the beat. The problem again seems to be solved and Jimi continues to play. He doesn't seem to let it bother him, riding the song out with some theatrical showmanship, playing the guitar between his legs and performing an extended solo with his teeth. "You all wanna hear all those little songs, man? Damn man, we was trying to get some other things together. I just woke up about two minutes ago... I think we'll play, play something a little more familiar. 'Cause I ain't came yet myself, I don't know about you, but I ain't came, you know. There, I came, thank you very much, good night!" Jimi continues with 'Message To Love', after which he adjusts his uni-vibe for 'Land Of The New Rising Sun'. In the second verse, his improvised lines, "Coming back to England, thank you baby for making so easy," suggest that he must have been pleased with his first concert in England for almost 18 months. Bringing the song to a rather abrupt end, Mitch starts the drum intro for 'Ezy Ryder', after which it's straight into a real crowd-pleaser – 'Hey Joe' – which included snatches of 'Satisfaction' and 'English Country Garden'. Jimi draws the concert to a close with 'Purple Haze' and 'Voodoo Child (Slight Return)' and, finally, another relatively new song, 'In From The Storm'. During this song, Jimi was looking very tired as he tried to squeeze notes from his guitar. Then, after an hour and fifty minutes, it was all over. "Thank you for being so patient. Maybe one of these days [we'll] smoke a joint again, I really hope so, right? Thank you very much. And peace and happiness and all the other good shit." With that, Jimi takes his guitar off over his head and lets it fall to the floor with a crash.

August 31
Monday
Stora Scenen, Grona Lund, Tivoli Gardens, Stockholm

Jimi opens up with: "I hope everybody feels all right?" The audience shouts back a resounding "Yeah!" Jimi: "Yeah, right, right. You all look good. Power to the people and all that good shit. I'll tell you what, give us a minute, about one minute just to tune up and, er, you know, check ourselves out and see where we're really at. Yeah, on bass we have Billy Cox, as the cat said. We've got Mitch Mitchell on drums, and yours truly on public saxophone. How's about a cigarette? I guess they didn't have any name on it... (Referring to joints)" Jimi plays a couple of chords. "Yeah, expect more where that came from." The first song of the evening is 'Lover Man'. Then: "Yeah, thank you very much. What's the name of this? (Asking Mitch) Oh yeah." The next song

1970 August 169

is a very short instrumental version of 'Catfish Blues' followed by 'Midnight Lightning'. Going into the next song, Jimi shouts the title to the audience – 'Ezy Ryder'. Up to this point, considering Jimi's condition, the playing has been quite good, but this song starts to breaks down a little in places. Jimi comments after the song: "Wow-wee that's really far out, I didn't think you was going to stay that long, great, great. Right now I'd like to loosen up a little bit..." The audience start screaming out songs for Jimi to play. "Oh man hell, I know what I'm gonna do. Hey listen, when I say toilet paper, that's when you all come rolling out, okay?" The audience continues shouting out requests. "As we ignore the primitive forces over there by the Amen section, we have our own minds to make up... a blues, a thing called 'Red House'."

for you, a thing called 'A Room Full Of Mirrors' [sic]. I'm sure, er, we've been through that, one way or another. All I can see is me, one of them kind of scenes. But then the cat broke his mirror... and now he's trying to make another mirror... We'd like to thank all the Swedish people for coming too..." The audience again starts shouting out, this time for 'Fire'. Jimi replies with: "Fuck you, fuck you, come up and play the guitar..." Then he proceeds to thrust the neck of his guitar out into the audience. He makes an obscure comment to someone on the side of the stage – "Something we'd often do" – and continues with 'A Room Full Of Mirrors'. Then: "Ah let me tune my guitar there again... I'd like to do this other thing there... What would you play? (Asking Mitch) I'm glad you said that, 'cause I ain't in the mood for nobody." An argument with the promoter prior to the show is clearly still on Jimi's mind. "I hope you all don't mind us doing a slow, very slow jam, a little bit. You know,

the problem out with the promoter. The argument was clearly quite heated, because he returns to the stage minus his headband. He announces to the audience: "Sorry for the intermission but like, er, I had to get a load off of my mind. I feel a little bit lighter now, so I'd like to do a thing called 'Message To Love'." It is clear, however, that nothing has been resolved, and if anything the set-to has made him feel worse. Jimi's heart is clearly not in his performance. This version of 'Message To Love' is very sloppy, with lots of mistakes and uninspired playing almost to the point that Jimi sounds like an amateur. Afterwards he comments: "Sorry about the tuning up, just give us another minute, and you can have all your money back. We'd like, er, before you all go home and all that, for all the cats who get laid and all the girls that get paid... You wanna be careful, this might be you all along, baby. Matter of fact, we dedicate this song to

As the song ends, it appears that the radio interference has followed him from the Isle Of Wight. This times, however, it seems to be sorted out a lot more quickly. Without any introduction, Jimi continues with 'Come On (Part One)'. After the song finishes, he comments: "Thank you anyway. I'd like to do this little song

we're just gonna mess around with it, okay, it only takes about four minutes. If you can't take that, dig into it."

During the next song, 'Land Of the New Rising Sun', Jimi just can't seem to get the argument out of mind and he eventually walks off stage. Mitch has to fill in with an extra-long drum solo. Meanwhile, Jimi goes backstage to sort

you. The one over there, with the pink underwear, yeah, yeah you... Ah, yeah, we're gonna do this thing called 'Machine Gun'..."

After 'Machine Gun', and without a pause or any introduction, it's straight into 'Voodoo Child (Slight Return)', followed by 'In From The Storm' and

'Purple Haze'. Then Jimi's back to announce: "Somebody said they want to turn off the guitar. One more time, thank you very much Sweden, you've all been outta site, and the honour of Lund. We're all gonna play one more last number to yer, and I'd like to say thanks for everything man, you've all been really sweet at the Lund. Cat back here is freaking out because like, er, it's past his bed time..." Jimi had played for almost 110 minutes, much to the promoter's anger. "Yeah this is a song we love to do... like I said before, this song is dedicated to all the girls who get laid, and, em, all the little girls back there with those little yellow, orange, pink and turquoise panties, that they keep throwing on the stage. It's close to Mother's Day, anybody that [wants to] be a mother, come backstage. Thank you very much and good night – 'Foxy Lady'." Jimi brings the song and the concert to an end with a few bars of 'The Star Spangled Banner' before announcing finally: "Thank you, goodbye."

September 1
Tuesday
Stora Scenen, Liseberg Nojespark, Gothenberg, Sweden

Jimi starts off the concert with an apology for the band's lateness on stage: "We're very sorry for the delay. We're very, very sorry for the delay, but we'll see if we can pay it back to you with some sounds." Starting off the concert with the introduction to 'Land Of The New Rising Sun', he quickly changes the tempo for 'Spanish Castle Magic'. During the song, there is the ever-present problem of radio interference coming through the speakers. "We can call this one 'Killing Floor'. Yeah, I should have quit you a long time ago baby. Before you put me crawling on the killing floor." Jimi hadn't played this song since January 1969. After this number he continues the set with a very melodic version of 'Getting My Heart Back Together Again'. Then he announces: "I'd like to do this thing called, er, 'Message To Love'. During the song, Jimi appears to be having a problem with one of the amplifiers and stops playing, leaving Mitch and Billy to continue with the song. Billy stops playing shortly after and Mitch fills in with a drum solo; in the meantime, Jimi's amplifier is being changed. Jimi comes in on the drum solo to a thunderous cheer of the audience, to play out the rest of the song. Jimi slows the tempo down to end with some beautiful melodic playing, and continues in the same vain for 'Land Of The New Rising Sun'. This is one the most moving versions of the song Jimi ever plays.

After the song is finished, Jimi thanks his audience and directs Mitch to start his drum introduction for 'In From The Storm'. After thanking the audience again at the end of this song, he continues with 'Hey Joe', ending it with a few bars of 'English Country Garden'. At the end of the song, Jimi suffers the irritation of more radio interference from an opera singer. He makes a comment to the audience about "their answer to new music". Then: "Yeah, we should really do another thing called 'Foxy Lady'. By this time she should've had three kids by now. We'll dedicate it to her children. 'Cause she IS worn out, baby." When the band finish, Jimi tells the audience: "We've a slow one, we've got a very slow song this time, as I say, a slow one. Free to relax. I'm just gonna unplug yer. We'll give you some more money's worth. This is dedicated to er..." Jimi continues with 'Red House' and 'A Room Full Of Mirrors'. Next, he announces: "We got another song... Something like, er, you know, power to the people and freedom to the soul and everybody, you know, do their own thing and all that kind of stuff. We got one that goes something like that, that's, em, 'Have You Heard', 'Straight Ahead', 'scuse me." After the song Jimi announces "Thank you very much and good night. Thank you very much and good night, you've been really nice. You've been very pleasant" before playing the last two songs in the concert: 'Purple Haze' and 'Voodoo Child (Slight Return)' which include snippets of Cream's 'The Sunshine Of Your Love' and 'Cat Squirrel'. Jimi then thanks the audience once again. He seems a lot more relaxed during this concert – The problems from the previous evening have clearly left his mind. He is back to his old self, playing superbly and enjoying it.

September 2
Wednesday
Vejlby-Risskov Hallen, Arhus, Denmark

Cry Of Love are supported by Blue Sun.

Jimi's show is scheduled for 19:00. However, when he is finally persuaded to go on for his performance, he has to actually be helped onto the stage by the roadies.

Jimi opens up with: "I said are you doing alright?" "Yeah," shouts the audience, but it was plain to see that he wasn't. "Thank God, thank God. I'll tell you what, give us a minute to, er, try and to tune up, okay? One minute." Jimi seems to tune his guitar easily enough and announces, "Welcome to the electric circus. Our first song will be called 'Freedom'." He struggles somewhat with

1970 August/September

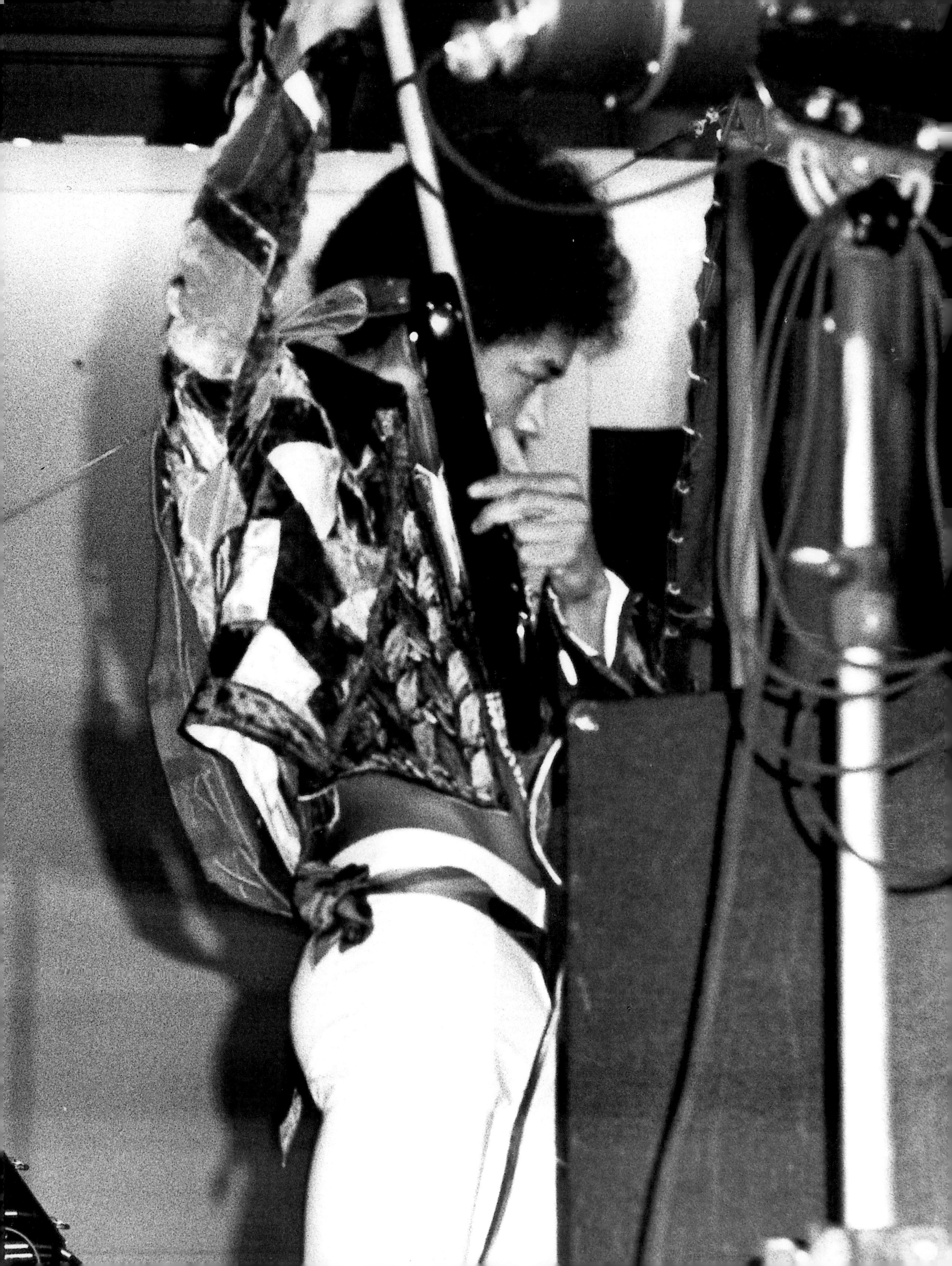

the intro but manages to sing the vocals reasonably well. However, he starts to miss words and whole verses here and there. The song comes to a messy end. Jimi's face clearly reveals that he is aware of the situation – his playing simply wasn't good enough. "Yeah, that's, that's where, er, that's where freedom is at, yeah, right on. Dig, we'd like to do a thing dedicated to the land and world and er, galaxy and peace. Thing called, em, let's see now. If I can get it right." Jimi then proceeds to count the frets of his guitar: "Five, six, seven. Lost count, wait a minute," much to the audience's amusement. He then decides to change guitars. After some delay, the audience starts to slow handclap. "Actually forgot what I was here for. Oh yeah, it was, er, 'Message To Love' right, 'Message To Love'? Yeah." Considering how Jimi is feeling at this particular point, he manages to play the song reasonably well, even adding parts of 'Power Of Soul' as he goes along. Nevertheless, some of the song becomes a little messy in places and again he misses out much of the vocals.

The song comes to a thunderous end, but Jimi finds that his guitar is out of tune. He proceeds with 'Land Of The New Rising Sun', without really taking the time to properly tune up. For many, this song is one of Jimi's most melodic haunting pieces, but he struggles amateurishly with it here. Mitch seems to sense that something is drastically wrong and tries to save the day by going into a very long and complicated drum solo. During Mitch's showcase, Jimi leaves the stage on the verge of collapse, and has to be carried to the dressing room. It is announced that there will be a five-minute intermission, but Jimi is in no fit state to return. The show end prematurely. Jimi was reported as saying, "I've been dead a long time" on the night, but no firm evidence of this quote has ever appeared.

September 3
Thursday
K.B. Hallen, Copenhagen, Denmark
Cry Of Love are supported by Blue Sun.

The show is scheduled for 19:00. Just after 8:45, Jimi comes on stage to a thunderous reception. Flashing a peace sign to the audience, he comments: "Right, right On," and starts off the concert with 'Stone Free'. Bringing the song to an end with screaming feedback he continues with 'Foxy Lady', singing, "Here I come baby, FINALLY, coming to get you", during the last verse. This comment is possibly aimed at Kirsten who was in the audience. Then: "Like to do one for all our brothers and sisters and all everybody else... A thing called 'Message To Love', for everybody."

Finishing the song, he slows the tempo down for a very haunting version of 'Land Of The New Rising Sun'. Jimi only sings one verse of the song, probably because the audience was being a little noisy and was not paying attention to what he was playing. He therefore speeds up the tempo to go straight into 'All Along The Watchtower'. When the song is over, Jimi announces: "Like to do this one dedicated to all the people fighting, for their own cause and their own rights. Fighting for those problems in their head, those mental blocks. Oh yes, and the cats in Vietnam and all the brothers that are fighting this and that. Fighting for freedom." Jimi continues with excellent versions of 'Machine Gun' and 'Spanish Castle Magic', which includes snippets of 'We Gotta Live Together' and 'Satisfaction'.

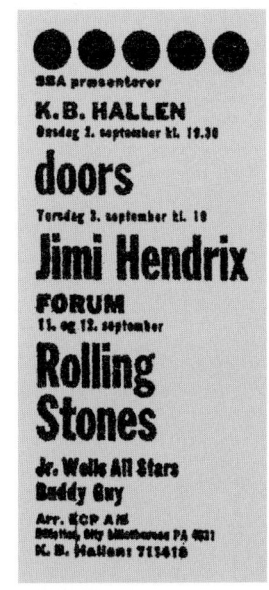

Jimi then leaves the stage and Mitch launches into a long drum solo. When he returns, Jimi shouts out to Mitch that the next song is 'Ezy Ryder'. When the song finishes, he announces: "Like to do another song that we might put on our new LP. A thing called 'Freedom'."

1970 September 173

After this number, Jimi goes straight into 'Red House' and 'In From The Storm'. Jimi obviously felt that his performance had been of a good standard – so far it had indeed been one of the best performances on this tour. Jimi continued with a shorter than normal 'Purple Haze', but more than makes up for that during 'Voodoo Child (Slight Return)', in which he includes a taste of 'The Sunshine Of Your Love' for good measure. Bringing the song back to 'Voodoo Child' he plays a wah-wah dead string chucka-chuck rhythm while introducing the members of the band. "Thank you very much, thank you very much. We have Billy Cox on bass. Mitch Mitchell on drums and, er, yours truly on public saxophone." He finally brings the song to an end by playing the solo with his teeth. The group leaves the stage and the audience responds with whistles. The whole audience are now up on their feet, clapping their hands and stamping their feet in time with each other.
Jimi returns to the stage for an encore, to the audience's delight. "Thank you very much, you're all really outta site man. Let's see if we can get it together in style." Someone in the audience shouts out for 'Hey Joe', Jimi responds with, "Oh yeah". He has now changed his guitar and, after tuning up, plays the requested 'Hey Joe'. "Yeah, I want everybody to help me out. Have some fun." Finally, Jimi closes the show with 'Fire'.

September 4
Friday
**Super Concert 70,
Deutschlandhalle, Berlin, Germany**

Cry Of Love are supported by Canned Heat, Procul Harum, Ten Years After, Cat Mother, Cold Blood and Murphy Blend.

Jimi starts his 19:00 concert off with the introduction to 'Land Of The New Rising Sun', then goes into 'Straight Ahead'. He continues with 'Spanish Castle Magic', 'The Sunshine Of Your Love' and 'Land Of The New Rising Sun'. During the song, the audience all starts to whistle, though it is not evident from the concert tape what is going on. However, something is clearly up, as Jimi only bothers to sing one verse of the song before bringing it to a sudden end. Without any introduction, he continues with 'Message To Love'. He then announces: "I'd like to do a thing called 'Machine Gun'." After an excellent eleven-minute version, he ends the song with a melodic version of 'The Breeze And I' before launching into 'Purple Haze'. He continues the set with 'Red House', 'Foxy Lady', 'Ezy Ryder', 'Hey Joe' and 'Power Of Soul', the last a song which he hadn't played since the Band Of Gypsys concert on New Year's Eve at the Fillmore. This version, however, was very much shorter. Jimi finishes off his performance with 'Lover Man'. He has not really been very communicative during the previous shows on this tour, and was even less so during this one. The performance however was probably one of the best so far. There had been no equipment trouble, and Jimi played fluently throughout.

September 6
Sunday
**Love And Peace Festival,
Isle Of Fehmarn, Germany**

Alexis Korner introduces Jimi to the stage around 13:00, by which time the sun has come out and the weather has improved considerably from earlier, although the wind is still very strong. Jimi now has to face an outburst of abuse from the audience who starts whistling and jeering "Go home, go home," as he comes on stage. This outburst was due to the concert being cancelled the previous evening. Jimi had never experienced a welcome like this before and comments: "Peace anyway, peace." This does not seem to make any difference and the audience continues to boo. Jimi then decides to boo back to the audience. "I don't give a fuck if you boo, long as you boo in key, you mothers." This is met with more shouts of "Go home, go home". Jimi seems a little upset at this reaction, and tries apologising for cancelling the previous evening's performance. "We got Billy Cox on bass, and Mitch Mitchell on drums and, er, yours truly on public saxophone. We'd like to play some music for you and, er, we hope you can dig it. Because we're sorry we couldn't come on last night, but it's just unbearable man, we couldn't make it together like that, you know. Long as you can dig it. Give us a minute to get in tune and everything." Jimi proceeds to tune up and plays the opening riff to the Kingsmen's 'Louie, Louie' then goes into 'Killing Floor'. The line 'I should have quit you a long time ago' is delivered as if he really means it this time.

After the song is over there is cheering and clapping. Jimi has won the German audience over effortlessly in the end. "Yeah, thank you very much man, thank you. We'd like to go on to another thing... we'd like to, er... do a thing called 'Spanish Castle Magic' and get back into the heavens." Jimi tunes his guitar after the song, and the audience starts chanting for 'Hey Joe'. Jimi responds: "We'll do it, we'll do it man, give us a chance, you know, we wanna try to see if we can get into other things too. We'd like to do a little thing here that goes something like this." Jimi continues with 'All Along The Watchtower', 'Hey Joe' and 'Land Of The New Rising Sun'. Again, Jimi only bothers to play the first verse to this song before announcing: "I'd like to dedicate this song to everybody out there [laughs] in Disneyland. It's a thing called 'A Message To Love'." Jimi has noticed some fighting that is going on in the audience and also remarks, "Everybody pick up on those things." He continues with 'Message To Love', then announces a song "Dedicated to the girl sitting over there with that big old thing across her chest. Thank you." Jimi continues with 'Foxy Lady'. After he ends the song, he changes guitars to his Gibson Flying V. "I'd like to do, er, a slow blues for yer, slow blues. One of those days." While Jimi plays 'Red House,' the wind has started to get stronger and the rain has started to fall quite heavily. However, Jimi seems unperturbed and continues to play in the rain. The audience by this time has all covered themselves and Jimi is now playing to a sea of plastic sheeting. Jimi sings: "Yeah, well I got a bad, bad feeling. [Laughing] YEAH, THE WEATHER IS TELLING YOU SOMETHING." By the time Jimi plays his solo, the rain is coming down with a vengeance. He continues to improvise the lyrics – "Way over yonder across the hill, AWAY FROM THOSE RAINY CLOUDS..." "If my baby don't LOVE ME HERE, I KNOW. Lord I know good and well, THE HEAVEN THERE KNOWS, [laughing] her sister will." Rather than allowing the weather to spoil his performance, Jimi seems amused to think that the heavens had been on his side by quashing the fighting as everyone ran for cover. 'Ezy Ryder' is next, followed by 'Freedom'. Jimi changes guitars back to his Stratocaster while Billy Cox takes off on a bass solo followed by an extended drum solo by Mitch Mitchell. Jimi finally steps in again, bringing it all together for 'A Room Full Of Mirrors'. After a quick tune up and without any introduction, he launches in 'Purple Haze'.

By the time he starts his last number, 'Voodoo Child,' (slight return) the fighting has commenced again and is now getting closer to the stage. Jimi continued, but sings only the first verse, ending it with, 'cause I'm a Voodoo Child, Lord knows I'm a Voodoo Child. Yeah I can't say it right now though."

Ironically, the last words Jimi would ever sing in public were. "If I don't see you no more in this world, well I'll meet you in the next one and don't be late, don't be late. Cause I'm a Voodoo Child, Lord knows I'm a Voodoo Child."

September 13
Sunday
De Doelen, Rotterdam, Holland
Due to Billy Cox not in a position to continue with the tour, this concert had to be cancelled.

September 16
Wednesday
Ronnie Scotts Club, Frith Street, London
Meanwhile, Eric Burdon and War continued their week at Ronnie Scotts Jazz Club. Jimi watched as they played their recent hits of 'Paint It Black', 'Spill The Wine' and 'Train'. After the interval Jimi decided to sit in with the group on 'Mother Earth' and 'Tobacco Road'. Jimi loved to jam like this, but on this occasion he seems reluctant, just playing quietly in the background. Sadly, this was to be the last time that Jimi Hendrix would ever play his guitar in public.

Mojo presenteert op
ZONDAG 13 SEPTEMBER
om 19.00 en 22.30 uur in
DE DOELEN - ROTTERDAM.

JIMI HENDRIX
EXPERIENCE

Kaarten à ƒ 15, ƒ 20, ƒ 25, ƒ 30, en ƒ 35,-

Verkrijgbaar aan de kassa's van
De Doelen (10-4 uur) Tel. 132490
Dankers - Coolsingel
Disk - Oldebarneveldplaats

Amsterdam
Nwe. Muziekhandel - Leidsestraat
T.V. Vilters - Rembrandtpleingalerij

Utrecht
NOZ - Amsterdamse Straatweg 309

Den Haag
Caminada - Plaats 25

ACKNOWLEDGEMENTS

I would first like to thank Chris Charlesworth and all the staff at *Omnibus Press* for all their encouragement and allowing me to share my life's work on Jimi Hendrix.

I would also very much like to thank all the new friends I have made on the *Hey Joe Internet* digest for all the contributions they have made during the research of this book. I would especially like to thank the following people who, like myself, have spent many, many years researching the life of Jimi Hendrix: Keith Altham, Charlie Angel, Eric Barrett, Eric Burdon, Neville Chester, Ian Coomber, Billy Cox, Bob Elliott, Kathy Etchingham, Michael Fairchild, Dan Foster, Gary Geldeart, Caesar Glebbeek, Ray Rae Goldman, Jess Hansen, Colin Hartridge, Ayako Hendrix, James Allen Hendrix, Leon Hendrix, Kees De Lang, Larry Lee, John McDermott, Buddy Miles, Mitch Mitchell, Kirsten Nefer, Bill Nitopi, Hakan Persson, Bill Pooton, John Price, Noel Redding, Steve Roby, Steve Rodham, Harry Shapiro, Gerry Stickells, Trixi Sullivan, Juma Sultan, Ben Valkhoff, Ken Voss, Al (Baby Boo) Young.

Copyright © 1999 Omnibus Press
(A Division of Book Sales Limited)

Edited by Chris Charlesworth.
Cover & book designed by Michael Bell Design.
Picture research by Nikki Russell & Tony Brown.

ISBN 0.7119.75108
Order No. OP 48104

All rights reserved. No part of this book may be reproduced in any form or by any electronic or mechanical means, including information storage or retrieval systems, without permission in writing from the publisher, except by a reviewer who may quote brief passages.

Exclusive Distributors:
Book Sales Limited
8/9 Frith Street, London W1V 5TZ, UK.
Music Sales Corporation
257 Park Avenue South, New York, NY 10010, USA.
The Five Mile Press
22 Summit Road, Noble Park, Victoria 3174, Australia.

To the Music Trade only:
Music Sales Limited
8/9 Frith Street, London W1V 5TZ, UK.

Photo credits:
Cover photo: LFI; Bob Baker/Redferns: 41t&b; Glen A.Baker Archives/Redferns: 53, 124c; Mike Barrich: 157; ChuckBoyd/Redferns 4, 5, 18, 22, 81, 102, 114bl, 145, 155; Tony Brown Collection: 60, 66, 77, 82, 164, 165; Mike Charity/Camera Press: 20, 38; Bob Cianci/Tony Brown Collection: 89; Tom Copi/Tony Brown Collection: 57l&r; Tony Gale/Pictorial Press: 5, 26, 31, 32, 73; Harry Goodwin: 4, 16, 25, 33, 35l, 47; G.Howe/Camera Press: 39; Hulton Getty: 58, 79r, 168; ITC: 94, 95; K&K Gunter Zint/Redferns: 42; K&K Studios/Redferns: 43; Alan Koss: 149, 150; Elliot Landy/Redferns: 4/5, 6/7, 79l, 90, 114br, 118/119, 121, 127, 175; Barry Levine/Redferns: 20tl; Rob Lewis Collection: 116b, 117, 120b, 156; Lincolnshire Free Press: 51; LFI: 1, 5, 11, 48, 49t&b, 50, 55, 68l&r, 70, 75, 93t&b, 95t, r&b, 114tl, 106, 110, 126b, 127t&r, 128, 132l, 133, 134, 135; Petra Niemeier/Redferns: 5, 9, 34, 35r&b, 36b, 124b; Knud Neilsen: 171; Tom Nyerges: 100, 139; Michael Ochs Archive/Redferns: 4, 8, 10, 12/13, 27, 114/115, 125, 126/127; Jan Olofsson/Redferns: 21, 116, 176; Pictorial Press: 59, 113, 120tr; Barry Plummer: 69; Popperfoto:17, 36t; David Redfern: 120c; Redferns: back cover, 91; Rex: 2/3, 5, 9c, 37, 44, 52, 56, 74l&r, 76, 78, 114tr, 122/123, 127br, 144, 147l&r; S &G Press/Redferns: 132r; Jorgen Sangsta: 172; Sigurgeir Sigurjonsson: 170; David Sygall: 85; Laurens Van Houten: 5, 152, 166, 167, 169; Val Wilmer/Redferns: 4, 14; Bill Zygmant/Rex: 129, 136.

Every effort has been made to trace the copyright holders of the photographs in this book but one or two were unreachable. We would be grateful if the photographers concerned would contact us.

Printed in Singapore.

A catalogue record for this book is available from the British Library.

Visit Omnibus Press on the web at
www.omnibuspress.com